T0138652

Foundations of Fuzzy Logic and Semantic Web Languages

Chapman & Hall/CRC
Studies in Informatics Series

SERIES EDITOR

G. Q. Zhang

Department of EECS
Case Western Reserve University
Cleveland, Ohio, U.S.A.

PUBLISHED TITLES

Stochastic Relations: Foundations for Markov Transition Systems
Ernst-Erich Doberkat

Conceptual Structures in Practice
Pascal Hitzler and Henrik Schärfe

Context-Aware Computing and Self-Managing Systems
Waltenegus Dargie

Introduction to Mathematics of Satisfiability
Victor W. Marek

Ubiquitous Multimedia Computing
Qing Li and Timothy K. Shih

Mathematical Aspects of Logic Programming Semantics
Pascal Hitzler and Anthony Seda

Agent-Based Modeling and Simulation with Swarm
Hitoshi Iba

Foundations of Fuzzy Logic and Semantic Web Languages
Umberto Straccia

Chapman & Hall/CRC
Studies in Informatics Series

Foundations of Fuzzy Logic and Semantic Web Languages

Umberto Straccia

CRC Press
Taylor & Francis Group
Boca Raton London New York

CRC Press is an imprint of the
Taylor & Francis Group, an **informa** business
A CHAPMAN & HALL BOOK

CRC Press
Taylor & Francis Group
6000 Broken Sound Parkway NW, Suite 300
Boca Raton, FL 33487-2742

© 2014 by Taylor & Francis Group, LLC
CRC Press is an imprint of Taylor & Francis Group, an Informa business

No claim to original U.S. Government works

Printed on acid-free paper
Version Date: 20130715

International Standard Book Number-13: 978-1-4398-5347-4 (Hardback)

Visit the Taylor & Francis Web site at
http://www.taylorandfrancis.com

and the CRC Press Web site at
http://www.crcpress.com

To

my wife Maria Pia,
and my parents Carmine and Gerardina.

Contents

Preface

The primary purpose of this book is to provide a rigorous and succinct description of the mathematical methods and tools about the foundations of representing fuzzy information and reasoning with it within Semantic Web Languages. As such it may also be seen as a compendium on the matter.

The development covers the three main streams of Semantic Web languages: namely, triple languages RDF & RDFS, conceptual languages OWL, OWL 2 and their profiles (OWL EL, OWL QL and OWL RL), and rule-based languages such as RIF.

No previous knowledge of fuzzy set theory or fuzzy logic is required for an understanding of the material in this text, although I assume that the reader is familiar with the basic notions of classical (non fuzzy) set theory and classical (two-valued) logic.

All the theoretical and logical aspects of classical (two-valued) Semantic Web Languages are covered in the first six chapters, which are designated with Part I. Part II is then devoted to generalizing these languages to cope with fuzzy set theory and fuzzy logic and covers the remaining five chapters.

The two parts together may help both the non-fuzzy set theory and fuzzy logic expert to get an insight into Fuzzy Semantic Web Languages, while on the other hand may help the non Semantic Web Languages expert to get a better understanding of the theoretical fundamentals of Semantic Web Languages.

The book also contains an extensive bibliography, which covers virtually all relevant books and papers published by 2012, which may help the younger readers in keeping track of previous work.

Umberto Straccia
February 16th, 2013
Pisa, Italy

List of Figures

List of Tables

Chapter 1

The Quest for Fuzzy Logic in Semantic Web Languages

Semantic Web Languages (SWLs), such as *triple languages* RDF & RDFS [77] (*Resource Description Framework*), *conceptual languages* of the OWL 2 family (*Ontology Web Language*) [340] and *rule languages* of the RIF (*Rule Interchange Format*) family [365], are languages to provide a formal description of concepts, terms, and relationships within a given knowledge domain and to be used as well to write the metadata that typically annotates any kind of web-data.

A large body of work has been carried out addressing various aspects, such as computational complexity, reasoning algorithms, and scalability. Moreover, the standardization of languages such as RDFS and OWL 2, together with the emergence of various implemented tools, allows us to access in a computer processable and uniform way, large bodies of general purpose and/or domain depended knowledge spread over the Web, that can be used, *e.g.*, to infer new knowledge (which may be injected back on the Web).

However, the restriction of SWLs to classical, two-valued/bivalent logic has limitations related to its inability to semantically cope with the inherent "imperfection" of web-data. That is, the inability to deal with *e.g.*,

Inconsistency: One may easily find, *e.g.*, different Gross Domestic Product (GDP) values for a specific country such as illustrated by Wikipedia[1], in which *e.g.*, the GDP according to the United Nations[2] and the International Monetary Fund[3] differ.

Trust: Software agents may gather pieces of data from various information sources on the Web to collect them together and/or infer new knowledge. As we filter information that we think wasn't derived in a scientifically viable way and we have the ability to trust and distrust sources, so should software agents as well. The missing indication of the degree of trustworthiness of the sources and the inferred knowledge may lead to the propagation of "unreliable" information.

Non-monotonicity: The major problem that monotonic knowledge bases

---

[1]http://en.wikipedia.org/wiki/List_of_countries_by_GDP_(nominal)
[2]http://www.un.org
[3]http://www.imf.org/external/index.htm

face is that of inconsistency. Here it is assumed that if a true statement s can be derived from a set $\mathcal{K}$ of statements, then s can also be derived from every larger set $\mathcal{K}'$ that contains $\mathcal{K}$. This seems an appealing assumption to make, because it allows reasoning to be local and to only take into account the rules and facts that are immediately necessary to infer a new statement. But it is also an unrealistic assumption to make, because the world, even the formalized one, is full of contradictions and, typically, the increase of information at hand and assumptions made previously may become invalid. For instance, from the statement "usually I'm in office during office time" one may infer that "I will be at the office Monday morning." However, if later on I become aware of the fact that Monday I will be travelling, the inferred statement becomes invalid.

Uncertainty: A severe issue related to SWLs is the inability to deal with the inherent uncertainty in the gathered data. With uncertainty we mean the scenario in which any statement is true or false, but due to the limited knowledge we have access to, we are unable to exactly establish whether the statement is either true or false.

For instance, the GDP is the market value of all officially recognized final goods and services produced within a country in a given period and the GDP per capita is often considered an indicator of a country's standard of living. Now, one method to determine the GDP is the sum of private consumption, gross investment, government spending, and the difference among exports and imports, *i.e.*,

$$GDP = C + I + G + (X - M) \ .$$

Now, very likely the values of C, I, G, X and M cannot be gathered (by humans and/or software agents) exactly and, thus, can only be approximated. We may also provide an estimation of the probability of *e.g.*, being the value of C the approximated value v_C. That is, we may further provide the measure $Pr(C = v_C)$. Therefore, the exact value of the GDP is approximated with v_{GDP} as well and accompanied with the probability of the statement s "the GDP is v_{GDP}" being true, *i.e.*, $p = Pr(GDP = v_{GDP})$. The point now is that the correct annotation of the statement "the GDP is v_{GDP}" with the probability p of being this statement true cannot be done properly in current SWLs. This may cause a loss of information once these values are put back on the Web and further processed automatically by a software agent to determine, *e.g.*, an indicator of a country's standard of living. In fact, we may become unaware again of the degree of reliability on the inferred information.

Fuzziness: Natural language in general, and web-data specifically, are pervaded with concepts that are vague, specifically fuzzy, in the sense that statements, such as "the indicator of a country's standard of living is low", cannot always to be determined to be either true or false because it is unclear how to define exactly the involved term "low GDP". In a similar fashion, we face difficulties to figure out the answers to a request such as "find me the countries with a low GDP" (as an exercise, try to give an answer to the query for countries with low GDP listed in Wikipedia, say, according to the UN ranking). Concepts such as, low, high, warm, cold, dry, humid, *etc.*, are called fuzzy concepts and rely on fuzzy set theory. That is, while in classical set theory a set has crisp boundaries, *i.e.*, an object is either a member of a set S or it is not, in fuzzy set theory instead, an object may be member of a set to some more fine grained degree; usually a degree taken from the unit interval $[0, 1]$. Therefore, statements and answers are graded.

Incorporating all the above dimensions has not yet been worked out, even though there has been extensive research on each of them.

> *In this book, we will focus on fuzziness only, which may address some interesting application scenarios as succinctly illustrated below.*

Ontology-based Information Retrieval. In *Ontology-based Information Retrieval* (OBIR), one may determine the degree to which a web site, a Web page, a text passage, an image region, a video segment, database records, *etc.*, is *relevant* to an information need expressed using a domain specific ontology. In a fuzzy setting the notion of "relevance" or "aboutness" is indeed context dependent and subjective. That is, the notions of relevance and aboutness are fuzzy concepts and specific similarity functions are defined to implement such notions. Here the top-k retrieval problem, *i.e.*, the retrieval of the top-k ranked answers, where each answer is ranked according to the degree to which it satisfies the query, becomes an important one (see also *e.g.*, [65, 126, 320, 344, 386, 392, 404, 409, 410, 414, 417, 420, 421, 434, 435]). An illustrative example query may be: "find top-k cheapest hotels close to the train station".

A more general case consists of the so-called *Distributed Ontology-based Information Retrieval* (DOBIR) scenario, as depicted in Figure 1.1 (see [433]).

In DIR, a software agent has to perform *automatically* the following steps:

1. The agent has to select a subset of *relevant* resources $S' \subseteq S$, as it is not reasonable to access and to query all resources (using techniques of *resource selection/resource discovery*);

2. For every selected source $S_i \in S'$ the agent has to reformulate its information need Q_A into the query language $\mathcal{L}_i$ provided by the resource (using techniques of *schema mapping/ontology alignment*);

3. The relevant results from the selected resources have to be merged together (using techniques of *data fusion/rank aggregation*).

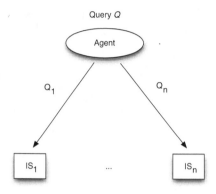

FIGURE 1.1: Distributed information retrieval scenario.

Concerning point 1, both the determination of the *relevant* source involves fuzziness as well the representation of the score of the degree of relevance of each source associated to a query. For point 2, a schema mapping can roughly be seen as a graded relation about the relatedness among the terms of the query and the ones of the sources' vocabulary, while in point 3 one needs to represented the score of the individual items that have been retrieved.

Ontology-based Matchmaking. In *Ontology-based Matchmaking* typically a buyer specifies his graded preferences over the product he wants to buy, while on the other hand sellers specifies theirs. The objective of the software agent here is to find the best possible agreement (called Pareto optimal solution or Nash equilibrium) between a buyer and the sellers (see *e.g.*, [48, 355, 356, 357, 358, 359, 360, 99, 430, 431, 432]). An excerpt may be the following (see also Figure 1.2). A car seller sells the car Audi TT for € 31500, as from the catalogue price. A buyer is looking for a sports car, but wants to pay no more than around € 30000. In classical set theory the problem relies on the crisp conditions on price. A more fine grained approach consists of considering prices as vague constraints, *i.e.*, fuzzy sets, as usual in negotiation (moreover, the notion of a sports car is vague as well);

1. The seller may sell above € 31500, but can go down to € 30500;

2. The buyer prefers to spend less than € 30000, but can go up to € 32000;

So the highest degree of matching is 0.75 and the car may be sold at € 31250.

Ontology-based Multi-Criteria Decision Making. *Multi-Criteria Decision Making* (MCDM) is among one of the most well known branches of decision-making. Roughly, MCDM is the study of identifying and choosing alternatives based on the values and preferences of the decision maker. Making a decision implies that there are alternative choices to be considered and

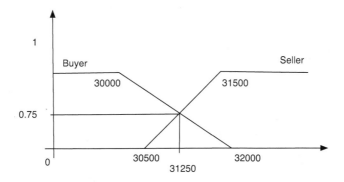

FIGURE 1.2: Matchmaking.

to choose the one that best fits our goals, objectives, desires, values, and so on [445] (see also [418]).

Usually, *alternatives* represent different choices of action available to the decision maker and is assumed to be finite in our case. The *decision criteria* represent the different dimensions from which the alternatives can be viewed (decision criteria are also referred to as *goals* or *attributes*). Most of the MCDM methods require the criteria to be assigned *decision weights* of importance. Usually, these weights are normalized to add up to one.

A standard feature of MCDM methods is that a MCDM problem can be expressed by means of a *decision matrix*, as shown below

		Criteria				
		w_1	w_2	.	.	w_m
Alternatives		C_1	C_2	.	.	C_m
s_1	A_1	a_{11}	a_{12}	.	.	a_{1m}
s_2	A_2	a_{21}	a_{22}	.	.	a_{2m}
.	.	.	.	.	.	.
.	.	.	.	.	.	.
s_n	A_n	a_{n1}	a_{n2}	.	.	a_{nm}

$$(1.1)$$

In the matrix each column belongs to a criterion C_j and each row describes the performance of an alternative A_i. The value a_{ij} describes the performance of alternative A_i against criterion C_j. Weight w_j reflects the relative importance of criteria C_j to the decision. The weights of the criteria are usually determined on a subjective basis and may also be seen as a kind of profit of the criteria. They may represent the opinion of a single decision maker or synthesize the opinions of a group of experts. Eventually, s_i is the overall score of alternative A_i computed using some aggregation method using the weights w_{ij} and performance values a_{ij} $(1 \leq j \leq m)$.

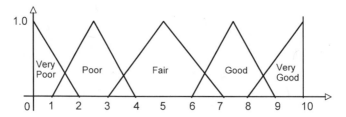

FIGURE 1.3: Fuzzy numbers.

Here, fuzziness arises naturally in the description of the criteria, offers, the relative importance of the criteria and the performance of each alternative against each criteria (see, *e.g.*, the area of *fuzzy* MCDM [225, 443]).

For instance, assume that we have to decide which offer to choose for the development of a public school (see matrix representation below):

Offer	Cost	DeliveryTime	Quality
	Fair	Low	High
A_1	VeryPoor	Fair	Good
A_2	Good	VeryGood	Poor
A_3	Fair	Fair	Poor

- There are three offers A_i (alternatives), described using the terms of an ontology, which have been evaluated manually or semi-automatically by one or more experts, or fully automatically by one or more software agents, according to three criteria

  – Cost, DeliveryTime, Quality

- The performance values of the alternatives w.r.t. a criteria are also vague, *i.e.*, are expressed in terms of qualitative degrees (*e.g.*, fuzzy numbers [242], see also Figure 1.3) such as

  – Very Poor, Poor, Fair, Good, Very Good

- The relative importance of each criteria is also expressed using fuzzy numbers such as

  – Very Low, Low, Fair, High, Very High

Then a key aspect concerns the problem of determining the score of each alternative and computing the top-k ranked alternatives.

Ontology-based Data Mining. In *Ontology-based Data Mining* (OBDM), the goal is to discover structured knowledge from an ontology-based and

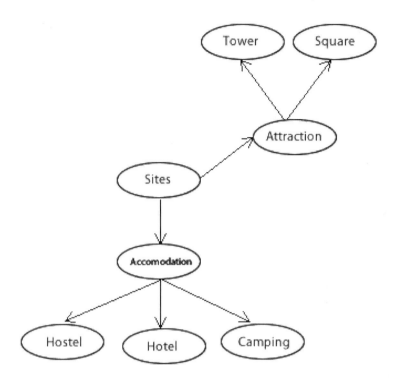

FIGURE 1.4: Excerpt of an ontology about interesting sites in a city.

usually large data set, where the ontology represents the background information on the domain. Here, fuzzy approaches play an important role, because they may provide human comprehensible, *i.e.*, better interpretable, results [246, 260, 261].

For instance, consider the case of hotel finding in a possible tourism application, where an ontology is used to describe the meaningful entities of the domain[4] (see also Figure 1.4).

Now, one may fix a city, say Pisa, extract the characteristic of the hotels from web sites and the *graded* hotel judgements of the users *e.g.*, from Trip Advisor[5] and ask about what characterizes *good* hotels. Then one may learn that, *e.g.*, that "a hotel having a *high* price is a *good* hotel [260, 261]". In this case, the notion of high price has been determined automatically form the data (see Figure 1.5).

---

[4]http://donghee.info/research/SHSS/ObjectiveConceptsOntology(OCO).html
[5]http://www.tripadvisor.com

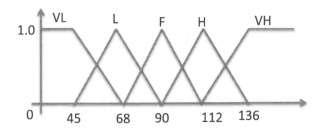

FIGURE 1.5: Very low, low, fair, high, and very high hotel prices.

We refer the interested reader to the FOIL-DL system[6], for further insights.

Ontology-based Geographic Information System. *Geographic Information Systems* (GISS) are widely used nowadays. It is quite obvious, however, that many spatial features often do not have clearly defined boundaries, and concepts like moderate slope, strong elevation, close to a lake, near to a major road, located in a dry region, *etc.*, can better be expressed with degrees of membership to a fuzzy set than with a binary yes/no classification [226, 419, 438].

The above mentioned areas, besides many more, may hopefully convince the reader that fuzzy set theory and fuzzy logic may contribute positively to make knowledge, expressed via SWLs, besides being mechanically processable, more suitable for human reading and information interchange.

---

[6]http://nmis.isti.cnr.it/~straccia/software/FOIL-DL/index.html

Part I

Semantic Web Languages Basics

Chapter 2

Introduction

The Semantic Web is a "web of data" whose goal is to enable machines to understand the semantics, or meaning, of information on the World Wide Web. In rough terms, it should extend the network of hyperlinked human-readable Web pages by inserting machine-readable *metadata*[1] about pages and how they are related to each other, enabling automated agents to access the Web more intelligently and perform tasks on behalf of users.

Semantic Web Languages (SWLs) are the languages used to provide a formal description of concepts, terms, and relationships within a given knowledge domain to be used to write the metadata. There are essentially three family of languages: namely,

- *Triple languages* RDF & RDFS [77] (*Resource Description Framework*);

- *Conceptual languages* of the OWL 2 family (*Ontology Web Language*) [340]; and

- *Rule languages* of the RIF family (*Rule Interchange Format*) [365].

While their syntactic specification is based on XML [463], their semantics is based on logical formalisms (see Fig. 2.1): briefly,

- RDFS is a logic having intensional semantics and the logical counterpart is ρdf [325];

- OWL 2 is a family of languages that relate to *Description Logics* (DLs) [19];

- RIF relates to the *Logic Programming* (LP) paradigm [263].

Both OWL 2 and RIF have an extensional semantics.

Of course, having standard languages to represent and reason about domain knowledge is of little use if we cannot appropriately query it. To this purpose, the query language SPARQL has been defined [380, 381], and considered as one of the key technologies of the Semantic Web.

---

[1]Obtained manually, semi-automatically, or automatically.

FIGURE 2.1: SWLs from a logical perspective.

2.1   RDF & RDFS

The basic ingredients of *RDF* are *triples* of the form (s, p, o), such as $(umberto, likes, tomato)$, stating that *subject s* has *property p* with *value o*. In *RDF Schema* (RDFS), which is an extension of RDF, additionally some special keywords may be used as properties to further improve the expressivity of the language. For instance we may also express that the class of tomatoes are a subclass of the class of vegetables $(tomato, \mathsf{sc}, vegetable)$, while Zurich is an instance of the class of cities $(zurich, \mathsf{type}, city)$.

From a computational point of view, one computes the so-called *closure* (denoted $cl(\mathcal{K})$) of a set of triples $\mathcal{K}$. That is, one infers all possible triples using inference rules [307, 325, 362], such as

$$\frac{(A, \mathsf{sc}, B), (X, \mathsf{type}, A)}{(X, \mathsf{type}, B)}$$

"if A subclass of B and X instance of A then infer that X is instance of B",

and then store all inferred triples into a relational database to be used then for querying. We recall also that there are several ways to store the closure $cl(\mathcal{K})$ in a database (see [1, 211]). Essentially, either we may store all the triples in table with three columns *subject, predicate, object,* or we use a table for each predicate, where each table has two columns *subject, object*. The latter approach seems to be better for query answering purposes. Note that making all implicit knowledge explicit is viable due to the low complexity of the closure computation, which is $\mathcal{O}(|\mathcal{K}|^2)$ in the worst case.

2.2 The OWL Family

The Web Ontology Language *OWL* [338] and its successor *OWL 2* [101, 340] are "object-oriented" languages for defining and instantiating Web ontologies. Ontology (see, *e.g.*, [174]) is a term borrowed from philosophy that refers to the science of describing the kinds of entities in the world and how they are related. An OWL ontology may include descriptions of classes, properties, and their instances, such as

> class   Person partial Human
>
>   restriction (hasName someValuesFrom String)
>
>   restriction (hasBirthPlace someValuesFrom Geoplace)

> "The class Person is a subclass of class Human and has two attributes: hasName having a string as value, and hasBirthPlace whose value is an instance of the class Geoplace".

Given such an ontology, the OWL formal semantics specifies how to derive its logical consequences. For example, if an individual Peter is an instance of the class Student, and Student is a subclass of Person, then one can derive that Peter is also an instance of Person in a similar way as it happens for RDFS. However, OWL is much more expressive than RDFS, as the decision problems for OWL are in higher complexity classes [345] than for RDFS. In Fig. 2.2 we report the various OWL languages and as subscript the DL they relate to [19, 125].

OWL 2 [101, 340] is an update of OWL 1 adding several new features, including an increased expressive power. OWL 2 also defines several *OWL 2 profiles, i.e.*, OWL 2 language subsets that may better meet certain computational complexity requirements or may be easier to implement. The choice of which profile to use in practice will depend on the structure of the ontologies and the reasoning tasks at hand. The OWL 2 profiles are:

OWL 2 EL is particularly useful in applications employing ontologies that contain very large numbers of properties and/or classes (basic reasoning problems can be performed in time that is polynomial with respect to the size of the ontology [13, 18]). The EL acronym reflects the profile's basis in the $\mathcal{EL}$ family of description logics [13, 18].

OWL 2 QL is aimed at applications that use very large volumes of instance data, and where query answering is the most important reasoning task.

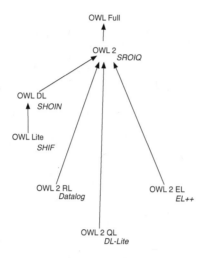

FIGURE 2.2: OWL family.

In OWL 2 QL, conjunctive query answering can be implemented using conventional relational database systems. Using a suitable reasoning technique, sound and complete conjunctive query answering can be performed in LogSpace with respect to the size of the data (assertions) [12, 87]. The QL acronym reflects the fact that query answering in this profile can be implemented by rewriting queries into a standard relational query language such as SQL [449].

OWL 2 RL is aimed at applications that require scalable reasoning without sacrificing too much expressive power. OWL 2 RL reasoning systems can be implemented using rule-based reasoning engines, as a mapping to *Logic Programming* [263], specifically *Datalog* [449], exists. The RL acronym reflects the fact that reasoning in this profile can be implemented using a standard rule language [173]. The computational complexity is the same as for Datalog [113] (polynomial in the size of the data, ExpTime w.r.t. the size of the knowledge base).

2.3   The RIF Family

The *Rule Interchange Format* (RIF) aims at becoming a standard for exchanging rules, such as

---

Forall ?Buyer ?Item ?Seller
    buy(?Buyer ?Item ?Seller) :– sell(?Seller ?Item ?Buyer)

"Someone buys an item from a seller if the seller sells that item to the buyer"

among rule systems, in particular among Web rule engines. RIF is in fact a family of languages, called *dialects*, among which the most significant are:

RIF-BLD The *Basic Logic Dialect* is the main logic-based dialect. Technically, this dialect corresponds to Horn logic with various syntactic and semantic extensions. The main syntactic extensions include the frame syntax and predicates with named arguments. The main semantic extensions include datatypes and externally defined predicates.

RIF-PRD The *Production Rule Dialect* aims at capturing the main aspects of various production rule systems. Production rules, as they are currently practiced in mainstream systems like Jess[2] or JRules[3], are defined using ad hoc computational mechanisms, which are not based on a logic. For this reason, RIF-PRD is not part of the suite of logical RIF dialects and stands apart from them. However, significant effort has been extended to ensure as much sharing with the other dialects as possible. This sharing was the main reason for the development of the RIF Core dialect.

RIF-Core The *Core Dialect* is a subset of both RIF-BLD and RIF-PRD, thus enabling limited rule exchange between logic rule dialects and production rules. RIF-Core corresponds to Horn logic without function symbols (*i.e.*, Datalog [2, 449]) with a number of extensions to support features such as objects and frames as in F-logic [238].

RIF-FLD The *Framework for Logic Dialects* is not a dialect in its own right, but rather a general logical extensibility framework. It was introduced in order to drastically lower the amount of effort needed to define and verify new logic dialects that extend the capabilities of RIF-BLD.

2.4 The Query Language SPARQL

Strictly speaking, SPARQL [381, 380] is a query language for data that is stored natively as RDF or viewed as RDF via middleware. From a logical point of view, its logical counterpart is the well-known notion of *conjunctive/disjunctive* query. As such, we may see SPARQL essentially as a query language for databases and, indeed, has much in common with SQL.

While SPARQL was originally proposed to query RDFS graphs only, in the meanwhile, by relying on the representation of OWL and RIF in RDFS,

---

[2]http://www.jessrules.com/
[3]http://www.ilog.com/products/jrules/

SPARQL was used to query OWL 2 and RIF ontologies as well, via the definition of the so-called *entailment regimes*. In fact, what correct answers to a SPARQL query are depends on the used entailment regime [379] and the vocabulary from which the resulting answers can be taken.

As an illustrative example, the following is a SPARQL query

```
SELECT ?p ?c
WHERE { (?p, type, ebayEmp)
        OPTIONAL {(?p, hasCar, ?c) }
      }
```

whose answers are Ebay employees that optionally owned a car. Note that the basic ingredients of the query are triples.

Chapter 3

Resource Description Language RDF & RDF Schema

3.1 Introduction

The *Resource Description Framework* (RDF) is a language for representing information about resources in the World Wide Web [304, 361] and has become a quite popular Semantic Web representation formalism. It is particularly intended for representing metadata about Web resources, such as the title and author of a Web page. However, by generalizing the concept of a "Web resource," RDF can also be used to represent information about things that can be identified on the Web, even when they cannot be directly retrieved on the Web. For our purposes we can think of it as anything we can identify.

RDF is based on the idea of identifying things using identifiers (called *Uniform Resource Identifiers*, or URIs) and describing resources in terms of simple properties and property values. RDF properties may be thought of as attributes of resources and in this sense correspond to traditional attribute-value pairs. This enables RDF to represent a simple statement about resources as a *triple* (s, p, o), such as $(umberto, likes, tomato)$, stating that *subject s* has *property p* with *value o*. Triples may also be represented as graphs, where nodes represent resources or values and arcs represent properties, as shown in Figure 3.1. In *RDF Schema* (RDFS) [77], which is an extension of RDF, additionally some special keywords may be used as properties to further improve the expressivity of the language. For instance (see Figure 3.1) we may also express that the class of "tomatoes are a subclass of the class of vegetables", while Zurich is an instance of the class of cities.

In what follows, we will describe the essential features of RDFS from a syntax, semantics, and a reasoning point of view that are necessary for our discussions later in Chapter 9 when we introduce fuzzy RDFS. Our exposition is along the line followed by [177, 307, 325] to describe syntax, semantics, and inference system for the "core" part of RDFS, called ρdf [325].

We refer the reader to Appendix A for a complete formal definition of the semantics of RDFS using the notion of interpretation defined here.

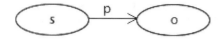

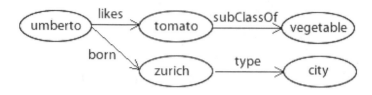

FIGURE 3.1: Triples as graph.

3.2 RDF and RDFS

Syntax. Consider pairwise disjoint alphabets **U**, **B**, and **L** denoting, respectively, *URI references*, *blank nodes*, and *literals*. We assume **U**, **B**, and **L** fixed, and for ease we will denote unions of these sets simply concatenating their names. We call the elements in **UBL** (**B**) *terms* (*variables*, denoted x, y, z).

An *RDF triple* is a triple τ of the form

$$(s, p, o) \in \mathbf{UBL} \times \mathbf{U} \times \mathbf{UBL} \ .$$

We call s the *subject*, p the *predicate*, and o the *object*. Note that as in [325] we allow literals for s. A *graph* G is a set of triples, a *subgraph* is a subset of a graph, the *universe* of G, *universe*(G), is the set of elements in **UBL** that occur in the triples of G, the *vocabulary* of G, *voc*(G), is *universe*$(G) \cap \mathbf{UL}$.

For our purposes, we rely on a fragment of RDFS, called ρdf [325], that covers essential features of RDFS (read rho-df, the ρ from restricted RDF). ρdf is defined as the following subset of the RDFS vocabulary:

$$\rho\mathrm{df} = \{\mathsf{sp}, \mathsf{sc}, \mathsf{type}, \mathsf{dom}, \mathsf{range}\} \ ,$$

where the keywords in ρdf may be used in triples as properties. Informally,

- (p, sp, q) means that property p is a *sub-property* of property q;
- (c, sc, d) means that class c is a *subclass* of class d;
- (a, type, b) means that a is of *type* b;
- (p, dom, c) means that the *domain* of property p is c; and
- (p, range, c) means that the *range* of property p is c.

Remark 1. *In a First-Order Logic (FOL) setting, we may interpret classes as unary predicates, and (RDF) predicates as binary predicates. Then*

1. *a subclass relation between class c and d may be encoded as the formula*

$$\forall x.c(x) \rightarrow d(x)$$

2. *a subproperty relation between property p and q may be encoded as*

$$\forall x \forall y.p(x, y) \rightarrow q(x, y)$$

3. *domain and range properties may be represented as:*

$$\forall x \forall y.p(x, y) \rightarrow c(x) \quad and \quad \forall x \forall y.p(x, y) \rightarrow c(y)$$

4. *the transitivity of a property can be represented as*

$$\forall x \forall y \exists z.(p(x, z) \wedge p(z, y)) \rightarrow p(x, y) \ .$$

Although this remark is trivial, we will see that it will play an important role in the formalization of fuzzy RDFS.

In what follows we define a *map* or (*variable assignment*) as a function $\mu :$ **UBL** $\rightarrow$ **UBL** preserving URIs and literals, *i.e.*, $\mu(t) = t$, for all $t \in$ **UL**. Given a graph G, we define $\mu(G) = \{(\mu(s), \mu(p), \mu(o)) \mid (s, p, o) \in G\}$. We speak of a map μ from G_1 to G_2, and write $\mu : G_1 \rightarrow G_2$, if μ is such that $\mu(G_1) \subseteq G_2$.

A *grounding* G' of graph G is obtained, as usual, by replacing variables in G with terms in **UL**. A graph G without variables is called *ground*.

Example 1. *The following is a graph (partially represented in Figure 3.1)*

$$
\begin{aligned}
G \quad = \{ \quad & (umberto, likes, tomato), (umberto, born, zurich), \\
& (tomato, \mathsf{type}, edibleFruit), (edibleFruit, \mathsf{sc}, fruit), \\
& (born, \mathsf{dom}, person), (born, \mathsf{range}, city) \ \} \ .
\end{aligned}
$$

Note that G is ground.

Semantics. An *interpretation* $\mathcal{I}$ over a vocabulary V is a tuple

$$\mathcal{I} = \langle \Delta_R, \Delta_P, \Delta_C, \Delta_L, P[\![\cdot]\!], C[\![\cdot]\!], \cdot^{\mathcal{I}} \rangle \ ,$$

where $\Delta_R, \Delta_P, \Delta_C, \Delta_L$ are the interpretation domains of $\mathcal{I}$, which are finite non-empty sets, and $P[\![\cdot]\!], C[\![\cdot]\!], \cdot^{\mathcal{I}}$ are the interpretation functions of $\mathcal{I}$. They have to satisfy:

1. Δ_R are the resources (the domain or universe of $\mathcal{I}$);

TABLE 3.1: Semantic conditions for classical ρdf interpretations.

Simple:	1. for each $(s, p, o) \in G$, $p^{\mathcal{I}} \in \Delta_P$ and $(s^{\mathcal{I}}, o^{\mathcal{I}}) \in P[\![p^{\mathcal{I}}]\!]$;
Subproperty:	1. $P[\![\mathsf{sp}^{\mathcal{I}}]\!]$ is transitive over Δ_P;
	2. if $(p, q) \in P[\![\mathsf{sp}^{\mathcal{I}}]\!]$ then $p, q \in \Delta_P$ and $P[\![p]\!] \subseteq P[\![q]\!]$;
Subclass:	1. $P[\![\mathsf{sc}^{\mathcal{I}}]\!]$ is transitive over Δ_C;
	2. if $(c, d) \in P[\![\mathsf{sc}^{\mathcal{I}}]\!]$ then $c, d \in \Delta_C$ and $C[\![c]\!] \subseteq C[\![d]\!]$;
Typing I:	1. $x \in C[\![c]\!]$ if and only if $(x, c) \in P[\![\mathsf{type}^{\mathcal{I}}]\!]$;
	2. if $(p, c) \in P[\![\mathsf{dom}^{\mathcal{I}}]\!]$ and $(x, y) \in P[\![p]\!]$ then $x \in C[\![c]\!]$;
	3. if $(p, c) \in P[\![\mathsf{range}^{\mathcal{I}}]\!]$ and $(x, y) \in P[\![p]\!]$ then $y \in C[\![c]\!]$;
Typing II:	1. for each $e \in \rho$df, $e^{\mathcal{I}} \in \Delta_P$
	2. if $(p, c) \in P[\![\mathsf{dom}^{\mathcal{I}}]\!]$ then $p \in \Delta_P$ and $c \in \Delta_C$
	3. if $(p, c) \in P[\![\mathsf{range}^{\mathcal{I}}]\!]$ then $p \in \Delta_P$ and $c \in \Delta_C$
	4. if $(x, c) \in P[\![\mathsf{type}^{\mathcal{I}}]\!]$ then $c \in \Delta_C$

2. Δ_P are property names (not necessarily disjoint from Δ_R);

3. $\Delta_C \subseteq \Delta_R$ are the classes;

4. $\Delta_L \subseteq \Delta_R$ are the literal values and contains $\mathbf{L} \cap V$;

5. $P[\![\cdot]\!]$ is a function $P[\![\cdot]\!]\colon \Delta_P \to 2^{\Delta_R \times \Delta_R}$;

6. $C[\![\cdot]\!]$ is a function $C[\![\cdot]\!]\colon \Delta_C \to 2^{\Delta_R}$;

7. $\cdot^{\mathcal{I}}$ maps each $t \in \mathbf{UL} \cap V$ into a value $t^{\mathcal{I}} \in \Delta_R \cup \Delta_P$, and such that $\cdot^{\mathcal{I}}$ is the identity for plain literals and assigns an element in Δ_R to each element in $\mathbf{L}$.

An interpretation $\mathcal{I}$ is a *model* of a ground graph G, denoted $\mathcal{I} \models G$, if and only if $\mathcal{I}$ is an interpretation over the vocabulary ρdf $\cup$ *universe*(G) that satisfies the conditions in Table 3.1.

Entailment, denoted $G \models H$, among ground graphs G and H is as usual: a ground graph G *entails* a ground graph H if and only if any model of G is also a model of H. The generalization to non-necessarily ground graphs is as follows: a graph G *entails* a graph H, denoted $G \models H$, if and only if for any grounding G' of G there is a grounding H' of H such that $G' \models H'$.

Remark 2 (Reflexivity issue). *In [325], the authors define two variants of the semantics: the default one includes reflexivity of $P[\![\mathsf{sp}^{\mathcal{I}}]\!]$ (resp. $C[\![\mathsf{sc}^{\mathcal{I}}]\!]$) over Δ_P (resp. Δ_C). Here we are only considering the alternative semantics presented in [325, Definition 4] which omits this requirement. Thus, we do not support entailment of triples such as*

$(a, \mathsf{sc}, a), (\mathsf{sp}, \mathsf{sp}, \mathsf{sp}), (\mathsf{sc}, \mathsf{sp}, \mathsf{sc}), (\mathsf{type}, \mathsf{sp}, \mathsf{type}), (\mathsf{dom}, \mathsf{sp}, \mathsf{dom}),$ *and* $(\mathsf{range}, \mathsf{sp}, \mathsf{range}),$ *that depend on the reflexivity and are of marginal interest anyway. See [325] (cf. p. 59) for a more in depth discussion on this issue.*

Let us denote with $\models^{\mathsf{rx}}$ the entailment relation $\models$ of ρdf in which we include also the reflexivity of $P[\![\mathsf{sp}^{\mathcal{I}}]\!]$ and $C[\![\mathsf{sc}^{\mathcal{I}}]\!]$. Then it can be shown that

Proposition 1 ([325]). *Let G and H be ρdf graphs. Assume that H does not contain triples of the form (a, sp, a) nor (a, sc, a) for $a \in \mathbf{UL}$, nor triples of the form (x, sp, y) nor (x, sc, y) for $x \in \mathbf{B}$ or $y \in \mathbf{B}$. Then,*

$$G \models H \text{ if and only if } G \models^{\mathsf{rx}} H \ .$$

Essentially the above theorem states that the only use of reflexive restrictions in RDFS models is the entailment of triples of the form $(a, \mathsf{sp}, b), (a, \mathsf{sc}, b)$, or their existential versions replacing the subject or object by variables (blank nodes).

The next proposition shows that $\models^{\mathsf{rx}}$ retains the original semantics of RDFS. Let $\models_{\mathsf{RDFS}}$ be the RDFS entailment relation defined in [307, 362] (see Appendix A).

Proposition 2 ([325]). *Let G and H be graphs that do not mention RDFS vocabulary outside ρdf. Then*

$$G \models_{\mathsf{RDFS}} H \text{ if and only if } G \models^{\mathsf{rx}} H \ .$$

Combining Propositions 1 and 2 we may characterize our entailment relation $\models$ in ρdf with respect to full RDFS semantics as follows.

Corollary 1. *Let G and H be graphs that do not mention RDFS vocabulary outside ρdf. Assume that H does not contain triples of the form (a, sp, a) nor (a, sc, a) for $a \in \mathbf{UL}$, nor triples of the form (x, sp, y) nor (x, sc, y) for $x \in \mathbf{B}$ or $y \in \mathbf{B}$. Then,*

$$G \models_{\mathsf{RDFS}} H \text{ if and only if } G \models H \ .$$

Remark 3 (Axiomatic triples). *Note that in ρdf models we do not impose the a priori satisfaction of any axiomatic triple. Indeed, ρdf models do not satisfy any of the RDFS axiomatic triples in [307, 362] (see Appendix A, Table A.2), because all of them mention RDFS vocabulary outside ρdf. This is also the reason for the inclusion of the "Typing II" conditions in ρdf models that capture the semantics restrictions imposed syntactically by the RDFS axiomatic triples* $(\mathsf{dom}, \mathsf{dom}, \mathsf{prop}), (\mathsf{dom}, \mathsf{range}, \mathsf{class}), (\mathsf{range}, \mathsf{dom}, \mathsf{prop}), (\mathsf{range}, \mathsf{range}, \mathsf{class}),$ *and* $(\mathsf{type}, \mathsf{range}, \mathsf{class}),$ *and the fact that every element in ρdf must be interpreted as a property.*

Another property of $\models$ is that it does not entail axiomatic triples:

Proposition 3 ([325]). *There is no ρdf triple τ such that $\models \tau$.*

As we will see, Corollary 1 and Proposition 3 simplify the reasoning machinery for ρdf significantly.

We conclude this section with an example.

Example 2. *Consider the graph G in Example 1. Then the following entailment relations hold:*

$$
\begin{aligned}
G &\models (tomato, \mathsf{type}, fruit) \\
G &\models (umberto, \mathsf{type}, person) \\
G &\models (zurich, \mathsf{type}, city) \ .
\end{aligned}
$$

For instance, concerning $G \models (tomato, \mathsf{type}, fruit)$, informally the argument is as follows. A tomato is an edible fruit, edible fruits are fruits and, thus, a tomato is a fruit. Concerning $G \models (zurich, \mathsf{type}, city)$, we have that umberto is born in Zurich, if someone is born somewhere then this latter is a city and, thus, Zurich is a city. The case $G \models (umberto, \mathsf{type}, person)$ is similar.

3.3   Conjunctive Queries

Concerning query answering, we are inspired by [177] and the logic programming setting [263] and we assume that a RDFS graph G is *ground*. That is, blank nodes have been skolemized, *i.e.*, replaced with terms in **UL**.

A *conjunctive query* is of the rule-like form

$$q(\mathbf{x}) \leftarrow \exists \mathbf{y}.\varphi(\mathbf{x}, \mathbf{y}) \tag{3.1}$$

where $q(\mathbf{x})$ is the *head* and $\exists \mathbf{y}.\varphi(\mathbf{x}, \mathbf{y})$ is the *body* of the query, which is a conjunction (we use the symbol "," to denote conjunction in the rule body) of triples τ_i $(1 \leq i \leq n)$. $\mathbf{x}$ is a vector of variables occurring in the body, called the *distinguished variables*, $\mathbf{y}$ are so-called *non-distinguished variables* and are distinct from the variables in $\mathbf{x}$, each variable occurring in τ_i is either a distinguished or a non-distinguished variable. If clear from the context, we may omit the existential quantification $\exists \mathbf{y}$.

A query example is:

$$q(x, y) \leftarrow (y, created, x), (y, \mathsf{type}, Italian), (x, exhibitedAt, Uffizi)$$

having intended meaning to retrieve all the artifacts x created by Italian artists y, being exhibited at Uffizi Gallery.

In order to define an *answer* to a conjunctive query we introduce the following definitions. Given a vector $\mathbf{x} = \langle x_1, \dots, x_k \rangle$ of variables, a *substitution* over $\mathbf{x}$ is a vector of terms $\mathbf{t}$ replacing variables in $\mathbf{x}$ with terms of **UBL**. Then, given a query $q(\mathbf{x}) \leftarrow \exists \mathbf{y}.\varphi(\mathbf{x}, \mathbf{y})$, and two substitutions $\mathbf{t}, \mathbf{t}'$ over $\mathbf{x}$

and $\mathbf{y}$, respectively, the *query instantiation* $\varphi(\mathbf{t}, \mathbf{t}')$ is derived from $\varphi(\mathbf{x}, \mathbf{y})$ by replacing $\mathbf{x}$ and $\mathbf{y}$ with $\mathbf{t}$ and $\mathbf{t}'$, respectively.

Note that a query instantiation $\varphi(\mathbf{t}, \mathbf{t}')$ is an RDF graph.

Given a ground graph G, a query $q(\mathbf{x}) \leftarrow \exists \mathbf{y}.\varphi(\mathbf{x}, \mathbf{y})$, and a vector $\mathbf{t}$ of terms in $universe(G)$, we say that $q(\mathbf{t})$ is *entailed* by G, denoted $G \models q(\mathbf{t})$, if and only if there is a vector $\mathbf{t}'$ of terms in $universe(G)$ such that in any model $\mathcal{I}$ of G, $\mathcal{I}$ is a model of the query instantiation $\varphi(\mathbf{t}, \mathbf{t}')$.

If $G \models q(\mathbf{t})$ then $\mathbf{t}$ is called an *answer* to q. The *answer set* of q w.r.t. G is defined as $ans(G, q) = \{\mathbf{t} \mid G \models q(\mathbf{t})\}$.

3.4   Reasoning

In what follows, we provide a sound and complete deductive system (for the graph entailment problem) for our language derived from [325]. The complete RDFS inference rules are presented in Appendix A.

The system is arranged in groups of rules that capture the semantic conditions of models. In every rule, A, B, C, X, and Y are meta-variables representing elements in **UBL** and D, E represent elements in **UL**. The rules are described in Table 3.2.

Remark 4 (On rules (5a) and (5b)). *As noted in [307, 440], the set of rules presented in [362] is not complete for RDFS entailment. The problem is produced when a blank node X is implicitly used as standing for a property in triples like $(a, \mathsf{sp}, X), (X, \mathsf{dom}, b)$, or (X, range, c). Here we solve the problem following the elegant solution proposed by [307] adding just two new rules of implicit typing (rules 5 above).*

Remark 5 (Rules for reflexivity). *A reader familiar with [325] will notice that these rules are as rules 1-5 of [325] (which has 7 rules). We excluded the rules handling reflexivity (rules 6-7) that are not needed in our setting.*

Furthermore, as noted in [325], the "Implicit Typing" rules are a necessary addition to the rules presented in [362] for complete RDFS entailment. These represent the case when variable A in (D, sp, A) and (A, dom, B) or (A, range, B), is a property implicitly represented by a blank node.

For completeness, we recap the missing rules 6-7 of [325] below:

6. Subproperty Reflexivity:

TABLE 3.2: Inference rules for ρdf.

---

1. Simple:

    (a) $\frac{G}{G'}$ for a map $\mu : G' \to G$

    (b) $\frac{G}{G'}$ for $G' \subseteq G$

2. Subproperty:

    (a) $\frac{(A,\mathsf{sp},B),(B,\mathsf{sp},C)}{(A,\mathsf{sp},C)}$

    (b) $\frac{(D,\mathsf{sp},E),(X,D,Y)}{(X,E,Y)}$

3. Subclass:

    (a) $\frac{(A,\mathsf{sc},B),(B,\mathsf{sc},C)}{(A,\mathsf{sc},C)}$

    (b) $\frac{(A,\mathsf{sc},B),(X,\mathsf{type},A)}{(X,\mathsf{type},B)}$

4. Typing:

    (a) $\frac{(D,\mathsf{dom},B),(X,D,Y)}{(X,\mathsf{type},B)}$

    (b) $\frac{(D,\mathsf{range},B),(X,D,Y)}{(Y,\mathsf{type},B)}$

5. Implicit Typing:

    (a) $\frac{(A,\mathsf{dom},B),(D,\mathsf{sp},A),(X,D,Y)}{(X,\mathsf{type},B)}$

    (b) $\frac{(A,\mathsf{range},B),(D,\mathsf{sp},A),(X,D,Y)}{(Y,\mathsf{type},B)}$

   (a) $\frac{(X,A,Y)}{(A,\mathsf{sp},A)}$

   (b) $\frac{(A,\mathsf{sp},B)}{(A,\mathsf{sp},A),(B,\mathsf{sp},B)}$

   (c) $\frac{}{(p,\mathsf{sp},p)}$ *for* $p \in \rho df$

   (d) $\frac{(A,p,X)}{(A,\mathsf{sp},A)}$ *for* $p \in \{\mathsf{dom, range}\}$

7. Subclass Reflexivity:

   (a) $\frac{(A,\mathsf{sc},B)}{(A,\mathsf{sc},A)}$

   (b) $\frac{(A,\mathsf{sc},B)}{(B,\mathsf{sc},B)}$

   (c) $\frac{(X,p,A)}{(A,\mathsf{sc},A)}$ *for* $p \in \{\mathsf{dom, range, type}\}$

An instantiation of a rule is a uniform replacement of the metavariables occurring in the triples of the rule by elements of **UBL**, such that all the triples obtained after the replacement are well-formed RDF triples.

A *proof* is defined in the usual way. Let G and H be graphs. Then $G \vdash H$ iff there is a sequence of graphs $P_1, \ldots, P_k$ with $P_1 = G$ and $P_k = H$, and for each j $(2 \leq j \leq k)$ one of the following holds:

1. there exists a map $\mu : P_j \to P_{j-1}$ (rule (1a));

2. $P_j \subseteq P_{j-1}$ (rule (1b));

3. there is an instantiation $\frac{R}{R'}$ of one of the rules (2)(5), such that $R \subseteq P_{j-1}$ and $P_j = P_{j-1} \cup R'$.

The sequence of rules used at each step (plus its instantiation or map), is called a *proof* of H from G.

Example 3. *Consider Example 1. The following is a proof of $G \vdash$ (tomato, type, fruit):*

(1) $(tomato, \mathsf{type}, edibleFruit)$ *Rule (1b)*
(2) $(edibleFruit, \mathsf{sc}, fruit)$ *Rule (1b)*
(3) $(tomato, \mathsf{type}, fruit)$ *Rule (3b) applied to (1) and (2)* .

The following proposition shows that our proof mechanism is sound and complete w.r.t. the ρdf semantics:

Proposition 4 (Soundness and Completeness [325]). *Inference $\vdash$ based on rules 1-5 is sound and complete for $\models$, that is,*

$$G \vdash H \text{ if and only if } G \models H .$$

Proposition 5 ([325]). *Assume $G \vdash G'$ then there is a proof of G' from G where the rule (1a) is used at most once and at the end.*

Corollary 2 ([325]). *Define the proof system $\vdash^{rx}$ as for ρdf by adding also the rules of reflexivity (rules (6) and (7)). Then for graphs G and H,*

$$G \models^{rx} H \text{ if and only if } G \vdash^{rx} H .$$

Corollary 3 ([325]). *Assume $G \vdash^{rx} H$ then there is a proof of H from G where the rule (1a) is used at most once and at the end.*

For notational convenience, we denote with $\{\tau_1, \ldots, \tau_n\} \vdash_{\mathsf{RDFS}} \tau$ that the consequence τ is obtained from the premise $\tau_1, \ldots, \tau_n$ by applying one of the inference rules with the exclusion of rules (1a) and (1b).

The *closure* of a graph G is defined as $cl(G) = \{\tau \mid G \vdash^* \tau\}$, where $\vdash^*$ is as $\vdash$ except that rule (1a) is excluded. Note that the size of the closure of G is polynomial in the size of G and that the closure is *unique*.

Example 4. *Consider the graph G in Example 1. Then the closure of G is:*

$$
\begin{aligned}
cl(G) \quad = G \cup \{ \quad & (tomato, \mathsf{type}, fruit), \\
& (umberto, \mathsf{type}, person), \\
& (zurich, \mathsf{type}, city) \quad \} .
\end{aligned}
$$

Using the closure, we may immediately prove that

Proposition 6. *Any graph G has a model.*

More importantly, from a practical point of view, it can be proven that:

Proposition 7 ([325]). *$G \vdash H$ if and only if $H \subseteq cl(G)$ or H is obtained from $cl(G)$ by applying rule (1a).*

Finally, note that a simple method to determine $G \models \tau$, where both G and τ are ground, consists in computing $cl(G)$, where the size of the closure of G is $\mathcal{O}(|G|^2)$, and check whether τ is included in $cl(G)$ [325]. [325] provides also an alternative method to test $G \models \tau$ that runs in time $\mathcal{O}(|G| \log |G|)$.

There also several ways to store the closure $cl(G)$ in a database (see [1, 211]). Essentially, either we may store all the triples in a table with three columns *subject, predicate, object*, or we use a table for each predicate, where each table has two columns *subject, object*. The latter approach seems to be better for query answering purposes.

Example 5. *Consider Example 2. Then the one table variant to store $cl(G)$ is:*

closure		
subject	predicate	object
umberto	*likes*	*tomato*
umberto	*born*	*zurich*
tomato	type	*edibleFruit*
edibleFruit	sc	*fruit*
born	dom	*person*
born	range	*city*
tomato	type	*fruit*
umberto	type	*person*
zurich	type	*city*

On the other hand, in case we use one table for each predicate we have the tables:

likes	
subject	object
umberto	*tomato*

born	
subject	object
umberto	*zurich*

type	
subject	object
tomato	*edibleFruit*
tomato	*fruit*
umberto	*person*
zurich	*city*

sc	
edibleFruit	*fruit*

dom	
born	*person*

range	
born	*city*

We have also the following complexity result:

Proposition 8 ([440]). *Entailment for RDFS is decidable, NP-complete, and in P if the target graph does not contain blank nodes.*

We conclude the chapter by showing how to compute the answer set of a conjunctive query (see Section 3.3). The following can be shown:

Proposition 9. *Given a ground graph G, $\mathbf{t}$ is an* answer *to q if and only if there exists an instantiation $\varphi(\mathbf{t}, \mathbf{t}')$ that is true in the closure of G (i.e., all triples in $\varphi(\mathbf{t}, \mathbf{t}')$ are in $cl(G)$).*

Therefore, we have a simple method to determine $ans(G, q)$. Namely, compute the closure $cl(G)$ of G and store it into a database, *e.g.*, using the method [210]. It is easily verified that any query can be mapped into an SQL query over the underlying database schema. Hence, $ans(G, q)$ can be determined by issuing such an SQL query to the database.

Chapter 4

Web Ontology Language OWL

4.1 Introduction

The Web Ontology Language *OWL* [338] and its successor *OWL 2* [101, 340] are languages for defining and instantiating Web ontologies. Ontology (see, *e.g.*, [174]) is a term borrowed from philosophy that refers to the science of describing the kinds of entities in the world and how they are related.

An OWL ontology may include descriptions of classes, properties, and their instances. Given such an ontology, the OWL formal semantics specifies how to derive its logical consequences, *i.e.*, facts not literally present in the ontology, but entailed by the semantics. An OWL ontology is a formal conceptualization of a domain of interest and consists of the following three different syntactic categories:

- Entities, such as classes, properties, and individuals, are identified by URIs and can be thought of as primitive terms or names. Entities represent basic elements of the domain being modelled. For example, a *class* Person can be used to model the set of all people. Similarly, the *object property* parentOf can be used to model the parent-child relationship. Finally, the *individual* Peter can be used to represent a particular person called "Peter".

- Expressions represent complex notions in the domain being modelled. For example, a *class expression* describes a set of individuals in terms of the restrictions on the individuals' features.

- Axioms are statements that are asserted to be true in the domain being modelled. For example, using a *subclass axiom*, one can state that the class Student is a subclass of the class Person.

These three syntactic categories are used to express the logical part of OWL ontologies – that is, they are interpreted under a precisely defined semantics that allows useful inferences to be drawn. For example, if an individual Peter is an instance of the class Student, and Student is a subclass of Person, then from the OWL semantics one can derive that Peter is also an instance of Person in a similar way as it happens for RDFS. However, OWL is much more expressive than RDFS, as we will see later on, as the decision problems for OWL are in higher complexity classes [345] than for RDFS.

We recall that the OWL language provides three increasingly expressive sublanguages designed for use by specific communities of implementers and users.

- *OWL Lite* supports those users primarily needing a classification hierarchy and simple constraint features. For example, while OWL Lite supports cardinality constraints, it only permits cardinality values of 0 or 1. It should be simpler to provide tool support for OWL Lite than its more expressive relatives, and provide a quick migration path for thesauri and other taxonomies. Deciding entailment in OWL Lite is ExpTime-complete.

- *OWL DL* supports those users who want the maximum expressiveness without losing computational completeness (all entailments are guaranteed to be computed) and decidability (all computations will finish in finite time) of reasoning systems. More precisely, deciding entailment in OWL DL is NExpTime-complete. OWL DL includes all OWL language constructs with restrictions such as type separation (a class cannot also be an individual or property, a property cannot also be an individual or class). OWL DL is so named due to its correspondence with *Description Logics* (DLs) [19, 125], a family of FOL fragments.

- *OWL Full* is meant for users who want maximum expressiveness and the syntactic freedom of RDF with no computational guarantees. For example, in OWL Full a class can be treated simultaneously as a collection of individuals and as an individual in its own right. Deciding entailment in OWL full is undecidable.

Each of these sublanguages is an extension of its simpler predecessor, both in what can be legally expressed and in what can be validly concluded. The following set of relations hold. Their inverses do not.

1. Every OWL Lite ontology is an OWL DL ontology.

2. Every OWL DL ontology is an OWL Full ontology.

3. Every OWL Lite conclusion is an OWL DL conclusion.

4. Every OWL DL conclusion is an OWL Full conclusion.

OWL 2 [101, 340] is an update of OWL adding several new features, including an increased expressive power—mainly w.r.t. properties, extended support for datatypes, simple meta modelling capabilities, extended annotation capabilities, database style keys. OWL 2 also defines several *OWL 2 profiles*, *i.e.*, OWL 2 language subsets that may better meet certain computational complexity requirements or may be easier to implement. The choice of which profile to use in practice will depend on the structure of the ontologies and the reasoning tasks at hand. The OWL 2 profiles are:

- *OWL 2 EL* is particularly useful in applications employing ontologies that contain very large numbers of properties and/or classes. This profile captures the expressive power used by many such ontologies and is a subset of OWL 2 for which the basic reasoning problems can be performed in time that is polynomial with respect to the size of the ontology [13, 178]. Dedicated reasoning algorithms for this profile are available and have been demonstrated to be implementable in a highly scalable way. The $\mathcal{EL}$ acronym reflects the profile's basis in the $\mathcal{EL}$ family of description logics [13], logics that provide only *existential* quantification (see later on).

- *OWL 2 QL* is aimed at applications that use very large volumes of instance data, and where query answering is the most important reasoning task. In OWL 2 QL, conjunctive query answering can be implemented using conventional relational database systems. Using a suitable reasoning technique, sound and complete conjunctive query answering can be performed in LogSpace with respect to the size of the data (assertions) [12, 87]. As in OWL 2 EL, polynomial time algorithms can be used to implement the ontology consistency and class expression subsumption reasoning problems. The expressive power of the profile is necessarily quite limited, although it does include most of the main features of conceptual models such as UML class diagrams and ER diagrams. The QL acronym reflects the fact that query answering in this profile can be implemented by rewriting queries into a standard relational query language such as SQL [449].

- *OWL 2 RL* is aimed at applications that require scalable reasoning without sacrificing too much expressive power. It is designed to accommodate OWL 2 applications that can trade the full expressivity of the language for efficiency, as well as RDFS applications that need some added expressivity. OWL 2 RL reasoning systems can be implemented using rule-based reasoning engines, as a mapping to *Logic Programming* [263], specifically *Datalog* [449], exists. The ontology consistency, class expression satisfiability, class expression subsumption, instance checking, and conjunctive query answering problems can be solved in time that is polynomial with respect to the size of the set of facts. The RL acronym reflects the fact that reasoning in this profile can be implemented using a standard rule language. The design of OWL 2 RL was inspired by the Horn-DL family, also called *Description Logic Programs* (DLPs) in [173] and pD^* [440].

4.2   Description Logics Basics

Description Logics (DLs) [19, 125] play a fundamental role for the OWL family of languages as they are the theoretical/logical counterpart of them. In fact, as OWL languages can be mapped into DLs, algorithms and computational complexity results found for DLs are then applied to the OWL family. For the sake of clarifying the concept, in Figure 2.2 we resume the OWL family of languages, the related computational complexity of reasoning within them[1] and the DL that they refer to: specifically,

- OWL 2 refers to the DL $\mathcal{SROIQ}$ [101, 203]

- OWL 1 DL refers to the DL $\mathcal{SHOIN}$ [201, 204, 205, 207, 208]

- OWL 1 Lite refers to the DL $\mathcal{SHIF}$ [204, 205]

- OWL 2 QL refers to the DL-Lite family, specifically DL-Lite$_{\mathcal{R}}$ [12, 87]

- OWL 2 EL refers to the DL $\mathcal{EL}$ family, specifically $\mathcal{EL}^{++}$ [13, 18, 178].

- OWL 2 RL refers to the Horn-DL family [173, 440].

We recall that each DL is usually identified with a string of calligraphic letters, each of which indicates that the *basic* DL, $\mathcal{AL}$ has been extended with a specific constructor [19].

DLs are a logical reconstruction of the so-called frame-based knowledge representation languages, with the aim of providing a simple well-established Tarski-style declarative semantics to capture the meaning of the most popular features of structured representation of knowledge. The basic syntactic building blocks are atomic concepts (unary predicates), atomic roles (binary predicates), and individuals (constants). The expressive power of the language is restricted in that it uses a rather small set of constructors for building complex concepts and roles. Specifically, a DL assumes three alphabets of symbols, for *concepts*, *roles*, and *individuals*. A concept may be understood as a unary predicate (a class), while a role may be seen as a binary predicate (property/attribute of a class). In each DL, complex concepts and roles can be built using different concept, and role constructors and classes may be organized into a hierarchy.

4.2.1   The Basic Description Language $\mathcal{AL}$

Elementary descriptions are *atomic concepts*, also called *concept names* (denoted A) and *atomic roles* (denoted R). Complex *concepts* (denoted C) can be built from them inductively with concept constructors.

---

[1]See http://www.cs.man.ac.uk/~ezolin/dl/

The basic DL is called $\mathcal{AL}$ ($\mathcal{A}$ttributive $\mathcal{L}$anguage) [371]. *Concepts* in $\mathcal{AL}$ are formed according to the following syntax rule:

$$
\begin{array}{rll}
C, D \;\; \rightarrow & A & | \quad \text{(atomic concept)} \\
& \top & | \quad \text{(universal concept)} \\
& \bot & | \quad \text{(bottom concept)} \\
& \neg A & | \quad \text{(atomic negation)} \\
& C \sqcap D & | \quad \text{(concept conjunction)} \\
& \forall R.C & | \quad \text{(universal restriction)} \\
& \exists R.\top & \quad\;\; \text{(unqualified existential restriction)}
\end{array}
$$

Note that, in $\mathcal{AL}$, negation can only be applied to atomic concepts, and only the top concept is allowed in the scope of an existential quantification over a role. Also, the sublanguage of $\mathcal{AL}$ obtained by disallowing atomic negation is called $\mathcal{FL}$ (*Frame Description Language*) and the sublanguage of $\mathcal{FL}$ obtained by disallowing limited existential quantification is called $\mathcal{FL}_0$ [76].

The table below provides an informal First-Order Logic (FOL) reading of concepts and relative concept expression examples.

	Syntax		FOL translation	Example
$C, D \;\rightarrow$	A	|	$A(x)$	Person
	$\top$	|	$\top(x)$	
	$\bot$	|	$\bot(x)$	
	$\neg A$	|	$\neg A(x)$	¬Femal
	$C \sqcap D$	|	$C(x) \wedge D(x)$	Person ⊓ Femal
	$\forall R.C$	|	$\forall y.R(x,y) \rightarrow C(x)$	Person ⊓ ∀hasChild.Femal
	$\exists R.\top$	||	$\exists y.R(x,y)$	Person ⊓ ∃hasChild.⊤

For instance, Person ⊓ ∀hasChild.Femal will denote those persons all of whose children are female. Using the bottom concept, we can also describe those persons without a child by the concept Person ⊓ ∀hasChild. ⊥.

We will often use the abbreviation $\exists R$ in place of the unqualified existential restriction $\exists R.\top$.

A *TBox* $\mathcal{T}$, or *Ontology*, consists of a finite set of *General Concept Inclusion axioms* (GCIs) $C \sqsubseteq D$, where C and D are concepts (read it as "all instances of C are instances of D"). The FOL view of a GCI $C \sqsubseteq D$ is informally $\forall x.C(x) \rightarrow D(x)$. For ease, we use $C = D \in \mathcal{T}$ in place of $C \sqsubseteq D, D \sqsubseteq C \in \mathcal{T}$. Given an atomic concept A and concept C, we call a GCI of the form $A \sqsubseteq C$ *primitive* and call a GCI of the form $A = C$ *definitional*. An example of GCI is Male $\sqsubseteq$ ¬Female.

An *ABox* $\mathcal{A}$ consists of a finite set of *concept and role assertion axioms* $a{:}C$ and $(a, b){:}R$, respectively, where a and b are individuals. Examples of assertion axioms are tim:Person ("tim is a person") and (tim, pat):hasChild. ("tim has pat as child").

A *knowledge base* $\mathcal{K} = \langle \mathcal{T}, \mathcal{A} \rangle$ consists of a TBox $\mathcal{T}$ and an ABox $\mathcal{A}$. For ease, sometimes we write $\mathcal{K}$ as well as $\mathcal{K} = \mathcal{T} \cup \mathcal{A}$.

Example 6. *A simple $\mathcal{AL}$ KB is*

$$\mathcal{K} = \{ \quad \text{tim:Person}, (\text{tim}, \text{pat}):\text{hasChild}, \text{pat}:\neg\text{Male},$$
$$\text{Male} = \neg\text{Female}, \text{Person} \sqsubseteq \forall\text{hasChild.Person},$$
$$\text{MalePerson} = \text{Person} \sqcap \text{Male}, \text{FemalPerson} = \text{Person} \sqcap \text{Femal} \quad \}.$$

From a semantics point of view, an *interpretation* $\mathcal{I}$ is a pair $\mathcal{I} = (\Delta^{\mathcal{I}}, \cdot^{\mathcal{I}})$ consisting of a non-empty set $\Delta^{\mathcal{I}}$ (called the *domain*) and of an *interpretation function* $\cdot^{\mathcal{I}}$ that assigns to each atomic concept a subset of $\Delta^{\mathcal{I}}$, to each role a subset of $\Delta^{\mathcal{I}} \times \Delta^{\mathcal{I}}$ and to each individual a an element in $\Delta^{\mathcal{I}}$ such that $a^{\mathcal{I}} \neq b^{\mathcal{I}}$ if $a \neq b$ (this assumption is called *Unique Name Assumption* - UNA).

The mapping $\cdot^{\mathcal{I}}$ is extended to concepts as follows:

$$
\begin{aligned}
\top^{\mathcal{I}} &= \Delta^{\mathcal{I}} \\
\bot^{\mathcal{I}} &= \emptyset \\
(C \sqcap D)^{\mathcal{I}} &= C^{\mathcal{I}} \cap D^{\mathcal{I}} \\
(\neg A)^{\mathcal{I}} &= \Delta^{\mathcal{I}} \setminus A^{\mathcal{I}} \\
(\forall R.C)^{\mathcal{I}} &= \{x \in \Delta^{\mathcal{I}} \mid R^{\mathcal{I}}(x) \subseteq C^{\mathcal{I}}\} \\
(\exists R.\top)^{\mathcal{I}} &= \{x \in \Delta^{\mathcal{I}} \mid R^{\mathcal{I}}(x) \neq \emptyset\}
\end{aligned}
$$

where $R^{\mathcal{I}}(x) = \{y \colon \langle x, y \rangle \in R^{\mathcal{I}}\}$.

The *satisfiability* of an axiom E in an interpretation $\mathcal{I} = (\Delta^{\mathcal{I}}, \cdot^{\mathcal{I}})$, denoted $\mathcal{I} \models E$, is defined as follows: $\mathcal{I} \models C \sqsubseteq D$ iff $C^{\mathcal{I}} \subseteq D^{\mathcal{I}}$, $\mathcal{I} \models a{:}C$ iff $a^{\mathcal{I}} \in C^{\mathcal{I}}$, and $\mathcal{I} \models (a, b){:}R$ iff $\langle a^{\mathcal{I}}, b^{\mathcal{I}} \rangle \in R^{\mathcal{I}}$.

For a finite set of axioms $\mathcal{E}$, we say that $\mathcal{I}$ *satisfies* $\mathcal{E}$ iff $\mathcal{I}$ satisfies each element in $\mathcal{E}$. If $\mathcal{I} \models E$ (resp. $\mathcal{I} \models \mathcal{E}$) we say that $\mathcal{I}$ is a *model* of E (resp. $\mathcal{E}$). $\mathcal{I}$ *satisfies* (is a *model* of) a knowledge base $\mathcal{K} = \langle \mathcal{T}, \mathcal{A} \rangle$, denoted $\mathcal{I} \models \mathcal{K}$, iff $\mathcal{I}$ is a model of each component $\mathcal{T}$ and $\mathcal{A}$, respectively. An axiom E is a *logical consequence* of a knowledge base $\mathcal{K}$, denoted $\mathcal{K} \models E$, iff every model of $\mathcal{K}$ satisfies E. Determining whether $\mathcal{K} \models a{:}C$ is called the *instance checking problem*, while determining whether $\mathcal{K} \models C \sqsubseteq D$ is called the *subsumption problem*.

Given $\mathcal{K}$, we say that two concepts C and D are *equivalent*, denoted $C \equiv_{\mathcal{K}} D$ iff in any model $\mathcal{I}$ of $\mathcal{K}$, $C^{\mathcal{I}} = D^{\mathcal{I}}$. We say that C is *coherent* iff there is a model $\mathcal{I}$ of $\mathcal{K}$ such that $C^{\mathcal{I}} \neq \emptyset$. If the knowledge base is empty, we simply omit $\mathcal{K}$ as subscript.

Example 7. *Consider the KB in Example 6. It can be verified that the KB is satisfiable and that*

$$\mathcal{K} \models \text{MalePerson} \sqsubseteq \neg\text{FemalPerson}$$
$$\mathcal{K} \models \text{pat:FemalPerson} .$$

Informally, e.g., $\mathcal{K} \models$ pat:FemalPerson holds because Pat is not male and, thus, is female. Tim is a person, a person has a person as child, and, thus, Pat, which is a child of Tim, is a person, too. Therefore, Pat is a female person.

4.2.2 The DL Family

We next provide an overview of the major logics belonging to the DL family.

4.2.2.1 DLs Naming Convention

DLs are a family of logics that can be identified by the constructs they use. Typically, most constructs have a letter to identify them and their use will be denoted by adding the letter to the basic description language $\mathcal{AL}$. For instance, the DL $\mathcal{ALC}$, is obtained from $\mathcal{AL}$ by adding the construct identified by $\mathcal{C}$ (concept complement) to $\mathcal{AL}$. Below, a list of major DL constructors, where C, D are concepts and $\mathcal{I}$ is an interpretation.

$\mathcal{C}$: Concept negation, denoted $\neg C$, and semantics

$$(\neg C)^{\mathcal{I}} = \Delta^{\mathcal{I}} \setminus C^{\mathcal{I}} .$$

Note that $\neg\neg C \equiv C$.

$\mathcal{U}$: Concept disjunction, denoted $C \sqcup D$, and semantics

$$(C \sqcup D)^{\mathcal{I}} = C^{\mathcal{I}} \cup D^{\mathcal{I}} .$$

Note that $C \sqcup D \equiv \neg(\neg C \sqcap \neg D)$. Also, a GCI $C \sqsubseteq D$ is the same as $\top \sqsubseteq \neg C \sqcup D$.

$\mathcal{E}$: Qualified existential restriction, $\exists R.C$, and semantics

$$(\exists R.C)^{\mathcal{I}} = \{x \in \Delta^{\mathcal{I}} \mid R^{\mathcal{I}}(x) \cap C^{\mathcal{I}} \neq \emptyset\} .$$

Note that $\exists R.C \equiv \neg\forall R.C$.

$\mathcal{O}$: Nominals (singleton class), denoted $\{a\}$, and semantics

$$\{a\}^{\mathcal{I}} = \{a^{\mathcal{I}}\} .$$

Note that $a{:}C$ can be expressed as $\{a\} \sqsubseteq C$, while $(a,b){:}R$ can be expressed as $\{a\} \sqsubseteq \exists R.\{b\}$.

$\mathcal{N}$: Number restrictions, denoted $(\geq n\ R)$ and $(\leq n\ R)$, and semantics

$$\begin{aligned}
(\geq n\ R)^{\mathcal{I}} &= \{x \in \Delta^{\mathcal{I}} \mid \sharp R^{\mathcal{I}}(x) \geq n\} \\
(\leq n\ R)^{\mathcal{I}} &= \{x \in \Delta^{\mathcal{I}} \mid \sharp R^{\mathcal{I}}(x) \leq n\} ,
\end{aligned}$$

where $\sharp S$ is the cardinality of a set S. Note that $(\leq n\ R) \equiv \neg(\geq n{+}1\ R)$.

$\mathcal{Q}$: Qualified number restrictions, denoted $(\geq n\ R.C)$ and $(\leq n\ R.C)$, and semantics

$$(\geq n\ R.C)^{\mathcal{I}} = \{x \in \Delta^{\mathcal{I}} \mid \sharp(R^{\mathcal{I}}(x) \cap C^{\mathcal{I}}) \geq n\}$$
$$(\leq n\ R.C)^{\mathcal{I}} = \{x \in \Delta^{\mathcal{I}} \mid \sharp(R^{\mathcal{I}}(x) \cap C^{\mathcal{I}}) \leq n\}\ .$$

Note that $(\leq n\ R.C) \equiv \neg(\geq n+1\ R.C)$.

$\mathcal{I}$: Inverse role, denote R^-, and semantics

$$(R^-)^{\mathcal{I}} = \{\langle y, x \rangle \mid \langle x, y \rangle \in R^{\mathcal{I}}\}\ .$$

Note that $(R^-)^-$ is the same as R. Sometimes we write R^- with the intended meaning that $R^- = P^-$ if $R = P$, and $R^- = P$, if $R = P^-$.

$\mathcal{F}$: Local functional role, denoted $(\leq 1\ R)$, and semantics

$$(\leq 1\ R)^{\mathcal{I}} = \{x \in \Delta^{\mathcal{I}} \mid \sharp R^{\mathcal{I}}(x) \leq 1\}\ .$$

$\mathcal{F}_g$: Global functional role axiom, denoted $\mathsf{fun}(S)$, and semantics

$$\mathcal{I} \models \mathsf{fun}(S)\ \text{iff for all } x \in \Delta^{\mathcal{I}}.\ \sharp S^{\mathcal{I}}(x) \leq 1\ .$$

$\mathcal{H}$: Role inclusion axiom, denoted $R_1 \sqsubseteq R_2$, and semantics

$$\mathcal{I} \models R_1 \sqsubseteq R_2\ \text{iff } R_1^{\mathcal{I}} \subseteq R_2^{\mathcal{I}}\ .$$

$\mathcal{R}$: Complex role inclusion axiom, denoted $R \circ S \sqsubseteq R$ and $R \circ S \sqsubseteq S$, and semantics

$$\mathcal{I} \models R \circ S \sqsubseteq R\ \text{iff } R^{\mathcal{I}} \circ S^{\mathcal{I}} \subseteq R^{\mathcal{I}}$$
$$\mathcal{I} \models R \circ S \sqsubseteq S\ \text{iff } R^{\mathcal{I}} \circ S^{\mathcal{I}} \subseteq S^{\mathcal{I}}\ .$$

Note that $R \circ S \sqsubseteq R$ ($R \circ S \sqsubseteq S$) is also denoted as $RS \sqsubseteq R$ ($RS \sqsubseteq S$).

$\mathcal{R}_+$: Transitive role axiom, denoted $\mathsf{trans}(R)$, and semantics

$$\mathsf{trans}(R)^{\mathcal{I}}\ \text{iff } R^{\mathcal{I}}\ \text{transitive}\ .$$

Note that $\mathsf{trans}(R)$ can be expressed as $R \circ R \sqsubseteq R$.

$\mathcal{S}$: Used for $\mathcal{ALC}$ with transitive roles, *i.e.*, the DL $\mathcal{ALCR}_+$.

We will also use the following shorthands:

- $C_1 \to C_2$ for $\neg C_1 \sqcup C_2$;

- $C_1 \leftrightarrow C_2$ for $(C_1 \rightarrow C_2) \sqcap (C_2 \rightarrow C_1)$;

- $\mathsf{dom}(R, C)$, called *domain restriction* axiom, for $\exists R.\top \sqsubseteq C$;

- $\mathsf{ran}(R, C)$, called *range restriction* axiom, for $\top \sqsubseteq \forall R.C$;

- $\mathsf{disj}(C, D)$, called *disjointness* axiom, for $C \sqcap D \sqsubseteq \bot$;

- $(= n\ R.C)$ for $(\geq n\ R.C) \sqcap (\leq n\ R.C)$;

- $(= n\ R)$ for $(= n\ R.\top)$.

4.2.2.2 Concrete Domains

Concrete domains [21, 294, 295] are used to extend DL languages to deal with datatypes, such as strings and integers. The elementary ingredients are as follows. We assume a set of *data values*, a set of *elementary datatypes*, and a set of *datatype predicates*, where each datatype predicate has a predefined arity $n \geq 1$. A *datatype* is an elementary datatype or a finite set of data values. A *datatype theory* $\mathbf{D} = \langle \Delta^{\mathbf{D}}, \cdot^{\mathbf{D}} \rangle$ consists of a datatype domain $\Delta^{\mathbf{D}}$ and a mapping $\cdot^{\mathbf{D}}$ that assigns to each data value an element of $\Delta^{\mathbf{D}}$, to each elementary datatype a subset of $\Delta^{\mathbf{D}}$, and to each datatype predicate p of arity n a relation over $\Delta^{\mathbf{D}}$ of arity n. We extend $\cdot^{\mathbf{D}}$ to all datatypes by $\{v_1, \ldots\}^{\mathbf{D}} = \{v_1^{\mathbf{D}}, \ldots\}$. For example, over the integers, $\geq_{20}$ may be a unary predicate denoting the set of integers greater or equal to 20. Concerning roles, a role R is either an *object property* or a *datatype property*. An interpretation maps an *object property* into a subset of $\Delta^{\mathcal{I}} \times \Delta^{\mathcal{I}}$, while maps a *datatype property* into a subset of $\Delta^{\mathcal{I}} \times \Delta^{\mathbf{D}}$. A datatype property does not have an inverse. For instance,

$$\mathsf{Person} \sqcap \exists \mathsf{age}.\geq_{20} \tag{4.1}$$

is a concept denoting the set of people whose age is at least 20.

We also use an alphabet for concrete individuals, denoted v, and extend an interpretation to concrete individuals by mapping them into $\Delta^{\mathbf{D}}$. As for individuals, we adopt the UNA, *i.e.*, $v_1^{\mathcal{I}} \neq v_2^{\mathcal{I}}$ if $v_1 \neq v_2$.

Example 8. *Consider $\mathcal{K}$ with*

$$\begin{aligned}
&\mathsf{AdultPerson} = \mathsf{Person} \sqcap \exists \mathsf{age}.\geq_{20} \\
&\mathsf{fun}(\mathsf{age}) \\
&\mathsf{tom}{:}\mathsf{Person} \\
&(\mathsf{tom}, 34){:}\mathsf{age}
\end{aligned}$$

Then

$$\mathcal{K} \models \mathsf{tom}{:}\mathsf{AdultPerson}\ .$$

Informally, Tom is a person whose age is 34. Since an adult people is identified as a person having an age no less than 20, Tom is an adult person, too.

To indicate that a DL language $\mathcal{L}$ has been extended with concrete domains, the convention is to append the label $(\mathbf{D})$ to $\mathcal{L}$. For instance, $\mathcal{ALC}(\mathbf{D})$ denotes the DL language $\mathcal{ALC}$ extended with the concrete domain $\mathbf{D}$.

Eventually, for an n-ary concrete predicate p, for functional datatype properties $f_1, \ldots f_n$, we will use the expression

$$p(f_1, \ldots, f_n)$$

as concept expression with semantics

$$p(f_1, \ldots, f_n)^{\mathcal{I}} = \{x \in \Delta^{\mathcal{I}} \mid \exists y_i \in \Delta^{\mathbf{D}}, f_i(x) = y_i, \langle y_1, \ldots, y_n \rangle \in p^{\mathbf{D}}, i = 1 \ldots n\} \,.$$

For instance, the concept expression 4.1 can also be written as

$$\text{Person} \sqcap \geq_{20}(\text{age}) \,.$$

4.2.2.3   The $\mathcal{AL}$ Family and $\mathcal{SROIQ}(\mathbf{D})$

In the $\mathcal{AL}$ family we have essentially all languages obtained from $\mathcal{AL}$ by adding the construct identified by some letter described above. Prominent representatives are

$\mathcal{ALC}$. The DL $\mathcal{ALC}$ [371] is the reference DL language and is typically used whenever new ideas and extensions are explored. $\mathcal{ALC}$ is also closely related to *Hybrid Logics* [11], which are roughly modal logics allowing to talk about the worlds. This is not surprising due to the close relationship between $\mathcal{ALC}$ and Propositional Multimodal Logic $\mathbf{K}$ [370] (intuitively, $\forall R.C \mapsto \Box_R C$ and $\exists R.C \mapsto \Diamond_R C$ and $a{:}C \mapsto @_a C$ and $\top \sqsubseteq C \mapsto \Box_U C$, where U is an universal accessibility relation[2]). From a computational complexity point of view, *e.g.*, the knowledge base satisfiability problem is ExpTime-complete [131].

$\mathcal{SHIF}$. The importance of the DL $\mathcal{SHIF}$ is due to the fact that it is the logical counterpart of the OWL 1 Lite [204, 205]. With that we mean that OWL 1 Lite constructs can be mapped into the DL $\mathcal{SHIF}(\mathbf{D})$. Note that in number restrictions, only so-called *simple roles* (*i.e.*, which are neither transitive nor have a transitive subrole) are allowed. From a computational complexity point of view, *e.g.*, the knowledge base satisfiability problem is ExpTime-complete [193, 442].

$\mathcal{SHOIN}$. The importance of the DL $\mathcal{SHOIN}$ is due to the fact that it is the logical counterpart of the OWL 1 DL [201, 204, 205, 207, 208], *i.e.*, OWL 1 DL constructs can be mapped into the DL $\mathcal{SHOIN}(\mathbf{D})$. As for $\mathcal{SHIF}$, in number restrictions, only *simple roles* are allowed. From a computational complexity point of view, *e.g.*, the knowledge base satisfiability problem is NExpTime-complete [171, 441, 442].

---

[2]For all worlds w, w', $U(w, w')$ holds.

$\mathcal{SROIQ}$. The importance of the DL $\mathcal{SROIQ}$ is due to the fact that it is the logical counterpart of the OWL 2 [101, 203], *i.e.*, OWL 2 constructs can be mapped into the DL $\mathcal{SROIQ}(\mathbf{D})$. In number restrictions, only *simple roles* are allowed, the set of complex role inclusions (and ordinary role inclusions) is supposed to be acyclic (in a non-standard way), and there are some other features, such as disjoint roles, reflexive and irreflexive roles, asymmetric roles, etc. From a computational complexity point of view, *e.g.*, the knowledge base satisfiability problem is 2NExpTime-complete [228].

For the sake of completeness, we recap here $\mathcal{SROIQ}(\mathbf{D})$ [203]. The constructs are illustrated in Table 4.1, where we use the following notation:

- C, D are concepts

- A is an atomic concept

- R is an object property

- S is a simple object property (also, called simple role, defined below)

- T is a datatype property

- a, b are individuals, v is a concrete individual

- $\mathbf{d}$ is a concrete predicate

- m is a natural number

Note that $\mathsf{trans}(R)$ is the same as $RR \sqsubseteq R$, and $\mathsf{sym}(R)$ is the same as $R^- \sqsubseteq R$.

The notion of simple role is defined as follows. We start with the definition of a (regular) role hierarchy whose definition involves a certain ordering on object properties, called *regular*. A strict partial order $\prec$ on a set A is an irreflexive and transitive relation on A. A strict partial order on the set of an object properties R and their inverse R^- is called a *regular order* if satisfies, additionally, $S \prec R$ iff $S^- \prec R^-$, for all object properties R and S. Note, in particular, that the irreflexivity ensures that neither $S \prec S^-$ nor $S^- \prec S$ hold. Now, let $\prec$ be a regular order. A *role inclusion axiom* (RIA for short) is an expression of the form $w \sqsubseteq R$, where w is a finite string of object properties not including the universal role U, and $R \neq U$ is an object property. A RIA $w \sqsubseteq R$, is $\prec$-regular if

1. $w = RR$, or

2. $w = R^-$, or

3. $w = S_1 \ldots S_n$ and $S_i \prec R$, for all i, or

4. $w = RS_1 \ldots S_n$ and $S_i \prec R$, for all i, or

5. $w = S_1 \ldots S_n R$ and $S_i \prec R$, for all i.

TABLE 4.1: Syntax and semantics of the DL $\mathcal{SROIQ}(\mathbf{D})$.

Concepts	Syntax (C)	FOL Reading of $C(x)$
(C1)	A	$A(x)$
(C2)	$\top$	1
(C3)	$\bot$	0
(C4)	$C \sqcap D$	$C(x) \wedge D(x)$
(C5)	$C \sqcup D$	$C(x) \vee D(x)$
(C6)	$\neg C$	$\neg C(x)$
(C7)	$\forall R.C$	$\forall y.R(x,y) \to C(y)$
(C8)	$\exists R.C$	$\exists y.R(x,y) \wedge C(y)$
(C9)	$\forall T.\mathbf{d}$	$\forall v.T(x,v) \to \mathbf{d}(v)$
(C10)	$\exists T.\mathbf{d}$	$\exists v.T(x,v) \wedge \mathbf{d}(v)$
(C11)	$\{a\}$	$x = a$
(C12)	$(\geq m\ S.C)$	$\exists y_1 \ldots \exists y_m . \bigwedge_{i=1}^{m}(S(x,y_i) \wedge C(y_i)) \wedge \bigwedge_{1 \leq j < k \leq m} y_j \neq y_k$
(C13)	$(\leq m\ S.C)$	$\forall y_1 \ldots \forall y_{m+1} . \bigwedge_{i=1}^{m}(S(x,y_i) \wedge C(y_i)) \to \bigvee_{1 \leq j < k \leq m} y_j = y_k$
(C14)	$(\geq m\ T.\mathbf{d})$	$\exists v_1 \ldots \exists v_m . \bigwedge_{i=1}^{m}(T(x,v_i) \wedge \mathbf{d}(v_i)) \wedge \bigwedge_{1 \leq j < k \leq m} v_j \neq v_k$
(C15)	$(\leq m\ T.\mathbf{d})$	$\forall v_1 \ldots \forall v_{m+1} . \bigwedge_{i=1}^{m}(T(x,v_i) \wedge \mathbf{d}(v_i)) \to \bigvee_{1 \leq j < k \leq m} v_j = v_k$
(C16)	$\exists S.\mathsf{Self}$	$S(x,x)$
Roles	**Syntax (R)**	**Semantics of $R(x,y)$**
(R1)	R	$R(x,y)$
(R2)	R^-	$R(y,x)$
(R3)	U	1
Axiom	**Syntax (E)**	**Semantics ($\mathcal{I}$ satisfies E if …)**
(A1)	$a{:}C$	$C(a)$
(A2)	$(a,b){:}R$	$R(a,b)$
(A3)	$(a,b){:}\neg R$	$\neg R(a,b)$
(A4)	$(a,v){:}T$	$T(a,v)$
(A5)	$(a,v){:}\neg T$	$\neg T(a,v)$
(A6)	$C \sqsubseteq D$	$\forall x.C(x) \to D(x)$
(A7)	$R_1 \ldots R_n \sqsubseteq R$	$\forall x_1 \forall x_{n+1} \exists x_2 \ldots$
		$\quad \exists x_n.(R_1(x_1,x_2) \wedge \ldots \wedge R_n(x_n,x_{n+1})) \to R(x_1,x_{n+1})$
(A8)	$T_1 \sqsubseteq T_2$	$\forall x \forall v.T_1(x,v) \to T_2(x,v)$
(A9)	$\mathsf{trans}(R)$	$\forall x \forall y \forall z.R(x,z) \wedge R(z,y) \to R(x,y)$
(A10)	$\mathsf{disj}(S_1,S_2)$	$\forall x \forall y.S_1(x,y) \wedge S_2(x,y) = 0$
(A11)	$\mathsf{disj}(T_1,T_2)$	$\forall x \forall v.T_1(x,v) \wedge T_2(x,v) = 0$
(A12)	$\mathsf{ref}(R)$	$\forall x.R(x,x)$
(A13)	$\mathsf{irr}(S)$	$\forall x.\neg S(x,x)$
(A14)	$\mathsf{sym}(R)$	$\forall x \forall y.R(x,y) = R(y,x)$
(A15)	$\mathsf{asy}(S)$	$\forall x \forall y,\ S(x,y) \to \neg S(y,x)$

An *RBox*, denoted $\mathcal{R}$, consists of a finite set of axioms of the form $(A7)-(A15)$ in Table 4.1 and a $\mathcal{SROIQ}(\mathbf{D})$ knowledge base is now a triple $\mathcal{K} = \langle \mathcal{T}, \mathcal{A}, \mathcal{R} \rangle$, where $\mathcal{R}$ is *regular* and *simple*. $\mathcal{R}$ is *regular* if there is a regular order $\prec$ such that all RIAs in $\mathcal{R}$ are $\prec$-regular. Essentially, regularity prevents a role hierarchy from containing cyclic dependencies. Eventually, *simple* roles are defined inductively as follows:

- a role is simple if it does not occur on the right-hand side of a RIA in $\mathcal{R}$

- an inverse role R^- is simple if R is, and

- if R occurs on the right hand side of an RIA in $\mathcal{R}$, then R is simple if, for each $w \sqsubseteq R \in \mathcal{R}$, $w = S$ for a simple role S.

Then $\mathcal{R}$ is *simple* if all roles occurring in role axioms of the form $(A9) - (A15)$ are simple.

With $sub(\mathcal{K})$ we denote the set of (sub)concept expressions occurring in $\mathcal{K}$.

4.2.2.4 The $\mathcal{EL}$ Family

The importance of the $\mathcal{EL}$ DL family [13, 18, 178] is due to the fact that it is the logical counterpart of the OWL 2 EL profile [341], *i.e.*, OWL 2 EL constructs can be mapped into the DL $\mathcal{EL}^{++}(\mathbf{D})$. We recall that it enables polynomial time algorithms for all the standard reasoning tasks, *i.e.*, the ontology satisfiability problem, the subsumption problem, and the instance checking problem and, thus, it is particularly suitable for applications where very large ontologies are needed, and where expressive power can be traded for performance guarantees.

We next recap succinctly the DL $\mathcal{EL}$ [17] and then extend it to $\mathcal{EL}^{++}(\mathbf{D})$ [13, 18]. Specifically, in $\mathcal{EL}$ [17] concept expressions are restricted to be of the form

$$
\begin{aligned}
C, D \quad \rightarrow \quad & A & | & \quad \text{(atomic concept)} \\
& \top & | & \quad \text{(universal concept)} \\
& C \sqcap D & | & \quad \text{(concept conjunction)} \\
& \exists R.C & & \quad \text{(qualified existential restriction)}
\end{aligned}
$$

and a TBox consists of definitional GCIs of the form $A = C$ only.

$\mathcal{EL}^{++}(\mathbf{D})$, which extends $\mathcal{EL}$, has been presented in [13] and then further extend in [18]. $\mathcal{EL}^{++}(\mathbf{D})$ as from [13], extends $\mathcal{EL}$ by allowing (*i*) the bottom concept $\bot$, nominal $\{a\}$, and concrete concept expressions of the form $p(f_1, \ldots, f_n)$; (*ii*) GCIs of the general form $C \sqsubseteq D$; and (*iii*) RIAs. Eventually, [18] allows further domain and range restrictions axioms and reflexive role axioms. Note that transitive role axioms, $\mathsf{trans}(R)$, are supported via $RR \sqsubseteq R$. Note also that disjointness axioms, $\mathsf{disj}(C, D)$, are supported via $C \sqcap D \sqsubseteq \bot$.

For the sake of ease of presentation, we summarize here $\mathcal{EL}^{++}(\mathbf{D})$ as from [18] in Table 4.2.

Eventually, the DL $\mathcal{EL}^+$ [15, 25] is as $\mathcal{EL}$, except that inclusion axioms have a more general form than in $\mathcal{EL}$: namely, general inclusion axioms are of the form $C \sqsubseteq D$, where C, D are $\mathcal{EL}$ concepts, while role inclusion axioms are of the form $R_1 \cdots R_n \sqsubseteq R$, where R_i and R are role names.

4.2.2.5 The DL-Lite Family

The importance of the DL-Lite DL family [12, 82, 83, 87] is due to the fact that it is the logical counterpart of the OWL 2 QL profile [341], *i.e.*, OWL 2 QL constructs can be mapped into the DL DL-Lite$_{\mathcal{R}}(\mathbf{D})$, which, we recall, was designed so that sound and complete query answering is in LogSpace (more precisely, in AC^0) with respect to the size of the data (assertions), while providing many of the main features necessary to express conceptual models such as UML class diagrams and ER diagrams.

TABLE 4.2: Syntax of $\mathcal{EL}^{++}(\mathbf{D})$.

Concept expressions:	$\top$
	$\bot$
	$\{a\}$
	$C \sqcap D$
	$\exists R.C$
	$p(f_1, \ldots, f_n)$
Axioms:	$C \sqsubseteq D$
	$R_1 \cdots R_n \sqsubseteq R$
	$\mathsf{dom}(R) \sqsubseteq C$
	$\mathsf{ran}(R) \sqsubseteq C$
	$\mathsf{ref}(R)$
	$a{:}C$
	$(a,b){:}R$

We next recap succinctly the DL DL-Lite DL family [87]. We start with the language DL-Lite$_{core}$ that is the core language for the whole family. Concepts and roles are formed according to the following syntax (A is an atomic concept, P is an atomic role, and P^- is its inverse):

$$
\begin{aligned}
B &\longrightarrow A \mid \exists R \\
C &\longrightarrow B \mid \neg B \\
R &\longrightarrow P \mid P^- \\
E &\longrightarrow R \mid \neg R .
\end{aligned}
$$

B denotes a *basic concept*, that is, a concept that can be either an atomic concept or a concept of the form $\exists R$, where R denotes a *basic role*, that is, a role that is either an atomic role or the inverse of an atomic role. Finally, C denotes a concept, which can be a basic concept or its negation, whereas E denotes a role, which can be a basic role or its negation. Sometimes we write $\neg C$ (resp., $\neg E$) with the intended meaning that $\neg C = \neg A$ if $C = A$ (resp., $\neg E = \neg R$ if $E = R$), and $\neg C = A$, if $C = \neg A$ (resp., $\neg E = R$, if $E = \neg R$)[3].

Inclusion axioms are of the form

$$B \sqsubseteq C$$

We might include $B_1 \sqcup B_2$ in the constructs for the left-hand side of inclusion axioms and $C_1 \sqcap C_2$ in the constructs for the right-hand side. In this way, however, we would not extend the expressive capabilities of the language, since these constructs can be simulated by considering that $B_1 \sqcup B_2 \sqsubseteq C$ is equivalent to the pair of assertions $B_1 \sqsubseteq C$ and $B_2 \sqsubseteq C$, and that $B \sqsubseteq C_1 \sqcap C_2$ is equivalent to $B \sqsubseteq C_1$ and $B \sqsubseteq C_2$. Similarly, we might add $\bot$ to the constructs for the left-hand side and $\top$ to those for the right-hand side.

---

[3]Of course, for any interpretation $\mathcal{I}$, $(\neg R)^{\mathcal{I}} = \Delta^{\mathcal{I}} \times \Delta^{\mathcal{I}} \setminus R^{\mathcal{I}}$.

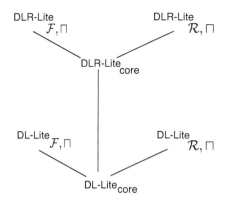

FIGURE 4.1: Excerpt of the DL-Lite family.

Assertion axioms are, as usual of the form $a{:}A$ and $(a,b){:}P$. Note that an assertion $a{:}C$ can be simulated in DL-Lite$_{core}$ by adding $A \sqsubseteq C$ to the TBox, and $a{:}A$ to the ABox, where A is a new atomic concept. Similarly, assertion axioms of the form $(a,b){:}E$ can be simulated, with the same mechanisms, in those extensions of DL-Lite$_{core}$ that allow for inclusion axioms on roles (see below).

DL-Lite$_{\mathcal{R}}$ is now obtained by extending DL-Lite$_{core}$ with the ability of specifying inclusion axioms between roles of the form

$$R \sqsubseteq E .$$

where R and E are defined as above, DL-Lite$_\sqcap$ is obtained by extending DL-Lite$_{core}$ allowing the conjunction of basic concepts on the left-hand side of concept inclusions, and DL-Lite$_{\mathcal{F}}$ is obtained by extending DL-Lite$_{core}$ with global functional roles. Worth mentioning is also $\mathcal{DLR}$ [19, Chapter 16] and the $\mathcal{DLR}$-Lite family [83, 84, 85, 86, 89], which is the extension of DL-Lite family to the case in which the predicates are no more unary (concepts) or binary (roles), but n-ary in general (see Figure 4.1 for an excerpt of the DL-Lite family). For a more detailed description of the DL-Lite family we refer the reader to [12].

We refer to assertions of the form $B_1 \sqsubseteq B_2$ (resp. $R_1 \sqsubseteq R_2$) as *positive inclusion assertions* (PIs), and to assertions of the form $B_1 \sqsubseteq \neg B_2$ (resp. $R_1 \sqsubseteq \neg R_2$) as *negative inclusion assertions* (NIs).

Note also that in fact, DL-Lite$_{\mathcal{R}}$ might be enhanced with the capability of managing qualified existential quantification on the right-hand side of inclusion assertions on concepts [83]. This construct, however, can be simulated by suitably making use of inclusions between roles and unqualified existential quantification of concepts in inclusions between concepts (see Appendix B).

4.2.2.6   The Horn-DL Family

The importance of the *Horn*-DL family [173, 440] is due to the fact that it is related to the logical counterpart of the OWL 2 RL profile [341]. Specifically, OWL 2 RL constructs can be mapped into a Horn-DL. This is achieved by defining a syntactic subset of OWL 2, which is amenable to implementation using rule-based technologies. Essentially, the restrictions are designed so as to avoid the need to infer the existence of individuals not explicitly present in the knowledge base, and to avoid the need for nondeterministic reasoning. Here we report the DL specification of OWL 2 RL. Specifically, concepts are formed according to the following syntax (A is an atomic concept, $m \in \{0, 1\}$, l is a value of the concrete domain, R is an object property, a individual, T is a datatype property):

$$
\begin{aligned}
B &\longrightarrow A \mid \{a\} \mid B_1 \sqcap B_2 \mid B_1 \sqcup B_2 \mid \exists R.B \mid \exists T.\mathbf{d} \\
C &\longrightarrow A \mid C_1 \sqcap C_2 \mid \neg B \mid \forall R.C \mid \exists R.\{a\} \mid \forall T.\mathbf{d} \mid \\
  &\qquad (\leq m\, S.B) \mid (\leq m\, S) \mid (\leq m\, T.\mathbf{d}) \\
D &\longrightarrow \exists R.\{a\} \mid \exists T. =_l \mid D_1 \sqcap D_2 \\
R &\longrightarrow P \mid P^-
\end{aligned}
$$

Axioms have the form

$$
\begin{aligned}
B &\sqsubseteq C \\
A &= D \\
R_1 &\sqsubseteq R_2 \\
R_1 &= R_2
\end{aligned}
$$

and

$$
\begin{aligned}
&\mathsf{disj}(B_1, B_2) \\
&\mathsf{dom}(R, C) \\
&\mathsf{ran}(R, C) \\
&\mathsf{dom}(T, C) \\
&\mathsf{fun}(R) \\
&\mathsf{irr}(R) \\
&\mathsf{sym}(R) \\
&\mathsf{asy}(R) \\
&\mathsf{trans}(R) \\
&\mathsf{disj}(R_1, R_2)
\end{aligned}
$$

Assertion axioms are as for $\mathcal{SROIQ}(\mathbf{D})$, except that for in concept assertions the concept has to be of the form C above: *i.e.*,

$$
a{:}C, (a, b){:}R, (a, b){:}\neg R, (a, v){:}T, (a, v){:}\neg T \ .
$$

For completeness, Appendix B describes OWL 2 and its profiles and the mapping to the appropriate DL.

4.3 Conjunctive Queries

As for RDFS, we introduce the notion of conjunctive query (see Section 3.3).

A *conjunctive query* is, similarly to RDFS (see Equation (3.1)) a rule-like expression of the form

$$q(\mathbf{x}) \leftarrow \exists \mathbf{y}.\varphi(\mathbf{x}, \mathbf{y}) \qquad (4.2)$$

where now the rule body $\varphi(\mathbf{x}, \mathbf{y})$ is a conjunction[4] of unary or binary predicates $P_i(\mathbf{z}_i)$ $(1 \le i \le n)$, where P_i is either an atomic concept A or an atomic role R, and $\mathbf{z}_i$ is a vector of distinguished or non-distinguished variables. If P_i is an atomic concept (resp., a role) then $\mathbf{z}_i$ is unary (resp., binary) tuple.

For instance, by referring to Example 8,

$$q(x, y) \leftarrow \mathsf{AdultPerson}(x), \mathsf{age}(x, y)$$

is a conjunctive query, whose intended meaning is to retrieve all adult people and their age.

Given a vector $\mathbf{x} = \langle x_1, \ldots, x_k \rangle$ of variables, a *substitution* over $\mathbf{x}$ is a vector of individuals $\mathbf{t}$ replacing variables in $\mathbf{x}$ with individuals. Then, given a query $q(\mathbf{x}) \leftarrow \exists \mathbf{y}.\varphi(\mathbf{x}, \mathbf{y})$, and two substitutions $\mathbf{t}, \mathbf{t}'$ over $\mathbf{x}$ and $\mathbf{y}$, respectively, the *query instantiation* $\varphi(\mathbf{t}, \mathbf{t}')$ is derived from $\varphi(\mathbf{x}, \mathbf{y})$ by replacing $\mathbf{x}$ and $\mathbf{y}$ with $\mathbf{t}$ and $\mathbf{t}'$, respectively. Note that a query instantiation $\varphi(\mathbf{t}, \mathbf{t}')$ is an ABox.

We adopt here the following notion of entailment. Given a knowledge base $\mathcal{K}$, a query $q(\mathbf{x}) \leftarrow \exists \mathbf{y}.\varphi(\mathbf{x}, \mathbf{y})$, and a vector $\mathbf{t}$ of individuals occurring in $\mathcal{K}$, we say that $q(\mathbf{t})$ is *entailed* by $\mathcal{K}$, denoted $\mathcal{K} \models q(\mathbf{t})$, if and only if there is a vector $\mathbf{t}'$ of individuals occurring in $\mathcal{K}$ such that in any model $\mathcal{I}$ of $\mathcal{K}$, $\mathcal{I}$ is a model of any atom in the query instantiation $\varphi(\mathbf{t}, \mathbf{t}')$.

If $\mathcal{K} \models q(\mathbf{t})$ then $\mathbf{t}$ is called a *answer* to q. We call these kinds of answers also *certain answers*. The *answer set* of q w.r.t. $\mathcal{K}$ is defined as

$$ans(\mathcal{K}, q) = \{ \mathbf{t} \mid \mathcal{K} \models q(\mathbf{t}) \} \ .$$

Remark 6. *Note that there is a subtle difference with the usual definition of answer, stated as follows:*

> *Given a knowledge base $\mathcal{K}$, a query $q(\mathbf{x}) \leftarrow \exists \mathbf{y}.\varphi(\mathbf{x}, \mathbf{y})$, and a vector $\mathbf{t}$ of individuals occurring in $\mathcal{K}$, we say that $q(\mathbf{t})$ is entailed by $\mathcal{K}$, denoted $\mathcal{K} \models q(\mathbf{t})$, if and only if for any model $\mathcal{I}$ of $\mathcal{K}$, $\mathcal{I}$ is a model of the FOL formula $\exists \mathbf{y}.\varphi(\mathbf{t}, \mathbf{y})$, according to the standard definitions of first-order logic. We denote the answer set according to this definition as $ans^{FOL}(\mathcal{K}, q)$.*

---

[4]Again we use the symbol ",″ to denote conjunction in the rule body.

The following example shows the difference among our definition of answer set and the usual one according to Remark 6. So, consider the simple knowledge base

$$\mathcal{K} = \{(a,c):R, b:\exists R\}$$

and the conjunctive query

$$q(x) \leftarrow R(x,y) .$$

Then it is easily verified that

$$\begin{aligned} ans(\mathcal{K},q) &= \{a\} \\ ans^{FOL}(\mathcal{K},q) &= \{a,b\} . \end{aligned}$$

The difference is due to the fact that in our case the instantiation of the non-distinguished variables has to be *known* independently from any model of $\mathcal{K}$, while according to Remark 6, for any model $\mathcal{I}$ of $\mathcal{K}$, the non-distinguished variables **y** may be substituted with domain elements depending on $\mathcal{I}$. Of course,

$$ans(\mathcal{K},q) \subseteq ans^{FOL}(\mathcal{K},q)$$

holds.

In general, our definition is amenable to a more efficient implementation and typically the former has lower computational complexity than the latter. In fact, while determining whether $a \in ans(\mathcal{K},q)$ inherits the computational complexity of the complexity of entailment in the underlying DL (assuming the size of q bounded by the size of $\mathcal{K}$), this may not be the case under Remark 6, e.g., determining whether $a \in ans^{FOL}(\mathcal{K},q)$ for $\mathcal{ALCI}$ is 2ExpTime-complete [296] (see, *e.g.*, [88, 145, 334, 335, 337, 336] for other results), while entailment can be decided in ExpTime [442].

Specifically, note that a simple procedure to determine the answer set $ans(\mathcal{K},q)$ consists in computing off-line the instances of all atomics concepts and roles occurring in $\mathcal{K}$, store them into a relational database $DB_{\mathcal{K}}$, convert q into and SQL query q_{SQL} and submit q_{SQL}. As q_{SQL} can be determined in *LogSpace*, determining whether $a \in ans(\mathcal{K},q)$ is in *LogSpace*$^{\mathcal{C}}$, where $\mathcal{C}$ is the complexity of checking entailment in the underlying DL.

We conclude by defining a *disjunctive query* **q** as usual as a finite set of conjunctive queries in which all the rules have the same head. Intuitively, the answers to a disjunctive query are the *union* of the answers of the conjunctive queries. That is, for a disjunctive query $\mathbf{q} = \{q_1, \ldots, q_m\}$, $\mathcal{K}$ *entails* **q** (denoted $\mathcal{K} \models \mathbf{q}$) iff $\mathcal{K} \models q_i$ for some $q_i \in \mathbf{q}$.

4.4 Reasoning

There are various reasoning problems to be addressed within DLs. The typical ones are resumed here (see, *e.g.*, [19]).

Consistency problem:

- Is $\mathcal{K}$ satisfiable? $\mapsto$ Is there some model $\mathcal{I}$ of $\mathcal{K}$?
- Is C coherent? $\mapsto$ $C^{\mathcal{I}} \neq \emptyset$ for some model $\mathcal{I}$ of $\mathcal{K}$?

Subsumption problem:

- $\mathcal{K} \models C \sqsubseteq D$? $\mapsto$ Is it true that $C^{\mathcal{I}} \subseteq D^{\mathcal{I}}$ for all models $\mathcal{I}$ of $\mathcal{K}$?

Equivalence problem:

- $\mathcal{K} \models C = D$? $\mapsto$ Is it true that $C^{\mathcal{I}} = D^{\mathcal{I}}$ for all models $\mathcal{I}$ of $\mathcal{K}$?

Instance checking problem:

- $\mathcal{K} \models a{:}C$? $\mapsto$ Is it true that $a^{\mathcal{I}} \in C^{\mathcal{I}}$ for all models $\mathcal{I}$ of $\mathcal{K}$?

Instance retrieval problem:

- Compute the set $\{a \mid \mathcal{K} \models a{:}C\}$

Typically, all the above problems can be reduced to the knowledge base satisfiability problem as long as the below presented reductions are supported by the underlying DL language (if not, then specific algorithms have been developed). Indeed, we have

- C is coherent w.r.t. $\mathcal{K}$ iff $\mathcal{K} \cup \{a{:}C\}$ is satisfiable, where a is a new individual;

- $\mathcal{K} \models C \sqsubseteq D$ iff $\mathcal{K} \cup \{a{:}C \sqcap \neg D\}$ is not satisfiable, where a is a new individual;

- $\mathcal{K} \models C = D$ iff $\mathcal{K} \models C \sqsubseteq D$ and $\mathcal{K} \models D \sqsubseteq C$;

- $\mathcal{K} \models a{:}C$ iff $\mathcal{K} \cup \{a{:}\neg C\}$ is not satisfiable.

On the other hand, in order to determine whether

$$\mathcal{K} \models (a,b){:}R ,$$

we may reduce it to the instance problem, as

$$\mathcal{K} \models (a,b){:}R \text{ iff } \mathcal{K} \cup \{b{:}B\} \models a{:}\exists R.B ,$$

where B is a new concept.

4.4.1   The Case of the $\mathcal{AL}$ Family

We succinctly describe here the major reasoning frameworks within the $\mathcal{AL}$ family, namely *tableau algorithms*. To do so, we describe a tableau algorithm deciding the knowledge base satisfiability problem for the DL $\mathcal{ALC}$ (see [19, 209, 206] and the paper [371] that originally has introduced this method), which is sufficiently expressive to illustrate the main characteristic of the tableau method.

Let $\mathcal{K} = \langle \mathcal{T}, \mathcal{A} \rangle$ be an $\mathcal{ALC}$ knowledge base. At first, we transform any concept in $\mathcal{K}$ into *negation normal form* (NNF), *i.e.*, negation occurs only in front of atomic concepts. To do so, we push all negation signs as far as possible into the description, using de Morgan's rules and the usual rules for quantifiers: that is, we iteratively apply the following transformation rules

$$
\begin{aligned}
\neg\neg C &\mapsto C \\
\neg(C \sqcap D) &\mapsto \neg C \sqcup \neg D \\
\neg(C \sqcup D) &\mapsto \neg C \sqcap \neg D \\
\neg \exists R.C &\mapsto \forall R.\neg C \\
\neg \forall R.C &\mapsto \exists R.\neg C \ .
\end{aligned}
\tag{4.3}
$$

With $nnf(C)$ we denote the negation normal form of C, obtained by applying the rules above.

Then, we try to construct a (finite) model $\mathcal{I}$ of $\mathcal{K}$ via a tableau algorithm. Essentially, the tableau algorithm is a terminating algorithm that, starting from an ABox, tries to build a clash-free forest of trees (called completion-forest). If it succeeds then $\mathcal{K}$ is satisfiable and from the forest a model can be build. Otherwise, $\mathcal{K}$ is not satisfiable.

4.4.1.1   The Case with Empty TBox

Let $\mathcal{K}$ be a KB in NNF with empty TBox. A *completion-forest* $\mathcal{F}$ for $\mathcal{K}$ is a collection of trees whose distinguished roots are arbitrarily connected by edges. Each node v is labelled with a set $\mathcal{L}(v)$ of concepts $C \in sub(\mathcal{K})$. The intuition here is that v is an instance of C. Each edge $\langle v, w \rangle$ is labelled with a set $\mathcal{L}(\langle v, w \rangle)$ of roles R occurring in $\mathcal{K}$ indicating that $\langle v, w \rangle$ and instance of R.

If nodes v and w are connected by an edge $\langle v, w \rangle$ with $R \in \mathcal{L}(\langle v, w \rangle)$ then w is called an *R-successor* of v and v is called an *R-predecessor* of w. As usual, *ancestor* is the transitive closure of *predecessor*.

For a node v, $\mathcal{L}(v)$ is said to contain a *clash* iff $\{A, \neg A\} \subseteq \mathcal{L}(v)$. A completion-forest is called *clash-free* iff none of its nodes contain a clash; it is called *complete* iff none of the expansion rules in Table 4.3 is applicable.

Now, the algorithm initializes a forest $\mathcal{F}$ as follows:

- $\mathcal{F}$ contains a root node v_0^i, for each individual a_i occurring in $\mathcal{A}$;

- $\mathcal{F}$ contains an edge $\langle v_0^i, v_0^j \rangle$, for each assertion axiom $(a_i, a_j){:}R \in \mathcal{A}$;

TABLE 4.3: The tableau rules for $\mathcal{ALC}$ with empty TBox.

($\sqcap$). If *(i)* $C_1 \sqcap C_2 \in \mathcal{L}(v)$ and *(ii)* $\{C_1, C_2\} \not\subseteq \mathcal{L}(v)$, then add C_1 and C_2 to $\mathcal{L}(v)$.

($\sqcup$). If *(i)* $C_1 \sqcup C_2 \in \mathcal{L}(v)$ and *(ii)* $\{C_1, C_2\} \cap \mathcal{L}(v) = \emptyset$, then add some $C \in \{C_1, C_2\}$ to $\mathcal{L}(v)$.

($\forall$). If *(i)* $\forall R.C \in \mathcal{L}(v)$ and $R \in \mathcal{L}(\langle v, w \rangle)$ with $C \notin \mathcal{L}(w)$, then add C to $\mathcal{L}(w)$.

($\exists$). If *(i)* $\exists R.C \in \mathcal{L}(v)$ and *(ii)* there is no $R \in \mathcal{L}(\langle v, w \rangle)$ with $C \in \mathcal{L}(w)$, then create a new node w, add R to $\mathcal{L}(\langle v, w \rangle)$ and add C to $\mathcal{L}(w)$.

- for each assertion $a_i{:}C \in \mathcal{A}$, we add C to $\mathcal{L}(v_0^i)$;

- for each $(a_i, a_j){:}R \in \mathcal{A}$, we add R to $\mathcal{L}(\langle v_0^i, v_0^j \rangle)$.

Then the completion-forest $\mathcal{F}$ is then expanded by repeatedly applying the completion rules described in Table 4.3 and answers "$\mathcal{K}$ is satisfiable" iff the completion rules can be applied in such a way that they yield a complete and clash-free completion-forest. Note that the only non-deterministic rule is ($\sqcup$).

We point out that it is relatively easy to build a model $\mathcal{I}$ from a complete and clash-free completion-forest. Informally,

- the domain of $\mathcal{I}$ are the nodes of the forest;

- the interpretation of individual a_i is v_0^i;

- if $R \in \mathcal{L}(\langle v, w \rangle)$, then $\langle v, w \rangle \in R^{\mathcal{I}}$;

- if $A \in \mathcal{L}(v)$, then $v \in A^{\mathcal{I}}$.

Now, termination, soundness, and completeness of the algorithm have been shown.

Proposition 10. *For each knowledge base* $\mathcal{K} = \langle \emptyset, \mathcal{A} \rangle$,

1. *the tableau algorithm terminates;*

2. *if the expansion rules can be applied in such a way that they yield a complete and clash-free completion-forest, then $\mathcal{K}$ has a finite model;*

3. *if $\mathcal{K}$ has a model, then the expansion rules can be applied in such a way that they yield a complete and clash-free completion-forest for $\mathcal{K}$;*

4. *the KB satisfiability problem is PSpace-complete [24, 16].*

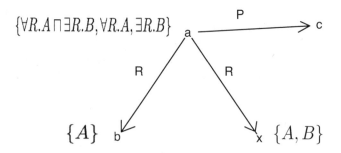

FIGURE 4.2: Clash-free complete completion-forest from ABox.

Example 9. *Consider*

$$\mathcal{K} = \{a{:}\forall R.A \sqcap \exists R.B, (a,b){:}R, (a,c){:}P\} \ .$$

$\mathcal{K}$ is satisfiable as there is a clash-free completion-forest (see Figure 4.2). The model build from the forest is:

- $\Delta^{\mathcal{I}} = \{a,b,c,x\}$;

- *the interpretation of individuals is the identity function;*

- $R^{\mathcal{I}} = \{\langle a,b\rangle, \langle a,x\rangle\}$, $P^{\mathcal{I}} = \{\langle a,c\rangle\}$;

- $A^{\mathcal{I}} = \{b,x\}$, $B^{\mathcal{I}} = \{x\}$.

4.4.1.2   The Case of Acyclic TBox

In this section, we show how to extend the tableau calculus if we restrict the form of a TBox to so-called *acyclic* TBoxes. Specifically, let $\mathcal{T}$ be a Tbox in which the GCIs have one of the following forms

$$A \ \sqsubseteq \ C$$
$$A \ = \ C$$

where A is a concept name, C is a concept. That is, the TBox consists only of primitive and definitional GCIs.

We say that A is the head of these axioms and C is the body. Furthermore, we also assume that no concept name A is in the head of more than one axiom. This further restriction allows to avoid that a GCI $C \sqsubseteq D$ may be introduced indirectly, *e.g.*, via

$$A \ = \ C$$
$$B \ = \ D$$
$$A \ \sqsubseteq \ B \ .$$

Now, we say that

- concept name A *directly uses* concept name B w.r.t. $\mathcal{T}$, denoted $A \to_{\mathcal{T}} B$, if A is the head of some axiom $E \in \mathcal{T}$ such that B occurs in the body of E;

- concept name A *uses* concept name B w.r.t. $\mathcal{T}$, denoted $A \leadsto_{\mathcal{T}} B$, if there exist concept names $A_1, \dots, A_n$, such that $A_1 = A$, $A_n = B$ and, for every $1 \le i < n$, it holds that $A_i \to_{\mathcal{T}} A_{i+1}$.

Eventually, we say that a TBox $\mathcal{T}$ is *cyclic* (*acyclic*) if there is (no) A such that $A \leadsto_{\mathcal{T}} A$.

An interesting feature of an acyclic KBs is that an acyclic TBox is eliminated by systematically replacing any defined atom by means of its definition (this procedure is called *unfolding*) and, then we may apply the reasoning method for a KB with empty TBox (see Section 4.4.1). Note, however, that the unfolding method is inherently intractable as the unfolded KB may become of exponential size [326].

We also present here an alternative method, called *lazy unfolding* [20, 19, 202], which it has been shown to be more efficient and that does not require the unfolding step. To do so, we first replace any axiom $A \sqsubseteq C \in \mathcal{T}$ with $A = C \sqcap A'$, where A' is a new concept name. Then, we extend out calculus in Table 4.3 with the rules in Table 4.4.

TABLE 4.4: The tableau rules to deal with acyclic TBox.

$(=_1)$. If *(i)* $A = C \in \mathcal{T}$, *(ii)* $A \in \mathcal{L}(v)$, and *(iii)* $C \notin \mathcal{L}(v)$ then add C to $\mathcal{L}(v)$.

$(=_2)$. If *(i)* $A = C \in \mathcal{T}$, *(ii)* $\neg A \in \mathcal{L}(v)$, and *(iii)* $nnf(\neg C) \notin \mathcal{L}(v)$ then add $nnf(\neg C)$ to $\mathcal{L}(v)$.

The construction of a model $\mathcal{I}$ from a complete and clash-free completion-forest is as for the empty TBox case.

As before, it can be shown that

Proposition 11. *For each knowledge base $\mathcal{K} = \langle \mathcal{T}, \mathcal{A} \rangle$ with acyclic $\mathcal{T}$,*

1. *the tableau algorithm terminates;*

2. *if the expansion rules can be applied in such a way that they yield a complete and clash-free completion-forest, then $\mathcal{K}$ has a finite model;*

3. *if $\mathcal{K}$ has a model, then the expansion rules can be applied in such a way that they yield a complete and clash-free completion-forest for $\mathcal{K}$.*

4. *the KB satisfiability problem is PSpace-complete [24, 16].*

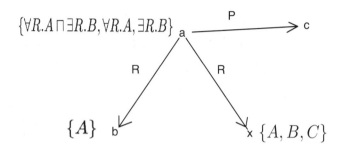

FIGURE 4.3: Clash-free complete completion-forest for acyclic KB.

Example 10. *Consider the KB as in Example 10 augmented with the GCI*

$$B = C \ .$$

$\mathcal{K}$ *is satisfiable as there is a clash-free complete completion-forest (see Figure 4.3).*

The model build from the forest is:

- $\Delta^{\mathcal{I}} = \{a, b, c, x\}$;

- *the interpretation of individuals is the identity function;*

- $R^{\mathcal{I}} = \{\langle a, b \rangle, \langle a, x \rangle\}$, $P^{\mathcal{I}} = \{\langle a, c \rangle\}$;

- $A^{\mathcal{I}} = \{b, x\}$, $B^{\mathcal{I}} = \{x\}$, $C^{\mathcal{I}} = \{x\}$.

4.4.1.3   The Case with General TBox

Eventually, we show here how we may deal with the case in which the GCIs in the TBox are of the general form $C \sqsubseteq D$. At first, note that we may assume, without loss of generality (w.l.o.g.), that any GCI is of the form $\top \sqsubseteq D$ as $C \sqsubseteq D$ is equivalent to $\top \sqsubseteq \neg C \sqcup D$. Now, let us consider the rules in Table 4.3 extended with the rule for GCIs in Table 4.5.

($\sqsubseteq$). If *(i)* $\top \sqsubseteq D \in \mathcal{T}$ and *(ii)* $D \notin \mathcal{L}(v)$, then add D to $\mathcal{L}(v)$.

While the calculus is still sound and complete, termination is not guaranteed as shown by the following example.

Example 11. *Consider the KB*

$$\mathcal{K} = \{a{:}A, A \sqsubseteq \exists R.A\}$$

It can readily be shown that there are infinitely many applications of the ($\exists$) *and* ($\sqsubseteq$) *rules, building an infinite completion-forest (tree).*

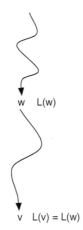

w   L(w)

v   L(v) = L(w)

FIGURE 4.4: Blocking in $\mathcal{ALC}$.

To cope with the non-termination problem, the notion of *blocking* has been introduced.

Specifically, a node v is *directly blocked* iff none of its ancestors are blocked and there exists an ancestor w such that[5]

$$\mathcal{L}(v) = \mathcal{L}(w) \ .$$

In this case we say that w *directly blocks* v. A node v is *indirectly blocked* iff one of its ancestors are blocked. Finally a node v is *blocked* iff it is not a root node and it is either directly or indirectly blocked (see Figure 4.4).

Now, the calculus is as described above except that the rules are not applied to blocked nodes. Specifically, the rules are described in Table 4.5.

Note that a model $\mathcal{I}$ from a complete and clash-free completion-forest is built informally as follows

- the domain of $\mathcal{I}$ are the nodes of the forest that are not blocked;

- the interpretation of individual a_i is v_0^i;

- if $A \in \mathcal{L}(v)$, then $v \in A^{\mathcal{I}}$;

- if $R \in \mathcal{L}(\langle v, w \rangle)$ and v, w not blocked, then $\langle v, w \rangle \in R^{\mathcal{I}}$;

- if $R \in \mathcal{L}(\langle v, w \rangle)$ and w blocked by w', then $\langle v, w' \rangle \in R^{\mathcal{I}}$.

It can be shown that using the rules in Table 4.5

Proposition 12. *For each knowledge base* $\mathcal{K} = \langle \mathcal{T}, \mathcal{A} \rangle$

---

[5]To be more precise, for $\mathcal{ALC}$, the condition $\mathcal{L}(v) \subseteq \mathcal{L}(w)$ suffices.

TABLE 4.5: The tableau rules for $\mathcal{ALC}$ KBs with GCIs.

($\sqcap$). If *(i)* $C_1 \sqcap C_2 \in \mathcal{L}(v)$, *(ii)* $\{C_1, C_2\} \not\subseteq \mathcal{L}(v)$, and *(iii)* node v is not indirectly blocked, then add C_1 and C_2 to $\mathcal{L}(v)$.

($\sqcup$). If *(i)* $C_1 \sqcup C_2 \in \mathcal{L}(v)$, *(ii)* $\{C_1, C_2\} \cap \mathcal{L}(v) = \emptyset$, and *(iii)* node v is not indirectly blocked, then add some $C \in \{C_1, C_2\}$ to $\mathcal{L}(v)$.

($\forall$). If *(i)* $\forall R.C \in \mathcal{L}(v)$, *(ii)* $R \in \mathcal{L}(\langle v, w \rangle)$ with $C \notin \mathcal{L}(w)$, and *(iii)* node v is not indirectly blocked, then add C to $\mathcal{L}(w)$.

($\exists$). If *(i)* $\exists R.C \in \mathcal{L}(v)$, *(ii)* there is no $R \in \mathcal{L}(\langle v, w \rangle)$ with $C \in \mathcal{L}(w)$, and *(iii)* node v is not blocked, then create a new node w, add R to $\mathcal{L}(\langle v, w \rangle)$ and add C to $\mathcal{L}(w)$.

($\sqsubseteq$). If *(i)* $\top \sqsubseteq D \in \mathcal{T}$, *(ii)* $D \notin \mathcal{L}(v)$, and *(iii)* node v is not indirectly blocked, then add D to $\mathcal{L}(v)$.

1. *the tableau algorithm terminates;*

2. *if the expansion rules can be applied in such a way that they yield a complete and clash-free completion-forest, then $\mathcal{K}$ has a finite model;*

3. *if $\mathcal{K}$ has a model, then the expansion rules can be applied in such a way that they yield a complete and clash-free completion-forest for $\mathcal{K}$;*

4. *the KB satisfiability problem is ExpTime-complete [131, 442].*

Example 12. *Consider Example 11. $\mathcal{K}$ is satisfiable as there is a clash-free completion-forest (see Figure 4.5). Note that node y is blocked by x.*
  The model build from the forest is:

- $\Delta^{\mathcal{I}} = \{a, x\}$;

- *the interpretation of individuals is the identity function;*

- $R^{\mathcal{I}} = \{\langle a, x \rangle, \langle x, x \rangle\}$;

- $A^{\mathcal{I}} = \{a, x\}$.

It is not our purpose to present here the tableau rules for more expressive languages of the $\mathcal{AL}$ family, *e.g.*, for $\mathcal{SHOIN}, \mathcal{SROIQ}$. We refer the reader to *e.g.*, [203, 206, 207]. However, let us note that besides adding a rule for each construct, the blocking condition is extended as well to a more sophisticated definition, as *e.g.*, $\mathcal{SHIF}$ does not employ the finite model property anymore.

Nevertheless, as an illustrative example, in Appendix C we recall the tableau calculus for $\mathcal{SHIF}_g$.

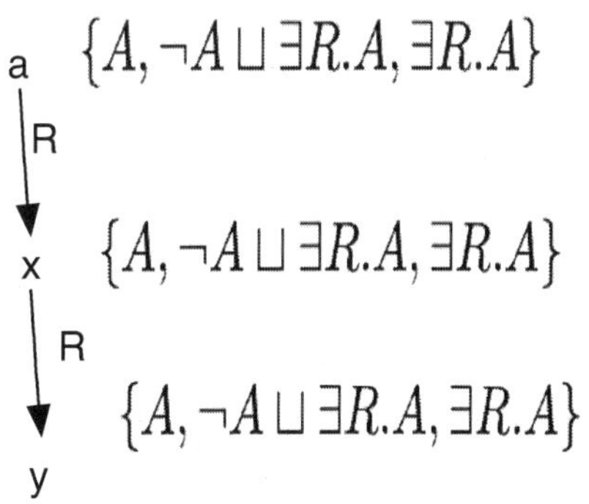

a $\quad \{A, \neg A \sqcup \exists R.A, \exists R.A\}$

$\Big| R$

$\blacktriangledown$

x $\quad \{A, \neg A \sqcup \exists R.A, \exists R.A\}$

$\Big| R$

$\blacktriangledown \quad \{A, \neg A \sqcup \exists R.A, \exists R.A\}$

y

FIGURE 4.5: Clash-free completion-forest from $\mathcal{ALC}$ KB.

4.4.1.4   A Classification Algorithm

For completeness, we provide here also the typical ontology classification algorithm for the $\mathcal{AL}$-family. The algorithm is as from [20, 22, 23]. For a more recent account on it, see [170].

We first introduce some definitions. For some pre-order $\leq$ (reflexive, transitive relation) on some set P, let $\prec$ be the *precedence relation* of $\leq$, *i.e.*, $\prec$ is the smallest relation such that its reflexive, transitive closure is $\leq$, except for pairs of "equivalent" objects, *i.e.*, where $a \leq b$ and $b \leq a$ holds. Obviously, $x \prec y$ iff $x \leq y$ and there is no z different from x and y such that $x \leq z \leq y$. The intuition here is that $x \leq y$ means y subsumes x, while $x \prec y$ means that y subsumes x and there is no other z subsumed by y and subsuming x. $\leq$ is intended to represent the subsumption relation and $\prec$ is intended to represent the hierarchy of concept names in $\mathcal{T}$, which we want to compute. If $x \leq y$ then x is a *successor* of y and y is a *predecessor* of x. Similarly, if $x \prec y$ then x is an *immediate successor* of y and y is an *immediate predecessor* of x.

Note that as $\leq$ (subsumption) is a pre-order, there may be two distinct concepts c, c', such that $c \leq c'$ and $c' \leq c$ holds, *i.e.*, c and c' are logically equivalent. As it cannot be $c \prec c' \prec c$, we will assume that for any two equivalent concept names c, c', only one is considered to occur in $\prec$.

A concept name hierarchy $\prec$ is represented as a directed acyclic graph where a node is labelled with a set of logically equivalent concept names and an edge corresponds to the immediate predecessor relation, *i.e.*, there is a link from node v_2 to node v_1 if $x \prec y$ and x and y are in the label of v_1 and v_2, respectively.

A simple classification algorithm. The algorithm is incremental. Suppose we want to classify the concept names in X. Assume we have determined the precedence relation $\prec_i$ for a set $X_i \subseteq X$ of concept names. Initially, $X_0 =$

$\{\bot, \top\}$ and $\bot \prec_0 \top$. Consider a concept name $c \in X \setminus X_i$. We determine a method to compute the precedence relation $\prec_{i+1}$ for set $X_{i+1} = X_i \cup \{c\}$. To do so, we compute c's immediate predecessors (procedure *topSearch*), PX_i^c, and immediate successors (procedure *bottomSearch*), SX_i^c, w.r.t. concept names in X_i. Let

$$PX_i^c = \{x \in X_i \mid c \prec x\}$$
$$SX_i^c = \{x \in X_i \mid x \prec c\}.$$

Given the set PX_i^c and SX_i^c, and $\prec_i$, it is possible to compute $\prec_{i+1}$ on $X_{i+1} = X_i \cup \{c\}$ in linear time. In fact, one just needs to add $c \prec x$ for $x \in PX_i^c$, $x \prec c$ for $x \in SX_i^c$, and eventually remove $x \prec y$, for $x \in SX_i^c$ and $y \in PX_i^c$, i.e.,

$$\prec_{i+1} = (\prec_i \cup \{c \prec x \mid x \in PX_i^c\} \cup \{x \prec c \mid x \in SX_i^c\})$$
$$\setminus \{x \prec_i y \mid x \in SX_i^c, y \in PX_i^c\}.$$

Specifically, we compute

$$TX_i^c = \{x \in X_i \mid c \leq x \text{ and } c \not\leq y \text{ for all } y \prec_i x\} \qquad (4.4)$$
$$BX_i^c = \{x \in X_i \mid x \leq c \text{ and } y \not\leq c \text{ for all } x \prec_i y\}. \qquad (4.5)$$

TX_i^c and BX_i^c are almost PX_i^c and SX_i^c, respectively. There is only a special case if c is equivalent to some $x \in X_i$, i.e., $c \leq x$ and $x \leq c$. In that case, PX_i^c is empty and $TX_i^c = \{x\}$ contains the concept x with $c \leq x$. In this case, we test $x \leq c$. If the test is positive, c is equivalent to x and it suffices to add c to the node label containing x.

The procedure *SimpleClassify*($\mathcal{K}$) is as follows [20, 22, 23]:

SimpleClassify($\mathcal{K}$)

    1. Let
        (a) X be the set of concept names in $\mathcal{T}$
        (b) $X_0 := \{\bot, \top\}$ and $\bot \prec_0 \top$
    2. If $(X \setminus X_i) = \emptyset$ return $\langle X_i, \prec_i \rangle$ and exit
    3. Select $c \in X \setminus X_i$
    4. Compute TX_i^c
    5. If $TX_i^c = \{x\}$ and $x \leq c$ then add c to the node label containing x, and go to step 2.
    6. Compute BX_i^c
    7. Set

$$X_{i+1} := X_i \cup \{c\}$$
$$\prec_{i+1} := (\prec_i \cup \{c \prec x \mid x \in TX_i^c\} \cup \{x \prec c \mid x \in BX_i^c\})$$
$$\setminus \{x \prec_i y \mid x \in BX_i^c, y \in TX_i^c\}.$$

8. Increment i and go to step 2.

We next show how to compute TX_i^c and BX_i^c. We first address TX_i^c. The other case is dual.

To start with, we assume that the elements in X_i are represented as a concept hierarchy, as explained previously. To determine TX_i^c, our procedure, called *topSearch*, starts with $\top \in X_i$ and visits the concept hierarchy X_i in a top-down breadth-first fashion. That is,

$$TX_i^c := topSearch(c, \top) \ .$$

For each concept name $x \in X_i$ under consideration, it determines whether x has an immediate successor y satisfying $c \leq y$. If there are such successors, they are considered as well. Otherwise, x is added to the result list of the *topSearch* algorithm.

To avoid multiple visits of elements of X_i and multiple comparisons of the same element c, *topSearch* employs the label "visited" and another label "positive" if the subsumption test has been made. The procedure *topSearch* gets two concepts as input, the concept c, which have to be inserted and the element $x \in X_i$ currently under consideration. For x, we already know that $c \leq x$ and we look at direct successors of x w.r.t. $\prec_i$. For each direct successor y of x, we have to check whether y subsumes c. This is done with the procedure *enhancedTopSubs*. The direct successors for which the test was positive are collected in a list *PosSucc*. If the list remains empty, x is added to the result list; otherwise *topSearch* is called for each positive successor, if not already visited.

The $topSearch(c, x)$ algorithm is as follows:

topSearch(c,x)

1. Visited$(c, x) := true$

2. For all y with $y \prec_i x$ do: if $enhancedTopSubs(y, c)$ then $PosSucc := PosSucc \cup \{y\}$

3. If $PosSucc = \emptyset$ then $Result := \{x\}$ and go to step 5.

4. For all $y \in PosSucc$ do: if not Visited(c, y) then $Result := Result \cup topSearch(c, y)$

5. Return $Result$.

The $enhancedTopSubs(y, c)$ algorithm is as follows:

enhancedTopSubs(y,c)

1. if SubsFlag$(y, c) = $ "positive" then $Result := true$ and go to step 5.

2. If SubsFlag$(y, c) = $ "negative" then $Result := false$ and go to step 5.

3. If for all z with $y \prec_i z$ it holds that $enhancedTopSubs(z, c)$ and $c \leq y$ then SubsFlag(y, c) := "positive" , $Result := true$ and go to step 5.

4. SubsFlag(y, c) := "negative", $Result := false$

5. Return $Result$.

Note that in step 3, before testing the subsumption $c \leq y$ we apply the following heuristics using *negative information* [20, 22, 23]:

> If for some predecessor z of y the test $c \leq z$ has failed, we can conclude that $c \not\leq y$ without performing the expensive test $c \leq y$. To gain maximum advantage, all predecessors of y should have been tested before the test is performed on y, which is obtained by recursive calls.

[20, 22, 23] address also the use of *positive information*: before checking $c \leq y$, check if there is some successor z of y that has passed the test $c \leq z$ and in this case $c \leq y$ holds without performing the expensive test $c \leq y$. However, [20, 22, 23] show that the use of negative information is much better than the use of positive information.

We next show how to compute BX_i^c, which is dual to the *topSearch* procedure and is performed by the *bottomSearch* algorithm. We have that

$$BX_i^c := bottomSearch(c, \bot)$$

bottomSearch(c,x)

1. Visited(c, x):= $true$

2. For all y with $x \prec_i y$ do: if $enhancedBottomSubs(c, y)$ then $PosPrec := PosPrec \cup \{y\}$

3. If $PosPrec = \emptyset$ then $Result := \{x\}$ and go to step 5.

4. For all $y \in PosPrec$ do: if not Visited(c, x) then $Result := Result \cup bottomSearch(c, y)$

5. Return $Result$.

The *enhancedBottomSubs*(c, y) algorithm is as follows:

enhancedBottomSubs(c,y)

1. if SubsFlag(c, y) = "positive" then $Result := true$ and go to step 5.

2. If SubsFlag(c, y) = "negative" then $Result := false$ and go to step 5.

3. If for all z with $z \prec_i y$ it holds that $enhancedBottomSubs(c, z)$ and $y \leq c$ then SubsFlag(c, y) := "positive" , $Result := true$ and go to step 5.

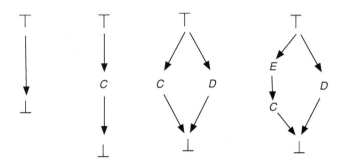

FIGURE 4.6: A DL classification run.

4. SubsFlag$(c, y) :=$ "negative", $Result := false$

5. Return $Result$.

Note that in step 3, before testing the subsumption $y \leq c$ we apply the following heuristics using *negative information* [20, 22, 23]:

> If for some successor z of y the test $z \leq c$ has failed, we can conclude that $y \not\leq c$ without performing the expensive test $y \leq c$. To gain maximum advantage, all successors of y should have been tested before the test was performed on y, which is obtained by recursive calls.

Example 13 ([170]). *Consider the KB*

$$\mathcal{K} = \{C \sqsubseteq \exists R.D, \exists R \sqsubseteq E\} .$$

Figure 4.6 illustrates a classification run.

Optimizing classical classification via told subsumers. Consider a KB $\mathcal{K} = \langle \mathcal{T}, \mathcal{A} \rangle$. We introduce the notion of *told subsumer* [19].

1. If $\mathcal{T}$ contains $A \sqsubseteq C$ or $A = C$ then C is called a *told subsumer* of A, denoted $A \rightarrow_{ts} C$.

2. If $D \sqsubseteq C_1 \sqcap \ldots \sqcap C_n \in \mathcal{T}$ then for all i, $D \rightarrow_{ts} C_i$.

3. If $A = C_1 \sqcap \ldots \sqcap C_n \in \mathcal{T}$ then for all i, $A \rightarrow_{ts} C_i$.

4. If $C_1 \sqcup \ldots \sqcup C_n \sqsubseteq D \in \mathcal{T}$ then for all i, $C_i \rightarrow_{ts} D$.

5. If $A = C_1 \sqcup \ldots \sqcup C_n \in \mathcal{T}$ then for all i, $C_i \rightarrow_{ts} A$.

6. $\rightarrow_{ts}$ is transitive

Now, we may exploit the notion of told subsumers by applying the following heuristics:

Remark 7. *Before classifying concept A, all of its told subsumers which have already been classified, and all their subsumers, can be marked as subsumers of A. Subsumption test for these atoms are, thus, unnecessary. That is, in the procedure SimpleClassify, we have another initialization step:*

$$\text{if } A \rightarrow_{ts} B \text{ then set } SubsFlag(B, A) = \text{'positive'}.$$

To maximize the effect of told subsumer optimization, atoms should be classified in *definitional order*. This means that a concept A is not to classify until all of its told subsumer have been classified. Specifically:

Remark 8. *In procedure SimpleClassify, in step 3, select concept $c \in X \setminus X_i$ only if all of its told subsumer have been classified. That is,*

$$\text{if } A \rightarrow_{ts} B \text{ then classify } B \text{ before } A.$$

Therefore, we get a preference order on the atoms in X.

The acyclic KBs case. Consider an acyclic KB $\mathcal{K} = \langle \mathcal{T}, \mathcal{A} \rangle$. For acyclic KBs we may take advantage of the heuristics developed previously, concerning told subsumers. Specifically, apply the *SimpleClassify* procedure with the two heuristics described in Remark 7 and 8. Then the ordering induced by Remark 8 can be exploited by omitting the bottom search phase for primitive concept names and assuming that they only subsume (concepts equivalent) to $\bot$. This is possible because, with an acyclic KB, a primitive concept can only subsume concepts for which it is a told subsumer. Therefore, as concepts are classified in definition order, a primitive concept will always be classified before any of the concepts it subsumes (and, thus, the bottom search phase is redundant).

Note that this additional optimization cannot be used with a general KB because, in the presence of general GCIs, it can no longer be guaranteed that a primitive concept will only subsume concepts for which it is a told subsumer. E.g., for

$$\mathcal{T} = \{A \sqsubseteq \exists R.C, \exists R.C \sqsubseteq B\} \,,$$

B is not a told subsumer of A, but B subsumes A.

4.4.2   The Case of the $\mathcal{EL}$ Family

For the sake of ease of presentation, we provide here the calculus for $\mathcal{EL}^{++}$ (we refer the reader to [13, 18] for $\mathcal{EL}^{++}(\mathbf{D})$ and its extensions). Essentially, we drop from $\mathcal{EL}^{++}(\mathbf{D})$ the concrete concept expressions of the form $p(f_1, \ldots, f_n)$.

We have seen that for the $\mathcal{AL}$-family the classification algorithm is built on top of the subsumption test algorithm. The main feature of the reasoning algorithm of $\mathcal{EL}^{++}$ is instead the fact that it is a polynomial-time subsumption algorithm that actually directly classifies a given TBox $\mathcal{T}$, *i.e.*, simultaneously computes all subsumption relationships between the concept names occurring in $\mathcal{T}$, which makes it particularly useful for large size ontologies.

Note also that the other decision problems can be reduced to the subsumption problem as well [14]. Let $\mathcal{K} = \langle \mathcal{A}, \mathcal{T} \rangle$ be an $\mathcal{EL}^{++}$ KB. Then

- C is coherent iff $\mathcal{K} \models a{:}C$, for a new individual a;

- $\mathcal{K}$ is satisfiable iff $\mathcal{K} \not\models a{:}\bot$;

- Concerning the instance problem, we convert an ABox $\mathcal{A}$ into a concept $C_\mathcal{A}$ as follows

$$C_\mathcal{A} := \prod_{a:A \in \mathcal{A}} \exists U.(\{a\} \sqcap C) \sqcap \prod_{(a,b):R \in \mathcal{A}} \exists U.(\{a\} \sqcap \exists R.b)$$

where U is a new role not occurring in $\mathcal{A}$. Then

$$\mathcal{K} \models a{:}C \text{ iff } \mathcal{T} \models \{a\} \sqcap C_\mathcal{A} \sqsubseteq C .$$

So, in the following we consider the subsumption problem only w.r.t. a TBox $\mathcal{T}$.

The algorithm proceeds in four steps:

1. Normalise the TBox.

2. Translate the normalized TBox into a graph.

3. Complete the graph using completion rules.

4. Read off the subsumption relationships from the normalized graph.

Remark 9. *Please, note that [243, 244] has shown that the TBox classification calculus for $\mathcal{EL}^{++}$, as illustrated in [13, 18], is incomplete in the presence of nominals in the TBox, e.g., given the TBox [229], (but see also [244] for other examples)*

$$\mathcal{T} = \{ \quad A \sqsubseteq \exists R.(B \sqcap \{o\})$$
$$A \sqsubseteq \exists S.\{o\}$$
$$\exists S.B \sqsubseteq B \} ,$$

this TBox entails $A \sqsubseteq B$, because if A is not empty then o is an instance of B, but the algorithm in [13, 18] is not able to infer it (the problem is in the (CR6) illustrated later on).

For further insights we refer the reader to [229, 230, 243, 244, 245, 297], and specifically to [230, 229] for a complete and similar to [13, 18] calculus.

However, even if incomplete, it is still illustrative to present the work as from [13, 18].

TABLE 4.6: NNF transformation rules for $\mathcal{EL}^{++}$ TBoxes.

NF1 $R_1 \circ \cdots \circ R_n \sqsubseteq S \mapsto \{R_1 \circ \cdots \circ R_{n-1} \sqsubseteq U, U \circ R_n \sqsubseteq S\}$

NF2 $C \sqcap \tilde{D} \sqsubseteq E \mapsto \{\tilde{D} \sqsubseteq A, C \sqcap A \sqsubseteq E\}$

NF3 $\exists R.\tilde{C} \sqsubseteq D \mapsto \{\tilde{C} \sqsubseteq A, \exists R.A \sqsubseteq D\}$

NF4 $\bot \sqsubseteq D \mapsto \emptyset$

NF5 $\tilde{C} \sqsubseteq \tilde{D} \mapsto \{\tilde{C} \sqsubseteq A, A \sqsubseteq \tilde{D}\}$

NF6 $B \sqsubseteq \exists R.\tilde{C} \mapsto \{B \sqsubseteq \exists R.A, A \sqsubseteq \tilde{C}\}$

NF7 $B \sqsubseteq C \sqcap D \mapsto \{B \sqsubseteq C, B \sqsubseteq D\}$

where $\tilde{C}, \tilde{D} \notin B_{\mathcal{T}}$, U new role name, and A new concept name.

So, let $B_{\mathcal{T}}$ to denote the smallest set of concept descriptions that contains the top concept $\top$, all concept names used in $\mathcal{T}$, and all concept descriptions of the form $\{a\}$.

We say that a $\mathcal{T}$ is *normalized* if

1. it only contains GCIs of the following form:

$$A \sqsubseteq B, \quad A_1 \sqcap A_2 \sqsubseteq B, \quad A \sqsubseteq \exists R.B, \quad \exists R.A \sqsubseteq B \ ,$$

   where $A, A_i \in B_{\mathcal{T}}$ and $B \in B_{\mathcal{T}} \cup \{\bot\}$;

2. all role inclusions are of the form $R \sqsubseteq S$ or $R_1 \circ R_2 \sqsubseteq S$.

By introducing new concept and role names, any TBox $\mathcal{T}$ can be turned into a normalized TBox $\mathcal{T}'$ that is a *conservative extension* of $\mathcal{T}$, *i.e.*, every model of $\mathcal{T}'$ is also a model of $\mathcal{T}$, and every model of T can be extended to a model of $\mathcal{T}'$ by appropriately choosing the interpretations of the additional concept and role names and it is shown that this transformation can actually be done in linear time [14]. The conversion into normal form is done using the translation rules shown in Table 4.6 in two phases:

1. exhaustively apply rules $(NF1) - (NF4)$;[6]

2. exhaustively apply rules $(NF5) - (NF7)$.

So, let us now assume that $\mathcal{T}$ is normalized. When developing the subsumption algorithm for normalized $\mathcal{EL}^{++}$ TBoxes, we can restrict our attention to subsumption between concept names. In fact, $\mathcal{T} \models C \sqsubseteq D$ iff $\mathcal{T}' \models A \sqsubseteq B$, where

---

[6]Note that in phase 1, the rule $(NF2)$ is applied modulo commutativity of conjunction.

$\mathcal{T}' = \mathcal{T} \cup \{A \sqsubseteq C, D \sqsubseteq B\}$, with A, B new concept names. The subsumption algorithm not only computes subsumption between two given concept names w.r.t. the normalized input TBox $\mathcal{T}$; it rather classifies $\mathcal{T}$, *i.e.*, it simultaneously computes the subsumption relationships between all pairs of concept names occurring in $\mathcal{T}$.

So, let $R_{\mathcal{T}}$ to denote the set of all role names used in $\mathcal{T}$. The algorithm computes a mapping $\mathcal{S}$ from $B_{\mathcal{T}}$ to a subset of $B_{\mathcal{T}} \cup \{\top, \bot\}$, and a mapping $\mathcal{R}$ from $R_{\mathcal{T}}$ to a binary relation on $B_{\mathcal{T}}$. The intuition is that these mappings make implicit subsumption relationships explicit in the following sense:

- $D \in \mathcal{S}(C)$ implies that $\mathcal{T} \models C \sqsubseteq D$;

- $(C, D) \in \mathcal{R}(P)$ implies $\mathcal{T} \models C \sqsubseteq \exists P.D$.

These mapping are initialized as follows:

- $\mathcal{S}(C) := \{C, \top\}$ for each $C \in B_{\mathcal{T}}$;

- $\mathcal{R}(P) := \emptyset$ for each $P \in R_{\mathcal{T}}$.

Then the sets $\mathcal{S}(C)$ and $\mathcal{R}(P)$ are extended by applying the completion rules shown in Table 4.7 until no more rule applies. Some of the rules use abbreviations that still need to be introduced. Indeed, $(CR6)$ uses the relation $\leadsto_{\mathcal{R}} \subseteq B_{\mathcal{T}} \times B_{\mathcal{T}}$, which is defined as follows: $C \leadsto_{\mathcal{R}} D$ iff there are $C_1, \ldots, C_k \in B_{\mathcal{T}}$ such that

- $C_1 = C$ or $C_1 = \{b\}$ for some b;

- $(C_j, C_{j+1}) \in \mathcal{R}(R_j)$ for some $R_j \in R_{\mathcal{T}}$ $(1 \leq j < k)$;

- $C_k = D$.

The following can be shown [13].

Proposition 13. *For a normalized TBox $\mathcal{T}$,*

1. *the rules of Table 4.7 can only be applied a polynomial number of times, and each rule application is polynomial;*

2. *Let $\mathcal{S}$ be the mapping obtained after the application of the rules of Table 4.7 to $\mathcal{T}$ has terminated, and let A, B be concept names occurring in $\mathcal{T}$, then $\mathcal{T} \models A \sqsubseteq B$ if [7] one of the following two conditions holds:*

   - $\mathcal{S}(A) \cap \{B, \bot\} \neq \emptyset$;
   - *there is $\{a\} \in B_{\mathcal{T}}$ such that $\bot \in \mathcal{S}(\{a\})$.*

We refer the reader to [293] for a conjunctive query answering procedure for $\mathcal{EL}$.

---

[7]The other direction does not hold as from Remark 9, but holds if nominals are missing in the TBox.

TABLE 4.7: Completion rules for $\mathcal{EL}^{++}$.

$(CR1)$ If $C' \in \mathcal{S}(C), C' \sqsubseteq D \in \mathcal{T}$, and $D \notin \mathcal{S}(C)$ then add D to $\mathcal{S}(C)$;

$(CR2)$ If $C_1, C_2 \in \mathcal{S}(C), C_1 \sqcap C_2 \sqsubseteq D \in \mathcal{T}$, and $D \notin \mathcal{S}(C)$ then add D to $\mathcal{S}(C)$;

$(CR3)$ If $C' \in \mathcal{S}(C), C' \sqsubseteq \exists P.D \in \mathcal{T}$, and $(C, D) \notin \mathcal{R}(P)$ then add (C, D) to $\mathcal{R}(P)$;

$(CR4)$ If $(C, D) \in \mathcal{R}(P), D' \in \mathcal{S}(D), \exists P.D' \sqsubseteq E \in \mathcal{T}$, and $E \notin \mathcal{S}(C)$ then add E to $\mathcal{S}(C)$;

$(CR5)$ If $(C, D) \in \mathcal{R}(P), \bot \in \mathcal{S}(D)$, and $\bot \notin \mathcal{S}(C)$ then add $\bot$ to $\mathcal{S}(C)$;

$(CR6)$ If $\{a\} \in \mathcal{S}(C) \cap \mathcal{S}(D), C \rightsquigarrow_{\mathcal{R}} D$, and $\mathcal{S}(D) \nsubseteq \mathcal{S}(C)$ then join $\mathcal{S}(D)$ to $\mathcal{S}(C)$;

$(CRR1)$ If $(C, D) \in \mathcal{R}(P), P \sqsubseteq S \in \mathcal{T}$, and $(C, D) \notin \mathcal{R}(S)$ then add (C, D) to $\mathcal{R}(S)$;

$(CRR2)$ If $(C, D) \in \mathcal{R}(R_1), (D, E) \in \mathcal{R}(R_2), R_1 \circ R_2 \sqsubseteq R_3 \in \mathcal{T}$, and $(C, E) \notin \mathcal{R}(R_3)$ then add (C, E) to $\mathcal{R}(R_3)$.

Example 14. *Consider the KB of Example 13, i.e.,*

$$\mathcal{K} = \{C \sqsubseteq \exists R.D, \exists R.\top \sqsubseteq E\} \ .$$

Note that $\mathcal{K}$ is already normalized. The following illustrates a classification run.

1. *Initialization:*

$$
\begin{aligned}
\mathcal{S}(C) &:= \{C, \top\} \\
\mathcal{S}(D) &:= \{D, \top\} \\
\mathcal{S}(E) &:= \{E, \top\} \\
\mathcal{R}(R) &:= \emptyset \ .
\end{aligned}
$$

2. *Application of rule $(CR3)$:*

$$\mathcal{R}(R) := \mathcal{R}(R) \cup \{(C, D)\} \ .$$

3. *Application of rule $(CR4)$:*

$$\mathcal{S}(C) := \mathcal{S}(C) \cup \{E\} \ .$$

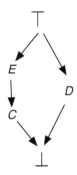

FIGURE 4.7: An $\mathcal{EL}^{++}$ classification example.

4. Stop. Figure 4.7 illustrates the final classification, which coincides with the one in Figure 4.6.

4.4.3 The Case of the DL-Lite Family

We recall that DL-Lite-family [12, 82, 83, 87] has been specifically tailored to capture some basic ontology language features, while keeping a low complexity of reasoning. Reasoning means not only computing the subsumption relationships between concepts, and checking satisfiability, but also answering complex queries (*i.e.*, conjunctive queries) over a huge set of instances.

In the following, we restrict our attention to DL-Lite$_{core}$ [82], which is sufficient to highlight the main concepts for reasoning within the DL-Lite-family.

Consider a DL-Lite$_{core}$ KB $\mathcal{K} = \langle \mathcal{T}, \mathcal{A} \rangle$ and a conjunctive query $q(\mathbf{x}) \leftarrow \exists \mathbf{y}.\varphi(\mathbf{x}, \mathbf{y})$. The main reasoning tasks related to $\mathcal{K}$ and q are:

- Knowledge base satisfiability problem;

- Subsumption checking;

- Concept coherence;

- Instance checking;

- Query answering, *i.e.*, computing the answer set $ans(\mathcal{K}, q)$.

In the following, define an *r*-concept as any concept that can occur on the right-hand side of a concept inclusion.

Note that the subsumption problem can be reduced to the KB unsatisfiability problem. In fact, for a DL-Lite$_{core}$ axiom $C \sqsubseteq D$, in order to determine whether $\mathcal{K} \models C \sqsubseteq D$, consider a new concept name A, a new individual a, and set $\mathcal{K}' = \langle \mathcal{T}', \mathcal{A}' \rangle$, where

$$\mathcal{T}' \quad := \quad \mathcal{T} \cup \{A \sqsubseteq C, A \sqsubseteq \neg D\}$$
$$\mathcal{A}' \quad := \quad \mathcal{A} \cup \{a{:}A\} \ .$$

Then, it is easy to see that $\mathcal{K} \models C \sqsubseteq D$ iff $\mathcal{K}'$ is not satisfiable.

Determining whether a r-concept C is coherent can be reduced to the KB satisfiability problem as follows: consider a new concept name A, a new individual a, and set $\mathcal{K}' = \langle \mathcal{T}', \mathcal{A}' \rangle$, where

$$\mathcal{T}' \quad := \quad \mathcal{T} \cup \{A \sqsubseteq C\}$$
$$\mathcal{A}' \quad := \quad \mathcal{A} \cup \{a{:}A\} \ .$$

Then, it is easy to see that C is coherent iff $\mathcal{K}'$ is satisfiable.

Concerning instance checking, *i.e.*, determining whether $\mathcal{K} \models a{:}C$ for r-concept C, consider a new concept name A and set $\mathcal{K}' = \langle \mathcal{T}', \mathcal{A}' \rangle$, where

$$\mathcal{T}' \quad := \quad \mathcal{T} \cup \{A \sqsubseteq \neg C\}$$
$$\mathcal{A}' \quad := \quad \mathcal{A} \cup \{a{:}A\} \ .$$

Then, it is easy to see that $\mathcal{K} \models a{:}C$ iff $\mathcal{K}'$ is not satisfiable.

Therefore, it remains to address the KB satisfiability problem and the query answering problem. At first, however, we need a KB normalization step.

Knowledge Base normalization. The *normalization* of $\mathcal{K} = (\mathcal{T}, \mathcal{A})$ is obtained by transforming $\mathcal{K}$ as follows. The ABox $\mathcal{A}$ is expanded by adding to $\mathcal{A}$ the assertions $a{:}\exists R$ and $b{:}\exists R^-$, for each $(a, b){:}R \in \mathcal{A}$.

Then $\mathcal{T}$ is expanded by closing it with respect to the following inference rule: if $B_1 \sqsubseteq B_2 \in \mathcal{T}$ and either $B_2 \sqsubseteq \neg B_3 \in \mathcal{T}$ or $B_3 \sqsubseteq \neg B_2 \in \mathcal{T}$ then add $B_1 \sqsubseteq \neg B_3$ to $\mathcal{T}$. It can be shown that after computing the above closure we have that $\mathcal{T} \models B_1 \sqsubseteq \neg B_2$ iff either $B_1 \sqsubseteq \neg B_2 \in \mathcal{T}$ or $B_2 \sqsubseteq \neg B_1 \in \mathcal{T}$.

Now we store $\mathcal{A}$ in a relational database. That is, (i) for each basic concept B occurring in $\mathcal{A}$, we define a relational table tab_B of arity 1, such that $\langle a \rangle \in tab_B$ iff $a{:}B \in \mathcal{A}$; and (ii) for each role P occurring in $\mathcal{A}$, we define a relational table tab_P of arity 2, such that $\langle a, b \rangle \in tab_P$ iff $(a, b){:}P \in \mathcal{A}$. We denote with $\mathrm{DB}(\mathcal{A})$ the relational database thus constructed.

Knowledge base satisfiability. To check the satisfiability of a normalized KB $\mathcal{K} = (\mathcal{T}, \mathcal{A})$, we verify the following condition: there exists $B_1 \sqsubseteq \neg B_2 \in \mathcal{T}$ and a constant a such $\{a{:}B_1, a{:}B_2\} \subseteq \mathcal{A}$. If this condition above holds, then $\mathcal{K}$ is not satisfiable. Otherwise, $\mathcal{K}$ is satisfiable. Note that the algorithm can verify this condition by posing to $\mathrm{DB}(\mathcal{A})$ a simple conjunctive query expressed in SQL query, *i.e.*, $\mathcal{K}$ is not satisfiable iff

$$q(x) \leftarrow tab_{B_1}(x), tab_{B_2}(x)$$

has non-empty answer in $\mathrm{DB}(\mathcal{A})$.

Notice that the algorithm does not consider the PIs (positive inclusions) occurring in $\mathcal{T}$ during its execution. Indeed, it can be shown that PIs do not affect the satisfiability of a DL-Lite KB, if the TBox is normalized [82].

It can be shown that the above described algorithm decides the KB satisfiability problem in polynomial time [82].

Query answering. We show now how to determine the answers of a conjunctive query over $\mathcal{K}$. To this end:

1. We have to check if $\mathcal{K}$ is satisfiable, as querying a non-satisfiable KB is undefined in our case.

2. By considering $\mathcal{T}$ only, the user query q is *reformulated* into a set of conjunctive queries $r(q, \mathcal{T})$. Informally, the basic idea is that the reformulation procedure closely resembles a top-down resolution procedure for logic programming, where each inclusion axiom $B_1 \sqsubseteq B_2$ is seen as a logic programming rule of the form $B_2(x) \leftarrow B_1(x)$. For instance, given the query $q(x, s) \leftarrow A(x)$ and suppose that $\mathcal{T}$ contains the inclusion axioms $B_1 \sqsubseteq A$ and $B_2 \sqsubseteq A$, then we can reformulate the query into two queries $q(x, s) \leftarrow B_1(x)$ and $q(x, s) \leftarrow B_2(x)$, exactly as it happens for top-down resolution methods in logic programming.

3. The reformulated queries in $r(q, \mathcal{T})$ are then *evaluated* over $\mathcal{A}$ only (which is stored in a database), producing the requested answer set $ans(\mathcal{K}, q)$.

The query reformulation step is as follows. We say that a variable in a conjunctive query is *bound* if it corresponds to either a distinguished variable or a shared variable, *i.e.*, a variable occurring at least twice in the query body (inclusive the scoring function), or a constant, while we say that a variable is *unbound* if it corresponds to a non-distinguished non-shared variable (as usual, we use the symbol "_" to represent non-distinguished non-shared variables). Note that an atom of the form $(\exists P)(x)$ (resp. $(\exists P^-)(x)$) has the same meaning as $P(x, \_)$ (resp. $P(\_, x)$). For ease of exposition, in the following we will use the latter form only.

An axiom τ is *applicable* to an atom $B(x)$, if τ has B in its right-hand side, and τ is applicable to an atom $P(x_1, x_2)$, if either (*i*) $x_2 = \_$ and the right-hand side of τ is $\exists P$, or (*ii*) $x_1 = \_$ and the right-hand side of τ is $\exists P^-$. We indicate with $gr(g; \tau)$ the atom obtained from the atom g by applying the inclusion axiom τ. Specifically, if $g = B_1(x)$ (resp., $g = P_1(x, \_)$ or $g = P_1(\_, x)$) and $\tau = B_2 \sqsubseteq B_1$ (resp., $\tau = B_2 \sqsubseteq \exists P_1$ or $\tau = B_2 \sqsubseteq \exists P_1^-$), we have:

- $gr(g, \tau) = A(x)$, if $B_2 = A$, where A is an atomic concept;

- $gr(g, \tau) = P_2(x, \_)$, if $B_2 = \exists P_2$;

- $gr(g, \tau) = P_2(\_, x)$, if $B_2 = \exists P_2^-$.

We are now ready to present the query reformulation algorithm. Given a conjunctive query q and a set of axioms $\mathcal{T}$, the algorithm reformulates q in terms of a set of conjunctive queries $r(q, \mathcal{T})$, which then can be evaluated over DB($\mathcal{A}$).

Algorithm 1 QueryRef$(q, \mathcal{T})$

Input: Conjunctive query q, normalized KB $\mathcal{K}$.
Output: Set of reformulated conjunctive queries $r(q, \mathcal{T})$.
1: $r(q, \mathcal{T}) := \{q\}$
2: **repeat**
3:     $S = r(q, \mathcal{T})$
4:     **for all** $q \in S$ **do**
5:         **for all** $g \in q$ **do**
6:             **if** $\tau \in \mathcal{T}$ is applicable to g **then**
7:                 $r(q, \mathcal{T}) := r(q, \mathcal{T}) \cup \{q[g/gr(g, \tau)]\}$
8:             **for all** $g_1, g_2 \in q$ **do**
9:                 **if** g_1 and g_2 unify **then**
10:                    $r(q, \mathcal{T}) := r(q, \mathcal{T}) \cup \{\kappa(reduce(q, g_1, g_2))\}$
11: **until** $S = r(q, \mathcal{T})$
12: **return** $r(q, \mathcal{T})$

In the algorithm, $q[g/g']$ denotes the query obtained from q by replacing the atom g with a new atom g'. At step 8, for each pair of atoms g_1, g_2 that unify, the algorithm computes the query $q' = reduce(q, g_1, g_2)$, by applying to q the most general unifier between g_1 and g_2.[8] Due to the unification, variables that were bound in q may become unbound in q'. Hence, inclusion axioms that were not applicable to atoms of q, may become applicable to atoms of q' (in the next executions of step (5)). Function κ applied to q' replaces with _ each unbound variable in q'.

The main property of the query reformulation algorithm is as follows. It can be shown that

$$ans(\mathcal{K}, q) = \{\mathbf{c} \mid q_i \in r(q, \mathcal{T}), \mathcal{A} \models q_i(\mathbf{c})\} \ .$$

The above property dictates that the set of reformulated queries $q_i \in r(q, \mathcal{T})$ can be used to find the answers, by evaluating them over the set of instances $\mathcal{A}$ only, without referring to the ontology $\mathcal{T}$ anymore. Note, however, that the size of $r(q, \mathcal{T})$ may be exponential w.r.t. $\mathcal{T}$.

It can be shown that the above described algorithm computes correctly the answer set of a conjunctive query.

From a computational complexity point of view, it can be shown that

Proposition 14 ([82]). *Satisfiability of a KB $\mathcal{K}$ can be decided in time polynomial in the size of $\mathcal{K}$. Conjunctive query answering is in LogSpace in data complexity, while is NP-complete in combined complexity.*

Proposition 14 extends also to the case of disjunctive queries, to DL-Lite$_{\mathcal{F}, \sqcap}$, DL-Lite$_{\mathcal{R}, \sqcap}$, $\mathcal{DLR}$-Lite$_{\mathcal{F}, \sqcap}$ and $\mathcal{DLR}$-Lite$_{\mathcal{R}, \sqcap}$ [83].

---

[8]We say that two atoms $g_1 = r(x_1, \ldots, x_n)$ and $g_2 = r(y_1, \ldots, y_n)$ *unify*, if for all i, either $x_i = y_i$ or $x_i = \_$ or $y_i = \_$. If g_1 and g_2 unify, then the unification of g_1 and g_2 is the atom $r(z_1, \ldots, z_n)$, where $z_i = x_i$ if $x_i = y_i$ or $y_i = \_$, otherwise $z_i = y_i$ [80].

Example 15 ([410]). *Suppose we have the following information about hotels and conferences.*

$$
\begin{array}{rcl}
\texttt{Accommodation} & \sqsubseteq & \exists\texttt{HasALoc} \\
\texttt{Accommodation} & \sqsubseteq & \exists\texttt{HasAPrice} \\
\texttt{Conference} & \sqsubseteq & \exists\texttt{HasCLoc} \\
\texttt{Hotel} & \sqsubseteq & \texttt{Accommodation} \\
\texttt{Hotel}\star & \sqsubseteq & \texttt{Accommodation} \\
\texttt{Hotel}\star\star & \sqsubseteq & \texttt{Accommodation} \\
& \vdots & \\
\texttt{Hotel}\star\star\star\star\star & \sqsubseteq & \texttt{Accommodation}
\end{array}
$$

HasALoc		HasCLoc		HasHPrice	
AID	HasLoc	ConfID	HasLoc	AID	Price
a1	hl1	c1	cl1	a1	150
a2	hl2	c2	cl2	a2	200
⋮	⋮	⋮	⋮	⋮	⋮

We may ask to find accommodations, their location, and price. The query may be expressed as

$$q(a, hl, p) \leftarrow \texttt{Accomodation}(a), \texttt{HasHLoc}(a, hl), \texttt{HasHPrice}(a, p) \ .$$

Then the following is the set of query rewritings $r(q, \mathcal{T})$:

$$
\begin{array}{rcl}
q(a, hl, p) & \leftarrow & \texttt{Accomodation}(a), \texttt{HasHLoc}(a, hl), \texttt{HasHPrice}(a, p) \\
q(a, hl, p) & \leftarrow & \texttt{Hotel}(a), \texttt{HasHLoc}(a, hl), \texttt{HasHPrice}(a, p) \\
q(a, hl, p) & \leftarrow & \texttt{Hotel}\star(a), \texttt{HasHLoc}(a, hl), \texttt{HasHPrice}(a, p) \\
& \vdots & \\
q(a, hl, p) & \leftarrow & \texttt{Hotel}\star\star\star\star\star(a), \texttt{HasHLoc}(a, hl), \texttt{HasHPrice}(a, p) \ .
\end{array}
$$

4.4.4 The Case of the Horn-DLs Family

A main feature of the Horn-DL family is its close relationship with logic programming and, indeed, reasoning is performed via a translation of Horn-DL statements into a logic programming language. In fact, [339] shows how OWL 2 RL can be implemented using the rule language RIF (Core).[9]

For the sake of ease of presentation, we are not going to present the whole mapping for Horn-DL, but for a significant subset only that is sufficient to illustrate the main idea behind this translation. The Horn-DL language we consider here is

$$
\begin{array}{rcl}
B & \longrightarrow & A \mid B_1 \sqcap B_2 \mid B_1 \sqcup B_2 \mid \exists R.B \\
C & \longrightarrow & A \mid C_1 \sqcap C_2 \mid \neg B \mid \forall R.C \\
R & \longrightarrow & P \mid P^-
\end{array}
$$

where inclusion axioms have the form

---

[9]A partial mapping is provided also in [341].

$$B \sqsubseteq C$$
$$R_1 \sqsubseteq R_2 \ .$$

Assertions are of the form $a{:}C, (a, b){:}R$.

Our mapping follows [173]. In the following, a *rule* [263] is as a conjunctive query with the exception that an unary or binary predicate occurs in the rule head. A *fact* is a rule $F \leftarrow$ with empty body. Facts are denoted F as well (omitting the symbol $\leftarrow$).[10]

We now define a recursive mapping function σ which takes inclusions axioms and assertions and maps then into the following expressions:

$$
\begin{aligned}
\sigma(R_1 \sqsubseteq R_2) &\mapsto \sigma_{role}(R_2, x, y) \leftarrow \sigma_{role}(R_1, x, y) \\
\sigma_{role}(R, x, y) &\mapsto R(x, y) \\
\sigma_r(R^-, x, y) &\mapsto R(y, x)
\end{aligned}
$$

$$
\begin{aligned}
\sigma(B \sqsubseteq C) &\mapsto \sigma_h(C, x) \leftarrow \sigma_b(B) \\
\sigma_h(A, x) &\mapsto A(x) \\
\sigma_h(C_1 \sqcap C_2, x) &\mapsto \sigma_h(C_1, x) \wedge \sigma_h(C_2, x) \\
\sigma_h(\forall R.C, x) &\mapsto \sigma_h(C, x) \leftarrow \sigma_{role}(R, x, y) \\
\sigma_b(A, x) &\mapsto A(x) \\
\sigma_b(C_1 \sqcap C_2, x) &\mapsto \sigma_b(C_1, x) \wedge \sigma_b(C_2, x) \\
\sigma_b(C_1 \sqcup C_2, x) &\mapsto \sigma_b(C_1, x) \vee \sigma_b(C_2, x) \\
\sigma_b(\exists R.C, x) &\mapsto \sigma_{role}(R, x, y) \wedge \sigma_b(C, y)
\end{aligned}
$$

$$
\begin{aligned}
\sigma(a{:}C) &\mapsto \sigma_h(C, a) \leftarrow \\
\sigma((a, b){:}R) &\mapsto \sigma_{role}(R, a, b) \leftarrow
\end{aligned}
$$

where y is a new variable.

We then transform the above generated expressions into rules by applying recursively the following mapping:

$$
\begin{aligned}
\sigma_r((H \wedge H') \leftarrow B) &\mapsto \sigma_r(H \leftarrow B), \sigma_r(H' \leftarrow B) \\
\sigma_r((H \leftarrow H') \leftarrow B) &\mapsto \sigma_r(H \leftarrow (B \wedge H')) \\
\sigma_r(H \leftarrow (B_1 \vee B_2)) &\mapsto \sigma_r(H \leftarrow B_1), \sigma_r(H \leftarrow B_2)
\end{aligned}
$$

Eventually, if none of the above three rules can be applied then

$$\sigma_r(H \leftarrow B) \mapsto H \leftarrow B \ .$$

---

[10]See Chapter 5.

For instance, the GCI

$$A \sqcap \exists R.C \sqsubseteq B \sqcap \forall P.D$$

is first mapped into the expression (via σ)

$$B(x) \wedge (D(x) \leftarrow P(x,z)) \leftarrow A(x) \wedge R(x,y) \wedge C(y)$$

that then is transformed into the two rules (via σ_r)

$$
\begin{aligned}
B(x) &\leftarrow A(x), R(x,y), C(y) \\
D(z) &\leftarrow A(x), R(x,y), C(y), P(x,z) \ .
\end{aligned}
$$

It can be shown that

Proposition 15 ([173])**.** *The above described transformation preserves semantic equivalence. That is, let $\mathcal{K}$ be a KB and $\mathcal{P}_{\mathcal{K}}$ be the rule set that results from applying the transformation to all axioms in $\mathcal{K}$, then $\mathcal{P}_{\mathcal{K}}$ is logically equivalent to $\mathcal{K}$ w.r.t. the semantics of FOL $\mathcal{P}_{\mathcal{K}}$ has the same set of models and entailed conclusions as $\mathcal{K}$.*

Hence, reasoning in Horn-DL can be reduced to reasoning within logic programming (see Chapter 5).

4.4.5 Reasoning Complexity Summary

We resume in Table 4.8 here the complexity of various reasoning task for the OWL family.

TABLE 4.8: The complexity of various reasoning task for the OWL family.

Language	Taxonomic Complexity	Data Complexity	Combined Complexity
OWL 2	2NExpTime-complete	Decidable	2NExpTime-complete
OWL 2 EL	PTime-complete	PTime-complete	PTime-complete
OWL 2 QL	NLogSpace-complete	AC^0	NLogSpace-complete
OWL 2 RL	PTime-complete	PTime-complete	PTime-complete
OWL DL	2NExpTime-complete	Decidable	NExpTime-complete

Chapter 5

Rule Languages

5.1 Introduction

The *Rule Interchange Format* (RIF) [365] is the third building block of the infrastructure for the Semantic Web, along with (principally) SPARQL, RDF, and OWL. Although originally envisioned by many as a rules layer for the Semantic Web, in reality the design of RIF is based on the observation that there are many rules languages in existence, and what is needed is to exchange rules between them. That is, RIF focuses on exchange rather than trying to develop a single one-fits-all rule language because, in contrast to other Semantic Web standards, such as RDF, OWL, and SPARQL, it was immediately clear that a single language would not satisfy the needs of many popular paradigms for using rules in knowledge representation and business modelling (see also the case of RuleML [63]).

A *rule* is perhaps one of the simplest notions in computer science, specifically FOL: it is an IF - THEN construct, *i.e.*, a *Horn* formula (named after the logician Alfred Horn). If some condition (the IF part) that is checkable in some dataset holds, then the conclusion (the THEN part) is processed. Deriving somewhat from its roots in Logic, rule systems use a notion of predicates that hold or not of some data object or objects. For example, the fact that two people are married might be represented with predicates as $Married(lisa, john)$. *Married* is a predicate that can be said to hold between individuals *lisa* and *john*. Adding the notion of variables, a rule could be something like:

$$\text{if } Married(x, y) \text{ then } Loves(x, y) \ .$$

We would expect that for every pair of $\langle x, y \rangle$ (*e.g.*, *lisa* and *john*) for which the *Married* predicate holds, using this rule we would conclude that the *Loves* predicate holds for that pair as well.

As pointed out in Section 2.3, RIF includes three dialects, a *Core* dialect that is extended into a *Basic Logic Dialect* (BLD) and *Production Rule Dialect* (PRD).

RIF-Core RIF-Core corresponds to Horn logic without function symbols (*i.e.*, Datalog [449]) with a number of extensions to support features such as objects and frames as in F-logic [238]. RIF-Core is a subset of RIF-BLD and RIF-PRD.

RIF-BLD From a theoretical perspective, RIF-BLD corresponds to the language of definite Horn rules with equality and a standard first-order semantics [93]. RIF-Core is a a specialization of RIF-BLD.

RIF-PRD It aims at capturing the main aspects of various production rule systems. Production rules have an if part, or condition, and a then part, or action. The condition is like the condition part of logic rules (as covered by RIF-Core and its basic logic dialect extension, RIF-BLD). The then part contains actions. An action can assert facts, modify facts, retract facts, and have other side effects. In general, an action is different from the conclusion of a logic rule, which contains only a logical statement. However, the conclusion of rules interchanged using RIF-Core can be interpreted, according to RIF-PRD operational semantics, as actions that assert facts in the knowledge base.

As we did for RDFS and OWL 2, where we were looking at the logical foundations of these languages, we present here the logical foundations behind RIF, too. Specifically, we present here Datalog [2, 449] with concrete datatypes (compare with OWL 2 concrete domains in Section 4.2.2.2), which is at the heart of RIF-Core, the common ingredient between RIF-BLD and RIF-PRD, and is sufficient to illustrate the main characteristics of the RIF family.

Appendix D describes RIF-Core and the mapping of a significant sublanguage of RIF-Core to Datalog.

5.2   Datalog Basics

Datalog is a rule and query language for deductive databases that syntactically is a subset of *Logic Programs* [263] and became prominent as a separate area around 1977 when Hervé Gallaire and Jack Minker organized a workshop on logic and databases [166]. David Maier is credited with coining the term Datalog [2].

A *knowledge base* $\mathcal{K} = \langle \mathcal{F}, \mathcal{P} \rangle$ consists of a finite *facts component* $\mathcal{F}$ and a finite *LP component* $\mathcal{P}$, which are both defined below.

Facts Component. F is a finite set of *atoms* of the form

$$p(c_1, \ldots, c_n) \ ,$$

where p is an n-ary relation and every c_i is an individual (also called *constant*). For each p, we represent the facts $p(c_1, \ldots, c_n)$ in $\mathcal{F}$ by means of a relational n-ary table T_p, containing the records $\langle c_1, \ldots, c_n \rangle$. We assume that there cannot be two records representing the same tuple (if there are, then we remove one of them).

Example 16 ([358]). *Suppose we have a car-selling site, and we would like to buy a car. The facts are the cars, which belong to the relation CarTable shown below.*

					CarTable				
ID	*MODEL*	*TYPE*	*PRICE*	*KM*	*COLOR*	*AIR BAG*	*AIR COND*	*ENG FUEL*	*DISCOUNT*
455	*MAZDA 3*	*Sedan*	*12500*	*18000*	*Red*	*0*	*1*	*Gasoline*	*0.1*
34	*ALFA 156*	*Sedan*	*12000*	*17000*	*Black*	*1*	*0*	*Diesel*	*0.2*
1812	*FORD FOCUS*	*Estate*	*13000*	*16000*	*Gray*	*1*	*1*	*Gasoline*	*0.2*

Rule Component. $\mathcal{P}$ is a finite set of *rules*, which are similar as conjunctive RDFS and DL queries (See Sections 3.3, 4.3 and 6), and are of the form

$$p(\mathbf{x}) \leftarrow \exists \mathbf{y}.\varphi(\mathbf{x}, \mathbf{y}) \;, \tag{5.1}$$

where now $\varphi(\mathbf{x}, \mathbf{y})$ is a conjunction[1] of n-ary predicates $p_i(\mathbf{z}_i)$ and $\mathbf{z}_i$ is a vector of distinguished or non-distinguished variables. Specifically, we say that $p(\mathbf{x})$ is the *head* and $\exists \mathbf{y}.\varphi(\mathbf{x}, \mathbf{y})$ is the *body* of the rule, $\mathbf{x}$ is a vector of variables occurring in the body, called the *distinguished variables*, $\mathbf{y}$ are so-called *non-distinguished variables* and are distinct from the variables in $\mathbf{x}$, each variable occurring in p_i is either a distinguished or a non-distinguished variable. If clear from the context, we may omit the existential quantification $\exists \mathbf{y}$. We also assume that predicate names in a rule body are distinct, *i.e.*, $p_i \neq p_j$ for $i \neq j$. The intended meaning of a rule such as (5.1) is that the head $p(\mathbf{x})$ is true whenever the body $\mathbf{y}.\varphi(\mathbf{x}, \mathbf{y})$ is true.

We also assume that relations occurring in $\mathcal{F}$ do not occur in the head of rules (so, we do not allow that the fact relations occurring in $\mathcal{F}$ can be redefined by $\mathcal{P}$). As usual in deductive databases, the relations in $\mathcal{F}$ are called *extensional* relations, while the others are *intensional* relations.

Example 17. *Consider again Example 16. An excerpt of the domain ontology is described below and partially encodes the web directory behind the car selling site www. autos. com.*

$\texttt{Vehicles}(x) \leftarrow \texttt{Cars}(x)$	$\texttt{Cars}(x) \leftarrow \texttt{Estate}(x)$
$\texttt{Vehicles}(x) \leftarrow \texttt{Trucks}(x)$	$\texttt{PassengerCars}(x) \leftarrow \texttt{MidSizeCars}(x)$
$\texttt{Vehicles}(x) \leftarrow \texttt{Vans}(x)$	$\texttt{PassengerCars}(x) \leftarrow \texttt{SportyCars}(x)$
$\texttt{Cars}(x) \leftarrow \texttt{LuxuryCars}(x)$	$\texttt{PassengerCars}(x) \leftarrow \texttt{CompactCars}(x)$
$\texttt{Cars}(x) \leftarrow \texttt{PassengerCars}(x)$	$\texttt{hasPrice}(x_1, x_4) \leftarrow \texttt{CarTable}(x_1, \ldots, x_9)$
$\texttt{Cars}(x_1) \leftarrow \texttt{CarTable}(x_1, \ldots, x_9)$	$\texttt{hasKm}(x_1, x_5) \leftarrow \texttt{CarTable}(x_1, \ldots, x_9)$
$\texttt{Cars}(x) \leftarrow \texttt{Sedan}(x)$	$\texttt{FuelType}(x_1, x_9) \leftarrow \texttt{CarTable}(x_1, \ldots, x_9)$

Remark 10. *Note that we impose relations p_i in a rule body to be distinct. This is not a limitation as we may rewrite, e.g.,*

$$p(x) \leftarrow q(x, y), q(y, z)$$

as

---

[1]Again we use the symbol "," to denote conjunction in the rule body.

$$p(x) \leftarrow q(x,y), p'(y,z)$$
$$p'(y,z) \leftarrow q(y,z)$$

for a new relation symbol p'.

We may write a fact $p(\mathbf{c})$ also as a rule of the form

$$p(\mathbf{c}) \leftarrow 1 \ , \tag{5.2}$$

where 1 in the body is a ground atom, which is always interpreted as true.

Semantics. From a semantics point of view, given $\mathcal{K} = \langle \mathcal{F}, \mathcal{P} \rangle$, the notions of *Herbrand universe* $H_\mathcal{K}$ (the set of all constants occurring in $\mathcal{K}$) and *Herbrand base* $B_\mathcal{K}$ of $\mathcal{K}$ (the set of all ground atoms that can be formed using constants in $H_\mathcal{K}$ and atoms occurring in $\mathcal{K}$) are as usual.

Additionally, given $\mathcal{K}$, the set of ground rules $\mathcal{K}^*$ derived from the grounding of $\mathcal{K}$ is constructed as follows:

1. set $\mathcal{K}^*$ to be $\{p(\mathbf{c}) \leftarrow 1 \mid p(\mathbf{c}) \in \mathcal{F}\}$;

2. add to $\mathcal{K}^*$ the set of all ground instantiations of rules in $\mathcal{P}$.

An *interpretation* $\mathcal{I}$ for $\mathcal{K}$ is a subset of $B_\mathcal{K}$. Given $\mathcal{K}$, we say that $\mathcal{I}$ *satisfies* (*is a model of*)

- the ground atom 1, denoted $\mathcal{I} \models 1$;

- a ground atom $A \in B_\mathcal{K}$, denoted $\mathcal{I} \models A$, iff $A \in \mathcal{I}$;

- a ground rule body ϕ of a rule $A \leftarrow \phi \in \mathcal{K}^*$, denoted $\mathcal{I} \models \phi$, iff $\mathcal{I}$ is a model of all atoms in ϕ;

- a ground rule $r \in \mathcal{K}^*$, denoted $\mathcal{I} \models r$, iff $\mathcal{I}$ is a model of the head of r whenever $\mathcal{I}$ is a model of the body of r;

- $\mathcal{K}^*$, denoted $\mathcal{I} \models \mathcal{K}^*$, iff $\mathcal{I}$ satisfies all rules $r \in \mathcal{K}^*$;

- $\mathcal{K}$, denoted $\mathcal{I} \models \mathcal{K}$, if $\mathcal{I}$ is a model of $\mathcal{K}^*$.

Let $\mathbf{I}_\mathcal{K} = 2^{B_\mathcal{K}}$ be the set of all interpretations (there are $2^{|B_\mathcal{K}|}$ many). Now, for $\mathcal{I}_1, \mathcal{I}_2 \in \mathbf{I}_\mathcal{K}$, we write $\mathcal{I}_1 \leq \mathcal{I}_2$ iff $\mathcal{I}_1 \subseteq \mathcal{I}_2$. It is easy to see that $\langle \mathbf{I}_\mathcal{K}, \leq \rangle$ is a finite complete lattice.

Among all the models, one model plays a special role: namely the $\leq$-least model $M_\mathcal{K}$ of $\mathcal{K}$. The existence, finiteness, and uniqueness of the minimal model $M_\mathcal{K}$ is guaranteed to exist by the following argument (see, *e.g.*, [263]).

Consider the function $T_\mathcal{K} \colon \mathbf{I}_\mathcal{K} \to \mathbf{I}_\mathcal{K}$ defined as

$$T_\mathcal{K}(\mathcal{I}) := \{A \mid A \leftarrow \phi \in \mathcal{K}^* \text{ s.t. } \mathcal{I} \models \phi\} \ . \tag{5.3}$$

Then, it can be shown that $T_\mathcal{K}$ is monotone on $\mathbf{I}_\mathcal{K}$, *i.e.*, if $\mathcal{I}_1 \leq \mathcal{I}_2$ then $T_\mathcal{K}(\mathcal{I}_1) \leq T_\mathcal{K}(\mathcal{I}_2)$. By the well-known Tarski-Knaster fixed-point theorem [439] for monotone functions over complete lattices, we get immediately:

Proposition 16. *For a knowledge base $\mathcal{K}$, there exists a unique minimal model $M_{\mathcal{K}}$ that is the least fixed point of the function $T_{\mathcal{K}}$. $M_{\mathcal{K}}$ can be obtained as the limit of the $\leq$-monotone sequence, $\mathcal{I}_0, \ldots, \mathcal{I}_i, \ldots$, where*

$$\begin{aligned} \mathcal{I}_0 &= \mathcal{F} \\ \mathcal{I}_{i+1} &= T_{\mathcal{K}}(\mathcal{I}_i) . \end{aligned} \tag{5.4}$$

The minimal model is attained in at most $2^{|B_{\mathcal{K}}|}$ $T_{\mathcal{K}}$ iterations.

5.3 Concrete Domains

Similarly to DLs (see Section 4.2.2.2), we may extend Datalog with *concrete domains*, to deal with datatypes, such as strings and integers. The formalization is similar to DLs, *i.e.*, we assume a set of constants that are *data values* and a set of *datatype predicates*, where each datatype predicate has a predefined arity $n \geq 1$. A *datatype theory* $\mathbf{D} = \langle \Delta^{\mathbf{D}}, \cdot^{\mathbf{D}} \rangle$ consists of a finite datatype domain $\Delta^{\mathbf{D}}$ and a mapping $\cdot^{\mathbf{D}}$ that assigns to each data value an element of $\Delta^{\mathbf{D}}$ and to each datatype predicate p of arity n a relation over $\Delta^{\mathbf{D}}$ of arity n.

A *concrete atom* is an expression of the form $\mathbf{d}(\mathbf{z})$, where $\mathbf{z}$ is a vector of variables or data values. We extend an interpretation $\mathcal{I}$ to concrete atoms by saying that $\mathcal{I}$ *satisfies* (*is a model of*) a ground concrete atom $\mathbf{d}(\mathbf{v})$, denoted $\mathcal{I} \models \mathbf{d}(\mathbf{v})$ iff $\mathbf{v} \in \mathbf{d}^{\mathbf{D}}$. For instance, $\geq_{20}$ may be a unary predicate denoting the set of integers greater or equal to 20. For convenience, we write "functional predicates"[2] as *assignments* of the form $x := f(\mathbf{z})$ and assume that the function $f(\mathbf{z})$ is safe.

Rules are then extended by allowing concrete atoms to occur in a rule body with the condition that the concrete atom is *safe*, *i.e.*, a variable occurring in a concrete atom does also occur in non-concrete atoms, of the same rule. For instance, the

$$GoodHotel(x, r, p) \leftarrow Hotel(x), HasRoomPrice(x, r, p), \leq_{80}(p) \tag{5.5}$$

has intended meaning to define a good hotel as one having a room with a price not larger than 80€.

Next, let us extend both the Herbrand universe as $H_{\mathcal{K}}^{\mathbf{D}} := H_{\mathcal{K}} \cup \Delta^{\mathbf{D}}$ and the Herbrand base $B_{\mathcal{K}}^{\mathbf{D}}$ to the set of all ground atoms and ground concrete atoms that can be formed from the constants in the Herbrand universe.

An interpretation $\mathcal{I}$ is extended by being a subset of $B_{\mathcal{K}}^{\mathbf{D}}$ with the additional condition that $\mathbf{d}(\mathbf{v}) \in \mathcal{I}$ iff $\mathcal{I} \models \mathbf{d}(\mathbf{v})$. Of course, $\langle 2^{B_{\mathcal{K}}^{\mathbf{D}}}, \leq \rangle$ is still a finite complete lattice (recall that $\Delta^{\mathbf{D}}$ is finite).

---

[2] A predicate $p(\mathbf{x}, y)$ is functional if for any $\mathbf{v}$ there is *unique* v' for which $p(\mathbf{v}, v')$ is true.

Now, the notions of *satisfaction* (*is model of*) are extended in the obvious way to rules including concrete atoms. It is then straightforward to see that the analogue of Proposition 16 still applies to interpretations over $B_{\mathcal{K}}^{D}$ in place of $B_{\mathcal{K}}$.

5.4   Conjunctive Queries

A *query* is a rule

$$q(\mathbf{x}) \leftarrow \exists \mathbf{y}.\varphi(\mathbf{x},\mathbf{y}) \; , \tag{5.6}$$

and the *answer set* of a query q w.r.t. a set $\mathcal{K}$ of facts and rules (denoted $ans(\mathcal{K},q)$) is the set of tuples $\mathbf{t}$ such that there exists $\mathbf{t}'$ such that the instantiation $\varphi(\mathbf{t},\mathbf{t}')$ of the query body is satisfied by the *minimal model* of $\mathcal{K}$, which is guaranteed to exist by Proposition 16.

Example 18. *Consider the following rules:*

$$r_1 : \text{path}(x,y) \quad \leftarrow \quad \text{edge}(x,y) \tag{5.7}$$
$$r_2 : \text{path}(x,y) \quad \leftarrow \quad \text{path}(x,z), \text{edge}(z,y) \tag{5.8}$$

The knowledge base $\mathcal{K}$ contains the rules above and the extensional database of edges as shown in the relational table T_{edge} below:

T_{edge}	
c	b
a	c
b	a
a	b

It can be verified that the set of answers of predicate path *is given by:*

$ans(\mathcal{K},\text{path})$					
a	a	b	a	c	a
a	b	b	b	c	b
a	c	b	c	c	c

For instance, informally $\langle a,a \rangle \in ans(\mathcal{K},\text{path})$ as there is an edge from a to b and, thus, there is a path from a to b. Therefore, as there is and edge from b to a as well, there is a path from a to a.

In order to verify the whole, below we report the computation of the minimal model $M_{\mathcal{K}}$ according to Proposition 16. We report only the restriction of $\mathcal{I}_i$ to the predicate path, *denoted as $\mathcal{I}_i(\text{path}) = \{\mathbf{t} \mid \text{path}(\mathbf{t}) \in \mathcal{I}_i\}$.*[3]

---

[3]The analogous value of $\mathcal{I}_i(\text{edge})$ remains constantly equal to the tuples in $\mathcal{F}$.

$$
\begin{aligned}
\mathcal{I}_0(\texttt{path}) &= \emptyset \\
\mathcal{I}_1(\texttt{path}) &= \mathcal{F} \\
\mathcal{I}_2(\texttt{path}) &= \mathcal{I}_1(\texttt{path}) \cup \{\langle c, a\rangle, \langle b, c\rangle, \langle b, b\rangle, \langle a, a\rangle\} \\
\mathcal{I}_3(\texttt{path}) &= \mathcal{I}_2(\texttt{path}) \cup \{\langle c, c\rangle\} \\
\mathcal{I}_4(\texttt{path}) &= \mathcal{I}_3(\texttt{path}) \;.
\end{aligned}
$$

So, the least fixed point, i.e., minimal model is attained after four $T_{\mathcal{P}}$ iterations.

5.5 Reasoning

The major reasoning task is to compute the answer set $ans(\mathcal{K}, q)$ of a query q, given a KB $\mathcal{K}$.

A simple query answering procedure to determine $ans(\mathcal{K}, q)$ is:

1. Convert $\mathcal{K}$ into $\mathcal{K}^*$;

2. Compute the minimal model $M_{\mathcal{K}}$ of $\mathcal{K}^*$;

3. Store the minimal model $M_{\mathcal{K}}$ of $\mathcal{K}^*$ in a database;

4. Translate the query q into an SQL statement;

5. Execute the SQL query over the relational database.

A bottleneck of this approach is that $M_{\mathcal{K}}$ may be huge, in the worst case exponential in the size of $\mathcal{K}$ (note that if $k = |H_{\mathcal{K}}|$ and p is an n-ary predicate then there are n^k ground instances of p). To overcome this problem, the LP community has developed numerous alternative approaches [2, 263, 449], notably SLD-Resolution [147, 263] and *memoing* techniques (also called *tabulation/tabulation/magic sets*) –see, *e.g.*, [95, 461].

We present them here as they are two major representatives, and which broadly belongs to the family of so-called *query driven answering procedures*.

5.5.1 SLD-Resolution Driven Query Answering

SLD-Resolution (Selective Linear Definite clause resolution) is the basic inference rule used in logic programming (see, *e.g.*, [263]). It is a refinement of resolution (see *e.g.*, [67, 93, 158, 167, 378]), which is both sound and refutation complete for Horn clauses and was introduced first in [147].

The basic principle underlying the method is as follows. We first illustrate the propositional case and the FOL case.

The propositional SLD inference rule is as follows: assume we have propositional rules

$$
\begin{array}{ll}
\text{From} & A \leftarrow A_1, \dots, C, \dots, A_k \\
\text{and} & B \leftarrow B_1, \dots, B_m \\
\text{and} & B = C \\
\hline
\text{infer} & A \leftarrow A_1, \dots, B_1, \dots, B_m, \dots, A_k
\end{array}
\tag{5.9}
$$

where the inferred rule is obtained from $A \leftarrow A_1, \dots, C, \dots, A_k$ by replacing atom C with the atoms $B_1, \dots, B_m$. The propositional atom B is called the *selected* atom.

In the FOL case the atoms B and C, which may contain variables, need not be equal. However, it is required that B and C have a *most general unifier* (mgu) (see,*e.g.*, [263]), that is a substitution θ of the variables in B and C such that the application of the substitution to B and C make the two atoms equal.

Specifically, a *substitution* θ is a finite set of the form

$$
\theta = \{x_1/t_1, \dots, x_n/t_n\} \, ,
$$

where each x_i is variable, each t_i is either a variable or constant distinct from x_i, and the variables $x_1, \dots, x_n$ are distinct. Each element x_i/t_i is called a *binding* for x_i. θ is called *ground* if all t_i are constants. θ is called a *variable substitution* iff all t_i are variables.

Given an atom A and a substitution $\theta = \{x_1/t_1, \dots, x_n/t_n\}$, with $A\theta$ we denote the atom obtained from A by replacing simultaneously all variables x_i with t_i. Given two substitutions $\theta = \{x_1/t_1, \dots, x_n/t_n\}$ and $\sigma = \{y_1/s_1, \dots, y_m/s_m\}$, then the *composition* $\theta\sigma$ of θ and σ is the substitution obtained from the set

$$
\{x_1/t_1\sigma, \dots, x_n/t_n\sigma, y_1/s_1, \dots, y_m/s_m\}
$$

by deleting the bindings $x_i/t_i\sigma$ for which $x_i = t_i\sigma$ and deleting any binding y_j/s_j for which $y_j \in \{x_1, \dots, x_n\}$.

The substitution ϵ given by the empty set is called *identity substitution*.

Two atoms A and B are variants iff there is a substitution θ and σ such that $A = B\theta$ and $B = A\sigma$.

A variable substitution $\theta = \{x_1/y_1, \dots, x_n/y_n\}$ is called a *renaming* of A if given that

- V is the set of variables occurring in A;

- all x_i are in V;

- all y_i are distinct,

then

$$
(V \setminus \{x_1, \dots, x_n\}) \cap \{y_1, \dots, y_n\} = \emptyset \, .
$$

Let $S = \{A_1, \dots, A_n\}$ be a set of atoms A_i, we say that a substitution θ is an *unifier* for S iff $S\theta = \{A_1\theta, \dots, A_n\theta\}$ is a singleton set. An unifier of S is called *most general unifier* (mgu) for S if, for each unifier σ of S there exists a non-empty substitution γ such that $\sigma = \theta\gamma$. We say that two atoms A and B *unify* iff there is an mgu for $\{A, B\}$. We refer the reader to, *e.g.*, [263, 308], for unification algorithms.

We are now ready to illustrate the SLD-resolution rule for Datalog rules:

$$
\begin{array}{ll}
\text{From} & A \leftarrow A_1, \ldots, C, \ldots, A_k \\
\text{and} & B \leftarrow B_1, \ldots, B_m \\
\text{and} & \theta \text{ as a mgu of } \{B, C\} \\
\hline
\text{infer} & A\theta \leftarrow A_1\theta, \ldots, B_1\theta, \ldots, B_m\theta \ldots, A_k\theta
\end{array}
\qquad (5.10)
$$

in which we assume that all atoms in the second rule have been renamed in order not to share any variable with the first one.

We have also a specialized case that involves a fact

$$
\begin{array}{ll}
\text{From} & A \leftarrow A_1, \ldots, C, \ldots, A_k \\
\text{and fact} & B \\
\text{and} & \theta \text{ as a mgu of } \{B, C\} \\
\hline
\text{infer} & A\theta \leftarrow A_1\theta, \ldots, 1, \ldots, A_k\theta
\end{array}
\qquad (5.11)
$$

Now, consider a KB $\mathcal{K}$ and a query rule

$$ q(\mathbf{x}) \leftarrow \phi . $$

An *SLD-derivation* of q w.r.t. $\mathcal{K}$ consists of a finite sequence of rules $r_1, \ldots, r_n$, each of which has q as head, r_1 is the query rule, each rule r_{i+1} is inferred from r_i via SLD-resolution, and r_n is the rule

$$ q(\mathbf{x})\theta \leftarrow \mathbf{1} $$

telling us that indeed $q(\mathbf{x})\theta$ is always true. In that case, we say that the restriction of the substitution θ to the variables in $\mathbf{x}$ is a *computed answer* for q. With $\theta_{|\mathbf{x}}$ we denote the vector $\langle x_1\theta, \ldots, x_n\theta \rangle$.

It can be shown that

Proposition 17 (Soundness & Completeness [263]). *Given a KB $\mathcal{K}$ and a query q of the form $q(\mathbf{x}) \leftarrow \phi$, then*

1. *every computed answer is an answer, i.e., if θ is a computed answer of q w.r.t. $\mathcal{K}$, then $\theta_{|\mathbf{x}} \in ans(\mathcal{K}, q)$;*

2. *for every answer $\mathbf{c} \in ans(\mathcal{K}, q)$, there is a computed answer θ of q w.r.t. $\mathcal{K}$ such $\theta_{|\mathbf{x}} = \mathbf{c}$.*

Hence in order to compute the answer set $ans(\mathcal{K}, q)$ via SLD-derivation, it suffices to determine (carefully, to avoid non-termination) all computed answers of q w.r.t. $\mathcal{K}$.

Example 19. *Consider Example 18 and the query*

$$q(x, y) \leftarrow \mathsf{path}(x, y) \ .$$

The following is an SLD-derivation of q w.r.t. $\mathcal{K}$:

$$
\begin{aligned}
q(x, y) &\leftarrow \mathsf{path}(x, y) & & \\
q(x, y) &\leftarrow \mathsf{path}(x, z), \mathsf{edge}(z, y) & \theta_{|\langle x, y \rangle} &= \langle \rangle \\
q(x, y) &\leftarrow \mathsf{path}(x, z_1), \mathsf{edge}(z_1, z), \mathsf{edge}(z, y) & \theta_{|\langle x, y \rangle} &= \langle -, - \rangle \\
q(x, y) &\leftarrow \mathsf{edge}(x, z_1), \mathsf{edge}(z_1, z), \mathsf{edge}(z, y) & \theta_{|\langle x, y \rangle} &= \langle -, - \rangle \\
q(c, y) &\leftarrow 1, \mathsf{edge}(b, z), \mathsf{edge}(z, y) & \theta_{|\langle x, y \rangle} &= \langle c, - \rangle \\
q(c, y) &\leftarrow 1, 1, \mathsf{edge}(a, y) & \theta_{|\langle x, y \rangle} &= \langle c, - \rangle \\
q(c, c) &\leftarrow 1, 1, 1 & \theta_{|\langle x, y \rangle} &= \langle c, c \rangle \ .
\end{aligned}
$$

Note that indeed $\theta_{|\langle x, y \rangle} = \langle c, c \rangle \in ans(\mathcal{K}, q)$ is an answer computed by this SLD-derivation.

Note that Example 19 exhibits also a potential non-terminating issue, if we apply the SLD-resolution always to the first atom of the query rule body. To this end appropriate atom selection strategies are required to avoid such a problem. We will not address them here. We instead present an alternative method that does not exhibit this issue, as illustrated next.

5.5.2   Tabling like Query Driven Query Answering

The algorithm we present here is an improved query driven query evaluation algorithm based on the *Semi Naive Evaluation Algorithm* for Datalog (see [33, 437, 449]) and may fall under the label of *memoing* technique (also called *tabling/tabulation*) –see, *e.g.*, [95, 461].

To start with, we recall that the *Semi-Naive Evaluation Algorithm* for Datalog[4] is a well-known query answering algorithm, whose basic idea is quite simple and has the advantage to be implemented on top of a relational database system to which to submit SQL queries.

Basically, as we do not want to rely on grounding $\mathcal{K}$, we collect the answers to a query incrementally together: roughly the method is as follows:

1. start by assuming all IDB (intensional database) relations empty;

2. repeatedly evaluate the rules using the EDB (extensional database) and the previous IDB, to get a new IDB;

3. stop when there is no change to IDB.

---

[4]http://infolab.stanford.edu/~ullman/fcdb/aut07/slides/dlog.ppt

Of course, since the EDB never changes, on each round we only get new IDB tuples if we use at least one IDB tuple that was obtained on the previous round. This allows us to save work by avoiding rediscovering most known facts.

To start with, we use the usual relation "directly depends on" among relation symbols, *i.e.*, given $\mathcal{K}$, we say that relation symbol p *directly depends on* relation symbol q if there is a rule in $\mathcal{K}$ such that p occurs in the head of it and q occurs in the body of it. The relation *depends on* is the transitive closure of "directly depends on". The *dependency graph* of $\mathcal{K}$ is a directed graph where nodes are relation symbols and the set of edges is the "directly depends on" relation. The KB is *recursive* if there is a cycle in the dependency graph (*i.e.*, there is p depending on p).

The query answering method we present is called *query driven* as we restrict the computation to predicates that depend on a query only.

At first, consider a general rule of the form $p(\mathbf{x}) \leftarrow \varphi(\mathbf{x}, \mathbf{y})$. Assume that $\varphi(\mathbf{x}, \mathbf{y})$ depends on the predicates $p_1, \ldots, p_k$, which occur in the rule body $\varphi(\mathbf{x}, \mathbf{y})$. Assume that $\Delta_{p_1}, \ldots, \Delta_{p_k}$ are the answers collected so far for the predicates $p_1, \ldots, p_k$. Let us consider a procedure $eval(p, \Delta_{p_1}, \ldots, \Delta_{p_k})$, which computes the set of answers $\mathbf{c}$ of p, by evaluating the body $\varphi(\mathbf{x}, \mathbf{y})$ over the data provided by $\Delta_{p_1}, \ldots, \Delta_{p_k}$. Of course, if the predicate p is in the head of more than one rule, then $eval(p, \Delta_{p_1}, \ldots, \Delta_{p_k})$ is the *union* of all the evaluations over the rules having p as head. Note also that $eval(p, \Delta_{p_1}, \ldots, \Delta_{p_k})$ is monotone in its arguments.

For instance, consider Example 18. Assume that both Δ_{edge} and Δ_{path} are given by $\mathcal{T}_{\mathrm{edge}}$. Then $eval(\mathrm{path}, \Delta_{\mathrm{edge}}, \Delta_{\mathrm{path}})$ returns the set of answers $\Delta'_{\mathrm{path}} = \mathcal{I}_2(\mathrm{path})$. Note that $eval(\mathrm{path}, \Delta_{\mathrm{edge}}, \Delta_{\mathrm{path}})$ can be obtained using relational algebra as:

$$ tab_{\Delta_{\mathrm{edge}}} \cup \pi_{1,4}(tab_{\Delta_{\mathrm{edge}}} \bowtie_{2=3} tab_{\Delta_{\mathrm{path}}}) \ . \tag{5.12} $$

In substance *eval* revises the set of answers for **path**. Note that with respect to Example 18, $tab_{\Delta'_{\mathrm{path}}}$ does not have the record $\langle c, c \rangle$. However, we obtain the answers after reiterating the evaluation step once more. That is, $eval(\mathrm{path}, \Delta_{\mathrm{edge}}, \Delta'_{\mathrm{path}})$ returns all answers of **path**. Note also that the union in Eq. (5.12) is due to the fact that **path** is in the head of two rules.

We are not going to further investigate the implementation details of the $eval(p, \Delta_{p_1}, \ldots, \Delta_{p_k})$ procedure, though it has to be carefully written to minimize the number of table look-ups and relational algebraic operations such as joins. It can be obtained by means of a combination of SQL statements over the tables and the application of the truth combination functions occurring in the rule body of p.

We point out that $eval(p, \Delta_{p_1}, \ldots, \Delta_{p_k})$ can also be seen as a query to a database made out by the relations $tab_{\Delta_{p_1}}, \ldots, tab_{\Delta_{p_k}}$ and that any successive evaluation step corresponds to the execution of the *same* query over an updated database. We refer the reader to, *e.g.*, [128, 129, 130, 259] concerning the problem of repeatedly evaluating the same query to a database that is being updated between successive query requests. In this situation, it may be possible to use the difference between successive database states and the answer to the query in one state to reduce the cost of evaluating the query in the next state.

We describe now our query answering procedure (see Algorithm 2). Assume we are interested in determining all answers of $q(\mathbf{x})$. We start with putting the predicate symbol q in the *active* set of predicate symbols A. At each iteration step we select a new predicate p from A and evaluate it using the *eval* function with respect to the answers gathered so far. If the evaluation leads to a better answer set for p ($\Delta_p > \mathbf{v}(p)$), we update the current answer set $\mathbf{v}(p)$ and add all predicates p', whose rule body contains p (the parents of p), to A, *i.e.*, all predicate symbols that might depend on p are put in the active set to be examined. At some point (even if cyclic definitions are present) A will become empty, as the truth space is finite, and we have actually found all answers of $q(\mathbf{x})$.

Algorithm 2 uses some auxiliary functions, data structures, and order definition:

- for two sets of tuples Δ_1 and Δ_2, we define

$$\Delta_1 > \Delta_2 \quad \text{iff} \quad \Delta_2 \subset \Delta_1 ; \qquad (5.13)$$

  As $eval(p_i, \mathbf{v}(p_{i_1}), ..., \mathbf{v}(p_{i_{k_i}}))$ is monotone, an optimized version of $eval(p_i, \mathbf{v}(p_{i_1}), ..., \mathbf{v}(p_{i_{k_i}}))$ may return only the newly retrieved tuples w.r.t. $\mathbf{v}(p_i)$. In that case, steps 10 and 11 have to be replaced with

  if $\Delta_{p_i} \neq \emptyset$ **then** $\mathbf{v}(p_i) := \mathbf{v}(p_i) \cup \Delta_{p_i}$, $\mathsf{A} := \mathsf{A} \cup (\mathbf{p}(p_i) \cap \mathbf{dg})$

- for predicate symbol p_i, $\mathbf{s}(p_i)$ is the set of predicate symbols occurring in the rule body of a rule having p_i as head, *i.e.*, the *sons* of p_i;

- for predicate symbol p_i, $\mathbf{p}(p_i) = \{p_j : p_i \in \mathbf{s}(p_j)\}$, *i.e.*, the *parents* of p_i;

- in step 9, $p_{i_1}, \ldots, p_{i_{k_i}}$ are all predicate symbols occurring in the rule bodies having p_i in its head, *i.e.*, the sons $\mathbf{s}(p_i) = \{p_{i_1}, \ldots, p_{i_{k_i}}\}$ of p_i;

- the variable $\mathbf{dg}$ collects the predicate symbols that may influence the result of the query predicates;

- the array variable $\mathbf{exp}$ traces the rule bodies that have been "expanded" (the predicate symbols occurring in the rule bodies are put into the active list);

- the variable $\mathbf{in}$ keeps track of the predicate symbols that have been put into the active list so far due to an expansion (to avoid, to put the same predicate symbol multiple times in the active list due to rule bodies expansion).

Algorithm 2 *Answer*$(\mathcal{K}, q)$

Input: Knowledge base $\mathcal{K}$, query q.
Output: A mapping v such that it contains all answers of q.
1: A $:= \{q\}$, dg $:= \{q\}$, in $:= \emptyset$.
2: **for all** predicate symbols p in $\mathcal{P}$ **do**
3:     v$(p) = \emptyset$, exp$(p) = $ false
4: **while** A $\neq \emptyset$ **do**
5:     **select** $p_i \in$ A, A $:=$ A $\setminus \{p_i\}$, dg $:=$ dg $\cup$ s(p_i)
6:     **if** $(p_i$ extensional predicate$) \wedge (\text{v}(p_i) = \emptyset)$ **then**
7:         v$(p_i) := tab_{p_i}$
8:     **if** p_i intensional predicate **then**
9:         $\Delta_{p_i} := eval(p_i, \text{v}(p_{i_1}), ..., \text{v}(p_{i_{k_i}}))$
10:     **if** $\Delta_{p_i} > \text{v}(p_i)$ **then**
11:         v$(p_i) := \Delta_{p_i}$, A $:=$ A $\cup$ (p$(p_i) \cap$ dg$)$
12:     **if not** exp(p_i) **then**
13:         exp$(p_i) = $ true, A $:=$ A $\cup$ (s$(p_i) \setminus$ in$)$, in $:=$ in $\cup$ s(p_i)
14: **return** v

From a computational complexity point of view, we recall that there are two main kinds of complexity connected to plain Datalog [452]:

- the *data complexity* is the complexity of checking whether $\langle \mathcal{F}, \mathcal{P} \rangle \models A$ when the set of rules $\mathcal{P}$ is fixed, whereas input databases $\mathcal{F}$ and ground atom A are an *input*;

- the *combined complexity* is the complexity of checking whether $\langle \mathcal{F}, \mathcal{P} \rangle \models A$ when input database $\mathcal{F}$, the set of rules $\mathcal{P}$, and ground atoms A are an input.

Grounding $\mathcal{P}$ on an input database $\mathcal{F}$ yields polynomially many clauses in the size of $\mathcal{F}$; hence, the complexity of propositional logic programming, which is linear (see, *e.g.*, [113, 132, 452]), is an upper bound for the data complexity. We thus get

Proposition 18 ([113, 453]). *Deciding whether* $\mathbf{t} \in ans(\mathcal{K}, q)$ *is P-complete in data complexity. The program complexity is exponentially higher: deciding whether* $\mathbf{t} \in ans(\mathcal{K}, q)$ *is ExpTime-complete in combined complexity.*

Example 20. *Consider Example 18. Let us compute all answers of predicate* path. *So, let* $q = $ path. *The execution of Answer*$(\mathcal{K}, q)$ *is shown in Table 5.1, which also reports* Δ_{p_i} *and* $\text{v}(p_i)$ *at each iteration* i.

TABLE 5.1: Query driven computation related to Example 20.

1.	$A := \{path\}, p_i := path, A := \emptyset, dg := \{path, edge\}, \Delta_{path} := \emptyset$
	$exp(path) := true, A := \{path, edge\}, in := \{path, edge\}$
2.	$p_i := path, A := \{edge\}, \Delta_{path} := \emptyset$
3.	$p_i := edge, A := \emptyset, v(edge) = \emptyset, v(edge) := tab_{edge}, A := \{path\}, exp(edge) := true$
4.	$p_i := path, A := \emptyset, \Delta_{path} > v(path), v(path) := \Delta_{path}, A := \{path\}$
5.	$p_i := path, A := \emptyset, \Delta_{path} > v(path), v(path) := \Delta_{path}, A := \{path\}$
6.	$p_i := path, A := \emptyset, \Delta_{path} > v(path), v(path) := \Delta_{path}, A := \{path\}$
7.	$p_i := path, A := \emptyset, \Delta_{path} = v(path)$
8.	stop. return $v(path)$

$Iter\_i$	Δ_{p_i}		$v(p_i)$
0.	—		$v(edge) = v(path) = \emptyset$
1.	$\Delta_{path} = \emptyset$		—
2.	$\Delta_{path} = \emptyset$		—
3.	—		$v(edge) = \Delta_{edge}$
4.	$\Delta_{path} = \{\langle a,b\rangle, \langle b,a\rangle, \langle a,c\rangle, \langle c,b\rangle\}$		$v(path) = \Delta_{path}$
5.	$\Delta_{path} = \{$	$\langle a,a\rangle, \langle a,b\rangle, \langle a,c\rangle,$ $\langle b,a\rangle, \langle b,b\rangle, \langle b,c\rangle,$ $\langle c,a\rangle, \langle c,b\rangle \}$	$v(path) = \Delta_{path}$
6.	$\Delta_{path} = \{$	$\langle a,a\rangle, \langle a,b\rangle, \langle a,c\rangle,$ $\langle b,a\rangle, \langle b,b\rangle, \langle b,c\rangle,$ $\langle c,a\rangle, \langle c,b\rangle, \langle c,c\rangle \}$	$v(path) = \Delta_{path}$
7.	$\Delta_{path} = \{$	$\langle a,a\rangle, \langle a,b\rangle, \langle a,c\rangle,$ $\langle b,a\rangle, \langle b,b\rangle, \langle b,c\rangle,$ $\langle c,a\rangle, \langle c,b\rangle, \langle c,c\rangle \}$	—

Chapter 6

Query Languages for SWL-based Knowledge Bases

6.1 Introduction

SPARQL [380, 381] is a query language and a protocol for data that is stored natively as RDF or viewed as RDF via middleware. The main mechanism for computing query results in SPARQL is subgraph matching: RDF triples in both the queried RDF data and the query pattern are interpreted as nodes and edges of directed graphs, and the resulting query graph is matched to the data graph using variables as wild cards. Various W3C standards, including RDF and OWL, provide semantic interpretations for RDF graphs that allow additional RDF statements to be inferred from explicitly given assertions. Many applications that rely on these semantics require a query language such as SPARQL, but in order to use SPARQL, basic graph pattern matching has to be defined using semantic entailment relations instead of explicitly given graph structures. There are different possible ways of defining a basic graph pattern matching extension for an entailment relation. [379] specifies one such way for a range of standard Semantic Web entailment relations. Such extensions of the SPARQL semantics are called *entailment regimes*. An entailment regime defines not only which entailment relation is used, but also which queries and graphs are well-formed for the regime, how the entailment is used (since there are potentially different meaningful ways to use the same entailment relation), or what kinds of errors can arise.

We are not going into the details of SPARQL specification, as we did not go into the details of RDFS, OWL 2, and RIF specification, but rather look at it from a logical perspective.

Specifically, we first introduce the notions of *conjunctive / disjunctive query* for KBs based on RDFS, Description Logics, and Logic Programs. Conjunctive queries have already been introduced in the previous chapters, though here we give a more involved version, which will be useful later on in this book. We then provide the formal definition of SPARQL 1.1.

6.2   Conjunctive and Disjunctive Queries

The RDFS case. We assume that a RDFS graph G is *ground*, that is blank nodes have been skolemized, *i.e.*, replaced with terms in **UL**. We recap here and extend the definitions of Section 3.3. So, an RDFS *query* is of the rule-like form

$$q(\mathbf{x}) \leftarrow \exists \mathbf{y}.\varphi(\mathbf{x}, \mathbf{y})$$

where we additionally allow built-in triples of the form (s, p, o), where p is a built-in predicate taken from a reserved vocabulary and having a *fixed interpretation*. We generalize the built-ins to any n-ary predicate p, where p's arguments may be ρdf variables, values from **UL**, and p has a fixed interpretation. We will assume that the evaluation of the predicate can be decided in finite time. For convenience, we write "functional predicates"[1] as *assignments* of the form $x := f(\mathbf{z})$ and assume that the function $f(\mathbf{z})$ is safe. We also assume that a non-functional built-in predicate $p(\mathbf{z})$ should be safe as well. For instance,

$$q(x_1, x_2) \leftarrow (x, worksFor, google), (x, hasSalary, s), (s, <, 23000)$$

is an RDFS query asking for Google employees earning less than 23000. Here $<$ is a built-in predicate.

The notions of *answer* and *answer set* of q w.r.t. G, *i.e.*,

$$ans(G, q) = \{\mathbf{t} \mid G \models q(\mathbf{t})\} \,,$$

are as from Section 3.3.

As next, we extend the query language by allowing so-called aggregates to occur in a query. Essentially, aggregates may be like the usual SQL aggregate functions such as SUM, AVG, MAX, MIN.

For instance, suppose we are looking for employees that work for some company. We would like to know the average salary of their employment. Such a query may be expressed as

$$
\begin{aligned}
q(x, avgS) \leftarrow \ & (x, worksFor, y), (x, hasSalary, s), \\
& \mathsf{GroupedBy}(x), \\
& avgS := \mathsf{AVG}[s] \,.
\end{aligned}
$$

Essentially, we group by the employee, consider for each employee the salaries, and compute the average salary value for each group. That is, if $g = \{\langle t, t_1 \rangle, \dots, \langle t, t_n \rangle\}$ is a group of tuples with the same value t for employee x, and value t_i for s, then the value of $avgL$ for the group g is $(\sum_i t_i)/n$.

---

[1] A predicate $p(\mathbf{x}, y)$ is functional if for any $\mathbf{t}$ there is *unique* t' for which $p(\mathbf{t}, t')$ is true.

Formally, let @ be an aggregate function with

$$@ \in \{\mathsf{SUM}, \mathsf{AVG}, \mathsf{MAX}, \mathsf{MIN}, \mathsf{COUNT}\}$$

then a query with aggregates is of the form

$$
\begin{aligned}
q(\mathbf{x}, \alpha) \quad \leftarrow \quad & \exists \mathbf{y}. \varphi(\mathbf{x}, \mathbf{y}), \\
& \mathsf{GroupedBy}(\mathbf{w}), \\
& \alpha := @[f(\mathbf{z})]
\end{aligned}
\qquad (6.1)
$$

where $\mathbf{w}$ are variables in $\mathbf{x}$ or $\mathbf{y}$, each variable in $\mathbf{x}$ occurs in $\mathbf{w}$ and any variable in $\mathbf{z}$ occurs in $\mathbf{y}$.

From a semantics point of view, we say that $\mathcal{I}$ *is a model of* (*satisfies*) $q(\mathbf{t}, a)$, denoted $\mathcal{I} \models q(\mathbf{t}, a)$ if and only if

> $a = @[a_1, \ldots, a_k]$ where $g = \{\langle \mathbf{t}, \mathbf{t}_1 \rangle, \ldots, \langle \mathbf{t}, \mathbf{t}_k \rangle\}$,
> is a group of k tuples with identical projection
> on the variables in $\mathbf{w}$, $\varphi(\mathbf{t}, \mathbf{t}_r)$ is true in $\mathcal{I}$
> and $a_r = f(\mathbf{t})$ where $\mathbf{t}_r$ is the projection of $\mathbf{t}_r$
> on the variables $\mathbf{z}$.

Now, the notion of $G \models q(\mathbf{t}, a)$ is as usual, *i.e.*, any model of G is a model of $q(\mathbf{t}, a)$.

Eventually, we further allow to order answers according to some ordering functions. For instance, assume that additionally would like to order the employee according to the average salary of employment. Then such a query will be expressed as

$$
\begin{aligned}
q(x, avgS) \quad \leftarrow \quad & (x, worksFor, y), (x, hasSalary, s), \\
& \mathsf{GroupedBy}(x), \\
& avgS := \mathsf{AVG}[s], \\
& \mathsf{OrderBy}(avgS) \ .
\end{aligned}
$$

Formally, a query with ordering is of the form

$$q(\mathbf{x}, z) \quad \leftarrow \quad \exists \mathbf{y}. \varphi(\mathbf{x}, \mathbf{y}), \mathsf{OrderBy}(z)$$

or, in case grouping is allowed as well, it is of the form

$$
\begin{aligned}
q(\mathbf{x}, z, \alpha) \quad \leftarrow \quad & \exists \mathbf{y}. \varphi(\mathbf{x}, \mathbf{y}), \\
& \mathsf{GroupedBy}(\mathbf{w}), \\
& \alpha := @[f(\mathbf{z})], \\
& \mathsf{OrderBy}(z) \ .
\end{aligned}
\qquad (6.2)
$$

From a semantics point of view, the notion of $G \models q(\mathbf{t}, z, a)$ is as before, but the notion of answer set has to be enforced with the fact that the answers are now ordered according to the assignment to the variable z. Of course, we require that the set of values over which z ranges can be ordered (like string, integers, reals). Finally, note that the additional of the SQL-like statement $\mathsf{LIMIT}(k)$ can be added straightforwardly.

It is obvious that we may devise the same query answering method as seen in Section 3.4, by computing the closure, store it into a database, and then using SQL queries with the appropriate support of built-in predicates.

Proposition 19. *Given a ground graph G, $\mathbf{t}$ is an* answer *to q if and only if there exists an instantiation $\varphi(\mathbf{t}, \mathbf{t}')$ that is true in the closure of G (i.e., all triples in $\varphi(\mathbf{t}, \mathbf{t}')$ are in $cl(G)$). The answer set can be computed in LogSpace w.r.t. the size of $cl(G)$.*

We conclude by defining a *disjunctive query* $\mathbf{q}$ as usual as a finite set of conjunctive queries in which all the rules have the same head. Intuitively, the answers to a disjunctive query are the *union* of the answers of the conjunctive queries. That is, for a disjunctive query $\mathbf{q} = \{q_1, \dots, q_m\}$, G *entails* $\mathbf{q}(\mathbf{t})$ (denoted $G \models \mathbf{q}(\mathbf{t})$) iff $G \models q_i(\mathbf{t})$ for some $q_i \in \mathbf{q}$.

The notion of answer and answer set of a disjunctive query is a straightforward extension of the ones for conjunctive queries. Also, it is straightforward to see that the answer set of a disjunctive query can be computed similarly as for conjunctive queries.

The OWL 2 and RIF cases. It is pretty obvious that the notion introduced for conjunctive RDFS queries straightforwardly extends to the cases of OWL 2 and RIF. Essentially in the query body we have to replace triple expressions with FOL predicates, which are unary or binary in case of OWL 2 (that is in the DLs case), and n-ary in case of RIF (that is in the LPs case).

6.3   SPARQL

Our introduced query language so far allows for conjunctive and disjunctive queries with aggregates, which may be seen as the logical counterpart of SQL. In this section we will present now SPARQL, which has some specific features not covered so far.

We recall that SPARQL [380, 381] is the W3C recommended query language for RDF.

A *SPARQL query* is defined by a triple $Q = (P, G, V)$, where P is a *graph pattern* (defined below) and the *dataset* G is an RDF graph and V is the *result form*. We will restrict ourselves to SELECT queries in this work so it is sufficient to consider the result form V as a list of variables.

Remark 11. *Note that, for presentation purposes, we simplify the notion of datasets by excluding named graphs and thus GRAPH queries. Our definitions can be straightforwardly extended to named graphs and we refer the reader to the SPARQL W3C specification [381] for details.*

We base our semantics of SPARQL on the semantics presented by Pérez *et al.* [348], extending the multiset semantics to lists, which are considered a multiset with "default" ordering.

RDF triples, possibly with variables in subject, predicate, or object positions, are called *triple patterns*. In the basic case, a *graph pattern* P is a set of triple patterns, also called *basic graph pattern* (BGP).

Let $\mathbf{U}$, $\mathbf{B}$, $\mathbf{L}$ be defined as for RDFS (Chapter 3) and let $\mathbf{V}$ denote a set of variables, disjoint from $\mathbf{UBL}$. We further denote by $var(P)$ the set of variables present in a graph pattern P.

Given a graph G and a BGP P, a *solution* [381, Section 12.3.1] θ for P over G is a mapping over a subset V of $var(P)$, *i.e.*, $\theta : V \rightarrow term(G)$ such that $G \models P\theta$ where $P\theta$ represents the triples obtained by replacing the variables in graph pattern P according to θ, and where $G \models P\theta$ means that any triple in $P\theta$ is entailed by G. We call V the *domain* of θ, denoted by $dom(\theta)$. For convenience, sometimes we will use the notation $\theta = \{x_1/t_1, \ldots, x_n/t_n\}$ to indicate that $\theta(x_i) = t_i$, *i.e.*, variable x_i is assigned to term t_i.

Two mappings θ_1 and θ_2 are considered *compatible* if for all $x \in dom(\theta_1) \cap dom(\theta_2), \theta_1(x) = \theta_2(x)$. We call the *evaluation* of a BGP P over a graph G, denoted $[\![P]\!]_G$, the set of solutions.

Remark 12. *Note that variables in the domain of θ play the role of distinguished variables in conjunctive queries and there are no non-distinguished variables.*

The notion of solution for BGPs is the same as the notion of answers for conjunctive queries:

Proposition 20. *Given a graph G and a BGP P, then the solutions of P are the same as the answers of the query $q(var(P)) \leftarrow P$ (where $var(P)$ is the vector of variables in P), i.e., $ans(G, q) = [\![P]\!]_G$.*

We present the syntax of SPARQL based on [348] and present *graph patterns* similarly. A *triple pattern* (s, p, o) is a graph pattern where $s, o \in \mathbf{ULV}$ and $p \in \mathbf{UV}$.[2] Sets of triple patterns are called *Basic Graph Patterns (BGPs)*. A generic *graph pattern* is defined in a recursive manner: any BGP is a graph pattern; if P and P' are graph patterns, R is a filter expression (see [381]), then $(P$ AND $P')$, $(P$ OPTIONAL $P')$, $(P$ UNION $P')$, $(P$ FILTER $R)$ are graph patterns. As noted in Remark 11 we do not consider GRAPH patterns.

Evaluations of more complex patterns including FILTERs, OPTIONAL patterns, AND patterns, UNION patterns, etc., are defined by an algebra that is built on top of this *basic graph pattern matching* (see [348, 381]).

The *SPARQL relational algebra* is defined as follows: Let Ω_1 and Ω_2 be sets of mappings: then

---

[2]We do not consider blank nodes in triple patterns since they can be considered as variables.

$$\Omega_1 \bowtie \Omega_2 = \{\theta_1 \cup \theta_2 \mid \theta_1 \in \Omega_1, \theta_2 \in \Omega_2, \theta_1 \text{ and } \theta_2 \text{ compatible}\}$$
$$\Omega_1 \uplus \Omega_2 = \{\theta \mid \theta \in \Omega_1 \text{ or } \theta \in \Omega_2\}$$
$$\Omega_1 - \Omega_2 = \{\theta_1 \in \Omega_1 \mid \text{ for all } \theta_2 \in \Omega_2, \theta_1 \text{ and } \theta_2 \text{ not compatible}\}$$
$$\Omega_1 \rightbowtie \Omega_2 = (\Omega_1 \bowtie \Omega_2) \uplus (\Omega_1 - \Omega_2) \ .$$

Now, let $\tau = (s, p, o)$ be a triple pattern, P, P_1, P_2 graph patterns and G an RDF graph, then the *evaluation* [348, Definition 2.2] $[\![\cdot]\!]_G$ is recursively defined as follows:

$$
\begin{aligned}
[\![t]\!]_G &= \{\theta \mid dom(\theta) = var(P) \text{ and } G \models \tau\theta\} \\
[\![P_1 \text{ FILTER } P_2]\!]_G &= [\![P_1]\!]_G \rightbowtie [\![P_2]\!]_G \\
[\![P_1 \text{ AND } P_2]\!]_G &= [\![P_1]\!]_G \bowtie [\![P_2]\!]_G \\
[\![P_1 \text{ UNION } P_2]\!]_G &= [\![P_1]\!]_G \uplus [\![P_2]\!]_G \\
[\![P_1 \text{ OPTIONAL } P_2]\!]_G &= [\![P_1]\!]_G \rightbowtie [\![P_2]\!]_G \\
[\![P \text{ FILTER } R]\!]_G &= \{\theta \in [\![P]\!]_G \mid R\theta \text{ is true }\} \ .
\end{aligned}
$$

Let R be a FILTER[3] expression, $u, v \in \mathbf{V} \cup \mathbf{UBL}$. The valuation of R on a substitution θ, written $R\theta$, is *true* if:

1. $R = \text{BOUND}(v)$ with $v \in dom(\theta)$;

2. $R = \text{isBLANK}(v)$ with $v \in dom(\theta)$ and $\theta(v) \in \mathbf{B}$;

3. $R = \text{isIRI}(v)$ with $v \in dom(\theta)$ and $\theta(v) \in \mathbf{U}$;

4. $R = \text{isLITERAL}(v)$ with $v \in dom(\theta)$ and $\theta(v) \in \mathbf{L}$;

5. $R = (u = v)$ with $u, v \in dom(\theta) \cup \mathbf{UBL} \wedge \theta(u) = \theta(v)$;

6. $R = (\neg R_1)$ with $R_1\theta$ is false;

7. $R = (R_1 \vee R_2)$ with $R_1\theta$ is true or $R_2\theta$ is true;

8. $R = (R_1 \wedge R_2)$ with $R_1\theta$ is true and $R_2\theta$ is true.

$R\theta$ yields an error (denoted ε), if:

1. $R = \text{isBLANK}(v)$, $R = \text{isIRI}(v)$, or $R = \text{isLITERAL}(v)$ and $v \notin dom(\theta) \cup T$;

2. $R = (u = v)$ with $u \notin dom(\theta) \cup T$ or $v \notin dom(\theta) \cup T$;

3. $R = (\neg R_1)$ and $R_1\theta = \varepsilon$;

4. $R = (R_1 \vee R_2)$ and $(R_1\theta \neq \top$ and $R_2\theta \neq \top)$ and $(R_1\theta = \varepsilon$ or $R_2\theta = \varepsilon)$;

5. $R = (R1 \wedge R2)$ and $R_1\theta = \varepsilon$ or $R_2\theta = \varepsilon$.

---

[3] For simplicity, we will omit from the presentation FILTERs such as comparison operators ('<', '>','≤','≥'), data type conversion and string functions and refer the reader to [381, Section 11.3] for details.

Otherwise $R\theta$ is *false*.

In order to make the presented semantics compliant with the SPARQL specification [381], we need to introduce an extension to consider unsafe FILTERs (also presented in [10]).

So, let P_1, P_2 be graph patterns R a FILTER expression. A mapping θ is in $[\![P_1 \text{ OPTIONAL } (P_2 \text{ FILTER } R)]\!]_{DS}$ if and only if:

1. $\theta = \theta_1 \cup \theta_2$, s.t. $\theta_1 \in [\![P_1]\!]_G$, $\theta_2 \in [\![P_2]\!]_G$ are compatible and $R\theta$ is true, or

2. $\theta \in [\![P_1]\!]_G$ and $\forall \theta_2 \in [\![P_2]\!]_G$, θ and θ_2 are not compatible, or

3. $\theta \in [\![P_1]\!]_G$ and $\forall \theta_2 \in [\![P_2]\!]_G$ s.t. θ and θ_2 are compatible, and $R\theta_3$ is false for $\theta_3 = \theta \cup \theta_2$.

We next extend our definitions to include variable assignments, aggregates, and solution modifiers. These are extensions similar to the ones presented related to assignments and aggregations for conjunctive queries (see Section 6.2).

So, let P be a graph pattern and G a graph, the evaluation of an ASSIGN statement is defined as:

$$[\![P \text{ ASSIGN } f(\mathbf{z}) \text{ AS } z]\!]_G = \{\theta \mid \theta_1 \in [\![P]\!]_G, \theta = \theta_1[z/f(\theta_1(\mathbf{z}))]\}$$

where

$$\theta[z/t] = \begin{cases} \theta \cup \{z/t\} & \text{if } z \notin dom(\theta) \\ (\theta \setminus \{z/t'\}) \cup \{z/t\} & \text{otherwise .} \end{cases}$$

Essentially, we assign to the variable z the value $f(\theta_1(\mathbf{z}))$, which is the evaluation of the function $f(\mathbf{z})$ with respect to a substitution $\theta_1 \in [\![P]\!]_G$.

For instance, using a built-in function we can retrieve for each employee the length of employment for any company:

```
SELECT ?x ?y ?z WHERE {
    (?x worksFor ?y),  (?x workingPeriod ?l)
    ASSIGN length(?l) AS ?z
}
```

Here, the *length* built-in predicate returns, given a temporal expression, *e.g.*, encoded in some way, the overall total length of the intervals.

Remark 13. *Note that this definition is more general than "SELECT expr AS ?var" project expressions in current SPARQL 1.1 [380] due to not requiring that the assigned variable be unbound.*

We introduce the ORDERBY clause where the evaluation of a $[\![P \text{ ORDERBY } ?x]\!]_G$ statement is defined as

$$[\![P \text{ ORDERBY } ?x]\!]_G = [\![P]\!]_{G\uparrow ?x}$$

where $\uparrow_{?x}$ means that the ordering of the solutions – for any $\theta \in \llbracket P \rrbracket_G$ – according to the values of $\theta(?x)$. The ordering follows the rules in [381, Section 9.1]. Likewise, the SQL-like statement $\mathsf{LIMIT}(k)$ can be added straightforwardly. Of course, similarly to ordering in the conjunctive query answering setting, we require that the set of values over which x ranges can be ordered and some linearization method for possible posets may be applied if necessary, such as [248].

We can further extend the evaluation of SPARQL queries with aggregate functions

$$@ \in \{\mathsf{SUM}, \mathsf{AVG}, \mathsf{MAX}, \mathsf{MIN}, \mathsf{COUNT}\}$$

as follows: the evaluation of a $\mathsf{GROUPBY}$ statement is defined as:[4]

$$\llbracket P \ \mathsf{GROUPBY}(\mathbf{w}) \ @\mathbf{f}(\mathbf{z}) \ AS \ \alpha \rrbracket_G = \{\theta \mid \theta_1 \ \text{in} \ \llbracket P \rrbracket_G,$$
$$\theta = \theta_1|_{\mathbf{w}}[\alpha_i/@_i f_i(\theta_i(\mathbf{z}_i))]\}_{\mathsf{DISTINCT}}$$

where the variables $\alpha_i \notin var(P)$, $\mathbf{z}_i \in var(P)$ and none of the $\mathsf{GROUPBY}$ variables $\mathbf{w}$ are included in the aggregation function variables $\mathbf{z}_i$. Here, we denote by $\theta|_{\mathbf{w}}$ the restriction of variables in θ to variables in $\mathbf{w}$. Using this notation, we can also straightforwardly introduce projection, *i.e.*, sub-SELECTs as an algebraic operator in the language covering another new feature of SPARQL 1.1: namely

$$\llbracket \mathsf{SELECT} \ \mathbf{V} \ \{P\} \rrbracket_G \ = \ \{\theta \mid \theta_1 \ \text{in} \ \llbracket P \rrbracket_G, \theta = \theta_1|_{\mathbf{v}}\} \ .$$

Remark 14. *Please note that the aggregator functions have a domain of definition and thus can only be applied to values of their respective domain. For example, SUM and AVG can only be used on numeric values, while $\mathsf{MAX}, \mathsf{MIN}$ are applicable to any total order. Resolution of type mismatches for aggregates is being defined in SPARQL 1.1 [380]. The COUNT aggregator can be used for any finite set of values.*

Remark 15. *Please note that, unlike the current SPARQL 1.1 syntax, assignment, solution modifiers (ORDER BY, LIMIT), and aggregation are standalone operators in our language and do not need to be tied to a sub-SELECT but can occur nested within any pattern. This may be viewed as syntactic sugar allowing for more concise writing than the current SPARQL 1.1 [380] draft.*

Example 21. *Suppose we want to know, for each employee, the average salary of their employments with different employers. Then such a query will be expressed as:*

```
SELECT ?x ?avgS WHERE {
    (?x worksFor ?y) (?x hasSalary ?s)
    GROUPBY(?x)
    AVG(?s) AS ?avgS
}
```

---

[4]In the expression, $@\mathbf{f}(\mathbf{z}) \ AS \ \alpha$ is a concise representation of n aggregations of the form $@_i f_i(\mathbf{z}_i) \ AS \ \alpha_i$.

Essentially, we group by the employee, consider for each employee its salaries and compute the average value for each group. That is, if $g = \{\langle t, t_1 \rangle, \ldots, \langle t, t_n \rangle\}$ is a group of tuples with the same value t for employee x, and value t_i for s, then the value of avgS for the group g is $(\sum_i t_i)/n$.

Proposition 21. *Assuming the built-in predicates are computable in finite time, the answer set of any SPARQL is finite and can also be computed in finite time.*

This proposition can be demonstrated by induction over all the constructs we allow in SPARQL.

Part II

Fuzzy Logics and Semantic Web Languages

Chapter 7

Introduction

There has been a long-lasting misunderstanding in the literature of artificial intelligence and uncertainty modelling, regarding the role of probability/possibility theory and vague/fuzzy theory. A clarifying paper is [143]. We will recall here salient notes, which may clarify the role of these theories for the inexpert reader and will move on to incorporate fuzziness within SWLs in the following chapters.

A standard example that points out the difference between degrees of uncertainty and degrees of truth is that of a bottle [143]. In terms of binary truth values, a bottle is viewed as full or empty. But if one accounts for the quantity of liquid in the bottle, one may, *e.g.*, say that the bottle is "almost-full." Under this way of speaking, "almost full" becomes a fuzzy predicate [472] and the degree of truth of "the bottle is almost full" reflects the amount of liquid in the bottle. The situation is quite different when expressing our ignorance about whether the bottle is either full or not full (we know that only one of the two situations is the true one). Saying that the probability that the bottle is full is 0.8 does not mean that the bottle is almost full.

We recall that under *uncertainty theory* fall all those approaches in which statements rather than being either true or false, are true or false to some *probability* or *possibility* (for example, "it will rain tomorrow"). That is, a statement is true or false in any world, but we are "uncertain" about which world to consider as the right one, and thus we speak about, *e.g.*, a probability distribution or a possibility distribution over the worlds. For example, we cannot exactly establish whether it will rain tomorrow or not, due to our *incomplete* knowledge about our world, but we can estimate to which degree this is probable, possible, or necessary.

As for the main differences between probability and possibility theory, the probability of an event is the sum of the probabilities of all worlds that satisfy this event, whereas the possibility of an event is the maximum of the possibilities of all worlds that satisfy the event. Intuitively, the probability of an event aggregates the probabilities of all worlds that satisfy this event, whereas the possibility of an event is simply the possibility of the "most optimistic" world that satisfies the event. Hence, although both probability and possibility theory allow for quantifying degrees of uncertainty, they are conceptually quite different from each other. That is, probability and possibility theory represent different facets of uncertainty.

On the other hand, under *vagueness/fuzziness theory* fall all those approaches in which statements (for example, "the tomato is ripe") are true to some degree, which is taken from a truth space. That is, an interpretation maps a statement to a truth degree, since we are unable to establish whether a statement is completely true or false due to the involvement of vague concepts, such as "ripe," which only have an *imprecise* definition. For example, we cannot exactly say whether a tomato is ripe or not, but rather can only say that the tomato is ripe to some degree. Usually, such statements involve so-called *vague/fuzzy predicates* [472].

Note that all vague/fuzzy statements are truth-functional, that is, the degree of truth of every statement can be calculated from the degrees of truth of its constituents, while uncertain statements cannot be a function of the uncertainties of their constituents [142]. More concretely, in probability theory, only the negation is truth-functional (see Equation. (E.1)), while in possibility theory, only the disjunction resp. conjunction is truth-functional in possibilities resp. necessities of events (see Equation (E.6)).

Furthermore, fuzzy logics are based on truly many-valued logical operators, while uncertainty logics are defined on top of standard binary logical operators.

We refer the interested reader to Appendix E for a formalization of a simple propositional probabilistic or possibilistic logic, which may help the reader to verify the differences to fuzziness.

Chapter 8

Fuzzy Sets and Mathematical Fuzzy Logic Basics

8.1 Fuzzy Sets Basics

The aim of this section is to introduce the basic concepts of fuzzy set theory. To distinguish between fuzzy sets and classical (nonfuzzy) sets, we refer to the latter as *crisp sets*. For an in-depth treatment we refer the reader to, *e.g.*, [139, 242].

8.1.1 From Crisp Sets to Fuzzy Sets

To better highlight the conceptual shift from classical sets to fuzzy sets, we start with some basic definitions and well-known properties of classical sets. In the following, let us denote with X the *universal set* containing all possible elements of concern in each particular context. The *power set*, denoted 2^A, of a set $A \subset X$, is the set of subsets of A, *i.e.*,

$$2^A = \{B \mid B \subseteq A\}.$$

Often sets are defined by specifying a property satisfied by its members, in the form

$$A = \{x \mid P(x)\} \, ,$$

where $P(x)$ is a statement of the form "x has property P" *that is either true or false* for any $x \in X$.

Example 22. *Examples of universe X and subsets $A, B \in 2^X$ may be*

$$X = \{x \mid x \text{ is a person}\}$$
$$A = \{x \mid x \text{ is an employee}\}$$
$$B = \{x \mid x \text{ is an employee and has salary equal or less than 23000}\} \, .$$

In the above case we have $B \subseteq A \subseteq X$.

The *characteristic function*, denoted χ_A, of a set $A \subseteq X$ is a function mapping elements of X into $\{0, 1\}$, *i.e.*,

$$\chi_A \colon X \to \{0, 1\}$$

and is defined as

$$\chi_A(x) = \begin{cases} 1 & \text{for } x \in A \\ 0 & \text{for } x \notin A . \end{cases}$$

Note that it is easily verified that for any sets $A, B \in 2^X$, we have that (the reader may verify it also in the case of Example 22)

$$A \subseteq B \text{ iff } \forall x \in X. \ \chi_A(x) \leq \chi_B(x) . \tag{8.1}$$

Note that $\langle \subseteq, 2^X \rangle$ is a *Boolean algebra*, or *Boolean lattice*, i.e., a complemented distributive lattice.

When clear from context, we denoted with $|A|$ the *cardinality* of a denumerable set $A \subseteq X$. The *complement* of a set A is denoted $\bar{A}$, i.e.,

$$\bar{A} = X \setminus A .$$

Of course, $\bar{\emptyset} = X$ and $\bar{X} = \emptyset$ and observe that

$$\forall x \in X. \ \chi_{\bar{A}}(x) = 1 - \chi_A(x) . \tag{8.2}$$

In a similar way, we may express set operations of intersection and union via the characteristic function as follows:

$$\forall x \in X. \ \chi_{A \cap B}(x) \quad = \quad \min(\chi_A(x), \chi_B(x)) \tag{8.3}$$

$$\forall x \in X. \ \chi_{A \cup B}(x) \quad = \quad \max(\chi_A(x), \chi_B(x)) . \tag{8.4}$$

The *Cartesian product*, $A \times B$, of two sets $A, B \in 2^X$ is defined as

$$A \times B = \{ \langle a, b \rangle \mid a \in A, b \in B \} .$$

The most fundamental properties of set operations are illustrated in Table 8.1 (where $A, B, C \subseteq X$).

As defined so far, the characteristic function of a crisp set A assigns a value of either 1 or 0 to each individual of the universe set and, thus, discriminating between being a member or not being a member of A.

However, in many cases this way to define sets is unsatisfactory, as illustrated below.

Example 23. *For instance, by referring to Example 22, let us try to define the set C of employees with a* low *salary, i.e.,*

$$C = \{ x \in A \mid x \text{ has low salary} \} .$$

The problem relies on the fact that, in order to define such a set precisely, we need to define when a salary is low and when it is not, i.e., we need a definition making the statement $P(x)$ "x has low salary" either true or false for any x. For instance, we may decide that $P(x)$ is true iff the salary is equal or less than €2000, or equivalently, using the characteristic function, define

$$\chi_C(x) = \begin{cases} 1 & \text{if salary of } x \text{ is equal or less than } €2000 \\ 0 & \text{otherwise} . \end{cases}$$

TABLE 8.1: Fundamental properties of crisp set operations.

Involution	$\bar{\bar{A}}$	$=$	A
Idempotence	$A \cup A$	$=$	A
	$A \cap A$	$=$	A
Commutativity	$A \cup B$	$=$	$B \cup A$
	$A \cap B$	$=$	$B \cap A$
Associativity	$(A \cup B) \cup C$	$=$	$A \cup (B \cup C)$
	$(A \cap B) \cap C$	$=$	$A \cap (B \cap C)$
Distributivity	$A \cap (B \cup C)$	$=$	$(A \cap B) \cup (A \cap C)$
	$A \cup (B \cap C)$	$=$	$(A \cup B) \cap (A \cup C)$
Absorption	$A \cup (A \cap B)$	$=$	A
	$A \cap (A \cup B)$	$=$	A
Identity	$A \cup X$	$=$	X
	$A \cap \emptyset$	$=$	$\emptyset$
	$A \cup \emptyset$	$=$	A
	$A \cap X$	$=$	A
Law of contradiction	$A \cap \bar{A}$	$=$	$\emptyset$
Law of excluded middle	$A \cup \bar{A}$	$=$	X
De Morgan's rule	$\overline{A \cup B}$	$=$	$\bar{A} \cap \bar{B}$
	$\overline{A \cap B}$	$=$	$\bar{A} \cup \bar{B}$

It becomes evident then that the selection of such a threshold may be rather subjective *and* context dependent. *It also becomes difficult to conceive that an employee having a salary of € 2001 does not* have a low salary.

The main point is that statements involving concepts, such as

$$low, \ medium, \ high \tag{8.5}$$

may not be a matter of true or false, but rather are *graded*, where the grade may be taken from a specified range and indicates the *membership degree* to which elements of the universe belong to the set in question. Larger values denote higher degrees of set membership.

This idea can be formalized [472] by generalizing characteristic functions in such a way that the values assigned to the elements of the universe fall within a specified range, which is not necessarily $\{0, 1\}$. Such a function is called *membership function*, the set so defined is called *fuzzy set*, concepts such as those in Equation (8.5) are called *fuzzy concepts*, and statements involving fuzzy concepts are called *fuzzy statements*.

The most commonly used range of membership function is $[0, 1]$, though other mathematical structures are used as well (see *e.g.*, [186, 241, 242]).

To what concerns us here, we will either use $[0,1]$ or, another typical setting based on the finite-valued set $(n \geq 3)$.

$$L_n = \{0, \frac{1}{n-1}, \ldots, \frac{n-2}{n-1}, 1\} . \tag{8.6}$$

For instance, for $n = 5$,

$$L_5 = \{0, 0.25, 0.5, 0.75, 1\} .$$

There are typically two distinct notations employed in the literature to denote the membership function: in one of them the membership function of A is denoted μ_A and is a function

$$\mu_A \colon X \to [0,1] ,$$

while in the other one this function is denoted A and, thus, is a function

$$A \colon X \to [0,1] .$$

Note that in the second case, the symbol A may have two roles, one to indicate the fuzzy set and another one to indicate the fuzzy membership function. We will use both notations and the second one only if no ambiguity about the role of the symbol A arises.

   With $\tilde{2}^X$ we denote the *fuzzy power set* over X, *i.e.*, the set of all fuzzy sets over X.

Example 24. *By referring to Example 23, we may define the membership function μ_C as, e.g.,*

$$\mu_C(x) = \begin{cases} 1 & \textit{if salary of } x \textit{ is equal or less than } € 2000 \\ (2500 - x)/500 & \textit{if salary of } x \textit{ is in between } € 2000 \textit{ and } € 2500 \\ 0 & \textit{otherwise} , \end{cases}$$

which is illustrated below.

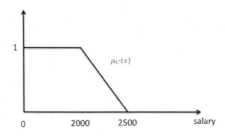

So, for instance, an employee having a salary of € 1500 definitely belongs to C (the degree is 1), one having a salary of € 2100 belongs to C to degree 0.8, while another one having a salary of € 2700 does not belong to C (the degree is 0).

As pointed out previously, the definition of the membership function depends on the context, *e.g.*, the definition of low salary may vary from country to country. Moreover, also the *shape* of such functions may quite be different. However, the trapezoidal (Fig. 8.1 (a)), the triangular (Figure 8.1 (b)), the *L*-function (left-shoulder function, Figure 8.1 (c)), and the *R*-function (right-shoulder function, Figure 8.1 (d)) are simple, but most frequently used to specify membership degrees.

The *trapezoidal function*, $trz(a, b, c, d)$, is defined as follows: let $a < b \le c < d$ be rational numbers then

$$trz(a, b, c, d)(x) = \begin{cases} 0 & \text{if } x \le a \\ (x - a)/(b - a) & \text{if } x \in (a, b] \\ 1 & \text{if } x \in (b, c] \\ (d - x)/(d - c) & \text{if } x \in (c, d] \\ 0 & \text{if } x > d \, . \end{cases}$$

A *triangular function*, $tri(a, b, c)$, is such that

$$tri(a, b, c)(x) = \begin{cases} 0 & \text{if } x \le a \\ (x - a)/(b - a) & \text{if } x \in (a, b] \\ (c - x)/(c - b) & \text{if } x \in (b, c] \\ 0 & \text{if } x > c \, . \end{cases}$$

Note that $tri(a, b, c) = trz(a, b, b, c)$. The *L*-function is defined as

$$ls(a, b)(x) = \begin{cases} 1 & \text{if } x \le a \\ (b - x)/(b - a) & \text{if } x \in (a, b] \\ 0 & \text{if } x > b \, . \end{cases}$$

Finally, the *R*-function is defined as

$$rs(a, b)(x) = \begin{cases} 0 & \text{if } x \le a \\ (x - a)/(b - a) & \text{if } x \in (a, b] \\ 1 & \text{if } x > b \, . \end{cases}$$

So, for instance, in Example 24, we defined the membership function of the employees with low salary as

$$\mu_C = ls(2000, 2500) \, .$$

Although fuzzy sets have a far greater expressive power than classical crisp sets, its usefulness depends critically on our capability to construct appropriate membership functions for various given concepts in different contexts. The problem of constructing meaningful membership functions is a difficult one and we refer the interested reader to, *e.g.*, [242, Chapter 10]. However, one easy and typically satisfactory method to define the membership functions is to uniformly partition the range of, *e.g.*, salary values (bounded by a minimum and maximum value), into 5 or 7 fuzzy sets using either trapezoidal functions (*e.g.*, as illustrated in Figure 8.2), or using triangular functions (as illustrated in Figure 8.3). The latter one is the more used one, as it has less parameters.

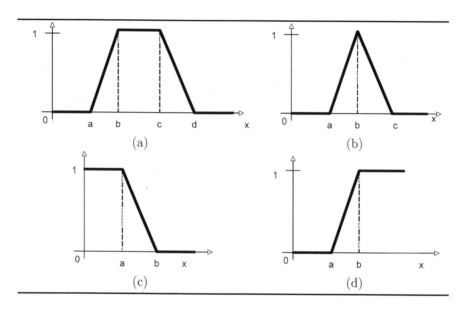

FIGURE 8.1: (a) Trapezoidal function $trz(a, b, c, d)$; (b) Triangular function $tri(a, b, c)$; (c) L-function $ls(a, b)$; and (d) R-function $rs(a, b)$.

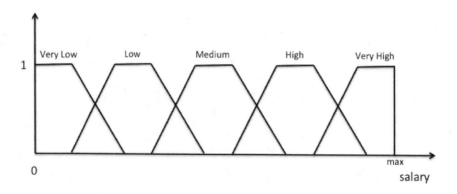

FIGURE 8.2: Fuzzy sets over salaries using trapezoidal functions.

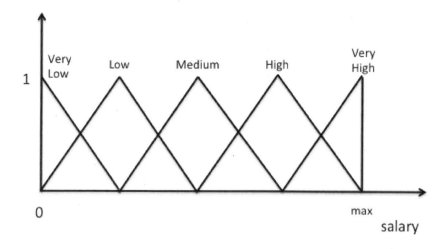

FIGURE 8.3: Fuzzy sets over salaries using triangular functions.

8.1.2 Standard Fuzzy Set Operations

We have seen that there are three basic operations on crisp sets, namely the complement, the intersection, and the union. There are many ways to generalize these operations to fuzzy sets, though, one particular generalization, called a *standard fuzzy set operation*, has been introduced originally in [472] and follow immediately as a generalization of the characteristic functions of crisp sets defined in the previous Section 8.1. In fact, inspired by Equations (8.2)–(8.4), for fuzzy sets $A, B \in \tilde{2}^X$, the standard fuzzy set operations are defined for any $x \in X$ as

$$
\begin{align}
\bar{A}(x) &= 1 - A(x) \tag{8.7} \\
(A \cap B)(x) &= \min(A(x), B(x)) \tag{8.8} \\
(A \cup B)(x) &= \max(A(x), B(x)) \ . \tag{8.9}
\end{align}
$$

In Figures 8.4 – 8.6 we show the graphical interpretation of standard fuzzy set operations for fuzzy sets with triangular membership function, where the grey part is the result of the operation.

The *standard inclusion* among fuzzy sets $A, B \in \tilde{2}^X$ is defined directly from Equation (8.1) as

$$
A \subseteq B \text{ iff } \forall x \in X. \ A(x) \leq B(x) \ . \tag{8.10}
$$

It is interesting to observe that under definition (8.10) of inclusion, in fact the inclusion relation is crisp and not fuzzy. We will see later on how one may generalise this. Furthermore, note that under standard fuzzy set operations, $\langle \subseteq, \tilde{2}^X \rangle$ is a complemented distributive lattice (a Boolean algebra/lattice). It

FIGURE 8.4: Graphical view of fuzzy set complement operation.

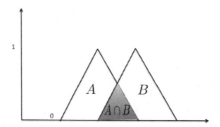

FIGURE 8.5: Graphical view of fuzzy set intersection operation.

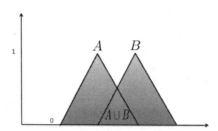

FIGURE 8.6: Graphical view of fuzzy set union operation.

satisfies all the properties listed in Table 8.1, except the law of contradiction and the law of excluded middle. In fact it is easily verified that, *e.g.*,

$$\min(A(x), 1 - A(x)) = 0$$

is violated for at least one $x \in X$. This is easy as it is violated for any $A(x) \in (0, 1)$, while it holds for $A(x) \in \{0, 1\}$. The argument showing that

$$\max(A(x), 1 - A(x)) = 1$$

is violated is the same.

8.1.3 Norm-Based Fuzzy Set Operations

In the previous section we introduced the standard fuzzy set operations, derived from their crisp analogue, and have seen that they behave exactly as the corresponding crisp operations if the range in $\{0, 1\}$ in place of $[0, 1]$.

8.1.3.1 T-Norms

Of course, standard fuzzy set operations are not the only ones that can be conceived to be suitable to generalize the classical Boolean operations. For each of the three types of operations there is a wide class of plausible fuzzy version. The most notable ones are characterized by the so-called class of *t-norms* (called *triangular norms*), *t-conorms* (also called *s-norm*), and *negation* (see, *e.g.*, [241]).

T-norms are used to define fuzzy set conjunction, t-conorms are used to define fuzzy set disjunction, while the negation operator is used to define the fuzzy set complement operation. Several t-norms, s-norms, and negation functions have been given in the literature. We will denote a t-norm with $\otimes$, an s-norm with $\oplus$, while will denote a negation with $\ominus$.

An important aspect of such functions is that they satisfy some properties that one expects to hold for the connectives as illustrated in Tables 8.2 and 8.3 $(a, b \in [0, 1])$.

TABLE 8.2: Axioms for t-norms and s-norms.

Axiom Name	T-norm	S-norm
Boundary condition	$a \otimes 1 = a$	$a \oplus 0 = a$
Commutativity	$a \otimes b = b \otimes a$	$a \oplus b = b \oplus a$
Associativity	$(a \otimes b) \otimes c = a \otimes (b \otimes c)$	$(a \oplus b) \oplus c = a \oplus (b \oplus c)$
Monotonicity	if $b \leq c$ then $a \otimes b \leq a \otimes c$	if $b \leq c$ then $a \oplus b \leq a \oplus c$

TABLE 8.3: Axioms for negation functions.

Axiom Name	Negation Function
Boundary condition	$\ominus 0 = 1$
	$\ominus 1 = 0$
Antitonicity	if $a \leq b$ then $\ominus a \geq \ominus b$

Note that from the axioms we get also that

$$
\begin{aligned}
a \otimes 0 &= 0 \\
a \oplus 1 &= 1 \\
a \otimes b &\leq a \\
a \oplus b &\geq a \, .
\end{aligned}
$$

Of course, due to commutativity, $\otimes$ and $\oplus$ are monotone also in the first argument.

For any $a \in [0,1]$, we say that a negation function $\ominus$ is *involutive* iff $\ominus \ominus a = a$ for any $a \in [0,1]$. Salient negation functions are:

Standard or Łukasiewicz negation: $\ominus_l a = 1 - a$;

Gödel negation: $\ominus_g a$ is 1 if $a = 0$, else is 0.

Of course, Lukasiewicz negation is involutive, while Gödel negation is not.
Salient t-norm functions are:

Gödel t-norm: $a \otimes_g b = \min(a, b)$;

Bounded difference or Łukasiewicz t-norm: $a \otimes_l b = \max(0, a + b - 1)$;

Algebraic product or product t-norm: $a \otimes_p b = a \cdot b$;

Drastic product: $a \otimes_d b = \begin{cases} 0 & \text{when } (a, b) \in [0, 1[\times [0, 1[\\ \min(a, b) & \text{otherwise} \end{cases}$

Salient s-norm functions are:

Gödel s-norm: $a \oplus_g b = \max(a, b)$;

Bounded sum or Łukasiewicz s-norm: $a \oplus_l b = \min(1, a + b)$;

Algebraic sum or product s-norm: $a \oplus_p b = a + b - ab$;

Drastic sum: $a \oplus_d b = \begin{cases} 1 & \text{when } (a, b) \in]0, 1] \times]0, 1] \\ \max(a, b) & \text{otherwise} \end{cases}$

We say that a t-norm $\otimes_1$ is *weaker* than a t-norm $\otimes_2$ (denoted $\otimes_1 \leq \otimes_2$) iff for all $(a, b) \in [0, 1]^2$ we have that $a \otimes_1 b \leq a \otimes_2 b$. Similarly, an s-norm $\oplus_1$ is *weaker* than an s-norm $\oplus_2$ (denoted $\oplus_1 \leq \oplus_2$) iff for all $(a, b) \in [0, 1]^2$ we have that $a \oplus_1 b \leq a \oplus_2 b$.

We say that $\otimes$ is *idempotent* iff $a \otimes a = a$ for all $a \in [0, 1]$, and *sub-idempotent* iff $a \otimes a < a$ for all $a \in [0, 1]$. Similarly, we say that $\oplus$ is *idempotent* iff $a \oplus a = a$ for all $a \in [0, 1]$, and *sup-idempotent* iff $a \oplus a > a$. An *idempotent element* is a value $a \in [0, 1]$ such that $a \otimes a = a$. So, 0 and 1 are idempotent elements. The numbers 0 and 1, which are idempotent elements for any $\otimes$, are called *trivial*.

The following important properties can be shown about t-norms.

Proposition 22 (See [241]).

1. *There is the following ordering among t-norms ($\otimes$ is any t-norm):*

$$\otimes_d \leq \otimes \leq \otimes_g$$
$$\otimes_d \leq \otimes_l \leq \otimes_p \leq \otimes_g .$$

2. *The only idempotent t-norm is $\otimes_g$.*

3. *The only t-norm satisfying $a \otimes a = 0$ for all $a \in [0, 1[$ is $\otimes_d$.*

There is also an analogue of Proposition 22 for s-norms.

Proposition 23 (See [241]).

1. *There is the following ordering among s-norms ($\oplus$ is any s-norm):*

$$\oplus_g \leq \oplus \leq \oplus_d$$
$$\oplus_g \leq \oplus_p \leq \oplus_l \leq \oplus_d .$$

2. *The only idempotent s-norm is $\oplus_g$.*

3. *The only s-norm satisfying $a \oplus a = 1$ for all $a \in]0, 1]$ is $\oplus_d$.*

Idempotent elements can be characterized as follows:

Proposition 24 ([241]). $a \in [0, 1]$ *is idempotent for $\otimes$ iff for all $b \in [a, 1]$, $a \otimes b = \min(a, b)$. If $\otimes$ is continuous then $a \in [0, 1]$ is idempotent for $\otimes$ iff for all $x \in [0, 1]$ we have that $a \otimes b = \min(a, b)$.*

A t-norm $\otimes$ is called *nilpotent* if it is continuous and each a in the open interval $(0, 1)$ is a *nilpotent element*, i.e., there is a natural number n such that $a \otimes \ldots \otimes a$ (n times) equals 0. $a \in (0, 1)$ is called a *zero divisor* of $\otimes$ if there exists $b \in (0, 1)$ such that $a \otimes b = 0$.

Remark 16.

1. *Each $a \in (0,1)$ is both a nilpotent element and a zero divisor of $\otimes_l$ and $\otimes_d$.*

2. *$\otimes_g$ has neither nilpotent nor zero divisors and $\otimes_l$ and $\otimes_d$ have only trivial idempotent elements.*

3. *The product $\otimes_p$ has neither non-trivial idempotent nor nilpotent elements nor zero divisors.*

4. *If a is an idempotent element, so is a^n, i.e., $a \otimes \ldots \otimes a$ (n times) and, thus, no element in $(0,1)$ can be both idempotent and nilpotent.*

5. *If a is nilpotent for $\otimes$ then it is also a zero divisor for $\otimes$ and there is always $b \in (0,1)$ such that $b \otimes b = 0$.*

6. *If $a \in (0,1)$ is nilpotent (a zero divisor) for $\otimes$ then each $(0,a)$ is also a nilpotent (a zero divisor) for $\otimes$. Therefore, the set for nilpotent elements and the set of zero divisors for $\otimes$ is either the empty set, as for $\otimes_g$ and $\otimes_p$, or an interval of the form $(0,c)$ or $(0,c]$.*

7. *$\otimes_l$ is nilpotent.*

Proposition 25 ([241]). *The following are equivalent:*

1. *$\otimes$ has zero divisors*

2. *$\otimes$ has idempotent elements*

A t-norm $\otimes$ is called *strict* if it is continuous and strictly monotone, *i.e.*, whenever $a > 0$ and $b < c$ then
$$a \otimes b < a \otimes c .$$
For instance, $\otimes_p$ is strict. It is known that:

Proposition 26 ([241]).

1. *If $\otimes$ is strictly monotone then it has only trivial idempotent elements.*

2. *If $\otimes$ is strictly monotone then it has no divisors (i.e., $x \otimes y = 0$ if either $x = 0$ or $y = 0$).*

8.1.3.2 Dual Norms

There is a well-known property that allows us to derive a related s-norm from any t-norm.

Proposition 27 (See [241]). *A function $\oplus$ is an s-norm iff there is a t-norm $\otimes$ such that for all $(a,b) \in [0,1]^2$ we have that*

$$a \oplus b = 1 - (1-a) \otimes (1-b) . \tag{8.11}$$

An s-norm as defined by Equation (8.11) is called the *dual* s-norm of $\otimes$. Vice versa, from any s-norm $\oplus$ we may define a t-norm $\otimes$ via

$$a \otimes b = 1 - (1 - a) \oplus (1 - b) . \tag{8.12}$$

A t-norm as defined by Equation (8.12) is called the *dual* t-norm of $\oplus$.

It is easily verified that for any of the t-norms $\otimes_i$ and s-norms $\oplus_i$ defined above ($i \in \{g, l, p, d\}$) we have that for all $(a, b) \in [0,1]^2$

$$a \oplus_i b = 1 - (1 - a) \otimes_i (1 - b) \tag{8.13}$$
$$a \otimes_i b = 1 - (1 - a) \oplus_i (1 - b) . \tag{8.14}$$

Given $\otimes, \oplus$, and $\ominus$, we call a tuple $\langle \otimes, \oplus, \ominus \rangle$ a *dual triple* iff for all $a, b \in [0, 1]$

$$\ominus(a \otimes b) = \ominus a \oplus \ominus b \tag{8.15}$$
$$\ominus(a \oplus b) = \ominus a \otimes \ominus b . \tag{8.16}$$

These equations describe the de Morgan's laws for fuzzy sets.

It is easily verified that

$$\langle \otimes_g, \oplus_g, \ominus_l \rangle$$
$$\langle \otimes_l, \oplus_l, \ominus_l \rangle$$
$$\langle \otimes_p, \oplus_p, \ominus_l \rangle$$
$$\langle \otimes_d, \oplus_d, \ominus_l \rangle$$

are dual triples. The following can be shown (see, *e.g.*, [242])

The following can be shown (see, *e.g.*, [242])

Proposition 28.

1. $\langle \otimes_g, \oplus_g, \ominus \rangle$ and $\langle \otimes_d, \oplus_d, \ominus_l \rangle$ are dual triples for any $\ominus$;

2. $\langle \otimes, \oplus, \ominus_l \rangle$ is a dual triple for any dual s-norm $\oplus$ of $\otimes$;

3. $\langle \otimes, \oplus, \ominus_l \rangle$ is a dual triple for any dual t-norm $\otimes$ of $\oplus$;

4. If $\langle \otimes, \oplus, \ominus \rangle$ is a dual triple satisfying the law of excluded middle and the law of contradiction, then $\langle \otimes, \oplus, \ominus \rangle$ does not satisfy the distributive laws.

8.1.3.3 Distributive Norms

Given $\otimes, \oplus$, we say that $\otimes$ is distributive over $\oplus$ iff for all $a, b, c \in [0, 1]$

$$a \otimes (b \oplus c) = (a \otimes b) \oplus (a \otimes c) \tag{8.17}$$

and that $\oplus$ is distributive over $\otimes$ iff for all $a, b, c \in [0, 1]$

$$a \oplus (b \otimes c) = (a \oplus b) \otimes (a \oplus c) . \tag{8.18}$$

If both $\otimes$ is distributive over $\oplus$ and $\oplus$ is distributive over $\otimes$ then the tuple $\langle \otimes, \oplus \rangle$ is called a *distributive pair*.

The following can be shown (see, *e.g.*, [242])

Proposition 29.

1. $\oplus$ *is distributive over* $\otimes$ *iff* $\otimes = \otimes_g$.

2. $\otimes$ *is distributive over* $\oplus$ *iff* $\oplus = \oplus_g$.

3. $\langle \otimes_g, \oplus_g \rangle$ *is the only distributive pair.*

8.1.3.4   T-Norm Representation Theorem

A major achievement about t-norms is the fact that any continuous t-norm is piece-vice isomorphic to either Gödel, Łukasiewicz, or product t-norm, making these three t-norms among the most important of the t-norm family. We address this property within this section.

A t-norm $\otimes$ is called *Archimedean* if it has the *Archimedean property*, *i.e.*, if for each a, b in the open interval $(0, 1)$ there is a natural number n such that $a \otimes \ldots \otimes a$ is less than or equal to b. Note that $\otimes_g$ is not Archimedian, while $\otimes_l$ and $\otimes_p$ are.

Proposition 30 ([241]).

1. *If $\otimes$ is right continuous and has only trivial idempotent elements then it is Archimedian.*

2. *If $\otimes$ is strict then it is Archimedian.*

3. *If each $a \in (0,1)$ is nilpotent for $\otimes$ then $\otimes$ is Archimedian.*

4. *If $\otimes$ is Archimedian then $\otimes$ is left-continuous iff $\otimes$ is continuous.*

5. *$\otimes$ is Archimedian iff the only idempotent elements are 0 and 1.*

6. *A continuous Archimedean t-norm is strict if 0 is its only nilpotent element; otherwise it is nilpotent.*

The following proposition characterizes Archimedian t-norms:

Proposition 31 ([241]).
Let $\otimes$ *be an Archimedian t-norm. The following are equivalent:*

1. *$\otimes$ is nilpotent.*

2. *There exists some nilpotent element for $\otimes$.*

3. *There exists some zero divisor for $\otimes$.*

4. *$\otimes$ is not strict.*

Now, note that for each continuous t-norm $\otimes$, the set E of its idempotents is a closed subset of $[0,1]$. Its complement, the set of all elements which are not idempotent, is therefore a union of a set $\mathcal{I}_{open}(E)$ of countably many non-overlapping open intervals $I \in \mathcal{I}(E)$. Let us define $\mathcal{I}(E)$ as the set:

$$[a,b] \in \mathcal{I}(E) \text{ iff } (a,b) \in \mathcal{I}_{open}(E) \ .$$

For $I \in \mathcal{I}(E)$, let us denote with $\otimes_{|I}$ the restriction of $\otimes$ to I. The following proposition characterizes fully continuous t-norms and is also called the Mostert–Shields theorem [321].[1]

Proposition 32 ([186, 241]). *Let $\otimes$ be continuous. Then*

    1. for each $I \in \mathcal{I}(E)$, $\otimes_{|I}$ is isomorphic to an Archimedian t-norm;

    2. if $a,b \in [0,1]$ are such that there is no $I \in \mathcal{I}(E)$ such that $a,b \in I$, then $a \otimes b = \min(a,b)$.

The above proposition tells us that any continuous t-norm $\otimes$ behaves as an Archimedian t-norm within an interval $I \in \mathcal{I}(E)$, while for two points not included within any interval $I \in \mathcal{I}(E)$, $\otimes$ is $\otimes_g$.

Now, it is well-known that

Proposition 33. *For any continuous Archimedian t-norm $\otimes$ we have that:*

    1. if $\otimes$ is strict then $\otimes$ is isomorphic to $\otimes_p$;

    2. if $\otimes$ is not strict, i.e., by Proposition 31, $\otimes$ is nilpotent, then $\otimes$ is isomorphic to $\otimes_l$.

Hence, combining Propositions 32 and 33 we get

Proposition 34 ([186, 241]). *Let $\otimes$ be continuous. Then*

    1. for each $I \in \mathcal{I}(E)$, $\otimes_{|I}$ is isomorphic to either product or Lukasiewicz t-norm;

    2. if $a,b \in [0,1]$ are such that there is no $I \in \mathcal{I}(E)$ such that $a,b \in I$, then $a \otimes b = \min(a,b)$.

Eventually, we conclude with the representation theorem of Mostert–Shields. So, let us introduce the notion of ordinal sum. Let $(\otimes_\alpha)_{\alpha \in A}$ be a family of t-norms and $((a_\alpha, b_\alpha))_{\alpha \in A}$ be a family for non-empty, pairwise disjoint open sub-intervals of $[0,1]$. Then the following function

$$a \otimes b = \begin{cases} a_\alpha + (b_\alpha - a_\alpha) \cdot \left(\frac{a-a_\alpha}{(b_\alpha-a_\alpha)} \otimes_\alpha \frac{b-a_\alpha}{(b_\alpha-a_\alpha)} \right) & \text{if } (a,b) \in (a_\alpha, b_\alpha) \times (a_\alpha, b_\alpha); \\ \min(a,b) & \text{otherwise} . \end{cases}$$

is a t-norm and is called the *ordinal sum* of *summands* $\langle a_\alpha, b_\alpha, \otimes_\alpha \rangle$, $\alpha \in A$.

Putting Propositions 32 - 34 we get the Mostert–Shields characterization of continuous t-norms:

---

[1] We say that a t-norm $\otimes_1$ is *isomorphic* to a t-norm $\otimes_2$ iff there is a strictly increasing function f such that $a \otimes_1 b = f^{-1}(f(a) \otimes_2 f(b))$.

Proposition 35 (Mostert–Shields t-norm characterization [241]). *The following are equivalent:*

1. $\otimes$ *is a continuous t-norm;*

2. $\otimes$ *is uniquely representable as an ordinal sum of continuous Archimedean t-norms;*

3. *there is a uniquely determined countable family* $((a_\alpha, b_\alpha))_{\alpha \in A}$ *of non-empty, pairwise disjoint open sub-intervals of* $[0, 1]$ *such that*

   (a) *if* $\otimes$ *is strict on* $I = (a_\alpha, b_\alpha)$ *then* $\otimes_{|I}$ *is isomorphic to product t-norm* $\otimes_p$;

   (b) *if* $\otimes$ *is not strict, i.e., nilpotent, on* $I = (a_\alpha, b_\alpha)$ *then* $\otimes_{|I}$ *is isomorphic to Łukasiewicz t-norm* $\otimes_l$;

   (c) *if* $a, b \in [0, 1]$ *are such that there is no* $I = (a_\alpha, b_\alpha)$ *such that* $a, b \in I$, *then* $a \otimes b = a \otimes_g b$.

We may quote the above proposition as:

> *"A t-norm is continuous iff it is isomorphic to an ordinal sum of Gödel, Łukasiewicz, and product t-norm"*,

which explains why Gödel, Łukasiewicz, and product t-norm are considered the most important ones with fuzzy logic. A similar characterization is not known for non-continuous t-norms.

We summarize:

- $\otimes_g$ is the only idempotent t-norm, and is neither Archimedian, nor strict nor nilpotent;

- $\otimes_l$ is Archimedian and nilpotent, and is neither idempotent, nor strict;

- $\otimes_p$ is Archimedian and strict, and is neither idempotent, nor nilpotent.

The above properties are summarized in the following Table 8.4:

TABLE 8.4: Some properties of t-norms.

t-norm	Archimedian	idempotent	nilpotent	strict
$\otimes_g$		•		
$\otimes_l$	•		•	
$\otimes_p$	•			•

TABLE 8.5: Properties for implication and negation functions.

Axiom Name	Implication Function
Boundary condition	$0 \Rightarrow b = 1$
	$a \Rightarrow 1 = 1$
	$1 \Rightarrow 0 = 0$
Antitonicity	if $a \leq b$, then $a \Rightarrow c \geq b \Rightarrow c$
Monotonicity	if $b \leq c$, then $a \Rightarrow b \leq a \Rightarrow c$

8.1.4 Fuzzy Implication

In fuzzy set theory and practice, an important notion is the concept of fuzzy implication. A *fuzzy implication*, denoted $\Rightarrow$, is a function

$$\Rightarrow: [0,1] \times [0,1] \rightarrow [0,1]$$

and corresponds to a generalization of the notion of logical implication over $\{0,1\}$ defined as $a \Rightarrow b$ is 1 (true) iff $a \leq b$.

As for t-norms, also for implication functions some axioms have to be satisfied and are illustrated in Table 8.5. Essentially, $\Rightarrow$ should be not increasing in its first argument, while not decreasing in its second argument.

In the literature, many implication functions have proposed (see, *e.g.*, [242], Section 11.2]), among which the salient ones are:

Gödel implication: $a \Rightarrow_g b = \begin{cases} 1 & \text{if } a \leq b \\ b & \text{otherwise} . \end{cases}$

Łukasiewicz implication: $a \Rightarrow_l b = \min(1, 1 - a + b)$.

Gougen or product implication: $a \Rightarrow_p b = \begin{cases} 1 & \text{if } a \leq b \\ \frac{b}{a} & \text{otherwise} . \end{cases}$

Kleene Dienes implication: $a \Rightarrow_{kd} b = \max(1 - a, b)$.

Reichebach implication: $a \Rightarrow_r b = 1 - a + ab$.

Drastic s-implication: $a \Rightarrow_{ds} b = \begin{cases} b & \text{if } a = 1 \\ 1 - a & \text{if } b = 0 \\ 1 & \text{otherwise} . \end{cases}$

Drastic r-implication: $a \Rightarrow_{dr} b = \begin{cases} b & \text{if } a = 1 \\ 1 & \text{otherwise} . \end{cases}$

Besides the possibility to define an implication function directly, there are methods to define them indirectly. One such method consists of departing from a s-norm and a negation function and defines

$$a \Rightarrow b = \ominus a \oplus b , \tag{8.19}$$

which generalizes the classical implication $\neg a \vee b$. These implications are called usually *s-implications* in the literature.

Remark 17. *It is easily verified that* $\Rightarrow_{kd}, \Rightarrow_r, \Rightarrow_l$ *and* $\Rightarrow_{ds}$ *are all s-implications, all based on standard fuzzy negation* $\ominus_l$ *and s-norms* $\oplus_g, \oplus_p, \oplus_l$ *and* $\oplus_d$*, respectively.*

Similarly as for t-norms, we say that an implication $\Rightarrow_1$ is *weaker* than $\Rightarrow_2$ iff $a \Rightarrow_1 b \leq a \Rightarrow_2 b$ for all $(a, b) \in [0, 1]^2$. It can be shown that

Proposition 36 ([242]).

1. *Given a negation* $\ominus$*, then for s-norms* $\oplus_1$ *and* $\oplus_2$ *such that* $\oplus_1 \leq \oplus_2$*. Let* $\Rightarrow_1$ *and* $\Rightarrow_2$ *their corresponding s-implications. Then* $\Rightarrow_1 \leq \Rightarrow_2$ *holds.*

2. *The following relation between S-implication holds:*

$$\Rightarrow_{kd} \leq \Rightarrow_r \leq \Rightarrow_a \leq \Rightarrow_{ds} .$$

Another method, based on a t-norm only, gives rise to so-called *r-implications* and is defined as follows. Let $\otimes$ be a continuous t-norm. Then the *r-implication* w.r.t. $\otimes$, is defined as

$$a \Rightarrow b = \sup\{c \mid a \otimes c \leq b\} . \tag{8.20}$$

Remark 18. *It is easily verified that* $\Rightarrow_g, \Rightarrow_l, \Rightarrow_p$ *and* $\Rightarrow_{dr}$ *are all r-implications, based on t-norms* $\oplus_g, \oplus_l, \oplus_p$ *and* $\oplus_d$*, respectively.* $\Rightarrow_l$ *is the only implication that is both an s-implication and an r-implication. Note also that* $a \Rightarrow b = 1$ *iff* $a \leq b$ *and that* $1 \Rightarrow b = b$*.*

It can be shown that

Proposition 37 ([242]).

1. *Given t-norms* $\otimes_1$ *and* $\otimes_2$ *such that* $\otimes_1 \leq \otimes_2$*. Let* $\Rightarrow_1$ *and* $\Rightarrow_2$ *their corresponding r-implications. Then* $\Rightarrow_1 \geq \Rightarrow_2$ *holds.*

2. *The following relation among r-implications holds:*

$$\Rightarrow_g \leq \Rightarrow_p \leq \Rightarrow_l \leq \Rightarrow_{dr} .$$

An important property of r-implication is the following [186].

Proposition 38. *For a given continuous t-norm $\otimes$ there is an unique implication $a \Rightarrow b$ satisfying, for all $a, b, c \in [0, 1]$, the condition*

$$a \otimes c \leq b \text{ iff } a \Rightarrow b \geq c \tag{8.21}$$

namely, the r-implication $a \Rightarrow b = \sup\{c \mid a \otimes c \leq c\}$.

We point out that in fact, given a continuous t-norm $\otimes$ and its r-implication $\Rightarrow$, then we have that

$$
\begin{align}
a \otimes_g b &= a \otimes (a \Rightarrow b) \tag{8.22} \\
a \oplus_g b &= ((a \Rightarrow b) \Rightarrow b) \otimes_g ((b \Rightarrow a) \Rightarrow a), \tag{8.23}
\end{align}
$$

which essentially allows us to define Gödel t-norm and s-norm, in terms of any continuous t-norm $\otimes$.

We also can define a negation function from an r-implication as

$$\ominus a = a \Rightarrow 0. \tag{8.24}$$

It easily verified that

- Łukasiewicz negation is obtained from Łukasiewicz r-implication;

- Gödel negation is obtained from Gödel, or product r-implication.

Additionally, we have the following inferences we will use extensively in this book: let $a \geq n$ and $a \Rightarrow b \geq m$. Then,

> With Kleene-Dienes implication, we have that "if $n > 1 - m$ then $b \geq m$".

More importantly, to what concerns our work, is that under an r-implication relative to a t-norm $\otimes$, we have that

$$\text{from } a \geq n \text{ and } a \Rightarrow b \geq m, \text{ we infer } b \geq n \otimes m. \tag{8.25}$$

To see this, as $a \geq n$ and $a \Rightarrow b = \sup\{c \mid a \otimes c \leq b\} = \bar{c} \geq m$ it follows that $b \geq a \otimes \bar{c} \geq n \otimes m$. In a similar way, under an r-implication relative to a t-norm $\otimes$, we have that

$$\text{from } a \Rightarrow b \geq n \text{ and } b \Rightarrow c \geq m, \text{ we infer that } a \Rightarrow c \geq n \otimes m. \tag{8.26}$$

A final concept related to implications is related to the definition of inclusion degree among a fuzzy sets. We have seen that the standard inclusion among a fuzzy sets $A, B \in \tilde{2}^X$ is crisp (see Equation (8.10)): either $A \subseteq B$ or $A \nsubseteq B$. We may fuzzify $\subseteq$ in the following way. Let $\Rightarrow$ be an implication functions.

TABLE 8.6: Some additional properties of combination functions of various t-norms.

Property	Lukasiewicz	Gödel	Product	Zadeh [472]
$x \otimes \ominus x = 0$	•	•	•	
$x \oplus \ominus x = 1$	•			
$x \otimes x = x$		•		•
$x \oplus x = x$		•		•
$\ominus \ominus x = x$	•			•
$x \Rightarrow y = \ominus x \oplus y$	•			•
$x \Rightarrow y = \ominus y \Rightarrow \ominus x$	•			•
$\ominus (x \Rightarrow y) = x \otimes \ominus y$	•			•
$\ominus (x \otimes y) = \ominus x \oplus \ominus y$	•	•	•	•
$\ominus (x \oplus y) = \ominus x \otimes \ominus y$	•	•	•	•
$x \otimes (y \oplus z) = (x \otimes y) \oplus (x \otimes z)$	•			•
$x \oplus (y \otimes z) = (x \oplus y) \otimes (x \oplus z)$	•			•

Then the *degree of inclusion* between fuzzy sets $A, B \in \tilde{2}^X$, denoted $A \precsim B$ is defined as

$$\inf_{x \in X} A(x) \Rightarrow B(x) . \tag{8.27}$$

We conclude this section with the following important remark. Table 8.6 recalls some salient properties of the various settings. In the table, the column name identifies the t-norm $\otimes$, from which the dual s-norm $\oplus$ is considered, according to Equation (8.11), and the negation function is determined via the r-implication by Equation (8.24). The "Zadeh" column is an exception and refers to the set of functions $\{\otimes_g, \oplus_g, \Rightarrow_{kd}, \ominus_l\}$.

As we may see, none of them satisfy all the properties. More important is the fact that a set $\langle \otimes, \oplus, \ominus \rangle$ of functions satisfying all the listed properties in the upper part has necessarily to collapse to the Boolean, two-valued, case $\{0,1\}$ [143]. As a note, [146] claimed that fuzzy logic collapses to Boolean logic, but didn't recognize that to prove it, all the properties of Table 8.6 had been used.

8.1.5   Fuzzy Relation

We say that a binary *fuzzy relation* is a fuzzy set $R \in \tilde{2}^{X \times X}$. The *inverse* of R has membership function $R^{-1}(y, x) = R(x, y)$, for every $x, y \in X$. The *composition* of two fuzzy relations R_1 and R_2 is defined as $(R_1 \circ R_2)(x, z) =$

$\sup_{y \in X} R_1(x, y) \otimes R_2(y, z)$. A fuzzy relation R is *transitive* iff $R(x, z) \geq (R \circ R)(x, z)$.

8.1.6 Aggregation Operators

Aggregation Operators (AOs) (see, *e.g.*, [443] and [242, Section 3.6]) are mathematical functions that are used to combine information. There exists a large number of different AOs that differ on the assumptions on the data (data types) and about the type of information that we can incorporate in the model. To what concerns us, an AO of dimension n is a mapping $@ : \mathbb{R}^n \to \mathbb{R}$ that satisfies:

1. $@(a) = a$ (idempotent if unary);

2. $@(0, \ldots, 0) = 0$ and $@(1, \ldots, 1) = 1$ (boundary conditions);

3. $@(a_1, \ldots, a_n) \leq @(b_1, \ldots, b_n)$ if $\forall i, a_i \leq b_i$ (monotone).

Note that we always have that

$$\min(a_1, \ldots, a_n) \leq @(a_1, \ldots, a_n) \leq \max(a_1, \ldots, a_n) .$$

Often, an AO $@$ is parameterized with a vector of n weights $W = [w_1, \ldots, w_n]$ such that $w_i \in [0, 1]$ and $\sum_i w_i = 1$. In that case we will denote the AO as $@_W$.

Examples of AOs are the *arithmetic mean*,

$$@^{\mathrm{avg}}(a_1, \ldots, a_n) = \frac{1}{n} \sum_i a_i , \qquad (8.28)$$

the *weighted sum*

$$@_W^{\mathrm{ws}}(a_1, \ldots, a_n) = \sum_i w_i a_i , \qquad (8.29)$$

and the *Ordered Weighted Averaging* (OWA) operators and the quantifier-guided OWAs that we shall present next.

The OWA operators [464, 466, 468] provide a parameterized class of mean type AOs. Formally, an OWA operator of dimension n is an AO such that

$$@_W^{\mathrm{owa}}(a_1, \ldots, a_n) = \sum_j w_j b_j , \qquad (8.30)$$

where b_j is the j-th largest of the a_i.

A fundamental aspect of these operators is the reordering step. In particular, a weight w_i is not associated with a specific argument but with an ordered position of the aggregate. By choosing different W we can implement different AOs. The OWA operator is a non-linear operator as a result of the process of determining the b_j. An OWA operator @ is a mean operator and is also symmetric and idempotent:

$$Symmetric : @(a_1, \ldots, a_n) = @(a_{\pi(1)}, \ldots, a_{\pi(n)})$$
$$Idempotent : @(a, \ldots, a) = a$$

where π is a permutation. Notable OWA operators are:

$$
\begin{aligned}
f(a_1, \ldots, a_n) &= \max(a_1, \ldots, a_n) \text{ for } W = [1, 0, \ldots, 0] \\
f(a_1, \ldots, a_n) &= \min(a_1, \ldots, a_n) \text{ for } W = [0, \ldots, 0, 1] \\
f(a_1, \ldots, a_n) &= \operatorname{avg}(a_1, \ldots, a_n) \text{ for } W = [1/n, 1/n, \ldots, 1/n] \\
f(a_1, \ldots, a_n) &= \operatorname{med}(a_1, \ldots, a_n) \text{ for } w_i = 0, \\
&\qquad n \text{ odd and } w_{(n+1)/2} = 1, \text{ or} \\
&\qquad n \text{ even and } w_{n/2} = 0.5 = w_{n/2+1}
\end{aligned}
$$

In the equations above, avg and med are the average and median value of the a_i, respectively.

Next we recap *quantifier aggregations* [242, 465, 466, 467]. Classical logic has two quantifiers, the universal $\forall$ and the existential $\exists$ quantifier. These are extremal ones between several other linguistic quantifiers such as *most, few, about half, some, many*, etc. Quantifiers can be seen as absolute of proportional (see, *e.g.*, [242]). To what concerns us, we consider the proportional ones. In this case, a proportional type quantifier, such as *most*, can be represented as a fuzzy subset $Q : [0, 1] \to [0, 1]$ such that for each $r \in [0, 1]$, the membership grade $Q(r)$ indicates the degree to which the proportion r satisfies the linguistic quantifier that Q represents. See Figure 8.7 for examples of fuzzy quantifiers.

An important class of quantifiers are the *monotone quantifiers* that satisfy the following conditions:

1. $Q(0) = 0$,

2. $Q(1) = 1$,

3. $Q(r_1) \leq Q(r_2)$ if $r_1 \leq r_2$.

Essentially, these quantifiers are characterized by the idea that as the proportion increases, the degree of satisfaction does not decrease. For two quantifiers Q_1, Q_2, we write $Q_1 \leq Q_2$ if for all r, $Q_1(r) \leq Q_2(r)$. We recall that the two classical quantifiers $\exists, \forall$ may be defined as the monotone quantifiers $Q_\forall(r) = 0$ if $r \neq 1$ and $Q_\exists(r) = 1$ if $r \neq 0$, respectively. Note that for any monotone quantifier Q, we have that

$$Q_\forall \leq Q \leq Q_\exists \tag{8.31}$$

dictating that $\forall$ and $\exists$ are indeed the lower and upper bounds of monotone quantifiers.

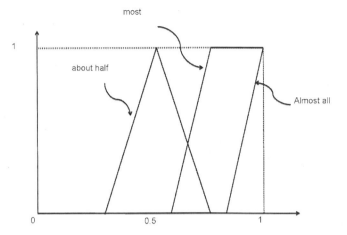

FIGURE 8.7: Some examples of fuzzy quantifiers.

To introduce quantifier-guided aggregation, we consider first the evaluation of quantified propositions. So, let Y be a (crisp) set of objects and B some fuzzy subset of Y. A quantified proposition is a statement of the form

$$QY\text{'s are } B \ .$$

An example of such a statement is "most students are young." Yager [465] suggested an approach to evaluate the truth of such quantified propositions using OWA. In the following we will assume that Q is a monotone quantifier. The first step consists in associating to Q an OWA weighting vector W_Q of dimension $n = |Y|$, where $|S|$ is the cardinality of a denumerable set S. The weights are obtained as

$$w_j = Q(\frac{j}{n}) - Q(\frac{j-1}{n}) \ . \tag{8.32}$$

Note that for Q monotone, $w_j \in [0,1]$ and $\sum_j w_j = 1$. Now, we can obtain the truth t of the statement "QY's are B" as

$$t = @_{W_Q}^{\text{owa}}(a_1, \ldots, a_n) \tag{8.33}$$

where $a_i = B(y_i)$, $y_i \in Y$ and $@_{W_Q}^{\text{owa}}$ is the OWA operator obtained using the weights W_Q found from Q as above.

We turn now to the issue of quantifier-guided aggregation, that has been shown to be useful for evaluating multi-criteria decision problems [38]. So, assume X to be a set of alternatives and we have a collection of n criteria A_i that are of concern in a given problem. For $x \in X$, with $A_i(x)$ we indicate the degree to which the i-th criterion is satisfied by alternative x. It is easily verified that the degree to which *all* criteria are satisfied by x can be determined by $D(x) = \min(A_1(x), \ldots, A_n(x))$ while the degree to which *some* criteria is satisfied by x can be determined by $D(x) = \max(A_1(x), \ldots, A_n(x))$. In general, for a monotone quantifier Q, the degree to which

$$Q \text{ of the criteria are satisfied by } x$$

can be formalized as

$$D(x) = @^{\text{owa}}_{W_Q}(A_1(x), \ldots, A_n(x)) \,, \tag{8.34}$$

where $@^{\text{owa}}_{W_Q}$ is the OWA operator obtained using the weights W_Q found from Q.

Thus, by selecting an appropriate weighting vector W, we are essentially implementing a kind of quantifier-guided aggregation.

We refer the reader to [443] for an in-depth discussion on the matter.

8.1.7   Matrix-Based Fuzzy Set Operations

We have seen that t-norms play an important role in the specification of fuzzy set operations such as intersection, union, and negation. A main feature is that they rely on some reasonable axioms one expects such fuzzy set operations should satisfy. In this section, we provide another setting, especially addressed by Hähnle [181, 182, 183, 184] related to many-valued logics, and appears to be particularly interesting for practical cases. In fact, we replace the set of membership degrees $[0, 1]$ with the finite one $L_n = \{0, \frac{1}{n-1}, \ldots, \frac{n-2}{n-1}, 1\}$ (see Equation (8.6)).

This is not surprising as usually computers cannot deal with $[0, 1]$, but rather with L_n for a reasonable large n.

In this setting, a fuzzy set operation, called *fuzzy combination function*, is simply defined as k-ary function

$$f \colon (L_n)^k \to L_n \,. \tag{8.35}$$

So, for instance, intersection and union (resp. $\otimes, \oplus$) may be seen as binary functions, which may be extended to the n-ary case, while set complement ($\ominus$) is an unary function.

As L_n is finite, one way to represent a fuzzy combination function f is by means of a matrix M_f with $k + 1$ columns and n^k rows, where the first k columns are the arguments of the function and the last column contains the evaluation of the function on the arguments. As for k arguments, each of which may have n values, the number of rows of the matrix is n^k. Of course, if the a binary function $f : L_n \times L_n$ is commutative, i.e., $f(x, y) = f(y, x)$ then we need not to represent all rows.

For instance, for $n = 5$, the matrix for standard negation is

$$M_{\ominus_l} = \begin{bmatrix} 0 & 1 \\ 0.25 & 0.75 \\ 0.5 & 0.5 \\ 0.75 & 0.25 \\ 1 & 0 \end{bmatrix}$$

Similarly, the t-norm $\otimes_l$ can be represented as

$$M_{\otimes_l} = \begin{bmatrix} 0 & 0 & 0 \\ 0 & 0.25 & 0 \\ 0 & 0.5 & 0 \\ 0 & 0.75 & 0 \\ 0 & 1 & 0 \\ 0.25 & 0 & 0 \\ 0.25 & 0.25 & 0 \\ 0.25 & 0.5 & 0 \\ 0.25 & 0.75 & 0 \\ 0.25 & 1 & 0.25 \\ 0.5 & 0 & 0 \\ 0.5 & 0.25 & 0 \\ 0.5 & 0.5 & 0 \\ 0.5 & 0.75 & 0.25 \\ 0.5 & 1 & 0.5 \\ 0.75 & 0 & 0 \\ 0.75 & 0.25 & 0 \\ 0.75 & 0.5 & 0.25 \\ 0.75 & 0.75 & 0.5 \\ 0.75 & 1 & 0.75 \\ 1 & 0 & 0 \\ 1 & 0.25 & 0.25 \\ 1 & 0.5 & 0.5 \\ 1 & 0.75 & 0.75 \\ 1 & 1 & 1 \end{bmatrix}$$

In a similar way, we can represent the t-norm $\oplus_g$, and the s-norms $\oplus_l$ and $\oplus_g$.

It is worth noting that the product t-norm $\otimes_p$ and s-norm $\oplus_p$ cannot be finitely represented, unless $n = 2$ (the product $\cdot$ is not closed on L_n for any $n \geq 3$). So, for $n \geq 3$ a matrix representation of the product is some approximation $x \cdot_n y$ of a real product $x \cdot y$, which is exactly what happens usually on computers. For instance, we may decide to approximate $\otimes_p$ via a rounding function, *e.g.*, we round $x \cdot y$ to the closest value in L_n and in case of a tie, we round to the lower value: specifically, for $x, y \in L_5$, we may define

$x \cdot_n y$ via the matrix

$$
M._n = \begin{bmatrix}
0 & 0 & 0 \\
0 & 0.25 & 0 \\
0 & 0.5 & 0 \\
0 & 0.75 & 0 \\
0 & 1 & 0 \\
0.25 & 0 & 0 \\
0.25 & 0.25 & 0 \\
0.25 & 0.5 & 0 \\
0.25 & 0.75 & 0.25 \\
0.25 & 1 & 0.25 \\
0.5 & 0 & 0 \\
0.5 & 0.25 & 0 \\
0.5 & 0.5 & 0.25 \\
0.5 & 0.75 & 0.25 \\
0.5 & 1 & 0.5 \\
0.75 & 0 & 0 \\
0.75 & 0.25 & 0.25 \\
0.75 & 0.5 & 0.25 \\
0.75 & 0.75 & 0.5 \\
0.75 & 1 & 0.75 \\
1 & 0 & 0 \\
1 & 0.25 & 0.25 \\
1 & 0.5 & 0.5 \\
1 & 0.75 & 0.75 \\
1 & 1 & 1
\end{bmatrix}
$$

Note that $\cdot_n$ is commutative, monotone, satisfies the boundary conditions, but is *not* associative, thus, $\cdot_n$ is *not* a t-norm: *e.g.*,

$$0.25 \cdot_n (0.75 \cdot_n 0.75) = 0 \neq 0.25 = (0.25 \cdot_n 0.75) \cdot_n 0.75 .$$

Another, more direct, approach to deal with fuzzy combination functions is to rely directly on built-in functions provided by an underlying computer system, rather than relying on matrix representation.

8.1.8   Fuzzy Modifiers

Fuzzy modifiers are an interesting feature of fuzzy set theory. Essentially, a fuzzy modifier, such as `very`, `more_or_less`, and `slightly`, apply to fuzzy sets to change their membership function.

Formally, a *fuzzy modifier* m represents a function

$$f_m \colon [0,1] \to [0,1] .$$

For example, we may define $f_{\texttt{very}}(x) = x^2$ and $f_{\texttt{slightly}}(x) = \sqrt{x}$. In this way, *e.g.*, by referring to Example 24, we may express the fuzzy set of employees having a *very* low salary by applying the modifier *very* to the fuzzy membership function of "low," *i.e.*,

$$\mu_{\texttt{very low}}(x) = f_{very}(\mu_{\texttt{low}}(x)) = (\mu_{\texttt{low}}(x))^2 = (ls(2000, 2500)(x))^2 .$$

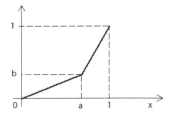

FIGURE 8.8: Linear modifier $lm(a, b)$.

The typical shape of modifiers we will consider here are so-called *linear modifiers*, as illustrated in Figure 8.8.

Note that such a modifier can be parameterized by means of one parameter c only, *i.e.*, $lm(a, b) = lm(c)$, where

$$a = c/(c+1) \ , \ b = 1/(c+1) \ .$$

8.2 Mathematical Fuzzy Logic Basics

Given that SWLs are grounded on mathematical logic, it is quite natural to look at *Mathematical Fuzzy Logic* [186] to get inspiration for a fuzzy logic extensions of SWLs. So far, we have put some effort on basic notions of fuzzy set theory. Mathematical fuzzy logic is based on fuzzy sets as much as classical logic is based on crisp set theory.

The aim of this section is to recap salient notions of mathematical fuzzy logic. An in-depth discussion can be found in [186].

8.2.1 From Classical Logic to Mathematical Fuzzy Logic

In the setting of many-valued logics (see also [172, 183]), the convention prescribing that a statement is either true or false is changed and is a matter of degree measured on an ordered scale that is no longer $\{0, 1\}$, but $[0, 1]$. The conceptual shift reflects the shift from classical crisp sets to fuzzy sets. For example, the compatibility of "tall" in the phrase "a tall man" with some individual of a given height is often graded: the man can be judged not quite tall, somewhat tall, rather tall, very tall, etc. Changing the usual true/false convention leads to a new concept of statements, whose compatibility with a given state of facts is a matter of degree and can be measured on an ordered scale $\mathcal{S}$ that is no longer $\{0, 1\}$, but, e.g., the unit interval $[0, 1]$. This leads to identifying "fuzzy statements" ϕ with a fuzzy set of possible states of affairs;

the degree of membership of a state of affairs to this fuzzy set evaluates the degree of fit between the statement and the state of facts it refers to. This degree of fit is called *degree of truth* of the statement ϕ in the interpretation $\mathcal{I}$ (state of affairs). Many-valued logics provide compositional calculi of degrees of truth, including degrees between "true" and "false that correspond to the fuzzy set operations of conjunction, union, and negation. So, a sentence is now not true or false only, but may have a truth degree taken from a *truth space* $\mathcal{S}$, usually $[0,1]$ or L_n for an integer $n \geq 3$. In the sequel, we assume $\mathcal{S} = [0,1]$.

In this section, *fuzzy statements* have the form $\langle \phi, r \rangle$, where $r \in [0,1]$ (see, *e.g.*, [183, 186]) and ϕ is a FOL statement, which encodes that the degree of truth of ϕ is *greater or equal r*. FOL statements are (see, *e.g.*, [67, 93, 158, 167, 378]), inductively defined from atomic formulae as usual (where ϕ and ψ are FOL formulae):

$$\phi \wedge \psi \ , \ \phi \vee \psi \ , \ \phi \to \psi \ , \ \phi \leftrightarrow \psi \ , \ \neg\phi \ ,$$

$$\exists x.\phi \ , \ \forall x.\phi \ .$$

Semantically, a *many-valued interpretation* $\mathcal{I}$ is similar to a classical interpretation, which rather than mapping any atomic statement into $\{0,1\}$, maps now maps each atomic formula A into $[0,1]$ and is then extended inductively to all statements as follows:

$$\begin{aligned}
\mathcal{I}(\phi \wedge \psi) &= \mathcal{I}(\phi) \otimes \mathcal{I}(\psi) \\
\mathcal{I}(\phi \vee \psi) &= \mathcal{I}(\phi) \oplus \mathcal{I}(\psi) \\
\mathcal{I}(\phi \to \psi) &= \mathcal{I}(\phi) \Rightarrow \mathcal{I}(\psi) \\
\mathcal{I}(\phi \leftrightarrow \psi) &= \mathcal{I}(\phi \to \psi) \otimes \mathcal{I}(\psi \to \phi) \\
\mathcal{I}(\neg\phi) &= \ominus \mathcal{I}(\phi) \\
\mathcal{I}(\exists x.\phi) &= \sup_{a \in \Delta^{\mathcal{I}}} \mathcal{I}_x^a(\phi) \\
\mathcal{I}(\forall x.\phi) &= \inf_{a \in \Delta^{\mathcal{I}}} \mathcal{I}_x^a(\phi) \ ,
\end{aligned} \qquad (8.36)$$

where $\Delta^{\mathcal{I}}$ is the domain of $\mathcal{I}$, the interpretation $\mathcal{I}_x^a$ is as $\mathcal{I}$ except that x is mapped into a, and now, not surprisingly, $\otimes$, $\oplus$, $\to$, and $\ominus$ are a *t-norm, s-norm, implication function*, and a *negation function*, respectively. This allows us to extend the classical Boolean conjunction, disjunction, implication, and negation, respectively, to the many-valued case. Often, the implication function $\Rightarrow$ is defined as *r-implication* (see Section 8.1.4), that is, $a \Rightarrow b = \sup\{c \mid a \otimes c \leq b\}$, but this need not be the case.

We also consider here the following abbreviations:

$$\phi \wedge_g \psi \ \overset{\text{def}}{=} \ \phi \wedge (\phi \to \psi) \qquad (8.37)$$

$$\phi \vee_g \psi \ \overset{\text{def}}{=} \ (\phi \to \psi) \to \phi) \wedge_g (\psi \to \phi) \to \psi) \qquad (8.38)$$

$$\neg_{\otimes}\phi \ \overset{\text{def}}{=} \ \phi \to 0 \ . \qquad (8.39)$$

$$\qquad (8.40)$$

TABLE 8.7: Combination functions of various fuzzy logics.

	Łukasiewicz Logic	Gödel Logic	Product Logic	SFL
$a \otimes b$	$\max(a + b - 1, 0)$	$\min(a, b)$	$a \cdot b$	$\min(a, b)$
$a \oplus b$	$\min(a + b, 1)$	$\max(a, b)$	$a + b - a \cdot b$	$\max(a, b)$
$a \Rightarrow b$	$\min(1 - a + b, 1)$	$\begin{cases} 1 & \text{if } a \le b \\ b & \text{otherwise} \end{cases}$	$\min(1, b/a)$	$\max(1 - a, b)$
$\ominus a$	$1 - a$	$\begin{cases} 1 & \text{if } a = 0 \\ 0 & \text{otherwise} \end{cases}$	$\begin{cases} 1 & \text{if } a = 0 \\ 0 & \text{otherwise} \end{cases}$	$1 - a$

In case $\Rightarrow$ is the r-implication based on $\otimes$, then $\wedge_g$ (resp. $\vee_g$) is interpreted as Gödel t-norm (resp. s-norm), while $\neg_\otimes$ is interpreted as the negation function related to $\otimes$ (see also Equation (8.24)).

As for fuzzy set theory, where we have seen that Łukasiewicz, Gödel, and product t-norm are the major players (see Proposition 35), in mathematical fuzzy logic, one usually distinguishes three different logics, namely *Łukasiewicz, Gödel*, and *product logics* [186], whose combination functions are reported in Table 8.7. In the table, we call *Standard Fuzzy Logic* (SFL), the logic with fuzzy combination functions $\otimes_g, \oplus_g, \ominus_l$ and $impf_{kd}$. By Equations (8.37) and (8.38), in fact standard fuzzy logic is entailed, *e.g.*, by Łukasiewicz logic, as $\min(a, b) = a \otimes_l (a \Rightarrow_l b)$ and $\max(a, b) = 1 - \min(1 - a, 1 - b)$ and, thus, is usually not considered in the mathematical fuzzy logic literature.

It is also worth nothing that these logics satisfy the same properties as illustrated in Table 8.6 and that there is no fuzzy logic satisfying all the properties listed in this table (otherwise it has to collapse to classical logic).

A fuzzy interpretation $\mathcal{I}$ *satisfies* a fuzzy statement $\langle \phi, r \rangle$ or $\mathcal{I}$ is a *model* of $\langle \phi, r \rangle$, denoted $\mathcal{I} \models \langle \phi, r \rangle$ iff $\mathcal{I}(\phi) \ge r$. We say that two formulae ϕ and ψ are *equivalent*, denoted $\psi \equiv \phi$, if for any fuzzy interpretation $\mathcal{I}$ we have that $\mathcal{I}(\phi) = \mathcal{I}(\psi)$. We say that $\mathcal{I}$ is a *model* of ϕ if $\mathcal{I}(\phi) = 1$ and ϕ is a *tautology* iff all fuzzy interpretations are models of ϕ, *i.e.*, $\psi \equiv 1$. A *fuzzy knowledge base* (or simply knowledge base, if clear from context) is a set of fuzzy statements and an interpretation $\mathcal{I}$ *satisfies* (is a *model* of) a knowledge base, denoted $\mathcal{I} \models \mathcal{K}$, iff it satisfies each element in it.

We say $\langle \phi, n \rangle$ is a *tight logical consequence* of a set of fuzzy statements $\mathcal{K}$ iff n is the infimum of $\mathcal{I}(\phi)$ subject to all models $\mathcal{I}$ of $\mathcal{K}$. Notice that the latter is equivalent to $n = \sup \{r \mid \mathcal{K} \models \langle \phi, r \rangle\}$. n is called the *best entailment degree* of ϕ w.r.t. $\mathcal{K}$ (denoted $bed(\mathcal{K}, \phi)$), *i.e.*,

$$bed(\mathcal{K}, \phi) = \sup \{r \mid \mathcal{K} \models \langle \phi, r \rangle\} . \tag{8.41}$$

On the other hand, the *best satisfiability degree* of ϕ w.r.t. $\mathcal{K}$ (denoted $bsd(\mathcal{K}, \phi)$) is

$$bsd(\mathcal{K}, \phi) = \sup_{\mathcal{I}} \{\mathcal{I}(\phi) \mid \mathcal{I} \models \mathcal{K}\} . \tag{8.42}$$

Of course, the properties of Table 8.6 immediately translate into equivalence among formulae. For instance, the following equivalences hold (in brackets we indicate the logic for which the equivalence holds)

$$
\begin{aligned}
\neg\neg\phi &\equiv \phi \;\; (\text{Ł}) \\
\phi \wedge \phi &\equiv \phi \;\; (G) \\
\neg(\phi \wedge \neg\phi) &\equiv 1 \;\; (\text{Ł}, G, \Pi) \\
\phi \vee \neg\phi &\equiv 1 \;\; (\text{Ł}) .
\end{aligned}
$$

We would like to point out some crucial difference between fuzzy logic and classical FOL, not illustrated so far.

Remark 19. *Unlike the classical case, in general, we do not have that $\forall x.\phi$ and $\neg\exists x.\neg\phi$ are equivalent. They are equivalent for Łukasiewicz logic and SFL (see later on, Remark 21), but are neither equivalent for Gödel nor for Product logic. For instance, under Gödel negation, just consider an interpretation $\mathcal{I}$ with domain $\{a\}$ and $\mathcal{I}(p(a)) = u$, with $0 < u < 1$. Then $\mathcal{I}(\forall x.p(x)) = u$, while $\mathcal{I}(\neg\exists x.\neg p(x)) = 1$ and, thus, $\forall x.p(x) \not\equiv \neg\exists x.\neg p(x)$.*
On the other hand, it can be shown that (see later on, Remark 21), e.g.,

$$\forall x.\neg\phi \equiv \neg\exists x.\phi .$$

We conclude, by pointing out that if the connective $\rightarrow$ is interpreted as r-implication w.r.t. the t-norm $\otimes$, then the following *graded deduction theorem* is valid:

$$\mathcal{K} \cup \{\langle\phi, r\rangle, \langle\phi \rightarrow \psi, s\rangle\} \models \langle\psi, r \otimes s\rangle . \tag{8.43}$$

In fact, consider an interpretation $\mathcal{I}$ satisfying $\mathcal{K}$, $\langle\phi, r\rangle$ and $\langle\phi \rightarrow \psi, s\rangle$. Then, from $r \leq \mathcal{I}(\phi)$, from $s \leq \mathcal{I}(\phi \rightarrow \psi) = \mathcal{I}(\phi) \Rightarrow \mathcal{I}(\psi)$, from the monotonicity of $\otimes$, and from Equation (8.21), we get

$$\mathcal{I}(\psi) \geq \mathcal{I}(\phi) \otimes s \geq r \otimes s .$$

This suggests also that the following *graded deduction rule* is correct:

$$\frac{\langle\phi, r\rangle, \langle\phi \rightarrow \psi, s\rangle}{\langle\psi, r \otimes s\rangle} . \tag{8.44}$$

8.2.1.1 On Witnessed Models

We say that a fuzzy interpretation $\mathcal{I}$ is a *witnessed interpretation* iff

$$I(\exists x.\phi) \;=\; I_x^a(\phi), \text{ for some } a \in \Delta^{\mathcal{I}} \tag{8.45}$$
$$I(\forall x.\phi) \;=\; I_x^a(\phi), \text{ for some } a \in \Delta^{\mathcal{I}}. \tag{8.46}$$

That is

$$I(\exists x.\phi) \;=\; \max_{a\in\Delta^{\mathcal{I}}} I_x^a(\phi)$$
$$I(\forall x.\phi) \;=\; \min_{a\in\Delta^{\mathcal{I}}} I_x^a(\phi).$$

These equations say that the supremum (resp. infimum) are attained at some point for a witnessed interpretation. Now, unlike the classical case, it may not be true that Equation (8.45) and Equation (8.46) hold for any $\mathcal{I}$, *i.e.*, $\mathcal{I}$ may not be witnessed. For instance, for $\mathcal{I}$ with domain the natural numbers and $\mathcal{I}_x^n(A(x)) = 1 - 1/n$, we have that

$$\mathcal{I}(\exists x.A(x)) = \sup_n \mathcal{I}_x^n(A(x)) = \sup_n 1 - 1/n = 1, \tag{8.47}$$

while in no point $\mathcal{I}_x^n(A(x))$ is 1. So, $\mathcal{I}$ is not witnessed (the argument for $\forall$ is similar).

The following important property can be shown (see, *e.g.*, [186, 188, 189, 190]).

Proposition 39. *In Łukasiewicz logic and, thus, in SFL, a fuzzy statement* $\langle \phi, r \rangle$ *has a witnessed fuzzy model iff it has a fuzzy model. This is not true for Gödel and product logic.*

This proposition says that, for Łukasiewicz logic, we may restrict our attention to witnessed models only. That is, Łukasiewicz has the so-called *witnessed model property* (there is a model iff there is witnessed model).

Of course, we also have that

Proposition 40. *If the truth space is finite then any fuzzy logic has the witnessed model property.*

Interesting is that (see [188])

$$\neg\forall x.A(x) \wedge \neg\exists x.\neg A(x) \tag{8.48}$$

has no classical model, but it has a fuzzy one, which has to be infinite. Indeed, in [188], it is shown that in Gödel logic it has no finite model, but it has an infinite fuzzy model. Of course, the above formula has no classical model. To see that it has a model under Gödel logic, consider the fuzzy interpretation $\mathcal{I}$ with domain the natural numbers and $\mathcal{I}_x^n(A(x)) = 1/(n+1)$. Then

$$\mathcal{I}(\forall x.A(x)) \;=\; \inf_n \mathcal{I}_x^n(A(x)) = 0, \text{ and, thus, } \mathcal{I}(\neg\forall x.A(x)) = 1$$
$$\mathcal{I}(\exists x.\neg A(x)) \;=\; \sup_n \mathcal{I}_x^n(\neg A(x)) = 0, \text{ and, thus, } \mathcal{I}(\neg\exists x.\neg A(x)) = 1.$$

Therefore, $\mathcal{I}$ is a model of ϕ.

8.2.2   Reasoning

We refer the reader to, *e.g.*, [182, 183, 186] for reasoning algorithms for fuzzy propositional and first-order logics. For the purposes of this book, we illustrate here some salient approaches that turn out to be useful later on. Except for Section 8.2.2.1, where we present Hilbert style axiomatizations, all the other methods will refer to the propositional case only, which however is sufficient to illustrate the main concepts behind the reasoning methods.

8.2.2.1   Axiomatizations

At first, we start with a the typical Hilbert style axiomatization approach [186]. The purpose of the axiomatization is to characterize tautologies, *i.e.*, ϕ is provable from the axioms iff ϕ is a tautology, that is $\phi \equiv 1$. The axioms have also the benefit to allow to get a better understanding of a fuzzy logic, but is unlikely suitable for any use in a practical scenario.

For the rest of this section, we restrict the logical connectives to $\wedge$ and $\rightarrow$, where $\wedge$ is interpreted as a t-norm $\otimes$ and $\rightarrow$ is its relative r-implication. $\neg\phi$ is a shorthand for $\phi \rightarrow 0$. Atomic formulae are restricted to be propositional letters. Additionally, a *theory* $\mathcal{T}$ is a set of formulae ϕ, a *model of* $\mathcal{T}$ is a fuzzy interoperation being a model of all formulae in $\mathcal{T}$, and $\mathcal{T}$ *entails* ϕ, denoted $\mathcal{T} \models \phi$, iff any model of $\mathcal{T}$ is a model of ϕ. Of course, we have that

$$\mathcal{T} \models \phi \text{ iff } \{\langle \psi, 1 \rangle \mid \psi \in \mathcal{T}\} \models \langle \phi, 1 \rangle \ .$$

Essentially, we focus our attention to fuzzy statements true to degree 1.

As usual, with $\mathcal{T} \vdash \phi$ we denote the fact that a formula can be derived from a theory using the theory, a set of axioms[2], and the deduction rule. With $\mathcal{T} \models_{cl} \phi$ we denote that the formula ϕ is classically entailed by $\mathcal{T}$.

Basic Logic BL. At first, consider the following axioms of the so-called *BL-logic*:

(A1) $(\phi \rightarrow \psi) \rightarrow ((\psi \rightarrow \chi) \rightarrow (\phi \rightarrow \chi))$

(A2) $(\phi \wedge \psi) \rightarrow \phi$

(A3) $(\phi \wedge \psi) \rightarrow (\psi \wedge \phi)$

(A4) $(\phi \wedge (\phi \rightarrow \psi)) \rightarrow (\psi \wedge (\psi \rightarrow \phi))$

(A5a) $(\phi \rightarrow (\psi \rightarrow \chi)) \rightarrow ((\phi \wedge \psi) \rightarrow \chi))$

(A5b) $((\phi \wedge \psi) \rightarrow \chi)) \rightarrow (\phi \wedge (\psi \rightarrow \chi))$

(A6) $(\phi \wedge (\psi \rightarrow \chi)) \rightarrow (((\psi \rightarrow \phi) \rightarrow \chi)) \rightarrow \chi)$

(A7) $0 \rightarrow \phi$

---

[2]The set of axioms may vary from case to case and is indicated via a subscript.

(Deduction rule) Modus ponens: from ϕ and $\phi \to \psi$ infer ψ.

We have that the following soundness and completeness result for BL-logic, where the t-norm can be arbitrary:

Proposition 41 ([186]). *Consider an arbitrary t-norm $\otimes$. Then $\mathcal{T} \vdash_{bl} \phi$ iff $\mathcal{T} \models \phi$. Also, if $\mathcal{T} \vdash_{bl} \phi$ then $\mathcal{T} \models_{cl} \phi$, but not vice versa (e.g., $\models_{cl} \phi \vee \neg\phi$, but $\not\models_{bl} \phi \vee \neg\phi$).*

Note also that

- $\mathcal{T} \vdash_{bl} (\phi \wedge \neg\phi) \to 0$

- $\mathcal{T} \vdash_{bl} \phi \to \neg\neg\phi$, but $\mathcal{T} \not\vdash_{BL} \neg\neg\phi \to \phi$, e.g., $\phi = p \vee \neg p$, t-norm is Gödel

- $\mathcal{T} \vdash_{bl} (\phi \to \psi) \to (\neg\psi \to \neg\phi)$, but not vice versa.

Łukasiewicz Logic Ł. We have seen that Proposition 41 provides us a soundness and completeness result for the BL-logic, in which we allow any t-norm to be considered to interpret the logical connective $\wedge$.

As next, let us *fix* the t-norm to be $\otimes_l$, *i.e.*, we are considering Łukasiewicz logic. Consider the following axiomatization:

(Axioms) Axioms of BL

(Ł) $\neg\neg\phi \to \phi$

(Deduction rule) Modus ponens: from ϕ and $\phi \to \psi$ infer ψ.

We have that the following soundness and completeness result for Łukasiewicz logic:

Proposition 42 ([186]). *Fix the t-norm to $\otimes_l$. Then $\mathcal{T} \vdash_l \phi$ iff $\mathcal{T} \models \phi$.*

Remark 20. *Note also that*

- $\vdash_l (\phi \to \psi) \leftrightarrow (\neg\psi \to \neg\phi)$

- $\vdash_l (\neg(\phi \wedge \psi)) \leftrightarrow (\neg\phi \vee \neg\psi)$

- $\vdash_l (\phi \to \psi) \leftrightarrow (\neg(\phi \wedge \neg\psi))$

- $\vdash_l (\phi \to \psi) \leftrightarrow (\neg\phi \vee \psi)$

- $\vdash_l (\neg(\phi \to \psi)) \leftrightarrow (\phi \wedge \neg\psi)$

- *SFL is entailed by Łukasiewicz logic.*

Product Logic Π. Let us *fix* the t-norm to be $\otimes_p$, *i.e.*, we are considering product logic. Consider the following axiomatization

(Axioms) Axioms of BL

(Π1) $\neg\neg\chi \to ((\phi \wedge \chi \to \psi \wedge \chi) \to (\phi \to \psi))$

(Π2) $(\phi \wedge_g \neg\phi) \to 0$

(Deduction rule) Modus ponens: from ϕ and $\phi \to \psi$ infer ψ.

We have that the following soundness and completeness result for product logic:

Proposition 43 ([186]). *Fix the t-norm to $\otimes_p$. Then $\mathcal{T} \vdash_p \phi$ iff $\mathcal{T} \models \phi$.*

Note also that

- $\vdash_p \neg(\phi \wedge \psi) \to \neg(\phi \wedge_g \psi)$

- $\vdash_p (\phi \to \neg\phi) \to \neg\phi$

- $\vdash_p \neg\phi \vee_g \neg\neg\phi.$

Gödel Logic G. Let us *fix* the t-norm to be $\otimes_g$, *i.e.*, we are considering Gödel logic. Consider the following axiomatization

(Axioms) Axioms of BL

(G) $\phi \to (\phi \wedge \phi)$

(Deduction rule) Modus ponens: from ϕ and $\phi \to \psi$ infer ψ.

We have that the following soundness and completeness result for Gödel logic:

Proposition 44 ([186]). *Fix the t-norm to $\otimes_g$. Then $\mathcal{T} \vdash_g \phi$ iff $\mathcal{T} \models \phi$.*

Note also that

- $\vdash_g (\phi \to \neg\phi) \to \neg\phi$

Boolean Logic. One may ask how the various axiomatizations relate to Boolean, classical, two-valued propositional logic. To this end, consider the following axiomatization

(Axioms) Axioms of BL

(B) $\phi \vee_g \neg\phi$

(Deduction rule) Modus ponens: from ϕ and $\phi \to \psi$ infer ψ.

We have that the following soundness and completeness result for classical Boolean logic:

Proposition 45 ([186]). *Fix interpretations to be classical, two-valued. Then* $\mathcal{T} \vdash_{bool} \phi$ *iff* $\mathcal{T} \models \phi$.

Note that Boolean logic extends Gödel logic as

- $\vdash_{bool} \phi \to (\phi \wedge \phi)$.

Note also that the union of any two of our three main logics turns out to be equivalent to the classical Boolean logic:

- Ł + G is equivalent to Boolean logic

- Ł + Π is equivalent to Boolean logic

- G + Π is equivalent to Boolean logic.

Rational Pavelka Logic RPL. So far, we considered only formulae and their absolute truth, *i.e.*, whether they have truth 1 in any model of a theory. In the following, we devise an axiomatization for the case of fuzzy statements, *i.e.*, statements of form $\langle \phi, r \rangle$ under Łukasiewicz-logic. To do so, we introduce the so-called *Rational Pavelka Logic* (RPL) [347].

In this setting, we fix the t-norm to be $\otimes_l$, and we extend the so far considered propositional language to include, besides 0 and 1, also any rational $r \in [0,1]$ as atom in a formula. We denote the set of rational numbers in $[0,1]$ with $[0,1]_{\mathbb{Q}}$. Hence, *e.g.*, $(0.3 \wedge \phi) \to 0.8$ is a formula. We extend interpretations to rationals in the obvious way: $\mathcal{I}(r) = r$. We also assume that any sub-formula in which rationals occur only is recursively replaced with its evaluation using:

$$r \wedge s \quad \mapsto \quad r \otimes_l s \tag{8.49}$$

$$r \to s \quad \mapsto \quad r \Rightarrow s \tag{8.50}$$

$$\neg r \quad \mapsto \quad 1 - r . \tag{8.51}$$

The axiomatizations of RPL is as for Łukasiewicz-logic and we have:

Proposition 46 (see [186]). *For RPL,* $\mathcal{T} \vdash_{rpl} \phi$ *iff* $\mathcal{T} \models \phi$.

The interesting point is the following observation: for any fuzzy interpretation $\mathcal{I}$, for any formula ϕ and rational $r \in [0,1]_{\mathbb{Q}}$

$$\mathcal{I}(\phi) \geq r \text{ iff } \mathcal{I}(r \to \phi) = 1$$
$$\mathcal{I}(\phi) \leq r \text{ iff } \mathcal{I}(\phi \to r) = 1 .$$

That is, $\mathcal{I}$ is a model of $\langle \phi, r \rangle$ iff it is a model of $r \to \phi$, and, similarly, $\mathcal{I}$ is a model of $\langle \neg \phi, r \rangle$ iff it is a model of $\phi \to (1 - r)$. As a consequence, from Proposition 46 we get immediately a sound and complete proof procedure for graded consequence under Łukasiewicz logic (and, thus, for SFL): for a set of fuzzy statements $\mathcal{K}$, let

$$\mathcal{T}_{\mathcal{K}} = \{r \to \psi \mid \psi \in \mathcal{K}\} .$$

Then

Proposition 47 (see [186]). *For a set of fuzzy statements $\mathcal{K}$,*

$$\mathcal{K} \models \langle \phi, r \rangle \text{ iff } \mathcal{T}_{\mathcal{K}} \vdash_{rpl} r \to \phi \ .$$

The analogue of Proposition 47 fails for product logic and Gödel logic (see [186]). We refer the reader to [148, 149] for more on this issue.

However, we may somewhat extend RPL, still guaranteeing soundness and completeness [186]. In fact, consider RPL extend with a binary logical combination operator $\wedge_p$ interpreted as product t-norm $\otimes_p$. Let RPL($\wedge_p$) this logic. Consider the evaluation of rationals as from Equations (8.49)–(8.51), plus the additional evaluation

$$r \wedge_p s \mapsto \quad r \otimes_p s \ ,$$

and, eventually, the axiomatization

(Axioms) Axioms of RPL

($R\Pi$1) $(\phi \to \psi) \to ((\phi \wedge_p \chi) \to (\psi \wedge_p \chi))$

($R\Pi$2) $(\phi \to \psi) \to ((\chi \wedge_p \phi) \to (\chi \wedge_p \psi))$

(Deduction rule) Modus ponens: from ϕ and $\phi \to \psi$ infer ψ

Then

Proposition 48 ([186]). *$\mathcal{T} \vdash_{pl(\wedge_p)} \phi$ iff $\mathcal{T} \models \phi$.*

Fuzzy First-Order Logic. Here we show how to provide an axiomatization of fuzzy FOL logic. In the following, we extend the propositional language by allowing predicates to occur as atomic formulae and quantified formulae are the form $\forall x.\phi$ and $\exists x.\phi$. A *term t* is either a variable or a constant.[3]

In the following, with $\mathcal{C}\forall$, where $\mathcal{C} \in \{$ BL, Ł, Π, G$\}$, we denote the fuzzy FOL in which the underlying logic is either the BL logic, the Łukasiewicz logic, the product logic or the Gödel logic. Now, consider the following axiomatization

(Axioms) Axioms of $\mathcal{C}$

($\forall$1) $\forall x.\phi(x) \to \phi(t)$ (*t* substitutable for *x* in $\phi(x)$)

($\exists$1) $\phi(t) \to \exists x.\phi(x)$ (*t* substitutable for *x* in $\phi(x)$)

($\forall$2) $\forall x.(\psi \to \phi) \to (\psi \to \forall x.\phi)$ (*x* not free in ψ)

($\exists$2) $\forall x.(\phi \to \psi) \to (\exists x.\phi \to \psi)$ (*x* not free in ψ)

---

[3]Note that we may introduce functions symbols as well, with crisp semantics (but is uninteresting), or we need to discuss also fuzzy equality (which we leave out here).

($\forall$3) $\forall x.(\phi \vee_g \psi) \to (\forall x.\phi) \vee_g \psi$ (x not free in ψ)

(Modus ponens) from ϕ and $\phi \to \psi$ infer ψ

(Generalization) from ϕ infer $\forall x.\phi$,

where the notions of "t substitutable for x in $\phi(x)$" and "x not free in ψ" are defined as for classical FOL (see, *e.g.*, [67, 93, 158, 167, 378]).[4]

We have that the following soundness and completeness result for the $\mathcal{C}\forall$ logic:

Proposition 49 ([186]). $\mathcal{T} \vdash_{\mathcal{C}} \phi$ *iff* $\mathcal{T} \models \phi$.

Remark 21. *Note that*

- $\vdash_{BL\forall} \exists x.\phi \to \neg\forall x.\neg\phi$

- $\vdash_{BL\forall} \neg\exists x.\phi \leftrightarrow \forall x.\neg\phi$

- $\vdash_{L\forall} \exists x.\phi \leftrightarrow \neg\forall x.\neg\phi$

- $\vdash_{BL\forall} (\forall x.\phi \to \phi) \leftrightarrow \phi \to (\forall x.\phi)$ *if x does not occur in ϕ*

- $\vdash_{BL\forall} (\exists x.\phi \to \phi) \leftrightarrow \phi \to (\exists x.\phi)$ *if x does not occur in ϕ* .

Predicate Rational Pavelka Logic (RPL$\forall$). The FOL variant is obtained from RPL in the obvious way: we fix Łukasiewicz t-norm and r-implication, formulae are as for L$\forall$, where rationals $r \in [0,1]_\mathbb{Q}$ may appear as atoms and, formulae with rationals are only evaluated according to Equations (8.49)–(8.51), and a sound and complete axiomatization is the one as for L$\forall$.

8.2.2.2 Operational Research-based

An important and application oriented approach for reasoning with fuzzy logic is based on Operational Research (OR). To this end, we first recap some salient definitions related to OR.

OR basics. In this section we recall basic notions related to Mixed Integer Linear Programming (MILP), Mixed Integer Quadratically Constrained Programming (MIQCP) and Mixed Integer Non Linear Programming (MINLP) optimization problems.

A general Mixed Integer Linear Programming (MILP) [366] problem consists in minimizing a linear function with respect to a set of constraints that are linear inequations in which rational and integer variables can occur. More precisely, let $x = \langle x_1, \ldots, x_k \rangle$ and $y = \langle y_1, \ldots, y_m \rangle$ be variables over $\mathbb{Q}$ and $\mathbb{Z}$ respectively, over the integers and let A, B be integer matrices and h an integer

---

[4]Roughly, a constant is always substitutable, and a variable y is substitutable into ϕ for x if the substitution does not make any free occurrence of x into a bound occurrence of y.

vector. The variables in y are called *control variables*. Let $f(x,y)$ be an $k+m$-ary linear function. Then the general MILP problem is to find $\bar{x} \in \mathbb{Q}^k, \bar{y} \in \mathbb{Z}^m$ such that $f(\bar{x},\bar{y}) = \min\{f(x,y) \mid Ax + By \geq h\}$.

The general case can be restricted to what concerns the paper as we can deal with *bounded* MILP (bMILP). That is, the rational variables usually range over $[0,1]$, while the integer variables range over $\{0,1\}$. It is well known that the bMILP problem is NP-complete (for the belonging to NP, guess the y and solve in polynomial time the linear system, NP-hardness follows from NP-Hardness of 0-1 Integer Programming). Furthermore, we say that $M \subseteq [0,1]^k$ is bMILP-representable iff there is a bMILP (A,B,h) with k real and m $0-1$ variables such that $M = \{x : \exists y \in \{0,1\}^m$ such that $Ax + By \geq h\}$.

In general, we require that every constructor is bMILP representable. For instance, classical logic, SFL, and Lukasiewicz connectives, are bMILP-representable, while Gödel negation is not. In general, connectives whose graph can be represented as the union of a finite number of convex polyhedra are bMILP-representable [216], however, discontinuous functions may not be bMILP representable.

There are a lot of available tools for solving these problems, such as Cbc[5], Gurobi[6] or lpsolve[7].

Concerning Mixed Integer Quadratically Constrained Programming (MIQCP), let $x = \langle x_1, \ldots, x_k \rangle$ and $y = \langle y_1, \ldots, y_m \rangle$ be variables over $\mathbb{Q}$ and $\mathbb{Z}$ respectively. Now, for all $i \in 0,1,\ldots,n$, let a_i be an integer vector of length k, b_i be an integer vector of length m, h_i be an integer number and $Q_i(x,y) = 1/2 \cdot (x+y)^T \cdot C_i \cdot (x+y)$, where C_i is a symmetric integer matrix of dimension $(k+m) \times (k+m)$. Let $f(x,y)$ be an $k+m$-ary linear function. The MICQP problem is to find $\bar{x} \in \mathbb{Q}^k, \bar{y} \in \mathbb{Z}^m$ such that $f(\bar{x},\bar{y}) = \min\{f(x,y) : a_0 \cdot x + b_0 \cdot y \geq h_0\}$ subject to a set of n constraints of the form: $a_i \cdot x + b_i \cdot y + Q_i(x,y) \geq h_i$ or $a_i \cdot x + b_i \cdot y + Q_i(x,y) \leq h_i$, for all $i = 1,\ldots,n$. Notice that the objective function is linear, while the restrictions can contain quadratic sections.

The general case may be restricted to the bounded MIQCP (bMIQCP), with rational variables ranging over $[0,1]$ and integer variables range over $\{0,1\}$. $M \subseteq [0,1]^k$ is bMICQP-representable iff there is a bMICQP (a_i,b_i,C_i,h_i) with k real and m $0-1$ variables such that $M = \{x : \exists y \in \{0,1\}^m$ such that $a_i \cdot x + b_i \cdot y + Q_i(x,y) \geq h_i$ or $a_i \cdot x + b_i \cdot y + Q_i(x,y) \leq h_i\}$.

This problem is known to be NP-Hard. Some examples of solvers are CPLEX[8] or Mosek[9].

Concerning Mixed Integer Non Linear Programming (MINLP), let $x = \langle x_1, \ldots, x_k \rangle$ and $y = \langle y_1, \ldots, y_m \rangle$ be variables over $\mathbb{Q}$ and $\mathbb{Z}$ respectively, and, for all $i \in 0,1,\ldots,n$, let h_i be an integer number, and $f_i(x,y)$ be

---

[5]http://www.coin-or.org/projects/Cbc.xml
[6]http://www.gurobi.com
[7]http://sourceforge.net/projects/lpsolve
[8]http://www.ilog.com/products/cplex/
[9]http://www.mosek.com/

an $k + m$-ary (possibly non linear) function. The Mixed Integer Non Linear Programming (MINLP) problem [160] is to find $\bar{x} \in \mathbb{Q}^k, \bar{y} \in \mathbb{Z}^m$ such that $f_0(\bar{x}, \bar{y}) = \min_{x \in \bar{x}, y \in \bar{y}} \{f_0(x, y)\}$ subject to a set of n constraints of the form: $f_i(x, y) \geq h_i$, for all $i = 1, \ldots, n$.

As in the previous cases, in the bounded MINLP (bMINLP), rational variables range over $[0, 1]$ and integer variables range over $\{0, 1\}$. The problem is NP-Hard, and there some available solvers, such as `Bonmin`[10].

OR-based decision algorithm. Now, unlike Section 8.2.2.1, we show here a simple method that allows to determine $bed(\mathcal{K}, \phi)$ and $bsd(\mathcal{K}, \phi)$ via Mixed Integer Linear Programming (MILP) for propositional Łukasiewicz logic and, thus, for SFL as well (see, *e.g.*, [359]). To this end, it can be shown that

$$bed(\mathcal{K}, \phi) \quad = \quad \min x. \text{ such that } \mathcal{K} \cup \{\langle \neg \phi, 1 - x \rangle\} \text{ satisfiable} \quad (8.52)$$
$$bsd(\mathcal{K}, \phi) \quad = \quad \max x. \text{ such that } \mathcal{K} \cup \{\langle \phi, x \rangle\} \text{ satisfiable} . \quad (8.53)$$

In fact, *e.g.*, concerning $bed(\mathcal{K}, \phi)$, suppose the minimal value of x is $\bar{n}$. We will know then that for any fuzzy interpretation $\mathcal{I}$ satisfying the knowledge base such that $\mathcal{I}(\phi) < \bar{n}$, the starting set is not satisfiable (otherwise $\bar{n}$ wouldn't be minimal) and, thus, $\mathcal{I}(\phi) \geq \bar{n}$ has to hold, which means that $bed(\mathcal{K}, \phi) = \bar{n}$.

Note that in effect Equation (8.52) is the same as

$$bed(\mathcal{K}, \phi) \quad = \quad \min x. \text{ such that } \mathcal{K} \cup \{\langle \phi \leq x \rangle\} \text{ satisfiable} . \quad (8.54)$$

Without loss of generalization, for Łukasiewicz logic, we may consider a formula ϕ in *Negation Normal Form* (NNF) (*i.e.*, negation may be in front of an atom only), which is obtained by applying recursively the rules

$$\neg 0 \quad = \quad 1$$
$$\neg 1 \quad = \quad 0$$
$$\neg \neg \phi \quad \mapsto \quad \phi$$
$$\neg(\phi \wedge \psi) \quad \mapsto \quad \neg \phi \vee \neg \psi$$
$$\neg(\phi \vee \psi) \quad \mapsto \quad \neg \phi \wedge \neg \psi$$
$$\neg(\phi \rightarrow \psi) \quad \mapsto \quad \phi \wedge \neg \psi .$$

With $nnf(\phi)$ we denote the NNF obtained from ϕ.

For a formula ϕ consider a variable x_ϕ (with intended meaning: the degree of truth of ϕ is greater or equal to x_ϕ). Now we apply the following transformation σ that generates a set of MILP in-equations:

$$bed(\mathcal{K}, \phi) = \min x. \text{ such that } x \in [0, 1],$$
$$x_{\neg \phi} \geq 1 - x, \sigma(\neg \phi), \quad (8.55)$$
$$\text{for all } \langle \psi, n \rangle \in \mathcal{K}, x_\psi \geq n, \sigma(\psi),$$

---

[10]http://www.coin-or.org/projects/Bonmin.xml

where the $\sigma(\cdot)$ is defined as follows:

$$\sigma(\phi) = \begin{cases} x_p \in [0,1] & \text{if } \phi = p \\[2mm] x_0 = 0 & \text{if } \phi = 0 \\[2mm] x_1 = 1 & \text{if } \phi = 1 \\[2mm] \begin{aligned} &x_\phi = 1 - x_{\phi'}, \\ &x_\phi \in [0,1] \end{aligned} & \text{if } \phi = \neg\phi' \\[4mm] \begin{aligned} &x_{\phi_1} \otimes x_{\phi_2} = x_\phi, \\ &\sigma(\phi_1), \sigma(\phi_2), x_\phi \in [0,1] \end{aligned} & \text{if } \phi = \phi_1 \wedge \phi_2 \\[4mm] \begin{aligned} &x_{\phi_1} \oplus x_{\phi_2} = x_\phi, \\ &\sigma(\phi_1), \sigma(\phi_2), x_\phi \in [0,1] \end{aligned} & \text{if } \phi = \phi_1 \vee \phi_2 \\[4mm] \begin{aligned} &(1 - x_{nnf(\neg\phi_1)}) \Rightarrow x_{\phi_2} = x_\phi, \\ &\sigma(nnf(\neg\phi_1)), \sigma(\phi_2), x_\phi \in [0,1] \end{aligned} & \text{if } \phi = \phi_1 \to \phi_2 \,. \end{cases}$$

In the definition above, the conditions $x_1 \oplus x_2 = z$, $x_1 \otimes x_2 = z$, $x_1 \Rightarrow x_2 = z$ with $0 \leq x_i, z \leq 1$, can be encoded as the sets of constraints:

- $x_1 \otimes_l x_2 = z \mapsto \{x_1 + x_2 - 1 \leq z, x_1 + x_2 - 1 \geq z - y, z \leq 1 - y, y \in \{0,1\}\}$, where y is a new variable.

- $x_1 \oplus_l x_2 = z \mapsto \{x_1 + x_2 \leq z + y, y \leq z, x_1 + x_2 \geq z, y \in \{0,1\}\}$, where y is a new variable.

- $x_1 \Rightarrow_l x_2 = z \mapsto \{(1 - x_1) \oplus_l x_2 = z\}$.

As the set of constraints is linearly bounded by $\mathcal{K}$ and as MILP satisfiability is NP-complete, we get the well-known result that determining the best entailment/satisfiability degree is NP-complete for propositional Łukasiewicz logic and SFL.

For completeness, we illustrate here also the equations for propositional SFL alone as well:

- $x_1 \otimes_g x_2 = z \mapsto \{z \leq x_1, z \leq x_2, x_1 \leq z + y, x_2 \leq z + (1-y), y \in \{0,1\}\}$, where y is a new variable.

- $x_1 \oplus_g x_2 = z \mapsto \{z \geq x_1, z \geq x_2, x_1 + y \geq z, x_2 + (1-y) \geq z, y \in \{0,1\}\}$, where y is a new variable.

- $x_1 \Rightarrow_{kd} x_2 = z \mapsto (1 - x_1) \oplus_g x_2 = z$.

Concerning the best satisfiability problem, in a similar way we derive

$$bsd(\mathcal{K}, \phi) = \max x. \text{ such that } x \in [0, 1],$$
$$x_\phi \geq x, \sigma(\phi), \tag{8.56}$$
$$\text{for all } \langle \psi, n \rangle \in \mathcal{K}, x_\psi \geq n, \sigma(\psi) ,$$

while we may determine whether a KB $\mathcal{K}$ is satisfiable by checking whether the set of constraints

$$sat(\mathcal{K}) = \{x_\psi \geq n, \sigma(\psi) \mid \langle \psi, n \rangle \in \mathcal{K}\} \tag{8.57}$$

has a solution.

It is illustrative to show that the method based on OR in which we *compile* a KB into a set of constraints, can be represented as well via an inference method on formulae, as illustrated by the L-ORFuzzySat algorithm (see Algorithm 3).

Then, it can be shown that

Proposition 50. *Let $\mathcal{K}$ be a propositional fuzzy KB $\mathcal{K}$ in Łukasiewicz logic. Then*

1. *The L-ORFuzzySat procedure terminates.*

2. *$\mathcal{K}$ is satisfiable iff the L-ORFuzzySat procedure returns* **true**.

Note that a model $\mathcal{I}$ of $\mathcal{K}$ can immediately be built from a solution by assigning to any atom p occurring in $\mathcal{K}$

$$\mathcal{I}(p) = \bar{x}_p ,$$

where $\bar{x}_p$ is the value of variable x_p is a solution to $\mathcal{C}_\mathcal{K}$. We also have in this model that

$$\mathcal{I}(\phi) = \bar{x}_\phi$$

for any formula ϕ occurring in $\mathcal{K}$.

We illustrated the method for the KB satisfiability problem. It is quite straightforward to adapt it to best entailment and the best satisfiability problems as well via Equations (8.55) and (8.56).

Example 25. *Consider*

$$\mathcal{K} = \{\langle p, 0.8 \rangle, \langle p \rightarrow q, 0.9 \rangle\} .$$

Let us show that

$$bed(\mathcal{K}, q) = 0.7 .$$

Algorithm 3 L-ORFuzzySat.

Input: A propositional fuzzy KB $\mathcal{K}$ in Łukasiewicz logic.

Output: Check if $\mathcal{K}$ satisfiable and if positive provide a model of $\mathcal{K}$

1. Transform a KB $\mathcal{K}$ into NNF, *i.e.*, by transforming the formulae in $\mathcal{K}$ into NNF;

2. Initialize the fuzzy theory $\mathcal{T}_\mathcal{K}$ and the initial set of constraints $\mathcal{C}_\mathcal{K}$ by

$$\mathcal{T}_\mathcal{K} = \{\phi \mid \langle \phi, n \rangle \in \mathcal{K}\}$$
$$\mathcal{C}_\mathcal{K} = \{x_\psi \geq n \mid \langle \phi, n \rangle \in \mathcal{K}\} \,.$$

3. Apply the following inference rules until no more rules can be applied. Of course, each rule instance is applied at most once.

   (var). For variable x_ϕ occurring in $\mathcal{C}_\mathcal{K}$ add $x_\phi \in [0,1]$ to $\mathcal{C}_\mathcal{K}$.

   (v\bar{a}r). For variable $x_{\neg\phi}$ occurring in $\mathcal{C}_\mathcal{K}$ add $x_\phi = 1 - x_{\neg\phi}$ to $\mathcal{C}_\mathcal{K}$.

   ($\bot$). If $0 \in \mathcal{T}_\mathcal{K}$ then $\mathcal{C}_\mathcal{K} := \mathcal{C}_\mathcal{K} \cup \{x_0 = 0\}$.

   ($\top$). If $1 \in \mathcal{T}_\mathcal{K}$ then $\mathcal{C}_\mathcal{K} := \mathcal{C}_\mathcal{K} \cup \{x_1 = 1\}$.

   ($\wedge$). If $\phi \wedge \psi \in \mathcal{T}_\mathcal{K}$, then

       (a) add ϕ and ψ to $\mathcal{T}_\mathcal{K}$

       (b) $\mathcal{C}_\mathcal{K} := \mathcal{C}_\mathcal{K} \cup \{x_\phi \otimes x_\psi = x_{\phi\wedge\psi}\}$.

   ($\vee$). If $\phi \vee \psi \in \mathcal{T}_\mathcal{K}$, then

       (a) add ϕ and ψ to $\mathcal{T}_\mathcal{K}$

       (b) $\mathcal{C}_\mathcal{K} := \mathcal{C}_\mathcal{K} \cup \{x_\phi \oplus x_\psi = x_{\phi\wedge\psi}\}$.

   ($\rightarrow$). If $\phi \rightarrow \psi \in \mathcal{T}_\mathcal{K}$, then

       (a) add $nnf(\neg\phi)$ and ψ to $\mathcal{T}_\mathcal{K}$

       (b) $\mathcal{C}_\mathcal{K} := \mathcal{C}_\mathcal{K} \cup \{(1 - x_{nnf(\neg\phi)}) \Rightarrow x_\psi = x_{\phi\rightarrow\psi}\}$.

4. Return that $\mathcal{K}$ is satisfiable, *i.e.*, **true**, iff the final set of constraints $\mathcal{C}_\mathcal{K}$ has a solution.

---

under Łukasiewicz logic. To do so, we need to determine

$$bed(\mathcal{K}, q) = \min x. \text{ such that } x \in [0,1],$$
$$x_{\neg q} \geq 1 - x,$$
$$1 - x_q = x_{\neg q},$$
$$x_p \geq 0.8,$$
$$x_{p\rightarrow q} \geq 0.9,$$
$$1 - x_p = x_{\neg p},$$
$$x_{\neg p} + x_q \leq x_{p\rightarrow q} + y,$$
$$y \leq x_{p\rightarrow q},$$
$$x_{\neg p} + x_q \geq x_{p\rightarrow q},$$
$$y \in \{0,1\} \,.$$

I can be verified that the minimal value of x is 0.7.

The case of L_n**.** We conclude this section by pointing out that the L-ORFuzzySat procedure can easily be adapted to a case in which we consider the set L_n as truth space in place of $[0, 1]$. In fact, we have to simply enforce that now, any $[0, 1]$-valued variable x takes values in L_n instead. Now,

$$x \in \{0, \frac{1}{n-1}, \ldots, \frac{n-2}{n-1}, 1\}$$

can be encoded as

$$\begin{aligned} z &= (n-1) \cdot x \\ z &\in \{0, 1, \ldots, n-1\} \end{aligned} \tag{8.58}$$

for a new integer variable z. Hence, for L_n we immediately have the analogue of Proposition 50:

Proposition 51. *Let* $\mathcal{K}$ *be a propositional fuzzy KB* $\mathcal{K}$ *under Łukasiewicz logic. Then*

1. *The L-ORFuzzySat procedure terminates.*

2. $\mathcal{K}$ *is satisfiable w.r.t.* L_n *iff the L-ORFuzzySat procedure returns* **true**, *in which in the final set of MILP constraints* $\mathcal{C}_{\mathcal{K}}$ *the* $[0, 1]$*-valued variables are enforced to take value in* L_n *as illustrated in Equation (8.58).*

It is yet unclear if the L-ORFuzzySat procedure can be adapted to the case in which other truth combination functions over L_n are considered. We do not address this further here.

8.2.2.3 Analytical Fuzzy Tableau

In this section we show that in fact there is a very simple decision procedure for the propositional KB satisfiability problem in SFL, without relying on OR. It is based on the following simple properties that hold in SFL:

- if $\mathcal{I}$ is model of $\langle \phi \wedge \psi, n \rangle$ then $\mathcal{I}$ is a model of both $\langle \phi, n \rangle$ and $\langle \psi, n \rangle$;

- if $\mathcal{I}$ is model of $\langle \phi \vee \psi, n \rangle$ then $\mathcal{I}$ is a model of either $\langle \phi, n \rangle$ or $\langle \psi, n \rangle$.

- $\mathcal{I}$ cannot be a model of both $\langle p, n \rangle$ and $\langle \neg p, m \rangle$ if $n > 1 - m$.

For the remainder of this section, w.l.o.g. we may consider SFL KBs in which any formula of the form $\phi \to \psi$ has been replaced with $\neg \phi \vee \psi$.

A *clash* is either

- a fuzzy statement $\langle 0, n \rangle$ with $n > 0$; or

- a pair of fuzzy statements $\langle p, n \rangle$ and $\langle \neg p, m \rangle$ with $n > 1 - m$.

A KB is *clash-free* iff it does not contain a clash.

The decision procedure for the KB satisfiability problem is illustrated by the SFD-TableauFuzzySat procedure described in Algorithm 4. It is easily verified that

---

Algorithm 4 SFD-TableauFuzzySat.

Input: A propositional fuzzy KB $\mathcal{K}$ under SFL.
Output: Check if $\mathcal{K}$ satisfiable.

1. Transform a KB $\mathcal{K}$ into NNF, *i.e.*, by transforming the formulae in $\mathcal{K}$ into NNF;

2. Initialize the *completion* $\mathcal{S}_\mathcal{K} = \mathcal{K}$;

3. Apply the following inference rules to $\mathcal{S}_\mathcal{K}$ until no more rules can be applied. We call a set of fuzzy statements $\mathcal{S}_\mathcal{K}$ complete iff none of the rules below can be applied to $\mathcal{S}_\mathcal{K}$. Note that rule ($\vee$) is non-deterministic.

   ($\wedge$). If $\langle \phi \wedge \psi, n \rangle \in \mathcal{S}_\mathcal{K}$ and $\{\langle \phi, n \rangle, \langle \psi, n \rangle\} \not\subseteq \mathcal{S}_\mathcal{K}$, then add both $\langle \phi, n \rangle$ and $\langle \psi, n \rangle$ to $\mathcal{S}_\mathcal{K}$.

   ($\vee$). If $\langle \phi \vee \psi, n \rangle \in \mathcal{S}_\mathcal{K}$ and $\{\langle \phi, n \rangle, \langle \psi, n \rangle\} \cap \mathcal{S}_\mathcal{K} = \emptyset$, then add *either* $\langle \phi, n \rangle$ or $\langle \psi, n \rangle$ to $\mathcal{S}_\mathcal{K}$

   ($\rightarrow$). If $\langle \phi \rightarrow \psi, n \rangle \in \mathcal{S}_\mathcal{K}$ and $\langle nnf(\neg \phi) \vee \psi, n \rangle \not\in \mathcal{S}_\mathcal{K}$, then add $\langle nnf(\neg \phi) \vee \psi, n \rangle$ to $\mathcal{S}_\mathcal{K}$

4. Return that $\mathcal{K}$ is satisfiable, *i.e.*, **true** iff we find a complete and clash-free completion $\mathcal{S}_\mathcal{K}$ of $\mathcal{K}$.

Proposition 52. *Let $\mathcal{K}$ be a propositional fuzzy KB $\mathcal{K}$. Then*

1. *The SFD-TableauFuzzySat procedure terminates.*

2. *$\mathcal{K}$ is satisfiable iff the SFD-TableauFuzzySat procedure returns* **true**.

Note that, unlike the Ł-ORFuzzySat procedure, the SFD-TableauFuzzySat procedure is *non-deterministic* as involves the non-deterministic rule ($\vee$) and, thus, in the worst case we have to generate exhaustively all possible (finite many) completions $\mathcal{S}_\mathcal{K}$ of $\mathcal{K}$.

Example 26. *Consider $\mathcal{K}$ of Example 25. Let us show that $\mathcal{K}$ is satisfiable under SFL. A clash-free completion of $\mathcal{K}$ is*

$$\mathcal{S}_\mathcal{K} = \{\langle p, 0.8 \rangle, \langle p \rightarrow q, 0.9 \rangle, \langle \neg p \vee q, 0.9 \rangle, \langle q, 0.9 \rangle\}$$

from which we immediately may build a model $\mathcal{I}$ with $\mathcal{I}(p) = 0.8$, $\mathcal{I}(q) = 0.9$.

It remains to show how to address the entailment problem, *i.e.*, to decide whether $\mathcal{K} \models \langle \phi, n \rangle$ holds. To this end, it is easily verified that

$$\mathcal{K} \models \langle \phi, n \rangle \text{ iff } \mathcal{K} \cup \{\langle \phi < n \rangle\} \text{ is not satisfiable,}$$

where an interpretation $\mathcal{I}$ is a model of the expression $\langle \phi < n \rangle$ iff $\mathcal{I}(\phi) < n$.

Given that we now have an additional construct, we will show that we have to ways to cope with it, that we will briefly illustrate.

The first method consists in extending the rules in the SFD-TableauFuzzySat procedure to deal with $<$ expressions. To this end, rather than using expressions of the form $(\phi < n)$, we allow expressions of the form

$$\langle \phi, n \rangle^+ \tag{8.59}$$

where $\mathcal{I}$ is a model of the expression $\langle \phi, n \rangle^+$ iff $\mathcal{I}(\phi) > n$. Then, of course,

$$\mathcal{K} \models \langle \phi, n \rangle \text{ iff } \mathcal{K} \cup \{\langle \neg \phi, 1 - n \rangle^+\} \text{ is not satisfiable} . \tag{8.60}$$

Now, we have to extend

1. the notion of clash; and

2. the inference rules to cope with expression of the form $\langle \phi, n \rangle^+$

That is, a *clash* is one of the following:

1. a fuzzy statement $\langle 0, n \rangle$ with $n > 0$;

2. a fuzzy statement $\langle 0, n \rangle^+$;

3. a fuzzy statement $\langle 1, 1 \rangle^+$;

4. a pair of fuzzy statements $\langle p, n \rangle$ and $\langle \neg p, m \rangle$ with $n > 1 - m$;

5. a pair of fuzzy statements $\langle p, n \rangle$ and $\langle \neg p, m \rangle^+$ with $n \geq 1 - m$;

6. a pair of fuzzy statements $\langle p, n \rangle^+$ and $\langle \neg p, m \rangle$ with $n \geq 1 - m$;

7. a pair of fuzzy statements $\langle p, n \rangle^+$ and $\langle \neg p, m \rangle^+$ with $n \geq 1 - m$.

The additional rules to be considered within the SFD-TableauFuzzySat procedure are:

$(\wedge)^+$. If $\langle \phi \wedge \psi, n \rangle^+ \in \mathcal{S}_{\mathcal{K}}$ and $\{\langle \phi, n \rangle^+, \langle \psi, n \rangle^+\} \not\subseteq \mathcal{S}_{\mathcal{K}}$, then add both $\langle \phi, n \rangle^+$ and $\langle \psi, n \rangle^+$ to $\mathcal{S}_{\mathcal{K}}$.

$(\vee)^+$. If $\langle \phi \vee \psi, n \rangle^+ \in \mathcal{S}_{\mathcal{K}}$ and $\{\langle \phi, n \rangle^+, \langle \psi, n \rangle^+\} \cap \mathcal{S}_{\mathcal{K}} = \emptyset$, then add *either* $\langle \phi, n \rangle^+$ *or* $\langle \psi, n \rangle^+$ to $\mathcal{S}_{\mathcal{K}}$.

$(\rightarrow)^+$. If $\langle \phi \rightarrow \psi, n \rangle^+ \in \mathcal{S}_{\mathcal{K}}$ and $\langle nnf(\neg \phi) \vee \psi, n \rangle^+ \notin \mathcal{S}_{\mathcal{K}}$, then add $\langle nnf(\neg \phi) \vee \psi, n \rangle^+$ to $\mathcal{S}_{\mathcal{K}}$.

We call the procedure with these rules and clash definition SFD-TableauFuzzySat+ and have:

Proposition 53. *Let $\mathcal{K}$ be a propositional fuzzy KB. Then $\mathcal{K} \models \langle \phi, n \rangle$ iff the SFD-TableauFuzzySat+ procedure returns* **true** *with input $\mathcal{K} \cup \{\langle \neg \phi, 1 - n \rangle^+\}$.*

We may also solve the best entailment degree problem by relying on the following important observation (see, *e.g.*, [394, 395, 396]). It has been shown that, in case of propositional SFL, from a set $\mathcal{K}$ of fuzzy statements of the form $\langle \phi, n \rangle$ it is possible to determine a finite set $N^{\mathcal{K}} \subset [0,1]$, where $|N^{\mathcal{K}}|$ is $O(|\mathcal{K}|)$, such that $bed(\mathcal{K}, \phi) \in N^{\mathcal{K}}$, *i.e.*, the best entailment degree of a formula ϕ w.r.t. $\mathcal{K}$ has to be an element of $N^{\mathcal{K}}$.

Proposition 54 ([394]). *Let $\mathcal{K}$ be a propositional fuzzy KB in NNF under SFL and let ϕ be a formula. Then $bed(\mathcal{K}, \phi) \in N^{\mathcal{K}}$ and $bsd(\mathcal{K}, \phi) \in N^{\mathcal{K}}$, where*

$$N^{\mathcal{K}} \;\;=\;\; \{0, 0.5, 1\} \;\cup\; \{n \mid \langle \phi, n \rangle \in \mathcal{K}\}.$$

Therefore, $bed(\mathcal{K}, \phi)$ can be determined by computing the greatest value $n \in N^{\mathcal{K}}$ such that $\mathcal{K} \models \langle \phi, n \rangle$. An easy way to search for this n is to order the elements of $N^{\mathcal{K}}$ and then to perform a binary search among these values by successive entailment tests. Similarly, $bsd(\mathcal{K}, \phi)$ can be determined by computing the greatest value $n \in N^{\mathcal{K}}$ such that $\mathcal{K} \cup \{\langle \phi, n \rangle\}$ satisfiable. Note that in this latter case we may rely on the SFD-TableauFuzzySat procedure.

Another method that does not require consideration of new constructs of the form $\langle \phi, n \rangle^+$, is to represent $\langle \phi, n \rangle^+$ with a fuzzy statement of the form $\langle \phi, n + \epsilon \rangle$, for a sufficiently small ϵ (this idea has been, *e.g.*, used in [390]). To choose such an ϵ, we may take advantage of Proposition 54. In fact, let us define

$$\bar{N}^{\mathcal{K}} = N^{\mathcal{K}} \cup \{1 - n \mid n \in N^{\mathcal{K}}\} . \tag{8.61}$$

Now, we define ϵ as half of the minimal absolute difference among the values in $\bar{N}^{KB}$. That is,

$$\epsilon = \min\{d/2 \mid n, m \in \bar{N}^{\mathcal{K}}, n \neq m, d = |n - m|\} . \tag{8.62}$$

Now we have that

Proposition 55. *Let $\mathcal{K}$ be a propositional fuzzy KB. Then for $n > 0$*

$$\mathcal{K} \models \langle \phi, n \rangle \;\; \text{iff} \;\; \mathcal{K} \cup \{\langle \neg\phi, 1 - n + \epsilon \rangle\} \;\; \text{is not satisfiable} .$$

Moreover, $\mathcal{K}$ is satisfiable iff it has a model over the truth set $\bar{N}^{\mathcal{K}}$.

Proposition 55 allows us now to use the SFD-TableauFuzzySat procedure in place of SFD-TableauFuzzySat+ to decide both the entailment problem and the best entailment degree problem.

Note also that a model $\mathcal{I}$ for $\mathcal{K}$ can be built as follows. Determine a clash-free completion $\mathcal{S}_{\mathcal{K}}$ of $\mathcal{K}$. Then build a model $\mathcal{I}$ by assigning $\mathcal{I}(p) = n$ if $\langle p, n \rangle \in \mathcal{S}_{\mathcal{K}}$ and for which there does not exist another $\langle p, m \rangle \in \mathcal{S}_{\mathcal{K}}$ with $m > n$.

We complete this section, by showing that in fact the SFD-TableauFuzzySat and SFD-TableauFuzzySat+ procedures can further be generalized to the Łukasiewicz logic case over L_n. The main idea is to revert all rules to non-deterministic rules in the following sense:

- if $\mathcal{I}$ is model of $\langle \phi \wedge \psi, n \rangle$ then $\mathcal{I}$ is a model of both $\langle \phi, n_1 \rangle$ and $\langle \psi, n_2 \rangle$ for some $n_1, n_2 \in L_n$ such that $n_1 \otimes_l n_2 = n$;

- if $\mathcal{I}$ is model of $\langle \phi \vee_l \psi, n \rangle$ then $\mathcal{I}$ is a model of both $\langle \phi, n_1 \rangle$ and $\langle \psi, n_2 \rangle$ for some $n_1, n_2 \in L_n$ such that $n_1 \oplus n_2 = n$.

Note the close relationship between the above properties and the ($\wedge$) and ($\vee$) rule in the L-ORFuzzySat procedure, in which we used variables x_ϕ and x_ψ in place of the values n_1 and n_2 instead.

In fact, the following proposition shows that, using the fuzzy operators of Łukasiewicz fuzzy logic to combine two truth degrees a and b, no new degrees can appear.

Proposition 56. *Let* $\frac{a}{n-1}, \frac{b}{n-1} \in L_n$. *Then, under the fuzzy operators of Łukasiewicz fuzzy logic,* $\ominus_l \frac{a}{n-1}, \frac{a}{n-1} \otimes_l \frac{b}{n-1}, \frac{a}{n-1} \oplus \frac{b}{n-1}, \frac{a}{n-1} \Rightarrow \frac{b}{n-1} \in L_n$ *[351].*

Let L-TableauFuzzySat procedure be as the SFD-TableauFuzzySat procedure, in which we replace the rules with

($\wedge$). If $\langle \phi \wedge \psi, n \rangle \in \mathcal{S}_\mathcal{K}$, $n_1, n_2 \in L_n$ such that $n_1 \otimes_l n_2 = n$ and $\{\langle \phi, n_1 \rangle, \langle \psi, n_2 \rangle\} \not\subseteq \mathcal{S}_\mathcal{K}$, then add both $\langle \phi, n_1 \rangle$ and $\langle \psi, n_1 \rangle$ to $\mathcal{S}_\mathcal{K}$.

($\vee$). If $\langle \phi \vee \psi, n \rangle \in \mathcal{S}_\mathcal{K}$, $n_1, n_2 \in L_n$ such that $n_1 \oplus_l n_2 = n$ and $\{\langle \phi, n_1 \rangle, \langle \psi, n_2 \rangle\} \not\subseteq \mathcal{S}_\mathcal{K}$, then add both $\langle \phi, n_1 \rangle$ and $\langle \psi, n_1 \rangle$ to $\mathcal{S}_\mathcal{K}$.

($\rightarrow$). If $\langle \phi \rightarrow \psi, n \rangle \in \mathcal{S}_\mathcal{K}$ and $\langle nnf(\neg\phi) \vee \psi, n \rangle \notin \mathcal{S}_\mathcal{K}$, then add $\langle nnf(\neg\phi) \vee \psi, n \rangle$ to $\mathcal{S}_\mathcal{K}$.

The L-TableauFuzzySat+ procedure is determined from the SFD-TableauFuzzySat+ procedure, by adapting additionally the ($\wedge$)$^+$ and ($\vee$)$^+$ rules in a similar way as we did above and we can show:

Proposition 57. *Let $\mathcal{K}$ be a propositional fuzzy KB $\mathcal{K}$. Then*

1. *The L-TableauFuzzySat procedure terminates.*

2. *$\mathcal{K}$ is satisfiable according to Łukasiewicz logic over L_n iff the L-TableauFuzzySat procedure returns* **true***.*

3. *$\mathcal{K} \models \langle \phi, n \rangle$ according to Łukasiewicz logic over L_n iff the L-TableauFuzzySat+ procedure returns* **true** *with input $\mathcal{K} \cup \{\langle \neg\phi, 1 - n \rangle^+\}$.*

Eventually, it is not difficult to see that indeed, the SFL-TableauFuzzySat can be modified to deal also with the case in which the truth combination functions are specified via a matrix, as illustrated in Section 8.1.7. Specifically, in line with Equation (8.35), let

$$f: (L_n)^k \rightarrow L_n$$

be a k-ary truth combination function, represented via a matrix M_f with $k + 1$ columns and n^k rows, where the first k columns are the arguments of the function and the last column contains the evaluation of the function on the arguments. At first, in the following, we use expressions of the form

$$\langle \phi, n \rangle^= \tag{8.63}$$

where $\mathcal{I}$ is a model of the expression $\langle \phi, n \rangle^=$ iff $\mathcal{I}(\phi) = n$.
   Now, we extend

1. the notion of clash; and

2. the inference rules to cope with expressions of the form $\langle \phi, n \rangle^=$.

A *clash* is a pair $\langle \phi, n_1 \rangle^=$ and $\langle \phi, n_2 \rangle^=$ with $n_1 \neq n_2$, while the additional rules to be considered are of the following form. For any k-ary truth combination function f

(M_f). If $\langle f(\phi_1, \ldots, \phi_k), n \rangle^= \in \mathcal{S}_\mathcal{K}$ and there are $n_i \in L_n$ $(1 \leq i \leq k)$ such that $f(n_1, \ldots, n_k) = n$ with $\langle \phi_i, n_i \rangle^= \notin \mathcal{S}_\mathcal{K}$, then add all $\langle \phi_i, n_i \rangle^=$ to $\mathcal{S}_\mathcal{K}$.

Of course, as the truth space L_n is finite, any rule (M_f) can be applied only finitely many times to an expression $\langle f(\phi_1, \ldots, \phi_k), n \rangle^= \in \mathcal{S}_\mathcal{K}$.
   Now, the $\mathcal{M}$-TableauFuzzySat procedure derived from the SFD-TableauFuzzySat procedure is described in Algorithm 5.

Algorithm 5 $\mathcal{M}$-TableauFuzzySat.

Input: A propositional fuzzy KB $\mathcal{K}$ with matrix-based truth combination functions.
Output: Check if $\mathcal{K}$ satisfiable.

1. Build non-deterministically a KB $\mathcal{K}'$ such that

   (a) $|\mathcal{K}'| \leq |\mathcal{K}|$
   (b) for each $\langle \phi, n \rangle \in \mathcal{K}$ there is $\langle \phi, n' \rangle^= \in \mathcal{K}'$ with $n' \geq n$.
   (c) there is no pair $\langle \phi, n \rangle$ and $\langle \phi, n' \rangle$ in $\mathcal{K}'$ such that $n' \neq n$.

2. Initialize the *completion* $\mathcal{S}_\mathcal{K} = \mathcal{K}'$;

3. Apply the following inference rules to $\mathcal{S}_{\mathcal{K}'}$ until no more rules can be applied. We call a set of fuzzy statements $\mathcal{S}_\mathcal{K}$ complete iff none of the rules below can be applied to $\mathcal{S}_\mathcal{K}$. Note that the rules are non-deterministic. For any k-ary truth combination function f, consider

   (M_f). If $\langle f(\phi_1, \ldots, \phi_k), n \rangle^= \in \mathcal{S}_\mathcal{K}$ and there are $n_i \in L_n$ $(1 \leq i \leq k)$ such that $f(n_1, \ldots, n_k) = n$ with $\langle \phi_i, n_i \rangle^= \notin \mathcal{S}_\mathcal{K}$, then add all $\langle \phi_i, n_i \rangle^=$ to $\mathcal{S}_\mathcal{K}$.

4. Return that $\mathcal{K}$ is satisfiable, *i.e.*, **true** iff we find a complete and clash-free completion $\mathcal{S}_\mathcal{K}$ of $\mathcal{K}$.

It is easily verified that

Proposition 58. *Let $\mathcal{K}$ be a propositional fuzzy KB $\mathcal{K}$ with matrix-based truth combination functions. Then*

1. *The $\mathcal{M}$-TableauFuzzySat procedure terminates.*

2. *$\mathcal{K}$ is satisfiable iff the $\mathcal{M}$-TableauFuzzySat procedure returns* **true***.*

3. *$\mathcal{K} \models \langle \psi, n \rangle$ iff the $\mathcal{M}$-TableauFuzzySat procedure returns* **false** *for all $\mathcal{K} \cup \{\langle \psi, n' \rangle^=\}$ with $n' < n$ and $n' \in L_n$. Here we assume that Step 1 of the $\mathcal{M}$-TableauFuzzySat procedure adds $\langle \psi, n' \rangle^=$ to $\mathcal{K}'$ as well.*

Note that procedure $\mathcal{M}$-TableauFuzzySat can straightforwardly be extended to any finite and arbitrary structured truth space L, such as a complete lattice, residuated lattice, etc.

Corollary 4. *Proposition 58 holds also in case matrix-based truth combination functions are defined over any finite and arbitrary structured truth space L in place of L_n.*

Of course, there is a high amount of non-determinism in $\mathcal{M}$-TableauFuzzySat and it remains to be seen if such a method is viable in practice (possibly involving several optimizations limiting the choices of the values).

8.2.2.4 Reduction to Classical Logic

In this section, our aim is to map both propositional SFL and Łukasiewicz logic knowledge bases into satisfiability and entailment preserving classical propositional knowledge bases. An immediate consequence is then that we can rely on already implemented crisp SAT reasoners to reason within these two propositional fuzzy logics fuzzy. This idea has been used *e.g.*, in [61, 396].

We illustrate first the case of SFL and then generalize it to Łukasiewicz logic.

Before we are going to formally present the mapping, we first illustrate the basic idea we rely on. Our mapping relies on ideas presented in [36, 37] for so-called regular multi-valued logics.

Assume we have a fuzzy KB

$$
\begin{aligned}
\mathcal{K} &= \{\alpha_1, \alpha_2, \alpha_3, \alpha_4\} \text{ with} \\
\alpha_1 &= \langle A, 0.4 \rangle, \\
\alpha_2 &= \langle \neg A, 0.3 \rangle, \\
\alpha_3 &= \langle \neg B, 0.8 \rangle, \\
\alpha_4 &= \langle \neg B, 0.9 \rangle \,.
\end{aligned}
$$

Let us introduce some new formulae, namely $A_{\geq 0.4}$, $A_{\leq 0.7}$, $B_{\leq 0.2}$ and $B_{\leq 0.1}$. Informally, the expression $A_{\geq 0.4}$ represents A is true to degree $c \geq 0.4$, while $A_{\leq 0.7}$ represents A is true to degree $c \leq 0.7$. Similarly, for the other formulae.

Of course, we have to consider also the relationships among the introduced formulae. For instance, $B_{\leq 0.1} \rightarrow B_{\leq 0.2}$. This formula dictates that if B's truth value is ≤ 0.1 then it is also ≤ 0.2. We may represent, thus, the fuzzy statements α_1 with the formula $A_{\geq 0.4}$. Similarly, α_2 may be mapped into $A_{\leq 0.7}$, α_3 may be mapped into $B_{\leq 0.2}$, while α_4 may be mapped into $B_{\leq 0.1}$. This illustrates our basic idea.

Formally we proceed as follows. Let $\mathcal{K}$ be propositional SFL KB in NNF in which all formulae of the form $\langle \phi \rightarrow \psi, n \rangle$ have been replaced with $\langle nnf(\neg\phi \vee \psi), n \rangle$.

Consider the set L_n. Without loss of generality, it can be assumed that L_n is ordered: $L_n = \{\gamma_1, \ldots, \gamma_n\}$ and $\gamma_i < \gamma_{i+1}, 1 \leq i \leq n - 1$. It is easy to see that $\gamma_1 = 0$ and $\gamma_n = 1$. We define $L_n^+ = \{c \in L_n : c \neq 0\}$.

Let $\mathbf{A}$ be the set of fuzzy atomic propositions occurring in $\mathcal{K}$. For each $\alpha, \beta \in L_n$ with $\alpha \in (0, 1]$ and $\beta \in [0, 1)$, for each $A \in \mathbf{A}$, two new atomic formulae $A_{\geq\alpha}, A_{>\beta}$ are introduced. $A_{\geq\alpha}$ represents the (non-fuzzy) proposition "A's truth is $\geq n$". $A_{>\beta}$ has similar meaning. The atomic elements $A_{>1}, A_{\geq 0}$ are not considered because they are not necessary, due to the restrictions on the allowed degree of the propositions in the fuzzy KB.

The intended semantics of these newly introduced atomic formulae is preserved by some implication formulae. For each $1 \leq i \leq n-1, 2 \leq j \leq n-1$ and for each $A \in \mathbf{A}$, $Crisp_{L_n}$ is the smallest set of classical formulae containing these two type of formulae:

$$A_{\geq\gamma_{i+1}} \rightarrow A_{>\gamma_i}$$

$$A_{>\gamma_j} \rightarrow A_{\geq\gamma_j}$$

(8.64)

As next, we need to map non-atomic fuzzy formulae into crisp variants. We do this by reflecting the semantics of the logical connective. For instance, $\langle A \wedge B, 0.25 \rangle$ will be mapped into $A_{\geq 0.25} \wedge A_{\geq 0.35}$ and similarly, *e.g.*, $\langle \neg A, 0.75 \rangle$ will be mapped into $\neg A_{>0.25}$.

Formally, the reduction of fuzzy formulae mapping ρ.

$$Crisp_{\mathcal{K}} = \{\rho(\phi, n) \mid \langle\phi, n\rangle \in \mathcal{K}\} \cup Crisp_{L_n},$$

(8.65)

where $\rho(\phi, n)$ is defined in Table 8.8:

It is easily verified that $|Crisp_{\mathcal{K}}|$ is linearly bounded by $|\mathcal{K}|$ and the following satisfiability preserving reduction property can be shown.

Proposition 59. *Let $\mathcal{K}$ be a propositional SFL KB. Then $\mathcal{K}$ is satisfiable iff $Crisp_{\mathcal{K}}$ is satisfiable, where $Crisp_{\mathcal{K}}$ is obtained according to Table 8.8.*

Concerning the entailment problem, we may easily reduce it to the satisfiability problem as, for $c > 0$, $\langle\neg\phi, 1 - c\rangle^+$ can be represented as $\langle\neg\phi, 1 - c^-\rangle$, where c^- is the next smaller value than c in L_n.

TABLE 8.8: Mapping of propositional SFL statements to crisp statements.

x	y	$\rho(x, y)$
$\top$	c	$\top$
$\bot$	0	$\top$
$\bot$	c	$\bot$ if $c > 0$
A	c	$A_{\geq c}$
$\neg A$	c	$\neg A_{>1-c}$
$\phi \wedge \psi$	c	$\rho(\phi, c) \wedge \rho(\psi, c)$
$\phi \vee \psi$	c	$\rho(\phi, c) \vee \rho(\psi, c)$

Therefore, by relying on Equation (8.60), for $c > 0$, we have

$$\mathcal{K} \models \langle \phi, c \rangle \text{ iff } \mathcal{K} \cup \{\langle \neg \phi, 1 - c^- \rangle\} \text{ is not satisfiable} , \qquad (8.66)$$

where c^- is the next smaller value than c in L_n and, thus, we may apply Proposition 59 to solve the entailment decision problem. Eventually, the best entailment degree problem can be reduced to calls to the entailment problem for various $c \in L_n$, similarly as described in Section 8.2.2.3.

We next show how the mapping above can be extended to the case of Łukasiewicz logic as well. To this end, we recall the property

- if $\mathcal{I}$ is model of $\langle \phi \wedge \psi, n \rangle$ then $\mathcal{I}$ is a model of both $\langle \phi, n_1 \rangle$ and $\langle \psi, n_2 \rangle$ for some $n_1, n_2 \in L_n$ such that $n_1 \otimes_l n_2 = n$.

The main difference now is we cannot simply map, *e.g.*, $\langle A \wedge B, 0.25 \rangle$ into $A_{\geq 0.25} \wedge A_{\geq 0.35}$, but we need to take into account all possible combinations of n_1 and n_2 such that $n_1 \otimes_l n_2 = 0.25$ and, thus, $\langle A \wedge B, 0.25 \rangle$ is rather mapped into

$$\bigvee_{c_1, c_2} A_{\geq c_1} \wedge B_{\geq c_2}$$

for $c_1, c_2 \in L_n^+$ such that $c_1 + c_2 - 1 = 0.25$.

The mapping is shown in Table 8.9.

Proposition 60. *Let $\mathcal{K}$ be a propositional Łukasiewicz logic KB. Then $\mathcal{K}$ is satisfiable iff $Crisp_{\mathcal{K}}$ is satisfiable, where $Crisp_{\mathcal{K}}$ is obtained according to Table 8.9.*

As for the SFL case, both the entailment and the best entailment degree problems can be reduced to the satisfiability problem (see Equation (8.66)).

Eventually, as for Section 8.2.2.3, we conclude by showing that the idea illustrated for Łukasiewicz logic can be adapted to the case of matrix-based truth-combination functions (see Section 8.1.7). At first, for $\gamma \in L_n$ we introduce atomic formulae of the form

$$A_{=\gamma}$$

TABLE 8.9: Mapping of propositional Łukasiewicz logic statements to crisp statements.

x	y	$\rho(x,y)$
$\top$	c	$\top$
$\bot$	0	$\top$
$\bot$	c	$\bot$ if $c > 0$
A	c	$A_{\geq c}$
$\neg A$	c	$\neg A_{>1-c}$
$\phi \wedge \psi$	c	$\bigvee_{c_1,c_2} \rho(\phi,c_1) \wedge \rho(\psi,c_2)$ for $c_1, c_2 \in L_n^+$ such that $c_1 + c_2 - 1 = c$.
$\phi \vee \psi$	c	$\rho(\phi,c) \vee \rho(\psi,c) \vee \bigvee_{c_1,c_2} \rho(\phi,c_1) \wedge \rho(\psi,c_2)$ for $c_1, c_2 \in L_n^+$ such that $c_1 + c_2 = c$.

Informally, the expression $A_{=\gamma}$ represents A is true to degree γ. Then, $Crisp_{L_n}$ is the smallest set of classical formulae containing:

$$\bigwedge_{\gamma_1 \neq \gamma_2} A_{=\gamma_1} \wedge A_{=\gamma_2} \to \bot \tag{8.67}$$

stating that A cannot have two different truth degrees. Now, the reduction of fuzzy formulae with truth combination functions defined via matrixes is defined as

$$Crisp_{\mathcal{K}} = \{\rho(\phi,n') \mid \langle \phi,n \rangle \in \mathcal{K}, n' \geq n\} \cup Crisp_{L_n}, \tag{8.68}$$

where $\rho(\phi,n)$ is defined in Table 8.10, and f is a k-ary truth combination function

$$f \colon (L_n)^k \to L_n .$$

Then we have that

TABLE 8.10: Mapping of matrix-based fuzzy propositional statements to crisp statements.

x	y	$\rho(x,y)$
$\top$	1	$\top$
$\top$	c	$\bot$ if $c < 1$
$\bot$	0	$\top$
$\bot$	c	$\bot$ if $c > 0$
A	c	$A_{=c}$
$f(\phi_1,\ldots,\phi_k)$	c	$\bigvee_{\langle c_1,\ldots,c_k \rangle} (\rho(\phi_1,c_1) \wedge \ldots \wedge \rho(\phi_k,c_k)))$ for $c_i \in L_n$ $(1 \leq i \leq k)$ such that $f(c_1,\ldots,c_k) = c$.

Proposition 61. *Let* $\mathcal{K}$ *be a propositional fuzzy KB with matrix-based truth combination functions. Then* $\mathcal{K}$ *is satisfiable iff* $Crisp_{\mathcal{K}}$ *is satisfiable, where* $Crisp_{\mathcal{K}}$ *is obtained according to Table 8.10.*

As for the SFL case, both the entailment and the best entailment degree problems can be reduced to the satisfiability problem (compare with Proposition 58).

Proposition 62. *Let* $\mathcal{K}$ *be a propositional fuzzy KB with matrix-based truth combination functions. Then* $\mathcal{K} \models \langle \psi, n \rangle$ *iff for all* $n' < n$ *with* $n' \in L_n$, $Crisp_{\mathcal{K}} \cup \{\rho(\psi, n')\}$ *is not satisfiable.*

Note that procedure $\mathcal{M}$-TableauFuzzySat can straightforwardly be extended to any finite and arbitrary structured truth space L, such as a complete lattice, residuated lattice, etc.

Corollary 5. *Proposition 58 holds also in case matrix-based truth combination functions are defined over any finite and arbitrary structured truth space* L *in place of* L_n.

8.2.3 Concrete Domains and Aggregation Operators

In this section, we will show how we may extend fuzzy logic endowed with so-called *fuzzy concrete domains* [359, 398]. Specifically, we introduce the logic $\mathcal{P}(\mathbf{D})$, a fuzzy propositional Łukasiewicz logic under extended with concrete domains in order to handle numerical, as well as non-numerical features, allowing to express, for instance, *e.g., I am searching for a passenger car costing about 25000€ yet if the car has a GPS system and more than two-year warranty I can spend up to 28000€.*

The notion is essentially an extension of the notion of concrete domains we have introduced for description logics (see Section 4.2.2.2).

For instance, we may be able to express

> *"I would like a passenger car with an alarm system if it costs more than 25000€"*

using the expression

$$\texttt{PassengerCar} \wedge ((\texttt{price} \geq_{25000}) \rightarrow \texttt{AlarmSystem})$$

In the formula above the expression ($\texttt{price} \geq_{25000}$) acts as a so-called concrete domain, *i.e.*, the atom $\texttt{price}$ has a fixed interpretation over a domain, in this case an integer $\mathcal{I}(\texttt{price})$ and ($\texttt{price} \geq_{25000}$) will be true under an interpretation $\mathcal{I}$ if $\mathcal{I}(\texttt{price}) \geq 25000$. Such expressions are called *hard constraints* in [359]. Similarly, we may express so-called *soft constraints* (or *fuzzy constraints*) [359], we instead may be satisfied to a certain degree. For instance, we may be able to express

> *"if a GPS system is mounted on the car she can spend up to 22000€ for a sedan. The less I spend the more I'm satisfied. I'm definitely satisfied if I spend less than 18000€"*

using the expression

$$\texttt{GPS\_system} \to (\texttt{price } ls(18000, 22000)) \ .$$

In the above expression, $ls(18000, 22000)$ is the well-known left-shoulder fuzzy set membership function we have seen in Section 8.1.1. Now, under un interpretation $\mathcal{I}$, the expression $(\texttt{price } ls(18000, 22000))$ will have a degree of truth $\mathcal{I}((\texttt{price } ls(18000, 22000)))$ determined by the evaluation of the left-shoulder function on the price, *i.e.*,[11]

$$\mathcal{I}((\texttt{price } ls(18000, 22000))) = ls(18000, 22000)(\mathcal{I}(\texttt{price})) \ .$$

We next provide the exact formulation. Similarly to Section 4.2.2.2, a *fuzzy concrete domain*, also called a *fuzzy datatype theory* $\mathbf{D} = \langle \Delta^{\mathbf{D}}, \cdot^{\mathbf{D}} \rangle$ consists of a datatype domain $\Delta^{\mathbf{D}}$ and a mapping $\cdot^{\mathbf{D}}$ that assigns to each data value an element of $\Delta^{\mathbf{D}}$, to each datatype into a function from $\Delta^{\mathbf{D}}$ to $[0, 1]$. The elementary datatypes we allow here are of two types: hard datatype and soft datatype. A *hard datatype* has one of the following forms: for any rational number n

$$\geq_n, \quad \leq_n, \quad =_n \ ,$$

with semantics

$$
\begin{aligned}
(\geq_n)^{\mathbf{D}}(x) &= \ 1 \text{ if } x \geq n, \text{ else } 0 \\
(\leq_n)^{\mathbf{D}}(x) &= \ 1 \text{ if } x \leq n, \text{ else } 0 \\
(=_n)^{\mathbf{D}}(x) &= \ 1 \text{ if } x = n, \text{ else } 0 \ .
\end{aligned}
$$

A *soft datatype* has one of the following form:

$$ls(a, b), \quad rs(a, b), \quad tri(a, b, c), \quad trz(a, b, c, d),$$

with semantics (see Section 8.1.1)

$$
\begin{aligned}
(ls(a, b))^{\mathbf{D}}(x) &= \ ls(a, b)(x) \\
(rs(a, b))^{\mathbf{D}}(x) &= \ rs(a, b)(x) \\
(tri(a, b, c))^{\mathbf{D}}(x) &= \ tri(a, b, c)(x) \\
(trz(a, b, c, d))^{\mathbf{D}}(x) &= \ trz(a, b, c, d)(x) \ .
\end{aligned}
$$

Now, let $\mathcal{F}$ be an alphabet of *feature names*, distinct from the alphabet of propositional letters. A *concrete atom* is an expression of the form

$$(f \ \mathbf{d}) \tag{8.69}$$

---

[11] Recall that $\mathcal{I}(\texttt{price})$ is an integer.

where f is a feature name and $\mathbf{d}$ is a datatype.

A *formula* is now inductively defined as follows:

1. every propositional letter is a formula;

2. every concrete atom is a formula;

3. if ψ and ϕ are formulae, then so are $\neg\psi$, $\psi \wedge \phi$, $\psi \vee \phi$, $\psi \rightarrow \phi$. As usual, we use $\psi \leftrightarrow \phi$ in place of $(\psi \rightarrow \phi) \wedge (\phi \rightarrow \psi)$;

4. if ϕ is a formula and $w \in [0,1]$, then $w \cdot \phi$ is a formula;

5. if $\psi_1, \ldots, \psi_k$ are formulae, then $w_1 \cdot \psi_1 + \ldots + w_k \cdot \psi_k$ is a formula, where $w_i \in [0,1]$ and $\sum_i w_i \leq 1$;

6. if ϕ is a formula, then $lm(a,b)(\phi)$ is a formula, where $lm(a,b)$ is a fuzzy modifier (see Section 8.1.8);

7. if @ is an aggregation function (see Section 8.1.6) and $\psi_1, \ldots, \psi_k$ are formulae, then $@(\psi_1, \ldots, \psi_k)$ is a formula.

A $\mathcal{P}(\mathbf{D})$ *fuzzy statement* is defined as follows:

- if ψ is a formula and $n \in (0,1]$ then $\langle \psi, n \rangle$ is a fuzzy statement of $\mathcal{P}(\mathbf{D})$. If n is omitted, then $\langle \psi, 1 \rangle$ is assumed.

Eventually, a $\mathcal{P}(\mathbf{D})$ *fuzzy knowledge base* is a set of $\mathcal{P}(\mathbf{D})$ fuzzy statements. A *fuzzy interpretation* $\mathcal{I}$ w.r.t. a concrete domain $\mathbf{D}$,

1. maps each propositional literal into $[0,1]$;

2. maps each feature name into $\Delta^{\mathbf{D}}$.

$\mathcal{I}$ is inductively extended to formulae as follows:

$$
\begin{aligned}
\mathcal{I}((f\ \mathbf{d})) &= \mathbf{d}^{\mathbf{D}}(\mathcal{I}(f)) \\
\mathcal{I}(\neg\psi) &= 1 - \mathcal{I}(\psi) \\
\mathcal{I}(\psi \wedge \phi) &= \mathcal{I}(\psi) \otimes_l \mathcal{I}(\phi) \\
\mathcal{I}(\psi \vee \phi) &= \mathcal{I}(\psi) \oplus_l \mathcal{I}(\phi) \\
\mathcal{I}(\psi \rightarrow \phi) &= \mathcal{I}(\psi) \rightarrow_l \mathcal{I}(\phi) \\
\mathcal{I}(w \cdot \phi) &= w \cdot \mathcal{I}(\phi) \\
\mathcal{I}(lm(a,b)(\phi)) &= lm(a,b)(\mathcal{I}(\phi)) \\
\mathcal{I}(w_1 \cdot \psi_1 + \ldots + w_k \cdot \psi_k) &= \sum_i w_i \cdot \mathcal{I}(\psi_i) \\
\mathcal{I}(@(\psi_1, \ldots, \psi_k)) &= @(\mathcal{I}(\psi_1), \ldots, \mathcal{I}(\psi_k)) \ .
\end{aligned}
$$

Eventually, the notions of a model of a fuzzy statement, of a knowledge base, and that of entailment, best entailment degree and best satisfiability degree are defined as in Section 8.2.1. For instance, $\mathcal{I}$ is a *model* (*satisfies*) of a fuzzy statement $\langle \psi, n \rangle$ iff $\mathcal{I}(\psi) \geq n$.

Example 27 ([48, 359]). *Assume, that a car seller sells a sedan car. A buyer is looking for a second-hand passenger car. Both buyers as well as sellers have preferences (restrictions). Our aim is to find the best agreement. The preferences are as follows. Concerning the buyer:*

1. *He does not want to pay more than 26000 euro (buyer reservation value).*

2. *If there is an alarm system in the car then he is completely satisfied with paying no more than 22300 euro, but he can go up to 22750 euro to a lesser degree of satisfaction.*

3. *He wants driver insurance and either theft insurance or fire insurance.*

4. *He wants air conditioning and the external color should be either black or gray.*

5. *Preferably the price is no more than 22000 euro, but he can go up to 24000 euro to a lesser degree of satisfaction.*

6. *The kilometers warranty is preferably at least 175000, but he may go down to 150000 to a lesser degree of satisfaction.*

7. *The weights of the preferences 2-6 are, (0.1, 0.2, 0.1, 0.2, 0.4). The higher the value the more important is the preference.*

Concerning the seller:

1. *He wants to sell no less than 22000 euro (seller reservation value)*

2. *If there is a navigator system in the car then he is completely satisfied with paying no less than 22750 euro, but he can go down to 22500 euro to a lesser degree of satisfaction.*

3. *Preferably the buyer buys the Insurance Plus package.*

4. *The kilometers warranty is preferably at most 100000, but he may go up to 125000 to a lesser degree of satisfaction.*

5. *The monthly warranty is preferably at most 60, but he may go up to 72 to a lesser degree of satisfaction.*

6. *If the color is black then the car has air conditioning.*

7. *The weights of the preferences 2-6 are, (0.3, 0.1, 0.3, 0.1, 0.2). The higher the value the more important is the preference.*

We have also some background theory about the domain:

1. *A sedan is a passenger car.*

2. *A satellite alarm system is an alarm system.*

3. *The navigator pack is a satellite alarm system with a GPS system.*

4. *The Insurance Plus package is a driver insurance together with a theft insurance.*

5. *The car colors are black or gray.*

Now, the background knowledge can be encoded as:

$$Sedan \to PassengerCar$$
$$SatelliteAlarm \to AlarmSystem$$
$$NavigatorPack \leftrightarrow (SatelliteAlarm \land GPS\_system)$$
$$InsurancePlus \leftrightarrow (DriverInsurance \land TheftInsurance)$$
$$ExColorBlack \lor ExColorGray$$
$$ExColorBlack \land ExColorGray \to 0$$

The buyer's preferences can be encoded as follows:

1. $B \leftrightarrow (PassengerCar \land (HasPrice \leq_{26000}))$

2. $B_1 \leftrightarrow (AlarmSystem \to (HasPrice\ ls(22300, 22750)))$

3. $B_2 \leftrightarrow (DriverInsurance \land (TheftInsurance \lor FireInsurance))$

4. $B_3 \leftrightarrow (Airconditioning \land (ExColorBlack \lor ExColorGray))$

5. $B_4 \leftrightarrow (HasPrice\ ls(22000, 24000))$

6. $B_5 \leftrightarrow (HasKMWarranty\ rs(15000, 175000))$

7. $Buy \leftrightarrow (B \land ((0.1 \cdot B_1) + (0.2 \cdot B_2) + (0.1 \cdot B_3) + (0.2 \cdot B_4) + (0.4 \cdot B_5)))$

Please note that the concept Buy collects all the buyer's preferences together in such a way that the higher the maximal degree of satisfiability of Buy (i.e., $bsd(\mathcal{K}, Buy)$), the more the buyer is satisfied.
The seller's preferences can be encoded as follows:

1. $S = (Sedan \land (HasPrice \geq 22000))$

2. $S_1 = (NavigatorPack \to (HasPrice\ rs(22500, 22750))$

3. $S_2 = InsurancePlus$

4. $S_3 = (HasKMWarranty\ ls(100000, 125000))$

5. $S_4 = (HasMWarranty\ ls(60, 72))$

6. $S_5 = (ExColorBlack \to AirConditioning)$

7. $Sell = (S \land ((0.3 \cdot S_1) + (0.1 \cdot S_2) + (0.3 \cdot S_3) + (0.1 \cdot S_4) + (0.2 \cdot S_5)))$

Similarly to the buyer case, the concept Sell collects all the seller's preferences together in such a way that the higher is the maximal degree of satisfiability of Sell (i.e., $bsd(\mathcal{K}, Sell)$), the more the seller is satisfied.
Now, it is clear that the best agreement among the buyer and the seller is

determined by the maximal degree of satisfiability of the conjunction Buy $\land$
Sell, i.e., we have to determine

$$bsd(\mathcal{K}, Buy \land Sell) \ .$$

In particular, in a model guaranteeing the maximal degree of satisfaction of
Buy $\land$ *Sell, we have that*

$$
\begin{aligned}
bsd(\mathcal{K}, Buy \land Sell) &= 0.7 \\
HasPrice &= 22000.0 \\
HasKMWarranty &= 175000.0 \\
HasMWarranty &= 0.0 \ .
\end{aligned}
$$

Reasoning. We extend the OR-based KB satisfiability decision algorithm (see Section 8.2.2.2, Algorithm L-ORFuzzySat) to deal with concrete domains and aggregates. The extension to the best entailment degree and best satisfiability degree problems is as for Section 8.2.2.2.

The crucial point is to show that we may map the additional constructs we have introduced here into sets of MILP constraints, that is, the newly introduced operators should be MILP representable, which is indeed the case. The rules can be found in Appendix F.

8.2.4   On Fuzzy IF-THEN Rules

One of the most important features of fuzzy logic is its ability to perform approximate reasoning [473], which involves inference rules with premises, consequences or both of them containing fuzzy propositions. A very popular formalism, due to their practical success, is a fuzzy rule-based system.

A fuzzy IF-THEN system [242] consists of a rule base (a set of IF-THEN rules) and a reasoning algorithm performing an inference mechanism such as Rete [161]. In general, the input of the system is the current value for the input variable and the output is a fuzzy set, which can be defuzzified into a single value. In a fuzzy IF-THEN rule, its antecedents, consequences, or both are fuzzy. Fuzzy IF-THEN rules are fired to a degree, which is a function of the degree of match between their antecedent and the input. The deduction rule is Generalised Modus Ponens.

Roughly speaking, given a rule "IF A THEN B", where A and B are fuzzy propositions, it is possible from a premise "A'" which matches A to some degree, to deduce "B'", which is similar to B.

One of the most popular IF-THEN systems is the Mamdani model [303]. In a Mamdani model, fuzzy rules have the form

$$\text{IF } X_1 \text{ IS } A_1 \text{ AND } \dots \text{ AND } X_n \text{ IS } A_n \text{ THEN } Y \text{ IS } B \ , \qquad (8.70)$$

where A_i and B are linguistic values defined by fuzzy sets on universes of discourse X_i and Y respectively, $i = 1, \dots n$.

For every clause in the antecedent of the rule, the matching degree between the current value of the variable and the linguistic label in the rule is computed (typically, using the minimum or another t-norm). If there exist several clauses, they are aggregated into a firing degree, using a fuzzy logic operator (typically, the maximum). Then, this firing degree is used for modifying the consequent of the rule using some function (typically the minimum). Sometimes this function is referred to in the literature as an implication function, but this is a misleading term which should be avoided (e.g., minimum is not an implication function) [187].

Rules are fired using some inference algorithm. The computed consequences related to the same variable are aggregated (typically, using the maximum). Then, the output variables can be defuzzified. Some examples of defuzzification methods are the LOM (Largest Of Maxima), SOM (Smallest Of Maxima), and MOM (Middle Of Maxima) [242]. More precisely, let B denote the fuzzy set to be defuzzified and let x be an arbitrary element of the universe. Then for all x:

- x_{LOM} is the LOM iff $\mu_B(x_{LOM}) \geq \mu_B(x)$ and, if $\mu_B(x_{LOM}) = \mu_B(x)$ then $x_{LOM} > x$.

- x_{SOM} is the SOM iff $\mu_B(x_{SOM}) \geq \mu_B(x)$ and, if $\mu_B(x_{SOM}) = \mu_B(x)$ then $x_{SOM} < x$.

- x_{MOM} is the MOM iff $x_{MOM} = (x_{LOM} + x_{SOM})/2$.

Now, we show here how to use $\mathcal{P}(\mathbf{D})$ (see Section 8.2.3) to represent Mamdani fuzzy IF-THEN rules and to reason with them (differently from [3], which only allows to represent fuzzy controllers). For more insights, we refer the reader to [186]. The interesting thing is that it is not only possible to represent a fuzzy control problem, but also background knowledge related to it.

In order to represent a fuzzy control problem we proceed as follows. Firstly, for each variable of the system, we define a concrete feature name f representing it and specify its range (a subset of the reals $[f_{\min}, f_{\max}]$). Then, we define the different linguistic labels, which will be used to describe the value of these variables, using triangular fuzzy sets.

Next, we define a formula resuming the rule base. It is well known [186] that a set $\{r_1, \ldots, r_p\}$ of Mamdani rules r_i of the form (8.70) can be transformed in a formula $Mamd$ of the form

$$Mamd \leftrightarrow \bigvee_{i \in \{1, \ldots, p\}} (A_{i_1} \wedge_g \ldots \wedge_g A_{i_n} \wedge_g B_i) \qquad (8.71)$$

An alternative [186] consists in involving an r-implication to represent a rule. That is, a set $\{r_1, \ldots, r_p\}$ of Mamdani rules r_i of the form (8.70) can be transformed in a formula $Rules$ of the form

$$Rules \leftrightarrow \bigwedge_{i \in \{1, \ldots, p\}} ((A_{i_1} \wedge \ldots \wedge A_{i_n}) \to B_i) \qquad (8.72)$$

Then, we represent the input of the system as fuzzy propositions.

Example 28 ([48]). *For the sake of concrete illustration, consider an adaption of the simple example available at http://en.wikipedia.org/wiki/Fuzzy_system. It considers the design of a fuzzy controller for an anti-lock braking system. The encoding in $\mathcal{P}(\mathbf{D})$ is shown in Table 8.11. The system has two input variables,* temperature *and* pressure, *which are used to compute an output value which will adjust the* throttle. *Specifically,*

- temperature *has 5 labels associated:* cold, cool, nominal, warm, *and* hot.

- pressure *has 5 labels:* weak, low, ok, strong, *and* high.

- throttle *has 7 labels:* N3 *(large negative),* N2 *(medium negative),* N1 *(small negative),* Z *(zero),* P1 *(small positive),* P2 *(medium positive), and* P3 *(large positive).*

The rules of the system are the following:

1. *IF temperature IS cool AND pressure IS weak, THEN throttle is P3.*

2. *IF temperature IS cool AND pressure IS low, THEN throttle is P2.*

3. *IF temperature IS cool AND pressure IS ok, THEN throttle is Z.*

4. *IF temperature IS cool AND pressure IS strong, THEN throttle is N2.*

The linguistic labels of the variables are defined using fuzzy concrete concepts. For example, $TempCool$, the label representing that the temperature is cool, can be defined as $tri(480, 500, 520)$, $ThrottleP2$ as $tri(10, 15, 20)$ and $ThrottleZ$ as $tri(15, 20, 25)$.

Now assume that the temperature is 489.6, which is represented as $(temperature =_{489.6})$. Then, $\mu_{cool}(481.92) = tri(480, 500, 520)(489.6) = 0.48$. We also assume that the pressure is 42.15, i.e., we have $(pressure = _{42.15})$, and that $\mu_{low}(42.15) = 0.57$, $\mu_{ok}(42.15) = 0.25$ and $\mu_{weak}(42.15) = \mu_{strong}(42.15) = \mu_{high}(42.15) = 0$. That is, the temperature is in the cool *state, the pressure is in the* low *and* ok *states, in such a way that only rules 2 and 3 are fired.*

Rule 2 is fired with a degree $\min\{0.48, 0.57\} = 0.48$, so throttle is P2 with degree 0.48. Rule 3 is fired with a degree $\min\{0.48, 0.25\} = 0.25$, so throttle is Z with degree 0.25. These two values for throttle are aggregated using the maximum.

Then, the defuzzification step is performed. It can be verified that $LOM = 17.6$, $MOM = 15$, and $SOM = 12.4$.

For concrete feature name throttle *representing an output variable of the system, LOM is implemented in the following steps (instruction $(defuzzify\text{-}lomMamd\ throttle)$ in Table 8.11).*

1. *Compute the maximum degree γ of satisfiability of $Mamd$, that is, we determine $\gamma = bsd(\mathcal{K}, Mamd)$.*

TABLE 8.11: Fragment of a $\mathcal{P}(\mathbf{D})$ fuzzy KB example for fuzzy control.

%feature names
temperature
pressure
throttle

% Labels for the variables
$TempCool := tri(480, 500, 520), \ldots$
$PressLow := tri(30, 40, 45)$
$PressOK := tri(40, 48.6, 57.2), \ldots$
$ThrottleP2 := tri(10, 15, 20),$
$ThrottleZ := tri(15, 20, 25), \ldots$

% Encoding of Mamdami Rules
$Rule_1 \leftrightarrow ((temperature\ TempCool) \wedge_g (pressure\ PressWeak) \wedge_g (throttle\ ThrottleP3))$
$Rule_2 \leftrightarrow ((temperature\ TempCool) \wedge_g (pressure\ PressLow) \wedge_g (throttle\ ThrottleP2))$
$Rule_3 \leftrightarrow ((temperature\ TempCool) \wedge_g (pressure\ PressOK) \wedge_g (throttle\ ThrottleZ))$
$Rule_4 \leftrightarrow ((temperature\ TempCool) \wedge_g (pressure\ PressStrong) \wedge_g (throttle\ ThrottleN2))$

% Encoding of Mamdami Rule base
$Mamd = (Rule_1 \vee_g Rule_2 \vee_g Rule_2 \vee_g Rule_3 \vee_g Rule_4)$

% Input to the controller
$(temperature\ =_{489.6})$
$(pressure\ =_{42.15})$

% Output of the controller
(defuzzify-lom? *Mamd throttle*)

2. *Ensure that Mamd is true equal or greater than γ, i.e., we add the fuzzy statement $\langle Mamd, \gamma \rangle$ to the KB.*

3. *Now, maximize the value of the (internal) variable $x_{throttle}$ representing the value of throttle, i.e., determine*

$$v_{throttle} := \max\ x_{throttle} \quad s.t. \quad \mathcal{K} \cup \{\langle Mamd, \gamma \rangle\}\ satisfiable\ .$$

4. *Output the result $v_{throttle}$.*

The SOM can be computed in a similar way, but minimizing the value of the (internal) variable $x_{throttle}$ representing the value of t. Finally, MOF can be computed as $(LOM + SOM)/2$.

Chapter 9

Fuzzy RDF & RDFS

9.1 Introduction

RDF [361] has become a quite popular Semantic Web representation formalism. The basic ingredients are triples of the form (s, p, o), such as $(tom, likes, tomato)$, stating that subject s has property p with value o.

However, under the classical semantics, RDF cannot represent vague information and, to this purpose, some *Fuzzy RDF* variants have been proposed [313, 314, 315, 429, 447, 448, 450]: essentially they allow us to state that a triple is true to some degree, *e.g.*, $(tom, likes, tomato)$ is true to degree at least 0.9.[1]

Our main goal of this part is to provide, under very general semantics, a minimal deductive system for fuzzy RDF, along the lines described by [325]. That is, we essentially fuzzify the RDFS sub-language ρdf, which is the core part of RDFS (see Chapter 3). To this end, the main conceptual shift parallels the one from crisp statements to fuzzy statements (see Chapter 8). Namely, rather than interpreting an RDFS triple (s, p, o) being either true or false, we associate to it a degree of truth taken from the truth space $[0, 1]$. Therefore, and not surprisingly, as we did for mathematical fuzzy logic (see Section 8.2), in which fuzzy statements were of the form $\langle \phi, n \rangle$ with $n \in [0, 1]$, in fuzzy RDFS we will have fuzzy triples of the form $\langle (s, p, o), n \rangle$ with the intended meaning "the degree of truth of the triple (s, p, o) is equal or greater than n."

9.2 Fuzzy RDF & RDFS

Syntax. To start with, we recall from Section 3.2 that a ρdf *triple* is a triple τ of the form

$$(s, p, o) \in \mathbf{UBL} \times \mathbf{U} \times \mathbf{UBL} \ ,$$

---

[1] We also refer the reader to [476, 265, 264, 427] to an even more general setting in which we may annotate a triple with an element of a so-called *annotation domain*, *i.e.*, an idempotent and commutative semi-ring and the relative SPARQL query language AnQL http://anql.deri.org/.

where ρdf is defined as the following subset of the RDFS vocabulary

$$\rho\text{df} = \{\text{sp}, \text{sc}, \text{type}, \text{dom}, \text{range}\} \ ,$$

supporting sub-property (sp), subclass (sc), typing (type), property domain restriction (dom), and property range restriction (range).

Now, a *fuzzy RDFS triple* is an expression

$$\langle \tau, n \rangle \ ,$$

where τ is a triple and $n \in [0, 1]$. The intended semantics is that the degree of truth of the fuzzy triple is not less than n. For instance, $\langle(audiTT, \text{type}, SportsCar), 0.8\rangle$ is a fuzzy triple, intending that AudiTT is almost a sports car. In a fuzzy triple $\langle \tau, n \rangle$, the truth value n may be omitted and, in that case, the value $n = 1$ is assumed.

A *fuzzy RDFS graph G* (or simply a fuzzy graph, or *fuzzy RDF Knowledge Base*) is a set of fuzzy RDF triples.

The notions of *universe* of a graph G, the *vocabulary* of G, *ground* graph, and *variable assignment* are as for the crisp case (see Section 3.2).

Without loss of generality we may also assume that there are not two fuzzy triples $\langle \tau, n \rangle$ and $\langle \tau, m \rangle$ in a fuzzy graph G. If this is the case, we may just remove the fuzzy triple with the lower score.

Semantics. The semantics is a natural extension of the crisp one, in which the interpretation of properties and classes become fuzzy sets instead of crisp sets.

In the remainder, let us fix a t-norm $\otimes$ and its dual $\oplus$. A *fuzzy interpretation $\mathcal{I}$* over a vocabulary V is a tuple

$$\mathcal{I} = \langle \Delta_R, \Delta_P, \Delta_C, \Delta_L, P[\![\cdot]\!], C[\![\cdot]\!], \cdot^{\mathcal{I}} \rangle \ ,$$

where $\Delta_R, \Delta_P, \Delta_C, \Delta_L$ are interpretation domains of $\mathcal{I}$ and $P[\![\cdot]\!], C[\![\cdot]\!], \cdot^{\mathcal{I}}$ are interpretation functions of $\mathcal{I}$.

They have to satisfy:

1. Δ_R is a nonempty finite set of resources, called the domain or universe of $\mathcal{I}$;

2. Δ_P is a finite set of property names (not necessarily disjoint from Δ_R);

3. $\Delta_C \subseteq \Delta_R$ is a distinguished subset of Δ_R identifying if a resource denotes a class of resources;

4. $\Delta_L \subseteq \Delta_R$, the set of literal values, Δ_L contains all plain literals in $\mathbf{L} \cap V$;

5. $P[\![\cdot]\!]$ maps each property name $p \in \Delta_P$ into a function $P[\![p]\!] : \Delta_R \times \Delta_R \to [0, 1]$, *i.e.*, assigns a degree to each pair of resources, denoting the degree of being the pair an instance of the property p;

6. $C[\![\cdot]\!]$ maps each class $c \in \Delta_C$ into a function $C[\![c]\!] : \Delta_R \to [0,1]$, *i.e.*, assigns a degree to every resource, denoting the degree of the resource being an instance of class c;

7. $\cdot^{\mathcal{I}}$ maps each $t \in \mathbf{UL} \cap V$ into a value $t^{\mathcal{I}} \in \Delta_R \cup \Delta_P$ and such that $\cdot^{\mathcal{I}}$ is the identity for plain literals and assigns an element in Δ_R to each element in $\mathbf{L}$.

Note that the only difference so far relies on points 5 and 6, in which the extension functions become now fuzzy membership functions.

The notion entailment is defined using the idea of *satisfaction* of a graph under certain interpretation. Intuitively a ground fuzzy triple $\langle (s, p, o), n \rangle$ in a fuzzy RDF graph G will be satisfied under the interpretation $\mathcal{I}$ if p is interpreted as a property name, s and o are interpreted as resources, and the interpretation of the pair (s, o) belongs to the extension of the property assigned to p to a degree not less than n.

Formally, an interpretation $\mathcal{I}$ is a *model* of an annotated ground graph G, denoted $\mathcal{I} \models G$, if and only if $\mathcal{I}$ is an interpretation over the vocabulary $\rho\mathrm{df} \cup universe(G)$ that satisfies the following conditions:

Simple:

1. $\langle (s, p, o), n \rangle \in G$ implies $p^{\mathcal{I}} \in \Delta_P$ and $P[\![p^{\mathcal{I}}]\!](s^{\mathcal{I}}, o^{\mathcal{I}}) \geq n$;

Subproperty:

1. $P[\![\mathsf{sp}^{\mathcal{I}}]\!](p, q) \otimes P[\![\mathsf{sp}^{\mathcal{I}}]\!](q, r) \leq P[\![\mathsf{sp}^{\mathcal{I}}]\!](p, r)$;
2. $P[\![p^{\mathcal{I}}]\!](x, y) \otimes P[\![\mathsf{sp}^{\mathcal{I}}]\!](p, q) \leq P[\![q^{\mathcal{I}}]\!](x, y)$;

Subclass:

1. $P[\![\mathsf{sc}^{\mathcal{I}}]\!](c, d) \otimes P[\![\mathsf{sc}^{\mathcal{I}}]\!](d, e) \leq P[\![\mathsf{sc}^{\mathcal{I}}]\!](c, e)$;
2. $C[\![c^{\mathcal{I}}]\!](x) \otimes P[\![\mathsf{sc}^{\mathcal{I}}]\!](c, d) \leq P[\![d^{\mathcal{I}}]\!](x)$;

Typing I:

1. $C[\![c]\!](x) = P[\![\mathsf{type}^{\mathcal{I}}]\!](x, c)$;
2. $P[\![\mathsf{dom}^{\mathcal{I}}]\!](p, c) \otimes P[\![p]\!](x, y) \leq C[\![c]\!](x)$;
3. $P[\![\mathsf{range}^{\mathcal{I}}]\!](p, c) \otimes P[\![p]\!](x, y) \leq C[\![c]\!](y)$;

Typing II:

1. For each $\mathsf{e} \in \rho\mathrm{df}$, $\mathsf{e}^{\mathcal{I}} \in \Delta_P$;
2. $P[\![\mathsf{sp}^{\mathcal{I}}]\!](p, q)$ is defined only for $p, q \in \Delta_P$;
3. $C[\![\mathsf{sc}^{\mathcal{I}}]\!](c, d)$ is defined only for $c, d \in \Delta_C$;
4. $P[\![\mathsf{dom}^{\mathcal{I}}]\!](p, c)$ is defined only for $p \in \Delta_P$ and $c \in \Delta_C$;

5. $P[\![\mathsf{range}^{\mathcal{I}}]\!](p,c)$ is defined only for $p \in \Delta_P$ and $c \in \Delta_C$;

6. $P[\![\mathsf{type}^{\mathcal{I}}]\!](s,c)$ is defined only for $c \in \Delta_C$.

It is easily verified that the classical setting is as the case in which the truth space is $L_2 = \{0,1\}$ in place of $[0,1]$ (the t-norm can be arbitrary).

It also easily verified that, *e.g.*, the condition 1 of the subclass condition encodes the fuzzy FOL statement

$$\langle \forall x.[(c(x) \to d(x)) \wedge (d(x) \to e(x))] \to (c(x) \to d(x)), 1 \rangle \,,$$

that, by the way, can be derived via axioms $(A1)$ and $(A5a)$ of the BL logic (see Section 8.2.2.1). The other conditions are derived similarly.

Finally, entailment among annotated ground fuzzy graphs G and H is as usual. Now, $G \models H$, where G and H may contain blank nodes, if and only if for any grounding G' of G there is a grounding H' of H such that $G' \models H'$.

Example 29. *Suppose we want to state the following: Skype collaborators are also Ebay collaborators to some degree since Ebay possesses 30% of Skype's shares, and also that Toivo is a part-time Skype collaborator:*

$$\langle (SkypeCollab, \mathsf{sc}, EbayCollab), 0.3 \rangle$$
$$\langle (toivo, \mathsf{type}, SkypeCollab), 0.5 \rangle$$

Then, e.g., under the product t-norm $\otimes_p$, we can infer the following triple:

$$\langle (toivo, \mathsf{type}, EbayCollab), 0.15 \rangle \,.$$

Informally, as Toivo is a Skype collaborator and a Skype collaborator is an Ebay collaborator, then Toivo is an Ebay collaborator, too. Concerning the degree to which this statement holds, by Equation (8.25), we have that Toivo is an Ebay collaborator to degree not smaller than $0.5 \otimes_p 0.3 = 0.15$.

Remark 22. *Note that we always have that $G \models \langle \tau, 0 \rangle$. Clearly, triples of the form $\langle \tau, 0 \rangle$ are uninteresting and, thus, in the following we do not consider them as part of the language.*

As for the crisp case, it can be shown that:

Proposition 63 ([429]). *Any fuzzy RDFS graph has a finite model.*

Therefore, we do not have to care about consistency.

9.3 Fuzzy Conjunctive Queries

Concerning query answering, we extend naturally the conjunctive queries defined in Section 3.3 and more extensively in Section 6.2 to the fuzzy setting.

As in Section 3.3, we assume that a fuzzy graph G is ground, that is blank nodes have been skolemized, *i.e.*, replaced with terms in **UL**.

Informally, queries are as for the classical case where triples are replaced with fuzzy triples in which *fuzzy variables* (taken from an appropriate alphabet and denoted Λ) may occur. We allow built-in triples of the form (s, p, o), where p is a built-in predicate taken from a reserved vocabulary and having a *fixed interpretation*, such as $(\lambda, \leq, l)$ stating that the value of λ has to be $\leq$ than the value $l \in L$. We generalize the built-ins to any n-ary predicate p, where p's arguments may be fuzzy variables, ρdf variables, domain values of $[0, 1]$, values from **UL**, and p has a fixed interpretation. We will assume that the evaluation of the predicate can be decided in finite time. As for the crisp case, for convenience, we write "functional predicates" as *assignments* of the form $x := f(\mathbf{z})$ and assume that the function $f(\mathbf{z})$ is safe. We also assume that a non-functional built-in predicate $p(\mathbf{z})$ should be safe as well.

To start with, a *fuzzy query* is of the form

$$\langle q(\mathbf{x}), \Lambda \rangle \leftarrow \exists \mathbf{y} \exists \mathbf{\Lambda}'.\varphi(\mathbf{x}, \Lambda, \mathbf{y}, \mathbf{\Lambda}') \tag{9.1}$$

in which $\varphi(\mathbf{x}, \Lambda, \mathbf{y}, \mathbf{\Lambda}')$ is a conjunction (as for the crisp case, we use "," as conjunction symbol) of fuzzy triples and built-in predicates, $\mathbf{x}$ and Λ are the distinguished variables, $\mathbf{y}$ and $\mathbf{\Lambda}'$ are the vectors of *non-distinguished variables* (existential quantified variables), and $\mathbf{x}$, Λ, $\mathbf{y}$ and $\mathbf{\Lambda}'$ are pairwise disjoint. Variable Λ and variables in $\mathbf{\Lambda}'$ can only appear in place of degrees of truth or built-in predicates. The query head contains at least one variable.

For instance, the query

$$\langle q(x), s \rangle \leftarrow \langle (x, \mathsf{type}, SportsCar), s_1 \rangle, (x, hasPrice, y), s := s_1 \cdot cheap(y) \ ,$$

where, *e.g.*, $cheap(p) = ls(10000, 1500)(x)$, has intended meaning to retrieve all cheap sports cars, where $ls(10000, 1500)$ is a left-shoulder fuzzy membership function (see Section 8.1.1). Any answer x is scored according to the product of being cheap and a sports car.

Given a fuzzy graph G, a query $\langle q(\mathbf{x}), \Lambda \rangle \leftarrow \exists \mathbf{y} \exists \mathbf{\Lambda}'.\varphi(\mathbf{x}, \Lambda, \mathbf{y}, \mathbf{\Lambda}')$, a vector $\mathbf{t}$ of terms in $universe(G)$ and a truth degree λ in $[0, 1]$, we say that $\langle q(\mathbf{t}), \lambda \rangle$ is *entailed* by G, denoted $G \models \langle q(\mathbf{t}), \lambda \rangle$, if and only if in any model $\mathcal{I}$ of G, there is a vector $\mathbf{t}'$ of terms in $universe(G)$ and a vector λ' of truth degrees in $[0, 1]$ such that $\mathcal{I}$ is a model of $\varphi(\mathbf{t}, \lambda, \mathbf{t}', \lambda')$. If $G \models \langle q(\mathbf{t}), \lambda \rangle$ then $\langle \mathbf{t}, \lambda \rangle$ is called an *answer* to q. The *answer set* of q w.r.t. G is

$$ans(G, q) = \{ \langle \mathbf{t}, \lambda \rangle \mid G \models \langle q(\mathbf{t}), \lambda \rangle, \lambda \neq 0 \text{ and}$$
$$\text{for any } \lambda' \neq \lambda \text{ such that } G \models \langle q(\mathbf{t}), \lambda' \rangle, \lambda' \leq \lambda \text{ holds} \} \ .$$

That is, for any tuple $\mathbf{t}$, the truth degree λ is as large as possible.

Disjunctive fuzzy queries with aggregation operators. As we did in Section 6.2, concerning crisp queries, we extend the notion of fuzzy conjunctive query to include aggregation operators as well.

As we have seen, aggregates may be like the usual SQL aggregate functions such as $\mathsf{SUM}, \mathsf{AVG}, \mathsf{MAX}, \mathsf{MIN}$. But now, we have also logic specific aggregates such as $\oplus$ and $\otimes$.

Formally, let @ be an aggregate function with

$$@ \in \{\mathsf{SUM}, \mathsf{AVG}, \mathsf{MAX}, \mathsf{MIN}, \mathsf{COUNT}, \oplus, \otimes\}$$

then a query with aggregates is of the form

$$
\begin{aligned}
\langle q(\mathbf{x}), \Lambda \rangle \quad \leftarrow \quad & \exists \mathbf{y} \exists \Lambda'.\varphi(\mathbf{x}, \mathbf{y}, \Lambda'), \\
& \mathsf{GroupedBy}(\mathbf{w}), \\
& \Lambda := @[f(\mathbf{z})] \,,
\end{aligned} \tag{9.2}
$$

where $\mathbf{w}$ are variables in $\mathbf{x}$ or $\mathbf{y}$ and each variable in $\mathbf{x}$ occurs in $\mathbf{w}$ and any variable in $\mathbf{z}$ occurs in $\mathbf{y}$ or Λ'.

From a semantics point of view, we say that $\mathcal{I}$ *is a model of* (*satisfies*) $q(\mathbf{t}, \lambda)$, denoted $\mathcal{I} \models \langle q(\mathbf{t}), \Lambda \rangle$ if and only if

$\lambda = @[\lambda_1, \ldots, \lambda_k]$ where $g = \{\langle \mathbf{t}, \mathbf{t}'_1, \lambda'_1 \rangle, \ldots, \langle \mathbf{t}, \lambda, \mathbf{t}'_k, \lambda'_k \rangle\}$,
is a group of k tuples with identical projection
on the variables in $\mathbf{w}$, $\varphi(\mathbf{t}, \mathbf{t}'_r, \lambda'_r)$ is true in $\mathcal{I}$
and $\lambda_r = f(\mathbf{t})$ where $\mathbf{t}$ is the projection of $\langle \mathbf{t}'_r, \lambda'_r \rangle$
on the variables $\mathbf{z}$.

Now, the notion of $G \models \langle q(\mathbf{t}), \Lambda \rangle$ is as usual: any model of G is a model of $\langle q(\mathbf{t}), \Lambda \rangle$.

We conclude by defining a *disjunctive query* $\mathbf{q}$ as usual as a finite set of conjunctive queries in which all the rules have the same head. Intuitively, the answers to a disjunctive query are the *union* of the answers of the conjunctive queries. That is, for a disjunctive query $\mathbf{q} = \{q_1, \ldots, q_m\}$, G *entails* $\mathbf{q}$ (denoted $G \models \mathbf{q}$) iff $G \models q_i$ for some $q_i \in \mathbf{q}$.

Top-k Retrieval. As now each answer to a query has a degree of truth (*i.e.*, *score*), the basic inference problem that is of interest is the top-k retrieval problem, formulated as follows.

Given a fuzzy graph G, and a query q, retrieve k answers $\langle \mathbf{t}, \lambda \rangle$ with maximal degree and rank them in decreasing order relative to the degree λ, denoted

$$ans_k(G, q) = \mathsf{Top}_k \ ans(G, q) \,.$$

We point the interested reader to Appendix G for a variant of the SPRQL query language for RDFS (see Section 6.3) allowing to query fuzzy RDFS graphs.

9.4 Reasoning

In what follows, we provide a sound and complete deductive system (for the graph entailment problem) for fuzzy ρdf (see [429]).

The most important feature of fuzzy RDFS is that we are able to provide a deductive system in the style of the one for classical RDFS (see Section 3.4). Moreover, only the support for the domain dependent $\otimes$ and $\oplus$ operations has to be provided and, thus, are amenable to an easy implementation on top of existing systems. The rules in Table 9.1 are arranged in groups that capture the semantic conditions of models, A, B, C, X, and Y are meta-variables representing elements in **UBL** and D, E represent elements in **UL**. The rule set contains two rules, $(1a)$ and $(1b)$, that are the same as for the crisp case, while rules $(2a)$ to $(5b)$ are the annotated rules homologous to the crisp ones. Finally, rule (6) is specific to the annotated case.

Please note that rule (6) is destructive *i.e.*, this rule removes the premises as the conclusion is inferred. We also assume that a rule is not applied if the consequence is of the form $\langle \tau, 0 \rangle$ (see Remark 22).

The reader may notice also that, except for rule $(1a), (1b)$ and (6), all rules apply the so-called graded deduction rule we have seen in Equation (8.44), related to mathematical fuzzy logic.

It can be shown that:

Proposition 64 (Soundness and completeness [429]). *For a fuzzy graph, the proof system $\vdash$ is sound and complete for $\models$, that is, (1) if $G \vdash \langle \tau, \lambda \rangle$ then $G \models \langle \tau, \lambda \rangle$ and (2) if $G \models \langle \tau, \lambda \rangle$ then there is $\lambda' \geq \lambda$ with $G \vdash \langle \tau, \lambda' \rangle$.*

We point out that rules $2 - 5$ can be represented concisely using the following inference rule:

$$(AG) \frac{\langle \tau_1, \lambda_1 \rangle, \ \ldots, \ \langle \tau_n, \lambda_n, \{\tau_1, \ldots \tau_n\} \vdash_{\mathsf{RDFS}} \tau \rangle}{\langle \tau, \bigotimes_i \lambda_i \rangle} \ . \tag{9.3}$$

Essentially, this rule says that if a classical RDFS triple τ can be inferred by applying a classical RDFS inference rule to triples $\tau_1, \ldots \tau_n$ (denoted $\{\tau_1, \ldots, \tau_n\} \vdash_{\mathsf{RDFS}} \tau$), then the degree of truth of τ will be $\bigotimes_i \lambda_i$, where λ_i is the degree of truth of triple τ_i. It follows immediately that, using rule (AG), in addition to rules (1) and (6) from the deductive system above, it is easy to extend these rules to cover the complete RDFS rule set.

Finally, like for the classical case, the *closure* is defined as $cl(G) = \{\langle \tau, \lambda \rangle \mid G \vdash^* \langle \tau, \lambda \rangle\}$, where $\vdash^*$ is as $\vdash$ without rule $(1a)$. Note again that the size of the closure of G is polynomial in $|G|$ and can be computed in polynomial time, provided that the computational complexity of operations $\otimes$ and $\oplus$ are polynomially bounded (from a computational complexity point of view, it is as for the classical case, plus the cost of the operations $\otimes$ and $\oplus$ in L).

TABLE 9.1: Inference rules for fuzzy ρdf.

1. **Simple:**

$$(a)\frac{G}{G'} \text{ for a map } \mu : G' \to G$$

$$(b)\frac{G}{G'} \text{ for } G' \subseteq G$$

2. **Subproperty:**

$$(a)\frac{\langle(A, \mathsf{sp}, B), \lambda_1\rangle, \langle(B, \mathsf{sp}, C), \lambda_2\rangle}{\langle(A, \mathsf{sp}, C), \lambda_1 \otimes \lambda_2\rangle}$$

$$(b)\frac{\langle(D, \mathsf{sp}, E), \lambda_1\rangle, \langle(X, D, Y), \lambda_2\rangle}{\langle(X, E, Y), \lambda_1 \otimes \lambda_2\rangle}$$

3. **Subclass:**

$$(a)\frac{\langle(A, \mathsf{sc}, B), \lambda_1\rangle, \langle(B, \mathsf{sc}, C), \lambda_2\rangle}{\langle(A, \mathsf{sc}, C), \lambda_1 \otimes \lambda_2\rangle}$$

$$(b)\frac{\langle(A, \mathsf{sc}, B), \lambda_1\rangle, \langle(X, \mathsf{type}, A), \lambda_2\rangle}{\langle(X, \mathsf{type}, B), \lambda_1 \otimes \lambda_2\rangle}$$

4. **Typing:**

$$(a)\frac{\langle(D, \mathsf{dom}, B), \lambda_1\rangle, \langle(X, D, Y), \lambda_2\rangle}{\langle(X, \mathsf{type}, B), \lambda_1 \otimes \lambda_2\rangle}$$

$$(b)\frac{\langle(D, \mathsf{range}, B), \lambda_1\rangle, \langle(X, D, Y), \lambda_2\rangle}{\langle(Y, \mathsf{type}, B), \lambda_1 \otimes \lambda_2\rangle}$$

5. **Implicit Typing:**

$$(a)\frac{\langle(A, \mathsf{dom}, B), \lambda_1\rangle, \langle(D, \mathsf{sp}, A), \lambda_2\rangle, \langle(X, D, Y), \lambda_3\rangle}{\langle(X, \mathsf{type}, B), \lambda_1 \otimes \lambda_2 \otimes \lambda_3\rangle}$$

$$(b)\frac{\langle(A, \mathsf{range}, B), \lambda_1\rangle, \langle(D, \mathsf{sp}, A), \lambda_2\rangle, \langle(X, D, Y), \lambda_3\rangle}{\langle(Y, \mathsf{type}, B), \lambda_1 \otimes \lambda_2 \otimes \lambda_3\rangle}$$

6. **Generalization:**

$$\frac{\langle(X, A, Y), \lambda_1\rangle, \langle(X, A, Y), \lambda_2\rangle}{\langle(X, A, Y), \lambda_1 \oplus \lambda_2\rangle}$$

Eventually, similar propositions as Propositions 5 and 7 hold. Specifically,

Proposition 65. $G \vdash H$ *if and only if* $H \subseteq cl(G)$ *or* H *is obtained from* $cl(G)$ *by applying rule* (1a).

Therefore, like the crisp case, a simple method to determine $G \models \tau$, where both G and τ is ground, consists in computing $cl(G)$, where the size of the closure of G is $\mathcal{O}(|G|^2)$, and check whether τ is included in $cl(G)$.

Now, under the above closure computation, we have, as for the crisp case [325]:

Proposition 66 (Size of Closure).

1. *The size of the closure of* G *is* $\mathcal{O}(|G|^2)$.

2. *The size of the closure of* G *is in the worst case no smaller than* $\Omega(|G|^2)$.

We conclude by showing how to compute the answer set of a fuzzy query. Essentially, it follows the same procedure as for the crisp case (see Section 3.4). In fact, we have that

Proposition 67. *Given a graph* G, $\langle \mathbf{t}, \lambda \rangle$ *is an* answer *to* q *if and only if* $\exists \mathbf{y} \exists \mathbf{\Lambda}'.\varphi(\mathbf{t}, \lambda, \mathbf{y}, \mathbf{\Lambda}')$ *is true in the closure of* G *and* λ *is* $\preceq$-*maximal.*[2]

By relying on Proposition 67, we may devise a similar query answering method as for the crisp case: a method to determine $ans_k(G, q)$ is as follows.

1. Compute the closure $cl(G)$ of G and store it into a database that supports top-k retrieval (*e.g.*, RankSQL [258][3]).

2. It can easily be verified that any fuzzy query can be mapped into a top-k SQL query [258] over the underlying database schema.

3. Hence, $ans_k(G, q)$ is determined by issuing these top-k SQL queries to the database.

Example 30. *Consider*

$$G = \{\langle (p, \mathsf{dom}, c), 0.5 \rangle, \langle (d, \mathsf{sc}, c), 0.4 \rangle, \langle (b, \mathsf{type}, d), 0.3 \rangle, \langle (a, p, b), 0.2 \rangle\}$$

under product logic. Then the closure of G *is*

$$cl(G) = G \cup \{\langle (b, \mathsf{type}, c), 0.12 \rangle, \langle (a, \mathsf{type}, c), 0.01 \rangle\}.$$

Therefore, for the query

$$\langle q(x), s \rangle \leftarrow \langle (x, \mathsf{type}, c), s \rangle$$

we have that

$$ans_1(G, q) = \{\langle (b, \mathsf{type}, c), 0.12 \rangle\}.$$

---

[2]$\exists \mathbf{y} \exists \mathbf{\Lambda}'.\varphi(\mathbf{t}, \lambda, \mathbf{y}, \mathbf{\Lambda}')$ is true in the closure of G if and only if for some $\mathbf{t}'$, λ' for all triples in $\varphi(\mathbf{t}, \lambda, \mathbf{t}', \lambda')$ there is a triple in $cl(G)$ that subsumes it and the built-in predicates are true, where an fuzzy triple $\langle \tau, \lambda_1 \rangle$ subsumes $\langle \tau, \lambda_2 \rangle$ if and only if $\lambda_2 \leq \lambda_1$.

[3]But, *e.g.*, Postgres http://www.postgresql.org/, MonetDB http://monetdb.cwi.nl/ may work as well.

Chapter 10

Fuzzy OWL

10.1 Introduction

In Chapter 4, we have introduced the Web Ontology Language *OWL* [338] and its successor *OWL 2* [101, 340], which together with RDFS (see Chapter 3) have become the most popular Semantic Web representation formalisms. We have also shown their relationship with the Description Logics family of logics.

The basic ingredients are the descriptions of classes, properties, and their instances, such as

- $a{:}C$, such as a:Person $\sqcap$ $\forall$hasChild.Femal, meaning that individual a is an instance of concept/class C (here C is seen as a unary predicate);

- $(a, b){:}R$, such as (tom, mary):hasChild, meaning that the pair of individuals $\langle a, b \rangle$ is an instance of the property/role R (here R is seen as a binary predicate);

- $C \sqsubseteq D$, such as Person $\sqsubseteq$ $\forall$hasChild.Person, meaning that the class C is a subclass of class D;

- $R \sqsubseteq P$, such as isContainedIn $\sqsubseteq$ isPartOf, meaning that the property R is a subproperty of the property P.

However, under the classical semantics, OWL cannot represent vague information, such as "tom likes apples to some grade," and, to this purpose, several *fuzzy* variants have been proposed: they can be classified according to

- the description logic resp. ontology language that they generalize [42, 49, 51, 52, 55, 138, 285, 286, 288, 287, 289, 291, 292, 367, 368, 369, 383, 391, 398, 399, 407, 415, 454, 471];

- the allowed fuzzy constructs [48, 220, 223, 222, 218, 219, 221, 217, 194, 195, 227, 299, 419];

- the underlying fuzzy logic [47, 45, 53, 188, 189, 397, 411, 405];

- applications [4, 114, 54, 262, 320, 386, 392, 393, 401, 406, 434, 435, 418, 430, 432, 431, 474];

- their reasoning algorithms and computational complexity results [40, 50, 41, 43, 27, 28, 64, 70, 72, 71, 68, 74, 69, 73, 75, 91, 92, 469, 342, 384, 390, 389, 395, 396, 404, 410, 425, 426, 412, 475].

We also refer the reader to [290, 416, 422] for a survey.

As DLs [19] (see Chapter 4) are the logical counterpart of the family of OWL languages, to illustrate the basic concepts of fuzzy OWL, it suffices to show the fuzzy DL case. Briefly, one starts from a classical DL, and attaches to the basic statements a degree $n \in [0, 1]$, similarly as we did for fuzzy RDFS in Chapter 9.

Our main goal of this part is to provide a very general semantics and deductive systems similarly as we did in Chapter 4.

10.2   Fuzzy Description Logics Basics

In general, fuzzy DLs allow expressions of the form $\langle a{:}C, n \rangle$, stating that a is an instance of concept C with degree at least n, *i.e.*, the FOL formula $C(a)$ is true to degree at least n. Similarly, $\langle C_1 \sqsubseteq C_2, n \rangle$ and $\langle R_1 \sqsubseteq R_2, n \rangle$ state vague subsumption relationships. Informally, $\langle C_1 \sqsubseteq C_2, n \rangle$ dictates that the FOL formula $\forall x.C_1(x) \to C_2(x)$ is always true to degree at least n. Essentially, *Fuzzy DLs* are then obtained by interpreting the statements as fuzzy FOL formulae and attaching a weight n to DL statements, thus, defining so *fuzzy DL statements*.

10.2.1   Syntax and Semantics

Let us consider the DL $\mathcal{SROIQ}$ without concrete domains (see Section 4.2.2.3 and Table 4.1). Consider $n \in [0, 1]$, and the crisp $\mathcal{SROIQ}$ axioms (A1) - (A17) in Table 4.1. Then the following are *fuzzy axioms* of *fuzzy $\mathcal{SROIQ}$*:

- *fuzzy GCIs* of the form $\langle C \sqsubseteq D, n \rangle$;

- *fuzzy concept assertions* of the form $\langle a{:}C, n \rangle$;

- *fuzzy role assertions* of the form $\langle (a, b){:}R, n \rangle$ and $\langle (a, b){:}\neg R, n \rangle$;

- *fuzzy RIAs* of the form $\langle R_1 \ldots R_n \sqsubseteq R, n \rangle$;

- axioms (A11), (A12), (A14)–(A17), *i.e.*, trans(R), dis(S_1, S_2), ref(R), irr(S), sym(R) and asy(S).

We will write fuzzy axioms also as $\langle \alpha, n \rangle$, where α is a GCI a RIA or an assertion. We will use interchangeably, if clear from context, α in place of $\langle \alpha, 1 \rangle$. We will say in this case that α is a classical axiom.

We make one change only to the concept constructs, by allowing graded singleton concept expressions of the form $\{n/a\}$, where n is a degree of truth, in place of the crisp variant $\{a\}$.

It is worth noting that one may find in fuzzy DLs also fuzzy statements of the form $\langle \alpha \geq n \rangle$, $\langle \alpha \leq n \rangle$, $\langle \alpha > n \rangle$, $\langle \alpha < n \rangle$, and $\langle \alpha = n \rangle$, stating that the degree of truth of axiom α is bounded by $\bullet n$, where $\bullet \in \{ \geq, \leq, >, <, = \}$. We stick here to the form $\langle \alpha, n \rangle$, *i.e.*, $\langle \alpha \geq n \rangle$, only (i) for uniformity among the various fuzzy Semantic Web Languages presented in the book; and (ii) as $\langle \alpha, n \rangle$ is the most used one. Besides, by reminding that graded statements are intended to be produced semi- or automatically, it is hardly conceivable that they may have, *e.g.*, the form $\langle \alpha \leq n \rangle$, $\langle \alpha > n \rangle$ or $\langle \alpha < n \rangle$. However, sometimes we will still use, if needed, expressions of the form $\langle \alpha \bullet n \rangle$.

A *fuzzy knowledge base* is now, similarly as for crisp $\mathcal{SROIQ}$, a triple $\mathcal{K} = \langle \mathcal{T}, \mathcal{A}, \mathcal{R} \rangle$, where now fuzzy axioms occur in place of classical axioms. $\mathcal{T}, \mathcal{A}$ and $\mathcal{R}$ are called now *fuzzy TBox*, *fuzzy ABox*, and *fuzzy RBox*, respectively.

Example 31. *Consider the following background knowledge about cars encoded as the fuzzy TBox* $\mathcal{T}^1$:

$$
\begin{aligned}
Car &\sqsubseteq \exists HasPrice.Price \\
Sedan &\sqsubseteq Car \\
Van &\sqsubseteq Car \\
CheapPrice &\sqsubseteq Price \\
ModeratePrice &\sqsubseteq Price \\
ExpensivePrice &\sqsubseteq Price \\
\langle CheapPrice &\sqsubseteq ModeratePrice, 0.7 \rangle \\
\langle ModeratePrice &\sqsubseteq ExpensivePrice, 0.4 \rangle \\
CheapCar &= Car \sqcap \exists HasPrice.CheapPrice \\
ModerateCar &= Car \sqcap \exists HasPrice.ModeratePrice \\
ExpensiveCar &= Car \sqcap \exists HasPrice.ExpensivePrice \\
\mathsf{fun}(HasPrice) &
\end{aligned}
$$

Essentially, the vague concepts here are $CheapPrice, ModeratePrice,$ *and* $ExpensivePrice$ *and the graded GCIs declare to which extent there is a relation ship among them.*

The facts about two specific cars a *and* b *are encoded with the following fuzzy ABox* $\mathcal{A}$:

$$
\begin{aligned}
\langle a{:}Sedan \sqcap \exists HasPrice.CheapPrice, 0.7 \rangle \\
\langle b{:}Van \sqcap \exists HasPrice.ModeratePrice, 0.8 \rangle \ .
\end{aligned}
$$

So, a is a sedan having a cheap price, while b is a van with a moderate price.

The semantics is a natural extension of the crisp one for DLs presented in Section 4, in which the interpretation of concepts and roles become fuzzy sets instead of crisp sets. Specifically, we consider the first order reading of the

---

[1]For the sake of clarity, here $\mathsf{fun}(R)$ is a macro for $\top \sqsubseteq (\leq 1\,R)$.

fuzzy DL constructs as from Section 4.2.2.3, specifically Table 4.1, and give them a fuzzy FOL semantics as illustrated in Section 8.2.

For our purposes, let us consider truth combination functions $\otimes, \oplus, \Rightarrow$ and $\ominus$ defined on a truth space L as from Chapter 8. Here, L may be $[0,1]$, $[0,1]_{\mathbb{Q}}$ or L_n (so, *e.g.*, $\otimes$ doesn't necessarily have to be a t-norm, see Section 8.1.7).

Then, a *fuzzy interpretation* $\mathcal{I} = (\Delta^{\mathcal{I}}, \cdot^{\mathcal{I}})$ consists of a nonempty set $\Delta^{\mathcal{I}}$ (the *domain*) and of a *fuzzy interpretation function* $\cdot^{\mathcal{I}}$ that assigns

- to each atomic concept A a function $A^{\mathcal{I}} \colon \Delta^{\mathcal{I}} \to L$;

- to each abstract role R a function $R^{\mathcal{I}} \colon \Delta^{\mathcal{I}} \times \Delta^{\mathcal{I}} \to L$;

- to each individual a an element $a^{\mathcal{I}} \in \Delta^{\mathcal{I}}$ such that $a^{\mathcal{I}} \neq b^{\mathcal{I}}$ if $a \neq b$ (UNA).

$C^{\mathcal{I}}$ denotes the membership function of the fuzzy concept C with respect to the fuzzy interpretation $\mathcal{I}$. For $x \in \Delta^{\mathcal{I}}$ $C^{\mathcal{I}}(x)$ gives us the degree of being x an element of the fuzzy concept C under $\mathcal{I}$. Similarly, $R^{\mathcal{I}}$ denotes the membership function of the fuzzy role R with respect to $\mathcal{I}$. For $x, y \in \Delta^{\mathcal{I}}$, $R^{\mathcal{I}}(x,y)$ gives us the degree of being (x,y) an element of the fuzzy role R.

Interpretations are extended to $\mathcal{SROIQ}$ constructs as illustrated in Table 10.1 (in Table 10.1, *e.g.*, the condition $(C3)$ has to be read as: $(C \sqcap D)^{\mathcal{I}}(x) = C^{\mathcal{I}}(x) \otimes D^{\mathcal{I}}(x)$).

We say that a fuzzy interpretation $\mathcal{I}$ *satisfies (is a model of)* a fuzzy KB $\mathcal{K} = \langle \mathcal{T}, \mathcal{A}, \mathcal{R} \rangle$ iff it satisfies each element in $\mathcal{A}$, $\mathcal{T}$ and $\mathcal{R}$. A fuzzy KB $\mathcal{K} = \langle \mathcal{T}, \mathcal{A}, \mathcal{R} \rangle$ *entails* an axiom E, denoted $\mathcal{K} \models E$, iff every model of $\mathcal{K}$ satisfies E. We say that two concepts C and D are *equivalent*, denoted $C \equiv_{\mathcal{K}} D$ iff in any model $\mathcal{I}$ of $\mathcal{K}$ and for all $x \in \Delta^{\mathcal{I}}$, $C^{\mathcal{I}}(x) = D^{\mathcal{I}}(x)$.

As for the fuzzy FOL case (see Section 8.2.1), for concept assertion, role assertion GCI or role inclusion axiom ϕ, we say that $\langle \phi, n \rangle$ is a *tight logical consequence* of $\mathcal{K}$ iff n is the infimum of $\phi^{\mathcal{I}}$ subject to all models $\mathcal{I}$ of $\mathcal{K}$. Notice that the latter is equivalent to $n = \sup \{r \mid \mathcal{K} \models \langle \phi, r \rangle\}$. n is called the *best entailment degree* of ϕ w.r.t. $\mathcal{K}$ (denoted $bed(\mathcal{K}, \phi)$), *i.e.*,

$$bed(\mathcal{K}, \phi) = \sup \{r \mid \mathcal{K} \models \langle \phi, r \rangle\} . \tag{10.1}$$

On the other hand, the *best satisfiability degree* of ϕ w.r.t. $\mathcal{K}$ (denoted $bsd(\mathcal{K}, \phi)$) is

$$bsd(\mathcal{K}, \phi) = \sup_{\mathcal{I}} \{\phi^{\mathcal{I}} \mid \mathcal{I} \models \mathcal{K}\} . \tag{10.2}$$

For a concept C, we also say that the *best satisfiability degree* of C w.r.t. $\mathcal{K}$ (denoted $bsd(\mathcal{K}, C)$) is

$$bsd(\mathcal{K}, C) = \sup_{\mathcal{I} \models \mathcal{K}} \ \sup_{x \in \Delta^{\mathcal{I}}} C^{\mathcal{I}}(x) .$$

TABLE 10.1: Syntax and semantics of the fuzzy DL $\mathcal{SROIQ}$.

Concepts	Syntax (C)	Semantics: truth value of $C^{\mathcal{I}}(x)$
(C1)	A	$A^{\mathcal{I}}(x)$
(C2)	$\top$	$\top^{\mathcal{I}}(x) = 1$
(C3)	$\bot$	$\bot^{\mathcal{I}}(x) = 0$
(C4)	$C \sqcap D$	$C^{\mathcal{I}}(x) \otimes D^{\mathcal{I}}(x)$
(C5)	$C \sqcup D$	$C^{\mathcal{I}}(x) \oplus D^{\mathcal{I}}(x)$
(C6)	$\neg C$	$\ominus C^{\mathcal{I}}(x)$
(C7)	$\forall R.C$	$\inf_{y \in \Delta^{\mathcal{I}}} \{ R^{\mathcal{I}}(x,y) \Rightarrow C^{\mathcal{I}}(y) \}$
(C8)	$\exists R.C$	$\sup_{y \in \Delta^{\mathcal{I}}} \{ R^{\mathcal{I}}(x,y) \otimes C^{\mathcal{I}}(y) \}$
(C11)	$\{n/a\}$	n if $x = a^{\mathcal{I}}$, 0 otherwise
(C12)	$(\geq m\ S.C)$	$\sup_{y_1,\dots,y_m \in \Delta^{\mathcal{I}}} [(\otimes_{i=1}^{m} \{ S^{\mathcal{I}}(x,y_i) \otimes C^{\mathcal{I}}(y_i) \}) \otimes (\otimes_{j<k\leq n} \{ y_j \neq y_k \})]$
(C13)	$(\leq m\ S.C)$	$\inf_{y_1,\dots,y_{n+1} \in \Delta^{\mathcal{I}}}$ $[(\otimes_{i=1}^{n+1} \{ S^{\mathcal{I}}(x,y_i) \otimes C^{\mathcal{I}}(y_i) \}) \Rightarrow (\oplus_{j<k\leq n+1} \{ y_j = y_k \})]$
(C16)	$\exists S.\text{Self}$	$S^{\mathcal{I}}(x,x)$
Roles	**Syntax (R)**	**Semantics of $R(x,y)$**
(R1)	R	$R^{\mathcal{I}}(x,y)$
(R2)	R^{-}	$R^{\mathcal{I}}(y,x)$
(R3)	U	1
Other	**Syntax (X)**	**Semantics: truth value of $X^{\mathcal{I}}$**
(X1)	$a{:}C$	$C^{\mathcal{I}}(a^{\mathcal{I}})$
(X2)	$(a,b){:}R$	$R^{\mathcal{I}}(a^{\mathcal{I}}, b^{\mathcal{I}})$
(X3)	$(a,b){:}\neg R$	$\ominus R^{\mathcal{I}}(a^{\mathcal{I}}, b^{\mathcal{I}})$
(X6)	$C \sqsubseteq D$	$\inf_{x \in \Delta^{\mathcal{I}}} C^{\mathcal{I}}(x) \Rightarrow D^{\mathcal{I}}(x)$
(X7)	$R_1 \dots R_n \sqsubseteq R$	$\sup_{x_1 \dots x_{n+1} \in \Delta^{\mathcal{I}}} \otimes [R_1^{\mathcal{I}}(x_1,x_2), \dots, R_n^{\mathcal{I}}(x_n,x_{n+1})] \Rightarrow R^{\mathcal{I}}(x_1,x_{n+1})$
Axiom	**Syntax (E)**	**Semantics ($\mathcal{I}$ satisfies E if ...)**
(A1)	$\langle a{:}C, n \rangle$	$C^{\mathcal{I}}(a^{\mathcal{I}}) \geq n$
(A2)	$\langle (a,b){:}R, n \rangle$	$R^{\mathcal{I}}(a^{\mathcal{I}}, b^{\mathcal{I}}) \geq n$
(A3)	$\langle (a,b){:}\neg R, n \rangle$	$\ominus R^{\mathcal{I}}(a^{\mathcal{I}}, b^{\mathcal{I}}) \geq n$
(A6)	$\langle C \sqsubseteq D, n \rangle$	$\inf_{x \in \Delta^{\mathcal{I}}} C^{\mathcal{I}}(x) \Rightarrow D^{\mathcal{I}}(x) \geq n$
(A7)	$\langle R_1 \dots R_n \sqsubseteq R, n \rangle$	$\sup_{x_1 \dots x_{n+1} \in \Delta^{\mathcal{I}}} \otimes [R_1^{\mathcal{I}}(x_1,x_2), \dots, R_n^{\mathcal{I}}(x_n,x_{n+1})]$ $\Rightarrow R^{\mathcal{I}}(x_1,x_{n+1}) \geq n$
(A9)	$\text{trans}(R)$	$\forall x,y \in \Delta^{\mathcal{I}}, R^{\mathcal{I}}(x,y) \geq \sup_{z \in \Delta^{\mathcal{I}}} R^{\mathcal{I}}(x,z) \otimes R^{\mathcal{I}}(z,y)$
(A10)	$\text{disj}(S_1, S_2)$	$\forall x,y \in \Delta^{\mathcal{I}}, S_1^{\mathcal{I}}(x,y) = 0$ or $S_2^{\mathcal{I}}(x,y) = 0$
(A12)	$\text{ref}(R)$	$\forall x \in \Delta^{\mathcal{I}}, R^{\mathcal{I}}(x,x) = 1$
(A13)	$\text{irr}(S)$	$\forall x \in \Delta^{\mathcal{I}}, S^{\mathcal{I}}(x,x) = 0,$
(A14)	$\text{sym}(R)$	$\forall x,y \in \Delta^{\mathcal{I}}, R^{\mathcal{I}}(x,y) = R^{\mathcal{I}}(y,x)$
(A15)	$\text{asy}(S)$	$\forall x,y \in \Delta^{\mathcal{I}}$, if $S^{\mathcal{I}}(x,y) > 0$ then $S^{\mathcal{I}}(y,x) = 0$.

Example 32. *Consider Example 31 under Gödel semantics. Then it can be shown that*

$$\mathcal{K} \models \langle a{:}ModerateCar, 0.7 \rangle$$
$$\mathcal{K} \models \langle b{:}ExpensiveCar, 0.4 \rangle .$$

Informally, in the former case the reasoning is as follows. As a is a sedan (at least to degree 0.7), it is a car (at least to degree 0.7) and, thus, a is a car with a cheap price (at least to degree 0.7). Therefore, by the definition of a cheap car, a is, thus, a cheap car (at least to degree 0.7). In the latter case, as b is a van (at least to degree 0.8), it is a car (at least to degree 0.8) and, thus, b is a car with a moderate price (at least to degree 0.8). Therefore, as a moderate price is to some degree an expensive price, b has, thus, an expensive price (at least to degree $\min(0.8, 0.4) = 0.4$). Eventually, by the definition of expensive car, b is, thus, an expensive car (at least to degree 0.4).

Remark 23. *Like for the fuzzy FOL case, for which $\forall$ and $\exists$ are not comple-mentary in general (see Remark 19), also for fuzzy DLs we have that $\forall R.C$ and $\neg \exists R.\neg C$ are not, unlike the classical case, equivalent. However, they are equivalent under Łukasiewicz logic and SFL.*

Remark 24 (On Number Restrictions). *In [49] it has been pointed out that, unlike the classical case (see Section 4.2.2.1), in the fuzzy case we do not have in general that $(\leq n \ R.C) \equiv \neg (\geq n+1 \ R.C)$ holds.*

For instance, in Łukasiewicz logic assume the following interpretation:

$$
\begin{aligned}
((tom, apple) : likes)^{\mathcal{I}} &= ((tom, banana) : likes)^{\mathcal{I}} \\
&= ((tom, orange) : likes)^{\mathcal{I}} \\
&= ((tom, peach) : likes)^{\mathcal{I}} = 0.5
\end{aligned}
$$

$$
\begin{aligned}
(apple{:}Fruit)^{\mathcal{I}} &= (banana{:}Fruit)^{\mathcal{I}} \\
&= (orange{:} Fruit)^{\mathcal{I}} \\
&= (peach{:}Fruit)^{\mathcal{I}} = 1 \ ,
\end{aligned}
$$

where $apple^{\mathcal{I}}, banana^{\mathcal{I}}, orange^{\mathcal{I}}, peach^{\mathcal{I}}$ are different.

Then, $(\leq 1 \ likes.Fruit)^{\mathcal{I}}(tom) = 1$. In this example, while one may expect tom not liking more than one fruit, he likes many more fruits x_i as long as they satisfy $((tom, x_i) : likes)^{\mathcal{I}} + (x_i{:}Fruit)^{\mathcal{I}} < 1$.

According to [49] the semantics of cardinality restrictions should satisfy the following properties instead:

- *If $(\leq n \ R.C)^{\mathcal{I}}(a) = 1$ then $|\{b \mid (R(a,b)^{\mathcal{I}} \otimes C(b))^{\mathcal{I}} > 0\}| \leq n$.*

- *$\exists R.C \equiv (\geq 1 \ R.C)$.*

- *$(\leq n \ R.C) \equiv \neg (\geq n+1 \ R.C)$.*

Therefore, [49] proposes the following semantics for number restrictions (using the equivalence $\forall x.\neg \phi \equiv \neg \exists x.\phi$, see Remark 19 and Remark 21):

$$
(\geq n \ R.C)^{\mathcal{I}}(x) = \sup_{y_1,\dots,y_n \in \Delta^{\mathcal{I}}} [\min_{i=1}^{n} \{R^{\mathcal{I}}(x, y_i) \otimes C^{\mathcal{I}}(y_i)\} \bigotimes (\otimes_{j < k \leq n} \{y_j \neq y_k\})]
$$

$$
(\leq n \ R.C)^{\mathcal{I}}(x) = \inf_{y_1,\dots,y_{n+1} \in \Delta^{\mathcal{I}}} [\min_{i=1}^{n+1} \{R^{\mathcal{I}}(x, y_i) \otimes C^{\mathcal{I}}(y_i)\} \Rightarrow (\oplus_{j < k \leq n+1} \{y_j = y_k\})]
$$

Note that, equivalences among fuzzy concepts are similar as for the fuzzy propositional case (see Table 8.6) as illustrated in Table 10.2.

10.2.2   Some Additional Constructs

It is also useful to introduce the following constructs:

- $C \to D$ with semantics $(C \to D)^{\mathcal{I}}(x) = C^{\mathcal{I}}(x) \Rightarrow D^{\mathcal{I}}(x)$;

TABLE 10.2: Some additional fuzzy concept equivalences.

Property	Łukasiewicz	Gödel	Product	SFL
$C \sqcap \neg C \equiv \bot$	•	•	•	
$C \sqcup \neg C \equiv \top$	•			
$C \sqcap C \equiv C$		•		•
$C \sqcup C \equiv C$		•		•
$\neg\neg C \equiv C$	•			•
$C \to D \equiv \neg C \sqcup D$	•			•
$C \to D \equiv \neg D \to \neg C$	•			•
$\neg(C \to D) \equiv C \sqcap \neg D$	•			•
$\neg(C \sqcap D) \equiv \neg C \sqcup \neg D$	•	•	•	•
$\neg(C \sqcup D) \equiv \neg C \sqcap \neg D$	•	•	•	•
$C \sqcap (D \sqcup E) \equiv (C \sqcap D) \sqcup (C \sqcap E)$		•		•
$C \sqcup (D \sqcap E) \equiv (C \sqcup D) \sqcap (C \sqcup E)$		•		•
$\exists R.C \equiv \neg\forall R.\neg C$	•			•

- $C \leftrightarrow D$ for $(C \to D) \sqcap (D \to C)$;

- $\min\{C, D\}$ for $C \sqcap (C \to D)$, and $\min\{C_1, \ldots, C_n\}$ for $\min\{\ldots \min\{C_1, C_2\}, \ldots\}$;

- $\max\{C, D\}$ for $\min((C \to D) \to D, (D \to C) \to C)$ and $\max\{C_1, \ldots, C_n\}$ for $\max\{\ldots \max\{C_1, C_2\}, \ldots\}$;

- for $x \in \{g, l, p, s\}$, $C \sqcap_x D$, $C \sqcup_x D$, $C \to_x D$, indicating that the concept operators $\sqcap_x$, $\sqcup_x$ and $\to_x$ are interpreted according the logic $x \in \{g, l, p, s\}$, where g, l, p, and s stand for Gödel logic, Łukasiewicz logic, product logic and SFL, respectively;

- $C_1 = C_2$ for the two axioms $C_1 \sqsubseteq C_2$ and $C_2 \sqsubseteq C_1$;

- $\langle C_1 = C_2, n \rangle$ for the axiom $\langle \top \sqsubseteq (C_1 \leftrightarrow C_2), n \rangle$;

- $\mathsf{dom}(R, C)$, called *domain restriction* axiom, for $\exists R.\top \sqsubseteq C$;

- $\mathsf{ran}(R, C)$, called *range restriction* axiom, for $\top \sqsubseteq \forall R.C$;

- $(= n \ R.C)$ for $(\geq n \ R.C) \sqcap (\leq n \ R.C)$;

- $(= n \ R)$ for $(= n \ R.\top)$.

Remark 25. *It is worth noting that, w.l.o.g., an axiom $\langle C \sqsubseteq D, n \rangle$ may be rewritten as $\langle \top \sqsubseteq C \to D, n \rangle$, an axiom $C_1 = C_2$ may be rewritten as $\top \sqsubseteq C_1 \leftrightarrow C_2$.*

Remark 26 (Fuzzy DLs under SFL). *[395], which presents fuzzy $\mathcal{ALC}$ under SFL, proposes a slightly different semantics for fuzzy GCIs. In fact, in [395] a fuzzy GCI is of the form $C \sqsubseteq D$ with semantics: $\mathcal{I}$ is a model of $C \sqsubseteq D$ iff for any $x \in \Delta^{\mathcal{I}}$ we have that $C^{\mathcal{I}}(x) \leq D^{\mathcal{I}}(x)$. This is the same of any fuzzy axiom of the form $\langle \top \sqsubseteq C \rightarrow_x D, 1 \rangle$, where $\rightarrow_x$ is an r-implication. To be compliant with [395] and most fuzzy DLs work developed later on under SFL, we will use expressions*

- $C \tilde{\sqsubseteq} D$ *with semantics: $\mathcal{I}$ is a model $C \tilde{\sqsubseteq} D$ iff for any $x \in \Delta^{\mathcal{I}}$ we have that $C^{\mathcal{I}}(x) \leq D^{\mathcal{I}}(x)$;*

- $A \tilde{=} C$ *with semantics: $\mathcal{I}$ is a model $A \tilde{=} C$ iff for any $x \in \Delta^{\mathcal{I}}$ we have that $A^{\mathcal{I}}(x) = C^{\mathcal{I}}(x)$;*

- $R \tilde{\sqsubseteq} S$ *with semantics: $\mathcal{I}$ is a model $R \tilde{\sqsubseteq} S$ iff for any $x, y \in \Delta^{\mathcal{I}}$ we have that $R^{\mathcal{I}}(x, y) \leq S^{\mathcal{I}}(x, y)$.*

10.2.3 Acyclic Fuzzy Ontologies

As for the crisp case (see Section 4.4.1.2), *acyclic fuzzy ontologies* play an important role in fuzzy DLs both as they occur often in practices as well as from a computational complexity point of view.

Specifically, let us also introduce a restricted form of TBoxes, *i.e.*, *acyclic* TBoxes. That is, let $\mathcal{T}$ be a Tbox in which the GCIs have one of the following form

$$
\begin{aligned}
A &\sqsubseteq_n C \\
A &\tilde{\sqsubseteq} C \\
A &=_n C \\
A &\tilde{=} C \,,
\end{aligned}
$$

where A is a concept name, C is a concept, and $A \sqsubseteq_n C$ is a shorthand for $\langle \top \sqsubseteq A \rightarrow C, n \rangle$ and $A =_n C$ is a shorthand for $\langle \top \sqsubseteq A \leftrightarrow C, n \rangle$. We call the former two GCIs *primitive* and call the latter two *definitional*.

We say that A is the head of these axioms and C is the body. Furthermore, we also assume that no concept name A is in the head of more than one axiom.

Now, we say that

- concept name A *directly uses* concept name B w.r.t. $\mathcal{T}$, denoted $A \rightarrow_{\mathcal{T}} B$, if A is the head of some axiom $\tau \in \mathcal{T}$ such that B occurs in the body of τ;

- concept name A *uses* concept name B w.r.t. $\mathcal{T}$, denoted $A \rightsquigarrow_{\mathcal{T}} B$, if there exist concept names $A_1, \ldots, A_n$, such that $A_1 = A$, $A_n = B$ and, for every $1 \leq i < n$, it holds that $A_i \rightarrow_{\mathcal{T}} A_{i+1}$.

Eventually, we say that a TBox $\mathcal{T}$ is *cyclic* (*acyclic*) if there is (no) A such that $A \rightsquigarrow_{\mathcal{T}} A$. We say also that a fuzzy TBox is *unfoldable* if it is an acyclic TBox which only contains inclusion axioms of the form $A \tilde{\sqsubseteq} C$ and $A \tilde{=} C$.

10.2.4 On Witnessed Models

By relying on Table 10.1, in a similar way as for fuzzy FOL (see Section 8.2.1.1), the use of infima (universal quantification $\forall$) and suprema (existential quantification $\exists$) may lead to counterintuitive behaviors (see also, *e.g.*, [186, 188, 189, 190]). For instance, consider the concept assertion

$$\langle a{:}\exists R.A, 1 \rangle \ .$$

Consider the interpretation $\mathcal{I}$ with domain $\mathbb{N}$, $a^{\mathcal{I}} = 1$, and for all $n, m \in \mathbb{N}$

$$A^{\mathcal{I}}(n) = 1 - \frac{1}{n}$$
$$R^{\mathcal{I}}(m, n) = 1 \ .$$

Then for any $n \in N$

$$R^{\mathcal{I}}(a^{\mathcal{I}}, n) \otimes A^{\mathcal{I}}(n) = A^{\mathcal{I}}(n) = 1 - \frac{1}{n} < 1$$

However,

$$(\exists R.A)^{\mathcal{I}}(a^{\mathcal{I}}) = \sup_{n \in \mathbb{N}} R^{\mathcal{I}}(a^{\mathcal{I}}, n) \otimes A^{\mathcal{I}}(n) = \sup_{n \in \mathbb{N}} A^{\mathcal{I}}(n) = \sup_{n \in \mathbb{N}} 1 - \frac{1}{n} = 1 \ .$$

That is, unlike the crisp case, notwithstanding there is no individual n of the domain of $\mathcal{I}$ satisfying

$$R^{\mathcal{I}}(a^{\mathcal{I}}, n) \otimes A^{\mathcal{I}}(n) = 1 \ ,$$

still, $\mathcal{I}$ satisfies the assertion $\langle a{:}\exists R.A, 1 \rangle$, which is the fuzzy DL analogue of Equation (8.47). Similar arguments apply to any of the expressions in Table 10.1 involving infima and suprema[2].

Additionally, in a similar way as for Equation (8.48), under Gödel logic we may build a fuzzy assertion, *e.g.*,

$$\langle a{:}\neg\forall R.A \sqcap \neg\exists R.\neg A, 1 \rangle$$

that has no classical model, but it has a fuzzy one, which has to be infinite and non-witnessed.

While such interpretations may exist in theory, we believe that they unlikely may model any practical knowledge representation and reasoning domain. Therefore, we will restrict out attention to *witnessed models* only in the sense of Section 8.2.1.1.

Specifically, a fuzzy interpretation $\mathcal{I}$ is *witnessed* iff the supremum of every expression in Table 10.1 coincides with the minimum and the infimum of every expression coincides with the maximum.

---

[2]That is, expressions of the form $(C7), (C8), (C12), (C13), (X6), (X7), (A6), (A7), (A9)$.

Note that it is obvious that all finite fuzzy interpretations (this means that $\Delta^\mathcal{I}$ is a finite set) are indeed witnessed but the opposite is not true. Note also that still Proposition 39 applies.

Eventually, to what concern us here, we recall from [39] the following property.

Proposition 68 ([39] Theorem 4.4.). *In Łukasiewicz logic, thus, in SFL, an acyclic knowledge base $\mathcal{K}$ is satisfiable iff $\mathcal{K}$ has a finite model.*

Proposition 68 is not true if we drop the acyclicity condition, *i.e.*, any GCI may occur in the TBox (see [39], Theorem 3.3). In fact, the following examples show that if we allow arbitrary knowledge bases, then the fuzzy DL $\mathcal{ALC}$ under Łukasiewicz and Product fuzzy logics do not verify the *Finite Model Property* (FPM) even if we restrict to witnessed models; in other words, finite satisfiability and witnessed satisfiability are different for arbitrary knowledge bases.

Remark 27 ([39]). *$\mathcal{K}$ is the fuzzy KB with the following axioms*

(1) $\langle a{:}A, 0.5 \rangle$

(2) $\top \sqsubseteq \exists R.\top$

(3) $(\forall R.A) \equiv (\exists R.A)$

(4) $A \equiv (\forall R.A) \sqcap (\forall R.A)$

Now, let $\mathcal{I}$ be a witnessed model of $\mathcal{K}$ under Łukasiewicz fuzzy logic. Then, it can be shown [39] that for every natural number n there are individuals $b_1, b_2, b_3, \ldots, b_n$ such that $0.5 = A^\mathcal{I}(b_1) < A^\mathcal{I}(b_2) < A^\mathcal{I}(b_3) < \cdots < A^\mathcal{I}(b_n) < 1$. Therefore, there is no finite model for $\mathcal{K}$ under Łukasiewicz fuzzy logic. Moreover, $\mathcal{K}$ is, under Łukasiewicz fuzzy logic, satisfiable by a witnessed model but not by a finite model. In fact, one witnessed model of $\mathcal{K}$ is the model $\mathcal{I}$ defined by

- $\Delta^\mathcal{I} = \{1, 2, 3, \ldots\} \cup \{\infty\}$,

- $R^\mathcal{I}$ *is the crisp relation* $\{(i, i+1) : i = 1, 2, 3, \ldots\} \cup \{(\infty, \infty)\}$,

- $A^\mathcal{I}(\infty) = 1$ *and* $A^\mathcal{I}(i) = (2^i - 1)/2^i$ *for every* $i = 1, 2, 3, \ldots$

- $a^\mathcal{I} = 1$.

Similar results hold for $\mathcal{K}$ under product logic: $\mathcal{K}$ is, under product fuzzy logic, satisfiable by a witnessed model but not by a finite model. In fact, one witnessed model of this fuzzy KB is the model $\mathcal{I}$ defined by

- $\Delta^\mathcal{I} = \{1, 2, 3, \ldots\}$,

- $R^\mathcal{I}$ *is the crisp relation* $\{(i, i+1) : i = 1, 2, 3, \ldots\}$,

- $A^{\mathcal{I}}(i) = \sqrt[2^{i-1}]{\left(\frac{1}{2}\right)}$ *for every* $i = 1, 2, 3, \ldots,$

- $a^{\mathcal{I}} = 1.$

Remark 28 ([39]). $\mathcal{K}'$ *is the fuzzy KB with the following axioms*

(1) $\langle a{:}A, 0.5 \rangle$

(2) $\top \sqsubseteq \exists R.\top$

(3) $(\forall R.A) \equiv (\exists R.A)$

(4) $A \equiv (\forall R.A) \sqcap (\forall R.A)$

(5) $\langle \top \sqsubseteq (\neg A), 0.1 \rangle$

Note that $\mathcal{K}'$ is obtained by adding axiom (5) to $\mathcal{K}$ in Example 27. In [39] it has been shown that $\mathcal{K}'$ is unsatisfiable both under Łukasiewicz fuzzy logic as well as under product logic.

We conclude by recalling the following interesting property.

Remark 29. *Let us point out that w.r.t. witnessed models, similarly to the classical case (see Section 4.4.1.2), if A is a concept name and $\otimes$ is continuous, and $\Rightarrow$ is the related r-implication, then an axiom $\langle A \sqsubseteq D, n \rangle$ may be rewritten as $\langle A = C \sqcap A', n \rangle$, where A' is a new concept name.*

Similarly, is it easily verified that any inclusion axiom $A \tilde{\sqsubseteq} C$ may be rewritten as $A \tilde{=} C \sqcap A'$, where A' is a new concept name.

Remark 30. *Under the conditions of Remark 29, we may assume that GCIs in an acyclic TBox have one of the forms*

$$A =_n C$$
$$A \tilde{=} C.$$

10.3 Salient Language Extensions

As we did for fuzzy FOL (see Section 8.2.3), next we describe some salient extension to fuzzy DLs, which make fuzzy DLs particularly attractive from an application point of view.

Fuzzy Concrete Domains. To start with, we discuss how one may provide *concrete domains* within fuzzy DLs. To do so, we rely on [398]. In general, similarly to Section 8.2.3 (see also Section 4.2.2.2), a *fuzzy concrete domain*, also called a *fuzzy datatype theory* $\mathbf{D} = \langle \Delta^{\mathbf{D}}, \cdot^{\mathbf{D}} \rangle$ consists of a datatype domain $\Delta^{\mathbf{D}}$ and a mapping $\cdot^{\mathbf{D}}$ that assigns to each data value an element of $\Delta^{\mathbf{D}}$, and assigns to every n-ary datatype predicate d an n-ary fuzzy relation over $\Delta_{\mathbf{D}}$. More specifically, fuzzy DLs do support unary datatypes only. Therefore, $\cdot^{\mathbf{D}}$ maps indeed each datatype predicate into a function from $\Delta^{\mathbf{D}}$ to $[0,1]$.

Typical examples of datatype predicates $\mathbf{d}$ are the well known fuzzy membership functions

$$\mathbf{d} \quad := \quad ls(a,b) \mid rs(a,b) \mid tri(a,b,c) \mid trz(a,b,c,d)$$

and the crisp membership functions

$$\mathbf{d} \quad := \quad \geq_v \mid \leq_v \mid =_v \ ,$$

where, *e.g.*, $ls(a,b)$ is the left-shoulder fuzzy membership function, while, *e.g.*, $\geq_v$ corresponds to the crisp set of data values that are greater than equal to the value v.

Concerning roles, a role R is either an *object property* or a *datatype property*. An interpretation maps an *object property* into a function $\Delta^{\mathcal{I}} \times \Delta^{\mathcal{I}} \rightarrow [0,1]$, while maps a *datatype property* into a function $\Delta^{\mathcal{I}} \times \Delta^{\mathbf{D}} \rightarrow \{0,1\}$. A datatype property does not have an inverse, but may be functional.

We also use an alphabet for concrete individuals, denoted v, and extend an interpretation to concrete individuals by mapping them into $\Delta^{\mathbf{D}}$. As for individuals, we adopt the UNA, *i.e.*, $v_1^{\mathcal{I}} \neq v_2^{\mathcal{I}}$ if $v_1 \neq v_2$.

We can now extend concept expressions according to the following syntax:

$$C, D \quad \rightarrow \quad \forall T.\mathbf{d} \mid \exists T.\mathbf{d} \ ,$$

where $\mathbf{d}$ is a datatype and T is a datatype property.

For instance, the expression

$$Human \sqcap \exists hasAge \geq_{18} \ ,$$

where the datatype property *hasAge* has been declared functional, will denote the crisp set of humans, which have an age less or equal than 18, while

$$Human \sqcap \exists hasAge.ls(10,30)$$

will denote the fuzzy set of young humans (their age is $ls(10,30)$).

Example 33. *According to the fuzzy wine ontology[3], we have the following inclusion*

$$SparklingWine \sqcap \exists hasSugar.ExtraDrySugarContentForSparklingWine$$
$$\sqsubseteq ExtraDrySparklingWine$$

where hasSugar is a functional role and

$$ExtraDrySugarContentForSparklingWine$$

---

[3]See http://nmis.isti.cnr.it/~straccia/software/FuzzyOWL/.

TABLE 10.3: From fuzzy $\mathcal{SROIQ}$ to fuzzy $\mathcal{SROIQ}(\mathbf{D})$.

Concepts	Syntax (C)	Semantics: truth value of $C^{\mathcal{I}}(x)$
(C9)	$\forall T.\mathbf{d}$	$\inf_{v\in\Delta\mathbf{D}}\, T^{\mathcal{I}}(x,v) \Rightarrow \mathbf{d}^{\mathbf{D}}(v)$
(C10)	$\exists T.\mathbf{d}$	$\sup_{v\in\Delta\mathbf{D}}\, T^{\mathcal{I}}(x,v) \otimes \mathbf{d}^{\mathbf{D}}(v)$
(C14)	$(\geq n\ T.\mathbf{d})$	$\sup_{v_1,\ldots,v_n\in\Delta\mathbf{D}}\, \otimes_{i=1}^{n}(T^{\mathcal{I}}(x,v_i)\otimes\mathbf{d}^{\mathbf{D}}(v_i)) \otimes \otimes_{1\le j<k\le n} v_j \ne v_k$
(C15)	$(\leq m\ T.\mathbf{d})$	$\sup_{v_1,\ldots,v_{n+1}\in\Delta\mathbf{D}}\, \cdot\, \otimes_{i=1}^{n+1}(T^{\mathcal{I}}(x,v_i)\otimes\mathbf{d}^{\mathbf{D}}(v_i)) \Rightarrow \oplus_{1\le j<k\le n+1} v_j = v_k$
Roles	**Syntax (R)**	**Semantics of $R(x,y)$**
(X4)	$(a,v){:}T$	$T^{\mathcal{I}}(a^{\mathcal{I}},v^{\mathcal{I}})$
(X5)	$(a,v){:}\neg T$	$\ominus T^{\mathcal{I}}(a^{\mathcal{I}},v^{\mathcal{I}})$
Axiom	**Syntax (E)**	**Semantics ($\mathcal{I}$ satisfies E if ...)**
(A4)	$\langle (a,v){:}T, n\rangle$	$T^{\mathcal{I}}(a^{\mathcal{I}},v^{\mathcal{I}}) \geq n$
(A5)	$(a,v){:}\neg T$	$\ominus T^{\mathcal{I}}(a^{\mathcal{I}},v^{\mathcal{I}}) \geq n$
(A8)	$T_1 \sqsubseteq T_2$	$\inf_{x\in\Delta^{\mathcal{I}},v\in\Delta\mathbf{D}}\, T_1^{\mathcal{I}}(x,v) \Rightarrow T_1^{\mathcal{I}}(x,v)$
(A11)	$\mathsf{dis}(T_1,T_2)$	$\forall x\in\Delta^{\mathcal{I}}, v\in\Delta\mathbf{D},\, T_1^{\mathcal{I}}(x,v)=0$ or $T_2^{\mathcal{I}}(x,v)=0$

is a fuzzy concrete domain whose definition is

$$tri(12,16,20)$$

in which the values represent the amount of sugar (grams per litre) a sparkling wine should have to be an extra dry sparkling wine. Informally, the closer the amount of sugar is around 12g/l or 20g/l, the less the sparkling wine is an extra dry one. Optimal is a sugar level of 16g/l.

We refer the reader to the fuzzy wine ontology for many more definitions of this type.

More generally, fuzzy $\mathcal{SROIQ}(\mathbf{D})$ is obtained from fuzzy $\mathcal{SROIQ}$ (see Table 10.1) by adding the constructs as illustrated in Table 10.3.

Modifiers. Fuzzy modifiers (see Section 8.1.8) such as `very` and `slightly`, apply to fuzzy concepts to change their membership function. We recall from Section 8.1.8 that a *fuzzy modifier* m represents a function (*e.g.*, $f_{\mathtt{very}}(x) = lm(c)(x)$, see Figure 8.8)

$$f_m \colon [0,1] \to [0,1]\ .$$

Now, we extend the language of fuzzy concept constructors by allowing to apply a modifier m to a concept C or a concrete domain predicate $\mathbf{d}$: *i.e.*,

$$C \quad \to \quad m(C) \mid \forall T.m(\mathbf{d}) \mid \exists T.m(\mathbf{d})$$

allowing, *e.g.*, to express the concept

$$Human \sqcap \exists hasAge.\mathtt{very}(ls(10,30))$$

denoting the fuzzy set of *very* young humans (their age is $\mathtt{very}(ls(10,30))$) (see also [48, 127, 194, 195, 196, 197, 198, 444]).

From a semantics point of view, we extend fuzzy interpretations in the obvious way

$$m(C)^{\mathcal{I}}(x) \;=\; f_m(C^{\mathcal{I}}(x))$$
$$m(\mathbf{d})^{\mathcal{I}}(x) \;=\; f_m(\mathbf{d}^{\mathbf{D}}(x)) \,.$$

Aggregation Operators. Eventually, as for the fuzzy propositional case (see Section 8.2.3), we may extend fuzzy DLs by allowing aggregation operators (see Section 8.1.6) to aggregate concepts, as illustrated, *e.g.*, in [58, 59]. So, let @ be an n-ary aggregation operator as defined in Section 8.1.6, then we extend the language of fuzzy concepts by allowing to apply @ to n concepts $C_1, \ldots, C_n$, *i.e.*,

$$C \;\rightarrow\; @(C_1, \ldots, C_n)$$

allowing, *e.g.*, to express the concept

$$0.7 \cdot ExpensiveHotel + 0.3 \cdot LuxuriousHotel$$

denoting the fuzzy set of expensive and luxurious hotels, whose membership function is the weighted sum of being an expensive and luxurious hotel.

From a semantics point of view, we extend fuzzy interpretations in the obvious way

$$@(C_1, \ldots, C_n)^{\mathcal{I}}(x) \;=\; @(C_1^{\mathcal{I}}(x), \ldots, C_n^{\mathcal{I}}(x)) \,.$$

We conclude this section by illustrating how we analogously may encode Example 27 in fuzzy DLs.

Example 34 ([48, 359]). *Consider Example 27 concerning the matching about a car seller and a buyer.*

To start with, the background knowledge can be encoded as:

$$Sedan \sqsubseteq PassengerCar$$
$$SatelliteAlarm \sqsubseteq AlarmSystem$$
$$NavigatorPack = (SatelliteAlarm \sqcap GPS\_system)$$
$$InsurancePlus = (DriverInsurance \sqcap TheftInsurance)$$
$$\top \sqsubseteq ExColorBlack \sqcup ExColorGray$$
$$ExColorBlack \sqcap ExColorGray \sqsubseteq \bot$$
$$\mathsf{fun}(HasAlarmSystem)$$
$$\mathsf{fun}(HasAirConditioning)$$
$$\mathsf{fun}(HasExColor)$$
$$\mathsf{fun}(HasNavigator)$$
$$\mathsf{fun}(HasMWarranty)$$
$$\mathsf{fun}(HasPrice)$$
$$\mathsf{fun}(HasKMWarranty)$$

The buyer's preferences can be encoded as follows:

1. $B = (PassengerCar \sqcap \exists HasPrice. \leq_{26000})$

2. $B_1 = (\exists HasAlarmSystem.AlarmSystem \rightarrow \exists HasPrice.ls(22300, 22750))$

3. $B_2 = (\exists HasInsurance.DriverInsurance \sqcap \exists HasInsurance.(TheftInsurance \sqcup FireInsurance))$

4. $B_3 = (\exists HasAirConditioning.Airconditioning \sqcap \exists HasExColor.(ExColorBlack \sqcup ExColorGray))$

5. $B_4 = (\exists HasPrice.ls(22000, 24000))$

6. $B_5 = (\exists HasKMWarranty.rs(15000, 175000))$

7. $Buy = (B \sqcap (0.1 \cdot B_1 + 0.2 \cdot B_2 + 0.1 \cdot B_3 + 0.2 \cdot B_4 + 0.4 \cdot B_5))$

In a similar way, the seller's preferences can be encoded as follows:

1. $S = (Sedan \sqcap \exists HasPrice. \geq_{22000})$

2. $S_1 = ((\exists HasNavigator.NavigatorPack) \rightarrow (\exists HasPrice.rs(22500, 22750))))$

3. $S_2 = (\exists HasInsurance.InsurancePlus)$

4. $S_3 = (\exists HasKMWarranty.ls(100000, 125000))$

5. $S_4 = (\exists HasMWarranty.ls(60, 72))$

6. $S_5 = ((\exists HasExColor.ExColorBlack) \rightarrow (\exists HasAirConditioning.AirConditioning))$

7. $Sell = (S \sqcap (0.3 \cdot S_1 + 0.1 \cdot S_2 + 0.3 \cdot S_3 + 0.1 \cdot S_4 + 0.2 \cdot S_5))$

Now, as for Example 27, the best agreement among the buyer and the seller is determined by the maximal degree of satisfiability of the concept conjunction $Buy \sqcap Sell$, i.e.,

$$bsd(\mathcal{K}, Buy \sqcap Sell) \ ,$$

for which we have the analogous results[4]

$$
\begin{aligned}
bsd(\mathcal{K}, Buy \sqcap Sell) &= 0.7 \\
HasPrice &= 22000.0 \\
HasKMWarranty &= 175000.0 \\
HasMWarranty &= 0.0 \ .
\end{aligned}
$$

It is easy to see that Example 28 can be encoded in fuzzy DLs in a similar way (see [48]).

10.4 Fuzzy Conjunctive Queries

Concerning query answering, we extend naturally the notion of fuzzy conjunctive queries defined in Section 9.3 for fuzzy RDFS (see Chapter 9) to the fuzzy DLs case.

---

[4]The values of a data property are the values of the data property corresponding to the individual that maximizes the degree of truth of the concept $Buy \sqcap Sell$.

Informally, fuzzy DL queries are as for fuzzy RDFS where fuzzy triples are replaced with fuzzy FOL assertions in which *fuzzy variables* (taken from an appropriate alphabet and denoted Λ) may occur and where the fuzzy predicates are either unary (for atoms) or binary (for roles).

To start with, a *fuzzy query* is of the form

$$\langle q(\mathbf{x}), \Lambda \rangle \leftarrow \exists \mathbf{y} \exists \mathbf{\Lambda}'.\varphi(\mathbf{x}, \Lambda, \mathbf{y}, \mathbf{\Lambda}') \tag{10.3}$$

in which $\varphi(\mathbf{x}, \Lambda, \mathbf{y}, \mathbf{\Lambda}')$ is a conjunction (as for the crisp case, we use "," as conjunction symbol) of fuzzy unary or binary fuzzy atoms and built-in predicates, $\mathbf{x}$ and Λ are the distinguished variables, $\mathbf{y}$ and $\mathbf{\Lambda}'$ are the vectors of *non-distinguished variables* (existential quantified variables), and $\mathbf{x}$, Λ, $\mathbf{y}$ and $\mathbf{\Lambda}'$ are pairwise disjoint. Variable Λ and variables in $\mathbf{\Lambda}'$ can only appear in place of degrees of truth or built-in predicates. The query head contains at least one variable.

For instance, the query

$$\langle q(x), s \rangle \leftarrow \langle SportsCar(x), s_1 \rangle, hasPrice(x,y), s := s_1 \cdot ls(10000, 1500)(x)$$

has intended meaning to retrieve all cheap sports cars. Any answer x is scored according to the product of being cheap and a sports car.

From a semantics point of view, we rely on the one for fuzzy RDFS and integrate one of the classical DLs, described in Section 4.3. So, given a fuzzy DL KB $\mathcal{K}$, a query $\langle q(\mathbf{x}), \Lambda \rangle \leftarrow \exists \mathbf{y} \exists \mathbf{\Lambda}'.\varphi(\mathbf{x}, \Lambda, \mathbf{y}, \mathbf{\Lambda}')$, a vector $\mathbf{t}$ of individuals occurring in $\mathcal{K}$ and a truth degree λ in $[0,1]$, we say that $\langle q(\mathbf{t}), \lambda \rangle$ is *entailed* by $\mathcal{K}$, denoted $\mathcal{K} \models \langle q(\mathbf{t}), \lambda \rangle$, if and only if there is a vector $\mathbf{t}'$ of individuals occurring $\mathcal{K}$ and a vector λ' of truth degrees in $[0,1]$ such that for any model $\mathcal{I}$ of $\mathcal{K}$, $\mathcal{I}$ is a model of all fuzzy atoms occurring in $\varphi(\mathbf{t}, \lambda, \mathbf{t}', \lambda')$. If $\mathcal{K} \models \langle q(\mathbf{t}), \lambda \rangle$ then $\langle \mathbf{t}, \lambda \rangle$ is called an *answer* to q. The *answer set* of q w.r.t. $\mathcal{K}$ is

$$ans(\mathcal{K}, q) = \{ \langle \mathbf{t}, \lambda \rangle \mid \mathcal{K} \models \langle q(\mathbf{t}), \lambda \rangle, \lambda \neq 0 \text{ and}$$
$$\text{for any } \lambda' \neq \lambda \text{ such that } \mathcal{K} \models \langle q(\mathbf{t}), \lambda' \rangle, \lambda' \leq \lambda \text{ holds} \} .$$

That is, for any tuple $\mathbf{t}$, the truth degree λ is as large as possible.

Please note that, similarly to Remark 6 we have:

Remark 31. *There is a subtle difference with the usual definition of answer, stated as follows:*

> *Given a knowledge base $\mathcal{K}$, a query $\langle q(\mathbf{x}), \Lambda \rangle \leftarrow \exists \mathbf{y} \exists \mathbf{\Lambda}'.\varphi(\mathbf{x}, \Lambda, \mathbf{y}, \mathbf{\Lambda}')$, and a vector $\mathbf{t}$ of individuals occurring in $\mathcal{K}$ and a truth degree λ in $[0,1]$, we say that $\langle q(\mathbf{t}), \lambda \rangle$ is entailed by $\mathcal{K}$, denoted $\mathcal{K} \models \langle q(\mathbf{t}), \lambda \rangle$, if and only if for any model $\mathcal{I}$ of $\mathcal{K}$, $\mathcal{I}$ is a model of the FOL formula $\exists \mathbf{y} \exists \mathbf{\Lambda}'.\varphi(\mathbf{t}, \mathbf{y})$, according to the standard definitions of first-order logic. We denote the answer set according to this definition as $ans^{FOL}(\mathcal{K}, q)$.*

The following example shows the difference between our definition of answer set and the usual one according to Remark 31. So, consider the simple knowledge base

$$\mathcal{K} \;=\; \{\langle (a,c){:}R, 0.7\rangle, \langle b{:}\exists R, 0.8\rangle\}$$

and the conjunctive query

$$\langle q(x), s\rangle \leftarrow \langle R(x,y), s\rangle\ .$$

Then it is easily verified that

$$
\begin{aligned}
ans(\mathcal{K}, q) &=' \{\langle a, 0.7\rangle\}\\
ans^{FOL}(\mathcal{K}, q) &= \{\langle a, 0.7\rangle, \langle b, 0.8\rangle\}\ .
\end{aligned}
$$

As for the crisp DL case, the difference is due to the fact that in our case the instantiation of the non-distinguished variables has to be *known* independently from any model of $\mathcal{K}$, while according to Remark 31, for any model $\mathcal{I}$ of $\mathcal{K}$, the non-distinguished variables $\mathbf{y}, \mathbf{\Lambda}'$ may be substituted with domain elements depending on $\mathcal{I}$. Of course,

$$ans(\mathcal{K}, q) \subseteq ans^{FOL}(\mathcal{K}, q)$$

holds. As for the crisp DL case, in general, our definition here is amenable to a more efficient implementation, as in fact, determining whether $a \in ans(\mathcal{K}, q)$ inherits the computational complexity of the complexity of entailment in the underlying fuzzy DL. Indeed, a simple procedure to determine the answer set $ans(\mathcal{K}, q)$ consists in computing off-line the instances of all atomics concepts and roles occurring in $\mathcal{K}$, store them into a relational database $DB_{\mathcal{K}}$, convert q into and SQL query q_{SQL} and submit q_{SQL}.

Disjunctive fuzzy queries with aggregation operators. As for the fuzzy RDFS case, we may extend conjunctive queries to disjunctive queries and to queries including aggregation operators as well.

Formally, let @ be an aggregate function with

$$@ \in \{\mathsf{SUM}, \mathsf{AVG}, \mathsf{MAX}, \mathsf{MIN}, \mathsf{COUNT}, \oplus, \otimes\}$$

then a query with aggregates is of the form

$$
\begin{aligned}
\langle q(\mathbf{x}), \mathbf{\Lambda}\rangle \;\leftarrow\; & \exists \mathbf{y} \exists \mathbf{\Lambda}'.\varphi(\mathbf{x}, \mathbf{y}, \mathbf{\Lambda}'),\\
& \mathsf{GroupedBy}(\mathbf{w}), \qquad\qquad (10.4)\\
& \mathbf{\Lambda} := @[f(\mathbf{z})]\ ,
\end{aligned}
$$

where $\mathbf{w}$ are variables in $\mathbf{x}$ or $\mathbf{y}$ and each variable in $\mathbf{x}$ occurs in $\mathbf{w}$ and any variable in $\mathbf{z}$ occurs in $\mathbf{y}$ or $\mathbf{\Lambda}'$.

From a semantics point of view, we say that $\mathcal{I}$ *is a model of* (*satisfies*) $\langle q(\mathbf{t}), \lambda \rangle$, denoted $\mathcal{I} \models \langle q(\mathbf{t}), \lambda \rangle$ if and only if

$$\lambda = @[\lambda_1, \ldots, \lambda_k] \text{ where } g = \{\langle \mathbf{t}, \mathbf{t}'_1, \lambda'_1 \rangle, \ldots, \langle \mathbf{t}, \lambda, \mathbf{t}'_k, \lambda'_k \rangle\},$$

is a group of k tuples with identical projection
on the variables in $\mathbf{w}$, $\varphi(\mathbf{t}, \mathbf{t}'_r, \lambda'_r)$ is true in $\mathcal{I}$
and $\lambda_r = f(\mathbf{t})$ where $\mathbf{t}$ is the projection of $\langle \mathbf{t}'_r, \lambda'_r \rangle$
on the variables $\mathbf{z}$.

Now, the notion of $\mathcal{K} \models \langle q(\mathbf{t}), \lambda \rangle$ is as usual: any model of $\mathcal{K}$ is a model of $\langle q(\mathbf{t}), \lambda \rangle$.

We conclude by defining a *disjunctive query* $\mathbf{q}$ as usual as a finite set of conjunctive queries in which all the rules have the same head. Intuitively, the answers to a disjunctive query are the *union* of the answers of the conjunctive queries. That is, for a disjunctive query $\mathbf{q} = \{q_1, \ldots, q_m\}$, $\mathcal{K}$ *entails* $\mathbf{q}$ (denoted $\mathcal{K} \models \mathbf{q}$) iff $\mathcal{K} \models q_i$ for some $q_i \in \mathbf{q}$.

The notion of answer and answer set of a disjunctive query is a straightforward extension of the ones for conjunctive queries.

Top-k Retrieval. As now each answer to a query has a degree of truth (*i.e.*, *score*), a basic inference problem that is of interest is the top-k retrieval problem, formulated as follows.

Given a fuzzy KB $\mathcal{K}$, and a query q, retrieve k answers $\langle \mathbf{t}, \lambda \rangle$ with maximal degree and rank them in decreasing order relative to the degree λ, denoted

$$ans_k(\mathcal{K}, q) = \texttt{Top}_k \ ans(\mathcal{K}, q) \ .$$

10.5   Representing Fuzzy OWL Ontologies in OWL

As pointed out in Section 4, OWL [338] and its successor OWL 2 [101, 340] are standard W3C languages for defining and instantiating Web ontologies whose logical counterpart are classical DLs. So far, several fuzzy extensions of DLs exists and some fuzzy DL reasoners have been implemented, such as FUZZYDL [48], DELOREAN [42] and FIRE [153, 385], SOFTFACTS [421] and DLMEDIA [435, 420].

Not surprisingly, each reasoner uses its own fuzzy DL language for representing fuzzy ontologies and, thus, there is a need for a standard way to represent such information.

A first possibility would be to adopt as a standard one of the fuzzy extensions of the languages OWL and OWL 2 that have been proposed, such as [168, 382, 383]. However, as it is not expected that a fuzzy OWL extension will become a W3C proposed standard in the near future, [54, 57, 60] identifies the syntactic differences that a fuzzy ontology language has to cope

FIGURE 10.1: Annotation property defining concept BuyerPreferences.

with, and proposes to use OWL 2 *itself* to represent fuzzy ontologies. More precisely, [60] uses OWL 2 annotation properties to encode fuzzy $\mathcal{SROIQ}(\mathbf{D})$ ontologies. The use of annotation properties makes it possible *(i)* to use current OWL 2 editors for fuzzy ontology representation, and *(ii)* that OWL 2 reasoners discard the fuzzy part of a fuzzy ontology, producing almost the same results as if it would not exist. In order to support this methodology for fuzzy ontology representation, [60] describes an implementation of a Protégé plug-in to edit fuzzy ontologies and some parsers that translate fuzzy ontologies represented using this methodology into the languages supported by some fuzzy DL reasoners.

Roughly, firstly, we can build the *core part* of the ontology by using any ontology editor supporting OWL 2, such as *Protégé* 4.1[5] [200, 333]. This allows reasoning with this part using standard ontology reasoners. Then, we can add the *fuzzy part* of the ontology by using annotation properties. Representing the fuzzy information using OWL 2 annotations can also be done with an OWL 2 ontology editor (see, *e.g.*, Figures 10.1 and 10.2).

---

[5]http://protege.stanford.edu/

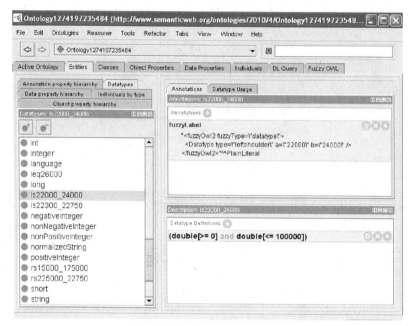

FIGURE   10.2:   Annotation   property   defining   fuzzy   datatype
$ls(22000, 24000)$.

However, typing the annotations is a tedious and error-prone task, so a
Protégé plug-in that makes the syntax of the annotations transparent to the
users has been developed. The Fuzzy OWL 2 plug-in is publicly available on
the Web [165]. Once installed, a new tab *Fuzzy OWL* enables the plug-in.
The plug-in has a menu with the available options (see Figure 10.3). The user
can choose to define fuzzy elements in the ontology (fuzzy datatypes, fuzzy
modified concepts, weighted concepts, weighted sum concepts, fuzzy nominals, fuzzy modifiers, fuzzy modified roles, fuzzy axioms, and fuzzy modified
datatypes), and he/she can specify the fuzzy logic used in the ontology.

Figure 10.4 illustrates how the plug-in works by showing how to create
a new fuzzy datatype. The user specifies the name of the datatype, and the
type of the membership function. Then, the plug-in asks for the necessary
parameters according to the type. A picture is displayed to help the user
recall the meaning of the parameters. Then, after some basic error checking,
the new datatype is created and can be used in the ontology.

Furthermore, the plug-in is integrated with the *fuzzyDL* [164] reasoner [41]
and makes it possible to submit queries to it. For the moment, such queries
must be expressed using the particular syntax supported by *fuzzyDL*.

We are not going into more detail here and refer the reader to [60] and
the FuzzyOWL2 web site [165], from which one may download some fuzzy

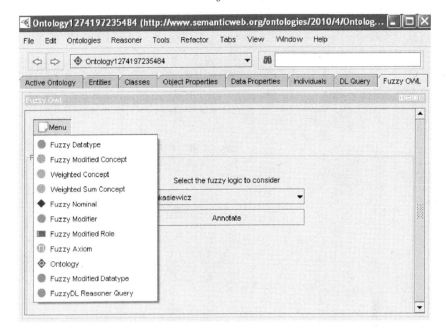

FIGURE 10.3: Menu options of the Fuzzy OWL 2 plug-in.

OWL 2 ontologies as well, such as a fuzzy wine ontology, an ontology for matchmaking, and multi-criteria decision making.

10.6 Reasoning

In Section 4.4 we have described the various reasoning problems of interest for crisp DLs such as the consistency problem, the subsumption problem, the instance checking problem, and the instance retrieval problem, which have their natural fuzzy analogue. Other major reasoning problems are the best entailment degree– and the best satisfiability degree problems (see Equation (10.1) and Equation (10.2) in Section 10.2.1).

In summary, in fuzzy DLs the following problems are of interest.

Consistency problem:

- Is $\mathcal{K}$ satisfiable?
- Is C coherent, *i.e.*, is $C^{\mathcal{I}}(x) > 0$ for some model $\mathcal{I}$ of $\mathcal{K}$ and $x \in \Delta^{\mathcal{I}}$?

Instance checking problem:

- Does $\mathcal{K} \models \langle a{:}C, n \rangle$ hold?

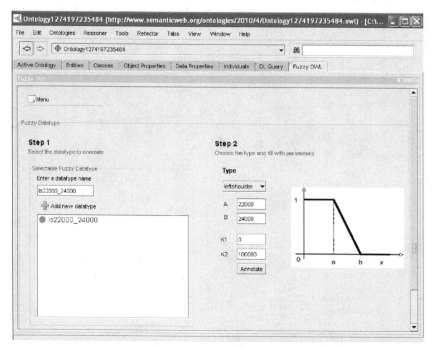

FIGURE 10.4: Creation of a fuzzy datatype with the Fuzzy OWL 2 plug-in.

Subsumption problem:

- Does $\mathcal{K} \models \langle C \sqsubseteq D, n \rangle$ hold?

Best entailment degree problem:

- What is $bed(\mathcal{K}, \phi)$?

Best satisfiability degree problem:

- What is $bsd(\mathcal{K}, \phi)$?

Instance retrieval problem:

- Compute the set $\{\langle a, n \rangle \mid n = bed(\mathcal{K}, a{:}C)\}$.

Note that, as for the crisp case in order to determine whether

$$\mathcal{K} \models \langle (a, b){:}R, n \rangle \ ,$$

we may reduce it to the instance problem, as

$$\mathcal{K} \models \langle (a, b){:}R, n \rangle \text{ iff } \mathcal{K} \cup \{\langle b{:}B, 1 \rangle\} \models \langle a{:}\exists R.B, n \rangle \ ,$$

where B is a new concept.

Similarly as for the crisp case, all the above problems can be reduced to satisfiability degree problems as long as the below presented reductions are supported by the underlying DL language (if not then specific algorithms have been developed): indeed, we have

Remark 32 (Fuzzy DL problem reductions). *The following problem reductions hold:*

- $\mathcal{K}$ *is satisfiable iff* $bsd(\mathcal{K}, a{:}\bot) > 0$, *where a is a new individual.*

- C *is coherent w.r.t.* $\mathcal{K}$ *iff one of the following holds:*

    - $\mathcal{K} \cup \{\langle a{:}C > 0 \rangle\}$ *is satisfiable, where a is a new individual;*
    - $\mathcal{K} \not\models \langle C \sqsubseteq \bot, 1 \rangle$;
    - $bsd(\mathcal{K}, a{:}C) > 0$, *where a is a new individual.*

- $\mathcal{K} \models \langle a{:}C, n \rangle$ *iff one of the following holds:*

    - $\mathcal{K} \cup \{\langle a{:}C < n \rangle\}$ *is not satisfiable;*
    - $bed(\mathcal{K}, a{:}C) \geq n$.

- $\mathcal{K} \models \langle C \sqsubseteq D, n \rangle$ *iff one of the following holds:*

    - $\mathcal{K} \cup \{\langle a{:}C \to D < n \rangle\}$ *is not satisfiable, where a is a new individual;*
    - $bed(\mathcal{K}, C \sqsubseteq D) \geq n$.

- *Similarly to the propositional fuzzy logic case (see Equation (8.53) and Equation (8.54)), we have that*

$$bed(\mathcal{K}, \phi) = \min x. \text{ such that } \mathcal{K} \cup \{\langle \phi \leq x \rangle\} \text{ satisfiable} \quad (10.5)$$
$$bsd(\mathcal{K}, \phi) = \max x. \text{ such that } \mathcal{K} \cup \{\langle \phi \geq x \rangle\} \text{ satisfiable}. (10.6)$$

10.6.1 The Case of the $\mathcal{AL}$ Family

We describe here the major reasoning frameworks within the fuzzy $\mathcal{AL}$ family. As for the crisp case (see Section 4.4.1), we describe here decision algorithms for the knowledge base satisfiability problem for the fuzzy DL $\mathcal{ALC}$, which is sufficiently expressive to illustrate the main characteristic of the methods, which follows to some extend those presented in Section 8.2.2 for the fuzzy propositional case.

But before we start, let us discuss some very important consequences of Remark 28. The literature contains several reasoning algorithms for Łukasiewicz [49, 425, 426], Product [47], or any left continuous t-norm fuzzy DLs [53, 387]) that claim to support GCIs. These algorithms restrict themselves to witnessed models. Unfortunately, these papers are implicitly assuming that the logic satisfies FMP. However, by Remark 28 we have shown that this assumption cannot be done.

The fuzzy KB $\mathcal{K}'$ is an example showing that some algorithms for Łukasiewicz logic [49, 425, 426] do not work properly. In fact, these algorithms say that $\mathcal{K}'$ is satisfiable, whereas it is not. More precisely, the blocking condition (see later on) of the algorithms fails due to an implicit assumption of the FMP: it makes the algorithms stop after having created individual b_2, whereas the inconsistency appears at individual b_3.

Similarly, $\mathcal{K}'$ is also a counterexample to the algorithm for product logic [47] and it is not difficult to obtain counterexamples for the algorithms that consider other t-norms [53, 387] by doing small modifications in $\mathcal{K}'$; it is only necessary to change the degree of truth used in axiom (5).

Consequently, the proofs of the correctness of the cited algorithms are only valid if we add some additional restrictions:

- [49, 425, 426] consider the fuzzy DL $\mathcal{ALC}$ under Łukasiewcz fuzzy logic. The proof is only valid in case we only consider acyclic KBs.

- [47] consider the fuzzy DL $\mathcal{ALC}$ under product fuzzy logic. Here, the proof is only valid if we only consider unfoldable KBs.

- [53] provides reasoning algorithms for the fuzzy DLs $\mathcal{ALC}$ defined by families of fuzzy operators corresponding to a left-continuous t-norm extended with an involutive negation[6]. This work restricts itself to acyclic KBs, so for instance $\mathcal{K}$ cannot be represented in the logic. Here, the proof is correct for Łukasiewicz logic, while the proof of the correctness of the algorithm for acyclic KBs in a fuzzy logic different from Łukasiewicz is not valid, while the proofs are correct for unfoldable KBs.

- [387] provides a reasoning algorithm for the fuzzy DLs $\mathcal{SI}$ defined by families of fuzzy operators corresponding to a left-continuous t-norm. Here, the semantics of GCIs is defined using Zadeh's set inclusion, but the proof of the correctness of the algorithm is only valid if we restrict to unfoldable KBs, or to acyclic KBs and Łukasiewicz fuzzy logic.

In the case of finite Łukasiewicz fuzzy logic (that is, if a finite set of degrees of truth is assumed), the algorithms [49, 425, 426] would not work properly either. As we have shown, the models of $\mathcal{K}$ require an infinite number of degrees of truth, so $\mathcal{K}$ is unsatisfiable under a finite number of degrees of truth. However, these algorithms would say that $\mathcal{K}$ is satisfiable.

Remark 33. *Finally, we would like to add a remark that should be taken into account in the algorithms for reasoning in fuzzy DLs that include GCIs and the weighted sum constructor [48]. It is not hard to see that, even in SFL, one*

---

[6]Here the fuzzy logic corresponding to a left continuous t-norm $\otimes$ is understood as based on the connectives given by the t-norm $\otimes$, its residuum, Łukasiewicz negation, and the dual t-conorm of $\otimes$. This is quite different than the logic of left-continuous t-norms as used in [186, 188, 189], and closer (except for the use of truth constants as concept constructors) to the framework in [169].

can simulate fuzzy KBs that do not satisfy the FMP if we take $\mathcal{K}$ and replace axiom (4) *in Example 27 with*

$$A \equiv (0.5 \cdot \forall R.A + 0.5 \cdot \forall R.A) \ .$$

Hence, in this case, we also need to restrict to unfoldable TBoxes to guarantee the FMP. In fact, the KB satisfiability problem in $\mathcal{ALC}$ under SFL with weighted sum constructor is indeed undecidable (see below).

The issues raised by [39] generated a series of undecidability results [26, 27, 28, 69, 74, 92] caused essentially by cyclic TBoxes (see [74] for a more detailed account) and non Gödelt-norms:

Proposition 69 ([74]). *Assume that fuzzy GCIs are restricted to be classical, i.e., of the form $\langle \alpha, 1 \rangle$ only. Then for the following fuzzy DLs, the KB satisfiability problem is undecidable:*

1. *$\mathcal{ELC}^7$ with classical axioms only under Łukasiewicz logic and product logic;*

2. *$\mathcal{ELC}$ under any non Gödelt-norm $\otimes$;*

3. *$\mathcal{ELC}$ with concept assertions of the form $\langle \alpha = n \rangle$ only under any non Gödelt-norm $\otimes$;*

4. *$\mathcal{AL}$ with concept implication operator $\to^8$ and concept assertions of the form $\langle \alpha = n \rangle$ only under any non Gödelt-norm $\otimes$.*

5. *$\mathcal{ELC}$ under SFL with weighted sum constructor.*

On the other hand it is remarkable to note that from the results in [46] it follows immediately that

Proposition 70 ([46]). *The KB (witnessed) satisfiability problem is decidable for the fuzzy DL $\mathcal{SROIQ}$ under Gödel logic, under SFL and any finitely valued truth space.*

As we will see later on, the result of Proposition 70 is obtained from the fact that under Gödel logic, under SFL and any finitely valued logic, the satisfiability problem of a fuzzy $\mathcal{SROIQ}$ KB can be reduced to a crisp $\mathcal{SROIQ}$ satisfiability problem, which is known to be decidable (see Section 4.2 and [203]).

---

[7]$\mathcal{EL}$ with complement.
[8]See Section 10.2.2.

10.6.1.1   Reduction to Classical Logic

To start with, let us show how one may reduce the KB satisfiability problem in fuzzy DLs into crisp KB satisfiability problems under Gödel logic, under SFL and any finitely valued logic. Besides obtaining decidability results, the method has also the advantage that classical DL reasoners can be used to reason within these fuzzy DLs. For instance, this is the method followed by the fuzzy DL reasoner DeLorean [42].

To illustrate the method, we recap [396], which first proposed the method, which then has been extended and improved in further works such as [41, 43, 44, 45, 46, 50, 56, 61, 383, 405]. Specifically,

- [396] proposed a reasoning preserving procedure for fuzzy $\mathcal{ALCH}$ into crisp $\mathcal{ALCH}$, under SFL;

- [405] extends [396] to the case of fuzzy $\mathcal{ALC}$ where the truth space is any finitely valued complete lattice;

- [44] extends [396] to the case of fuzzy $\mathcal{SROIQ}(\mathbf{D})$;

- [45] extends [396] to the case of fuzzy $\mathcal{SROIQ}(\mathbf{D})$ under Gödel logic;

- [61] extends [396] to the case of fuzzy $\mathcal{SROIQ}$ under finitely many-valued Łukasiewicz logic;

- [46] extends [44] to the case of fuzzy $\mathcal{SROIQ}(\mathbf{D})$ under Gödel logic and under SFL. The results extends immediately to any finitely valued fuzzy $\mathcal{SROIQ}(\mathbf{D})$ as well.

Before we formally present the method, we first illustrate the basic idea it relies on, which is based on the ideas presented in [36, 37] for so-called regular multi-valued logics and somewhat resembles the method proposed in Section 8.2.2.4 for fuzzy propositional logic.

Assume we have a $\mathcal{K} = \langle \emptyset, \mathcal{A} \rangle$, where $\mathcal{A}$ contains

$$\langle a{:}A, 0.6 \rangle$$
$$\langle a{:}\neg A, 0.7 \rangle \ .$$

Clearly, $\mathcal{K}$ is not satisfiable. Now, similarly to Equation (8.61), let $\bar{N}^{\mathcal{K}}$ be the set of truth degrees that occur in $\mathcal{K}$, their negation plus $\{0, 0.5, 1\}$, *i.e.*,

$$\bar{N}^{\mathcal{K}} = \{0, 0.3, 0.4, 0.5, 0.6, 0.7, 1\}$$

and define

$$N_+^{\mathcal{K}} = N^{\mathcal{K}} \setminus \{0\} \ .$$

The important point here is that $\mathcal{K}$ has a model iff $\mathcal{K}$ has a model based on the truth space $\bar{N}^{\mathcal{K}}$ and, thus, allows us to restrict our attention to the values in $\bar{N}^{\mathcal{K}}$ only.

Now, for each $\alpha \in \bar{N}^{\mathcal{K}}$ we introduce new concepts $A_{\geq \alpha}$. $A_{\geq \alpha}$ represents the crisp set of individuals which is an instance of A with degree higher or equal than α, *i.e.*, the α-cut of A. Of course, we have to consider also the relationships among the introduced concepts. so, *e.g.*, we need the axioms

$$A_{\geq 0.5} \sqsubseteq A_{\geq 0.4}$$
$$A_{\geq 0.6} \sqsubseteq A_{\geq 0.5} .$$

For instance, axiom $A_{\geq 0.5} \sqsubseteq A_{\geq 0.4}$ dictates that if a truth value is ≤ 0.5 then it is also ≥ 0.4. Now, we will map

$$\langle a{:}A, 0.6 \rangle \mapsto a{:}A_{\geq 0.6}$$
$$\langle a{:}\neg A, 0.7 \rangle \mapsto a{:}\neg A_{\geq 0.4} .$$

The argument behind the last map is that $\langle a{:}\neg A, 0.7 \rangle$ dictates that $\langle a{:}A \leq 0.3 \rangle$, which restricted to the truth space $\bar{N}^{\mathcal{K}}$ is the same as saying that a cannot be an instance of A to degree ≥ 0.4. This illustrates our basic idea.

Formally, consider fuzzy $\mathcal{ALCH}$ under SFL. We will assume that fuzzy KBs do not include fuzzy axioms of the form $\langle \alpha, 0 \rangle$, $\langle a{:}\neg C, 1 \rangle$. The reason is that they are always satisfied. Let $\mathcal{K} = \langle \mathcal{T}, \mathcal{A}, \mathcal{R} \rangle$ be fuzzy $\mathcal{ALCH}$ KB under SFL. Consider

$$X^{\mathcal{K}} = \{0, 0.5, 1\} \cup \{c \mid \langle \alpha, c \rangle \text{ occurs in } \mathcal{K}\} \tag{10.7}$$

from which we define

$$\bar{N}^{\mathcal{K}} = X^{\mathcal{K}} \cup \{1 - c \mid c \in X^{\mathcal{K}}\} \tag{10.8}$$
$$N_+^{\mathcal{K}} = \bar{N}^{\mathcal{K}} \setminus \{0\} . \tag{10.9}$$

Essentially, $\bar{N}^{\mathcal{K}}$ (which is finite) contains the truth degrees that occur in $\mathcal{K}$ and their negation. The important point here is that $\mathcal{K}$ has a model iff $\mathcal{K}$ has a model based on the truth space $\bar{N}^{\mathcal{K}}$ and, thus, allows us to restrict our attention to the values in $\bar{N}^{\mathcal{K}}$ only. This property derives directly from [395]:

Proposition 71. *A fuzzy $\mathcal{ALCH}$ KB $\mathcal{K}$ under Gödel logic and under SFL has a model iff it has a (witnessed) model over the truth space $\bar{N}^{\mathcal{K}}$.*

In the following, we may assume now that the truth space $\mathcal{N}$ is a finite chain of $p + 1$ elements: namely

$$\mathcal{N} = \{0 = \gamma_0 < \gamma_1 < \cdots < \gamma_p = 1\} ,$$

where $p \geq 2$, from which we define

$$\mathcal{N}_+ = \mathcal{N} \setminus \{\gamma_0\} .$$

For instance, in the case of fuzzy $\mathcal{ALCH}$ KB $\mathcal{K}$ under SFL,

$$\mathcal{N} := \bar{N}^{\mathcal{K}} . \tag{10.10}$$

Degrees of truth will be denoted as $\gamma \in \mathcal{N}$ and $\alpha \in \mathcal{N}_+$. We will also define $+\gamma_i = \gamma_{i+1}$, $-\gamma_i = \gamma_{i-1}$.

We will also use $\bowtie \in \{\geq, >, \leq, <\}$, $\rhd \in \{\geq, >\}$, $\lhd \in \{\leq, <\}$. The symmetric $\bowtie^-$, and the negation $\neg \bowtie$ of an operator $\bowtie$ are defined as follows:

$\bowtie$	$\bowtie^-$	$\neg \bowtie$
$\geq$	$\leq$	$<$
$>$	$<$	$\leq$
$\leq$	$\geq$	$>$
$<$	$>$	$\geq$

Now, let $\mathbf{A}$ be the set of atomic fuzzy concepts and $\mathbf{R}$ the set of atomic fuzzy roles in a fuzzy KB $\mathcal{K} = \langle \mathcal{T}, \mathcal{A}, \mathcal{R} \rangle$, respectively. For each $\alpha \in \mathcal{N}_+$, for each $A \in \mathbf{A}$, a new atomic concept $A_{\geq \alpha}$ is introduced. Similarly, for each $R_A \in \mathbf{R}$, a new atomic role $R_{A \geq \alpha}$ is created.

For each $1 \leq i \leq p-1$ and for each $A \in \mathbf{A}$, $T(\mathcal{N})$ is the smallest TBox containing these axioms:

$$A_{\geq \gamma_{i+1}} \sqsubseteq A_{\geq \gamma_i} . \tag{10.11}$$

Similarly, for each $R_A \in \mathbf{R}$, $R(\mathcal{N})$ is the smallest RBox containing:

$$R_{A \geq \gamma_{i+1}} \sqsubseteq R_{A \geq \gamma_i} . \tag{10.12}$$

Fuzzy concept and role expressions are reduced by using mapping ρ, as shown in Table 10.4. Given a fuzzy concept C, $\rho(C, \geq \alpha)$ is a crisp set containing all the elements which belong to C with a degree greater than or equal to α. The other cases $\rho(C, \bowtie \gamma)$ are similar. ρ is defined in a similar way for fuzzy roles and this equivalence also holds.

Axioms are reduced as in Table 10.5, where $\kappa(\tau)$ maps a fuzzy axiom τ into a set of crisp axioms. We note $\kappa(\mathcal{A})$ the union of the reductions of all the fuzzy axioms in $\mathcal{A}$. Analogously, $\kappa(\mathcal{T})$ is the union of the reductions of all fuzzy concepts in $\mathcal{T}$, where as $\kappa(\mathcal{R})$ is the union of the reductions of all fuzzy roles in $\mathcal{R}$.

Let $\mathsf{crisp}(\mathcal{K})$ denote the reduction of a fuzzy ontology $\mathcal{K}$. That is, a fuzzy KB $\mathcal{K} = \langle \mathcal{T}, \mathcal{A}, \mathcal{R} \rangle$ is reduced into a KB

$$\mathsf{crisp}(\mathcal{K}) = \langle T(\mathcal{N}) \cup \kappa(\mathcal{T}), \kappa(\mathcal{A}), R(\mathcal{N}) \cup \kappa(\mathcal{R}) \rangle .$$

Now, it can be shown that

Proposition 72 ([46, 396]). *A $\mathcal{ALCH}$ fuzzy KB $\mathcal{K}$ under SFL is satisfiable iff its crisp representation $\mathsf{crisp}(\mathcal{K})$ is satisfiable.*

A consequence of Proposition 72 is that

TABLE 10.4: Crisp mapping of concept and role expressions

$$\rho(\top, \rhd\gamma) = \top$$
$$\rho(\top, \lhd\gamma) = \bot$$
$$\rho(\bot, \rhd\gamma) = \bot$$
$$\rho(\bot, \lhd\gamma) = \top$$
$$\rho(A, \geq \gamma) = A_{\geq\gamma}$$
$$\rho(A, > \gamma) = A_{\geq+\gamma}$$
$$\rho(A, \leq \gamma) = \neg A_{\geq+\gamma}$$
$$\rho(A, < \gamma) = \neg A_{\geq\gamma}$$
$$\rho(\neg C, \bowtie \gamma) = \rho(C, \bowtie^{-} \ominus_Z \gamma)$$
$$\rho(C \sqcap D, \rhd\gamma) = \rho(C, \rhd\gamma) \sqcap \rho(D, \rhd\gamma)$$
$$\rho(C \sqcap D, \lhd\gamma) = \rho(C, \lhd\gamma) \sqcup \rho(D, \lhd\gamma)$$
$$\rho(C \sqcup D, \rhd\gamma) = \rho(C, \rhd\gamma) \sqcup \rho(D, \rhd\gamma)$$
$$\rho(C \sqcup D, \lhd\gamma) = \rho(C, \lhd\gamma) \sqcap \rho(D, \lhd\gamma)$$
$$\rho(\forall R.C, \geq \gamma) = \forall\rho(R, > \ominus\gamma).\rho(C, \geq \gamma)$$
$$\rho(\forall R.C, > \gamma) = \forall\rho(R, \geq \ominus\gamma).\rho(C, > \gamma)$$
$$\rho(\forall R.C, \lhd\gamma) = \exists\rho(R, \lhd^{-} \ominus \gamma).\rho(C, \lhd\gamma)$$
$$\rho(\exists R.C, \rhd\gamma) = \exists\rho(R, \rhd\gamma).\rho(C, \rhd\gamma)$$
$$\rho(\exists R.C, \lhd\gamma) = \forall\rho(R, \neg\lhd \gamma).\rho(C, \lhd\gamma)$$
$$\rho(R_A, \geq \gamma) = R_{A_{\geq\gamma}}$$
$$\rho(R_A, > \gamma) = R_{A_{\geq+\gamma}}$$

Proposition 73 ([46, 396]). *Given a $\mathcal{ALCH}$ fuzzy KB $\mathcal{K}$. Then under Gödel logic or SFL, $bed(\mathcal{K}, \alpha) \in \bar{N}^{\mathcal{K}}$. Moreover, given a fuzzy KB $\mathcal{K}$ over a finitely valued truth space $\mathcal{N}$, then $bed(\mathcal{K}, \alpha) \in \mathcal{N}$.*

Therefore, by a binary search on $\bar{N}^{\mathcal{K}}$ (reps. $\mathcal{N}$), the value of $bed(\mathcal{K}, \alpha)$ can be determined in at most $\log |\bar{N}^{\mathcal{K}}|$ entailment tests and, thus, crisp entailment tests. Therefore, the BED problem can be reduced to the crisp case as well.

The reductions for other logics such as Gödel logic or Łukasiewicz logic are based on a similar principle [46, 61]). For instance, under Gödel logic, we have,

TABLE 10.5: Crisp reduction of the fuzzy DL axioms

$$\kappa(\langle a{:}C, \gamma\rangle) = \{a{:}\rho(C, \geq \gamma)\}$$
$$\kappa(\langle (a,b){:}R, \gamma\rangle) = \{(a,b){:}\rho(R, \geq \gamma)\}$$
$$\kappa(\langle C \sqsubseteq D, n\rangle) = \{\rho(C, > \ominus\gamma) \sqsubseteq \rho(D, \geq \gamma)\}$$
$$\kappa(C \tilde{\sqsubseteq} D) = \bigcup_{\alpha \in \mathcal{N}_+}\{\rho(C, \geq \alpha) \sqsubseteq \rho(D, \geq \alpha)\}$$
$$\kappa(A \tilde{=} C) = \bigcup_{\alpha \in \mathcal{N}_+}\{\rho(A, \geq \alpha) = \rho(C, \geq \alpha)\}$$
$$\kappa(\langle R \sqsubseteq S, \gamma\rangle) = \{\rho(R, > \ominus\gamma) \sqsubseteq \rho(R, \geq \gamma)\}$$
$$\kappa(R \tilde{\sqsubseteq} S) = \bigcup_{\alpha \in \mathcal{N}_+}\{\rho(R, \geq \alpha) \sqsubseteq \rho(S, \geq \alpha)\}$$

e.g.,

$$\kappa(\langle C \sqsubseteq D, \gamma \rangle) = \bigcup_{\alpha \in \mathcal{N}_+ \;|\; \alpha \leq \gamma} \{\rho(C, \geq \alpha) \sqsubseteq \rho(D, \geq \alpha)\} \;,$$

while over finitely valued Łukasiewicz logic, we have, *e.g.*,

$$\kappa(\langle C \sqsubseteq D, \gamma \rangle) \;=\; \bigcup_{\gamma_1, \gamma_2} \{\rho(C, \geq \gamma_1) \sqsubseteq \rho(D, \geq \gamma_2)\}$$

for every pair $\gamma_1, \gamma_2 \in \mathcal{N}^+$ such that $\gamma_1 = \gamma_2 + 1 - \gamma$.

The mapping ρ also changes: *e.g.*, under Gödel logic, we have, *e.g.*,

$$\rho(\forall R.C, \geq \gamma) \;=\; \bigsqcap_{\alpha \in \mathcal{N}_+ \;|\; \alpha \leq \gamma} (\forall \rho(R, \geq \alpha).\rho(C, \geq \alpha)) \;,$$

while over finitely valued Łukasiewicz logic, we have, *e.g.*,

$$\rho(\forall R.C, \geq \gamma) \;=\; \bigsqcap_{\gamma_1, \gamma_2} \forall \rho(R, \geq \gamma_1).\rho(C, \geq \gamma_2)$$

for every pair $\gamma_1, \gamma_2 \in \mathcal{N}^+$ such that $\gamma_1 = \gamma_2 + 1 - \gamma$.

However, despite being the method simple to implement (see the DE-LOREAN [42]) and the size of the crisp KB linearly bounded by the size of $|\mathcal{T}||\bar{N}^{\mathcal{K}}|$ (resp., $|\mathcal{T}||\mathcal{N}|$), from a practical point of view the method does not scale yet, especially for the BED problem. For other logics, such as Gödel logicor Łukasiewicz logic, the reduction may become even exponential.

It is not hard to be convinced that the *crisp reduction* method can easily be extended to $\mathcal{SROIQ}(\mathbf{D})$ under any other finitely valued DL as well, as explained at the beginning of this section and, thus, proofs Proposition 70.

10.6.1.2 Analytical Fuzzy Tableau

We recall here the typical fuzzy tableau method employed for fuzzy DLs of the fuzzy $\mathcal{AL}$ family under SFL semantics, introduced in [395] for acyclic $\mathcal{ALC}$ and later on extend to fuzzy $\mathcal{ALC}$ with classical GCIs [390] and then extended to more expressive DLs as in, *e.g.*, [73, 384, 387, 389, 397, 405].

Specifically,

- [395] provides a tableau for acyclic fuzzy $\mathcal{ALC}$ KBs.

- [390] extents [395] to deal with $\mathcal{ALC}$ KBs with classical GCIs.

- [405] deals with acyclic $\mathcal{ALC}$ over finite complete lattices.

- [73] extends [405] to $\mathcal{SHI}$ with graded GCIs over finite complete residuated De Morgan lattices.

- [389] extends [395] to acyclic fuzzy $\mathcal{SHIN}$ KBs.

The method starts from the tableau algorithm for crisp DLs illustrated in Section 4.4.1 and applies the ideas developed for the analytical tableau for fuzzy propositional logic as from Section 8.2.2.3. So, let $\mathcal{K} = \langle \mathcal{T}, \mathcal{A} \rangle$ be an $\mathcal{ALC}$ knowledge base under SFL.

At first, we transform any concept in $\mathcal{K}$ into *negation normal form* (NNF), *i.e.*, negation occurs only in front of atomic concepts. To do so, as for the crisp case we push all negation signs as far as possible into the description, using de Morgan's rules and the usual rules for quantifiers: that is, we iteratively apply the transformation rules of Equation (4.3) for the crisp case, which indeed are semantics preserving under SFL (see Table 10.2):

$$
\begin{aligned}
\neg\neg C &\mapsto C \\
\neg(C \sqcap D) &\mapsto \neg C \sqcup \neg D \\
\neg(C \sqcup D) &\mapsto \neg C \sqcap \neg D \\
\neg \exists R.C &\mapsto \forall R.\neg C \\
\neg \forall R.C &\mapsto \exists R.\neg C \ .
\end{aligned}
$$

With $nnf(C)$ we denote the negation normal form of C, obtained by applying the rules above.

Next, as for the fuzzy propositional case (see Equation (8.62)), we define ϵ as half of the minimal absolute difference among the values in $\bar{N}^{KB}$. That is,

$$
\epsilon = \min\{d/2 \mid n, m \in \bar{N}^{KB}, d = |n - m|\} \ . \tag{10.13}
$$

Now we have that the analogue of Proposition 55

Proposition 74 ([395]). *Let $\mathcal{K}$ be a fuzzy KB in SFL. Then for $n > 0$ and $0 < n_1 \le 0.5 < n_2 \le 1$*

$$
\begin{aligned}
\mathcal{K} &\models \langle a{:}C, n \rangle & \text{iff} & \quad \mathcal{K} \cup \{\langle a{:}\neg C, 1 - n + \epsilon \rangle\} \text{ is not satisfiable} \\
\mathcal{K} &\models \langle C \sqsubseteq D, n \rangle & \text{iff} & \quad \mathcal{K} \cup \{\langle a{:}C \sqcap \neg D), 1 - n + \epsilon \rangle\} \text{ is not satisfiable} \\
\mathcal{K} &\models C \tilde{\sqsubseteq} D & \text{iff} & \quad \mathcal{K} \cup \{\langle a{:}C, n \rangle\} \models \langle a{:}D, n \rangle \text{ for } m \in \{n_1, n_2\} \\
\mathcal{K} &\models A \tilde{=} C & \text{iff} & \quad \mathcal{K} \models A \tilde{\sqsubseteq} C \text{ and } \mathcal{K} \models C \tilde{\sqsubseteq} A \ .
\end{aligned}
$$

Proposition 74, like for the fuzzy propositional case and contrary to the usual analytical fuzzy tableau methods such as [384, 387, 389, 390, 395, 397, 405], allows us now to use an analytical tableau procedure to decide the KB satisfiability problem and the entailment problem without requiring the use of fuzzy statements of the form $\langle \alpha \bullet n \rangle$ with $\bullet \in \{\le, <, >\}$, which simplifies the calculus.

Now, we try to construct a finite fuzzy model $\mathcal{I}$ of $\mathcal{K}$ via a tableau algorithm. Essentially, the tableau algorithm is a terminating algorithm that, starting from an ABox, tries to build a clash-free forest of trees (called completion-forest). If it succeeds then $\mathcal{K}$ is satisfiable and from the forest a model can be built. Otherwise, $\mathcal{K}$ is not satisfiable.

The Case with Empty TBox. As for the crisp case (see Section 4.4.1), we start with the case of an empty TBox. So, Let $\mathcal{K}$ be a KB in NNF with empty TBox. A *completion-forest* $\mathcal{F}$ for $\mathcal{K}$ is a collection of trees whose distinguished roots are arbitrarily connected by edges. Each node v is labelled with a set $\mathcal{L}(v)$ of expressions $\langle C, n \rangle$, where $n \in (0, 1]$ and $C \in sub(\mathcal{K})$. The intuition here is that v is an instance of C to degree greater or equal than n. We will always assume that there cannot be $\langle C, n \rangle \in \mathcal{L}(v)$ and $\langle C, m \rangle \in \mathcal{L}(v)$ with $m > n$. If there are, the expression with the lower degree is dropped from $\mathcal{L}(v)$.

Each edge $\langle v, w \rangle$ is labelled with a set $\mathcal{L}(\langle v, w \rangle)$ of expressions $\langle R, n \rangle$, where R occurs in $\mathcal{K}$, indicating that $\langle v, w \rangle$ and instance of R to degree greater than or equal to n. As for $\mathcal{L}(v)$, we will always assume that there cannot be $\langle R, n \rangle \in \mathcal{L}(\langle v, w \rangle)$ and $\langle R, m \rangle \in \mathcal{L}(\langle v, w \rangle)$ with $m > n$. If there are, the expression with the lower degree is dropped from $\mathcal{L}(\langle v, w \rangle)$.

If nodes v and w are connected by an edge $\langle v, w \rangle$ with $\langle R, n \rangle \in \mathcal{L}(\langle v, w \rangle)$ then w is called an R_n-*successor* of v and v is called an R_n-*predecessor* of w. *Ancestor* is the transitive closure of *predecessor*, where we omit the degrees.

For a node v, $\mathcal{L}(v)$ is said to contain a *clash* iff $\mathcal{L}(v)$ contains either

- an expression $\langle \bot, n \rangle$ with $n > 0$; or

- a pair of expressions $\langle A, n \rangle$ and $\langle \neg A, m \rangle$ with $n > 1 - m$.

A completion-forest is called *clash-free* iff none of its nodes contain a clash; it is called *complete* iff none of the expansion rules in Table 10.6 is applicable.

Now, the algorithm initializes a forest $\mathcal{F}$ as follows:

- $\mathcal{F}$ contains a root node v_0^i, for each individual a_i occurring in $\mathcal{A}$;

- $\mathcal{F}$ contains an edge $\langle v_0^i, v_0^j \rangle$, for each $\langle (a_i, a_j){:}R, n \rangle \in \mathcal{A}$;

- for each $\langle a_i{:}C, n \rangle \in \mathcal{A}$, we add $\langle C, n \rangle$ to $\mathcal{L}(v_0^i)$;

- for each $\langle (a_i, a_j){:}R, n \rangle \in \mathcal{A}$, we add $\langle R, n \rangle$ to $\mathcal{L}(\langle v_0^i, v_0^j \rangle)$.

Then the completion-forest $\mathcal{F}$ is then expanded by repeatedly applying the completion rules described in Table 10.6 and answers "$\mathcal{K}$ is satisfiable" iff the completion rules can be applied in such a way that they yield a complete and clash-free completion-forest. Note that it is relatively easy to build a model $\mathcal{I}$ from a complete and clash-free completion-forest. Informally,

- the domain of $\mathcal{I}$ are the nodes of the forest;

- the interpretation of individual a_i is v_0^i;

- if $\langle R, n \rangle \in \mathcal{L}(\langle v, w \rangle)$, then $R^{\mathcal{I}}(v, w) = n$;

- if $\langle A, n \rangle \in \mathcal{L}(v)$, then $A^{\mathcal{I}}(v) = n$.

TABLE 10.6: The tableau rules for fuzzy $\mathcal{ALC}$ with empty TBox.

($\sqcap$). If *(i)* $\langle C_1 \sqcap C_2, n \rangle \in \mathcal{L}(v)$ and *(ii)* $\{\langle C_1, n \rangle, \langle C_2, n \rangle\} \not\subseteq \mathcal{L}(v)$, then add $\langle C_1, n \rangle$ and $\langle C_2, n \rangle$ to $\mathcal{L}(v)$.

($\sqcup$). If *(i)* $\langle C_1 \sqcup C_2, n \rangle \in \mathcal{L}(v)$ and *(ii)* $\{\langle C_1, n \rangle, \langle C_2, n \rangle\} \cap \mathcal{L}(v) = \emptyset$, then add some $\langle C, n \rangle \in \{\langle C_1, n \rangle, \langle C_2, n \rangle\}$ to $\mathcal{L}(v)$.

($\forall$). If *(i)* $\langle \forall R.C, n \rangle \in \mathcal{L}(v)$, *(ii)* $\langle R, m \rangle \in \mathcal{L}(\langle v, w \rangle)$, $m > 1 - n$, and *(iii)* $\langle C, n \rangle \notin \mathcal{L}(w)$, then add $\langle C, n \rangle$ to $\mathcal{L}(w)$.

($\exists$). If *(i)* $\langle \exists R.C, n \rangle \in \mathcal{L}(v)$ and *(ii)* there is no $\langle R, n_1 \rangle \in \mathcal{L}(\langle v, w \rangle)$ with $\langle C, n_2 \rangle \in \mathcal{L}(w)$ such that $\min(n_1, n_2) \geq n$, then create a new node w, add $\langle R, n \rangle$ to $\mathcal{L}(\langle v, w \rangle)$ and add $\langle C, n \rangle$ to $\mathcal{L}(w)$.

Now, termination, soundness, and completeness of the algorithm have been shown.

Proposition 75 ([395]). *For each knowledge base* $\mathcal{K} = \langle \emptyset, \mathcal{A} \rangle$,

1. *the tableau algorithm terminates;*

2. *if the expansion rules can be applied in such a way that they yield a complete and clash-free completion-forest, then* $\mathcal{K}$ *has a finite model;*

3. *if* $\mathcal{K}$ *has a model, then the expansion rules can be applied in such a way that they yield complete and clash-free completion-forest for* $\mathcal{K}$*;*

4. *the KB satisfiability problem is PSpace-complete [395].*

Example 35. *Consider a fuzzy analogue of Example 9:*

$$\mathcal{K} = \{\langle a{:}\forall R.A \sqcap \exists R.B, 0.9 \rangle, \langle (a,b){:}R, 0.8 \rangle, \langle (a,c){:}P, 0.7 \rangle\} \ .$$

$\mathcal{K}$ *is satisfiable as there is a clash-free completion-forest (see Figure 10.5). The model build from the forest is:*

- $\Delta^{\mathcal{I}} = \{a, b, c, x\}$;

- *the interpretation of individuals is the identity function;*

- $R^{\mathcal{I}}(a,b) = 0.8, R^{\mathcal{I}}(a,x) = 0.9, P^{\mathcal{I}}(a,c) = 0.7$;

- $A^{\mathcal{I}}(b) = A^{\mathcal{I}}(x) = B^{\mathcal{I}}(x) = 0.9$.

The Case of Acyclic TBox. We next extend the previous algorithm to the case of *acyclic* TBoxes.

Similarly to Section 4.4.1.2, we also present here a method, called *lazy unfolding*. To do so, we extend our calculus in Table 10.6 with the rules in Table 10.7.

As for Proposition 75, it can be shown that

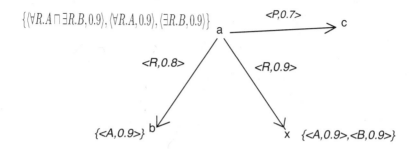

FIGURE 10.5: Clash-free complete completion-forest from fuzzy ABox.

Proposition 76. *For each knowledge base* $\mathcal{K} = \langle \mathcal{T}, \mathcal{A} \rangle$ *with acyclic* $\mathcal{T}$,

1. *the tableau algorithm terminates;*

2. *if the expansion rules can be applied in such a way that they yield a complete and clash-free completion-forest, then* $\mathcal{K}$ *has a finite model;*

3. *if* $\mathcal{K}$ *has a model, then the expansion rules can be applied in such a way that they yield a complete and clash-free completion-forest for* $\mathcal{K}$.

Example 36. *Consider Example 35, where we add*

$$B \sqsubseteq_{0.4} C$$

to $\mathcal{K}$. $\mathcal{K}$ *is satisfiable as there is a clash-free complete completion-forest (see Figure 10.6).*

TABLE 10.7: The tableau rules for fuzzy $\mathcal{ALC}$ with acyclic fuzzy KB.

($\sqsubseteq^A$) If $A \sqsubseteq_n C \in \mathcal{T}$, $\langle A, m \rangle \in \mathcal{L}(v)$ with $m > 1 - n$ and $\langle C, n \rangle \notin \mathcal{L}(v)$ then add $\langle C, n \rangle$ to $\mathcal{L}(v)$.

($\tilde{\sqsubseteq}^A$) If $A \tilde{\sqsubseteq} C \in \mathcal{T}$, $\langle A, n \rangle \in \mathcal{L}(v)$ and $\langle C, n \rangle \notin \mathcal{L}(v)$ then add $\langle C, n \rangle$ to $\mathcal{L}(v)$.

($=_1^A$) If $A =_n C \in \mathcal{T}$, $\langle A, m \rangle \in \mathcal{L}(v)$ with $m > 1 - n$ and $\langle C, n \rangle \notin \mathcal{L}(v)$ then add $\langle C, n \rangle$ to $\mathcal{L}(v)$.

($=_2^A$) If $A =_n C \in \mathcal{T}$, $\langle \neg A, m \rangle \in \mathcal{L}(v)$ with $m > 1 - n$ and $\langle nnf(\neg C), n \rangle \notin \mathcal{L}(v)$ then add $\langle nnf(\neg C), n \rangle$ to $\mathcal{L}(v)$.

($\tilde{=}_1^A$) If $A \tilde{=} C \in \mathcal{T}$, $\langle A, n \rangle \in \mathcal{L}(v)$ and $\langle C, n \rangle \notin \mathcal{L}(v)$ then add $\langle C, n \rangle$ to $\mathcal{L}(v)$.

($\tilde{=}_2^A$) If $A \tilde{=} C \in \mathcal{T}$, $\langle \neg A, n \rangle \in \mathcal{L}(v)$ and $\langle nnf(\neg C), n \rangle \notin \mathcal{L}(v)$ then add $\langle nnf(\neg C), n \rangle$ to $\mathcal{L}(v)$.

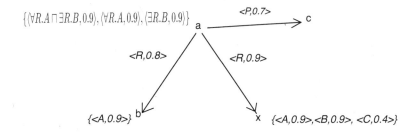

FIGURE 10.6: Clash-free and complete completion-forest from acyclic fuzzy KB.

The model built from the forest is:

- $\Delta^{\mathcal{I}} = \{a, b, c, x\}$;

- *the interpretation of individuals is the identity function;*

- $R^{\mathcal{I}}(a, b) = 0.8, R^{\mathcal{I}}(a, x) = 0.9, P^{\mathcal{I}}(a, c) = 0.7$;

- $A^{\mathcal{I}}(b) = A^{\mathcal{I}}(x) = B^{\mathcal{I}}(x) = 0.9, C^{\mathcal{I}}(x) = 0.4$.

The Case with General TBox. Eventually, we show here how we may deal with the case in which the GCIs in the TBox are of the general form $\langle C \sqsubseteq D, n \rangle$ and $C \tilde{\sqsubseteq} D$[9]. As we have seen in Remark 25, w.l.o.g. we may assume that the former GCIs have the form $\langle \top \sqsubseteq C', n \rangle$.

Like for the crisp case, to cope with the non-termination problem, a notion of *blocking* has to be introduced, which is the same as for the crisp case: we say that a node v is *directly blocked* iff none of its ancestors is blocked and there exists an ancestor w such that

$$\mathcal{L}(v) = \mathcal{L}(w) .$$

In this case we say that w *directly blocks* v. A node v is *indirectly blocked* iff one of its ancestors is blocked. Finally a node v is *blocked* iff it is not a root node and it is either directly or indirectly blocked.

Now, the calculus is as described above except that the rules are not applied to blocked nodes. Specifically, the rules are described in Table 10.8. As before, it can be shown that using the rules in Table 10.8

Proposition 77. *For each knowledge base $\mathcal{K} = \langle \mathcal{T}, \mathcal{A} \rangle$*

1. *the tableau algorithm terminates;*

2. *if the expansion rules can be applied in such a way that they yield a complete and clash-free completion-forest, then $\mathcal{K}$ has a finite model;*

---

[9]Axioms of the form $A \tilde{=} C$ are replaced with $A \tilde{\sqsubseteq} C$ and $C \tilde{\sqsubseteq} A$.

TABLE 10.8: The tableau rules for fuzzy $\mathcal{ALC}$ with GCIs.

($\sqcap$). If *(i)* $\langle C_1 \sqcap C_2, n \rangle \in \mathcal{L}(v)$, *(ii)* $\{\langle C_1, n \rangle, \langle C_2, n \rangle\} \not\subseteq \mathcal{L}(v)$, and *(iii)* node v is not indirectly blocked, then add $\langle C_1, n \rangle$ and $\langle C_2, n \rangle$ to $\mathcal{L}(v)$.

($\sqcup$). If *(i)* $\langle C_1 \sqcup C_2, n \rangle \in \mathcal{L}(v)$, *(ii)* $\{\langle C_1, n \rangle, \langle C_2, n \rangle\} \cap \mathcal{L}(v) = \emptyset$, and *(iii)* node v is not indirectly blocked, then add some $\langle C, n \rangle \in \{\langle C_1, n \rangle, \langle C_2, n \rangle\}$ to $\mathcal{L}(v)$.

($\forall$). If *(i)* $\langle \forall R.C, n \rangle \in \mathcal{L}(v)$, *(ii)* $\langle R, m \rangle \in \mathcal{L}(\langle v, w \rangle)$ with $m > 1 - n$, *(iii)* $\langle C, n \rangle \notin \mathcal{L}(w)$, and *(iv)* node v is not indirectly blocked, then add $\langle C, n \rangle$ to $\mathcal{L}(w)$.

($\exists$). If *(i)* $\langle \exists R.C, n \rangle \in \mathcal{L}(v)$, *(ii)* there is no $\langle R, n_1 \rangle \in \mathcal{L}(\langle v, w \rangle)$ with $\langle C, n_2 \rangle \in \mathcal{L}(w)$ such that $\min(n_1, n_2) \geq n$, and *(iii)* node v is not blocked, then create a new node w, add $\langle R, n \rangle$ to $\mathcal{L}(\langle v, w \rangle)$ and add $\langle C, n \rangle$ to $\mathcal{L}(w)$.

($\sqsubseteq$). If *(i)* $\langle \top \sqsubseteq D, n \rangle \in \mathcal{T}$, *(ii)* $\langle D, n \rangle \notin \mathcal{L}(v)$, and *(iii)* node v is not indirectly blocked, then add $\langle D, n \rangle$ to $\mathcal{L}(v)$.

($\tilde{\sqsubseteq}$). If *(i)* $C \tilde{\sqsubseteq} D \in \mathcal{T}$, *(ii)* for some $n \in N_+^{\mathcal{K}}$, $\{\langle nnf(\neg C), 1 - n + \epsilon \rangle, \langle D, n \rangle\} \cap \mathcal{L}(v) = \emptyset$, and *(iii)* node v is not indirectly blocked, then add E to $\mathcal{L}(v)$ for some $E \in \{\langle nnf(\neg C), 1 - n + \epsilon \rangle, \langle D, n \rangle\}$.

   3. if $\mathcal{K}$ has a model, then the expansion rules can be applied in such a way that they yield a complete and clash-free completion-forest for $\mathcal{K}$.

Example 37. *Consider a fuzzy variant of Example 12.*

$$\mathcal{K} = \{\langle a{:}A, 0.7 \rangle, \langle A \sqsubseteq \exists R.A, 0.6 \rangle\} \ .$$

$\mathcal{K}$ is satisfiable as there is a clash-free and complete completion-forest (see Figure 10.7). Note that node y is blocked by x.

   The model build from the forest is:

- $\Delta^{\mathcal{I}} = \{a, x\}$;

- *the interpretation of individuals is the identity function;*

- $R^{\mathcal{I}}(a, x) = R^{\mathcal{I}}(x, x) = 0.6$;

- $A^{\mathcal{I}}(a) = 0.7, A^{\mathcal{I}}(x) = 0.6$.

As for the crisp case, it is not our purpose to present here the tableau rules for more expressive languages of the fuzzy $\mathcal{AL}$ family.

   We refer the reader to, *e.g.*, [389]. However, let us note that besides adding a rule for each construct, the blocking condition is extended as well to a more sophisticated definition, as, *e.g.*, $\mathcal{SHIF}$ does not employ the finite model property anymore.

   Nevertheless, in Appendix H we recall the tableau calculus for fuzzy $\mathcal{SHIF}_g$ under SFL.

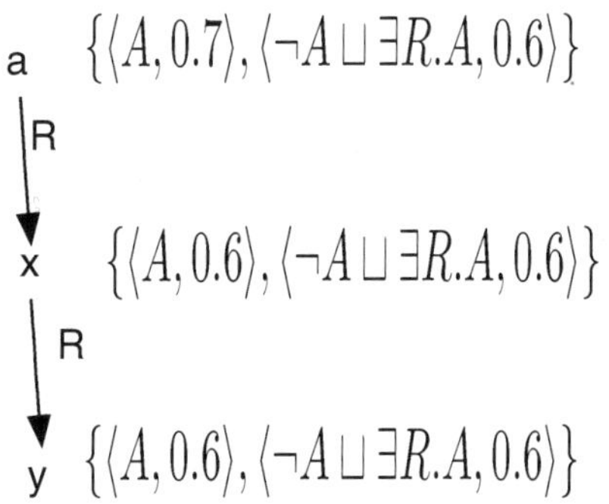

$$a \quad \{\langle A, 0.7\rangle, \langle \neg A \sqcup \exists R.A, 0.6\rangle\}$$

$$\downarrow R$$

$$x \quad \{\langle A, 0.6\rangle, \langle \neg A \sqcup \exists R.A, 0.6\rangle\}$$

$$\downarrow R$$

$$y \quad \{\langle A, 0.6\rangle, \langle \neg A \sqcup \exists R.A, 0.6\rangle\}$$

FIGURE 10.7: Clash-free and complete completion-forest from fuzzy $\mathcal{ALC}$ KB.

10.6.1.3 Fuzzy Tableau for Finite-Valued DLs

We have seen in Section 8.2.2.3, Algorithm 5, that in fact an analytical fuzzy tableau for propositional fuzzy logic can be adapted to the case in which the truth combination functions are defined via arbitrary matrix over a finite-truth space such as $L_n = \{0, \frac{1}{n-1}, \ldots, \frac{n-2}{n-1}, 1\}$ (see Section 8.1.7).

Next, we show that the tableau calculus illustrated in the previous Section 10.6.1.2 can be adapted to this case in an analogous way [73].

The tableau algorithm is quite similar than the one described for fuzzy $\mathcal{ALC}$ with GCIs, except that now all inference rules and the completion-forest initialization phase become non-deterministic.

Specifically, consider a fuzzy $\mathcal{ALC}$ KB with GCIs, truth-space $L_n = \{0, \frac{1}{n-1}, \ldots, \frac{n-2}{n-1}, 1\}$ and truth-combination functions $\otimes, \oplus, \Rightarrow$ and $\ominus$ defined over L_n.

The notions of completion-forest, R_n-successor, R_n-predecessor, and ancestor is as for Section 10.6.1.2. However, we will interpret $\langle C, n\rangle \in \mathcal{L}(v)$ as a statement of the form: "v is an instance of C to degree *exactly equal to* n". The case for role expressions $\langle R, n\rangle \in \mathcal{L}(\langle v, w\rangle)$ is similar. The notion of clash is adjusted as for the fuzzy propositional case and is as follows. For nodes v and w,

- $\mathcal{L}(v)$ is said to contain a *clash* iff $\mathcal{L}(v)$ contains either

  - an expression $\langle \bot, n\rangle$ with $n > 0$; or
  - a pair of expressions $\langle A, n\rangle$ and $\langle A, m\rangle$ with $n \neq m$;

- $\mathcal{L}(\langle v, w\rangle)$ is said to contain a *clash* iff $\mathcal{L}(v)$ contains

  - a pair of expressions $\langle R, n\rangle$ and $\langle R, m\rangle$ with $n \neq m$.

Now, the algorithm initializes a forest $\mathcal{F}$ *non-deterministically* as follows:

- $\mathcal{F}$ contains a root node v_0^i, for each individual a_i occurring in $\mathcal{A}$;

- $\mathcal{F}$ contains an edge $\langle v_0^i, v_0^j \rangle$, for each $\langle (a_i, a_j):R, n \rangle \in \mathcal{A}$;

- for each $\langle a_i:C, m \rangle \in \mathcal{A}$, we add $\langle C, m' \rangle$ to $\mathcal{L}(v_0^i)$ for *some* $m' \in L_n$ with $m' \geq m$;

- for each $\langle (a_i, a_j):R, m \rangle \in \mathcal{A}$, we add $\langle R, m' \rangle$ to $\mathcal{L}(\langle v_0^i, v_0^j \rangle)$ for *some* $m' \in L_n$ with $m' \geq m$.

Then the completion-forest $\mathcal{F}$ is then expanded by repeatedly applying the completion rules described in Table 10.9 and answers "$\mathcal{K}$ is satisfiable" iff the completion rules can be applied in such a way that they yield a complete and clash-free completion-forest. It can be shown that using the rules in Table 10.9

Proposition 78 ([73]). *For each knowledge base $\mathcal{K} = \langle \mathcal{T}, \mathcal{A} \rangle$ with a finitely valued truth space L_n*

1. *the tableau algorithm terminates;*

2. *if the expansion rules can be applied in such a way that they yield a complete and clash-free completion-forest, then $\mathcal{K}$ has a finite model;*

3. *if $\mathcal{K}$ has a model, then the expansion rules can be applied in such a way that they yield a complete and clash-free completion-forest for $\mathcal{K}$.*

Of course, the method can be adapted to any truth space as well, as long as it is finite.

In Appendix H.2 we extend it to fuzzy $\mathcal{SHIF}_g$.

10.6.1.4   Operational Research-based Fuzzy Tableau

Similarly as we have seen in Section 8.2.2.2 and Appendix F for the fuzzy propositional case, an important and application oriented approach for reasoning with fuzzy DLs is based on Operational Research (OR) [47, 48, 51, 52, 53, 55, 58, 59, 62, 398, 399, 419, 418, 425, 426].

We will illustrate here the method under SFL. We refer to, *e.g.*, [47, 53, 399] to other semantics.

As for the analytical tableau case, we will assume here that all concepts are in NNF.

The Case with Empty TBox. In the following, we will assume that the TBox in a knowledge base is empty. Like the tableau algorithm presented for crisp DLs such as [206, 209] our algorithm works on *completion-forests* since an ABox might contain several individuals with arbitrary roles connecting them. Our method combines appropriate DL tableaux rules, which constructs

TABLE 10.9: The tableau rules for finitely valued fuzzy $\mathcal{ALC}$ with GCIs.

($\sqcap$). If *(i)* $\langle C_1 \sqcap C_2, m \rangle \in \mathcal{L}(v)$, *(ii)* there are $m_1, m_2 \in L_n$ such that $m_1 \otimes m_2 = m$ with $\{\langle C_1, m_1 \rangle, \langle C_2, m_2 \rangle\} \not\subseteq \mathcal{L}(v)$, and *(iii)* node v is not indirectly blocked, then add $\langle C_1, m_1 \rangle$ and $\langle C_2, m_2 \rangle$ to $\mathcal{L}(v)$.

($\sqcup$). If *(i)* $\langle C_1 \sqcup C_2, m \rangle \in \mathcal{L}(v)$, *(ii)* there are $m_1, m_2 \in L_n$ such that $m_1 \oplus m_2 = m$ with $\{\langle C_1, m_1 \rangle, \langle C_2, m_2 \rangle\} \cap \mathcal{L}(v) = \emptyset$, and *(iii)* node v is not indirectly blocked, then add some $\langle C, k \rangle \in \{\langle C_1, m_1 \rangle, \langle C_2, m_2 \rangle\}$ to $\mathcal{L}(v)$.

($\neg$). If *(i)* $\langle \neg C, m \rangle \in \mathcal{L}(v)$ with $\langle C, \ominus m \rangle \not\in \mathcal{L}(v)$ and *(ii)* node v is not indirectly blocked, then add $\langle C, \ominus m \rangle$ to $\mathcal{L}(v)$.

($\to$). If *(i)* $\langle C_1 \to C_2, m \rangle \in \mathcal{L}(v)$, *(ii)* there are $m_1, m_2 \in L_n$ such that $m_1 \Rightarrow m_2 = m$ and $\{\langle C_1, m_1 \rangle, \langle C_2, m_2 \rangle\} \not\subseteq \mathcal{L}(v)$, and *(iii)* node v is not indirectly blocked, then add $\langle C_1, m_1 \rangle$ and $\langle C_2, m_2 \rangle$ to $\mathcal{L}(v)$.

($\forall$). If *(i)* $\langle \forall R.C, m \rangle \in \mathcal{L}(v)$, *(ii)* $\langle R, m_1 \rangle \in \mathcal{L}(\langle v, w \rangle)$, *(iii)* there is $m_2 \in L_n$ such that $m_1 \Rightarrow m_2 \geq m$ with $\langle C, m_2 \rangle \not\in \mathcal{L}(w)$, and *(iv)* node v is not indirectly blocked, then add $\langle C, m_2 \rangle$ to $\mathcal{L}(w)$.

($\exists$). If *(i)* $\langle \exists R.C, m \rangle \in \mathcal{L}(v)$, *(ii)* there are $m_1, m_2 \in L_n$ such that $m_1 \otimes m_2 = m$, *(iii)* there is no $\langle R, m_1 \rangle \in \mathcal{L}(\langle v, w \rangle)$ with $\langle C, m_2 \rangle \in \mathcal{L}(w)$, and *(iv)* node v is not blocked, then create a new node w, add $\langle R, m_1 \rangle$ to $\mathcal{L}(\langle v, w \rangle)$ and add $\langle C, m_2 \rangle$ to $\mathcal{L}(w)$.

($\exists'$). If *(i)* $\langle \exists R.C, m \rangle \in \mathcal{L}(v)$, *(ii)* $\langle R, m_1 \rangle \in \mathcal{L}(\langle v, w \rangle)$, *(iii)* there is $m_2 \in L_n$ such that $m_1 \otimes m_2 \leq m$ with $\langle C, m_2 \rangle \not\in \mathcal{L}(w)$, and *(iv)* node v is not indirectly blocked, then add $\langle C, m_2 \rangle$ to $\mathcal{L}(w)$.

($\forall'$). If *(i)* $\langle \forall R.C, m \rangle \in \mathcal{L}(v)$, *(ii)* there are $m_1, m_2 \in L_n$ such that $m_1 \Rightarrow m_2 = m$, *(iii)* there is no $\langle R, m_1 \rangle \in \mathcal{L}(\langle v, w \rangle)$ with $\langle C, m_2 \rangle \in \mathcal{L}(w)$, and *(iv)* node v is not blocked, then create a new node w, add $\langle R, m_1 \rangle$ to $\mathcal{L}(\langle v, w \rangle)$ and add $\langle C, m_2 \rangle$ to $\mathcal{L}(w)$.

($\sqsubseteq$). If *(i)* $\langle C \sqsubseteq D, m \rangle \in \mathcal{T}$, *(ii)* there are $m_1, m_2 \in L_n$ such that $m_1 \Rightarrow m_2 \geq m$, *(iii)* $\{\langle C, m_1 \rangle, \langle D, m_2 \rangle\} \not\subseteq \mathcal{L}(v)$, and *(iv)* node v is not indirectly blocked, then add $\langle C, m_1 \rangle$ and $\langle D, m_2 \rangle$ to $\mathcal{L}(v)$.

($\tilde{\sqsubseteq}$). If *(i)* $C \tilde{\sqsubseteq} D \in \mathcal{T}$, *(ii)* there are $m_1, m_2 \in L_n$ such that $m_1 \leq m_2$, *(iii)* $\{\langle C, m_1 \rangle, \langle D, m_2 \rangle\} \not\subseteq \mathcal{L}(v)$, and *(iv)* node v is not indirectly blocked, then add $\langle C, m_1 \rangle$ and $\langle D, m_2 \rangle$ to $\mathcal{L}(v)$.

the completion-forest with methods developed have seen in Section 8.2.2.2 and Appendix F.

So, let $\mathcal{K}$ be a fuzzy KB with empty TBox. A *completion-forest* $\mathcal{F}$ for $\mathcal{K}$ is a collection of trees whose distinguished roots are arbitrarily connected by edges. Each node v is labelled with a set $\mathcal{L}(v)$ of concepts $C \in sub(\mathcal{K})$. If $C \in \mathcal{L}(v)$ then we consider a variable $x_{v:C}$. The intuition here is that v is an instance of C to degree equal or greater than the value of the variable $x_{v:C}$. Each edge $\langle v, w \rangle$ is labelled with a set $\mathcal{L}(\langle v, w \rangle)$ of roles $R \in \mathbf{R}_{\mathcal{K}}$ and if $R \in \mathcal{L}(\langle v, w \rangle)$ then we consider a variable $x_{(v,w):R}$ representing the degree of being $\langle v, w \rangle$ and instance of R.

If nodes v and w are connected by an edge $\langle v, w \rangle$ with $R \in \mathcal{L}(\langle v, w \rangle)$ then w is called an *R-successor* of v.

The forest has associated a set $\mathcal{C}_{\mathcal{F}}$ of constraints c of the form $l \leq l', l = l'$, where l, l' are linear expressions. Essentially the constraints are added by the application of rules to concept expressions to reflect the semantics of the connectives. Intuitively, if for a node v, $\mathcal{L}(v)$ contains $C_1 \sqcup C_2$ and $\mathcal{C}_{\mathcal{F}}$ contains $x_{v:C_1 \sqcup C_2} \geq 0.7$ (dictating that v is an instance of $C_1 \sqcup C_2$ to degree at least 0.7), then the application of the ($\sqcup$) rule to $C_1 \sqcup C_2$ will add the concepts C_1 and C_2 to $\mathcal{L}(v)$ and the constraints, encoding $x_{v:C_1} \oplus x_{v:C_2} \geq x_{v:C_1 \sqcup C_2}$, to $\mathcal{C}_{\mathcal{F}}$. Any assignment to the variables that satisfies these constraints, guarantees then also that indeed v is an instance of $C_1 \sqcup C_2$ to degree at least 0.7.

We refer the reader to Section 8.2.2.2 and Appendix F for the encoding of the truth combination functions. In what follows, we will be using the expressions $z \leq x_1 \oplus x_2$, $z \leq x_1 \otimes x_2$ and $z \geq x_1 \otimes x_2$ both to denote the inequality with respect to a t-norm (t-conorm) operation and the set of constraints they are equivalent to.

Now, given $\mathcal{K} = \langle \emptyset, \mathcal{A} \rangle$, the algorithm initializes a forest $\mathcal{F}$ as follows:

- $\mathcal{F}$ contains a root node v_0^i, for each individual a_i occurring in $\mathcal{A}$;

- $\mathcal{F}$ contains an edge $\langle v_0^i, v_0^j \rangle$, for each assertion axiom $\langle (a_i, a_j) : R, n \rangle \in \mathcal{A}$;

- for each $\langle a_i : C, n \rangle \in \mathcal{A}$, we add both C to $\mathcal{L}(v_0^i)$ and $x_{v_0^i:C} \geq n$ to $\mathcal{C}_{\mathcal{F}}$;

- for each $\langle (a_i, a_j) : R, n \rangle \in \mathcal{A}$, we add both R to $\mathcal{L}(\langle v_0^i, v_0^j \rangle)$ and $x_{(v_0^i, v_0^j):R} \geq n$ to $\mathcal{C}_{\mathcal{F}}$.

The completion-forest $\mathcal{F}$ is then expanded by repeatedly applying the completion rules described below. The completion-forest is *complete* when none of the completion rules is applicable. Then, the bMILP (bounded Mixed Integer Linear Programming) problem on the set of constraints $\mathcal{C}_{\mathcal{F}}$ is solved. We will show that if there is a solution to $\mathcal{C}_{\mathcal{F}}$ then $\mathcal{K}$ is satisfiable and vice versa.

We also assume a fixed rule application strategy as the order of rules below, such that the rule for ($\exists$) is applied as last. Also, all expressions in node labels are processed according to the order they are introduced into the completion-forest $\mathcal{F}$.

The rules for Ł-$\mathcal{ALC}$ are in Table 10.10.

Note that, despite that $|sub(\mathcal{K})|$ is $O(|\mathcal{K}|)$, we may well have that $|\mathcal{C}_{\mathcal{F}}|$ is $O(2^{|\mathcal{K}|})$, as the completion-forest $\mathcal{F}$ may contain exponentially many nodes.

TABLE 10.10: The OR-based tableau rules for fuzzy $\mathcal{ALC}$ with empty TBox.

(var). For variable $x_{v:C}$ occurring in $\mathcal{C}_{\mathcal{F}}$ add $x_{v:C} \in [0,1]$ to $\mathcal{C}_{\mathcal{F}}$. For variable $x_{(v,w):R}$ occurring in $\mathcal{C}_{\mathcal{F}}$ add $x_{(v,w):R} \in [0,1]$ to $\mathcal{C}_{\mathcal{F}}$.

$(\bot)$. If $\bot \in \mathcal{L}(v)$ then $\mathcal{C}_{\mathcal{F}} := \mathcal{C}_{\mathcal{F}} \cup \{x_{v:\bot} = 0\}$.

$(\top)$. If $\top \in \mathcal{L}(v)$ then $\mathcal{C}_{\mathcal{F}} := \mathcal{C}_{\mathcal{F}} \cup \{x_{v:\top} = 1\}$.

$(\bar{A})$. If $\neg A \in \mathcal{L}(v)$ then add A to $\mathcal{L}(v)$, and $\mathcal{C}_{\mathcal{F}} := \mathcal{C}_{\mathcal{F}} \cup \{x_{v:A} \leq 1 - x_{v:\neg A}\}$.

$(\sqcap)$. If *(i)* $C_1 \sqcap C_2 \in \mathcal{L}(v)$ and *(ii)* the rule has not been already applied to this concept, then add C_1 and C_2 to $\mathcal{L}(v)$, and $\mathcal{C}_{\mathcal{F}} := \mathcal{C}_{\mathcal{F}} \cup \{x_{v:C_1} \otimes x_{v:C_2} \geq x_{v:C_1 \sqcap C_2}\}$.

$(\sqcup)$. If *(i)* $C_1 \sqcup C_2 \in \mathcal{L}(v)$ and *(ii)* the rule has not been already applied to this concept, then add C_1 and C_2 to $\mathcal{L}(v)$, and $\mathcal{C}_{\mathcal{F}} := \mathcal{C}_{\mathcal{F}} \cup \{x_{v:C_1} \oplus x_{v:C_2} \geq x_{v:C_1 \sqcup C_2}\}$.

$(\forall)$. If *(i)* $\forall R.C \in \mathcal{L}(v)$, $R \in \mathcal{L}(\langle v, w \rangle)$ and *(ii)* the rule has not been already applied to this concept, then add C to $\mathcal{L}(w)$, and $\mathcal{C}_{\mathcal{F}} := \mathcal{C}_{\mathcal{F}} \cup \{x_{w:C} \geq x_{v:\forall R.C} \otimes x_{(v,w):R}\}$.

$(\exists)$. If *(i)* $\exists R.C \in \mathcal{L}(v)$ and *(ii)* the rule has not been already applied to this concept, then create a new node w, add R to $\mathcal{L}(\langle v, w \rangle)$, add C to $\mathcal{L}(w)$, and $\mathcal{C}_{\mathcal{F}} := \mathcal{C}_{\mathcal{F}} \cup \{x_{(v,w):R} \otimes x_{w:C} \geq x_{v:\exists R.C}\}$.

Indeed, consider a knowledge base containing only the assertion α

$$a{:}\exists R.C_1^1 \sqcap \exists R.C_2^1 \sqcap$$
$$\forall R.(\exists R.C_1^2 \sqcap \exists R.C_2^2 \sqcap$$
$$\forall R.(\exists R.C_1^3 \sqcap \exists R.C_2^3 \sqcap$$
$$\dots$$
$$\forall R.(\exists R.C_1^n \sqcap \exists R.C_2^n)\dots) .$$

It is not difficult to see that the completion-forest $\mathcal{F}$ is a binary tree of depth n consisting of $O(2^n)$ nodes and that $\mathcal{C}_{\mathcal{F}}$ contains both $O(2^n)$ variables taking values in $\{0,1\}$ as well as $O(2^n)$ variables taking values in $[0,1]$. In determining whether a MILP problem has a solution is an NP-complete problem [216] we get an NexpTime upper bound for the satisfiability problem (guess the assignment to the binary variables and solve the system of linear in-equations in exponential time).

Now, it can be shown that

Proposition 79 ([53]). *For each knowledge base $\mathcal{K} = \langle \emptyset, \mathcal{A} \rangle$,*

1. the tableau algorithm terminates;

2. *if the expansion rules can be applied to a knowledge base* $\mathcal{K} = \langle \emptyset, \mathcal{A} \rangle$
   such that they yield a complete completion-forest $\mathcal{F}$ *such that* $\mathcal{C}_{\mathcal{F}}$ *has a
   solution, then* $\mathcal{K}$ *has a (finite) model;*

3. *if a knowledge base* $\mathcal{K} = \langle \emptyset, \mathcal{A} \rangle$ *has a (finite) model, then the application
   of the expansion rules yields a complete completion-forest for* $\mathcal{K}$ *such
   that* $\mathcal{C}_{\mathcal{F}}$ *has a solution.*

Example 38. *Consider Example 35. A complete completion-forest* $\mathcal{F}$ *is as for
the crisp case (see Figure 4.2). The constraint set* $\mathcal{C}_{\mathcal{F}}$ *contains the following
inequations:*

$$x_{a:\forall R.A \sqcap \exists R.B} \geq 0.9,$$
$$x_{(a,b):R} \geq 0.8,$$
$$x_{(a,c):P} \geq 0.7,$$
$$x_{a:\forall R.A} \otimes x_{a:\exists R.B} \geq x_{a:\forall R.A \sqcap \exists R.B} \,,$$
$$x_{b:A} \geq x_{a:\forall R.A} \otimes x_{(a,b):R} \,,$$
$$x_{(a,x):R} \otimes x_{x:B} \geq x_{a:\exists R.B} \,,$$
$$x_{x:A} \geq x_{a:\forall R.A} \otimes x_{(a,x):R} \,,$$

from which we may build, e.g., the same model as in Example 35.

The Case of Acyclic TBox. We next extend the previous algorithm to the
case of *acyclic* TBoxes.

Similarly to the analytical fuzzy tableau case, we present here the method
based on lazy unfolding. We recall that $A \sqsubseteq_n C$ is the same as $\langle \top \sqsubseteq A \rightarrow C, n \rangle$
and $A =_n C$ is the same as $\langle \top \sqsubseteq A \leftrightarrow C, n \rangle$ (note that $A \rightarrow C \equiv \neg A \sqcup C$ and
$A \leftrightarrow C \equiv ((A \rightarrow C) \sqcap (C \rightarrow A)))$ and, thus, as we have seen in Remark 25,
w.l.o.g. we may assume that the GCIs in an acyclic TBox have the form
$\langle \top \sqsubseteq D, n \rangle$, where D is of the form $A \rightarrow C$ or $A \leftrightarrow C$.

Now, we extend our calculus in Table 10.10 with the rules in Table 10.11.
As for Proposition 79, it can be shown that

Proposition 80 ([53]). *For each knowledge base* $\mathcal{K} = \langle \mathcal{T}, \mathcal{A} \rangle$ *with acyclic* $\mathcal{T}$,

1. *the tableau algorithm terminates;*

2. *if the expansion rules can be applied to a knowledge base* $\mathcal{K} = \langle \mathcal{T}, \mathcal{A} \rangle$
   such that they yield a complete completion-forest $\mathcal{F}$ *such that* $\mathcal{C}_{\mathcal{F}}$ *has a
   solution, then* $\mathcal{K}$ *has a (finite) model;*

3. *if a knowledge base* $\mathcal{K} = \langle \mathcal{T}, \mathcal{A} \rangle$ *has a (finite) model, then the application
   of the expansion rules yields a complete completion-forest for* $\mathcal{K}$ *such that
   $\mathcal{C}_{\mathcal{F}}$ *has a solution.*

TABLE 10.11: The OR-based tableau rules for fuzzy $\mathcal{ALC}$ with acyclic fuzzy KBs.

($\sqsubseteq_A$). Assume $\langle \top \sqsubseteq D, n \rangle \in \mathcal{T}$, D is of the form $A \to C$ or $A \leftrightarrow C$, v is a node to which this rule has not yet been applied and $A \in \mathcal{L}(v)$, then add D to $\mathcal{L}(v)$ and set $\mathcal{C}_{\mathcal{F}} := \mathcal{C}_{\mathcal{F}} \cup \{x_{v:D} \geq n\}$.

($\tilde{\sqsubseteq}^A$) If $A \tilde{\sqsubseteq} C \in \mathcal{T}$, v is a node to which this rule has not yet been applied and $A \in \mathcal{L}(v)$, then add C to $\mathcal{L}(v)$ and set $\mathcal{C}_{\mathcal{F}} := \mathcal{C}_{\mathcal{F}} \cup \{x_{v:A} \leq x_{v:C}\}$.

($\tilde{=}_1^A$) If $A \tilde{=} C \in \mathcal{T}$, v is a node to which this rule has not yet been applied and $A \in \mathcal{L}(v)$ then add C to $\mathcal{L}(v)$ and set $\mathcal{C}_{\mathcal{F}} := \mathcal{C}_{\mathcal{F}} \cup \{x_{v:A} = x_{v:C}\}$.

($\tilde{=}_2^A$) If $A \tilde{=} C \in \mathcal{T}$, v is a node to which this rule has not yet been applied and $\neg A \in \mathcal{L}(v)$ then add $nnf(\neg C)$ to $\mathcal{L}(v)$ and set $\mathcal{C}_{\mathcal{F}} := \mathcal{C}_{\mathcal{F}} \cup \{x_{v:\neg A} = x_{v:\neg C}\}$.

Example 39. *Note that by referring to Example 36, a complete completion-forest is as for Example 4.3 in which $\neg B$ is added to the node label of x. The set of constraints can be worked out easily from Example 36, by adding*

$$x_{x:\neg B \sqcup C} \geq 0.4 \ ,$$
$$x_{x:\neg B} \oplus x_{x:C} \geq x_{x:\neg B \sqcup C} \ ,$$
$$x_{x:B} \leq 1 - x_{x:\neg B} \ ,$$

from which we may build, e.g., the same model as in Example 36.

The Case with General TBox. Eventually, we show here how we may deal with the case in which the GCIs in the TBox are of the general form $\langle C \sqsubseteq D, n \rangle$ and $C \tilde{\sqsubseteq} D$[10]. As we have seen in Remark 25, w.l.o.g. we may assume that the former GCIs have the form $\langle \top \sqsubseteq C', n \rangle$.

Like for the crisp and analytical fuzzy table case, to cope with the non-termination problem, a notion of *blocking* has to be introduced, which is the same as for the crisp case: we say that a node v is *directly blocked* iff none of its ancestors are blocked and there exists an ancestor w such that

$$\mathcal{L}(v) = \mathcal{L}(w) \ .$$

In this case we say that w *directly blocks* v. A node v is *indirectly blocked* iff one of its ancestors is blocked. Finally a node v is *blocked* iff it is not a root node and it is either directly or indirectly blocked.

---

[10]Axioms of the form $A \tilde{=} C$ are replaced with $A \tilde{\sqsubseteq} C$ and $C \tilde{\sqsubseteq} A$.

TABLE 10.12: The OR-based tableau rules for fuzzy $\mathcal{ALC}$ with GCIs.

(var). For variable $x_{v:C}$ occurring in $\mathcal{C_F}$ add $x_{v:C} \in [0,1]$ to $\mathcal{C_F}$. For variable $x_{(v,w):R}$ occurring in $\mathcal{C_F}$ add $x_{(v,w):R} \in [0,1]$ to $\mathcal{C_F}$.

$(\bot).$ If $\bot \in \mathcal{L}(v)$ then $\mathcal{C_F} := \mathcal{C_F} \cup \{x_{v:\bot} = 0\}$.

$(\top).$ If $\top \in \mathcal{L}(v)$ then $\mathcal{C_F} := \mathcal{C_F} \cup \{x_{v:\top} = 1\}$.

$(\bar{A}).$ If $\neg A \in \mathcal{L}(v)$ then add A to $\mathcal{L}(v)$, and $\mathcal{C_F} := \mathcal{C_F} \cup \{x_{v:A} \le 1 - x_{v:\neg A}\}$.

$(\sqcap).$ If *(i)* $C_1 \sqcap C_2 \in \mathcal{L}(v)$, *(ii)* the rule has not been already applied to this concept, and *(iii)* node v is not indirectly blocked, then add C_1 and C_2 to $\mathcal{L}(v)$, and $\mathcal{C_F} := \mathcal{C_F} \cup \{x_{v:C_1} \otimes x_{v:C_2} \ge x_{v:C_1 \sqcap C_2}\}$.

$(\sqcup).$ If *(i)* $C_1 \sqcup C_2 \in \mathcal{L}(v)$ and *(ii)* the rule has not been already applied to this concept, and *(iii)* node v is not indirectly blocked, then add C_1 and C_2 to $\mathcal{L}(v)$, and $\mathcal{C_F} := \mathcal{C_F} \cup \{x_{v:C_1} \oplus x_{v:C_2} \ge x_{v:C_1 \sqcup C_2}\}$.

$(\forall).$ If *(i)* $\forall R.C \in \mathcal{L}(v)$, $R \in \mathcal{L}(\langle v,w \rangle)$ and *(ii)* the rule has not been already applied to this concept, and *(iii)* node v is not indirectly blocked, then add C to $\mathcal{L}(w)$, and $\mathcal{C_F} := \mathcal{C_F} \cup \{x_{w:C} \ge x_{v:\forall R.C} \otimes x_{(v,w):R}\}$.

$(\exists).$ If *(i)* $\exists R.C \in \mathcal{L}(v)$ and *(ii)* the rule has not been already applied to this concept, and *(iii)* node v is not blocked then create a new node w, add R to $\mathcal{L}(\langle v,w \rangle)$, add C to $\mathcal{L}(w)$, and $\mathcal{C_F} := \mathcal{C_F} \cup \{x_{(v,w):R} \otimes x_{w:C} \ge x_{v:\exists R.C}\}$.

$(\sqsubseteq).$ If *(i)* $\langle \top \sqsubseteq D, n \rangle \in \mathcal{T}$, *(ii)* v is a node to which this rule has not yet been applied, and *(iii)* node v is not indirectly blocked, then add D to $\mathcal{L}(v)$ and set $\mathcal{C_F} := \mathcal{C_F} \cup \{x_{v:D} \ge n\}$.

$(\tilde{\sqsubseteq}).$ If *(i)* $C \tilde{\sqsubseteq} D \in \mathcal{T}$, *(ii)* v is a node to which this rule has not yet been applied, and *(iii)* node v is not indirectly blocked, then add $nnf(\neg C)$ and D to $\mathcal{L}(v)$ and set $\mathcal{C_F} := \mathcal{C_F} \cup \{x_{v:nnf(\neg C)} \oplus_l x_{v:D} \ge 1\}$.

Now, the calculus is as described above except that the rules are not applied to blocked nodes. Specifically, the rules are described in Table 10.12[11].

As before, it can be shown that using the rules in Table 10.12

Proposition 81. *For each knowledge base* $\mathcal{K} = \langle \mathcal{T}, \mathcal{A} \rangle$

1. *the tableau algorithm terminates;*

2. *if the expansion rules can be applied to a knowledge base* $\mathcal{K} = \langle \mathcal{T}, \mathcal{A} \rangle$

---

[11]Note that in the $(\tilde{\sqsubseteq})$ rule we use the fact that $C \tilde{\sqsubseteq} D$ is the same as $\top \sqsubseteq C \rightarrow_l D$, i.e., $\top \sqsubseteq \neg C \sqcup_l D$.

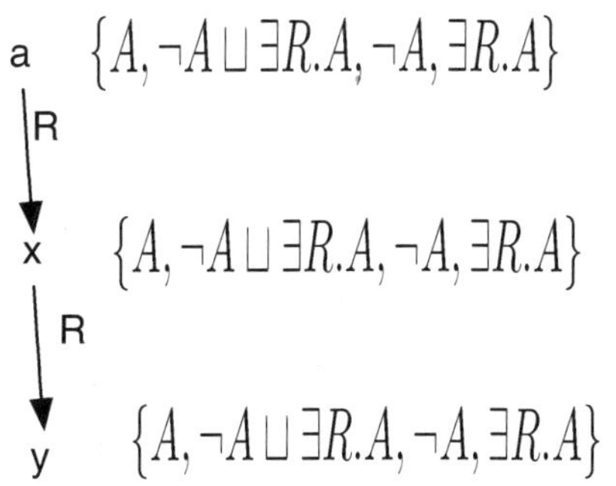

$$a \quad \{A, \neg A \sqcup \exists R.A, \neg A, \exists R.A\}$$

R

$$x \quad \{A, \neg A \sqcup \exists R.A, \neg A, \exists R.A\}$$

R

$$y \quad \{A, \neg A \sqcup \exists R.A, \neg A, \exists R.A\}$$

FIGURE 10.8: OR-based complete completion-forest from fuzzy $\mathcal{ALC}$ KB.

such that they yield a complete completion-forest $\mathcal{F}$ such that $\mathcal{C}_{\mathcal{F}}$ has a solution, then $\mathcal{K}$ has a (finite) model;

3. *if a knowledge base $\mathcal{K} = \langle \mathcal{T}, \mathcal{A} \rangle$ has a (finite) model, then the application of the expansion rules yields a complete completion-forest for $\mathcal{K}$ such that $\mathcal{C}_{\mathcal{F}}$ has a solution.*

In Appendix H we recall the OR-based tableau calculus for fuzzy $\mathcal{SHIF}_g$ under SFL.

Example 40. *Consider Example 37. A complete completion-forest is as in Figure 10.8.*

It can be verified that the constraint set contains

$$x_{a:A} \geq 0.7 ,$$

$$x_{a:\neg A \sqcup \exists R.A} \geq 0.6 ,$$
$$x_{a:\neg A} \oplus x_{a:\exists R.A} \geq x_{a:\neg A \sqcup \exists R.A} ,$$
$$x_{a:A} \leq 1 - x_{a:\neg A} ,$$
$$x_{(a,x):R} \otimes x_{x:A} \geq x_{a:\exists R.A} ,$$

$$x_{x:\neg A \sqcup \exists R.A} \geq 0.6 ,$$
$$x_{x:\neg A} \oplus x_{x:\exists R.A} \geq x_{x:\neg A \sqcup \exists R.A} ,$$
$$x_{x:A} \leq 1 - x_{x:\neg A} ,$$
$$x_{(x,y):R} \otimes x_{y:A} \geq x_{y:\exists R.A} ,$$

$$x_{y:\neg A \sqcup \exists R.A} \geq 0.6 ,$$
$$x_{y:\neg A} \oplus x_{y:\exists R.A} \geq x_{y:\neg A \sqcup \exists R.A} ,$$
$$x_{y:A} \leq 1 - x_{y:\neg A} .$$

It can be verified that from this constraint set one may construct, e.g., a model as in Example 37.

10.6.1.5   A Fuzzy Classification Algorithm

As for the crisp DL case (see Section 4.4.1.4), we provide here also an ontology classification algorithm for the fuzzy $\mathcal{AL}$-family.

So, let X be the finite set of concept names we want to classify. At first, let us fix a t-norm $\otimes$ on which the subsumption relationship is based on.

As in the fuzzy case, the subsumption relationship is graded, we are only interested in the case where the subsumption relationship is non-zero and maximal, *i.e.*, we consider a subsumption relationship of degree n among atoms A and B if $n = bed(\mathcal{K}, A \sqsubseteq B) \in (0,1]$. So, let $\leq^n \subseteq X \times X$ be such a graded subsumption relation among concept names, where $A \leq^n B$ iff $n = bed(\mathcal{K}, A \sqsubseteq B) \in (0,1]$.

The order is *reflexive* as for any $a \in X$

$$a \leq^1 a \ .$$

The order is also max-$\otimes$ *transitive* (or simply *transitive*), *i.e.*,

$$a \leq^k c \ , \text{ where } k = \max\{n \otimes m \mid \exists b \in X \text{ s.t. } a \leq^n b \leq^m c\} \ .$$

Therefore, we call $\leq^n$ also a *pre-order*. Note that max-$\otimes$ transitivity ensures that we cannot have $a \leq^n b$ and $a \leq^m b$ with $n \neq m$. Therefore, $\leq^{(\cdot)}$ can also be seen as a function $X \times X \to (0,1]$. Also, as for the classical case, $\leq^n$ is not antisymmetric and, thus, is not a partial order. Specifically, we may well have $a \leq^n b$ and $b \leq^m a$ with both $a \neq b$ and $n \neq m$.

We call $a, b \in X$ *equivalent* (denoted $a \equiv b$) iff both $a \leq^1 b$ and $b \leq^1 a$ hold. We call $a, b \in X$ *quasi-equivalent* (denoted $a \equiv^n_m b$) iff both $a \leq^n b$ and $b \leq^m a$ hold. Of course, equivalent concepts are quasi-equivalent ($n = m = 1$).

Remark 34. *Note that if* $a_1 \leq^{n_1} a_2 \leq^{n_2} \ldots \leq^{n_k} a_k \leq^{n_{k+1}} a_1$ *then not necessarily all the* a_i *are pairwise quasi-equivalent. In fact, consider* $a_1 \leq^{n_1} a_2 \leq^{n_2} a_3 \leq^{n_3} a_1$. *Then one may think that* $a_1 \equiv^{n_1}_{n_2 \otimes n_3} a_2$, *but this is true only if* $n_2 \otimes n_3 \neq 0$, *which is not always the case (e.g.,, $a_1 \leq^{0.1} a_2 \leq^{0.2} a_3 \leq^{0.3} a_1$ and Łukasiewicz t-norm). However, if $\otimes$ is strict then all the a_i are pairwise quasi-equivalent.*

With $eq(a)$ we denote the set of equivalent objects to a without a itself, *i.e.*,

$$eq(a) = \{b \mid a \equiv b, a \neq b\} \ .$$

while with $[a]$ we denote the equivalence class of a, *i.e.*,

$$[a] = \{b \mid a \equiv b\} \ .$$

Of course, $eq(a) = [a] \setminus \{a\}$ and $[a] = [b]$ if $a \equiv b$.

Remark 35. *Note that $c \leq^n a$ iff $c \leq^n x$ for all $x \in [a]$ and, similarly, $a \leq^n c$ iff $x \leq^n c$ for all $x \in [a]$.*

With $qe(a)$ we denote the set of quasi-equivalent objects to a without a itself, *i.e.*,

$$qe(a) = \{b \mid a \equiv^n_m b, a \neq b\} \ .$$

Remark 36. *Note that $b, c \in qe(a)$ does not imply that b and c are quasi-equivalent. However, in general $b \in qe(a)$ iff $a \in qe(b)$. But, if $\otimes$ is strict then b and c are quasi-equivalent (by Remark 34).*

Remark 37. *Note that if $c \not\leq^n a$ then it is still possible that $c \leq^m x$ for some $x \in qe(a)$ and, similarly, if $a \not\leq^n c$ then it is still possible that $x \leq^m c$ for some $x \in qe(a)$. However, if $\otimes$ is strict then $c \not\leq^n a$ iff $c \not\leq^m x$ for all $x \in qe(a)$ and similarly, $a \not\leq^n c$ then $x \leq^m c$ for all $x \in qe(a)$ (the cases $c \leq^n a$ and $a \leq^n c$ are similar).*

Given the previous observations, we are going to represent $\leq^{(\cdot)}$ via a possibly *cyclic* directed graph, where in a node we collect the equivalent concepts for a representative concept a, as for the classical case. There are cycles in the graph if quasi-equivalent concepts exist.

We call $\prec^{(\cdot)}$ a *precedence relation* of $\leq^{(\cdot)}$, iff $\prec^{(\cdot)}$ is the smallest relation such that

1. its reflexive, transitive closure is $\leq^{(\cdot)}$, except for pairs of equivalent objects, *i.e.*, pairs of objects a, b such that $a \equiv b$;

2. for quasi-equivalent concepts a, b, if $a \equiv^n_m b$ then $a \prec^n b$ and $b \prec^m a$.

Note that if $x \prec^k y$ then $x \leq^k y$ and there is no $z \notin qe(x) \cup qe(y)$ such that $x \leq^n z \leq^m y$ for some $n, m \in (0, 1]$.

$\prec$ is intended to represent the concept name relationships in a TBox $\mathcal{T}$, which we want to compute. If $x \leq^n y$ then x is a *successor* of y and y is a *predecessor* of x. Similarly, if $x \prec^n y$ then x is an *immediate successor* of y and y is an *immediate predecessor* of x.

A concept name *hierarchy graph* $\prec^{(\cdot)}$ is represented as a directed, labelled graph, where

- there is a node a for an equivalence class $[a], a \in X$, such that there are not two nodes a, b for equivalent concepts a and b;

- a node a is labelled with the set $eq(a)$ of logically equivalent concept names;

- there is an edge e from node b to node a, labelled with degree n if $a \prec^n b$.

In few words: a node a is a place holder for the equivalence class $[a]$, while an edge between a and b represents the subsumption relationship among a and b.

Note that $a \prec^n b$ iff $x \prec^m b$ for any equivalent $x \in eq(a)$. Similarly, $a \prec^n b$ iff $a \prec^m x$ for any equivalent $x \in eq(b)$.

A simple classification algorithm. Our algorithm proceeds similarly as for the classical case (see Section 4.4.1.4), but some special care has to be given to quasi-equivalent concepts and to cycles.

So, assume we have determined the precedence relation $\prec_i^{(\cdot)}$ for a set $X_i \subseteq X$ of concept names. Initially, $X_0 = \{\bot, \top\}$ and $\bot \prec_0^1 \top$. Consider a concept name $c \in X \setminus X_i$. We determine a method to compute the precedence relation $\prec_{i+1}^{(\cdot)}$ for set $X_{i+1} = X_i \cup \{c\}$. To do so, we compute c's immediate predecessors (procedure $topFuzzySearch$), TX_i^c as from Equation (4.4), and immediate successors (procedure $bottomFuzzySearch$), BX_i^c as from Equation (4.5), w.r.t. concept names in X_i and determine $\prec_{i+1}^{(\cdot)}$ as

$$\prec_{i+1}^{(\cdot)} = (S_1 \cup S_2 \cup S_3) \setminus S_4$$

where

$$
\begin{aligned}
S_1 &= \prec_i^{(\cdot)} \\
S_2 &= \{c \prec^n p \mid p \in TX_i^c\} \\
S_3 &= \{s \prec^n c \mid s \in BX_i^c\} \\
S_4 &= \{s \prec_i^k p \mid s \in BX_i^c, p \in TX_i^c, s, p \text{ not quasi-equivalent,} \\
&\qquad s \prec^n c \prec^m p \text{ and } k = n \otimes m\}\,.
\end{aligned}
$$

As for the classical case, there is a special case if c is equivalent to some $x \in X_i$, i.e., $c \leq^1 x$ and $x \leq^1 c$. In that case, $TX_i^c = \{x\}$ dictating $c \leq^n x$. In this case, if $n = 1$ we test also if $x \leq^1 c$. If the test is positive, c is equivalent to x and we add c to $eq(x)$.

The procedure $SimpleFuzzyClassify(\mathcal{K})$ is as follows:

SimpleFuzzyClassify($\mathcal{K}$)

1. Let
    (a) X be the set of concept names in $\mathcal{T}$
    (b) $X_0 := \{\bot, \top\}$. Create two nodes $\bot$ and $\top$ with empty label, and add an edge dictating $\bot \prec^1 \top$
2. If $(X \setminus X_i) = \emptyset$ return $\langle X_i, \prec_i \rangle$ and exit
3. Select $c \in X \setminus X_i$
4. Compute TX_i^c
5. If $TX_i^c = \{x\}$ and $c \leq^1 x$, then test $x \leq^1 c$ and if test is positive add c to $eq(x)$, and go to step 2.
6. Compute BX_i^c

7. Set

$$X_{i+1} \quad := \quad X_i \cup \{c\}$$

$$\prec_{i+1}^{(\cdot)} \quad = \quad (S_1 \cup S_2 \cup S_3) \setminus S_4$$

where

$$
\begin{aligned}
S_1 &= \prec_i^{(\cdot)} \\
S_2 &= \{c \prec^n p \mid p \in TX_i^c\} \\
S_3 &= \{s \prec^n c \mid s \in BX_i^c\} \\
S_4 &= \{s \prec_i^k p \mid s \in BX_i^c, p \in TX_i^c, s, p \text{ not quasi-equivalent}, \\
&\qquad s \prec^n c \prec^m p \text{ and } k = n \otimes m\} \ .
\end{aligned}
$$

Note that $c \prec^n p$ is given by the value $n := SubsFlag(c, p)$, where the variable $SubsFlag(., .)$ is updated in the procedure *enhancedFuzzyTopSubs*.

8. Increment i and go to step 2.

We next show how to compute TX_i^c and BX_i^c in the fuzzy setting. We first address TX_i^c. The other case is dual.

To start with, we assume that the elements in X_i are represented as a concept hierarchy, as explained previously. To determine TX_i^c, our procedure, called *topFuzzySearch*, starts with $\top \in X_i$ and visits the concept hierarchy X_i in a top-down breadth-first fashion. That is,

$$TX_i^c := topFuzzySearch(c, \top) \ .$$

Some care has to be given to cycles to avoid visiting the same node twice.

For each concept name $x \in X_i$ under consideration, it determines whether x has an immediate successor y satisfying $c \leq^n y$. If there are such successors, they are considered as well. Otherwise, x is added to the result list of the *topSearch* algorithm.

To avoid multiple visits of elements of X_i and multiple comparisons of the same element c, *topFuzzySearch* employs the label "visited" and another label $n \in [0, 1]$ if the subsumption test has been made and the degree of subsumption is n.

The procedure *topFuzzySearch* gets two concepts as input, the concept c, which has to be inserted and the element $x \in X_i$ currently under consideration. For x, we already know that $c \leq^n x$ and we look at direct successors of x w.r.t. $\prec_i^{(\cdot)}$. For each direct successor y of x, we have to check to which degree $n_y \in [0, 1]$, y subsumes c. This is done with the procedure *enhancedFuzzyTopSubs*. The direct successors y for which the test was positive ($n_y > 0$) are collected in a list *PosSucc*. If the list remains empty, x is added to the result list; otherwise *topFuzzySearch* is called for each positive successor, if not already visited.

The *topFuzzySearch*(c, x) algorithm is as follows:

topFuzzySearch(c,x)

1. Visited$(c, x) := true$
2. For all y with $y \prec_i^m x$ do: if *enhancedFuzzyTopSubs*(y, c) then $PosSucc := PosSucc \cup \{y\}$
3. If $PosSucc = \emptyset$ then $Result := \{x\}$ and go to step 5.
4. For all $y \in PosSucc$ do: if not Visited(c, y) then $Result := Result \cup$ *topFuzzySearch*(c, y)
5. Return *Result*.

The *enhancedFuzzyTopSubs*(y, c) algorithm is as follows:

enhancedFuzzyTopSubs(y,c)

1. If $SubsFlag(y, c) > 0$ then $Result := true$ and go to step 6.
2. If $SubsFlag(y, c) = 0$ then $Result := false$ and go to step 6.
3. If $\otimes$ is a strict t-norm then
   - if for all z with $y \prec_i^{m_y} z$ it holds that *enhancedFuzzyTopSubs*(z, c) and $c \leq^n y$ then $SubsFlag(y, c) := n, Result := true$ and go to step 6.
4. If $\otimes$ is not a strict t-norm and $c \leq^n y$ then $SubsFlag(y, c) := n, Result := true$ and go to step 6.
5. $SubsFlag(y, c) := 0, Result := false$
6. Return *Result*.

Note that in step 3, before testing the subsumption $c \leq^n y$ we apply the following heuristics using *negative information* [20, 22, 23], which works for strict t-norms only:

> If $\otimes$ is a strict t-norm and if for some predecessor z of y the test $c \leq^m z$ has failed, we can conclude that $c \not\leq^n y$ without performing the expensive test $c \leq^n y$. To gain maximum advantage, all predecessor of y should have been tested before the test is performed on y, which is obtained by recursive calls.

We next show how to compute BX_i^c, which is dual to the *topFuzzySearch* procedure and is performed by the *bottomFuzzySearch* algorithm. We have that

$$BX_i^c := bottomFuzzySearch(c, \perp)$$

bottomFuzzySearch(c,x)

1. Visited$(c, x) :=$ *true*

2. For all y with $x \prec_i^m y$ do: if *enhancedFuzzyBottomSubs*(c, y) then $PosPrec := PosPrec \cup \{y\}$

3. If $PosPrec = \emptyset$ then $Result := \{x\}$ and go to step 5.

4. For all $y \in PosPrec$ do: if not Visited(c, x) then $Result := Result \cup$ *bottomFuzzySearch*(c, y)

5. Return $Result$.

The *enhancedFuzzyBottomSubs*(c, y) algorithm is as follows:

enhancedFuzzyBottomSubs(c,y)

1. if $SubsFlag(c, y) > 0$ then $Result := true$ and go to step 6.

2. If $SubsFlag(c, y) = 0$ then $Result := false$ and go to step 6.

3. If $\otimes$ is a strict t-norm then

   • If for all z with $z \prec_i^{m_z} y$ it holds that *enhancedFuzzyBottomSubs*(c, z) and $y \leq^n c$ then $SubsFlag(c, y) := n$, $Result := true$ and go to step 6.

4. If $\otimes$ is not a strict t-norm and $y \leq^n c$ then $SubsFlag(c, y) := n$, $Result := true$ and go to step 6.

5. $SubsFlag(c, y) := 0$, $Result := false$

6. Return $Result$.

Note that in step 3, before testing the subsumption $y \leq^n c$ we apply the following heuristics using *negative information* [20, 22, 23], which works for strict t-norms only:

> If $\otimes$ is a strict t-norm and if for some successor z of y the test $z \leq^m c$ has failed, we can conclude that $y \not\leq^n c$ without performing the expensive test $y \leq^n c$. To gain maximum advantage, all successors of y should have been tested before the test is performed on y, which is obtained by recursive calls.

Example 41. *Consider a fuzzy analogue of Example 13 under product logic:*

$$\mathcal{K} = \{\langle C \sqsubseteq \exists R.D, 0.7 \rangle, \langle \exists R \sqsubseteq E, 0.8 \rangle\} .$$

Figure 10.9 illustrates a classification run.

Optimising fuzzy classification via told subsumers. We extend the notion of a told subsumer introduced in Section 4.4.1.4 to the fuzzy case. Consider a KB $\mathcal{K} = \langle \mathcal{T}, \mathcal{A} \rangle$.

1. If $\mathcal{T}$ contains $\langle A \sqsubseteq C, m \rangle$ then C is called a *told subsumer* of A to degree m, denoted $A \rightarrow_{ts}^m C$.

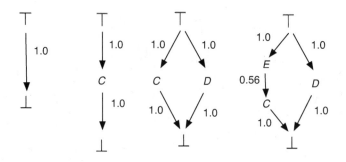

FIGURE 10.9: A fuzzy DL classification run.

2. If $\mathcal{T}$ contains $A = C$ then C is called a *told subsumer* of A to degree 1, denoted $A \rightarrow^1_{ts} C$.

3. If $\langle D \sqsubseteq C_1 \sqcap \ldots \sqcap C_n, m \rangle \in \mathcal{T}$ then for all i, $D \rightarrow^m_{ts} C_i$.

4. If $A = C_1 \sqcap \ldots \sqcap C_n \in \mathcal{T}$ then for all i, $A \rightarrow^1_{ts} C_i$.

5. If $\langle C_1 \sqcup \ldots \sqcup C_n \sqsubseteq D, m \rangle \in \mathcal{T}$ then for all i, $C_i \rightarrow^m_{ts} D$.

6. If $A = C_1 \sqcup \ldots \sqcup C_n \in \mathcal{T}$ then for all i, $C_i \rightarrow^1_{ts} A$.

7. $\rightarrow_{ts}$ is $\max - \otimes$-transitive.

We say that B is a *told subsumer* of A iff $A \rightarrow^n_{ts} B$ with $n > 0$. Note that if $\otimes$ is strict and $A \rightarrow^n_{ts} B$ then $n > 0$ and, thus, B is a told subsumer of A.

Remark 38. *Note that if $A \rightarrow^n_{ts} B$ with $n > 0$ we know that $\mathcal{K} \models \langle A \sqsubseteq B, n \rangle$. Unfortunately, n is not necessarily the maximal degree of subsumption, e.g., for*

$$\langle A \sqsubseteq B, 0.5 \rangle$$
$$\langle A \sqsubseteq C, 1 \rangle$$
$$\langle C \sqcap D \sqsubseteq B, 1 \rangle$$
$$D = \top$$

we have that $A \rightarrow^{0.5}_{ts} B$, though $\mathcal{K} \models \langle A \sqsubseteq B, 1 \rangle$.

Now, the analogous of Remark 7 is not true.

Remark 39. *Before classifying concept A, all of its told subsumers which have already been classified, and all their subsumers, can be marked as subsumers of A, though the maximal degree of subsumption may not be known, without the subsumption test. That is:*

if $A \rightarrow^n_{ts} B$ with $n > 0$ then we know that $A \leq^m B$ with $m \geq n$.

However, the analogous of Remark 8 is true.

Remark 40. *In procedure $SimpleFuzzyClassify$, in step 3, select concept $c \in X \setminus X_i$ only if all of its told subsumer have been classified. That is,*

$$\text{if } A \to_{ts}^n B \text{ with } n > 0 \text{ then classify } B \text{ before } A$$

Therefore, we get a preference order on the atoms in X.

Fuzzy acyclic KBs case. This is like the crisp case: consider an acyclic KB $\mathcal{K} = \langle \mathcal{T}, \mathcal{A} \rangle$. For acyclic KBs we may take advantage of the heuristics developed in the previous paragraph concerning told subsumers and the following remark that works for acyclic KBs only.

Remark 41. *Before classifying concept A, all of its told subsumers which have already been classified, and all their subsumers, can be marked as subsumers of A. Subsumption test for these atoms are, thus, unnecessary. That is, in the procedure $SimpleFuzzyClassify$, we have another initialization step:*

$$\text{if } A \to_{ts}^n B \text{ with } n > 0 \text{ then set } SubsFlag(B, A) = n.$$

So, for acyclic KBs if $A \to_{ts}^n B$ with $n > 0$ then $A \leq^n B$ holds.

Specifically, apply the $SimpleFuzzyClassify$ procedure with the two heuristics described in Remark 41 and 40. Then the ordering induced by Remark 40 can be exploited by omitting the bottom search phase for primitive concept names and assuming that they only subsume (concepts equivalent) to $\bot$. This is possible because, with an acyclic KB, a primitive concept can only subsume concepts for which it is a told subsumer. Therefore, as concepts are classified in definition order, a primitive concept will always be classified before any of the concepts it subsumes (and, thus, the bottom search phase is redundant).

10.6.2 The Case of Fuzzy $\mathcal{EL}$

We describe here a polynomial fuzzy classification algorithm for fuzzy $\mathcal{EL}^+$ (see Section 4.2.2.4 for the definition of crisp $\mathcal{EL}^+$) under Gödel logic [388, 475], which is the only reasoning algorithm within the $\mathcal{EL}$ family known so far, though it is expected that fuzzy calculi involving different t-norms and/or fuzzy calculi in the style of [229, 230, 243, 244, 245, 297] (see Remark 9) will appear in the near future.

So, in $\mathcal{EL}^+$ concepts have the form as for $\mathcal{EL}$, namely

$$
\begin{array}{rcll}
C, D & \to & A & \mid \text{(atomic concept)} \\
 & & \top & \mid \text{(universal concept)} \\
 & & C \sqcap D & \mid \text{(concept conjunction)} \\
 & & \exists R.C & \text{(qualified existential restriction)}
\end{array}
$$

General inclusion axioms are of the form $\langle C \sqsubseteq D, n \rangle$, where C, D are $\mathcal{EL}^+$

TABLE 10.13: Normalization rules for fuzzy $\mathcal{EL}^+$ TBoxes.

NF1 $R_1 \circ \cdots \circ R_k \sqsubseteq S \mapsto \{R_1 \circ \cdots \circ R_{k-1} \sqsubseteq U, U \circ R_k \sqsubseteq S\}$

NF2 $\langle C_1 \sqcap \ldots \sqcap \tilde{C} \sqcap \ldots \sqcap C_k \sqsubseteq C, n \rangle \mapsto \{\langle \tilde{C} \sqsubseteq A, n \rangle, \langle C_1 \sqcap \ldots A \ldots \sqcap C_k \sqsubseteq C, n \rangle\}$

NF3 $\langle \exists R.\tilde{C} \sqsubseteq D, n \rangle \mapsto \{\langle \tilde{C} \sqsubseteq A, n \rangle, \langle \exists R.A \sqsubseteq D, n \rangle\}$

NF4 $\langle \tilde{C} \sqsubseteq \tilde{D}, n \rangle \mapsto \{\langle \tilde{C} \sqsubseteq A, n \rangle, \langle A \sqsubseteq \tilde{D}, n \rangle\}$

NF5 $\langle B \sqsubseteq \exists R.\tilde{C}, n \rangle \mapsto \{\langle B \sqsubseteq \exists R.A, n \rangle, \langle A \sqsubseteq \tilde{C}, n \rangle\}$

NF6 $\langle B \sqsubseteq C \sqcap D, n \rangle \mapsto \{\langle B \sqsubseteq C, B \sqsubseteq D, n \rangle\}$

where $\tilde{C}, \tilde{D} \notin CN_{\mathcal{T}}^{\top}$, $B \in CN_{\mathcal{T}}^{\top}$ U new role name, and A new concept name.

concepts, while role inclusion axioms are of the form $R_1 \cdots R_n \sqsubseteq R$, where R_i and R are role names (note that the degree in role inclusions axioms is 1, *i.e.*, role inclusion axioms are classical).

Now, before applying the polynomial algorithm for classification, a fuzzy $\mathcal{EL}^+$ TBox needs to be normalized [15, 25] in a similar way as we did for $\mathcal{EL}^{++}$ in Section 4.4.2 (see also [388]). Specifically, let $CN_{\mathcal{T}}^{\top}$ (resp. $CN_{\mathcal{T}}$) denote the set of concept names occurring in $\mathcal{T}$ with (resp. without) the top concept $\top$. We say that a fuzzy $\mathcal{EL}^+$ Tbox $\mathcal{T}$ is *normalized* if

1. it only contains GCIs of the following form:

$$\langle A_1 \sqcap \ldots \sqcap A_k \sqsubseteq B, n \rangle, \quad \langle A \sqsubseteq \exists R.B, n \rangle, \quad \langle \exists R.A \sqsubseteq B, n \rangle,$$

where $A, A_i \in CN_{\mathcal{T}}^{\top}$ and $B \in CN_{\mathcal{T}}$.

2. all role inclusions are of the form $R \sqsubseteq S$ or $R_1 \circ R_2 \sqsubseteq S$.

As shown in [388], ant fuzzy $\mathcal{EL}^+$ TBox $\mathcal{T}$ can be turned in linear time into a satisfiability preserving normalized TBox $\mathcal{T}'$ by exhaustively applying proper normalization rules (see Table 10.13), which introduce new concept and role names in the TBox.

As next, we assume that a TBox is normalized. Similarly to crisp $\mathcal{EL}^{++}$, when developing the subsumption algorithm for normalized $\mathcal{EL}^+$ TBoxes, we can restrict our attention to subsumption between concept names. In fact, $\mathcal{T} \models \langle C \sqsubseteq D, n \rangle$ iff $\mathcal{T}' \models \langle A \sqsubseteq B, n \rangle$, where $\mathcal{T}' = \mathcal{T} \cup \{\langle A \sqsubseteq C, n \rangle, \langle D \sqsubseteq B, n \rangle\}$, with A, B new concept names. Now, let $R_{\mathcal{T}}$ to denote the set of all role names used in $\mathcal{T}$.

The algorithm computes a mapping $\mathcal{S}$ from $CN_{\mathcal{T}}$ to a subset of $CN_{\mathcal{T}}^{\top} \times [0, 1]$, and a mapping $\mathcal{R}$ from $R_{\mathcal{T}}$ to a subset of $CN_{\mathcal{T}}^{\top} \times CN_{\mathcal{T}}^{\top} \times [0, 1]$. The intuition is that these mappings make implicit subsumption relationships explicit in the following sense:

TABLE 10.14: Completion rules for fuzzy $\mathcal{EL}^+$.

$(CR1)$ If for $1 \leq i \leq k$, $\langle A_i, n_i \rangle \in \mathcal{S}(X), \langle A_1 \sqcap \ldots \sqcap A_k \sqsubseteq B, n \rangle \in \mathcal{T}$, and $\langle B, m \rangle \notin \mathcal{S}(X)$, where $m = \min(n_1, \ldots n_k, n)$ then add $\langle B, m \rangle$ to $\mathcal{S}(X)$;

$(CR2)$ If $\langle A, n \rangle \in \mathcal{S}(X), \langle A \sqsubseteq \exists P.B, k \rangle \in \mathcal{T}$, and $\langle X, B, m \rangle \notin \mathcal{R}(P)$, where $m = \min(n, k)$ then add $\langle X, B, m \rangle$ to $\mathcal{R}(P)$;

$(CR3)$ If $\langle X, Y, n_1 \rangle \in \mathcal{R}(P), \langle A, n_2 \rangle \in \mathcal{S}(Y), \langle \exists P.A \sqsubseteq B, n_3 \rangle \in \mathcal{T}$, and $\langle B, m \rangle \notin \mathcal{S}(X)$, where $m = \min(n_1, n_2, n_3)$ then add $\langle B, m \rangle$ to $\mathcal{S}(X)$;

$(CR4)$ If $\langle X, Y, n \rangle \in \mathcal{R}(P), P \sqsubseteq S \in \mathcal{T}$, and $\langle X, Y, n \rangle \notin \mathcal{R}(S)$ then add $\langle X, Y, n \rangle$ to $\mathcal{R}(S)$;

$(CR5)$ If $\langle X, Y, n_1 \rangle \in \mathcal{R}(R_1), \langle Y, Z, n_2 \rangle \in \mathcal{R}(R_2), R_1 \circ R_2 \sqsubseteq R_3 \in \mathcal{T}$, and $\langle X, Z, m \rangle \notin \mathcal{R}(R_3)$, where $m = \min(n_1, n_2)$ then add $\langle X, Z, m \rangle$ to $\mathcal{R}(R_3)$.

- $\langle B, n \rangle \in \mathcal{S}(A)$ implies that $\mathcal{T} \models \langle A \sqsubseteq B, n \rangle$;

- $\langle A, B, n \rangle \in \mathcal{R}(P)$ implies $\mathcal{T} \models \langle A \sqsubseteq \exists P.B, n \rangle$.

These mapping are initialized as follows:

- $\mathcal{S}(A) := \{\langle A, 1 \rangle, \langle \top, 1 \rangle\}$ for each $A \in CN_{\mathcal{T}}$;

- $\mathcal{R}(P) := \emptyset$ for each $P \in R_{\mathcal{T}}$.

Then, the sets $S(A)$ and $R(P)$ are extended by applying the completion rules shown in Table 10.14 until no more rules are applied.

Now, it can be shown that by appropriately optimizing the application of the completion rules (see [15, 25, 388])

Proposition 82 ([388]). *For a normalized $\mathcal{EL}^+$ TBox $\mathcal{T}$,*

1. *the rules of Table 10.14 can only be applied a polynomial number of times, and each rule application is polynomial;*

2. *Let S be the mapping obtained after the application of the rules of Table 10.14 to $\mathcal{T}$ has terminated, and let A, B be concept names occurring in $\mathcal{T}$, then for $n \in (0, 1]$ we have that $\mathcal{T} \models \langle A \sqsubseteq B, n \rangle$ iff $\langle B, n' \rangle \in S(A)$ for some $n' \geq n$.*

Example 42. *Let us consider $\mathcal{K}$ in Example 41 under Gödel logic.*
Note that $\mathcal{K}$ is already normalized. The following illustrates a classification run.

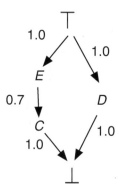

FIGURE 10.10: A fuzzy $\mathcal{EL}^{++}$ classification example.

1. *Initialization:*

$$
\begin{aligned}
\mathcal{S}(C) &:= \{\langle C,1\rangle, \langle\top,1\rangle\} \\
\mathcal{S}(D) &:= \{\langle D,1\rangle, \langle\top,1\rangle\} \\
\mathcal{S}(E) &:= \{\langle E,1\rangle, \langle\top,1\rangle\} \\
\mathcal{R}(R) &:= \emptyset \ .
\end{aligned}
$$

2. *Application of rule* $(CR2)$:

$$
\mathcal{R}(R) := \mathcal{R}(R) \cup \{\langle C,D,0.7\rangle\} \ .
$$

3. *Application of rule* $(CR3)$:

$$
\mathcal{S}(C) := \mathcal{S}(C) \cup \{\langle E,0.7\rangle\} \ .
$$

4. *Stop. Figure 10.10 illustrates the final classification, which coincides with the one in Figure 10.9, except to the subsumption degree among E and C.*

10.6.3   The Case of Fuzzy DL-Lite

In Section 4.2.2.5 we described the crisp DL-Lite family, while in Section 4.4.3 we described a conjunctive query answering procedure for crisp DL-Lite$_{core}$. As query answering is the major reasoning task of the DL-Lite family, we do so here the same and describe indeed a top-k query answering procedure of DL-Lite$_{core}$ under Gödel logic with involute negation and which find its application in [344, 99, 420, 430, 431, 432, 435] (see, *e.g.*, [289, 342, 343, 404, 410, 424, 434] for similar reasoning algorithms related to the DL-Lite family).

So, we recall that in fuzzy DL-Lite$_{core}$ concepts and roles have the following syntax

$$\begin{aligned} B &\longrightarrow A \mid \exists R \\ C &\longrightarrow B \mid \neg B \\ R &\longrightarrow P \mid P^- . \end{aligned}$$

Fuzzy inclusion axioms are classical, *i.e.*, of the form

$$B \sqsubseteq C$$

and fuzzy assertion axioms are, as usual of the form $\langle a{:}A, n\rangle$ and $\langle (a, b){:}P, n\rangle$.

As for the crisp case (see Section 4.4.3), we have a normalization step.

Knowledge Base normalisation. That is, the *normalisation* of $\mathcal{K} = (\mathcal{T}, \mathcal{A})$ is obtained by transforming $\mathcal{K}$ as follows. The ABox $\mathcal{A}$ is expanded by adding to $\mathcal{A}$ the assertions $\langle a{:}\exists R, n\rangle$ and $\langle b{:}\exists R^-, n\rangle$, for each $\langle (a, b){:}R, n\rangle \in \mathcal{A}$. From $\mathcal{A}$ we remove all fuzzy assertions $\langle a{:}B, n\rangle$ if there is another $\langle a{:}B, m\rangle$ in $\mathcal{A}$ with degree $m > n$. We do the same for fuzzy role assertions. Then $\mathcal{T}$ is expanded by closing it with respect to the following inference rule: if $B_1 \sqsubseteq B_2 \in \mathcal{T}$ and either $B_2 \sqsubseteq \neg B_3 \in \mathcal{T}$ or $B_3 \sqsubseteq \neg B_2 \in \mathcal{T}$ then add $B_1 \sqsubseteq \neg B_3$ to $\mathcal{T}$. It can be shown that after computing the above closure we have that $\mathcal{T} \models B_1 \sqsubseteq \neg B_2$ iff either $B_1 \sqsubseteq \neg B_2 \in \mathcal{T}$ or $B_2 \sqsubseteq \neg B_1 \in \mathcal{T}$.

Now we store $\mathcal{A}$ in a relational database. That is, (*i*) for each basic concept B occurring in $\mathcal{A}$, we define a relational table tab_B of arity 2, such that $\langle a, n\rangle \in tab_B$ iff $\langle a{:}B, n\rangle \in \mathcal{A}$; and (*ii*) for each role P occurring in $\mathcal{A}$, we define a relational table tab_P of arity 3, such that $\langle a, b, n\rangle \in tab_P$ iff $\langle (a, b){:}P, n\rangle \in \mathcal{A}$. We denote with DB($\mathcal{A}$) the relational database thus constructed.

Knowledge Base satisfiability. Before we start to query the KB, once and for all, we check whether the KB is satisfiable. To check the satisfiability of a normalized KB $\mathcal{K} = (\mathcal{T}, \mathcal{A})$, we verify the following condition: there exists $B_1 \sqsubseteq \neg B_2 \in \mathcal{T}$ and a constant a such $\{\langle a{:}B_1, n\rangle, \langle a{:}B_2, m\rangle\} \subseteq \mathcal{A}$ with $n > 1 - m$. If this condition above holds, then $\mathcal{K}$ is not satisfiable. Otherwise, $\mathcal{K}$ is satisfiable.

Note that the algorithm can verify this condition by posing to DB($\mathcal{A}$) a simple fuzzy conjunctive query expressed in SQL query, *i.e.*, $\mathcal{K}$ is not satisfiable iff

$$q(x) \leftarrow tab_{B_1}(x, s_1), tab_{B_2}(x, s_2), s_1 > 1 - s_2$$

has a non-empty answer in DB($\mathcal{A}$). As for the crisp case, it can be shown that the above described algorithm decides the KB satisfiability problem in polynomial time.

Top-k Query answering. To determine the answers of a top-k conjunctive query over $\mathcal{K}$ is essentially similar to the case of the crisp case. To this end:

1. We have to check if $\mathcal{K}$ is satisfiable, as querying a non-satisfiable KB is undefined in our case.

2. By considering $\mathcal{T}$ only, the user query q is *reformulated* into a set of fuzzy conjunctive queries $r(q, \mathcal{T})$.

3. The reformulated queries in $r(q, \mathcal{T})$ are then *evaluated* over $\mathcal{A}$ only (which is stored in a database), producing the requested answer set $ans(\mathcal{K}, q)$.

Now, let us consider a fuzzy conjunctive query without ranking aggregation functions. The procedure is similar to the crisp case. Specifically, we have the following. An axiom τ is *applicable* to an atom $\langle B(x), s \rangle$ in a query body, if τ has B in its right-hand side, and τ is applicable to an atom $\langle P(x_1, x_2), s \rangle$ in a query body, if either (*i*) $x_2 = \_$ and the right-hand side of τ is $\exists P$, or (*ii*) $x_1 = \_$ and the right-hand side of τ is $\exists P^-$. We indicate with $gr(g; \tau)$ the expression obtained from the atom g by applying the inclusion axiom τ. Formally, if $g = \langle B_1(x), s \rangle$ (resp., $g = \langle P_1(x, \_), s \rangle$ or $g = \langle P_1(\_, x), s \rangle$) and $\tau = B_2 \sqsubseteq B_1$ (resp., $\tau = B_2 \sqsubseteq \exists P_1$ or $\tau = B_2 \sqsubseteq \exists P_1^-$), we have:

- $gr(g, \tau) = \langle A(x), s \rangle$, if $B_2 = A$, where A is an atomic concept;

- $gr(g, \tau) = \langle P_2(x, \_), s \rangle$, if $B_2 = \exists P_2$;

- $gr(g, \tau) = \langle P_2(\_, x), s \rangle$, if $B_2 = \exists P_2^-$.

Now, the query reformulation algorithm, that given a conjunctive query q and a set of axioms $\mathcal{T}$, reformulates q in terms of a set of conjunctive queries $r(q, \mathcal{T})$, which then can be evaluated over $\mathsf{DB}(\mathcal{A})$ is exactly as for the crisp case (see Algorithm 1) and we have that

$$ans_k(\mathcal{K}, q) = \mathsf{Top}_k\{\langle \mathbf{t}, \lambda \rangle \mid q_i \in r(q, \mathcal{T}), \mathcal{A} \models \langle q_i(\mathbf{t}), \lambda \rangle\} \ .$$

The above property dictates that the set of reformulated queries $q_i \in r(q, \mathcal{T})$ can be used to find the top-k answers, by evaluating them over the set of instances $\mathcal{A}$ only, *i.e.*, over the database, without referring to the ontology $\mathcal{T}$ anymore. As for the crisp case, note, however, that the size of $r(q, \mathcal{T})$ may be exponential w.r.t. $\mathcal{T}$.

In the following, we show how to find the top-k answers of the union of the answer sets of conjunctive queries $q_i \in r(q, \mathcal{T})$.

A naive solution would be: we compute for all $q_i \in r(q, \mathcal{T})$ the whole answer set $ans(q_i, \mathcal{A}) = \{\langle \mathbf{t}, \lambda \rangle \mid \mathcal{A} \models \langle q_i(\mathbf{t}), \lambda \rangle\}$, then we compute the union, $\bigcup_{q_i \in r(q, \mathcal{T})} ans(q_i, \mathcal{T})$, of these answer sets, order it in descending order of the scores and then we take the top-k tuples. We note that each conjunctive query $q_i \in r(q, \mathcal{T})$ can easily be transformed into a top-k SQL query expressed over $\mathsf{DB}(\mathcal{A})$, *i.e.*, the database encoding $\mathcal{A}$. The transformation is conceptually simple.

Example 43 ([410]). *Let us consider Example 15. We may ask to find* cheap *accommodations, their location, and price. Such a query may be expressed as*

$$\langle q(a, hl, p), s\rangle \leftarrow \texttt{Accomodation}(a), \texttt{HasHLoc}(a, hl),$$
$$\texttt{HasHPrice}(a, p), s := ls(50, 80)(p) \ .$$

Then the following is the set of query rewritings $r(q, \mathcal{T})$:

$$\langle q(a, hl, p), s\rangle \quad \leftarrow \quad \texttt{Accomodation}(a), \texttt{HasHLoc}(a, hl),$$
$$\texttt{HasHPrice}(a, p), s := ls(50, 80)(p)$$

$$\langle q(a, hl, p), s\rangle \quad \leftarrow \quad \texttt{Hotel}(a), \texttt{HasHLoc}(a, hl),$$
$$\texttt{HasHPrice}(a, p), s := ls(50, 80)(p)$$

$$\langle q(a, hl, p), s\rangle \quad \leftarrow \quad \texttt{Hotel}\star(a), \texttt{HasHLoc}(a, hl),$$
$$\texttt{HasHPrice}(a, p), s := ls(50, 80)(p)$$

$$\vdots \quad \vdots \quad \vdots$$

$$\langle q(a, hl, p), s\rangle \quad \leftarrow \quad \texttt{Hotel} \star \star \star \star\star(a), \texttt{HasHLoc}(a, hl),$$
$$\texttt{HasHPrice}(a, p), s := ls(50, 80)(p) \ .$$

A major drawback of this solution is the fact that there might be too many tuples with non-zero score and hence for any query $q_i \in r(q, \mathcal{O})$, all these scores should be computed and the tuples should be retrieved. This may *not be feasible* in practice [424]. Indeed, in [424] it is shown that in some cases this approach didn't work at all due to main memory problems and motivated the algorithm described next, called *Disjunctive Threshold Algorithm*, initially proposed in [410], that does address the case for top-k join queries (queries without ranking aggregates) and then has been extended to the case of queries with ranking aggregates in [424].

The DTA for top-k join queries. An immediate method to compute $ans_k(\mathcal{K}, q)$ for top-k join queries is to compute for all $q_i \in r(q, \mathcal{T})$, the top-$k$ answers $ans_k(\mathcal{A}, q_i)$. If both k and the number, $n_q = |r(q, \mathcal{T})|$, of reformulated queries are reasonable, then we may compute the union,

$$U(q, \mathcal{K}) = \bigcup_{q_i \in r(q, \mathcal{T})} ans_k(\mathcal{A}, q_i) \ ,$$

of these top-k answer sets, order it in descending order w.r.t. score and then we take the top-k tuples.

As an alternative, we can avoid computing the whole union $U(q, \mathcal{K})$, so further improving the answering procedure, by relying on a *disjunctive* variant [410] of the so-called *Threshold Algorithm* (TA) [152], called *Disjunctive TA* (DTA).

We recall that the TA has been developed to compute the top-k answers of a conjunctive query without joins and with monotone score combination function. In the following we show that we can use the same principles of the TA to compute the top-k answers of the union of conjunctive queries *without* ranking aggregates:

1. First, we compute for all $q_i \in r(q, \mathcal{T})$, the top-$k$ answers $ans_k(\mathcal{A}, q_i)$, using top-k rank-based relational database engine. Now, let us assume that the tuples in the top-k answer set $ans_k(\mathcal{A}, q_i)$ are sorted in decreasing order with respect to the score.

2. Then we process each top-k answer set $ans_k(\mathcal{A}, q_i)$ ($q_i \in r(q, \mathcal{T})$) according to some criteria (*e.g.*, in parallel, or alternating fashion, or by selecting the next tuple from the answer set with highest threshold θ_i defined below), and top-down (*i.e.*, the higher scored tuples in $ans_k(\mathcal{A}, q_i)$ are processed before the lower scored tuples in $ans_k(\mathcal{A}, q_i)$).

   (a) For each processed tuple **t**, if its score is one of the k highest we have already computed, then remember tuple **t** and its score $s_{\mathbf{t}}$ (ties are broken arbitrarily, so that only k tuples and their scores need to be remembered at any time).

   (b) For each answer set $ans_k(\mathcal{A}, q_i)$, let θ_i be the score of the last tuple processed in this set. Define the threshold value θ to be

   $$\theta = \max(\theta_1, ..., \theta_{n_q}) \ .$$

   (c) As soon as at least k tuples have been processed whose score is at least equal to θ, then halt (indeed, any successive retrieved tuple will have score $\leq \theta$).

   (d) Let Y be the set containing the k tuples that have been processed with the highest scores. The output is then the set $\{\langle \mathbf{t}, s_{\mathbf{t}} \rangle \mid \mathbf{t} \in Y\}$. This set is $ans_k(\mathcal{K}, q)$.

It is not difficult to see that the DTA determines the top-k answers. Indeed, if at least k tuples have been processed whose score is at least equal to θ then any new not yet processed tuple **t** will have score bounded by θ and, thus, it cannot make it into the top-k. Hence, we can stop and the top-k tuples are among those already processed.

Example 44 ([424]). *Suppose we are interested in retrieving the top-3 answers of the disjunctive query* **q** *that has been rewritten as* $\{q_3, q_4, q''\}$. *We have seen that it suffices to find the top-3 answers of the union of the answers to* q_3, q_4 *and to* q''. *Let us show how the DTA works. First, we submit* q_3, q_4 *and* q'' *to a rank-based relational database engine, to compute the top-3 answers. Let us assume that*

$$\begin{aligned}
ans_3(\mathcal{F}, q_3) &= [\langle 0, 1.0 \rangle, \langle 3, 0.7 \rangle, \langle 4, 0.6 \rangle] \\
ans_3(\mathcal{F}, q_4) &= [\langle 1, 0.9 \rangle, \langle 2, 0.8 \rangle, \langle 5, 0.5 \rangle] \\
ans_3(\mathcal{F}, q'') &= [\langle 2, 0.84 \rangle, \langle 3, 0.64 \rangle, \langle 4, 0.36 \rangle] \ .
\end{aligned}$$

The lists are in descending order w.r.t. the score from left to right. Now we process alternatively $ans_k(\mathcal{F}, q_3)$, then $ans_k(\mathcal{F}, q_4)$ and then $ans_k(\mathcal{F}, q'')$ in decreasing order of the score. The table below summarizes the execution of our DTA algorithm. The ranked list column contains the list of tuples processed.

Step	Tuple	θ_{q_3}	θ_{q_4}	$\theta_{q''}$	θ	Ranked List
1	$\langle 0, 1.0 \rangle$	1.0	-	-	-	$\langle 0, 1.0 \rangle$
2	$\langle 1, 0.9 \rangle$	1.0	0.9	-	-	$\langle 0, 1.0 \rangle, \langle 1, 0.9 \rangle$
3	$\langle 2, 0.84 \rangle$	1.0	0.9	0.84	1.0	$\langle 0, 1.0 \rangle, \langle 1, 0.9 \rangle, \langle 2, 0.84 \rangle$
4	$\langle 3, 0.7 \rangle$	0.7	0.9	0.84	0.9	$\langle 0, 1.0 \rangle, \langle 1, 0.9 \rangle, \langle 2, 0.84 \rangle \langle 3, 0.7 \rangle$
5	$\langle 2, 0.8 \rangle$	0.7	0.8	0.84	0.84	$\langle 0, 1.0 \rangle, \langle 1, 0.9 \rangle, \langle 2, 0.84 \rangle \langle 3, 0.7 \rangle$

At step 5 we stop as the ranked list already contains three tuples above the threshold $\theta = 0.84$. So, the final output is $ans_k(\mathcal{F}, q_3) = [\langle 0, 1.0 \rangle, \langle 1, 0.9 \rangle, \langle 2, 0.84 \rangle]$. Note that not all tuples have been processed.

Proposition 83 ([410, 424]). *Given $\mathcal{K} = \langle \mathcal{A}, \mathcal{T} \rangle$ and a conjunctive query q without ranking aggregates, then the DTA determines $ans_k(\mathcal{K}, q)$ in linear time w.r.t. the size of $\mathcal{A}$.*

Proposition 83 extends also to the case of disjunctive queries, to DL-Lite$_{\mathcal{F}, \sqcap}$, DL-Lite$_{\mathcal{R}, \sqcap}$, $\mathcal{DLR}$-Lite$_{\mathcal{F}, \sqcap}$ and $\mathcal{DLR}$-Lite$_{\mathcal{R}, \sqcap}$ [424].

We remark that in case a ranking aggregate occurs in a query, the DTA has to be modified as illustrated in [424]. We do not report it here and refer the reader to [424] for an in-depth description and its experimentation. We just recall that Proposition 83 extends also to disjunctive queries, to DL-Lite$_{\mathcal{F}, \sqcap}$, DL-Lite$_{\mathcal{R}, \sqcap}$, $\mathcal{DLR}$-Lite$_{\mathcal{F}, \sqcap}$, and $\mathcal{DLR}$-Lite$_{\mathcal{R}, \sqcap}$, in which a ranking aggregate @ $\in \{\mathsf{MIN}, \mathsf{AVG}, \mathsf{SUM}, \mathsf{MAX}\}$ may occur in a query.

10.6.4   The Case of Fuzzy Horn-DLs

In Section 4.4.4, we have seen that reasoning in Horn-DLs may be performed by a reduction to logic programming. We will show here that this is indeed the case as well as for fuzzy Horn-DLs under Gödel logic (for other logics the transformation still needs to be worked out). Specifically, we show that a fuzzy Horn-DL KB $\mathcal{K}$ can be reduced to a reasoning preserving fuzzy logic program $\mathcal{P}_\mathcal{K}$ (fuzzy logic programs are described in Chapter 11).

So, in the following consider a fuzzy Horn-DL based on the Gödel t-norm $\otimes$ and let $\mathcal{K} = \langle \mathcal{T}, \mathcal{A} \rangle$ be a KB in which concepts have the form

$$
\begin{aligned}
B &\longrightarrow A \mid B_1 \sqcap B_2 \mid B_1 \sqcup B_2 \mid \exists R.B \\
C &\longrightarrow A \mid C_1 \sqcap C_2 \mid \neg B \mid \forall R.C \\
R &\longrightarrow P \mid P^-
\end{aligned}
$$

where for $n \in (0, 1]$ inclusion axioms have the form

$$
\begin{aligned}
&\langle B \sqsubseteq C, n \rangle \\
&\langle R_1 \sqsubseteq R_2, n \rangle
\end{aligned}
$$

and fuzzy assertions are of the form $\langle a{:}C, n \rangle, \langle (a, b){:}R, n \rangle$.

Our mapping to fuzzy logic programming follows close the one described in Section 4.4.4.

We anticipate informally (see Chapter 11), that a fact in fuzzy logic programming is of the form

$$p(c_1, \ldots, c_n) \leftarrow n \ ,$$

where p is an n-ary relation, every c_i is a constant, and $n > 0$ is a rational in $[0, 1]_{\mathbb{Q}}$ (meaning that the degree of truth of $p(c_1, \ldots, c_n)$ is no less than n), while a fuzzy rule (to what concerns us here) is of the form

$$p(\mathbf{x}) \leftarrow f(p_1(\mathbf{z}_1), \ldots, p_n(\mathbf{z}_k)) \ ,$$

where f is a k-ary monotone function $f : [0, 1]^{k \rightarrow [0,1]}$, whose meaning is

"if n_i is the degree of truth of $p_i(\mathbf{z}_i)$ then the degree of truth of $p(\mathbf{x})$ is no less than $f(n_1, \ldots, n_k)$".

We now define a recursive mapping function σ which takes a inclusion axioms and assertions and maps it into the following expressions:

$$
\begin{aligned}
\sigma(\langle R_1 \sqsubseteq R_2, n \rangle) &\mapsto \sigma_{role}(R_2, x, y) \leftarrow \sigma_{role}(R_1, x, y) \otimes n \\
\sigma_{role}(R, x, y) &\mapsto R(x, y) \\
\sigma_r(R^-, x, y) &\mapsto R(y, x)
\end{aligned}
$$

$$
\begin{aligned}
\sigma(\langle B \sqsubseteq C, n \rangle) &\mapsto \sigma_h(C, x) \leftarrow \sigma_b(B) \otimes n \\
\sigma_h(A, x) &\mapsto A(x) \\
\sigma_h(C_1 \sqcap C_2, x) &\mapsto \sigma_h(C_1, x) \wedge \sigma_h(C_2, x) \\
\sigma_h(\forall R.C, x) &\mapsto \sigma_h(C, x) \leftarrow \sigma_{role}(R, x, y) \\
\sigma_b(A, x) &\mapsto A(x) \\
\sigma_b(C_1 \sqcap C_2, x) &\mapsto \sigma_b(C_1, x) \otimes \sigma_b(C_2, x) \\
\sigma_b(C_1 \sqcup C_2, x) &\mapsto \sigma_b(C_1, x) \oplus \sigma_b(C_2, x) \\
\sigma_b(\exists R.C, x) &\mapsto \sigma_{role}(R, x, y) \otimes \sigma_b(C, y)
\end{aligned}
$$

$$
\begin{aligned}
\sigma(\langle a{:}C, n \rangle) &\mapsto \sigma_h(C, a) \leftarrow n \\
\sigma(\langle (a, b){:}R, n \rangle) &\mapsto \sigma_{role}(R, a, b) \leftarrow n
\end{aligned}
$$

where y is a new variable.

We then transform the above generated expressions into rules by applying recursively the following mapping:

$$
\begin{aligned}
\sigma_r((H \wedge H') \leftarrow B) &\mapsto \sigma_r(H \leftarrow B), \sigma_r(H' \leftarrow B) \\
\sigma_r((H \leftarrow H') \leftarrow B) &\mapsto \sigma_r(H \leftarrow (B \wedge H')) \\
\sigma_r(H \leftarrow (B_1 \vee B_2)) &\mapsto \sigma_r(H \leftarrow B_1), \sigma_r(H \leftarrow B_2)
\end{aligned}
$$

Eventually, if none of the above three rules can be applied then

$$\sigma_r(H \leftarrow B) \quad \mapsto \quad H \leftarrow B \ .$$

For instance, the GCI

$$\langle A \sqcap \exists R.C \sqsubseteq B \sqcap \forall P.D, n \rangle$$

is first mapped into the expression (via σ)

$$B(x) \wedge (D(x) \leftarrow P(x,z)) \leftarrow A(x) \otimes R(x,y) \otimes C(y) \otimes n$$

that then is transformed into the two rules (via σ_r)

$$
\begin{aligned}
B(x) \quad &\leftarrow \quad A(x) \otimes R(x,y) \otimes C(y) \otimes n \\
D(z) \quad &\leftarrow \quad A(x) \otimes R(x,y) \otimes C(y) \otimes P(x,z) \otimes n \ .
\end{aligned}
$$

It can be shown that

Proposition 84. *The above described transformation preserves semantic equivalence. That is, let $\mathcal{K}$ be a fuzzy Horn-DL KB and $\mathcal{P_K}$ be the rule set that results from applying the transformation to all axioms in $\mathcal{K}$, then $\mathcal{P_K}$ is logically equivalent to $\mathcal{K}$ w.r.t. the semantics of FOL $\mathcal{P_K}$ has the same set of models and entailed conclusions as $\mathcal{K}$.*

Hence, reasoning in fuzzy Horn-DL can be reduced to reasoning within fuzzy logic programming (see Chapter 11).

10.6.5 The Case of Concrete Domains and Aggregation Operators

A major ingredient of fuzzy DLs is the capability to deal with fuzzy concrete domains and aggregation operators (see Section 8.2.3 for the fuzzy propositional case), as illustrated in Section 10.3.

In Section 8.2.3 we have shown that indeed one may reason in the presence of concrete domain and aggregation operators by relying on an OR-based decision procedure, by mapping the constraints imposed by the concrete domain and aggregation functions into set of inequations (see Appendix F). It is, thus, not surprising that this approach may be followed also in the case of fuzzy DLs [48, 51, 53, 58, 59, 398, 399]. We refer the reader to Appendix H.4 for the detailed description of the inference rules.

We also remark that under SFL one may also map fuzzy DLs with concept modifiers and concrete fuzzy concepts $\mathbf{d} \in \{rs(a,b), tri(a,b,c), trz(a,b,c,d)\}$ into crisp fuzzy DLs, as illustrated in [45] and this is the method followed by the DELOREAN [42] reasoner. However, it is unknown whether this approach can be adapted to aggregation operators.

Chapter 11

Fuzzy Rule Languages

11.1 Introduction

In logic programming, the management of imperfect information has attracted the attention of many researchers and numerous frameworks have been proposed. Addressing all of them is almost impossible, due to both the large number of works published in this field (early works date back to early 80's [376], see also [416]) and the different approaches proposed. Like for the DL case, essentially they differ in the underlying notion of uncertainty theory and vagueness theory (probability theory, possibilistic logic, fuzzy logic and multi-valued logic) and how uncertainty/vagueness values, associated to rules and facts, are managed.

We report below a list of references and the underlying fuzziness and uncertainty theory in logic programming frameworks. The list of references is by no means intended to be all-inclusive. The author apologizes both to the authors and with the readers for all the relevant works, which are not cited here.

Probability theory: [29, 30, 34, 35, 102, 117, 119, 115, 116, 118, 163, 352, 353, 354, 232, 233, 231, 252, 250, 254, 255, 278, 279, 280, 281, 282, 282, 283, 310, 322, 327, 328, 329, 330, 349, 350, 455, 462]

Possibilistic logic: [5, 6, 7, 96, 137, 179, 331]

Fuzzy set theory: [309, 31, 32, 79, 90, 97, 144, 192, 214, 240, 176, 175, 309, 324, 323, 346, 363, 375, 376, 377, 298, 436, 451, 458, 456, 459, 460, 470]

Multi-valued logic: [65, 81, 103, 104, 105, 112, 110, 106, 107, 108, 109, 112, 121, 120, 124, 122, 123, 154, 155, 156, 157, 159, 180, 234, 235, 236, 239, 247, 249, 251, 253, 266, 267, 268, 269, 270, 271, 272, 273, 274, 300, 302, 301, 305, 311, 312, 318, 318, 316, 317, 319, 364, 372, 373, 374, 402, 400, 403, 408, 409, 414, 413, 429, 446]

While there is a large literature related to the management of fuzziness in logic programs, there are frameworks that are general enough to cover a large amount of them (see, *e.g.*, [289, 400, 416, 456]). Roughly, rules are of the form

$$A \leftarrow f(B_1, ..., B_n) \ ,$$

where A, B_i are atoms and f is a total function $f : \mathcal{S}^n \to \mathcal{S}$ over a truth space $\mathcal{S}$. Computationally, given an assignment/interpretation $\mathcal{I}$ of values to the B_i, the value of A is computed by stating that A is at least as true as $f(\mathcal{I}(B_1), ..., \mathcal{I}(B_n))$.

The form of the rules is sufficiently expressive to encompass many approaches to many-valued logic programming. [289] provides an even more general setting as the function f may also depend on the variables occurring in the rule body. On the other hand there are also some extensions to many-valued disjunctive logic programs [311, 312, 403]. In some cases, *e.g.*, [253] there is also a function g, which dictates how to aggregate the truth values in case an atom is head of several rules.

Most works deal with logic programs without negation and some may provide some technique to answer queries in a top-down manner, as *e.g.*, [104, 239, 253, 456, 402]. On the other hand, there are very few works dealing with normal logic programs [107, 154, 155, 266, 267, 268, 269, 270, 271, 272, 311, 400, 403, 408, 413, 288], and little is know about top-down query answering procedures. The only exceptions are [400, 408, 413].

Another rising problem is the problem to compute the top-k ranked answers to a query, without computing the score of all answers. This allows to answer queries such as "find the top-k closest hotels to the conference location." Solutions to this problem can be found in [289, 409, 414, 428].

In the following, we will address the foundational part of rule-based languages.

11.2   Fuzzy Datalog Basics

As for Mathematical Fuzzy Logic, the main idea is that an atom $p(\mathbf{t})$, rather than being interpreted as either true or false, will be mapped into a truth value (or score) r in $[0, 1]_\mathbb{Q}$ (examples of other truth spaces can be found in, *e.g.*, [103, 250, 402]).

A *knowledge base* $\mathcal{K} = \langle \mathcal{F}, \mathcal{P} \rangle$ consists of a finite *facts component* $\mathcal{F}$ and a finite *LP component* $\mathcal{P}$, which are both defined below.

Facts Component. $\mathcal{F}$ is a finite set of expressions of the form

$$\langle p(c_1, \ldots, c_n), r \rangle \ ,$$

where p is an n-ary relation, every c_i is a constant, and $r > 0$ is a rational in $[0, 1]_\mathbb{Q}$.

The underlying meaning of such an expression is that the degree of truth of $p(c_1, \ldots, c_n)$ is equal to or greater than r. For each p, we represent the facts $\langle p(c_1, \ldots, c_n), r \rangle$ in $\mathcal{F}$ by means of a relational $n + 1$-ary table T_p, containing the records $\langle c_1, \ldots, c_n, r \rangle$. As usual, we assume that there cannot be two records $\langle c_1, \ldots, c_n, r_1 \rangle$ and $\langle c_1, \ldots, c_n, r_2 \rangle$ in T_p with $r_1 < r_2$ (if there are, then we remove the one with the lower score). We assume each table sorted in descending order with respect to the scores. For ease, we may omit the score component and in such cases the value 1 is assumed.

Rule Component. $\mathcal{P}$ is a finite set of *rules*, which are similar as fuzzy conjunctive RDFS and DL queries (See Sections 9.3 and 10.4), and are of the form (where $\mathbf{s} = \langle s_1, \ldots, s_n \rangle$, $n \geq 0$)

$$\langle p(\mathbf{x}), s \rangle \leftarrow \exists \mathbf{y}. \langle p_1(\mathbf{z}_1), s_1 \rangle, \ldots, \langle p_n(\mathbf{z}_n), s_n \rangle, s := f(\mathbf{s}, \mathbf{z}) \,, \qquad (11.1)$$

where

1. p is an n-ary relation, every p_i is an n_i-ary relation;

2. $\mathbf{x}$ are the *distinguished variables*;

3. $\mathbf{y}$ are existentially quantified variables called the *non-distinguished variables*;

4. $\mathbf{z}$ and every $\mathbf{z}_i$ is a tuple of constants or variables in $\mathbf{x}$ or $\mathbf{y}$;

5. s and elements in $\mathbf{s}$ are called *scoring terms*. Scoring terms are either rational numbers in $[0,1]_\mathbb{Q}$ or variables, called *scoring* variables;

6. all variables in $\mathbf{x}$, $\mathbf{y}$, and variables in $\{s, s_1, \ldots, s_n\}$ are pairwise disjoint and all variables in $\mathbf{x}$ occur in at least one of the $\mathbf{z}_i$;

7. f is a *scoring* function $f \colon [0,1]_\mathbb{Q}^l \to [0,1]_\mathbb{Q}$, which computes the overall *score* to be assigned to the rule head. We assume that f is *monotone*, that is, for each $\mathbf{v}, \mathbf{v}' \in [0,1]_\mathbb{Q}^l$ such that $\mathbf{v} \leq \mathbf{v}'$, it holds $f(\mathbf{v}) \leq f(\mathbf{v}')$, where $(v_1, \ldots, v_l) \leq (v_1', \ldots, v_l')$ iff $v_i \leq v_i'$ for all i. We also assume that the computational cost of f is bounded by l.

Similar to the crisp Datalog case, we call $\langle p(\mathbf{x}), s \rangle$ the *head* and $\exists \mathbf{y}. \langle p_1(\mathbf{z}_1), s_1 \rangle, \ldots, \langle p_n(\mathbf{z}_n), s_n \rangle, s := f(\mathbf{s}, \mathbf{z})$ the *body* of the rule; if clear from the context, we may omit the existential quantification $\exists \mathbf{y}$; as for the crisp case, we assume that predicate names in a rule body are distinct, *i.e.*, $p_i \neq p_j$ for $i \neq j$; we also assume that relations occurring in $\mathcal{F}$ do not occur in the head of rules (so, we do not allow that the fact relations occurring in $\mathcal{F}$ can be redefined by $\mathcal{P}$); and the relations in $\mathcal{F}$ are called *extensional* relations, while the others are *intensional* relations. We further call $s := f(\mathbf{s}, \mathbf{z})$ a *scoring atom* and an expression $\langle p(\mathbf{z}), s \rangle$ a *fuzzy atom*.

Remark 42. *In the following we will make the following convention: if a scoring term is omitted then the value 1 is assumed and if the scoring term in the rule head is a rational $r \in [0,1]_\mathbb{Q}$, then the scoring atom is of the form $r := f(\ldots)$. For ease of presentation, if there is at least one fuzzy atom in the rule body, we may omit a scoring atom of the form $r := r$, for $r \in [0,1]_\mathbb{Q}$.*

An example of fuzzy rule is the following:

$$\langle GoodHotel(x), s \rangle \leftarrow Hotel(x), \langle Cheap(x), s_1 \rangle,$$
$$\langle CloseToVenue(x), s_2 \rangle, \langle Comfortable(x), s_3 \rangle,$$
$$s := 0.3 \cdot s_1 + 0.5 \cdot s_2 + 0.2 \cdot s_3 \qquad (11.2)$$

The intended meaning is to retrieve good hotels, where the degree of goodness is a function of the degree of being cheap, close to the venue, and comfortable.

Remark 43. *Note also that a classical LP rule*

$$p(\mathbf{x}) \leftarrow p_1(\mathbf{z}_1), \ldots, p_n(\mathbf{z}_n) \ ,$$

is nothing else than a special case of fuzzy rules, and, e.g., is the same as writing

$$\langle p(\mathbf{x}), 1 \rangle \leftarrow \langle p_1(\mathbf{z}_1), 1 \rangle, \ldots, \langle p_n(\mathbf{z}_n), 1 \rangle \ .$$

So, e.g., all rules of Example 17 are fuzzy rules as well.

Remark 44. *In the following, a fuzzy rule*

$$\langle p(\mathbf{x}), s \rangle \leftarrow \exists \mathbf{y}. \langle p_1(\mathbf{z}_1), s_1 \rangle, \ldots, \langle p_n(\mathbf{z}_n), s_n \rangle, s := f(\mathbf{s}) \ ,$$

in which the scoring function in the scoring atom depends on the scores of the atoms in the body only (and all s, s_i are scoring variables), is represented succinctly as

$$p(\mathbf{x}) \leftarrow f(p_1(\mathbf{z}_1), \ldots, p_n(\mathbf{z}_n)) \ .$$

According to Remark 44, the rule in Equation (11.2) can be represented as well as

$$GoodHotel(x) \leftarrow \min(Hotel(x), 0.3 \cdot Cheap(x)$$
$$+ 0.5 \cdot CloseToVenue(x) + 0.2 \cdot Comfortable(x)) \ .$$

Semantics. From a semantics point of view, given $\mathcal{K} = \langle \mathcal{F}, \mathcal{P} \rangle$, the notions of *Herbrand universe* $H_\mathcal{K}$ (the set of all constants occurring in $\mathcal{K}$) and *Herbrand base* $B_\mathcal{K}$ of $\mathcal{K}$ (the set of all ground atoms that can be formed using constants in $H_\mathcal{K}$ and atoms occurring in $\mathcal{K}$) are as usual.

Similarly to the crisp case, given $\mathcal{K}$, the (possibly infinite) set of ground rules $\mathcal{K}^*$ derived from the grounding of $\mathcal{K}$ is constructed as follows:

1. set $\mathcal{K}^*$ to be $\{\langle p(\mathbf{t}), n \rangle \leftarrow n := n \mid \langle p(\mathbf{t}), n \rangle \in \mathcal{F}, r \in [0,1]_\mathbb{Q}\}$;

2. add to $\mathcal{K}^*$ the set of all ground instantiations of rules in $\mathcal{K}$, in which we do also replace scoring variables with rational values in $[0,1]_\mathbb{Q}$.

Remark 45. *Note that in $\mathcal{K}^*$ we replace scoring variables with rational values in $[0,1]_\mathbb{Q}$. Therefore, $\mathcal{K}^*$ does not consists of a finite set of rules iff at least one scoring variable is present in $\mathcal{P}$.*

An *interpretation* $\mathcal{I}$ for $\mathcal{K}$ is a function $I \colon B_\mathcal{K} \to [0, 1]_\mathbb{Q}$. Given $\mathcal{K}$, we say that $\mathcal{I}$ *satisfies* (*is a model of*)

- a ground fuzzy atom $\langle A, r \rangle$, where $A \in B_\mathcal{K}$, denoted $\mathcal{I} \models \langle A, r \rangle$, iff $\mathcal{I}(A) \geq r$;

- a ground scoring atom $r := f(\mathbf{v})$ iff $r = f(\mathbf{v})$. For ease, we use f both denoting the logical function symbol as well as the interpreted function;

- a ground rule body ϕ of a rule $\psi \leftarrow \phi \in \mathcal{K}^*$, denoted $\mathcal{I} \models \phi$, iff $\mathcal{I}$ is a model of all atoms in ϕ;

- a ground rule $r \in \mathcal{K}^*$, denoted $\mathcal{I} \models r$, iff $\mathcal{I}$ is a model of the head of r whenever $\mathcal{I}$ is a model of the body of r;

- $\mathcal{K}^*$, denoted $\mathcal{I} \models \mathcal{K}^*$, iff $\mathcal{I}$ satisfies all rules $r \in \mathcal{K}^*$;

- $\mathcal{K}$, denoted $\mathcal{I} \models \mathcal{K}$, if $\mathcal{I}$ is a model of $\mathcal{K}^*$.

Example 45. *Consider $\mathcal{K}$ as follows:*

$$\mathcal{F} = \{ \quad \langle p(a), 0.2 \rangle,$$
$$\langle p(b), 0.5 \rangle \quad \}$$

$$\mathcal{P} = \{ \quad \langle q(x), s \rangle \leftarrow \langle p(x), s' \rangle, s := f(s')$$

where for $r \in [0, 1]_\mathbb{Q}$

$$f(r) = \begin{cases} 0 & \text{if } r \leq 0.3 \\ r & \text{otherwise.} \end{cases}$$

Then

$$H_\mathcal{K} = \{a, b\}$$

$$B_\mathcal{K} = \{p(a), p(b), q(a), q(b)\}$$

$$\mathcal{K}^* = \{ \langle p(a), r \rangle \leftarrow r := 0.2 \mid r \in [0, 1]_\mathbb{Q}\} \cup$$
$$\langle p(b), r \rangle \leftarrow r := 0.5 \mid r \in [0, 1]_\mathbb{Q}\} \cup$$
$$\langle q(a), r \rangle \leftarrow \langle p(a), r' \rangle, r := f(r') \mid r, r' \in [0, 1]_\mathbb{Q}\} \cup$$
$$\langle q(b), r \rangle \leftarrow \langle p(b), r' \rangle, r := f(r') \mid r, r' \in [0, 1]_\mathbb{Q}\} .$$

Now, consider the interpretations

$$\mathcal{I}_1(p(a)) = 0.4$$
$$\mathcal{I}_1(p(b)) = 0.7$$
$$\mathcal{I}_1(q(a)) = 0.5$$
$$\mathcal{I}_1(q(b)) = 0.8$$

and

$$\begin{aligned}
\mathcal{I}_2(p(a)) &= 0.4 \\
\mathcal{I}_2(p(b)) &= 0.7 \\
\mathcal{I}_2(q(a)) &= 0.5 \\
\mathcal{I}_2(q(b)) &= 0.6 \, .
\end{aligned}$$

Note that $\mathcal{I}_1$ and $\mathcal{I}_2$ differ only in the interpretation of $q(b)$. Now, it can be verified that $\mathcal{I}_1$ is a model of $\mathcal{K}^*$ and, thus, $\mathcal{K}$, while $\mathcal{I}_2$ is not. Specifically, $\mathcal{I}_2$ is not a model of the rule

$$\langle q(b), 0.7 \rangle \leftarrow \langle p(b), 0.7 \rangle, 0.7 := f(0.7)$$

because, $\mathcal{I}_2$ is a model of the rule body, but is not a model of the rule head.

Now, let us extend the $\leq$ relation from $[0, 1]$ to the set $\mathbf{I}_\mathcal{K}$ of all interpretations point-wise: (i) $\mathcal{I}_1 \leq \mathcal{I}_2$ iff $\mathcal{I}_1(A) \leq \mathcal{I}_2(A)$, for every ground atom $A \in B_\mathcal{K}$. With $\mathcal{I}_\perp$ we denote the bottom interpretation ($\mathcal{I}_\perp$ maps all atoms to $\perp$), while with $\mathcal{I}_\top$ we denote the top interpretation ($\mathcal{I}_\top$ maps all atoms to 1). It turns out that $\langle \mathbf{I}_\mathcal{K}, \leq \rangle$ is a complete lattice.

As for the crisp case, one model plays a special role: namely the $\leq$-least model $M_\mathcal{K}$ of $\mathcal{K}$. The existence, finiteness, and uniqueness of the minimal model $M_\mathcal{K}$ are guaranteed to exist by the following argument. Consider the function $T_\mathcal{K} \colon \mathbf{I}_\mathcal{K} \to \mathbf{I}_\mathcal{K}$ defined as follows: for all ground atoms $A \in B_\mathcal{K}$

$$T_\mathcal{K}(\mathcal{I})(A) = \sup\{r \mid \langle A, r \rangle \leftarrow \phi \in \mathcal{K}^* \text{ s.t. } \mathcal{I} \models \phi\} \, . \qquad (11.3)$$

Then, it can be shown that $T_\mathcal{K}$ is monotone on $\mathbf{I}_\mathcal{K}$, *i.e.*, if $\mathcal{I}_1 \leq \mathcal{I}_2$ then $T_\mathcal{K}(\mathcal{I}_1) \leq T_\mathcal{K}(\mathcal{I}_2)$. In fact, if $\mathcal{I}_1 \leq \mathcal{I}_2$, $\langle A, r \rangle \leftarrow \phi \in \mathcal{K}^*$ and $I_1 \models \phi$ then $I_2 \models \phi$ as well. Therefore,

$$\begin{aligned}
T_\mathcal{K}(\mathcal{I}_1)(A) &= \sup\{r \mid \langle A, r \rangle \leftarrow \phi \in \mathcal{K}^* \text{ s.t. } \mathcal{I}_1 \models \phi\} \\
&\leq \sup\{r \mid \langle A, r \rangle \leftarrow \phi \in \mathcal{K}^* \text{ s.t. } \mathcal{I}_2 \models \phi\} \\
&= T_\mathcal{K}(\mathcal{I}_2)(A) \, .
\end{aligned}$$

Therefore, by the well-known Tarski-Knaster fixed-point theorem [439] for monotone functions over complete lattices, we get immediately the analogue of Proposition 16:

Proposition 85. *For a knowledge base $\mathcal{K}$, there exists a unique minimal model $M_\mathcal{K}$ that is the least fixed point of the function $T_\mathcal{K}$. $M_\mathcal{K}$ can be obtained as the limit of the $\leq$-monotone sequence, $\mathcal{I}_0, \ldots, \mathcal{I}_i, \ldots$, where*

$$\begin{aligned}
\mathcal{I}_0 &= \mathcal{I}_\perp \\
\mathcal{I}_{i+1} &= T_\mathcal{K}(\mathcal{I}_i) \, .
\end{aligned} \qquad (11.4)$$

Example 46. *Consider Example 45. Let us illustrate the computation of the minimal model. We do only report the changes to the previous step.*

$$\mathcal{I}_0 \quad = \quad \mathcal{I}_\perp$$

$$\mathcal{I}_1(p(a)) \quad = \quad T_{\mathcal{K}}(\mathcal{I}_0)(p(a)) = 0.2$$
$$\mathcal{I}_1(p(b)) \quad = \quad T_{\mathcal{K}}(\mathcal{I}_0)(p(b)) = 0.5$$

$$\mathcal{I}_2(q(b)) \quad = \quad T_{\mathcal{K}}(\mathcal{I}_1)(q(b)) = 0.5$$

$$\mathcal{I}_3 \quad = \quad T_{\mathcal{K}}(\mathcal{I}_2) = \mathcal{I}_2 \ .$$

Therefore, $M_{\mathcal{K}} = \mathcal{I}_3$ *is the minimal model with*

$$M_{\mathcal{K}}(p(a)) \quad = \quad 0.2$$
$$M_{\mathcal{K}}(p(b)) \quad = \quad 0.5$$
$$M_{\mathcal{K}}(q(a)) \quad = \quad 0.0$$
$$M_{\mathcal{K}}(q(b)) \quad = \quad 0.5 \ .$$

Let us remark that however, a finite number of iterations may not suffice to compute the minimal model as illustrated by the following example (for similar examples, see, *e.g.*, [239, 456]).

Example 47. *Consider the score combination function* $f(x) = \frac{x+a}{2}$ *(0 < a ≤ 1), and* $\mathcal{K}_1$ *containing the rules:*

$$\langle p, s \rangle \quad \leftarrow \quad s := 0$$
$$\langle p, s \rangle \quad \leftarrow \quad \langle p, s' \rangle, s := f(s).$$

Then the minimal model is attained after ω *steps of* $T_{\mathcal{K}}$ *iterations starting from* $\mathcal{I}_\perp$ *and is* $M_{\mathcal{K}_1}(p) = a$.
Now, consider the (non-continuous) function $g(x) = 0$ *if* $x < a$, *and* $g(x) = 1$ *otherwise, and* $\mathcal{K}_2$ *containing only the rules*

$$\langle p, s \rangle \quad \leftarrow \quad s := 0$$
$$\langle p, s \rangle \quad \leftarrow \quad \langle p, s' \rangle, s := f(s)$$
$$\langle q, s \rangle \quad \leftarrow \quad \langle p, s' \rangle, s := g(s) \ .$$

Then the minimal model is attained after $\omega + 1$ *steps of* $T_{\mathcal{K}}$ *iterations starting from* $\mathcal{I}_\perp$ *and is* $M_{\mathcal{K}_2}(p) = a, M_{\mathcal{K}_2}(q) = 1$.

However, it can be shown that if all functions appearing in $\mathcal{P}$ are Scott-continuous, then at most ω steps are necessary to compute the minimal model [400, 402].

In any case, finiteness of the truth space, monotonicity of score combination functions together with the finiteness of the grounded program guarantees then that the minimal model can be computed in finite time by iterating $T_{\mathcal{K}}$ over $\mathcal{I}_\perp$.

Remark 46. *Note that the requirement of being the scoring functions monotone is crucial to guarantee the existence of a unique minimal model. For instance, the KB*

$$\mathcal{K} = \{ \quad \langle a, 0.2 \rangle,$$
$$\langle b, 0.3 \rangle,$$

$$a \leftarrow (1 - b),$$
$$b \leftarrow (1 - a)$$
$$\}$$

involving the non-monotone scoring function $1 - x$, *has two minimal models,* M^1 *and* M^2: *namely*

$$M_{\mathcal{K}}^1(a) = 0.7$$
$$M_{\mathcal{K}}^1(b) = 0.3$$

and

$$M_{\mathcal{K}}^2(a) = 0.2$$
$$M_{\mathcal{K}}^2(b) = 0.8 .$$

11.3   Concrete Domains

The notion of concrete domains naturally extends the one for crisp Datalog presented in Section 5.3 and is coherent with what proposed for the fuzzy propositional logic case (see Section 8.2.3), where now a concrete atom, rather being true or false only, is mapped into $[0, 1]_\mathbb{Q}$ (see, *e.g.*, [398]). Specifically, we assume a set of constants that are *data values* and a set of *datatype predicates*, where each datatype predicate has a predefined arity $n \geq 1$. A *datatype theory* $\mathbf{D} = \langle \Delta^{\mathbf{D}}, \cdot^{\mathbf{D}} \rangle$ consists of a finite datatype domain $\Delta^{\mathbf{D}}$ and a mapping $\cdot^{\mathbf{D}}$ that assigns to each data value an element of $\Delta^{\mathbf{D}}$ and assigns to each n-ary datatype predicate p a n-ary function $p^{\mathbf{D}} \colon \Delta^{\mathbf{D}} \times \ldots \times \Delta^{\mathbf{D}} \to [0, 1]_\mathbb{Q}$.

A *concrete atom* is an expression of the form $\mathbf{d}(\mathbf{z})$, where $\mathbf{z}$ is a vector of variables or data values. For instance, $ls(18000, 22000)$ is the well-known left-shoulder fuzzy set membership function we have seen in Section 8.1.1, which maps a data value into $[0,1]_\mathbb{Q}$. A concrete atom $\mathbf{d}(\mathbf{z})$ may occur in a rule body only in the form of a fuzzy atom expression $\langle \mathbf{d}(\mathbf{z}), s \rangle$.

As in Section 5.3, let us extend both the Herbrand universe as $H_\mathcal{K}^\mathbf{D} :=$ $H_\mathcal{K} \cup \Delta^\mathbf{D}$ and the Herbrand base $B_\mathcal{K}^\mathbf{D}$ to the set of all ground atoms and ground concrete atoms that can be formed from the constants in the Herbrand universe. Then, an *interpretation* $\mathcal{I}$ for $\mathcal{K}$ is a function $I : B_\mathcal{K}^\mathbf{D} \to [0,1]_\mathbb{Q}$ with the additional condition that $\mathbf{d}^\mathcal{I} = \mathbf{d}^\mathbf{D}$, for each datatype predicate $\mathbf{d}$.

Now, the notions of *satisfaction* (*is model of*) are extended in the obvious way to rules including concrete fuzzy atoms. For instance, an interpretation $\mathcal{I}$ is a model of a ground concrete fuzzy atom $\langle \mathbf{d}(\mathbf{v}), r \rangle$ iff $\mathbf{d}^\mathbf{D}(\mathbf{v}) \geq r$. It is then straightforward to see that the analogue of Proposition 85 still applies to interpretations over $B_\mathcal{K}^\mathbf{D}$ in place of $B_\mathcal{K}$.

11.4 Fuzzy Conjunctive Queries

Similarly to Section 5.4, a *fuzzy query* is a fuzzy rule

$$\langle q(\mathbf{x}), s \rangle \leftarrow \varphi(\mathbf{x}, \mathbf{y}, \mathbf{s}), s := f(\mathbf{x}, \mathbf{y}, \mathbf{s}) , \tag{11.5}$$

and the *answer set* of a query q w.r.t. a KB $\mathcal{K}$ (denoted $ans(\mathcal{K}, q)$) is the set of tuples $\langle \mathbf{t}, r \rangle$ such that $M_{\mathcal{K}'}(q(\mathbf{t})) = r > 0$, where $\mathcal{K}'$ is obtained from $\mathcal{K}$ by extending it with the query rule (11.5) ($M_{\mathcal{K}'}$ is guaranteed to exists by Proposition 85).

Example 48. *Given $\mathcal{K}$ with rule*

$$q(x) \leftarrow 0.5 \cdot p(x) + 0.7 \cdot r(x)$$

and facts

$$\langle p(a), 0.4 \rangle, \quad \langle p(b), 0.2 \rangle, \quad \langle r(b), 0.5 \rangle$$

then $ans(q, \mathcal{K}) = \{\langle a, 0.45 \rangle, \langle b, 0.2 \rangle\}$.

In the following, to ease the presentation, we will also say that a *fuzzy query* is of the form $q(\mathbf{x})$, intended as a question about the truth degree of the ground instances of $q(\mathbf{x})$ in the minimal model of $\mathcal{K}$.

11.5 Reasoning

We present here some methods to determine the answer set $ans(\mathcal{K}, q)$ of a query q, given a KB $\mathcal{K}$. The first one is a generalization of the one SLD-resolution methods presented in Section 5.5.1, the second one maps fuzzy LPs into crisp LPs, while the third one addresses a rather novel problem in the context of fuzzy LPs, namely the problem of determine the top-k answers [289, 409, 414, 428]:

Top-k retrieval. Given $\mathcal{K}$, retrieve top-k tuples of the answer set of q ranked in decreasing order relative to the score, denoted

$$ans_k(\mathcal{K}, q) = \text{Top}_k(ans(\mathcal{K}, q)) \ .$$

For the sake of illustrative purposes, we consider the following well-known example in which we define a path in a weighted graph.

Example 49 ([428]). *Consider the following rules*

$$r_1 : \text{path}(x, y) \quad \leftarrow \quad \text{edge}(x, y) \tag{11.6}$$
$$r_2 : \text{path}(x, y) \quad \leftarrow \quad \min(\text{path}(x, z), \text{edge}(z, y)) \tag{11.7}$$

and the facts

T_{edge}		
c	b	0.6
a	c	0.5
b	a	0.4
a	b	0.3

It can be verified that the set of answers of predicate **path** *is given by:*

$ans(\mathcal{K}, \text{path})$								
a	a	0.4	b	a	0.4	c	a	0.4
a	b	0.5	b	b	0.4	c	b	0.6
a	c	0.5	b	c	0.4	c	c	0.4

The top-3 answers for **path** *are instead:*

$$ans_k(\mathcal{K}, q) = \{\langle c, b, 0.6 \rangle, \langle a, b, 0.5 \rangle, \langle a, c, 0.5 \rangle\} \ .$$

We next introduce the following requirements.

Truth space. To always guarantee termination of the procedures presented here, we will assume that the truth space is $\mathcal{L} = \{\perp, 0, \frac{1}{n}, \ldots \frac{n-1}{n}, 1\}$, for some positive integer n. We will use the symbol $\perp$ to denote the truth "undefined" and extend the linear order $\leq$ over rational numbers by postulating $\perp < 0$. In the rules, we assume that the scoring function is such that $f(\ldots, \perp, \ldots) = \perp$. We assume that for a fact $\langle p(\mathbf{t}), r \rangle$, $r > \perp$ holds. The semantics is a straightforward adaption of the one presented in Section 11.2 and Proposition 85 extends easily to this setting as well:

Proposition 86 ([428]). *Given a truth space $\mathcal{L} = \{\perp, 0, \frac{1}{n}, \ldots \frac{n-1}{n}, 1\}$, then for a knowledge base $\mathcal{K}$, there exists a unique minimal model $M_{\mathcal{K}}$ that is the least fixed point of the function $\mathcal{T}_{\mathcal{K}}$. $M_{\mathcal{K}}$ can be obtained as the limit of the $\leq$-monotone sequence, $\mathcal{I}_0, \ldots, \mathcal{I}_i, \ldots,$, where*

$$
\begin{aligned}
\mathcal{I}_0 &= \mathcal{I}_{\perp} \\
\mathcal{I}_{i+1} &= \mathcal{T}_{\mathcal{K}}(\mathcal{I}_i) .
\end{aligned}
\tag{11.8}
$$

in which the interpretation $\mathcal{I}_{\perp}$ maps all ground atoms to $\perp$. Furthermore, the number of iterations is bounded by $|\mathcal{L}|$.

From a practical point of view the finiteness of $\mathcal{L}$ is a limitation we can live with especially taking into account that computers have finite resources, and thus, only a finite set of truth degrees can be represented. For other conditions that guarantee termination, we refer the reader to, *e.g.*, [103, 104, 105, 111, 112, 239, 400, 402].

Remark 47. *Note that we have introduced $\perp$ to distinguish the case where a tuple $\mathbf{t}$ may be retrieved, even though the score is 0, from the case where a tuple is not retrieved, since it does not satisfy the query. In particular, if a tuple does not belong to an extensional relation, then its score is assumed to be undefined ($\perp$), while if $\mathcal{I}$ would be defined on $\{0, \frac{1}{n}, \ldots \frac{n-1}{n}, 1\}$, then the score of this tuple would be 0. The semantics is inspired by [289, 428].*

To further illustrate the case, consider the following example.

Example 50. *Consider again Example 48. Then, w.r.t. $\mathcal{L} = \{\perp, 0, \frac{1}{10}, \ldots \frac{9}{10}, 1\}$, $ans(q, \mathcal{K}) = \{\langle b, 0.2 \rangle\}$. Please, note that $\langle a, 0.45 \rangle \notin ans(q, \mathcal{K})$ since $M_{\mathcal{K}}(r(a)) = \perp$ and $0.5 \cdot 0.9 + 0.7 \cdot \perp = \perp$, by definition of scoring functions.*

Eventually, it is not difficult to see that, w.l.o.g. we may assume that all fuzzy rules are of the form

$$
\langle p(\mathbf{x}), s \rangle \leftarrow \exists \mathbf{y}. \langle p_1(\mathbf{z}_1), s_1 \rangle, \ldots, \langle p_n(\mathbf{z}_n), s_n \rangle, s := f(\mathbf{s}, \mathbf{z}) ,
\tag{11.9}
$$

in which all scoring terms s, s_i are scoring variables, and all variables occurring in the rule occur in the scoring function as well. This may easily achieved by observing that

- a fuzzy atom $\langle p_i(\mathbf{z}), r \rangle$ occurring in the rule body with $r \in [0, 1]_{\mathbb{Q}}$, may be replaced with a fuzzy atom $\langle p_i(\mathbf{z}), s' \rangle$, where s' is a new scoring variable and where the scoring function $f(\mathbf{s}, \mathbf{z})$ is replaced with

$$
g(\mathbf{s}, \mathbf{z}, s') = \begin{cases} f(\mathbf{s}, \mathbf{z}) & \text{if } s' \geq r \\ \perp & \text{otherwise;} \end{cases}
$$

- a fuzzy atom $\langle p(\mathbf{z}), r \rangle$ in the head with $r \in [0, 1]_{\mathbb{Q}}$, may be replaced with a fuzzy atom $\langle p(\mathbf{z}), s' \rangle$, where s' is a new scoring variable and where the scoring atom $r := f(\mathbf{s}, \mathbf{z})$ is replaced with $s := g(\mathbf{s}, \mathbf{z})$, where

$$g(\mathbf{s}, \mathbf{z}) = \begin{cases} r & \text{if } f(\mathbf{s}, \mathbf{z}) = r \\ \bot & \text{otherwise;} \end{cases}$$

- if a variable z' occurring in the rule and not being the scoring variable in the head, does not occur in the scoring function, then the scoring function $f(\mathbf{s}, \mathbf{z})$ is replaced with

$$g(\mathbf{s}, \mathbf{z}, z') = f(\mathbf{s}, \mathbf{z}) \ .$$

For instance, note that a rule[1]

$$\langle p, 0.7 \rangle \leftarrow \langle q, 0.5 \rangle$$

is replaced with the rule

$$\langle p, s \rangle \leftarrow \langle q, s' \rangle, s := g(s') \tag{11.10}$$

where

$$g(s') = \begin{cases} 0.7 & \text{if } s' \geq 0.5 \\ \bot & \text{otherwise.} \end{cases}$$

In fact, in the rule

$$\langle p, 0.7 \rangle \leftarrow \langle q, 0.5 \rangle, 0.7 := 0.7$$

by replacing $\langle q, 0.5 \rangle$ the rule becomes

$$\langle p, 0.7 \rangle \leftarrow \langle q, s' \rangle, 0.7 := f(s')$$

where

$$g(s') = \begin{cases} 0.7 & \text{if } s' \geq 0.5 \\ \bot & \text{otherwise} \end{cases}$$

and then by replacing $\langle p, 0.7 \rangle$ we obtain the rule in Equation (11.10).

In the following, we will assume that the answer set of a query q w.r.t. $\mathcal{K}$ is defined as the set $ans(q, \mathcal{K})$ of tuples $\langle \mathbf{t}, r \rangle \in H_{\mathcal{K}} \times \ldots \times H_{\mathcal{K}} \times \mathcal{L}$ such that $M_{\mathcal{K}}(q(\mathbf{t})) = r > \bot$ (the score of $\mathbf{t}$ is $r > \bot$ in the minimal model).

We conclude this section by recalling the notion of recursive / non-recursive KB from Section 5.5.2, *i.e.*, given $\mathcal{K}$, we say that relation symbol p *directly depends on* relation symbol q if there is a rule in $\mathcal{K}$ such that p occurs in the head of it and q occurs in the body of it. The relation *depends on* is the transitive closure of "directly depends on." The *dependency graph* of $\mathcal{K}$ is a directed graph where nodes are relation symbols and the set of edges is the "directly depends on" relation. The KB is *recursive* if there is a cycle in the dependency graph (*i.e.*, there is p depending on p).

---

[1] Recall that the scoring atom $0.7 := 0.7$ is omitted.

11.5.1 SLD-Resolution Driven Query Answering

The method proposed here naturally generalizes the one presented in Section 5.5.1 to the fuzzy case and is inspired to [104, 239, 456]. We first present the propositional case and extend it to the FOL case.

The propositional fuzzy SLD inference rule is as follows: assume we have propositional rules in which we assume that all scoring variables in the second rule have been renamed in order not to share any variable with the first one.

$$
\begin{array}{ll}
\text{From} & \langle A, s \rangle \leftarrow \langle A_1, s_1 \rangle, \dots, \langle A_j, s_j \rangle, \dots, \langle A_k, s_k \rangle, s := f(\mathbf{s}) \\
\text{and} & \langle B, s' \rangle \leftarrow \langle B_1, s'_1 \rangle, \dots, \langle B_m, s'_m \rangle, s' := g(\mathbf{s}') \\
\text{and} & B = A_j \\
\hline
\text{infer} & \langle A, s \rangle \leftarrow \langle A_1, s_1 \rangle, \dots, \langle A_{j-1}, s_{j-1} \rangle, \\
& \quad \langle B_1, s'_1 \rangle, \dots, \langle B_m, s'_m \rangle, \\
& \quad \langle A_{j+1}, s_{j+1} \rangle \dots, \langle A_k, s_k \rangle, \\
& \quad s := f(s_1, \dots, s_{j-1}, g(\mathbf{s}'), s_{j+1}, \dots, s_k) \, .
\end{array}
\tag{11.11}
$$

The propositional atom B is called the *selected* atom. Essentially, we replace the fuzzy atom $\langle A_j, s_j \rangle$ with the fuzzy atoms $\langle B_1, s'_1 \rangle, \dots, \langle B_m, s'_m \rangle$ and accordingly replace the scoring variable s_j occurring in the scoring function f with $g(\mathbf{s}')$.

When the second rule is replaced with a fact, the specialized fuzzy SLD inference rule is:

$$
\begin{array}{ll}
\text{From} & \langle A, s \rangle \leftarrow \langle A_1, s_1 \rangle, \dots, \langle A_j, s_j \rangle, \dots, \langle A_k, s_k \rangle, s := f(\mathbf{s}) \\
\text{and} & \langle B, r \rangle \\
\text{and} & B = A_j \\
\hline
\text{infer} & \langle A, s \rangle \leftarrow \langle A_1, s_1 \rangle, \dots, \langle A_{j-1}, s_{j-1} \rangle, \\
& \quad \langle A_{j+1}, s_{j+1} \rangle \dots, \langle A_k, s_k \rangle, \\
& \quad s := f(s_1, \dots, s_{j-1}, r, s_{j+1}, \dots, s_k) \, .
\end{array}
\tag{11.12}
$$

In the above inference rules, we assume that the scoring function is evaluated as soon as all required parameters are ground.

A *fuzzy SLD-derivation* of q w.r.t. $\mathcal{K}$ consists of a finite sequence of rules $r_1, \dots, r_n$, each of which has q as head, each rule r_{i+1} is inferred from r_i via fuzzy SLD-resolution, and r_n is the rule

$$\langle q, s \rangle \leftarrow s := r$$

telling us that indeed the truth of q in the minimal model is greater or equal than $r \in [0, 1]_{\mathbb{Q}}$. r is called a *computed answer* of q w.r.t. $\mathcal{K}$.

Example 51. *Consider the following KB $\mathcal{K}$ with rules*

$$
\begin{align}
\langle q, s \rangle &\leftarrow \langle p_1, s_1 \rangle, \langle p_2, s_2 \rangle, s := s_1 \cdot s_2 \tag{11.13} \\
\langle q, s' \rangle &\leftarrow \langle p_3, s_3 \rangle, s' := \max(0.5, s_3) \tag{11.14} \\
\langle p_3, s'' \rangle &\leftarrow \langle p_1, s_4 \rangle, \langle p_2, s_5 \rangle, s'' := 0.3 \cdot s_4 + 0.7 \cdot s_5 \tag{11.15}
\end{align}
$$

and facts

$$
\begin{align}
&\langle p_1, 0.7 \rangle \tag{11.16} \\
&\langle p_2, 0.6 \rangle \tag{11.17}
\end{align}
$$

Let us determine the truth of q in the minimal model of $\mathcal{K}$. The following are two fuzzy SLD-derivations of q w.r.t. $\mathcal{K}$:

$$\langle q, s \rangle \leftarrow \langle p_2, s_2 \rangle, s := 0.7 \cdot s_2 \quad via\ (11.13), (11.16) \tag{11.18}$$

$$\langle q, s \rangle \leftarrow s := 0.42 \quad via\ (11.18), (11.17) \tag{11.19}$$

$$\langle q, s' \rangle \leftarrow \langle p_1, s_4 \rangle, \langle p_2, s_5 \rangle, s' := \max(0.5, 0.3 \cdot s_4 + 0.7 \cdot s_5) \quad via\ (11.14), (11.15) \tag{11.20}$$

$$\langle q, s' \rangle \leftarrow \langle p_2, s_5 \rangle, s' := \max(0.5, 0.3 \cdot 0.7 + 0.7 \cdot s_5) \quad via\ (11.20), (11.16) \tag{11.21}$$

$$\langle q, s' \rangle \leftarrow s' := 0.63 \quad via\ (11.21), (11.17) \tag{11.22}$$

It is easily verified that there is no other fuzzy SLD-derivation of q ending with a higher score than 0.63.

It can be shown that

Proposition 87 (Soundness & Completeness [104, 239, 456]). *Given a KB $\mathcal{K}$ and a query q, then*

1. *if $r \in [0,1]_{\mathbb{Q}}$ is a computed answer of q w.r.t. $\mathcal{K}$ then $M_{\mathcal{K}}(q) \geq r$;*

2. *there is a (finite) fuzzy SLD-derivation such that $M_{\mathcal{K}}(q)$ is a computed answer of q w.r.t. $\mathcal{K}$.*

We next address the FOL case, which is essentially the same as the propositional case described above, except that now we have to take unification into account.

The inference rules are the following (as usual, we assume a variable renaming of the second input in the inference rules):

$$
\begin{array}{ll}
\text{From} & \langle A, s \rangle \leftarrow \langle A_1, s_1 \rangle, \ldots, \langle A_j, s_j \rangle, \ldots, \langle A_k, s_k \rangle, s := f(\mathbf{z}, \mathbf{s}) \\
\text{and} & \langle B, s' \rangle \leftarrow \langle B_1, s'_1 \rangle, \ldots, \langle B_m, s'_m \rangle, s' := g(\mathbf{z}', \mathbf{s}') \\
\text{and} & \theta \text{ as a mgu of } \{B, A_j\} \\
\hline
\text{infer} & \langle A\theta, s \rangle \leftarrow \langle A_1\theta, s_1 \rangle, \ldots, \langle A_{j-1}\theta, s_{j-1} \rangle, \\
& \quad \langle B_1\theta, s'_1 \rangle, \ldots, \langle B_m\theta, s'_m \rangle, \\
& \quad \langle A_{j+1}\theta, s_{j+1} \rangle \ldots, \langle A_k\theta, s_k \rangle, \\
& \quad s := f(\mathbf{z}, s_1, \ldots, s_{j-1}, g(\mathbf{z}', \mathbf{s}'), s_{j+1}, \ldots, s_k)\theta \ .
\end{array}
\tag{11.23}
$$

$$
\begin{array}{ll}
\text{From} & \langle A, s \rangle \leftarrow \langle A_1, s_1 \rangle, \ldots, \langle A_j, s_j \rangle, \ldots, \langle A_k, s_k \rangle, s := f(\mathbf{z}, \mathbf{s}) \\
\text{and} & \langle B, r \rangle \\
\text{and} & \theta \text{ as a mgu of } \{B, A_j\} \\
\hline
\text{infer} & \langle A\theta, s \rangle \leftarrow \langle A_1\theta, s_1 \rangle, \ldots, \langle A_{j-1}\theta, s_{j-1} \rangle, \\
& \quad \langle A_{j+1}\theta, s_{j+1} \rangle \ldots, \langle A_k\theta, s_k \rangle, \\
& \quad s := f(\mathbf{z}, s_1, \ldots, s_{j-1}, r, s_{j+1}, \ldots, s_k)\theta \ .
\end{array}
\tag{11.24}
$$

Now, a *fuzzy SLD-derivation* of a query q w.r.t. $\mathcal{K}$ consists of a finite sequence of rules $r_1, \ldots, r_n$, each of which has q as head, each rule r_{i+1} is inferred from r_i via fuzzy SLD-resolution, and r_n is the rule

$$\langle q(\mathbf{x})\theta, s \rangle \leftarrow s := r$$

telling us that indeed the truth of

$$q(\mathbf{x})\theta$$

in the minimal model is greater than or equal to $r \in [0,1]_{\mathbb{Q}}$. With $\theta_{|\mathbf{x}}$ we denote the vector $\langle x_1\theta, \ldots, x_n\theta \rangle$, *i.e.*, the restriction of the substitution θ to the variables in $\mathbf{x}$. In that case, we say $\langle \theta_{|\mathbf{x}}, r \rangle$ is a *computed answer* for q.

As for the propositional case (see Proposition 87), it can be shown that

Proposition 88 (Soundness & Completeness [104, 239, 456]). *Given a KB $\mathcal{K}$ and a query $q(\mathbf{x})$, then*

1. *if $\langle \mathbf{t}, r \rangle$ is a computed answer, then $M_{\mathcal{K}}(q(\mathbf{t})) \geq r$, i.e., there is an answer $\langle \mathbf{t}, r' \rangle \in ans(\mathcal{K}, q)$ such that $r' \geq r$;*

2. *if $\langle \mathbf{t}, r \rangle \in ans(\mathcal{K}, q)$, then there is a (finite) fuzzy SLD-derivation such that $\langle \mathbf{t}, r \rangle$ is a computed answer of $q(\mathbf{x})$ w.r.t. $\mathcal{K}$.*

Therefore, in order to compute the answer set $ans(\mathcal{K}, q)$ via fuzzy SLD-derivation, it suffices to determine all computed answers of q w.r.t. $\mathcal{K}$.

Example 52. *Let us consider a FOL variant of Example 51. Consider the following KB $\mathcal{K}$ with rules*

$$\langle q(x), s \rangle \quad \leftarrow \quad \langle p_1(x), s_1 \rangle, \langle p_2(x), s_2 \rangle, s := s_1 \cdot s_2 \qquad (11.25)$$

$$\langle q(x), s \rangle \quad \leftarrow \quad \langle p_3(x), s_3 \rangle, s := \max(0.5, s_3) \qquad (11.26)$$

$$\langle p_3(x'), s' \rangle \quad \leftarrow \quad \langle p_1(x'), s_4 \rangle, \langle p_2(x'), s_5 \rangle, s' := 0.3 \cdot s_4 + 0.7 \cdot s_5 \qquad (11.27)$$

and facts

$$\langle p_1(a), 0.7 \rangle \qquad (11.28)$$

$$\langle p_2(a), 0.6 \rangle \qquad (11.29)$$

Let us determine the answer set of q. The following are two fuzzy SLD-derivation of $q(x)$ w.r.t. $\mathcal{K}$:

$$\langle q(a), s \rangle \leftarrow \langle p_2(a), s_2 \rangle, s := 0.7 \cdot s_2 \quad (11.25), (11.28),$$
$$\theta_1 = \{x/a\} \qquad (11.30)$$

$$\langle q(a), s \rangle \leftarrow s := 0.42 \quad (11.30), (11.29) \qquad (11.31)$$

$$\langle q(x), s \rangle \leftarrow \langle p_1(x), s_4 \rangle, \langle p_2(x), s_5 \rangle, s := \max(0.5, 0.3 \cdot s_4 + 0.7 \cdot s_5) \quad (11.26), (11.27),$$
$$\theta_2 = \{x'/x\} \quad (11.32)$$

$$\langle q(a), s \rangle \leftarrow \langle p_2(a), s_5 \rangle, s := \max(0.5, 0.3 \cdot 0.7 + 0.7 \cdot s_5) \quad (11.32), (11.28),$$
$$\theta_2 = \{x'/x, x/a\} (11.33)$$

$$\langle q(a), s \rangle \leftarrow s := 0.63 \quad (11.33), (11.29) \quad (11.34)$$

Hence, we have two computed answers $\langle a, 0.42 \rangle$ and $\langle a, 0.63 \rangle$. It easily verified that no other computed answer $\langle a, r \rangle$ with $r > 0.63$ exists and, thus, $\langle a, 0.63 \rangle \in ans(\mathcal{K}, q)$ (specifically, we have $ans(\mathcal{K}, q) = \{\langle a, 0.63 \rangle\}$).

Example 53. *Consider Example 49 and the query*

$$\langle q(x,y),s\rangle \leftarrow \langle \texttt{path}(x,y),s_1\rangle, s:=s_1 .$$

The following is a SLD-derivation of q w.r.t. $\mathcal{K}$ (see also Example 19):

$$\langle q(x,y),s\rangle \leftarrow \langle \texttt{path}(x,y),s_1\rangle, s:=s_1$$
$$\langle q(x,y),s\rangle \leftarrow \langle \texttt{path}(x,z),s_1\rangle, \langle \texttt{edge}(z,y),s_2\rangle, s:=\min(s_1,s_2)$$
$$\langle q(x,y),s\rangle \leftarrow \langle \texttt{path}(x,z_1),s_1\rangle, \langle \texttt{edge}(z_1,z),s_2\rangle, \langle \texttt{edge}(z,y),s_3\rangle, s:=\min(s_1,s_2,s_3)$$
$$\langle q(x,y),s\rangle \leftarrow \langle \texttt{edge}(x,z_1),s_1\rangle, \langle \texttt{edge}(z_1,z),s_2\rangle, \langle \texttt{edge}(z,y),s_3\rangle, s:=\min(s_1,s_2,s_3)$$
$$\langle q(c,y),s\rangle \leftarrow \langle \texttt{edge}(b,z),s_2\rangle, \langle \texttt{edge}(z,y),s_3\rangle, s:=\min(0.6,s_2,s_3)$$
$$\langle q(c,y),s\rangle \leftarrow \langle \texttt{edge}(a,y),s_3\rangle, s:=\min(0.6,0.4,s_3)$$
$$\langle q(c,c),s\rangle \leftarrow s:=\min(0.6,0.4,0.5) .$$

$\langle\langle c,c\rangle,0.4\rangle$ *is an answer computed by this SLD-derivation.*

11.5.2 Reduction to Classical Logic

Another and simple way to reason with fuzzy rules consists in mapping them into crisp LP rules, if arithmetic built-in atoms are supported (which is often the case). Essentially, we map an n-ary fuzzy atom $\langle p(\mathbf{z}),r\rangle$ into an $n+1$-ary atom $p(\mathbf{z},r)$, *i.e.*,

$$\langle p(\mathbf{z}),r\rangle \mapsto p(\mathbf{z},r) \tag{11.35}$$

and use the additional slot as a place holder of the degree of truth of the fuzzy atom. So a fact is mapped as

$$\langle p(\mathbf{t}),r\rangle \mapsto p(\mathbf{t},r) ,$$

while the rules having the same predicate in the head,

$$\langle p(\mathbf{x}),s\rangle \leftarrow \varphi_1(\mathbf{x},\mathbf{y}_1,\mathbf{s}_1)$$
$$\vdots \quad \vdots \quad \vdots$$
$$\langle p(\mathbf{x}),s\rangle \leftarrow \varphi_k(\mathbf{x},\mathbf{y}_k,\mathbf{s}_k)$$

can be transformed as

$$p_1'(\mathbf{x},s) \leftarrow \varphi_1'(\mathbf{x},\mathbf{y}_1,\mathbf{s}_1)$$
$$\vdots \quad \vdots \quad \vdots$$
$$p_k'(\mathbf{x},s) \leftarrow \varphi_k'(\mathbf{x},\mathbf{y}_k,\mathbf{s}_k)$$
$$p(\mathbf{x},s) \leftarrow p_1'(\mathbf{x},s_1),\ldots,p_k'(\mathbf{x},s_k), s:=\max(s_1,\ldots,s_k) ,$$

where p'_i are new predicate symbols and $\varphi'_i(\mathbf{x}, \mathbf{y}_i, \mathbf{s}_i)$ is obtained from $\varphi_i(\mathbf{x}, \mathbf{y}_i, \mathbf{s}_i)$ by using the replacement schema of Equation (11.35), which concludes the transformation.

11.5.3 Top-k Query Answering

While there are many works addressing the top-k problem for vague queries in databases (cf. [78, 94, 150, 152, 212, 213, 258, 257, 306]), little is known for the corresponding problem in knowledge representation and reasoning [97, 98, 110, 111, 289, 224, 358, 360, 404, 409, 410, 414, 421, 457].

We note that retrieving the top-k answers of an extensional relation p is trivial as we have just to retrieve the first k tuples in the relational table T_p associated to p. Hence, we restrict top-k retrieval to intensional relations only. Note also that (i) $ans_k(\mathcal{K}, q)$ is not necessarily unique as there may be several tuples having the same score of the bottom ranked one in $ans_k(\mathcal{K}, q)$ (we assume in this case that ties are broken arbitrary); and (ii) there may be less than k tuples in $ans_k(\mathcal{K}, q)$ as there might not be k non-$\perp$ scored tuples in $ans(\mathcal{K}, q)$.

Furthermore, please note that having introduced the degree $\perp \in \mathcal{L}$ allows us to be compatible with top-k SQL retrieval over relational databases (see, *e.g.*, [258]), where it is understood and common practice not to retrieve tuples that do not satisfy the condition of the plain SQL query (that is, the SQL query where the function computing the score is left out), and, in particular, tuples not occurring in any relational table (see *e.g.*, Example 50).

In the following, we address first the top-k retrieval problem for non-recursive KBs [409] and then address the general case [423].

11.5.3.1 Top-k Retrieval for Non-Recursive KBs

Consider a non-recursive KB $\mathcal{K}$. Interestingly, for such case there is a simple procedure to determine the top-k answers of a query [409], which closely resembles the one for DL-Lite (see Section 10.6.3):

1. by considering the rule component, the user query q is *reformulated* into a set of conjunctive queries $r(q, \mathcal{K})$ using the fuzzy SLD-resolution rule;

2. the reformulated queries in $r(q, \mathcal{K})$ are then *evaluated* over the facts component, which is stored in a database, producing the requested top-k answer set $ans_k(\mathcal{K}, q)$.

Specifically, given the fuzzy SLD-resolution rule (11.23), let r, r', r'' be the first, second, and inferred rule, respectively. We say that rule r' is *applicable* to atom A_j occurring in rule r and we call r'' the *resolvent* of r and A_j, denoted $resolve(r', A_j)$.

The query reformulation algorithm (Algorithm 6) is is quite similar to the DL-Lite case (see Section 10.6.3). Given a query q and a KB $\mathcal{K}$, the algorithm reformulates q in terms of a set of conjunctive queries $r(q, \mathcal{K})$, which then can be evaluated over the facts component in $\mathcal{K}$.

Algorithm 6 $\texttt{QueryRef}(q, \mathcal{K})$

Input: query q, KB $\mathcal{K}$.
Output: Set of reformulated conjunctive queries $r(q, \mathcal{K})$.
1: $r(q, \mathcal{K}) := \{q(\mathbf{x}) \leftarrow \phi \mid q(\mathbf{x}) \leftarrow \phi \in \mathcal{K}\}$
2: **repeat**
3:    $S = r(q, \mathcal{K})$
4:    **for all** queries $q \in S$ **do**
5:       **for all** atoms $A_j \in q$ **do**
6:          **if** rule $r' \in \mathcal{K}$ is applicable to A_j **then**
7:             $r(q, \mathcal{K}) := r(q, \mathcal{K}) \cup \{resolve(r', A_j)\}$
8: **until** $S = r(q, \mathcal{K})$
9: **return** $r(q, \mathcal{K})$

The termination of the query reformulation step is guaranteed by the non-recursiveness of $\mathcal{K}$. This concludes the query reformulation step.

Example 54 ([409]). *Suppose the rule component $\mathcal{P}$ contains the rules r_1 and r_2:*

$$r_1 : \quad T(x,y) \quad \leftarrow \quad P(x,y)$$
$$r_2 : \quad R(x,y) \quad \leftarrow \quad B(x), C(y) .$$

We also assume that the fact component $\mathcal{F}$ is

P		B	C
0	1	1	1
3	2	2	3
4	5	5	2
6	8	7	4

Assume also that we have the rules

$$q' : \quad \langle q(x), s \rangle \quad \leftarrow \quad T(x,y), R(y,z), s := \max(0, 1 - x/10)$$
$$q'' : \quad \langle q(x), s \rangle \quad \leftarrow \quad C(x), s := \max(0, 1 - x/5) .$$

Now, it can be verified that, e.g.,

$$\mathcal{K} \models \langle q(3), 0.7 \rangle$$
$$\mathcal{K} \models \langle q(1), 0.8 \rangle , \quad and$$
$$\mathcal{K} \not\models \langle q(6), v \rangle \quad for \ any \ v \in [0,1] ,$$

The answer set is

$$ans(\mathcal{K}, q) = \{\langle 0, 1.0 \rangle, \langle 1, 0.8 \rangle, \langle 2, 0.6 \rangle, \langle 3, 0.7 \rangle, \langle 4, 0.6 \rangle\}$$

and, thus, that the top-3 answers are

$$ans_3(\mathcal{K}, q) = \{\langle 0, 1.0 \rangle, \langle 1, 0.8 \rangle, \langle 3, 0.7 \rangle\} .$$

It can also be verified that

$$r(q, \mathcal{K}) = \{q', q'', q_1, q_2\} \ ,$$

where

$$
\begin{aligned}
q_1 : &\quad \langle q(x), s \rangle \quad \leftarrow \quad P(x,y), R(y,z), s := \max(0, 1 - x/10) \\
q_2 : &\quad \langle q(x), s \rangle \quad \leftarrow \quad P(x,y), B(y), C(z), s := \max(0, 1 - x/10) \ .
\end{aligned}
$$

It is easily verified that now we have only to evaluate q'' and q_2 over the facts component of $\mathcal{K}$, as both q' and q_1 queried over the fact components provide empty results only. Specifically, we have that

$$
\begin{aligned}
ans(\mathcal{F}, q'') &= \{\langle 1, 0.8 \rangle, \langle 3, 0.4 \rangle, \langle 2, 0.6 \rangle, \langle 4, 0.2 \rangle\} \\
ans(\mathcal{F}, q_2) &= \{\langle 0, 1.0 \rangle, \langle 3, 0.7 \rangle, \langle 4, 0.6 \rangle\} \ .
\end{aligned}
$$

Hence, $ans(\mathcal{K}, q)$ is obtained from $ans(\mathcal{F}, q'') \cup ans(\mathcal{F}, q_2)$ from which we drop a tuple $\langle \mathbf{t}, r \rangle$ if there is another tuple $\langle \mathbf{t}, r' \rangle$ in it with $r' > r$.

The main property of the query reformulation algorithm is as follows. It can be shown that

Proposition 89 ([409]). *Given a KB $\mathcal{K} = \langle \mathcal{F}, \mathcal{P} \rangle$ and a query q, then*

$$ans_k(\mathcal{K}, q) = \mathrm{Top}_k \{\langle \mathbf{t}, v \rangle \mid q_i \in r(q, \mathcal{P}), \langle q_i(\mathbf{t}), v \rangle \in ans(\mathcal{F}, q_i)\} \ .$$

The above property dictates that in order to determine the top-k answers, we may reformulate the query q using the rule component $\mathcal{P}$ only, and then query the reformulated queries $q_i \in r(q, \mathcal{P})$ against the fact component $\mathcal{F}$ stored in a relational database. From the union of these answer sets we can find the top-k answers.

Of course, the size of the rewriting $r(q, \mathcal{P})$ may be exponential w.r.t. to the size of q and $\mathcal{P}$ in the worst case as the following simple example illustrates.

Example 55. *Consider the query*

$$q(x) \leftarrow A_0(x)$$

and a set of rules $\mathcal{P}$ of the form $(i = 0, 1, \ldots, k-1)$

$$
\begin{aligned}
A_i(x) &\quad \leftarrow \quad A_{i+1}(x), C_{i+1}(x) \\
A_i(x) &\quad \leftarrow \quad A_{i+1}(x), D_{i+1}(x) \ .
\end{aligned}
$$

Then $\{q\} \cup \mathcal{P}$ has $2k + 1$ rules, whose size (number of atoms) is bounded by 3. So, $|q| + |\mathcal{P}|$ is $\mathcal{O}(k)$. Now, it is easy to see that $r(q, \mathcal{P})$ consists instead of 2^{k+1} rules. The size of $r(q, \mathcal{P})$ is

$$\sum_{i=0}^{k} 2^i \cdot (i+2) = 2 \cdot \sum_{i=0}^{k} \cdot 2^i + \sum_{i=0}^{k} i \cdot 2^i = 2 \cdot 2^{k+1} + (k-1) \cdot 2^{k+1} + 2 = (k+1) \cdot 2^{k+1} + 2 \ ,$$

which is $\mathcal{O}(k \cdot 2^k)$ and, thus, is exponential w.r.t. $|q| + |\mathcal{P}|$.

We next show how to find the top-k answers of the union of the answer sets of queries $q_i \in r(q, \mathcal{P})$.

A naive solution to the top-k retrieval problem is as for the case of DL-Lite: we compute for all $q_i \in r(q, \mathcal{P})$ the whole answer set $ans(\mathcal{F}, q_i)$, then we compute the union of these answer sets, order it in descending order of the scores and then we take the top-k tuples.

A more effective solution consists in relying on existing top-k query answering algorithms for relational databases (see, *e.g.*, [94, 150, 258]). Like for DL-Lite, we may compute for all $q_i \in r(q, \mathcal{P})$, the top-$k$ answers $ans_k(\mathcal{F}, q_i)$, using *e.g.*, the system RankSQL [258]; and if both k and the number, $n_q = |r(q, \mathcal{P})|$, of reformulated queries is reasonable, then we may compute the union, of these top-k answer sets, order it in descending order w.r.t. score and then we take the top-k tuples.

We can further improve this solution by adopting the *Disjunctive Threshold Algorithm* (DTA) we have seen also for DL-Lite.

While computing $r(q, \mathcal{P})$ may require exponential time w.r.t. the size of q and $\mathcal{P}$ (see Example 55), computing the top-k answers of each query $q_i \in r(q, \mathcal{P})$ requires (sub) linear time w.r.t. the database size (using, *e.g.*, [94]), and, thus, so does the DTA.

11.5.3.2   Top-k Retrieval: The General Case

We address here now the more general case in which $\mathcal{P}$ may be recursive (see [428]).

Consider $\mathcal{K} = \langle \mathcal{F}, \mathcal{P} \rangle$, consisting of a facts component $\mathcal{F}$ and an LP component $\mathcal{P}$. $\mathcal{F}$ is a finite set of facts of the form $\langle p(c_1, \ldots, c_n), s \rangle$. We assume that all rules in $\mathcal{P}$ are of the form

$$p(\mathbf{x}) \leftarrow f(p_1(\mathbf{z}_1), \ldots, p_m(\mathbf{z}_m)) .$$

For our purposes, in the following, let $H_{\mathcal{K}}$ and $B_{\mathcal{K}}$ be the Herbrand universe and Herbrand base of $\mathcal{K}$, respectively. An interpretation $\mathcal{I}$ for $\mathcal{K}$ is a function $I \colon B_{\mathcal{K}} \to \mathcal{L}$, where $\mathcal{L} = \{\bot, 0, \frac{1}{n}, \ldots \frac{n-1}{n}, 1\}$ and

1. $\mathcal{I}(r) = r$, for $r \in \mathcal{L}$; and

2. $\mathcal{I}(f(A_1, \ldots, A_m)) = f(\mathcal{I}(A_1), \ldots, \mathcal{I}(A_m)))$.

With $\mathcal{I}_\bot$ we denote the bottom interpretation ($\mathcal{I}_\bot$ maps all atoms to $\bot$), while with $\mathcal{I}_\top$ we denote the top interpretation ($\mathcal{I}_\top$ maps all atoms to 1).

We recap that $\mathcal{I}$ is a model of $\mathcal{K}$ iff for all ground rules $A \leftarrow \varphi \in \mathcal{K}^*$, $\mathcal{I}(\varphi) \leq I(A)$ holds. Differently to Section 11.2, the existence, finiteness, and uniqueness of the minimal model $M_{\mathcal{K}}$ is guaranteed to exist by the following non usual argument.

Consider $\mathcal{K}$, the Herbrand base $B_{\mathcal{K}} = \{A_1, \ldots, A_n\}$ and $\mathcal{K}^*$. Note that both are finite and so is $\mathcal{K}^*$. Let us associate each atom $A_i \in B_{\mathcal{K}}$ with a variable x_i, which will take a value in $\mathcal{L}$ (sometimes we will refer to that variable with x_A as well). An interpretation $\mathcal{I}$ may be seen as an assignment of truth values to the variables $x_1, ..., x_n$ and vice versa. Now, for each ground fact $\langle A, r \rangle$ in $\mathcal{K}^*$, we consider the equation

$$x_A = r$$

while for each ground rule $A \leftarrow f(A_1, ..., A_m)$ in $\mathcal{K}^*$ we consider the equation

$$x_A = f(x_{A_1}, ..., x_{A_m})$$

if A is head of at most one rule, while we consider the equation

$$x_A = \max\{f(...) \mid A \leftarrow f(...) \in \mathcal{K}^*\}$$

if A is head of more than one rule.

Now, given $\mathcal{K}^*$, we have obtained the system of equations

$$
\begin{aligned}
x_1 &= f_1(x_{1_1}, ..., x_{1_{a_1}}) , \\
&\vdots \\
x_n &= f_n(x_{n_1}, ..., x_{n_{a_n}}) ,
\end{aligned}
\tag{11.36}
$$

where the variables inside the functions f_i belong to $\{x_1, ..., x_n\}$.

Each variable x_{i_k} will take a value in $\mathcal{L}$, each (monotone) function f_i determines the value of x_i (*i.e.*, A_i). We refer to the monotone system as in Equation (11.36) as the tuple $\mathcal{S} = \langle \mathcal{L}, V, \mathbf{f} \rangle$, where $V = \{x_1, ..., x_n\}$ are the variables and $\mathbf{f} = \langle f_1, ..., f_n \rangle$ is the tuple of functions.

Now, it can be verified that the minimal model of $\mathcal{K}^*$, *i.e.*, $M_{\mathcal{K}}$, is bijectively related to the least solution of the system (11.36). As it is well known (see, *e.g.*, [9]), a monotonic equation system as (11.36) (each function $f_i \colon \mathcal{L}^{a_i} \mapsto \mathcal{L}$ in Equation (11.36) is $\leq$-monotone) has a $\leq$-least solution, lfp($\mathbf{f}$), the $\leq$-least fixed-point of $\mathbf{f}$ is given as the least upper bound of the $\leq$-monotone sequence, $\mathbf{y}_0, ..., \mathbf{y}_i, ...$, where

$$
\begin{aligned}
\mathbf{y}_0 &= \perp \\
\mathbf{y}_{i+1} &= \mathbf{f}(\mathbf{y}_i) .
\end{aligned}
\tag{11.37}
$$

It is thus immediate that, as the truth space is *finite*, the above sequence converges in a *finite* number of steps and that the $\leq$-least model $M_{\mathcal{K}}$ of $\mathcal{K}$ is finite.

Computing top-k answers. We describe an incremental query driven top-k query answering algorithm.

A distinguishing feature of our query answering procedure is that we do not determine all answers, but collect, during the computation, answers incrementally together and we can stop as soon as we have gathered k answers greater or equal than a computed threshold δ.

For the ease of reading, we will proceed stepwise. In the next section, we will provide an algorithm answering ground queries. Additionally, we will see later on that the same algorithm can be used to compute the threshold we are going to use later on. Eventually, we will extend the latter procedure to compute the top-k answers only.

A query driven procedure for equational systems. It is illustrative to address the following specific problem. Consider an equational system $\mathcal{S} = \langle \mathcal{L}, V, \mathbf{f} \rangle$ and a variable x_i. How can we compute the value of variable x_i in the least fixed point of $\mathcal{S}$? The immediate way is to compute bottom-up the least fixed point as described in Equation (11.37), and then look for the value of x_i in the least fixed point. But, there is also a query driven method [9]. The method has been used then in [400] as a basis for a query driven ground query answering method for normal logic programs and has further been extended in [289, 413, 414]. This is not surprising, as we have seen in the previous section that the minimal model of $\mathcal{K}^*$, i.e., $M_{\mathcal{K}}$, is bijectively related to the least solution of a system of the form (11.36). Hence, if we want to know the truth value of a ground atom A in $M_{\mathcal{K}}$, it suffices to look at the value of the variable x_A in the least fixed point of the related equational system.

Formally, consider an equational system $\mathcal{S} = \langle \mathcal{L}, V, \mathbf{f} \rangle$ of the form (11.36). The procedure described in Algorithm 7 determines the value of a set of variables in Q in the least-fixed point, and is a slight refinement of the one presented in [9].

Algorithm 7 $Solve(\mathcal{S}, Q)$

Input: $\preceq$-monotonic system $\mathcal{S} = \langle \mathcal{L}, V, \mathbf{f} \rangle$, where $Q \subseteq V$ is the set of query variables
Output: A mapping $\mathbf{v}$ that equals lfp($\mathbf{f}$) on Q
1: A: $= Q$, dg: $= Q$, in: $= \emptyset$
2: **for all** $x \in V$ **do**
3:     $\mathbf{v}(x) = \bot$, $\texttt{exp}(x) = \texttt{false}$
4: **while** A $\neq \emptyset$ **do**
5:     select $x_i \in$ A, A: $=$ A $\setminus \{x_i\}$, dg: $=$ dg $\cup$ s(x_i)
6:     r: $= f_i(\mathbf{v}(x_{i_1}), ..., \mathbf{v}(x_{i_{a_i}}))$
7:     **if** $r > \mathbf{v}(x_i)$ **then**
8:         $\mathbf{v}(x_i)$: $= r$, A: $=$ A $\cup$ (p(x_i) $\cap$ dg)
9:         **if not** $\texttt{exp}(p_i)$ **then**
10:             $\texttt{exp}(x_i) = \texttt{true}$, A: $=$ A $\cup$ (s(x_i) $\setminus$ in), in: $=$ in $\cup$ s(x_i)
11: **return** $\mathbf{v}$

We next describe how it works. We use some auxiliary functions. $\mathbf{s}(x)$ denotes the set of *sons* of x, i.e.,

$$\mathbf{s}(x_i) = \{x_{i_1}, \ldots, x_{i_{a_i}}\}$$

(the set of variables appearing in the right-hand side of the definition of x_i in (11.36)). $\mathbf{p}(x)$ denotes the set of *parents* of x, i.e., the set

$$\mathbf{p}(x) = \{x_i \mid x \in \mathbf{s}(x_i)\}$$

(the set of variables depending directly on the value of x). We assume that each function $f_i : \mathcal{L}^{a_i} \mapsto \mathcal{L}$ in Equation (11.36) is $\preceq$-monotone. We also use f_x

in place of f_i, for $x = x_i$. Informally the algorithm works as follows. Assume we are interested in the value of x_0 in the least fixed point of the system. We associate to each variable x_i a marking $\mathbf{v}(x_i)$ denoting the current value of x_i (the mapping $\mathbf{v}$ contains the current value associated to the variables). Initially, $\mathbf{v}(x_i)$ is $\bot$.

We start with putting x_0 in the *active* set of variables $\mathbf{A}$, for which we evaluate whether the current value of the variable is identical to whatever its right-hand side evaluates to. When evaluating a right-hand side it might of course turn out that we do indeed need a better value of some sons (which are initialized with the value $\bot$) and put them on the set of active nodes to be examined. If it turns out that a variable changes its value (actually, it can only $\le$-increase) all variables that might depend on this variable are put in the active set to be re-examined. At some point (even if cyclic definitions are present) the active set will become empty, because of the finiteness of the truth space, and we have actually found part of the fixed point, sufficient to determine the value of the query x_0.

The variable $\mathbf{dg}$ collects the variables that may influence the value of the query variables, the array variable $\mathbf{exp}$ traces the equations that have been "expanded" (the body variables are put into the active set), while the variable $\mathbf{in}$ keeps track of the variables that have been put into the active set so far due to an expansion (to avoid putting the same variable multiple times in the active set due to function body expansion).

In [9], it is shown that the above algorithm behaves correctly.

Proposition 90 ([9]). *Given a monotone system of equations $\mathcal{S} = \langle \mathcal{L}, V, \mathbf{f} \rangle$, then after a finite number of steps, $Solve(\mathcal{S}, Q)$ determines a mapping $\mathbf{v}$ that equals to $lfp(\mathbf{f})$ on Q, i.e., $\mathbf{v}_{|Q} = lfp(\mathbf{f})_{|Q}$.*

See [428] for the computational complexity of the *Solve* procedure.

A query driven top-k procedure. We are ready now to describe the query driven top-k algorithm [428].

The procedure *TopAnswers* is detailed in Algorithm 8.[2] Basically, we will compute answers iteratively one by one together with a threshold δ such that if we have already collected k answers with a score greater than or equal to δ we can stop, as any not yet computed answer will have a score no greater than δ.

Roughly, we proceed as follows. Suppose q is the query. We start with putting the predicate symbol q in the *active* set of predicate symbols $\mathbf{A}$. At each iteration step we select a new predicate p from $\mathbf{A}$, look for the next highest scoring tuple for p (procedure *getNextTuple*), update the current answer set for p ($rankedList(p)$), add all predicates p', whose rule body contains p (the parents of p), to $\mathbf{A}$, i.e., all predicate symbols that might depend on p are put in the active set to be examined, and finally we update the threshold. If we

---

[2]The condition $\mathbf{rL'} = \mathbf{rankedList}$ means that the contents do not change.

have already gathered k answers for q whose score is greater than or equal to the threshold we stop. Our procedure uses also some auxiliary functions and data structures:

- for predicate symbol p_i, $s(p_i)$ is the set of predicate symbols occurring in the rule body of a rule having p_i in its head[3], *i.e.*, the *sons* of p_i, from which we exclude the extensional predicates. $p(p_i)$ denotes the parents of p_i, *i.e.*, $p(p_i) = \{p_j \mid p_i \in s(p_j)\}$;

- the variable `rankedList` contains, for each intensional relation p, the current ranked tuples together with their score;

- the variable `Q` is a global variable. It is used in the *getNextTuple* procedure and contains, for each intensional relation p, the next top-ranked tuple to be returned. The tuples in `Q`(p) are ranked in decreasing order with respect to the score s.

Algorithm 8 *TopAnswers*$(\mathcal{L}, \mathcal{K}, q, k)$

Input: Truth space $\mathcal{L}$, KB $\mathcal{K} = \langle \mathcal{F}, \mathcal{P} \rangle$, query relation q, $k \geq 1$.
Output: Mapping `rankedList` such that `rankedList`(q) contains top-k answers of q.
1: $\delta = 1$
2: **for all** predicates p in $\mathcal{P}$ **do**
3:     **if** p intensional **then**
4:         `rankedList`$(p) = \emptyset$, `Q`$(p) := \emptyset$
5:     **if** p extensional **then**
6:         `rankedList`$(p) = T_p$
7: **repeat**
8:     **if** `A` $= \emptyset$ **then**
9:         `A` $:= \{q\}$, `dg` $:= \{q\}$, `in` $:= \emptyset$, `rL'` $:=$ `rankedList`, initialise all pointers in the relations tables to point to the first record
10:         **for all** intensional predicates p **do**
11:           $\exp(p) = $ **false**
12:     **select** $p \in$ `A`, `A` $:=$ `A` $\setminus \{p\}$, `dg` $:=$ `dg` $\cup s(p)$
13:     $\langle t, s \rangle := getNextTuple(p)$
14:     **if** $\langle t, s \rangle \neq$ **null then**
15:         `rankedList`$(p) := $ `rankedList`$(p) \cup \{\langle t, s \rangle\}$, `A` $:=$ `A` $\cup (p(p) \cap$ `dg`$)$
16:     **if not** $\exp(p)$ **then**
17:         $\exp(p) = $ **true**, `A` $:=$ `A` $\cup (s(p) \setminus$ `in`$)$, `in` $:=$ `in` $\cup s(p)$
18:     Update threshold δ
19: **until** (`rankedList`(q) does contain k top-ranked tuples with score greater or equal than query rule threshold) **or** ((`rL'` $=$ `rankedList`) **and** `A` $= \emptyset$)
20: **return** top-k ranked tuples in `rankedList`(q)

Note that the termination of the algorithm is guaranteed by the finiteness of the knowledge base, the finiteness of the truth set, and the monotonicity of the score combination functions: each tuple may enter a ranked list at most $h = |\mathcal{L}| - 1$ times and we stop as soon as two successive loops in *TopAnswers* do not change the ranked lists and the queue `A` becomes empty.[4]

---

[3] Recall that there may be more than one rule having p_i in its head.
[4] (`rL'` $=$ `rankedList`) and `A` $= \emptyset$.

Algorithm 9 *getNextTuple(p)*

Input: Intensional relation symbol p.
Output: Next instance of p together with the score.
1: Consider set of rules $\mathcal{R} = \{r \mid r : p(\mathbf{x}) \leftarrow f(A_1, \ldots, A_n) \in \mathcal{P}\}$
2: Let p_i be the relation symbols occurring in A_i
3: **if** $\mathbb{Q}(p) \neq \emptyset$ **then**
4: $\quad \langle \mathbf{t}, s \rangle := getTop(\mathbb{Q}(p))$
5: $\quad$ remove $\langle \mathbf{t}, s \rangle$ from $\mathbb{Q}(p)$
6: $\quad$ **return** $\langle \mathbf{t}, s \rangle$
7: **repeat**
8: $\quad$ **for all** $r \in \mathcal{R}$ **do**
9: $\qquad$ Generate the set T of all new valid join tuples $\mathbf{t}$ for rule r, using tuples in rankedList(p_i) and square ripple join (see [212])
10: $\qquad$ **for all** $\mathbf{t} \in T$ **do**
11: $\qquad\quad$ $s :=$ compute the score of $p(\mathbf{t})$ using f
12: $\qquad\quad$ **if neither** $\langle \mathbf{t}, s' \rangle \in$ rankedList(p) **nor** $\langle \mathbf{t}, s' \rangle \in \mathbb{Q}(p)$ with $s \leq s'$ **then**
13: $\qquad\qquad$ insert $\langle \mathbf{t}, s \rangle$ into $\mathbb{Q}(p)$
14: **until** $\mathbb{Q}(p) \neq \emptyset$ **or** no new valid join tuple can be generated
15: **if** $\mathbb{Q}(p) \neq \emptyset$ **then**
16: $\quad \langle \mathbf{t}, s \rangle := getTop(\mathbb{Q}(p))$
17: $\quad$ remove $\langle \mathbf{t}, s \rangle$ from $\mathbb{Q}(p)$
18: $\quad$ **return** $\langle \mathbf{t}, s \rangle$
19: **else**
20: $\quad$ **return** null

We now describe the *getNextTuple* procedure (see Algorithm 9). Its main purpose is, given a relation symbol p and the rules $r_i : p(\mathbf{x}) \leftarrow \varphi_i$ having $p(\mathbf{x})$ as head, to get back the next tuple (and its score) satisfying the body conditions of some of these rules using the so far retrieved tuples for the relations occurring in φ_i.

Whenever we already have some join combinations for p in the queue $\mathbb{Q}(p)$ (obtained by a previous call) then we just return the top-ranked one. Otherwise, we take into account all rules r having p in its head. For each rule r, we try to generate join combinations for p, involving all seen tuples of the relations occurring in the rule body of r. For each join combination we compute its score. We put the results on the queue $\mathbb{Q}(p)$ and return the top-ranked one. As $\mathbb{Q}(p)$ may still contain answers for p, the next time we ask for a next tuple with respect to p, we access $\mathbb{Q}(p)$ directly.

Example 56 ([428]). *Consider the rule*

$$r : p(x, z) \leftarrow p_1(x, y) \cdot p_2(y, z) \ .$$

Assume that actually rankedList(p_1) *and* rankedList(p_2) *contain the following tuples.*

recId	rankedList(p_1)			rankedList(p_2)		
1	a	b	1.0	m	h	0.95
2	e	f	0.9	m	j	0.85
3	l	m	0.8	f	k	0.75
4	c	d	0.7	m	n	0.65
5	o	p	0.6	p	q	0.55

It can be verified that a call to getNextTuple(p), will put two join combinations $\langle l, h, 0.76 \rangle$ and $\langle l, j, 0.68 \rangle$ into Q(p). Therefore, the procedure will return $\langle l, h, 0.76 \rangle$ as the result and remove $\langle l, h, 0.76 \rangle$ from Q(p).

The second call of getNextTuple(p), we will return $\langle l, j, 0.68 \rangle$ as Q(p) is still non-empty, and remove this tuple from Q(p) (which makes it empty). The third call of getNextTuple(p), it will return $\langle e, f, 0.675 \rangle$. The fourth call of getNextTuple(p), it we return $\langle l, n, 0.52 \rangle$. Finally, in the fifth call of getNextTuple(p), it will return $\langle o, q, 0.33 \rangle$.

Threshold for querying an extensional knowledge base. Assume that we have a knowledge base in which the rule component consists of one rule only (the query rule) of the form

$$r : q(\mathbf{x}) \leftarrow f(p_1, p_2, \ldots, p_n) \ ,$$

where all p_i are extensional predicates. Example 56 is such a case. In this case, the threshold δ is determined as in [212], which we illustrate next.

Let $\mathbf{t}_i^r$ be the last tuple seen in rankedList(p_i) so far with respect to rule r, while let $\hat{\mathbf{t}}_i$ be the top ranked one in rankedList(p_i). With $\mathbf{t}.score$ we indicate the score of tuple $\mathbf{t}$.[5] Then we define δ^r as the maximum of the following n values:

$$\begin{aligned} \delta_1^r &= f(\mathbf{t}_1^r.score, \hat{\mathbf{t}}_2.score, \ldots, \hat{\mathbf{t}}_n.score) \\ \delta_2^r &= f(\hat{\mathbf{t}}_1.score, \mathbf{t}_2^r.score, \ldots, \hat{\mathbf{t}}_n.score) \\ &\vdots \quad \vdots \quad \vdots \\ \delta_n^r &= f(\hat{\mathbf{t}}_1.score, \hat{\mathbf{t}}_2.score, \ldots, \mathbf{t}_n^r.score) \ . \end{aligned}$$

Finally, we define the threshold to be used in the *TopAnswer* procedure as $\delta = \delta^r$. For instance, for

$$q(x) \leftarrow p_1(x, y) \cdot p_2(y, z)$$

we have

$$\begin{aligned} \delta_1^r &= \mathbf{t}_1^r.score \cdot \hat{\mathbf{t}}_2.score \\ \delta_2^r &= \hat{\mathbf{t}}_1.score \cdot \mathbf{t}_2^r.score \\ \delta^r &= \max(\delta_1^r, \delta_2^r) \ . \end{aligned}$$

Example 57 (Example 56 cont.). *After the first call of getNextTuple(p) we have that*

$\hat{\mathbf{t}}_1$	$\mathbf{t}_1^r$	$\hat{\mathbf{t}}_2$	$\mathbf{t}_2^r$
$\langle a, b, 1.0 \rangle$	$\langle l, m, 0.8 \rangle$	$\langle m, h, 0.95 \rangle$	$\langle m, j, 0.85 \rangle$

---

[5]If no tuple has been yet seen in p_i, then $\mathbf{t}.score = 1$ is assumed.

and, thus,

$$\delta_1^r = 0.8 \cdot 0.95 = 0.76$$
$$\delta_2^r = 1.0 \cdot 0.85 = 0.85$$
$$\delta^r = \max(0.76, 0.85) = 0.85 \ .$$

The important fact is now that whenever we consider a new join combination for rule r, its score will be *less than or equal to* δ^r. Indeed, if we consider a new join tuple using the next unseen tuple from $\mathtt{rankedList}(p_1)$ and a seen tuple in $\mathtt{rankedList}(p_2)$, its score will be less than or equal to δ_1^r, while if we consider a new join tuple using the next unseen tuple from $\mathtt{rankedList}(p_2)$ and a seen tuple in $\mathtt{rankedList}(p_1)$, its score will be less than or equal to δ_2^r. Therefore, overall the score will be less than or equal to δ^r.

Example 58 (Example 57 cont.). *In the second call to $getNextTuple(p)$, we get $\langle l, j, 0.68 \rangle$ and $0.68 \leq 0.85 = \delta^r$, in the third call to $getNextTuple(p)$, we get $\langle e, f, 0.675 \rangle$ and $0.675 \leq 0.85 = \delta^r$, in the fourth call to $getNextTuple(p)$, we get $\langle l, n, 0.52 \rangle$ and $0.52 \leq 0.76 = \delta^r$ (note that after the third call, $\delta^r = 0.76$), while the fifth call to $getNextTuple(p)$, we get $\langle o, q, 0.33 \rangle$ and $0.33 \leq 0.665 = \delta^r$ (after the fourth call, $\delta^r = 0.665$).*

As a consequence, whenever we have top-k answers for q with a score greater than or equal to δ^r, we can stop the retrieval process (see step 9 of *TopAnswers*).

This property can be generalized to n-ary joins (see [212], Theorem 4.2.1). The following result holds:

Proposition 91 ([428]). *For a knowledge base in which the rule component consists of one rule r only (the query rule) of the form $r : q(\mathbf{x}) \leftarrow f(p_1, p_2, \ldots, p_n)$, where all p_i are extensional predicates, then the threshold-based method correctly reports the top-k results ordered by the score.*

We next show that we may easily extend our threshold-based method to the case that for a query we have a knowledge base in which the rule component consists of $m \geq 1$ rules (the query rules) of the form

$$r_1 \quad : \quad q(\mathbf{x}) \leftarrow f_1(p_1^1, p_2^1, \ldots, p_{n_1}^1)$$
$$\vdots \qquad\qquad \vdots$$
$$r_m \quad : \quad q(\mathbf{x}) \leftarrow f_m(p_1^m, p_2^m, \ldots, p_{n_m}^m)$$

where all p_i^j are extensional predicates. In this case, let δ^{r_i} be the threshold for rule r_i, as computed previously. Now, let δ^q be

$$\delta^q = \max(\delta^{r_1}, \ldots, \delta^{r_m}) \ . \tag{11.38}$$

Finally, we define $\delta = \delta^q$.

It is easily verified that Proposition 91 holds for this more general case as well.

Proposition 92 ([428]). *For a knowledge base in which the rule compo-nent consists of rules $r_1, \ldots, r_m$ having $q(\mathbf{x})$ as their head (the query rules), where the arguments of the rules are extensional predicates and $\delta = \delta^q = \max(\delta^{r_1}, \ldots, \delta^{r_m})$, then the threshold-based method correctly reports the top-k results ordered by the score.*

Threshold for querying an intensional knowledge base. We address now the general case [428]. For this purpose consider the following example.

The solution provided by [428] is that we need to take into account a threshold for each intensional predicate related to the query as they may depend on each other.

Specifically, let us consider a knowledge base in which an intensional pred-icate is head of *one rule only* (we address the case p is head of more than one rule later on, similarly as we did previously). So, for an intensional predicate p heading exactly one rule r

$$r : p(\mathbf{x}) \leftarrow f(p_1(\mathbf{z}_1), \ldots, p_n(\mathbf{z}_n))$$

we consider a threshold variable δ^p. With $r.\mathbf{t}_{p_i}$ ($\hat{r}.\mathbf{t}_{p_i}$) we denote the last tuple seen (the top ranked one) in $\texttt{rankedList}(p_i)$ with respect to rule r. We assume that by default $\hat{r}.\mathbf{t}_{p_i}.score = 1$ if no tuple is $\texttt{rankedList}(p_i)$. For an intensional predicate p_i, we define

$$\begin{aligned} p_i^\top &= \max(\delta^{p_i}, \hat{r}.\mathbf{t}_{p_i}.score) \\ p_i^\perp &= \delta^{p_i}, \end{aligned}$$

while if p_i is an extensional predicate, we define

$$\begin{aligned} p_i^\top &= \hat{r}.\mathbf{t}_{p_i}.score \\ p_i^\perp &= r.\mathbf{t}_{p_i}.score. \end{aligned}$$

Now, for each rule r we consider the equation $\delta(r)$

$$\delta^p = \max(f(p_1^\perp, p_2^\top, \ldots, p_n^\top), f(p_1^\top, p_2^\perp, \ldots, p_n^\top), \ldots, f(p^\top, p^\top, \ldots, p_n^\perp)). \quad (11.39)$$

Eventually, for a knowledge base $\mathcal{K} = \langle \mathcal{F}, \mathcal{P} \rangle$, we consider the set Δ of all equations involving intensional predicates. Note that, if $\mathcal{K}$ has m intensional predicates, Δ consists of m equations and m variables. As all equations in-volve monotone functions only, the system of equations is monotone, Δ has a minimal solution, denoted $\bar{\Delta}$. Finally, for a query $q(\mathbf{x})$, the threshold δ of the *TopAnswers* algorithm is defined as

$$\delta = \bar{\delta}^q,$$

where $\bar{\delta}^q$ is the solution to variable δ^q in the minimal solution $\bar{\Delta}$ of the set of equations Δ.

Please note that $\bar{\Delta}$ and, thus, $\bar{\delta}^q$, can be computed iteratively as described in Equation 11.37. Of course, if specific functions are involved only (*e.g.*, linear functions), then better methods may be available to compute the minimal solution. We may also apply the $Solve(\Delta, \{\delta^q\})$ algorithm to compute $\bar{\delta}^q$ in a more effective and query driven manner.

In case an intensional relation p is in the head of more than one rule, *e.g.*,

$$\begin{aligned} r_1 : p(\mathbf{x}) &\leftarrow \varphi_1(\mathbf{x}, \mathbf{y}) \\ r_2 : p(\mathbf{x}) &\leftarrow \varphi_2(\mathbf{x}, \mathbf{y}) \end{aligned} \tag{11.40}$$

we proceed as previously in case of empty logic program in which now δ^p is the maximum among the thresholds computed for rule r_1 and r_2 according to Equation (11.39). That is, for two new relations p', p'', we define

$$\delta^p = \max(\delta^{p'}, \delta^{p''}) \tag{11.41}$$

where $\delta^{p'}, \delta^{p''}$ are the thresholds computed according to Equation (11.39) for the two rules

$$\begin{aligned} p'(\mathbf{x}) &\leftarrow \varphi_1(\mathbf{x}, \mathbf{y}) \\ p''(\mathbf{x}) &\leftarrow \varphi_1(\mathbf{x}, \mathbf{y}) \,. \end{aligned} \tag{11.42}$$

Example 59 (Example 49 cont.). *Let us determine top-3 answers for* path. *It can be verified that the equations for the threshold computation are:*

$$\delta^{\texttt{path}} = \max(\delta^{\texttt{path}'}, \delta^{\texttt{path}''})$$

$$\delta^{\texttt{path}'} = r_1.\mathbf{t}_{\texttt{edge}}.score$$

$$\delta^{\texttt{path}''} = \max(\min(\delta^{\texttt{path}}, \hat{r}_2.\mathbf{t}_{\texttt{edge}}.score), \min(\max(\delta^{\texttt{path}}, \hat{r}_2.\mathbf{t}_{\texttt{path}}.score), r_2.\mathbf{t}_{\texttt{edge}}.score))$$

The computation is shown below (we use the abbreviations p, p', p'', e *for* path, path', path'' *and* edge, *respectively*).

									scores			
Iter	A	p	$\langle \mathbf{t}, s \rangle$	rankedList(p)	$\delta^{\texttt{p}}$	$\delta^{\texttt{p}'}$	$\delta^{\texttt{p}''}$	$r_1.\mathbf{t}_{\texttt{e}}$	$\hat{r}_2.\mathbf{t}_{\texttt{p}}$	$r_2.\mathbf{t}_{\texttt{e}}$	$\hat{r}_2.\mathbf{t}_{\texttt{e}}$
Loop 1					1.0	1.0	1.0	1.0	1.0	1.0	1.0
1.	p	p'	$\langle c, b, 0.6 \rangle$	$\langle c, b, 0.6 \rangle$	1.0	0.6	1.0	0.6	1.0	1.0	1.0
2.	p	p	$\langle a, c, 0.5 \rangle$	$\langle c, b, 0.6 \rangle, \langle a, c, 0.5 \rangle$	0.5	0.5	0.5	0.5	0.6	0.4	0.6
3.	p	p	$\langle c, a, 0.4 \rangle$	$\langle c, b, 0.6 \rangle, \langle a, c, 0.5 \rangle,$ $\langle c, a, 0.4 \rangle$	0.5	0.5	0.5	0.5	0.6	0.4	0.6
4.	p	p	$\langle a, b, 0.5 \rangle$	$\langle c, b, 0.6 \rangle, \langle a, c, 0.5 \rangle,$ $\langle a, b, 0.5 \rangle, \langle c, a, 0.4 \rangle$	0.4	0.4	0.4	0.4	0.6	0.4	0.6
Stop, return $\langle c, b, 0.6 \rangle, \langle a, c, 0.5 \rangle, \langle a, b, 0.5 \rangle$											

TopAnswers

Note that further answers for path *have a score not greater than the threshold* $\delta^{\texttt{path}} = 0.4$.

Proposition 93 ([428]). *Given a knowledge base, the generalized threshold-based method correctly reports the top-k results ordered by the score.*

We refer the reader to [428] for further insights on the top-k retrieval algorithm and for the computational complexity analysis of the *TopAnswers* procedure.

Part III

Appendices

Appendix A

RDFS Semantics and Inference Rules

For the sake of completeness, we reproduce here the definitions and axioms of the normative semantics of RDFS [307, 362] consisting of a model theory and axiomatic triples. We also recap a complete inference rule set.

The set $rdfsV$ stands for the RDFS vocabulary and is illustrated in Table A.1 with the shortcuts we use in brackets. The first column shows built-in classes, and the second and third show built-in properties.

An *interpretation* $\mathcal{I}$ over a vocabulary V is a tuple

$$\mathcal{I} = \langle \Delta_R, \Delta_P, \Delta_C, \Delta_L, P[\![\cdot]\!], C[\![\cdot]\!], \cdot^{\mathcal{I}} \rangle ,$$

where $\Delta_R, \Delta_P, \Delta_C, \Delta_L$ are the interpretation domains of $\mathcal{I}$, which are finite non-empty sets, and $P[\![\cdot]\!], C[\![\cdot]\!], \cdot^{\mathcal{I}}$ are the interpretation functions of $\mathcal{I}$. They have to satisfy:

1. Δ_R are the resources (the domain or universe of $\mathcal{I}$);

2. Δ_P are property names (not necessarily disjoint from Δ_R);

3. $\Delta_C \subseteq \Delta_R$ are the classes;

4. $\Delta_L \subseteq \Delta_R$ are the literal values and contains $\mathbf{L} \cap V$;

5. $P[\![\cdot]\!]$ is a function $P[\![\cdot]\!]: \Delta_P \to 2^{\Delta_R \times \Delta_R}$;

TABLE A.1: RDFS vocabulary.

rdfs:Resource [res]	rdf:type [type]	rdfs:isDefinedBy [isDefined]
rdf:Property [prop]	rdfs:domain [dom]	rdfs:comment [comment]
rdfs:Class [class]	rdfs:range [range]	rdfs:label [label]
rdfs:Literal [literal]	rdfs:subClassOf [sc]	rdf:value [value]
rdfs:Datatype [datatype]	rdfs:subPropertyOf [sp]	rdf:nil [nil]
rdf:XMLLiteral [xmlLit]	rdf:subject [subj]	rdf:_1 [_1]
rdfs:Container [cont]	rdf:predicate [pred]	rdf:_2 [_2]
rdf:Statement [stat]	rdf:object [obj]	...
rdf:List [list]	rdfs:member [member]	rdf:_i [_i]
rdf:Alt [alt]	rdf:first [first]	...
rdf:Bag [bag]	rdf:rest [rest]	
rdf:Seq [seq]	rdfs:seeAlso [seeAlso]	
rdfs:ContainerMembershipProperty [contMP]		

TABLE A.2: RDFS axiomatic triples.

(type, type, prop)	(subj, type, prop)	(pred, type, prop)	(obj, type, prop)
(first, type, prop)	(rest, type, prop)	(value, type, prop)	(_1, type, prop)
(_2, type, prop)	...		
(nil, type, list)	(type, dom, res)	(dom, dom, prop)	(range, dom, prop)
(sp, dom, prop)	(sc, dom, class)	(subj, dom, stat)	(pred, dom, stat)
(obj, dom, stat)	(member, dom, res)	(first, dom, list)	(rest, dom, list)
(seeAlso, dom, res)	(isDefined, dom, res)	(comment, dom, res)	(label, dom, res)
(value, dom, res)	(type, range, class)	(dom, range, class)	(range, range, class)
(sp, range, prop)	(sc, range, class)	(subj, range, res)	(pred, range, res)
(obj, range, res)	(member, range, res)	(first, range, res)	(seeAlso, range, res)
(isDefined, range, res)	(comment, range, literal)	(label, range, literal)	(value, range, res)
(alt, sc, cont)	(bag, sc, cont)	(seq, sc, cont)	(contMP, sc, prop)
(isDefined, sp, seeAlso)	(xmlLit, type, datatype)	(xmlLit, sc, literal)	(datatype, sc, class)
(_1, type, contMP)	(_1, dom, res)	(_1, range, res)	(_2, type, contMP)
(_2, dom, res)	(_2, range, res)	...	

6. $C[\![\cdot]\!]$ is a function $C[\![\cdot]\!]: \Delta_C \to 2^{\Delta_R}$;

7. $\cdot^{\mathcal{I}}$ maps each $t \in \mathbf{UL} \cap V$ into a value $t^{\mathcal{I}} \in \Delta_R \cup \Delta_P$, and such that $\cdot^{\mathcal{I}}$ is the identity for plain literals and assigns an element in Δ_R to each element in $\mathbf{L}$.

An interpretation $\mathcal{I}$ is a *model* of a ground graph G, denoted $\mathcal{I} \models G$, if and only if $\mathcal{I}$ is an interpretation over the vocabulary $rdfsV \cup universe(G)$ that satisfies the RDFS axiomatic triples [307, 362] (see Table A.2) and the semantic conditions as in Table A.3.

A ground graph G *entails* a ground graph H if and only if any model of G is also a model of H. A graph G *entails* a graph H, denoted $G \models H$, if and only if for any grounding G' of G there is a grounding H' of H such that $G' \models H'$.

Next, we provide a sound and complete deductive system for RDFS. The system is arranged in groups of rules that capture the semantic conditions of models. In every rule, $A, B, C, X,$ and Y are meta-variables representing elements in **UBL** and D, E represent elements in **UL**. The rules are described below.

1. Simple:

    (a) $\frac{G}{G'}$ for a map $\mu: G' \to G$

    (b) $\frac{G}{G'}$ for $G' \subseteq G$

2. Subproperty:

    (a) $\frac{(A,\text{sp},B),(B,\text{sp},C)}{(A,\text{sp},C)}$

    (b) $\frac{(D,\text{sp},E),(X,D,Y)}{(X,E,Y)}$

    (c) $\frac{(A,\text{type},\text{contMP})}{(A,\text{sp},\text{member})}$

TABLE A.3: Semantic conditions for classical RDFS interpretations.

Simple:	1. for each $(s, p, o) \in G$, $p^{\mathcal{I}} \in \Delta_P$ and $(s^{\mathcal{I}}, o^{\mathcal{I}}) \in P[\![p^{\mathcal{I}}]\!]$;
RDF:	1. $p \in \Delta_P$ if and only if $(p, \mathsf{prop}^{\mathcal{I}}) \in P[\![\mathsf{type}^{\mathcal{I}}]\!]$;
	2. if $l \in universe(G)$ is a typed XML literal with lexical form w then $l^{\mathcal{I}}$ is the XML literal value of w, $l^{\mathcal{I}} \in \Delta_L$ and $(l^{\mathcal{I}}, \mathsf{xmlLit}^{\mathcal{I}}) \in P[\![\mathsf{type}^{\mathcal{I}}]\!]$;
RDFS:	1. $x \in \Delta_R$ if and only if $x \in C[\![\mathsf{res}^{\mathcal{I}}]\!]$;
	2. $x \in \Delta_C$ if and only if $x \in C[\![\mathsf{class}^{\mathcal{I}}]\!]$;
	3. $x \in \Delta_L$ if and only if $x \in C[\![\mathsf{literal}^{\mathcal{I}}]\!]$;
	4. if $c \in \Delta_C$ then $(c, \mathsf{res}^{\mathcal{I}}) \in P[\![\mathsf{sc}^{\mathcal{I}}]\!]$;
	5. if $x \in C[\![\mathsf{datatype}^{\mathcal{I}}]\!]$ then $(x, \mathsf{literal}^{\mathcal{I}}) \in P[\![\mathsf{sc}^{\mathcal{I}}]\!]$;
	6. if $x \in C[\![\mathsf{contMP}^{\mathcal{I}}]\!]$ then $(x, \mathsf{member}^{\mathcal{I}}) \in P[\![\mathsf{sp}^{\mathcal{I}}]\!]$;
Subproperty:	1. $P[\![\mathsf{sp}^{\mathcal{I}}]\!]$ is reflexive and transitive over Δ_P;
	2. if $(p, q) \in P[\![\mathsf{sp}^{\mathcal{I}}]\!]$ then $p, q \in \Delta_P$ and $P[\![p]\!] \subseteq P[\![q]\!]$;
Subclass:	1. $P[\![\mathsf{sc}^{\mathcal{I}}]\!]$ is reflexive and transitive over Δ_C;
	2. if $(c, d) \in P[\![\mathsf{sc}^{\mathcal{I}}]\!]$ then $c, d \in \Delta_C$ and $C[\![c]\!] \subseteq C[\![d]\!]$;
Typing:	1. $x \in C[\![c]\!]$ if and only if $(x, c) \in P[\![\mathsf{type}^{\mathcal{I}}]\!]$;
	2. if $(p, c) \in P[\![\mathsf{dom}^{\mathcal{I}}]\!]$ and $(x, y) \in P[\![p]\!]$ then $x \in C[\![c]\!]$;
	3. if $(p, c) \in P[\![\mathsf{range}^{\mathcal{I}}]\!]$ and $(x, y) \in P[\![p]\!]$ then $y \in C[\![c]\!]$;

3. Subclass:

(a) $\dfrac{(A,\mathsf{sc},B),(B,\mathsf{sc},C)}{(A,\mathsf{sc},C)}$

(b) $\dfrac{(A,\mathsf{sc},B),(X,\mathsf{type},A)}{(X,\mathsf{type},B)}$

(c) $\dfrac{(A,\mathsf{type},\mathsf{class})}{(A,\mathsf{sc},\mathsf{res})}$

(d) $\dfrac{(A,\mathsf{type},\mathsf{datatype})}{(A,\mathsf{sc},\mathsf{literal})}$

4. Typing:

(a) $\dfrac{(D,\mathsf{dom},B),(X,D,Y)}{(X,\mathsf{type},B)}$

(b) $\dfrac{(D,\mathsf{range},B),(X,D,Y)}{(Y,\mathsf{type},B)}$

(c) $\dfrac{(A,D,B)}{(D,\mathsf{type},\mathsf{prop})}$

(d) $\dfrac{(A,D,B)}{(A,\mathsf{type},\mathsf{res})}$

(e) $\dfrac{}{(l,\mathsf{type},\mathsf{xmlLit})}$ if $l \in universe(G)$ is a typed XML literal

5. Implicit Typing:

$$(a) \quad \frac{(A,\mathsf{dom},B),(D,\mathsf{sp},A),(X,D,Y)}{(X,\mathsf{type},B)}$$

$$(b) \quad \frac{(A,\mathsf{range},B),(D,\mathsf{sp},A),(X,D,Y)}{(Y,\mathsf{type},B)}$$

6. Subproperty Reflexivity:

$$\frac{(A,\mathsf{type},\mathsf{prop})}{(A,\mathsf{sp},A)}$$

7. Subclass Reflexivity:

$$\frac{(A,\mathsf{type},\mathsf{class})}{(A,\mathsf{sc},A)}$$

A *proof* is defined as follows. Let G and H be RDFS graphs. Then $G \vdash^{RDFS} H$ iff there is a sequence of graphs $P_1, \ldots, P_k$ with $P_1 = G \cup \{\tau \mid \tau$ is an RDFS axiom as in Table A.2 $\}$ and $P_k = H$, and for each j $(2 \leq j \leq k)$ one of the following holds:

1. there exists a map $\mu : P_j \to P_{j-1}$ (rule (1a));

2. $P_j \subseteq P_{j-1}$ (rule (1b));

3. there is an instantiation $\frac{R}{R'}$ of one of the rules (2)(5), such that $R \subseteq P_{j-1}$ and $P_j = P_{j-1} \cup R'$.

The sequence of rules used at each step (plus its instantiation or map), is called a *proof* of H from G. Now it can be shown that

Proposition 94 (Soundness and Completeness [307]). *For RDFS graphs G and H,*

$$G \models_{\mathsf{RDFS}} H \ \textit{if and only if} \ G \vdash^{RDFS} H \ .$$

Moreover, if $G \vdash^{RDFS} H$ then there is a proof of H from G where the rule (1a) is used at most once and at the end.

Appendix B

From OWL to Description Logics

B.1 The Case of OWL 2

The syntax of *OWL 2* expressions and the mapping to $\mathcal{SROIQ}(\mathbf{D})$ is essentially as follows. In the following, A is an *atom* (unary predicate), R is a *role* (binary predicate), R^- is the inverse of role R, S is a simple role, T is a datatype property, a, b are individuals, and l is a literal of the concrete domain supported by OWL 2. Symbols may have a subscript.

An object property R may also be the top relation U or the bottom relation $\perp_r$, with obvious extension $U^{\mathcal{I}} = \Delta^{\mathcal{I}} \times \Delta^{\mathcal{I}}$ and $\perp_r{}^{\mathcal{I}} = \emptyset$, respectively, for any interpretation $\mathcal{I}$.

Assertion axioms. Assertion axioms are of the form:

SameIndividual$(a, b) \mapsto a = b$. Note that in Section 4.2.2.3 we used UNA instead.
DifferentIndividuals$(a, b) \mapsto a \neq b$
ClassAssertion$(C, a) \mapsto a{:}C$
ObjectPropertyAssertion$(R, a, b) \mapsto (a, b){:}R$
NegativeObjectPropertyAssertion$(R, a, b) \mapsto (a, b){:}\neg R$
DataPropertyAssertion$(T, a, l) \mapsto (a, l){:}T$
NegativeDataPropertyAssertion$(T, a, l) \mapsto (a, l){:}\neg T$

Class Expressions. We recap here briefly the syntax of *OWL 2* class expressions.

$$
\begin{aligned}
C \quad \longrightarrow \quad & A \mid C_1 \sqcap C_2 \mid\mid C_1 \sqcup C_2 \mid \neg C \mid \{a\} \mid \\
& \exists R.C \mid \forall R.C \mid \exists R.\{a\} \mid \exists S.\mathsf{Self} \mid \\
& (\geq n \; S.C) \mid (\leq n \; S.C) \mid (= n \; S.C) \mid \\
& \exists T.\mathbf{d} \mid \forall T.\mathbf{d} \mid \exists T. =_l \mid \\
& (\geq n \; T.\mathbf{d}) \mid (\leq n \; T.\mathbf{d}) \mid (= n \; T.\mathbf{d})
\end{aligned}
$$

Class Axioms. The class axioms of OWL 2 are of the following form

SubClassOf$(C_1, C_2) \mapsto C_1 \sqsubseteq C_2$
EquivalentClasses$(C_1, C_2) \mapsto C_1 = C_2$
DisjointClasses$(C_1, C_2) \mapsto \mathsf{disj}(C_1, C_2)$
DisjointUnion$(C, C_1, C_2) \mapsto C = C_1 \sqcup C_2, \mathsf{disj}(C_1, C_2)$

Object Property Axioms. The object property axioms of OWL 2 are of the following form

$$\mathsf{SubObjectPropertyOf}(R_1, R_2, \ldots, R_n, R) \mapsto R_1 \ldots R_n \sqsubseteq R$$
$$\mathsf{EquivalentObjectProperties}(R_1, R_2) \mapsto R_1 \sqsubseteq R_2, R_2 \sqsubseteq R_1$$
$$\mathsf{DisjointObjectProperties}(S_1, S_2) \mapsto \mathsf{disj}(S_1, S_2)$$
$$\mathsf{InverseObjectProperties}(R_1, R_2) \mapsto \mathsf{EquivalentObjectProperties}(R_1, R_2^-)$$
$$\mathsf{ObjectPropertyDomain}(R, C) \mapsto \mathsf{dom}(R, C)$$
$$\mathsf{ObjectPropertyRange}(R, C) \mapsto \mathsf{ran}(R, C)$$
$$\mathsf{FunctionalObjectProperty}(S) \mapsto \mathsf{fun}(R)$$
$$\mathsf{InverseFunctionalObjectProperty}(S) \mapsto \mathsf{fun}(R^-)$$
$$\mathsf{ReflexiveObjectProperty}(R) \mapsto \mathsf{ref}(R)$$
$$\mathsf{IrreflexiveObjectProperty}(S) \mapsto \mathsf{irr}(R)$$
$$\mathsf{SymmetricObjectProperty}(R) \mapsto \mathsf{sym}(R)$$
$$\mathsf{AsymmetricObjectProperty}(S) \mapsto \mathsf{asy}(R)$$
$$\mathsf{TransitiveObjectProperty}(R) \mapsto \mathsf{trans}(R)$$

Data Property Axioms. The data property axioms of OWL 2 are of the following form

$$\mathsf{SubDataPropertyOf}(T_1, T_2) \mapsto T_1 \sqsubseteq T_2$$
$$\mathsf{EquivalentDataProperties}(T_1, T_2) \mapsto T_1 \sqsubseteq T_2, T_2 \sqsubseteq T_1$$
$$\mathsf{DisjointDataProperties}(T_1, T_2) \mapsto \mathsf{disj}(T_1, T_2)$$
$$\mathsf{DataPropertyDomain}(T, C) \mapsto \mathsf{dom}(T, C)$$
$$\mathsf{DataPropertyRange}(T, \mathbf{d}) \mapsto \mathsf{ran}(R, \mathbf{d})$$
$$\mathsf{FunctionalDataProperty}(T) \mapsto \mathsf{fun}(T)$$

Datatypes. We refer the reader to http://www.w3.org/TR/2008/WD-owl2-syntax-20081008/#Datatype_Maps concerning the datatypes supported by OWL 2.

Simple roles. An object property R is *composite* w.r.t. a set of object property axioms $\mathcal{R}$ iff

1. R is either $\top_r$ or $\bot_r$; or

2. $\mathcal{R}$ contains an axiom of the form

    (a) $\mathsf{SubObjectPropertyOf}(R_1, R_2, \ldots, R_n, R)$;

    (b) $\mathsf{SubObjectPropertyOf}(R_1, R_2, \ldots, R_n, R^-)$;

    (c) $\mathsf{TransitiveObjectProperty}(R)$;

    (d) $\mathsf{TransitiveObjectProperty}(R^-)$;

The relation $\rightarrow$ w.r.t. $\mathcal{R}$ is the smallest relation for which the following conditions hold:

1. If $\mathcal{R}$ contains SubObjectPropertyOf(R_1, R_2), then $R_1 \rightarrow R_2$;

2. If $\mathcal{R}$ contains EquivalentObjectProperties(R_1, R_2), then $R_1 \rightarrow R_2$ and $R_2 \rightarrow R_1$;

3. If $\mathcal{R}$ contains InverseObjectProperties(R_1, R_2), then $R_1 \rightarrow R_2^-$ and $R_2^- \rightarrow R_1$;

4. If $\mathcal{R}$ contains SymmetricObjectProperty(R), then $R \rightarrow R^-$;

5. If $R_1 \rightarrow R_2$ then $R_1^- \rightarrow R_2^-$.

Let $\rightarrow^*$ be the reflexive-transitive closure of $\rightarrow$.

An object property expression R is *simple* w.r.t. $\mathcal{R}$ if, for each object property R' such that $R' \rightarrow^* R$ holds, R' is not composite.

We also assume that no SubObjectPropertyOf axiom contains the universal role U property (similarly, no SubDataPropertyOf axiom contains the universal datatype property) and that $\mathcal{R}$ is regular (see Section 4.2.2.3).

B.2 The Case of OWL QL

The syntax of *OWL QL* expressions and the mapping to DL-Lite is essentially as follows. In the following, A is an *atom* (unary predicate), R is a *role* (binary predicate) and R^- is the inverse of role R. Symbols may have a subscript. The mapping to DL-Lite$_{\mathcal{R}}$ is derived from the one for OWL 2 (see Section B.1).

Assertions. Assertion axioms are of the form:

$$\text{ClassAssertion}(A, a)$$
$$\text{ObjectPropertyAssertion}(R, a, b)$$

Class Expressions. In OWL 2 QL, there are two types of class expressions. The B sub class production defines the class expressions that can occur as sub class expressions in *SubClassOf* axioms, and the C super class production defines the classes that can occur as super class expressions in *SubClassOf* axioms. Their syntax is:

$$B \longrightarrow A \mid \exists R$$
$$C \longrightarrow A \mid B_1 \sqcap C_2 \mid \neg B \mid \exists R.A$$

Class Axioms. The class axioms of OWL 2 QL are of the following form.

$$\text{SubClassOf}(B, C)$$
$$\text{EquivalentClasses}(B_1, B_2)$$
$$\text{DisjointClasses}(B_1, B_2)$$

Property Axioms. The property axioms of OWL 2 QL are of the following form

$$\mathsf{SubObjectPropertyOf}(R_1, R_2)$$
$$\mathsf{EquivalentObjectProperties}(R_1, R_2)$$
$$\mathsf{DisjointObjectProperties}(R_1, R_2)$$
$$\mathsf{InverseObjectProperties}(R_1, R_2)$$
$$\mathsf{ObjectPropertyDomain}(R, C)$$
$$\mathsf{ObjectPropertyRange}(R, C)$$
$$\mathsf{ReflexiveObjectProperty}(R)$$
$$\mathsf{SymmetricObjectProperty}(R)$$
$$\mathsf{AsymmetricObjectProperty}(R)$$

Note that there are some differences among DL-Lite$_\mathcal{R}$ and *OWL 2 QL*:

1. existential quantification to a class $\exists R.C$;

2. symmetric property axioms and asymmetric property axioms;

3. reflexive property axioms and irreflexive property axioms.

Notice that, although 1 and 2 are not natively supported by DL-Lite$_\mathcal{R}$, they are actually expressible in DL-Lite$_\mathcal{R}$ by suitably processing the intensional level of the ontology. Conversely, reflexivity and irreflexivity axioms are brand new features and require new inference mechanisms.

Native handling of qualified existential quantification. It is well known that an axiom τ of the form

$$B \sqsubseteq \exists R.A$$

can be replaced with the transformation

$$\tau \mapsto \{B \sqsubseteq \exists R_{aux}, R_{aux} \sqsubseteq R, \exists R_{aux}^- \sqsubseteq A\} \,,$$

where R_{aux} is a new role. We point out that [100] provides also a query reformulation method that does not require the translation.

Native handling of symmetric and asymmetric object property axioms.

1. each $\mathsf{SymmetricObjectProperty}(R)$ is managed by adding $R \sqsubseteq R^-$ to the DL component;

2. each $\mathsf{AsymmetricObjectProperty}(R)$ is managed by adding $R \sqsubseteq \neg R^-$ to the DL component;

Handling of reflexive and irreflexive object property axioms. It has been observed in [100] that since (i) the asymmetry axiom on a property implies the irreflexivity axiom on the same property; and (ii) the asymmetry axiom influences only the consistency check on the ontology; the irreflexivity axiom influences only the consistency check, too. [100] shows how to deal with irreflexivity axioms in the consistency checking phase.

On the other hand, reflexive role declarations impact the query reformulation phase, cannot be represented in DL-Lite$_R$, and they have to be dealt with specifically in the reformulation algorithm, though the solution is easy. Essentially, a reflexive role R means that $R(x,x)$ is always true, we have to appropriately drop any occurrence of $R(x,x)$ occurring in a query during the query reformulation procedure. We refer the reader to [100] for the details.

B.3 The Case of OWL EL

We recap here briefly the syntax of *OWL EL* class expressions. In the following, A is an *atom* (unary predicate), R is a *role* (binary predicate), S is a simple role, and T is a datatype property. Symbols may have a subscript.

The mapping to $\mathcal{EL}^{++}(\mathbf{D})$ is derived from the one for OWL 2 (see Section B.1).

Assertions.. Assertion axioms are of the form:

$$\mathsf{ClassAssertion}(A, a)$$
$$\mathsf{ObjectPropertyAssertion}(R, a, b)$$

Class Expressions. OWL 2 EL class expression are as follows:

$$C \longrightarrow A \mid C_1 \sqcap C_2 \mid \{a\} \mid \exists R.C \mid \exists R.\{a\} \mid \exists S.\mathsf{Self}$$
$$\exists T.\mathbf{d} \mid$$

Class Axioms. The class axioms of OWL 2 EL are of the following form

$$\mathsf{SubClassOf}(C_1, C_2)$$
$$\mathsf{EquivalentClasses}(C_1, C_2)$$
$$\mathsf{DisjointClasses}(C_1, C_2)$$

Property Axioms. The property axioms of OWL 2 QL are of the following form

$$\mathsf{SubObjectPropertyOf}(R_1, R_2)$$
$$\mathsf{EquivalentObjectProperties}(R_1, R_2)$$
$$\mathsf{ObjectPropertyDomain}(R, C)$$
$$\mathsf{ObjectPropertyRange}(R, C)$$
$$\mathsf{ReflexiveObjectProperty}(R)$$
$$\mathsf{TransitiveObjectProperty}(R)$$

B.4   The Case of OWL RL

We recap here briefly the syntax of *OWL RL* expressions. In the following, A is an *atom* (unary predicate), R is a *role* (binary predicate), S is a simple role, and T is a datatype property. Symbols may have a subscript.

The mapping to Horn-DL is derived from the one for OWL 2 (see Section B.1).

Assertions. Assertion axioms are of the form:

$$\mathsf{ClassAssertion}(C, a)$$
$$\mathsf{ObjectPropertyAssertion}(R, a, b)$$

Class Expressions. In OWL 2 RL, there are two types of class expressions. The sub class B production defines the class expressions that can occur as sub class expressions in *SubClassOf* axioms, and the C super class production defines the classes that can occur as super class expressions in *SubClassOf* axioms. The D class production defines the classes that can occur in concept definitions. Their syntax is ($m \in \{0, 1\}$):

$$
\begin{aligned}
B &\longrightarrow A \mid \{a\} \mid B_1 \sqcap B_2 \mid B_1 \sqcup B_2 \mid \exists R.B \mid \exists R.\{a\} \mid \exists T.\mathbf{d} \mid \exists T. =_l \\
C &\longrightarrow A \mid C_1 \sqcap C_2 \mid \neg B \mid \forall R.C \mid \exists R.\{a\} \mid \forall T.\mathbf{d} \mid \exists T. =_l \mid \\
&\qquad (\leq m\ S.B) \mid (\leq m\ S) \mid (\leq m\ T.\mathbf{d}) \\
D &\longrightarrow \exists R.\{a\} \mid \exists T. =_l \mid D_1 \sqcap D_2 \\
R &\longrightarrow P \mid P^-
\end{aligned}
$$

Class Axioms. The class axioms of OWL 2 RL are of the following form

$$\mathsf{SubClassOf}(B, C)$$
$$\mathsf{EquivalentClasses}(A, D)$$
$$\mathsf{DisjointClasses}(B_1, B_2)$$

Property Axioms. The property axioms of OWL 2 QL are of the following form

$$
\begin{aligned}
&\mathsf{SubObjectPropertyOf}(R_1, R_2) \\
&\mathsf{EquivalentObjectProperties}(R_1, R_2) \\
&\mathsf{DisjointObjectProperties}(S_1, S_2) \\
&\mathsf{InverseObjectProperties}(R_1, R_2) \\
&\mathsf{ObjectPropertyDomain}(R, C) \\
&\mathsf{ObjectPropertyRange}(R, C) \\
&\mathsf{FunctionalObjectProperty}(S) \\
&\mathsf{InverseFunctionalObjectProperty}(S) \\
&\mathsf{IrreflexiveObjectProperty}(S) \\
&\mathsf{SymmetricObjectProperty}(R) \\
&\mathsf{AsymmetricObjectProperty}(S) \\
&\mathsf{TransitiveObjectProperty}(R)
\end{aligned}
$$

Appendix C

A Tableau Calculus for $\mathcal{SHIF}_g$

The major issue introduced by functional roles is that together with inverse roles they may cause a concept to be satisfiable in an infinite model only.

Example 60. *Consider the following KB* $\mathcal{K} = \langle \mathcal{R}, \mathcal{T}, \mathcal{A} \rangle$ *with*

$$\begin{aligned} \mathcal{R} &= \emptyset \\ \mathcal{T} &= \{\top \sqsubseteq \exists S.A\} \\ \mathcal{A} &= \{a{:}\neg A\}\,, \end{aligned}$$

where the inverse of the role S is functional, i.e., $\mathsf{fun}(S^-)$*. Then,* $\mathcal{K}$ *has a model, but no finite one. Indeed, a model* $\mathcal{I}$ *of* $\mathcal{K}$ *is*

$$\begin{aligned} \Delta^{\mathcal{I}} &= \mathbb{N} \\ a^{\mathcal{I}} &= 1 \\ 1 &\notin A^{\mathcal{I}} \\ n &\in A^{\mathcal{I}} \text{ for all } n > 1 \\ (n, n+1) &\in S^{\mathcal{I}} \text{ for all } n \geq 1\,. \end{aligned}$$

This property is well-known for $\mathcal{SHIF}_g$. In order to cope with this issue, classical DLs have proposed the so-called notion of *pairwise blocking* to guarantee the correct termination of a tableau from which then we may build a possibly infinite model (see, *e.g.*, [209]).

With respect to $\mathcal{ALC}$, we need to extend some notions. The set of roles is the set of roles and their inverse. To avoid considering roles such as R^{--}, we define a function Inv such that $\mathsf{Inv}(R) = R^-$ if R is an atomic role, and $\mathsf{Inv}(R) = R_1$ if $R = R_1^-$. We also define a function $\mathsf{Trans}(R)$ to return true iff R is a transitive role, *i.e.*, $\mathsf{trans}(R)$ or $\mathsf{trans}(\mathsf{Inv}(R))$ (note that R is transitive iff $\mathsf{Inv}(R)$ is transitive).

We start with considering role axioms and role inclusion axioms. Given an RBox $\mathcal{R}$, we define the sub-role relation $\sqsubseteq_{\mathcal{R}}^*$ as the transitive-reflexive closure of $\sqsubseteq$ over $\mathcal{R}' = \mathcal{R} \cup \{\mathsf{Inv}(R_1) \sqsubseteq \mathsf{Inv}(R_2) \mid R_1 \sqsubseteq R_2 \in \mathcal{R}\}$, that is

1. if R occurs in $\mathcal{R}'$ then $R \sqsubseteq_{\mathcal{R}}^* R$;

2. if $R_1 \sqsubseteq R_2 \in \mathcal{R}'$ then $R_1 \sqsubseteq_{\mathcal{R}}^* R_2$;

3. if $R_1 \sqsubseteq R_2 \in \mathcal{R}'$ and $R_2 \sqsubseteq R_3 \in \mathcal{R}'$ then $R_1 \sqsubseteq_{\mathcal{R}}^* R_3$.

We extend an interpretation $\mathcal{I}$ to interpret $R_1 \sqsubseteq_{\mathcal{R}}^* R_2$ as $\mathcal{I} \models R_1 \sqsubseteq_{\mathcal{R}}^* R_2$ iff $\mathcal{I} \models R_1 \sqsubseteq R_2$. It is then easy to see that $\mathcal{K} \models R_1 \sqsubseteq_{\mathcal{R}}^* R_2$ iff $R_1 \sqsubseteq_{\mathcal{R}}^* R_2$. This provides us a simple procedure to determine whether $\mathcal{K} \models R_1 \sqsubseteq_{\mathcal{R}}^* R_2$.

Let $\mathcal{K}$ be a $\mathcal{SHIF}_g$ KB. Recall $\mathcal{SHIF}_g$ differs from $\mathcal{SHIF}$ as there are no local functional roles ($\leq 1\, R$) occurring in $\mathcal{K}$, but there are global functional roles $\mathsf{fun}(R)$ only.

Now, a *completion-forest* $\mathcal{F}$ for $\mathcal{K}$ is a collection of trees whose distinguished roots are arbitrarily connected by edges. Each node v is labelled with a set $\mathcal{L}(v)$ of concepts $C \in sub(\mathcal{K})$. The intuition here is that v is an instance of C. Each edge $\langle v, w \rangle$ is labelled with a set $\mathcal{L}(\langle v, w \rangle)$ of roles R occurring in $\mathcal{K}$ indicating that $\langle v, w \rangle$ and instance of R.

If nodes v and w are connected by an edge $\langle v, w \rangle$ then w is called a *successor* of v and v is called a *predecessor* of w. *Ancestor* is the transitive closure of predecessor, and *descendant* is the transitive closure of successor.

If nodes v and w are connected by an edge $\langle v, w \rangle$ with $R' \in \mathcal{L}(\langle v, w \rangle)$ and $R' \sqsubseteq_{\mathcal{R}}^* R$, then w is called an R-*successor* of v and v is called an R-*predecessor* of w. If node w is an R-successor of v or an $\mathsf{Inv}(R)$-predecessor of v, then w is called an R-*neighbor* of v.

For a node v, $\mathcal{L}(v)$ is said to contain a *clash* iff $\{A, \neg A\} \subseteq \mathcal{L}(v)$. A completion-forest is called *clash-free* iff none of its nodes contains a clash; it is called *complete* iff none of the expansion rules in Table C.1 is applicable.

Now, the algorithm initializes a forest $\mathcal{F}$ as follows:

- $\mathcal{F}$ contains a root node v_0^i, for each individual a_i occurring in $\mathcal{A}$;

- $\mathcal{F}$ contains an edge $\langle v_0^i, v_0^j \rangle$, for each assertion axiom $(a_i, a_j){:}R \in \mathcal{A}$;

- for each assertion $a_i{:}C \in \mathcal{A}$, we add C to $\mathcal{L}(v_0^i)$;

- for each $(a_i, a_j){:}R \in \mathcal{A}$, we add R to $\mathcal{L}(\langle v_0^i, v_0^j \rangle)$.

We also need a technical definition involving functional roles (see [295]). Let $\mathcal{F}$ be forest, R a functional role such that we have two edges $\langle v, w_1 \rangle$ and $\langle v, w_2 \rangle$ such that R occurs in $\mathcal{L}(\langle v, w_1 \rangle)$ and $\mathcal{L}(\langle v, w_2 \rangle)$, respectively. Then we call such a pair a *fork*. As R is functional, such a fork means that w_1 and w_2 have to be interpreted as the same individual. Such a fork can be deleted by adding both $\mathcal{L}(\langle v, w_2 \rangle)$ to $\mathcal{L}(\langle v, w_1 \rangle)$, and $\mathcal{L}(w_2)$ to $\mathcal{L}(w_1)$, and then deleting node w_2. Of course, as inverse roles are allowed these may also contribute to create a fork, *i.e.*, we have a fork if w_1 and w_2 are R-neighbors of v.

We assume that forks are eliminated as soon as they appear (as part of a rule application) with the proviso that newly generated nodes are replaced by older ones and not vice versa.

At the beginning, we check that there are no forks in the initial forest, otherwise the KB is not satisfiable (due to the unique name assumption, if we have $(a, b_1){:}R$ and $(a, b_2){:}R$ with $b_1 \neq b_2$ then R cannot be functional).

As next we define the notion of *pairwise blocking* (see Figure C.1). A node v is *blocked* iff it is not a root node and it is either *directly blocked* or *indirectly*

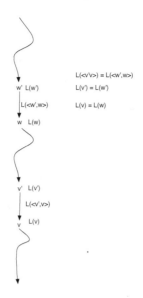

FIGURE C.1: Pairwise blocking in $\mathcal{SHIF}$.

blocked. A node v is *directly blocked* iff none of its ancestors are blocked, and it has ancestors v', w, w' such that

1. w is not a root node,

2. v is a successor of v',

3. w is a successor of w',

4. $\mathcal{L}(v) = \mathcal{L}(w)$,

5. $\mathcal{L}(v') = \mathcal{L}(w')$,

6. $\mathcal{L}(\langle v', v\rangle) = \mathcal{L}(\langle w', w\rangle)$.

The set of reasoning rules are shown in Table C.1.

Note that a model $\mathcal{I}$ from a complete and clash-free completion-forest can be built as follows [206]. The major problem now is that the model may be infinite. The main idea is that an individual in the domain $\Delta^{\mathcal{I}}$ intuitively corresponds to a *path*, in a complete completion-forest $\mathcal{F}$, from a root node to some node that is not blocked, and that goes only through non-root nodes. To obtain an infinite model, these paths may be *cyclic*. Instead of going to a direct blocked node, these path go "back" to the blocking node and this an infinite number of times. Thus, if blocking occurred while constructing a complete and clash-free completion-forest, we obtain an infinite domain. More precisely, a *path* is of the form

$$[\frac{v_0}{v'_0}, \ldots, \frac{v_n}{v'_n}] ,$$

TABLE C.1: The tableau rules for $\mathcal{SHIF}_g$.

($\sqcap$). If *(i)* $C_1 \sqcap C_2 \in \mathcal{L}(v)$, *(ii)* $\{C_1, C_2\} \not\subseteq \mathcal{L}(v)$ and *(iii)* node v is not indirectly blocked, then add C_1 and C_2 to $\mathcal{L}(v)$.

($\sqcup$). If *(i)* $C_1 \sqcup C_2 \in \mathcal{L}(v)$, *(ii)* $\{C_1, C_2\} \cap \mathcal{L}(v) = \emptyset$ and *(iii)* node v is not indirectly blocked, then add some $C \in \{C_1, C_2\}$ to $\mathcal{L}(v)$.

($\forall$). If *(i)* $\forall R.C \in \mathcal{L}(v)$, *(ii)* there is an R-neighbour w of v with $C \notin \mathcal{L}(w)$ and *(iii)* node v is not indirectly blocked, then add C to $\mathcal{L}(w)$.

($\exists$). If *(i)* $\exists R.C \in \mathcal{L}(v)$, *(ii)* there is no R-neighbour w of v with $C \in \mathcal{L}(w)$ and *(iii)* node v is not blocked, then create a new node w, add R to $\mathcal{L}(\langle v, w \rangle)$ and add C to $\mathcal{L}(w)$.

($\forall_+$). If *(i)* $\forall S.C \in \mathcal{L}(v)$, *(ii)* there is some R with $\mathsf{Trans}(R)$ and $R \sqsubseteq^*_{\mathcal{R}} S$, *(iii)* there is an R-neighbour w of v with $\forall R.C \notin \mathcal{L}(w)$ and *(iii)* node v is not indirectly blocked, then add $\forall R.C$ to $\mathcal{L}(w)$.

($\sqsubseteq$). If *(i)* $\top \sqsubseteq D \in \mathcal{T}$, *(ii)* $D \notin \mathcal{L}(v)$ and *(ii)* node v is not indirectly blocked, then add D to $\mathcal{L}(v)$.

where v_i, v_i' are nodes of $\mathcal{F}$. For such a path, we define $\mathsf{Tail}(p) = v_n$. With $[p \mid \frac{v_{n+1}}{v'_{n+1}}]$ we denote the path $[\frac{v_0}{v'_0}, \ldots, \frac{v_n}{v'_n}, \frac{v_{n+1}}{v'_{n+1}}]$. The set of paths $\mathsf{Path}(\mathcal{F})$ is defined inductively as follows:

1. for root nodes v_0^i in $\mathcal{F}$, $[\frac{v_0^i}{v_0^i}] \in \mathsf{Path}(\mathcal{F})$;

2. for a path $p \in \mathsf{Path}(\mathcal{F})$ and a node w in $\mathcal{F}$

   (a) if w is a successor of $\mathsf{Tail}(p)$ and w is neither blocked nor a root node, then $[p \mid \frac{w}{w}] \in \mathsf{Path}(\mathcal{F})$; or

   (b) if for some node v in $\mathcal{F}$, v is a successor of $\mathsf{Tail}(p)$ and w blocks v, then $[p \mid \frac{w}{v}] \in \mathsf{Path}(\mathcal{F})$.

Please note that, due to the construction of $\mathsf{Path}(\mathcal{F})$, for $p \in \mathsf{Path}(\mathcal{F})$ with $p = [p' \mid \frac{w}{v}]$, we have that w is not blocked, v is blocked iff $w \neq v$, and v is never indirectly blocked. Furthermore, $\mathcal{L}(w) = \mathcal{L}(v)$.

Now, let $\mathcal{F}$ be a complete and clash-free completion-forest constructed by the tableaux algorithm for $\mathcal{K}$.

- The domain of $\mathcal{I}$ are the paths of the forest, *i.e.*,

$$\Delta^{\mathcal{I}} = \mathsf{Path}(\mathcal{F}) .$$

- The interpretation of an individual a_i occurring in $\mathcal{K}$ is as follows:

$$a^{\mathcal{I}} = [\frac{v_0^i}{v_0^i}] .$$

- $\top^{\mathcal{I}} = \Delta^{\mathcal{I}}$, $\bot^{\mathcal{I}} = \emptyset$.

- The interpretation of an atom A is as follows:

$$A^{\mathcal{I}} = \{p \in \Delta^{\mathcal{I}} \mid v = \mathsf{Tail}(p), A \in \mathcal{L}(v)\} .$$

- The interpretation of a role R is as follows:

$$
\begin{aligned}
R^{\mathcal{I}} \;=\; & \{\langle p, q\rangle \in \mathsf{Path}(\mathcal{F}) \times \mathsf{Path}(\mathcal{F}) \mid \\
& \quad q = [p \mid \tfrac{v}{v'}] \text{ and } v' \text{ is a } R\text{-successor of } \mathsf{Tail}(p), or \\
& \quad p = [q \mid \tfrac{v}{v'}] \text{ and } v' \text{ is a } \mathsf{Inv}(R)\text{-successor of } \mathsf{Tail}(q)\} \cup \\
& \{\langle [\tfrac{v}{v}], [\tfrac{w}{w'}]\rangle \mid v, w \text{ are root nodes and } w \text{ is an } R\text{-neighbor of } v\} .
\end{aligned}
$$

It can be shown that:

Proposition 95 ([209]). *For each $\mathcal{SHIF}_g$ knowledge base $\mathcal{K}$*

1. *the tableau algorithm terminates;*

2. *if the expansion rules can be applied in such a way that they yield a complete and clash-free completion-forest, then $\mathcal{K}$ has a model;*

3. *if $\mathcal{K}$ has a model, then the expansion rules can be applied in such a way that they yield complete and clash-free completion-forest for $\mathcal{K}$;*

4. *the KB satisfiability problem is NExpTime-complete [442].*

Example 61. *Consider the KB in Example 60. $\mathcal{K}$ is satisfiable as there is a clash-free complete completion-forest (see Figure C.2). Note that nodes x, y, and z form a pairwise blocking condition, with $w' = x, w = y = v'$ and $v = z$.*

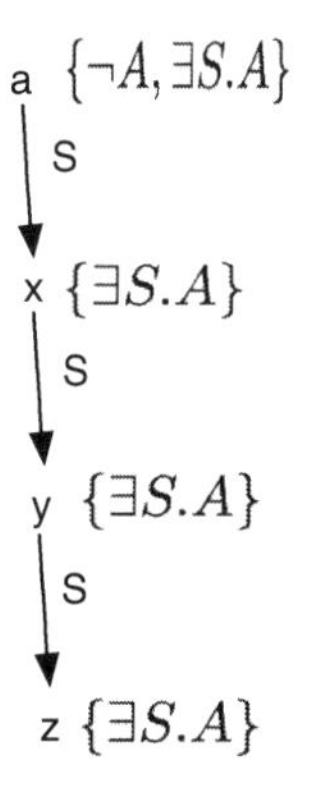

FIGURE C.2: Clash-free complete completion-forest for $\mathcal{SHIF}$ KB.

Appendix D

From RIF-Core to Datalog

In this appendix, we provide a mapping of a significant subset of RIF-Core statements into Datalog with concrete domains.

Syntax. To start with, a *term t* and *atoms* are defined as follows:

1. a *constant* is a term;

2. a *variable* is a term.

An *atomic formula* is of the form $p(t_1, \ldots, t_n)$, where t_i are terms. A *formula* ϕ has the following grammar (where A is an atom, p is a predicate symbol, and t_i are terms)

$$
\begin{array}{rcll}
\phi & \to & A & \mid \quad \text{(atom)} \\
& & \phi_1 \wedge \phi_2 & \mid \quad \text{(conjunction)} \\
& & \phi_1 \vee \phi_2 & \mid \quad \text{(disjunction)} \\
& & Ext(p(t_1, \ldots, t_n)) & \mid \quad \text{(external atom)} \\
& & \exists x.\phi & \quad \text{(existential formula)} \, .
\end{array}
$$

A *fact* is an atom (not necessarily ground), while a rule is of the form $(n \geq 1)$

$$ A_1 \wedge \ldots \wedge A_n \leftarrow \phi \, , \tag{D.1} $$

where A_i are atoms and ϕ is a formula.

Note that external atoms are used for representing built-in predicates as "procedurally attached" predicates, which might exist in various rule-based systems, but are not specified by RIF.

For a rule $A_1 \wedge \ldots \wedge A_n \leftarrow \phi$, $A_1 \wedge \ldots \wedge A_n$ is called, *head*, while ϕ is called the *body* of the rule. Rules have to be *safe*, that is any variable occurring in an external term or atom have to also occur in the same rule body within a non external atom. Rules and facts are considered as universally quantified. In a fact or rule, the universally quantified variables are called *distinguished variables*, while the existentially quantified variables in a rule body are the so-called *non-distinguished variables* and are distinct from the distinguished variables (note that there are non existential quantifications in facts).

A RIF-Core *knowledge base* is a pair $\mathcal{K} = \langle \mathcal{F}, \mathcal{P} \rangle$, where $\mathcal{F}$ is a finite set of facts and $\mathcal{P}$ is a finite set of rules.

Remark 48. *Let us note that RIF-Core [365] also provides some other forms of atoms, such as membership, equality, and frame atoms, which are however peculiar features of F-Logic and do not strictly belong to the Datalog realm as F-Logic is a Higher-Order Language. We refer the interested reader to [237, 238]. Examples of such atoms are*

1. *Frame atoms: $john[age \to x, spouse \to y]$, dictating that "the age of john is x, while his spouse is y". We may well use variables in place of the attributes (predicate) age and spouse and the constant john, which makes RIF-Core a higher order logic;*

2. *Membership term: $john\#Person$, dictating that "john is a Person". We may well use a variables in place of the constant john and the unary predicate symbol Person.*

Eventually, RIF-Core also employs "lists" as built-in terms and external function calls. Specifically

- *if $t_1, \ldots, t_n$ are terms, then $List(t_1, \ldots, t_n)$ is a so-called* closed list *term;*

- *if f is a function symbol, $t_1, \ldots, t_n$ are constants or variables then $Ext(f(t_1, \ldots, t_n))$ is an* externally defined term.

We do not address these types of terms and atoms here. Note that such external terms can be simulated anyway via an external atom $Ext(p_f(t_1, \ldots, t_n), x)$ for an appropriate external predicate p_f where x will hold the result of the application of f to the arguments $t_1, \ldots, t_n$.

Semantics. The semantics extend the one for Datalog with concrete domains (see Sections 5.2 and 5.3). Specifically, let $\mathcal{K} = \langle \mathcal{F}, \mathcal{P} \rangle$ be a knowledge base and consider a finite datatype theory $\mathbf{D} = \langle \Delta^{\mathbf{D}}, \cdot^{\mathbf{D}} \rangle$ including the support for all externally defined atoms occurring in $\mathcal{K}$.

The *Herbrand universe* $H_{\mathcal{K}}$ is the set of all constants occurring in $\mathcal{K}$ together with the values in $\Delta^{\mathbf{D}}$. The *Herbrand base* $B_{\mathcal{K}}$ of $\mathcal{K}$ is the set of all ground atoms that can be formed using constants in $H_{\mathcal{K}}$ and atoms occurring in $\mathcal{K}$.

The set of ground rules $\mathcal{K}^*$ derived from the grounding of $\mathcal{P}$ is constructed as follows (we extend the language by allowing the ground atomic formula 1, denoting the truth *true*, to occur in the rule body):

1. set $\mathcal{K}^*$ to be

$$\mathcal{K} := \{p(\mathbf{c}) \leftarrow 1 \mid p(\mathbf{c}) \in \mathcal{F}\} \cup \{p(\mathbf{c}) \leftarrow 1 \mid p(\mathbf{x}) \in \mathcal{F}, \mathbf{c} \in H_{\mathcal{K}}\} \ ;$$

2. add to $\mathcal{K}^*$ the set of all ground instantiations of rules in $\mathcal{K}$, *i.e.*, rules obtained by replacing distinguished and non-distinguished variables with

elements from the Herbrand universe $H_{\mathcal{K}}$ and from which we remove the existential quantification expression of the form $\exists \mathbf{x}$. Note that rule bodies of rules in $\mathcal{K}^*$ are Boolean propositional formulae.

An *interpretation* $\mathcal{I}$ for $\mathcal{K}$ is a subset of $B_{\mathcal{K}}$. Given $\mathcal{K}$, we say that $\mathcal{I}$ *satisfies* (*is a model of*)

- the ground atom 1, denoted $\mathcal{I} \models 1$;

- a ground atom $A \in B_{\mathcal{K}}$, denoted $\mathcal{I} \models A$, iff $A \in \mathcal{I}$;

- a ground formula ϕ, denoted $\mathcal{I} \models \phi$ iff (inductively)

  1. $\mathcal{I} \models A$ if ϕ is an atom A;
  2. $\mathcal{I} \models \phi_1$ and $\mathcal{I} \models \phi_2$ if ϕ is a conjunction $\phi_1 \wedge \phi_2$;
  3. $\mathcal{I} \models \phi_1$ or $\mathcal{I} \models \phi_2$ if ϕ is a disjunction $\phi_1 \vee \phi_2$;
  4. $\mathbf{t} \in p^{\mathbf{D}}$ if ϕ is an external atom $Ext(p(\mathbf{t}))$;

- a ground rule $r \in \mathcal{K}^*$, denoted $\mathcal{I} \models r$, iff $\mathcal{I}$ is a model of the head of r whenever $\mathcal{I}$ is a model of the body of r;

- $\mathcal{K}^*$, denoted $\mathcal{I} \models \mathcal{K}^*$, iff $\mathcal{I}$ satisfies all rules $r \in \mathcal{K}^*$;

- $\mathcal{K}$, denoted $\mathcal{I} \models \mathcal{K}$, if $\mathcal{I}$ is a model of $\mathcal{K}^*$.

Let $\mathbf{I}_{\mathcal{K}} = 2^{B_{\mathcal{K}}}$ be the set of all interpretations (there are $2^{|B_{\mathcal{K}}|}$ many). Now, for $\mathcal{I}_1, \mathcal{I}_2 \in \mathbf{I}_{\mathcal{K}}$, we write $\mathcal{I}_1 \leq \mathcal{I}_2$ iff $\mathcal{I}_1 \subseteq \mathcal{I}_2$. It is easy to see that $\langle \mathbf{I}_{\mathcal{K}}, \leq \rangle$ is a finite complete lattice.

The *minimal model* of $\mathcal{K}$, denoted $M_{\mathcal{K}}$, is the $\leq$-least model of $\mathcal{K}$. The existence, finiteness, and uniqueness of the minimal model $M_{\mathcal{K}}$ is guaranteed to exist using the same argument as for Datalog (see Proposition 16).

Mapping. The mapping of our RIF-Core sublanguage to Datalog is as follows. Facts are mapped as follows:

$$p(\mathbf{c}) \;\mapsto\; p(\mathbf{c})$$
$$p(\mathbf{x}) \;\mapsto\; p(\mathbf{c}) \text{ for all } \mathbf{c} \in H_{\mathcal{K}} \text{ .}$$

Concerning rules, consider a rule $A_1 \wedge \ldots \wedge A_n \leftarrow \phi$. First of all, we transform the rule body ϕ into a *Prenex Disjunctive Normal Form* (PDNF), which is of the form

$$\exists \mathbf{x}.(\phi_1 \vee \ldots \vee \phi_k) \text{ ,}$$

where each ϕ_i is a conjunction of atoms or external atoms. To do so, we apply recursively the following rules (we assume that $x \neq y$)[1]

$$\exists x.\phi_1 \wedge \exists y.\phi_2 \;\mapsto\; \exists x \exists y.(\phi_1 \wedge \phi_2)$$
$$\exists x.\phi_1 \wedge \exists x.\phi_2 \;\mapsto\; \exists x \exists y.(\phi_1 \wedge \phi_2[x/y]), \text{ where } y \text{ new variable}$$
$$\exists x.\phi_1 \vee \exists y.\phi_2 \;\mapsto\; \exists x \exists y.(\phi_1 \vee \phi_2)$$
$$\exists x.\phi_1 \vee \exists x.\phi_2 \;\mapsto\; \exists x \exists y.(\phi_1 \vee \phi_2[x/y]), \text{ where } y \text{ new variable}$$
$$\exists \mathbf{x}.(\phi_1 \wedge (\phi_2 \vee \phi_3)) \;\mapsto\; \exists \mathbf{x}.((\phi_1 \wedge \phi_2) \vee (\phi_1 \wedge \phi_3))$$

Now, consider a rule $A_1 \wedge \ldots \wedge A_n \leftarrow \phi$, where ϕ is in PDNF, we may eventually map it into a set of Datalog rules by applying the following two rules:

$$A_1 \wedge \ldots \wedge A_n \leftarrow \phi \;\mapsto\; A_1 \leftarrow \phi, \ldots, A_n \leftarrow \phi$$
$$A \leftarrow \exists \mathbf{x}.(\phi_1 \vee \ldots \vee \phi_k) \;\mapsto\; A \leftarrow \phi_1, \ldots, A \leftarrow \phi_k \;.$$

This concludes the mapping.

---

[1]With $\phi[x/y]$ we denote, as usual, the formula obtained from ϕ by replacing all free occurrences of x with y (see, *e.g.*, [93]). We also omit the rules obtained by commutativity of $\wedge$ and $\vee$.

Appendix E

Basic Logics to Deal with Uncertain Statements

The aim of this section is to illustrate typical logics to deal with uncertainty, *i.e.*, we illustrate a typical formalization of uncertain statements via a probabilistic and a possibilistic setting. Reasoning procedures are presented as well.

E.1 Probabilistic Logic

Probabilistic logic has its origin in philosophy and logic. Its roots can be traced back to Boole in 1854 [66]. There is a wide spectrum of formal languages that have been explored in probabilistic logic, ranging from constraints for unconditional and conditional events to rich languages that specify linear inequalities over events (see especially the work by Nilsson [332], Fagin et al. [151], Dubois and Prade et al. [8, 133, 134, 135], Frisch and Haddawy [162], and [275, 276, 284]; see also the survey on sentential probability logic by Hailperin [185]). Recently, non-monotonic generalizations of probabilistic logic have been developed and explored; see especially [277] for an overview. In this section, for illustrative purposes, we recall only the simple probabilistic logic described in [332].

We first define probabilistic formulas and probabilistic knowledge bases. We assume a set of *basic events* $\Phi = \{p_1, \ldots, p_n\}$ with $n \geq 1$. We use $\bot$ and $\top$ to denote *false* and *true*, respectively. We define *events* by induction as follows. Every element of $\Phi \cup \{\bot, \top\}$ is an event. If ϕ and ψ are events, then also $\neg\phi$, $(\phi \wedge \psi)$, $(\phi \vee \psi)$, and $(\phi \rightarrow \psi)$ are events. We adopt the usual conventions to eliminate parentheses.

A *probabilistic formula* is an expression of the form $\langle \phi, n \rangle$, where ϕ is an event, and n is a real number from the unit interval $[0, 1]$. Informally, $\langle \phi, n \rangle$ says that ϕ is true with a probability of at least n. For example, $\langle \mathtt{rain\_tomorrow}, 0.7 \rangle$ may express that it will rain tomorrow with a probability of at least 0.7. Notice also that $\langle \neg\phi, 1 - n \rangle$ encodes that ϕ is true with a probability of at most u. A *probabilistic knowledge base* $\mathcal{K}$ is a finite set of probabilistic formulas.

We next define worlds and probabilistic interpretations. A *world* I associates with every basic event in Φ a binary truth value. We extend I by induction to all events as usual. We denote by $\mathcal{I}_\Phi$ the (finite) set of all worlds for Φ.

A world I *satisfies* an event ϕ, or I is a *model* of ϕ, denoted $I \models \phi$, iff $I(\phi) = \textbf{true}$.

A *probabilistic interpretation* Pr is a probability function on $\mathcal{I}_\Phi$ (that is, a mapping $Pr \colon \mathcal{I}_\Phi \to [0,1]$ such that all $Pr(I)$ with $I \in \mathcal{I}_\Phi$ sum up to 1). Intuitively, $Pr(I)$ is the degree to which the world $I \in \mathcal{I}_\Phi$ is probable, that is, the probability function Pr encodes our "uncertainty" about which world is the right one, though, in any world a statement is either true or false.

The *probability* of an event ϕ in Pr, denoted $Pr(\phi)$, is the sum of all $Pr(I)$ such that $I \in \mathcal{I}_\Phi$ and $I \models \phi$. That is,

$$Pr(\phi) = \sum_{I \models \phi} Pr(I) \, .$$

The following proposition is an immediate consequence of the above definitions.

Proposition 96. *For all probabilistic interpretations Pr and events ϕ and ψ, the following relationships hold:*

$$
\begin{aligned}
Pr(\phi \wedge \psi) &= Pr(\phi) + Pr(\psi) - Pr(\phi \vee \psi)\,; \\
Pr(\phi \wedge \psi) &\leq \min(Pr(\phi), Pr(\psi))\,; \\
Pr(\phi \wedge \psi) &\geq \max(0, Pr(\phi) + Pr(\psi) - 1)\,; \\
Pr(\phi \vee \psi) &= Pr(\phi) + Pr(\psi) - Pr(\phi \wedge \psi)\,; \\
Pr(\phi \vee \psi) &\leq \min(1, Pr(\phi) + Pr(\psi))\,; \qquad\qquad \text{(E.1)} \\
Pr(\phi \vee \psi) &\geq \max(Pr(\phi), Pr(\psi))\,; \\
Pr(\neg\phi) &= 1 - Pr(\phi)\,; \\
Pr(\bot) &= 0\,; \\
Pr(\top) &= 1\,.
\end{aligned}
$$

A probabilistic interpretation Pr *satisfies* a probabilistic formula $\langle \phi, n \rangle$, or Pr is a *model* of $\langle \phi, n \rangle$, denoted $Pr \models \langle \phi, n \rangle$, iff $Pr(\phi) \geq n$. We say Pr *satisfies* a probabilistic knowledge base $\mathcal{K}$, or Pr is a model of $\mathcal{K}$, iff Pr satisfies all $F \in \mathcal{K}$. We say $\mathcal{K}$ is *satisfiable* iff a model of $\mathcal{K}$ exists.

A probabilistic formula F is a *logical consequence* of $\mathcal{K}$, denoted $\mathcal{K} \models F$, iff every model of $\mathcal{K}$ satisfies F. We say $\langle \phi, n \rangle$ is a *tight logical consequence* of $\mathcal{K}$ iff n is the infimum of $Pr(\phi)$ subject to all models Pr of $\mathcal{K}$. Notice that the latter is equivalent to $n = \sup \{r \mid \mathcal{K} \models \langle \phi, r \rangle\}$. n is called the *best entailment degree* of ϕ w.r.t. $\mathcal{K}$ (denoted $bed(\mathcal{K}, \phi)$), *i.e.*,

$$bed(\mathcal{K}, \phi) = \sup \{r \mid \mathcal{K} \models \langle \phi, r \rangle\} \, .$$

The main decision and optimization problems in probabilistic logic are deciding the satisfiability of probabilistic knowledge bases and logical consequences from probabilistic knowledge bases, as well as computing the best entailment degree from probabilistic knowledge bases, which can be done by deciding the solvability of a system of linear inequalities and by solving a linear optimization problem, respectively. In particular, column generation techniques from operations research have been successfully used to solve large problem instances in probabilistic logic; see especially the work by Jaumard et al. [215] and Hansen et al. [191].

For the sake of completeness, we provide here a simple procedure to solve the KB satisfiability problem as well as the best entailment problem. In the following, we use variable y_I as a placeholder for the value of $Pr(I)$. Then a probabilistic knowledge base $\mathcal{K}$ has a model Pr iff the following system of linear constraints over the variables y_I $(I \in \mathcal{I}_\Phi)$, is solvable:

$$\text{for all } y_I, \qquad y_I \geq 0$$

$$\sum_I y_I = 1 \qquad\qquad (\text{E.2})$$

$$\text{for all } \langle \phi', n \rangle \in \mathcal{K}, \qquad \sum_{I \models \phi'} y_I \geq n \ .$$

Specifically, if $\mathbf{y_I}$ is a solution to (E.2), then the probabilistic interpretation $Pr(I) := y_I$ (for all $I \in \mathcal{I}_\Phi$) is a probabilistic model of $\mathcal{K}$. If no solution to (E.2) exists then $\mathcal{K}$ has no model. Note that (E.2) has exponentially as many variables y_I, one for each possible classical interpretation I.

Similarly, the best entailment degree $bed(\mathcal{K}, \phi)$ can be computed as

$$\begin{aligned} &\text{minimize } \textstyle\sum_{I \models \phi} y_I \text{ subject to} \\ &\text{for all } y_I, \qquad\qquad\qquad\qquad y_I \geq 0 \\ &\qquad\qquad\qquad\qquad\qquad\quad \textstyle\sum_I y_I = 1 \qquad\qquad (\text{E.3}) \\ &\text{for all } \langle \phi', n \rangle \in \mathcal{K}, \qquad\qquad \textstyle\sum_{I \models \phi'} y_I \geq n \end{aligned}$$

We point out that $bed(\mathcal{K}, \phi)$ can be computed as well as

$$bed(\mathcal{K}, \phi) = \min x. \text{ such that } \mathcal{K} \cup \{\langle \neg\phi, 1 - x \rangle\} \text{ satisfiable.} \qquad (\text{E.4})$$

Informally, concerning the minimization in computing $bed(\mathcal{K}, \phi)$, suppose the minimal value of x is $\bar{n}$. We will know then that for any interpretation Pr satisfying the knowledge base such that $Pr(\phi) < \bar{n}$, the starting set is not satisfiable (otherwise $\bar{n}$ wouldn't be minimal) and, thus, $Pr(\phi) \geq \bar{n}$ has to hold. Which means that $bed(\mathcal{K}, \phi) = \bar{n}$.

Therefore, we may rewrite (E.3) as follows:

minimize x subject to $\quad\quad 0 \leq x \leq 1$

for all y_I, $\quad\quad\quad\quad\quad\quad y_I \geq 0$

$$\sum_I y_I = 1 \quad\quad\quad\quad (E.5)$$

$$\sum_{I \models \phi} y_I \leq x$$

for all $\langle \phi', n \rangle \in \mathcal{K}, \quad\quad \sum_{I \models \phi'} y_I \geq n$

In the above system we used the fact that

$$\sum_{I \models \phi} y_I + \sum_{I \models \neg\phi} y_I = 1$$

and, thus, the condition

$$\sum_{I \models \neg\phi} y_I \geq 1 - x$$

is the same as

$$\sum_{I \models \phi} y_I \leq x \ .$$

E.2   Possibilistic Logic

We next recall possibilistic logic; see especially [140]. The main syntactic and semantic differences to probabilistic logic can be summarized as follows. Syntactically, rather than using probabilistic formulas to constrain the probabilities of propositional events, we now use possibilistic formulas to constrain the necessities and possibilities of propositional events. Semantically, rather than having probability distributions on worlds, each of which associates with every event a unique probability, we now have possibility distributions on worlds, each of which associates with every event a unique possibility and a unique necessity. Differently from the probability of an event, which is the sum of the probabilities of all worlds that satisfy that event, the possibility of an event is the maximum of the possibilities of all worlds that satisfy the event. As a consequence, probabilities and possibilities of events behave quite differently from each other (see Equations (E.1) and (E.6)). These fundamental semantic differences between probabilities and possibilities can also be used as the main criteria for using either probabilistic logic or possibilistic logic in a given application involving uncertainty. In addition, possibilistic logic may especially be used for encoding user preferences, since possibility measures can actually be viewed as rankings (on worlds or also objects) along an ordinal scale.

The semantic differences between probabilities and possibilities are also reflected in the computational properties of possibilistic and probabilistic logic, since reasoning in probabilistic logic generally requires to solve linear optimisation problems, while reasoning in possibilistic logic does not, and thus can generally be done with less computational effort. Note that although possibility measures can be viewed as sets of upper probability measures [141], and possibility and probability measures can be translated into each other [136], no translations are known between possibilistic and probabilistic knowledge bases as described here.

We first define possibilistic formulas and knowledge bases. *Possibilistic formulas* have the form $\langle P\phi, n \rangle$ or $\langle N\phi, n \rangle$, where ϕ is an event, and n is a real number from $[0, 1]$. Informally, such formulas encode to what extent ϕ is *possibly* resp. *necessarily* true. For example, $\langle \texttt{Prain\_tomorrow}, 0.7 \rangle$ encodes that it will rain tomorrow is possible to degree 0.7, while $\langle \texttt{Nfather} \rightarrow \texttt{man}, 1 \rangle$ says that a father is necessarily a man. A *possibilistic knowledge base* $\mathcal{K}$ is a finite set of possibilistic formulas.

A *possibilistic interpretation* is a mapping $\pi \colon \mathcal{I}_\Phi \rightarrow [0, 1]$. Intuitively, $\pi(I)$ is the degree to which the world I is *possible*. In particular, every world I such that $\pi(I) = 0$ is *impossible*, while every world I such that $\pi(I) = 1$ is *totally possible*. We say π is *normalized* iff $\pi(I) = 1$ for some $I \in \mathcal{I}_\Phi$. Intuitively, this guarantees that there exists at least one world, which could be considered the real one.

The *possibility* of an event ϕ in a possibilistic interpretation π, denoted $Poss(\phi)$, is then defined by

$$Poss(\phi) = \max \{\pi(I) \mid I \models \phi\}$$

where $\max \emptyset = 0$. Intuitively, the possibility of ϕ is evaluated in the most possible world where ϕ is true. The dual notion to the possibility of an event ϕ is the *necessity* of ϕ, denoted $Nec(\phi)$, which is defined by

$$Nec(\phi) = 1 - Poss(\neg\phi) \ .$$

It reflects the lack of possibility of $\neg\phi$, that is, $Nec(\phi)$ evaluates to what extent ϕ is certainly true. The following theorem follows immediately from the above definitions.

Proposition 97. *For all possibilistic interpretations π and events ϕ and ψ,* *the following relationships hold:*

$$
\begin{aligned}
Poss(\phi \wedge \psi) &\leq \min(Poss(\phi), Poss(\psi)); \\
Poss(\phi \vee \psi) &= \max(Poss(\phi), Poss(\psi)); \\
Poss(\neg\phi) &= 1 - Nec(\phi); \\
Poss(\bot) &= 0; \\
Poss(\top) &= 1 \quad \textit{(in the normalized case)};
\end{aligned}
$$

$$
\begin{aligned}
Nec(\phi \wedge \psi) &= \min(Nec(\phi), Nec(\psi)); \\
Nec(\phi \vee \psi) &\geq \max(Nec(\phi), Nec(\psi)); \\
Nec(\neg\phi) &= 1 - Poss(\phi); \\
Nec(\bot) &= 0 \quad \textit{(in the normalized case)}; \\
Nec(\top) &= 1.
\end{aligned}
$$

(E.6)

A possibilistic interpretation π *satisfies* a possibilistic formula $\langle P\phi, n \rangle$ (resp., $\langle N\phi, n \rangle$), or π is a *model* of $\langle P\phi, n \rangle$ (resp., $\langle N\phi, n \rangle$), denoted $\pi \models \langle P\phi, n \rangle$ (resp., $\pi \models \langle N\phi, n \rangle$), iff $Poss(\phi) \geq n$ (resp., $Nec(\phi) \geq n$). The notions of satisfiability, logical consequence, tight logical consequence and best entailment degree for possibilistic knowledge bases are then defined as usual (in the same way as in the probabilistic case). Specifically, we recall

$$
\begin{aligned}
bed(\mathcal{K}, P\phi) &= \sup\{r \mid \mathcal{K} \models \langle P\phi, r \rangle\} \\
bed(\mathcal{K}, N\phi) &= \sup\{r \mid \mathcal{K} \models \langle N\phi, r \rangle\}.
\end{aligned}
$$

We refer the reader to [140, 199] for algorithms for possibilistic logic. However, for the sake of completeness, we provide here an analogous reasoning procedure as for the probabilistic case.

Similarly to the probabilistic case (see Equation (E.4)), it can be shown that

$$
bed(\mathcal{K}, P\phi) = \min x. \text{ such that } \mathcal{K} \cup \{P\phi \leq x\} \text{ satisfiable,} \qquad \text{(E.7)}
$$

where a possibility distribution π *satisfies* the expression $P\phi \leq x$ iff $Poss(\phi) \leq x$. The problem above can be solved by the mixed integer linear programming problem (see [216], how the problem below converts to a mixed integer linear programming problem) with variables x, y_I with $I \in \mathcal{I}_\Phi$:

$$
\min x. \text{ such that} \qquad 0 \leq x \leq 1
$$

$$
\text{for all } I, \qquad 0 \leq y_I \leq 1
$$

$$
\max\{y_I \mid I \models \phi\} \leq x \qquad \text{(E.8)}
$$

$$
\text{for all } \langle P\phi', n \rangle \in \mathcal{K}, \qquad \max\{y_I \mid I \models \phi'\} \geq n
$$

$$
\text{for all } \langle N\phi', n \rangle \in \mathcal{K}, \qquad \min\{1 - y_I \mid I \not\models \phi'\} \geq n.
$$

The case for $bed(\mathcal{K}, N\phi)$ can be addressed similarly:

$$
bed(\mathcal{K}, N\phi) = \min x. \text{ such that } \mathcal{K} \cup \{N\phi \leq x\} \text{ satisfiable,} \qquad \text{(E.9)}
$$

where a possibility distribution π *satisfies* the expression $\mathsf{N}\phi \leq x$ iff $Necc(\phi) \leq x$. Now, it suffices to change the third row in Equation (E.8) with

$$\min\{1 - y_I \mid I \not\models \phi\} \leq x \ .$$

Of course, a possibilistic KB $\mathcal{K}$ is satisfiable iff the system

$$\text{for all } I, \qquad\qquad\qquad 0 \leq y_I \leq 1$$

$$\text{for all } \langle \mathsf{P}\phi', n \rangle \in \mathcal{K}, \qquad \max\{y_I \mid I \models \phi'\} \geq n \qquad\qquad \text{(E.10)}$$

$$\text{for all } \langle \mathsf{N}\phi', n \rangle \in \mathcal{K}, \qquad \min\{1 - y_I \mid I \not\models \phi'\} \geq n$$

is satisfiable. Specifically, if $\mathbf{y_I}$ is a solution to (E.10), then the possibilistic interpretation $\pi(I) := y_I$ (for all $I \in \mathcal{I}_\Phi$) is a possibilistic model of $\mathcal{K}$. If no solution to (E.10) exists then $\mathcal{K}$ has no model.

Appendix F

OR-based Inference Rules for $\mathcal{P}(\mathbf{D})$

We restrict our presentation to the case in which the truth space is L_n. So, let the truth space be L_n and let us define

$$\epsilon = \frac{1}{2 \cdot (n-1)} . \tag{F.1}$$

For a feature name f, we assume that f's values are rational numbers, $[f_{\min}, f_{\max}]$ is the range of allowed values in the concrete domain $\mathbf{D}$ for values f may take. We assume that there is some natural number p, such that for any feature name f, the smallest positive value f may take is equal or greater than 10^{-p}. With p_ϵ we define the value

$$p_\epsilon = 10^{-(p+1)} . \tag{F.2}$$

We recall that any $[0, 1]$-valued variable x has to take values in L_n, *i.e.*,

$$x \in \{0, \frac{1}{n-1}, \ldots, \frac{n-2}{n-1}, 1\} ,$$

which can be encoded as

$$\begin{aligned} z &= (n-1) \cdot x \\ z &\in \{0, 1, \ldots, n-1\} \end{aligned} \tag{F.3}$$

for a new integer variable z.

The $\mathcal{P}(\mathbf{D})$ rules to be considered in the L-ORFuzzySat procedure (Section 8.2.2.2) are as follows.

(var). For variable x_ϕ occurring in $\mathcal{C}_\mathcal{K}$, set

$$\mathcal{C}_\mathcal{K} := \mathcal{C}_\mathcal{K} \cup \{x_\phi \in [0,1], z = (n-1) \cdot x, z \in \{0, 1, \ldots, n-1\}\} ,$$

where z is a new integer variable.

(var̄). For variable $x_{\neg\phi}$ occurring in $\mathcal{C}_\mathcal{K}$ add $x_\phi = 1 - x_{\neg\phi}$ to $\mathcal{C}_\mathcal{K}$.

($\perp$). If $0 \in \mathcal{T}_\mathcal{K}$ then $\mathcal{C}_\mathcal{K} := \mathcal{C}_\mathcal{K} \cup \{x_0 = 0\}$.

($\top$). If $1 \in \mathcal{T}_\mathcal{K}$ then $\mathcal{C}_\mathcal{K} := \mathcal{C}_\mathcal{K} \cup \{x_1 = 1\}$.

($\wedge$). If $\phi \wedge \psi \in \mathcal{T}_\mathcal{K}$, then

    1. add ϕ and ψ to $\mathcal{T}_\mathcal{K}$

    2. $\mathcal{C}_\mathcal{K} := \mathcal{C}_\mathcal{K} \cup \{x_\phi \otimes x_\psi = x_{\phi \wedge \psi}\}$.

($\vee$). If $\phi \vee \psi \in \mathcal{T}_\mathcal{K}$, then

    1. add ϕ and ψ to $\mathcal{T}_\mathcal{K}$

    2. $\mathcal{C}_\mathcal{K} := \mathcal{C}_\mathcal{K} \cup \{x_\phi \oplus x_\psi = x_{\phi \wedge \psi}\}$.

($\to$). If $\phi \to \psi \in \mathcal{T}_\mathcal{K}$, then

    1. add $nnf(\neg\phi)$ and ψ to $\mathcal{T}_\mathcal{K}$

    2. $\mathcal{C}_\mathcal{K} := \mathcal{C}_\mathcal{K} \cup \{(1 - x_{nnf(\neg\phi)}) \Rightarrow x_\psi = x_{\phi \to \psi}\}$.

($\to$). If $\phi \to \psi \in \mathcal{T}_\mathcal{K}$, then

    1. add $nnf(\neg\phi)$ and ψ to $\mathcal{T}_\mathcal{K}$

    2. $\mathcal{C}_\mathcal{K} := \mathcal{C}_\mathcal{K} \cup \{(1 - x_{nnf(\neg\phi)}) \Rightarrow x_\psi = x_{\phi \to \psi}\}$.

($\geq$). If $(f \geq_m) \in \mathcal{T}_\mathcal{K}$, then

$$
\begin{aligned}
\mathcal{C}_\mathcal{K} = \mathcal{C}_\mathcal{K} \cup \{\ & x_f \geq f_{\min} \cdot (1 - x_{(f \geq_m)}) + m \cdot x_{(f \geq_m)}, \\
& x_f \leq (m - p_\epsilon) \cdot (1 - x_{(f \geq_m)}) + f_{\max} \cdot x_{(f \geq_m)}, \\
& x_{(f \geq_m)} \in \{0, 1\}, x_f \in [f_{\min}, f_{\max}]\}\ .
\end{aligned}
$$

($\neg \geq$). If $\neg(f \geq_m) \in \mathcal{T}_\mathcal{K}$, then add $(f \geq_m)$ to $\mathcal{T}_\mathcal{K}$ and set

$$
\mathcal{C}_\mathcal{K} = \mathcal{C}_\mathcal{K} \cup \{x_{\neg(f \geq_m)} = 1 - x_{(f \geq_m)}\}\ .
$$

($\leq$). If $(f \leq_m) \in \mathcal{T}_\mathcal{K}$, then

$$
\begin{aligned}
\mathcal{C}_\mathcal{K} = \mathcal{C}_\mathcal{K} \cup \{\ & x_f \leq f_{\max} \cdot (1 - x_{(f \leq_m)}) + m \cdot x_{(f \leq_m)}, \\
& x_f \geq (m + p_\epsilon) \cdot (1 - x_{(f \leq_m)}) + f_{\min} \cdot x_{(f \leq_m)}, \\
& x_{(f \leq_m)} \in \{0, 1\}, x_f \in [f_{\min}, f_{\max}]\}\ .
\end{aligned}
$$

($\neg \leq$). If $\neg(f \leq_m) \in \mathcal{T}_\mathcal{K}$, then add $(f \leq_m)$ to $\mathcal{T}_\mathcal{K}$ and set

$$
\mathcal{C}_\mathcal{K} = \mathcal{C}_\mathcal{K} \cup \{x_{\neg(f \leq_m)} = 1 - x_{(f \leq_m)}\}\ .
$$

($=$). If $(f =_m) \in \mathcal{T}_\mathcal{K}$, then

$$
\begin{aligned}
\mathcal{C}_\mathcal{K} = \mathcal{C}_\mathcal{K} \cup \{\ & x_f \geq f_{\min} \cdot (1 - x_{(f =_m)}) + m \cdot x_{(f =_m)}, \\
& x_f \leq f_{\max} \cdot (1 - x_{(f =_m)}) + m \cdot x_{(f =_m)}, \\
& x_f \leq f_{\max} \cdot (1 - y_1) + (m - p_\epsilon) \cdot y_1, \\
& x_f \geq f_{\min} \cdot (1 - y_2) + (m + p_\epsilon) \cdot y_2, \\
& x_{(f =_m)} + y_1 + y_2 = 1, \\
& x_{(f =_m)} \in \{0, 1\}, y_i \in \{0, 1\}, x_f \in [f_{\min}, f_{\max}]\}\ ,
\end{aligned}
$$

where y_i are new variables.

$(\neg =)$. If $\neg(f =_m) \in \mathcal{T_K}$, then add $(f =_m)$ to $\mathcal{T_K}$ and set

$$\mathcal{C_K} = \mathcal{C_K} \cup \{x_{\neg(f =_m)} = 1 - x_{(f =_m)}\} .$$

(ls). If $(f\ ls(a,b)) \in \mathcal{T_K}$, then

$$\begin{aligned}
\mathcal{C_K} = \mathcal{C_K} \cup \{\ & x_f + (f_{\max} - a) \cdot y_1 \leq f_{\max}, \\
& x_{(f\ ls(a,b))} \geq y_1, \\
& x_f + (f_{\min} - a) \cdot y_2 \geq f_{\min}, \\
& x_f + (f_{\max} - b) \cdot y_2 \leq f_{\max}, \\
& x_f + x_{(f\ ls(a,b))} \cdot (b - a) \geq b - (b - f_{\min}) \cdot (1 - y_2), \\
& x_f + x_{(f\ ls(a,b))} \cdot (b - a) \leq b - (a - f_{\max}) \cdot (1 - y_2), \\
& x_f + (f_{\min} - b) \cdot y_3 \geq f_{\min}, \\
& x_{(f\ ls(a,b))} \leq 1 - y_3, \\
& y_1 + y_2 + y_3 = 1, \\
& y_i \in \{0, 1\}, x_f \in [f_{\min}, f_{\max}]\} ,
\end{aligned}$$

where y_i are new variables.

$(\neg ls)$. If $\neg(f\ ls(a,b)) \in \mathcal{T_K}$, then add $(f\ ls(a,b))$ to $\mathcal{T_K}$ and set

$$\mathcal{C_K} = \mathcal{C_K} \cup \{x_{\neg(f\ ls(a,b))} = 1 - x_{(f\ ls(a,b))}\} .$$

(rs). If $(f\ rs(a,b)) \in \mathcal{T_K}$, then

$$\begin{aligned}
\mathcal{C_K} = \mathcal{C_K} \cup \{\ & x_f + (f_{\max} - a) \cdot y_1 \leq f_{\max}, \\
& x_{(f\ rs(a,b))} \leq 1 - y_1, \\
& x_f + (f_{\min} - a) \cdot y_2 \geq f_{\min}, \\
& x_f + (f_{\max} - b) \cdot y_2 \leq f_{\max}, \\
& -x_f + x_{(f\ rs(a,b))} \cdot (b - a) \geq -a + (a - f_{\max}) \cdot (1 - y_2), \\
& -x_f + x_{(f\ rs(a,b))} \cdot (b - a) \leq -a + (b - f_{\min}) \cdot (1 - y_2), \\
& x_f + (f_{\min} - b) \cdot y_3 \geq f_{\min}, \\
& x_{(f\ rs(a,b))} \geq y_3, \\
& y_1 + y_2 + y_3 = 1, \\
& y_i \in \{0, 1\}, x_f \in [f_{\min}, f_{\max}]\} ,
\end{aligned}$$

where y_i are new variables.

$(\neg rs)$. If $\neg(f\ rs(a,b)) \in \mathcal{T_K}$, then add $(f\ rs(a,b))$ to $\mathcal{T_K}$ and set

$$\mathcal{C_K} = \mathcal{C_K} \cup \{x_{\neg(f\ rs(a,b))} = 1 - x_{(f\ rs(a,b))}\} .$$

(tri). If $(f\ tri(a,b,c)) \in \mathcal{T}_\mathcal{K}$, then

$$
\begin{aligned}
\mathcal{C}_\mathcal{K} = \mathcal{C}_\mathcal{K} \cup \{\ & x_f + (f_{\max} - a) \cdot y_1 \leq f_{\max}, \\
& x_{(f\ tri(a,b,c))} \leq 1 - y_1, \\
& x_f + (f_{\min} - a) \cdot y_2 \geq f_{\min}, \\
& x_f + (f_{\max} - b) \cdot y_2 \leq f_{\max}, \\
& -x_f + x_{(f\ tri(a,b,c))} \cdot (b - a) \geq -a + (a - f_{\max}) \cdot (1 - y_2), \\
& -x_f + x_{(f\ tri(a,b,c))} \cdot (b - a) \leq -a + (b - f_{\min}) \cdot (1 - y_2), \\
& x_f + (f_{\min} - b) \cdot y_3 \geq f_{\min}, \\
& x_f + (f_{\max} - c) \cdot y_3 \leq f_{\max}, \\
& x_f + x_{(f\ tri(a,b,c))} \cdot (c - b) \geq c - (c - f_{\min}) \cdot (1 - y_3), \\
& x_f + x_{(f\ tri(a,b,c))} \cdot (c - b) \leq c - (b - f_{\max}) \cdot (1 - y_3), \\
& x_f + (f_{\min} - c) \cdot y_4 \geq f_{\min}, \\
& x_{(f\ tri(a,b,c))} \leq 1 - y_4, \\
& y_1 + y_2 + y_3 + y_4 = 1, \\
& y_i \in \{0, 1\}, x_f \in [f_{\min}, f_{\max}]\}\ ,
\end{aligned}
$$

where y_i are new variables.

$(\neg tri)$. If $\neg(f\ tri(a,b,c)) \in \mathcal{T}_\mathcal{K}$, then add $(f\ tri(a,b,c))$ to $\mathcal{T}_\mathcal{K}$ and set

$$
\mathcal{C}_\mathcal{K} = \mathcal{C}_\mathcal{K} \cup \{x_{\neg(f\ tri(a,b,c))} = 1 - x_{(f\ tri(a,b,c))}\}\ .
$$

(trz). If $(f\ trz(a,b,c,d)) \in \mathcal{T}_\mathcal{K}$, then

$$
\begin{aligned}
\mathcal{C}_\mathcal{K} = \mathcal{C}_\mathcal{K} \cup \{\ & x_f + (f_{\max} - a) \cdot y_1 \leq f_{\max}, \\
& x_{(f\ trz(a,b,c,d))} \leq 1 - y_1, \\
& x_f + (f_{\min} - a) \cdot y_2 \geq f_{\min}, \\
& x_f + (f_{\max} - b) \cdot y_2 \leq f_{\max}, \\
& -x_f + x_{(f\ trz(a,b,c,d))} \cdot (b - a) \geq -a + (a - f_{\max}) \cdot (1 - y_2), \\
& -x_f + x_{(f\ trz(a,b,c,d))} \cdot (b - a) \leq -a + (b - f_{\min}) \cdot (1 - y_2), \\
& x_f + (f_{\min} - b) \cdot y_3 \geq f_{\min}, \\
& x_f + (f_{\max} - c) \cdot y_3 \leq f_{\max}, \\
& x_{(f\ trz(a,b,c,d))} \geq y_3, \\
& x_f + (f_{\min} - c) \cdot y_4 \geq f_{\min}, \\
& x_f + (f_{\max} - d) \cdot y_4 \leq f_{\max}, \\
& x_f + x_{(f\ trz(a,b,c,d))} \cdot (d - c) \geq d - (d - f_{\min}) \cdot (1 - y_4), \\
& x_f + x_{(f\ trz(a,b,c,d))} \cdot (d - c) \leq d - (c - f_{\max}) \cdot (1 - y_4),
\end{aligned}
$$

$$x_f + (f_{\min} - d) \cdot y_5 \geq f_{\min},$$
$$x_{(f\ trz(a,b,c,d))} \leq 1 - y_5,$$
$$y_1 + y_2 + y_3 + y_4 + y_5 = 1,$$
$$y_i \in \{0, 1\}, x_f \in [f_{\min}, f_{\max}] \ ,$$

where y_i are new variables.

$(\neg trz)$. If $\neg(f\ trz(a, b, c, d)) \in \mathcal{T}_{\mathcal{K}}$, then add $(f\ trz(a, b, c, d))$ to $\mathcal{T}_{\mathcal{K}}$ and set

$$\mathcal{C}_{\mathcal{K}} = \mathcal{C}_{\mathcal{K}} \cup \{x_{\neg(f\ trz(a,b,c,d))} = 1 - x_{(f\ trz(a,b,c,d))}\} \ .$$

(w). If $w \cdot \phi \in \mathcal{T}_{\mathcal{K}}$, then

    1. add ϕ to $\mathcal{T}_{\mathcal{K}}$

    2. $\mathcal{C}_{\mathcal{K}} := \mathcal{C}_{\mathcal{K}} \cup \{x_{w \cdot \phi} = w \cdot x_\phi\}$.

$(\neg w)$. If $\neg(w \cdot \phi) \in \mathcal{T}_{\mathcal{K}}$, then

    1. add $nnf(\neg\phi)$ to $\mathcal{T}_{\mathcal{K}}$

    2. $\mathcal{C}_{\mathcal{K}} := \mathcal{C}_{\mathcal{K}} \cup \{x_{w \cdot \phi} = w \cdot x_\phi\}$.

(ws). If $w_1 \cdot \psi_1 + \ldots + w_k \cdot \psi_k \in \mathcal{T}_{\mathcal{K}}$, then

    1. add all ψ_i to $\mathcal{T}_{\mathcal{K}}$

    2. $\mathcal{C}_{\mathcal{K}} := \mathcal{C}_{\mathcal{K}} \cup \{x_{w_1 \cdot \psi_1 + \ldots + w_k \cdot \psi_k} = \sum_i w_i \cdot x_\psi\}$.

$(\neg ws)$. If $\neg(w_1 \cdot \psi_1 + \ldots + w_k \cdot \psi_k) \in \mathcal{T}_{\mathcal{K}}$, then

    1. add all $\neg\psi_i$ to $\mathcal{T}_{\mathcal{K}}$

    2. $\mathcal{C}_{\mathcal{K}} := \mathcal{C}_{\mathcal{K}} \cup \{x_{\neg(w_1 \cdot \psi_1 + \ldots + w_k \cdot \psi_k)} = 1 - \sum_i w_i \cdot x_\psi\}$.

(lm). If $lm(a, b)(\phi) \in \mathcal{T}_{\mathcal{K}}$, then add ϕ to $\mathcal{T}_{\mathcal{K}}$ and set

$$
\begin{aligned}
\mathcal{C}_{\mathcal{K}} := \mathcal{C}_{\mathcal{K}} \cup \{ \ & x_\phi - y \leq a, \\
& x_\phi \geq a \cdot y, \\
& x_\phi + a/b \cdot y \geq a/b \cdot x_{lm(a,b)(\phi)}, \\
& x_\phi - y \leq a/b \cdot x_{lm(a,b)(\phi)}, \\
& (a-1) \cdot x_{lm(a,b)(\phi)} + (1-b) \cdot x_\phi \leq (a-b) \cdot y + 2(1-y), \\
& (a-1) \cdot x_{lm(a,b)(\phi)} + (1-b) \cdot x_\phi + 2(1-y) \geq (a-b) \cdot y, \\
& y \in \{0, 1\}\}
\end{aligned}
$$

where y is a new variable.

$(\neg lm)$. If $\neg lm(a, b)(\phi) \in \mathcal{T}_{\mathcal{K}}$, then

    1. add $lm(a, b)(\phi)$ to $\mathcal{T}_{\mathcal{K}}$

    2. $\mathcal{C}_{\mathcal{K}} := \mathcal{C}_{\mathcal{K}} \cup \{x_{\neg lm(a,b)(\phi)} = 1 - x_{lm(a,b)(\phi)}\}$.

(owa). If $@_W^{\mathrm{owa}}(\psi_1, \ldots, \psi_k) \in \mathcal{T}_{\mathcal{K}}$, then add all ψ_i to $\mathcal{T}_{\mathcal{K}}$ and set

$$\mathcal{C}_\mathcal{K} := \mathcal{C}_\mathcal{K} \ \cup \ \{x_{@_W^{owa}(\psi_1,\dots,\psi_k)} = \sum_{i=1}^{k} w_i \cdot y_i\} \ \cup \ perm(x_{\psi_1},\dots,x_{\psi_k}) \,,$$

where $W = \langle w_1, \dots, w_k \rangle$ and $perm(x_1,\dots,x_k)$ is the set of constraints ($N = \{1,\dots,k\}$ and $i,j \in N$)

$$perm(x_1,\dots,x_k) = \{ \quad y_1 \geq y_2, \dots, y_{k-1} \geq y_k,$$
$$y_i \leq x_j + 2z_{ij},$$
$$x_j \leq y_i + 2z_{ij},$$
$$\sum_{j=1}^{k} z_{ij} = k-1,$$
$$\sum_{i=1}^{k} z_{ij} = k-1,$$
$$y_i \in [0,1], z_{ij} \in \{0,1\} \quad \} \,,$$

where y_i, z_{ij} are new variables.

($\neg owa$). If $\neg @_W^{owa}(\psi_1,\dots,\psi_k) \in \mathcal{T}_\mathcal{K}$, then

    1. add $@_W^{owa}(\psi_1,\dots,\psi_k)$ to $\mathcal{T}_\mathcal{K}$

    2. $\mathcal{C}_\mathcal{K} := \mathcal{C}_\mathcal{K} \cup \{x_{\neg @_W^{owa}(\psi_1,\dots,\psi_k)} = 1 - x_{@_W^{owa}(\psi_1,\dots,\psi_k)}\}.$

($qowa$). If $@_{W_Q}^{owa}(\psi_1,\dots,\psi_k) \in \mathcal{T}_\mathcal{K}$, then add all ψ_i to $\mathcal{T}_\mathcal{K}$ and set

$$\mathcal{C}_\mathcal{K} := \mathcal{C}_\mathcal{K} \ \cup \ \{x_{@_{W_Q}^{owa}(\psi_1,\dots,\psi_k)} = \sum_{i} w_i \cdot y_i\} \ \cup \ perm(x_{\psi_1},\dots,x_{\psi_k}) \,,$$

where $W_Q = \langle w_1, \dots, w_k \rangle$ is such that

$$w_i = Q(\frac{i}{k}) - Q(\frac{i-1}{k})$$

and $perm(x_1,\dots,x_k)$ is as for the (owa) rule.

($\neg qowa$). If $\neg @_{W_Q}^{owa}(\psi_1,\dots,\psi_k) \in \mathcal{T}_\mathcal{K}$, then

    1. add $@_{W_Q}^{owa}(\psi_1,\dots,\psi_k)$ to $\mathcal{T}_\mathcal{K}$

    2. $\mathcal{C}_\mathcal{K} := \mathcal{C}_\mathcal{K} \cup \{x_{\neg @_{W_Q}^{owa}(\psi_1,\dots,\psi_k)} = 1 - x_{@_{W_Q}^{owa}(\psi_1,\dots,\psi_k)}\}.$

Some comments are in place.

Remark 49 (hard datatype rules). *For, e.g., the ($\geq$) rule, note that strict inequalities are not allowed, and hence, the inequality $x_f < m$ is expressed as $x_f \leq m - p_\epsilon$, for a sufficiently small $p_\epsilon \in (0,1]$.*

Remark 50 ((**ws**), (¬**ws**) rules). *For the* (*ws*) *and* (¬*ws*) *rules note the following:*

- *concerning* (*ws*), $w_1 \cdot \psi_1 + \ldots + w_k \cdot \psi_k$ *is equivalent to* $w_1 \cdot \psi_1 \vee \ldots \vee w_k \cdot \psi_k$;

- *concerning* (¬*ws*), $\neg(w_1 \cdot \psi_1 + \ldots + w_k \cdot \psi_k)$ *is the same as* $\neg w_1 \cdot \psi_1 \wedge \ldots \wedge \neg w_k \cdot \psi_k$, *and thus, we would*

  1. *add all* $\neg w_i \cdot C_i$ *to* $\mathcal{T}_{\mathcal{K}}$;
  2. *set* $\mathcal{C}_{\mathcal{K}} := \mathcal{C}_{\mathcal{K}} \cup \{\max(0, (\sum_i x_{\neg w_i \cdot \psi_i}) - (n-1)) = x_{\neg(w_1 \cdot \psi_1 + \cdots + w_k \cdot \psi_k)}\}$.

The above rules can then further be simplified by exploiting the fact that

$$x_{w_i \cdot \psi_i} = w_i \cdot x_{\psi_i}$$
$$x_{\neg w_i \cdot \psi_i} = 1 - x_{w_i \cdot \psi_i}$$

and applying the weighted sum rule.

Remark 51 ((**lm**) rule). *For the* (*lm*) *rule note the following:*

- *if* $x_\phi \leq a$ *the* $x_{lm(a,b)(\phi)} = \frac{b}{a} \cdot x_\phi$;

- *if* $x_\phi \geq a$ *the* $x_{lm(a,b)(\phi)} = \frac{b-1}{a-1} \cdot x_\phi + (1 - \frac{b-1}{a-1})$.

Remark 52 ((**owa**) rule). *The* (*owa*) *rule has been obtained directly from the encoding for Fuzzy DLs with aggregation operators [58], which we recap here.*

Yager [467] has shown that the maximization *of* $@_W^{owa}(x_1, \ldots, x_n)$ *can indeed be encoded as a MILP problem. However, this encoding does not work in our setting as we are not maximizing* $@_W^{owa}(x_1, \ldots, x_k)$, *but rather need to show that the set*

$$g(@_W^{owa}) = \{\langle x_1, \ldots, x_k, x \rangle \colon @_W^{owa}(x_1, \ldots, x_k) = x\}$$

is MILP representable. To this end, we need a different encoding.

So, let $N = \{1, \ldots, k\}$. *Similarly to [467], we introduce new* $[0,1]$-*valued variables* y_i ($i \in N$) *and impose*

$$y_1 \geq y_2 \geq \ldots \geq y_k \ . \tag{F.4}$$

The intuition is that y_i *will take the value of the i-th largest of the* x_j. *Hence, by definition of OWA,* y_i *has weight* w_i *and therefore, we add also the constraint*

$$\sum_i w_i \cdot y_i = x \ . \tag{F.5}$$

The remaining of the encoding concerns are now to establish which one among $x_1, \ldots, x_k$ *are the* y_i. *Consider the following set of equations: for* $i, j \in N$, *new binary variables* z_{ij}

$$y_i \leq x_j + 2z_{ij} \qquad x_j \leq y_i + 2z_{ij}$$

$$\sum_j z_{ij} = k - 1 \qquad \sum_i z_{ij} = k - 1 \qquad z_{ij} \in \{0,1\} \ . \tag{F.6}$$

It can be verified that (i) if $z_{ij} = 0$ then $y_i = x_j$ is imposed; (ii) for any y_i, there is only one x_j imposed to be equal to y_i; and (iii) for any x_j, there is only one y_i imposed to be equal to x_j. That is, there is a bijection among the y_j and the x_i, which together with Eq. (E.6) guarantees that the equations (E.6) - (F.6) correctly encode $@_W^{owa}(x_1, \ldots, x_k) = x$.

Appendix G

Fuzzy SPARQL: a Query Language for Fuzzy RDFS Graphs

The aim of this appendix is to introduce a fuzzy SPARQL, a fuzzy extension of SPARQL that is compliant with the crisp variant described in Section 6.3.

G.1 Fuzzy SPARQL

Fuzzy SPARQL [476, 264] extends SPARQL allowing to query fuzzy RDFS graphs.

A Fuzzy SPARQL has its counterpart in a generalization of fuzzy conjunctive queries, which are of the general form

$$
\begin{aligned}
q(\mathbf{x}, \mathbf{\Lambda}, \alpha, z) \quad \leftarrow \quad & \exists \mathbf{y} \exists \mathbf{\Lambda}'.\varphi(\mathbf{x}, \mathbf{\Lambda}, \mathbf{y}, \mathbf{\Lambda}'), \\
& \mathsf{GroupedBy}(\mathbf{w}), \\
& \alpha := @[f(\mathbf{z})], \\
& \mathsf{OrderBy}(z) \ .
\end{aligned}
$$

The semantics is a straightforward extension of the one that has been defined in Section 9.3 (see also [476]).

Now, the Fuzzy SPARQL query languages are defined as follows [476]. A *simple fuzzy SPARQL query* is defined – analogously to a SPARQL query – as a triple $Q = (P, G, V, A)$ with the differences that

- G is an fuzzy RDF graph;

- we allow fuzzy graph patterns and

- A is the set of fuzzy variables taken from an infinite set $\mathbf{A}$ (distinct from $\mathbf{V}$).

We further denote by $fvar(P)$ the set of fuzzy variables present in a graph pattern P.

Let λ be a fuzzy value from $[0, 1]$ or an fuzzy variable from $\mathbf{A}$. We call λ an *fuzzy label*. Triple patterns in fuzzy SPARQL are defined the same way as in SPARQL. For a triple pattern τ, we call $\langle \tau, \lambda \rangle$ an *fuzzy triple pattern* and sets of fuzzy triple patterns are called *basic fuzzy patterns* (BFP). A generic *fuzzy graph pattern* is defined in a recursive manner: any BFP is a fuzzy graph pattern; if P and P' are fuzzy graph patterns, R is a filter expression (see [381]), then $(P$ AND $P')$, $(P$ OPTIONAL $P')$, $(P$ UNION $P')$, $(P$ FILTER $R)$ are fuzzy graph patterns.

Example 62. *Suppose we are looking for rich people who own a sports car. This query can be posed as follows:*

```
SELECT ?p ?l1 ?c WHERE {
    <(?p type RichPerson), ?l1>
    OPTIONAL{<(?p hasSportsCar ?c), ?l2>}
}
```

Assuming our example dataset has the following triples:

$$\langle (toivo, \text{type}, RichPerson), 0.8 \rangle$$
$$\langle (toivo, hasSportsCar, ferrari), 1.0 \rangle$$
$$\langle (toivo, hasSportsCar, audiTT), 0.7 \rangle$$

we will get the following answers:

$$\theta_1 = \{?p/toivo, ?l1/0.8\}$$
$$\theta_2 = \{?p/toivo, ?l1/0.8, ?c/ferrari\}$$
$$\theta_3 = \{?p/toivo, ?l2/0.8, ?c/audiTT\} \ .$$

The first answer corresponds to the answer in which the OPTIONAL *pattern is not satisfied. In the second and third answers, the* OPTIONAL *pattern is also matched.*

From a semantics point of view, the semantics of fuzzy SPARQL queries extend the notion of SPARQL BGP matching. As for the SPARQL query language, we are going to define the notion of solutions for BFP as the equivalent notion of answers set of fuzzy conjunctive queries. Just as matching BGPs against RDF graphs is at the core of SPARQL semantics, matching BFPs against fuzzy RDF graphs is the heart of the evaluation semantics of fuzzy SPARQL.

We extend the notion of *substitution* to include a substitution of fuzzy variables in which we do not allow any assignment of a fuzzy variable to 0. A value of 0, although it is a valid answer for any triple, does not provide any additional information and thus is of minor interest. Furthermore this would contribute to increasing the number of answers unnecessarily.

Let P be a BFP and G an fuzzy RDF graph. We define *evaluation* $[\![P]\!]_G$ as the list of substitutions that are *solutions* of P, i.e., $[\![P]\!]_G = \{\theta \mid G \models \theta(P)\}$, and where $G \models \theta(P)$ means that any fuzzy triple in $\theta(P)$ is entailed by G.

As for SPARQL, we have:

Proposition 98. *Given a fuzzy graph G and a BFP P, the solutions of P are the same as the answers of the fuzzy query $q(var(P)) \leftarrow P$ (where $var(P)$ is the vector of variables in P), i.e., $ans(G, q) = [\![P]\!]_G$.*

For the extension of the SPARQL relational algebra to the fuzzy case we introduce – inspired by the definitions in [348] – definitions of compatibility and union of substitutions:

Two substitutions θ_1 and θ_2 are $\otimes$-*compatible* if and only if (i) θ_1 and θ_2 are compatible for all the non-fuzzy variables, *i.e.*, $\theta_1(x) = \theta_2(x)$ for any non-fuzzy variable $x \in dom(\theta_1) \cap dom(\theta_2)$; and (ii) $\theta_1(\lambda) \otimes \theta_2(\lambda) \neq 0$ for any fuzzy variable $\lambda \in dom(\theta_1) \cap dom(\theta_2)$.

Given two $\otimes$-compatible substitutions θ_1 and θ_2, the $\otimes$-*union* of θ_1 and θ_2, denoted $\theta_1 \otimes \theta_2$, is as $\theta_1 \cup \theta_2$, with the exception that any fuzzy variable $\lambda \in dom(\theta_1) \cap dom(\theta_2)$ is mapped to $\theta_1(\lambda) \otimes \theta_2(\lambda)$.

We now present the notion of evaluation for generic fuzzy SPARQL graph patterns. Let P be a BFP, P_1, P_2 fuzzy graph patterns, G an fuzzy graph and R a filter expression, then the evaluation $[\![\cdot]\!]_G$, *i.e.*, set of *answers*,[1] is recursively defined as:

- $[\![P]\!]_G = \{\theta \mid dom(\theta) = var(P) \text{ and } G \models \theta(P)\}$

- $[\![P_1 \text{ AND } P_2]\!]_G = \{\theta_1 \otimes \theta_2 \mid \theta_1 \in [\![P_1]\!]_G, \theta_2 \in [\![P_2]\!]_G, \theta_1 \text{ and } \theta_2 \otimes\text{-compatible}\}$

- $[\![P_1 \text{ UNION } P_2]\!]_G = [\![P_1]\!]_G \cup [\![P_2]\!]_G$

- $[\![P_1 \text{ FILTER } R]\!]_G = \{\theta \mid \theta \in [\![P_1]\!]_G \text{ and } R\theta \text{ is true}\}$

- $[\![P_1 \text{ OPTIONAL } P_2[R]]\!]_G =$
  $\{\theta \mid \text{ and } \theta \text{ meets one of the following conditions:}$

  1. $\theta = \theta_1 \otimes \theta_2$ if $\theta_1 \in [\![P_1]\!]_G, \theta_2 \in [\![P_2]\!]_G, \theta_1$ and $\theta_2 \otimes$-compatible, and $R\theta$ is true;

  2. $\theta = \theta_1 \in [\![P_1]\!]_G$ and $\forall \theta_2 \in [\![P_2]\!]_G$ such that θ_1 and θ_2 $\otimes$-compatible, $R(\theta_1 \otimes \theta_2)$ is true, and for all fuzzy variables $\lambda \in dom(\theta_1) \cap dom(\theta_2)$, $\theta_2(\lambda) \prec \theta_1(\lambda)$;

  3. $\theta = \theta_1 \in [\![P_1]\!]_G$ and $\forall \theta_2 \in [\![P_2]\!]_G$ such that θ_1 and θ_2 $\otimes$-compatible, $R(\theta_1 \otimes \theta_2)$ is false $\}$.

Let R be a FILTER expression and $x, y \in \mathbf{A} \cup L$, in addition to the FILTER expressions, we further allow the expressions presented next. The valuation of R on a substitution θ, denoted $R\theta$ is true if:[2]

- $R = (x \leq y)$ with $x, y \in dom(\theta) \cup L \wedge \theta(x) \leq \theta(y)$;

- $R = p(\mathbf{z})$ with $p(\mathbf{z})\theta = $ true if and only if $p(\theta(\mathbf{z})) = $ true, where p is a built-in predicate;

---

[1] Strictly speaking, we consider *sequences* of answers – note that SPARQL allows duplicates and imposes an order on solutions, see below for more discussion – but we stick with set *notation* representation here for illustration. Whenever we mean "real" sets where duplicates are removed we write $\{\ldots\}_{\text{DISTINCT}}$.

[2] We consider a simple evaluation of filter expressions where the "error" result is ignored, see [381, Section 11.3] for details.

- Otherwise $R\theta$ is false.

Remark 53. *For practical convenience, we retain in $\llbracket \cdot \rrbracket_G$ only "domain maximal answers." That is, let us define $\theta' \leq \theta$ if and only if (i) $\theta' \neq \theta$; (ii) $dom(\theta) = dom(\theta')$; (iii) $\theta(x) = \theta'(x)$ for any non-fuzzy variable x; and (iv) $\theta'(\lambda) \leq \theta(\lambda)$ for any fuzzy variable λ. Then, for any $\theta \in \llbracket P \rrbracket_G$ we remove any $\theta' \in \llbracket P \rrbracket_G$ such that $\theta' \leq \theta$.*

The following proposition shows that we have a conservative extension of SPARQL:

Proposition 99 ([476, 264]). *Let $Q = (P, G, V)$ be a SPARQL query over an RDF graph G. Let G' be obtained from G by annotating triples with 1.0. Then $\llbracket P \rrbracket_G$ under SPARQL semantics is in one-to-one correspondence to $\llbracket P \rrbracket_{G'}$ under fuzzy SPARQL semantics such that for any $\theta \in \llbracket P \rrbracket_G$ there is a $\theta' \in \llbracket P \rrbracket_{G'}$ with θ and θ' coinciding on $var(P)$.*

Next, we will present extensions to include variable assignments, aggregates, and solution modifiers. These extensions are similar to the ones presented in Section 6.3.

Let P be a fuzzy graph pattern and G a fuzzy graph, the evaluation of an ASSIGN statement is defined as:

$$\llbracket P \text{ ASSIGN } f(\mathbf{z}) \text{ AS } z \rrbracket_G = \{\theta \mid \theta_1 \in \llbracket P \rrbracket_G, \theta = \theta_1[z/f(\theta_1(\mathbf{z}))]\}$$

where

$$\theta[z/t] = \begin{cases} \theta \cup \{z/t\} & \text{if } z \notin dom(\theta) \\ (\theta \setminus \{z/t'\}) \cup \{z/t\} & \text{otherwise .} \end{cases}$$

Essentially, we assign to the variable z the value $f(\theta_1(\mathbf{z}))$, which is the evaluation of the function $f(\mathbf{z})$ with respect to a substitution $\theta_1 \in \llbracket P \rrbracket_G$.

Example 63 ([476]). *Using a built-in function we submit a query such as:*

```
SELECT ?p ?c ?z WHERE {
 <(?p type RichPerson), ?l1>
 <(?p hasSportsCar ?c), ?l2>
    ASSIGN ?l1 * ?l2 AS ?z
}
```

Fuzzy SPARQL also supports the ORDERBY clause where the evaluation of a $\llbracket P \text{ ORDERBY } ?x \rrbracket_G$ statement is defined as the ordering of the solutions – for any $\theta \in \llbracket P \rrbracket_G$ – according to the values of $\theta(?x)$. Ordering for non-fuzzy variables follows the rules in [381, Section 9.1].

In case the variable x is a fuzzy variable, the order is induced by $\leq$. In case the order is some partial order then we may use some linearization method for posets, such as [248]. Likewise, the SQL-like statement LIMIT(k) can be added straightforwardly.

We can further extend the evaluation of fuzzy SPARQL queries with aggregate functions

$$@ \in \{\mathsf{SUM}, \mathsf{AVG}, \mathsf{MAX}, \mathsf{MIN}, \mathsf{COUNT}, \oplus, \otimes\}$$

as follows:

The evaluation of a GROUPBY statement is defined as:[3]

$$[\![P \ \mathsf{GROUPBY}(\mathbf{w}) \ @\mathbf{f}(\mathbf{z}) \ AS \ \alpha]\!]_G = \{\theta \mid \theta_1 \ \text{in} \ [\![P]\!]_G,$$
$$\theta = \theta_1|_{\mathbf{w}}[\alpha_i/@_i f_i(\theta_i(\mathbf{z}_i))]\}_{\mathsf{DISTINCT}}$$

where the variables $\alpha_i \notin var(P)$, $\mathbf{z}_i \in var(P)$ and none of the GROUPBY variables $\mathbf{w}$ are included in the aggregation function variables $\mathbf{z}_i$. Here, we denote by $\theta|_{\mathbf{w}}$ the restriction of variables in θ to variables in $\mathbf{w}$. Using this notation, we can also straightforwardly introduce projection, *i.e.*, sub-SELECTs as an algebraic operator in the language covering another new feature of SPARQL 1.1:

$$[\![\mathsf{SELECT} \ \mathbf{V} \ \{P\}]\!]_G \ = \ \{\theta \mid \theta_1 \ \text{in} \ [\![P]\!]_G, \theta = \theta_1|_{\mathbf{v}}\} \ .$$

Remark 54. *Please note that the aggregator functions have a domain of definition and thus can only be applied to values of their respective domain. For example, SUM and AVG can only be used on numeric values, while MAX, MIN are applicable to any total order. Resolution of type mismatches for aggregates is currently being defined in SPARQL 1.1 [380] and we aim to follow those, as soon as the language is stable. The COUNT aggregator can be used for any finite set of values. The last two aggregation functions, namely $\oplus$ and $\otimes$, are defined by the fuzzy domain $[0,1]$ and thus can be used on any fuzzy variable.*

Example 64. *Suppose we want to know, for each person, the average score of being rich and having a sports car. Then such a query will be expressed as:*

```
SELECT ?x ?avgS WHERE {
  <(?p type RichPerson), ?l1>
  <(?p hasSportsCar ?c), ?l2>
    GROUPBY(?p)
    AVG(?l1 * ?l2) AS ?avgL
}
```

Proposition 100. *Assuming the built-in predicates are computable in finite time, the answer set of any fuzzy SPARQL is finite and can also be computed in finite time.*

---

[3] In the expression, $@\mathbf{f}(\mathbf{z}) \ AS \ \alpha$ is a concise representation of n aggregations of the form $@_i f_i(\mathbf{z}_i) \ AS \ \alpha_i$.

Appendix H

Tableau Calculi for Fuzzy $\mathcal{SHIF}_g$

As we have seen in Appendix C, the major issue introduced by functional roles is that together with inverse roles they may cause a concept to be satisfiable in an infinite model only as Example 60 illustrates. Of course, this property applies to fuzzy $\mathcal{SHIF}_g$ as well.

In order to cope with this issue, like for the crisp DLs case, we use the so-called notion of *pairwise blocking* to guarantee the correct termination of a tableau from which then we may build a possibly infinite model.

To start with, in this appendix, we restrict fuzzy RIAs in a fuzzy RBox $\mathcal{R}$ to be of the form $R_1 \tilde{\sqsubseteq} R_2$ only.

Then the definitions of $\mathsf{Inv}(R)$, $\mathsf{Trans}(R)$ and $\sqsubseteq^*_{\mathcal{R}}$ (the transitive-reflexive closure of $\tilde{\sqsubseteq}$ over $\mathcal{R}' = \mathcal{R} \cup \{\mathsf{Inv}(R_1) \tilde{\sqsubseteq} \mathsf{Inv}(R_2) \mid R_1 \tilde{\sqsubseteq} R_2 \in \mathcal{R}\}$) are as for the crisp case (see Appendix C).

H.1 Analytical Fuzzy Tableau under SFL

We now extend the analytical fuzzy tableau under SFL seen in Section 10.6.1.2 for fuzzy $\mathcal{ALC}$ to fuzzy $\mathcal{SHIF}_g$. So, let $\mathcal{K}$ be a $\mathcal{SHIF}_g$ KB. The notions of completion-forest, clash, and the initialization of a completion-forest is like Section 10.6.1.2.

If nodes v and w are connected by an edge $\langle v, w \rangle$ then w is called a *successor* of v and v is called a *predecessor* of w. *Ancestor* is the transitive closure of predecessor, and *descendant* is the transitive closure of successor.

If nodes v and w are connected by an edge $\langle v, w \rangle$ with $\langle R', n \rangle \in \mathcal{L}(\langle v, w \rangle)$ and $R' \sqsubseteq^*_{\mathcal{R}} R$, then w is called an R_n-*successor* of v and v is called an R_n-*predecessor* of w. If node w is an R_n-successor of v or an $\mathsf{Inv}(R)_n$-predecessor of v, then w is called an R_n-*neighbor* of v.

Similarly to the crisp case, we also need a technical definition involving functional roles. Let $\mathcal{F}$ be forest, R a functional role such that we have two edges $\langle v, w_1 \rangle$ and $\langle v, w_2 \rangle$ such that $\langle R, n_1 \rangle$ occurs in $\mathcal{L}(\langle v, w_1 \rangle)$ and $\langle R, n_2 \rangle$ occurs $\mathcal{L}(\langle v, w_2 \rangle)$, respectively. Then we call such a pair a *fork*. As R is functional, such a fork means that w_1 and w_2 have to be interpreted as the same individual. Such a fork can be deleted by adding both $\mathcal{L}(\langle v, w_2\rangle)$ to $\mathcal{L}(\langle v, w_1\rangle)$, and $\mathcal{L}(w_2)$ to $\mathcal{L}(w_1)$, and then deleting node w_2. Of course, as inverse roles are allowed these may also contribute to create a fork, *i.e.*, we have a fork if w_1 and w_2 are R-neighbors of v.

We assume that forks are eliminated as soon as they appear (as part of a rule application) with the proviso that newly generated nodes are replaced by older ones and not vice versa.

At the beginning, we check that there are no forks in the initial forest, otherwise the KB is not satisfiable (due to the unique name assumption, if we have $\langle(a, b_1){:}R, n_1\rangle$ and $\langle(a, b_2){:}R, n_2\rangle$ with $b_1 \neq b_2$ then R cannot be functional).

The notion of pairwise blocking, blocked node, directly blocked, and indirectly blocked is as for crisp $\mathcal{SHIF}_g$ (see Appendix C).

The set of reasoning rules are shown in Table H.1, where ϵ is given by Equation (10.13):

TABLE H.1: The tableau rules for fuzzy $\mathcal{SHIF}_g$.

($\sqcap$). If *(i)* $\langle C_1 \sqcap C_2, n\rangle \in \mathcal{L}(v)$, *(ii)* $\{\langle C_1, n\rangle, \langle C_2, n\rangle\} \not\subseteq \mathcal{L}(v)$ and *(iii)* node v is not indirectly blocked, then add $\langle C_1, n\rangle$ and $\langle C_2, n\rangle$ to $\mathcal{L}(v)$.

($\sqcup$). If *(i)* $\langle C_1 \sqcup C_2, n\rangle \in \mathcal{L}(v)$, *(ii)* $\{\langle C_1, n\rangle, \langle C_2, n\rangle\} \cap \mathcal{L}(v) = \emptyset$ and *(iii)* node v is not indirectly blocked, then add some $\langle C, n\rangle \in \{\langle C_1, n\rangle, \langle C_2, n\rangle\}$ to $\mathcal{L}(v)$.

($\forall$). If *(i)* $\langle \forall R.C, n\rangle \in \mathcal{L}(v)$, *(ii)* there is an R_m-neighbour w of v with $m > 1 - n$, *(iii)* $\langle C, n\rangle \not\in \mathcal{L}(w)$, and *(iv)* node v is not indirectly blocked, then add $\langle C, n\rangle$ to $\mathcal{L}(w)$.

($\forall_+$). If *(i)* $\langle \forall S.C, n\rangle \in \mathcal{L}(v)$, *(ii)* there is some R with $\mathsf{Trans}(R)$ and $R \sqsubseteq_{\mathcal{R}}^* S$, *(iii)* there is an R_m-neighbour w of v with $m > 1 - n$, *(iv)* $\langle \forall R.C, n\rangle \not\in \mathcal{L}(w)$ and *(iii)* and node v is not indirectly blocked, then add $\langle \forall R.C, n\rangle$ to $\mathcal{L}(w)$.

($\exists$). If *(i)* $\langle \exists R.C, n\rangle \in \mathcal{L}(v)$, *(ii)* there is no R_{n_1}-neighbour w of v with $\langle C, n_2\rangle \in \mathcal{L}(w)$ such that $\min(n_1, n_2) \geq n$, and *(iii)* node v is not blocked, then create a new node w, add $\langle R, n\rangle$ to $\mathcal{L}(\langle v, w\rangle)$ and add $\langle C, n\rangle$ to $\mathcal{L}(w)$.

($\sqsubseteq$). If *(i)* $\langle \top \sqsubseteq D, n\rangle \in \mathcal{T}$, *(ii)* $\langle D, n\rangle \not\in \mathcal{L}(v)$ and *(ii)* node v is not indirectly blocked, then add $\langle D, n\rangle$ to $\mathcal{L}(v)$.

($\tilde{\sqsubseteq}$). If *(i)* $C \tilde{\sqsubseteq} D \in \mathcal{T}$, *(ii)* for some $n \in N_+^{\mathcal{K}}$, $\{\langle nnf(\neg C), 1 - n + \epsilon\rangle, \langle D, n\rangle\} \cap \mathcal{L}(v) = \emptyset$ and *(iii)* node v is not indirectly blocked, then add E to $\mathcal{L}(v)$ for some $E \in \{\langle nnf(\neg C), 1 - n + \epsilon\rangle, \langle D, n\rangle\}$.

It can be shown in a similar way as in [389] that:

Proposition 101. *For each $\mathcal{SHIF}_g$ knowledge base $\mathcal{K}$*

1. *the tableau algorithm terminates;*

2. *if the expansion rules can be applied in such a way that they yield a complete and clash-free completion forest, then $\mathcal{K}$ has a model;*

3. *if $\mathcal{K}$ has a model, then the expansion rules can be applied in such a way that they yield complete and clash-free completion forest for $\mathcal{K}$.*

H.2 Fuzzy Tableau for Finite-Valued DLs

We shortly show how one may extend the tableau calculus illustrated in Section 10.6.1.3 for $\mathcal{ALC}$ to $\mathcal{SHIF}_g$ as well.

So, let $\mathcal{K}$ be a $\mathcal{SHIF}_g$ KB. The notions of completion-forest, successor, predecessor, ancestor, and neighbor and the management of forks are as in Section H.1. The notions of clash and the initialization of a completion-forest is like Section 10.6.1.3. The notion of *pairwise blocking* is as for the crisp case.

The set of reasoning rules are shown in Table H.2:

We have that

Proposition 102 ([73]). *For each $\mathcal{SHIF}_g$ knowledge base $\mathcal{K}$ with a finitely valued truth space L_n*

1. *the tableau algorithm terminates;*

2. *if the expansion rules can be applied in such a way that they yield a complete and clash-free completion forest, then $\mathcal{K}$ has a model;*

3. *if $\mathcal{K}$ has a model, then the expansion rules can be applied in such a way that they yield complete and clash-free completion forest for $\mathcal{K}$.*

Of course, the method can be adapted to any truth space as well, as long as it is finite.

H.3 Operational Research-based Fuzzy Tableau under SFL

We now extend the OR-based fuzzy tableau under SFL seen in Section 10.6.1.4 for fuzzy $\mathcal{ALC}$ to fuzzy $\mathcal{SHIF}_g$. So, let $\mathcal{K}$ be a $\mathcal{SHIF}_g$ KB. The notions of completion-forest, R-successor, R-predecessor, R-neighbor, successor, predecessor, neighbor, and ancestor are as for the crisp case (see Appendix C). As for $\mathcal{ALC}$, a forest has associated a set $\mathcal{C}_\mathcal{F}$ of mixed-integer

TABLE H.2: The tableau rules for finitely valued fuzzy $\mathcal{SHIF}_g$.

($\sqcap$). If *(i)* $\langle C_1 \sqcap C_2, m \rangle \in \mathcal{L}(v)$, *(ii)* there are $m_1, m_2 \in L_n$ such that $m_1 \otimes m_2 = m$ with $\{\langle C_1, m_1 \rangle, \langle C_2, m_2 \rangle\} \not\subseteq \mathcal{L}(v)$, and *(iii)* node v is not indirectly blocked, then add $\langle C_1, m_1 \rangle$ and $\langle C_2, m_2 \rangle$ to $\mathcal{L}(v)$.

($\sqcup$). If *(i)* $\langle C_1 \sqcup C_2, m \rangle \in \mathcal{L}(v)$, *(ii)* there are $m_1, m_2 \in L_n$ such that $m_1 \oplus m_2 = m$ with $\{\langle C_1, m_1 \rangle, \langle C_2, m_2 \rangle\} \cap \mathcal{L}(v) = \emptyset$, and *(iii)* node v is not indirectly blocked, then add some $\langle C, k \rangle \in \{\langle C_1, m_1 \rangle, \langle C_2, m_2 \rangle\}$ to $\mathcal{L}(v)$.

($\neg$). If *(i)* $\langle \neg C, m \rangle \in \mathcal{L}(v)$ with $\langle C, \ominus m \rangle \notin \mathcal{L}(v)$ and *(ii)* node v is not indirectly blocked, then add $\langle C, \ominus m \rangle$ to $\mathcal{L}(v)$.

($\rightarrow$). If *(i)* $\langle C_1 \rightarrow C_2, m \rangle \in \mathcal{L}(v)$, *(ii)* there are $m_1, m_2 \in L_n$ such that $m_1 \Rightarrow m_2 = m$ and $\{\langle C_1, m_1 \rangle, \langle C_2, m_2 \rangle\} \not\subseteq \mathcal{L}(v)$, and *(iii)* node v is not indirectly blocked, then add $\langle C_1, m_1 \rangle$ and $\langle C_2, m_2 \rangle$ to $\mathcal{L}(v)$.

($\forall$). If *(i)* $\langle \forall R.C, m \rangle \in \mathcal{L}(v)$, *(ii)* $\langle R, m_1 \rangle \in \mathcal{L}(\langle v, w \rangle)$, *(iii)* there is $m_2 \in L_n$ such that $m_1 \Rightarrow m_2 \geq m$ with $\langle C, m_2 \rangle \notin \mathcal{L}(w)$, and *(iv)* node v is not indirectly blocked, then add $\langle C, m_2 \rangle$ to $\mathcal{L}(w)$.

($\exists$). If *(i)* $\langle \exists R.C, m \rangle \in \mathcal{L}(v)$, *(ii)* there are $m_1, m_2 \in L_n$ such that $m_1 \otimes m_2 = m$, *(iii)* there is no $\langle R, m_1 \rangle \in \mathcal{L}(\langle v, w \rangle)$ with $\langle C, m_2 \rangle \in \mathcal{L}(w)$, and *(iv)* node v is not blocked, then create a new node w, add $\langle R, m_1 \rangle$ to $\mathcal{L}(\langle v, w \rangle)$ and add $\langle C, m_2 \rangle$ to $\mathcal{L}(w)$.

($\exists'$). If *(i)* $\langle \exists R.C, m \rangle \in \mathcal{L}(v)$, *(ii)* $\langle R, m_1 \rangle \in \mathcal{L}(\langle v, w \rangle)$, *(iii)* there is $m_2 \in L_n$ such that $m_1 \otimes m_2 \leq m$ with $\langle C, m_2 \rangle \notin \mathcal{L}(w)$, and *(iv)* node v is not indirectly blocked, then add $\langle C, m_2 \rangle$ to $\mathcal{L}(w)$.

($\forall'$). If *(i)* $\langle \forall R.C, m \rangle \in \mathcal{L}(v)$, *(ii)* there are $m_1, m_2 \in L_n$ such that $m_1 \Rightarrow m_2 = m$, *(iii)* there is no $\langle R, m_1 \rangle \in \mathcal{L}(\langle v, w \rangle)$ with $\langle C, m_2 \rangle \in \mathcal{L}(w)$, and *(iv)* node v is not blocked, then create a new node w, add $\langle R, m_1 \rangle$ to $\mathcal{L}(\langle v, w \rangle)$ and add $\langle C, m_2 \rangle$ to $\mathcal{L}(w)$.

($\forall_+$). If *(i)* $\langle \forall S.C, m \rangle \in \mathcal{L}(v)$, *(ii)* there is some R with $\mathsf{Trans}(R)$ and $R \sqsubseteq^*_\mathcal{R} S$, *(iii)* there is an R_{m_1}-neighbour w of v and $m_2 \in L_n$ such that $m_1 \Rightarrow m_2 \geq m$ *(iv)* $\langle \forall R.C, m_2 \rangle \notin \mathcal{L}(w)$, and *(iv)* and node v is not indirectly blocked, then add $\langle \forall R.C, m_2 \rangle$ to $\mathcal{L}(w)$.

($\sqsubseteq$). If *(i)* $\langle C \sqsubseteq D, m \rangle \in \mathcal{T}$, *(ii)* there are $m_1, m_2 \in L_n$ such that $m_1 \Rightarrow m_2 \geq m$, *(iii)* $\{\langle C, m_1 \rangle, \langle D, m_2 \rangle\} \not\subseteq \mathcal{L}(v)$, and *(iv)* node v is not indirectly blocked, then add $\langle C, m_1 \rangle$ and $\langle D, m_2 \rangle$ to $\mathcal{L}(v)$.

($\tilde{\sqsubseteq}$). If *(i)* $C \tilde{\sqsubseteq} D \in \mathcal{T}$, *(ii)* there are $m_1, m_2 \in L_n$ such that $m_1 \leq m_2$, *(iii)* $\{\langle C, m_1 \rangle, \langle D, m_2 \rangle\} \not\subseteq \mathcal{L}(v)$, and *(iv)* node v is not indirectly blocked, then add $\langle C, m_1 \rangle$ and $\langle D, m_2 \rangle$ to $\mathcal{L}(v)$.

linear programming constraints. The initialization of a completion-forest is like for $\mathcal{ALC}$ (see Section 10.6.1.4), too.

We assume that forks are eliminated as soon as they appear (as part of a rule application) with the proviso that newly generated nodes are replaced by older ones and not vice versa. At the beginning, we check that there are no forks in the initial forest, otherwise the KB is not satisfiable (due to the unique name assumption, if we have $\langle (a, b_1):R, n_1 \rangle$ and $\langle (a, b_2):R, n_2 \rangle$ with $b_1 \neq b_2$ then R cannot be functional).

The notion of pairwise blocking, blocked node, directly blocked, and indirectly blocked is as for crisp $\mathcal{SHIF}_g$ (see Appendix C).

The set of reasoning rules are shown in Table H.3:

Again, it can be shown that using the rules in Table H.3 we have that:

Proposition 103. *For each knowledge base $\mathcal{K} = \langle \mathcal{T}, \mathcal{A} \rangle$*

1. *the tableau algorithm terminates;*

2. *if the expansion rules can be applied to a knowledge base $\mathcal{K} = \langle \mathcal{T}, \mathcal{A} \rangle$ such that they yield a complete completion forest $\mathcal{F}$ such that $\mathcal{C}_{\mathcal{F}}$ has a solution, then $\mathcal{K}$ has a (witnessed) model;*

3. *if a knowledge base $\mathcal{K} = \langle \mathcal{T}, \mathcal{A} \rangle$ has a (witnessed) model, then the application of the expansion rules yields a complete completion-forest for $\mathcal{K}$ such that $\mathcal{C}_{\mathcal{F}}$ has a solution.*

H.4 Reasoning with Fuzzy Concrete Domains and Aggregation Operators under SFL

Fuzzy Concrete Domains. [398] first showed a general OR-based method to deal with concrete domains. Specifically, for a functional datatype property a fork is eliminated as soon as it appears, in the same way as for an object property (*i.e.*, role). For a datatype property T, we assume that T's values are rational numbers, $[T_{\min}, T_{\max}]$ is the range of allowed values that T-fillers may take. The OR-based inference rules related to concept expressions of the form

$$C, D \quad \rightarrow \quad \forall T.\mathbf{d} \mid \exists T.\mathbf{d}$$

are the datatype property analogue of the ($\forall$) and ($\exists$) rule in Table H.3, *i.e.*,

($\forall_{\mathbf{d}}$). If *(i)* $\forall T.\mathbf{d} \in \mathcal{L}(v)$, there is a T-neighbor w of v, *(ii)* the rule has not been already applied to this concept, and *(iii)* node v is not indirectly blocked, then add $\mathbf{d}$ to $\mathcal{L}(w)$, and $\mathcal{C}_{\mathcal{F}} := \mathcal{C}_{\mathcal{F}} \cup \{x_{w:\mathbf{d}} \geq x_{v:\forall T.\mathbf{d}} \otimes x_{(v,w):T}, T_{\min} \leq x_w \leq T_{\max}\}$.

TABLE H.3: The OR-based tableau rules for fuzzy $\mathcal{SHIF}_g$ with GCIs.

(var). For variable $x_{v:C}$ occurring in $\mathcal{C}_\mathcal{F}$ add $x_{v:C} \in [0,1]$ to $\mathcal{C}_\mathcal{F}$. For variable $x_{(v,w):R}$ occurring in $\mathcal{C}_\mathcal{F}$ add $x_{(v,w):R} \in [0,1]$ to $\mathcal{C}_\mathcal{F}$.

($\bot$). If $\bot \in \mathcal{L}(v)$ then $\mathcal{C}_\mathcal{F} := \mathcal{C}_\mathcal{F} \cup \{x_{v:\bot} = 0\}$.

($\top$). If $\top \in \mathcal{L}(v)$ then $\mathcal{C}_\mathcal{F} := \mathcal{C}_\mathcal{F} \cup \{x_{v:\top} = 1\}$.

($\bar{A}$). If $\neg A \in \mathcal{L}(v)$ then add A to $\mathcal{L}(v)$, and $\mathcal{C}_\mathcal{F} := \mathcal{C}_\mathcal{F} \cup \{x_{v:A} \le 1 - x_{v:\neg A}\}$.

($\sqcap$). If *(i)* $C_1 \sqcap C_2 \in \mathcal{L}(v)$, *(ii)* the rule has not been already applied to this concept, and *(iii)* node v is not indirectly blocked, then add C_1 and C_2 to $\mathcal{L}(v)$, and $\mathcal{C}_\mathcal{F} := \mathcal{C}_\mathcal{F} \cup \{x_{v:C_1} \otimes x_{v:C_2} \ge x_{v:C_1 \sqcap C_2}\}$.

($\sqcup$). If *(i)* $C_1 \sqcup C_2 \in \mathcal{L}(v)$ and *(ii)* the rule has not been already applied to this concept, and *(iii)* node v is not indirectly blocked, then add C_1 and C_2 to $\mathcal{L}(v)$, and $\mathcal{C}_\mathcal{F} := \mathcal{C}_\mathcal{F} \cup \{x_{v:C_1} \oplus x_{v:C_2} \ge x_{v:C_1 \sqcup C_2}\}$.

($\forall$). If *(i)* $\forall R.C \in \mathcal{L}(v)$, there is a R-neighbour w of v and *(ii)* the rule has not been already applied to this concept, and *(iii)* node v is not indirectly blocked, then add C to $\mathcal{L}(w)$, and $\mathcal{C}_\mathcal{F} := \mathcal{C}_\mathcal{F} \cup \{x_{w:C} \ge x_{v:\forall R.C} \otimes x_{(v,w):R}\}$.

($\forall_+$). If *(i)* $\forall S.C \in \mathcal{L}(v)$, *(ii)* there is some R with $\mathsf{Trans}(R)$, $R \sqsubseteq^*_\mathcal{R} S$ and $R \in \mathcal{L}(\langle v,w \rangle)$ and *(iii)* the rule has not been already applied to this concept, and *(iv)* node v is not indirectly blocked, then add $\forall R.C$ to $\mathcal{L}(w)$, and $\mathcal{C}_\mathcal{F} := \mathcal{C}_\mathcal{F} \cup \{x_{w:\forall R.C} \ge x_{v:\forall R.C} \otimes x_{(v,w):R}\}$.

($\exists$). If *(i)* $\exists R.C \in \mathcal{L}(v)$ and *(ii)* the rule has not been already applied to this concept and *(iii)* node v is not blocked then create a new node w, add R to $\mathcal{L}(\langle v,w \rangle)$, add C to $\mathcal{L}(w)$, and $\mathcal{C}_\mathcal{F} := \mathcal{C}_\mathcal{F} \cup \{x_{(v,w):R} \otimes x_{w:C} \ge x_{v:\exists R.C}\}$.

($\sqsubseteq$). If *(i)* $\langle \top \sqsubseteq D, n \rangle \in \mathcal{T}$, *(ii)* v is a node to which this rule has not yet been applied, and *(iii)* node v is not indirectly blocked, then add D to $\mathcal{L}(v)$ and set $\mathcal{C}_\mathcal{F} := \mathcal{C}_\mathcal{F} \cup \{x_{v:D} \ge n\}$.

($\tilde{\sqsubseteq}$). If *(i)* $C \tilde{\sqsubseteq} D \in \mathcal{T}$, *(ii)* v is a node to which this rule has not yet been applied, and *(iii)* node v is not indirectly blocked, then add $nnf(\neg C)$ and D to $\mathcal{L}(v)$ and set $\mathcal{C}_\mathcal{F} := \mathcal{C}_\mathcal{F} \cup \{x_{v:nnf(\neg C)} \oplus_l x_{v:D} \ge 1\}$.

($\exists_\mathbf{d}$). If *(i)* $\exists T.\mathbf{d} \in \mathcal{L}(v)$ and *(ii)* the rule has not been already applied to this concept and *(iii)* node v is not blocked then create a new node w, add T to $\mathcal{L}(\langle v,w \rangle)$, add $\mathbf{d}$ to $\mathcal{L}(w)$, and $\mathcal{C}_\mathcal{F} := \mathcal{C}_\mathcal{F} \cup \{x_{(v,w):T} \otimes x_{w:\mathbf{d}} \ge x_{v:\exists T.\mathbf{d}}, x_{(v,w):T} \in \{0,1\}, T_{\min} \le x_w \le T_{\max}\}$.

In the rules above, x_w is the variable representing the concrete value of a concrete predicate $\mathbf{d}$ *(e.g., see the case of ls below)*.

In the following we assume that a function L is MILP representable (see Section 8.2.2.2) and for L we consider the graph $g(L) = \{\langle x_1, x_2 \rangle \in [0,1] \times [0,1] \mid L(x_1) = x_2\}$. The general inference rules to deal with concrete domains are

(d). If $\mathbf{d} \in \mathcal{L}(w)$ and the rule has not been already applied to this concept then $\mathcal{C}_{\mathcal{F}} = \mathcal{C}_{\mathcal{F}} \cup \gamma(w, \mathbf{d})$, where the set $\gamma(w, \mathbf{d}))$ is obtained from the bMILP representation of $g(\mathbf{d})$ by replacing all occurrences of x_2 with $x_{w:\mathbf{d}}$ and x_1 with x_w.

(¬d). If $\neg\mathbf{d} \in \mathcal{L}(w)$ and the rule has not been already applied to this concept then add $\mathbf{d}$ to $\mathcal{L}(w)$ and set $\mathcal{C}_{\mathcal{F}} = \mathcal{C}_{\mathcal{F}} \cup \{x_{w:\neg\mathbf{d}} = 1 - x_{w:\mathbf{d}}\}$.

For instance, the inference rule for $ls(a, b) \in \mathcal{L}(w)$, where w is a T-successor of v, is obtained immediately from the (ls) rule for $\mathcal{P}(\mathbf{D})$ (Appendix F) in which we replace

- $f_{\max}$ and $f_{\min}$ with $T_{\max}$ and $T_{\min}$, respectively;

- x_f with x_w; and

- $x_{(f\ ls(a,b))}$ with $x_{w:ls(a,b)}$.

That is, the rules for $ls(a, b)$ are

(ls). If $ls(a, b) \in \mathcal{L}(w)$, the rule has not been already applied to this concept and w is a T-successor of v, then

$$\begin{aligned}
\mathcal{C}_{\mathcal{F}} = \mathcal{C}_{\mathcal{F}} \cup \{ \quad & x_w + (T_{\max} - a) \cdot y_1 \leq T_{\max}, \\
& x_{w:ls(a,b)} \geq y_1, \\
& x_w + (T_{\min} - a) \cdot y_2 \geq T_{\min}, \\
& x_w + (T_{\max} - b) \cdot y_2 \leq T_{\max}, \\
& x_w + x_{w:ls(a,b)} \cdot (b - a) \geq b - (b - T_{\min}) \cdot (1 - y_2), \\
& x_w + x_{w:ls(a,b)} \cdot (b - a) \leq b - (a - T_{\max}) \cdot (1 - y_2), \\
& x_w + (T_{\min} - b) \cdot y_3 \geq T_{\min}, \\
& x_{w:ls(a,b)} \leq 1 - y_3, \\
& y_1 + y_2 + y_3 = 1, \\
& y_i \in \{0, 1\}\}\ ,
\end{aligned}$$

where y_i are new variables.

$(\neg ls)$. If $\neg ls(a, b) \in \mathcal{L}(w)$ and the rule has not been already applied to this concept then add $ls(a, b)$ to $\mathcal{L}(w)$ and set $\mathcal{C}_{\mathcal{F}} = \mathcal{C}_{\mathcal{F}} \cup \{x_{w:\neg ls(a,b)} = 1 - x_{w:ls(a,b)}\}$.

The rules for $\mathbf{d} \in \{rs(a, b), tri(a, b, c), trz(a, b, c, d), \neg rs(a, b), \neg tri(a, b, c)$ and $\neg trz(a, b, c, d)\}$ occurring in $\mathcal{L}(w)$, where w is a T-successor of v, are obtained analogously from the $(\mathbf{d})$ rule for $\mathcal{P}(\mathbf{D})$ (Appendix F) in which we replace

- $f_{\max}$ and $f_{\min}$ with $T_{\max}$ and $T_{\min}$, respectively;

- x_f with x_w; and

- $x_{(f\ \mathbf{d})}$ with $x_{w:\mathbf{d}}$.

The inference rules for the cases $\mathbf{d} \in \{\geq_m, \leq_m, =_m\}$ can be worked out similarly. Indeed, let p_ϵ as determined in Appendix F. Then the inference rules for $\mathbf{d} \in \{\geq_m, \leq_m, =_m\}$ occurring in $\mathcal{L}(w)$, where w is a T-successor of v, are obtained immediately from the $(\mathbf{d})$ rule for $\mathcal{P}(\mathbf{D})$ in which we replace

- $f_{\max}$ and $f_{\min}$ with $T_{\max}$ and $T_{\min}$, respectively;

- x_f with x_w;

- $x_{(f\ \mathbf{d})}$ with $x_{w:\mathbf{d}}$.

Fuzzy Modifiers. We next show how to deal with fuzzy modifiers as described in Section 10.3. So, concept expressions are of the form

$$ C \quad \rightarrow \quad m(C) \mid \forall T.m(\mathbf{d}) \mid \exists T.m(\mathbf{d}) $$

where we further assume that m is a linear modifier. The rules for $lm(C)$ or $lm(\mathbf{d})$ occurring in $\mathcal{L}(w)$ can again easily be derived from the (lm) rule for $\mathcal{P}(\mathbf{D})$. Specifically, we have

(lm). If $lm(a,b)(E) \in \mathcal{L}(w)$, where E is a concept C or a concrete fuzzy predicate $\mathbf{d}$, the rule has not been already applied to this concept and if E is a concept then node w is not indirectly blocked, then add X to $\mathcal{L}(w)$ and set

$$
\begin{aligned}
\mathcal{C}_{\mathcal{F}} \quad :=\mathcal{C}_{\mathcal{F}} \cup \{ \quad & x_{w:E} - y \leq a, \\
& x_{w:E} \geq a \cdot y, \\
& x_{w:E} + a/b \cdot y \geq a/b \cdot x_{w:lm(a,b)(E)}, \\
& x_{w:E} - y \leq a/b \cdot x_{w:lm(a,b)(E)}, \\
& (a-1) \cdot x_{w:lm(a,b)(E)} + (1-b) \cdot x_{w:E} \leq (a-b) \cdot y + 2(1-y), \\
& (a-1) \cdot x_{w:lm(a,b)(E)} + (1-b) \cdot x_{w:E} + 2(1-y) \geq (a-b) \cdot y, \\
& y \in \{0,1\}\}
\end{aligned}
$$

where y is a new variable.

$(\neg lm_E)$. If $\neg lm(a,b)(E) \in \mathcal{L}(w)$, where E is a concept C or a concrete fuzzy predicate $\mathbf{d}$, the rule has not been already applied to this concept and if E is a concept then node w is not indirectly blocked, then add lm_E to $\mathcal{L}(w)$ and set $\mathcal{C}_{\mathcal{F}} = \mathcal{C}_{\mathcal{F}} \cup \{x_{w:\neg lm(a,b)(E)} = 1 - x_{w:lm(a,b)(E)}\}$.

Aggregation Operators. We start by showing how to reason with weighted sum concepts, *i.e.*, concept expressions of the form

$$ w_1 \cdot C_1 + \cdots + w_k \cdot C_k $$

where $m_i \in (0,1)$, $\sum_i m_i \leq 1$.

The inference rules are derived immediately from the corresponding one for $\mathcal{P}(\mathbf{D})$ in which we replace ψ_i with C_i and, thus, get

(ws). If $w_1 \cdot C_1 + \cdots + w_k \cdot C_k \in \mathcal{L}(v)$, the rule has not been already applied to this concept, and node v is not indirectly blocked, then

    1. add $C_1, \ldots, C_k$ to $\mathcal{L}(v)$;

    2. set $\mathcal{C_F} := \mathcal{C_F} \cup \{\sum_i w_i \cdot x_{v:C_i} = x_{v:w_1 \cdot C_1 + \cdots + w_k \cdot C_k}\}$.

($\neg ws$). If $\neg(w_1 \cdot C_1 + \cdots + w_k \cdot C_k) \in \mathcal{L}(v)$, and the rule has not been already applied to this concept, and node v is not indirectly blocked, then

    1. add $\neg C_1, \ldots, \neg C_k$ to $\mathcal{L}(v)$;

    2. set $\mathcal{C_F} := \mathcal{C_F} \cup \{1 - \sum_i w_i \cdot x_{v:C_i} = x_{v:\neg(w_1 \cdot C_1 + \cdots + w_k \cdot C_k)}\}$.

Remark 55. *Note that, by Remark 33, to guarantee decidability in presence of the weighted sum operator, we need to restrict the attention to acyclic KBs only.*

Eventually, we address how to deal with OWA and the quantifier-guided OWA (see Section 8.1.6 and Section 10.3). Not surpassingly, again the inference rules can immediately be derived from the (owa) and ($qowa$) rules for $\mathcal{P}(\mathbf{D})$ in which we replace ψ_i with C_i and, thus, get

(owa). If $@_W^{\mathrm{owa}}(C_1, \ldots, C_k) \in \mathcal{L}(v)$, the rule has not been already applied to this concept, and node v is not indirectly blocked, then

    1. add $C_1, \ldots, C_k$ to $\mathcal{L}(v)$;

    2. set

$$\mathcal{C_F} := \mathcal{C_F} \cup \{x_{v:@_W^{\mathrm{owa}}(C_1,\ldots,C_k)} = \sum_{i=1}^{k} w_i \cdot y_i\} \cup$$

$$perm(x_{v:C_1}, \ldots, x_{v:C_k}) ,$$

where $W = \langle w_1, \ldots, w_k \rangle$ and $perm(x_1, \ldots, x_k)$ is the set of constraints ($N = \{1, \ldots, k\}$ and $i, j \in N$)

$$
\begin{aligned}
perm(x_1, \ldots, x_k) = \{ \quad & y_1 \geq y_2, \ldots, y_{k-1} \geq y_k, \\
& y_i \leq x_j + 2z_{ij}, \\
& x_j \leq y_i + 2z_{ij}, \\
& \sum_{j=1}^{k} z_{ij} = k - 1, \\
& \sum_{i=1}^{k} z_{ij} = k - 1, \\
& y_i \in [0,1], z_{ij} \in \{0,1\} \quad \} ,
\end{aligned}
$$

where y_i, z_{ij} are new variables.

$(\neg ws)$. If $\neg @_W^{owa}(C_1, \ldots, C_k) \in \mathcal{L}(v)$, and the rule has not been already applied to this concept, and node v is not indirectly blocked, then

1. add $@_W^{owa}(C_1, \ldots, C_k)$ to $\mathcal{L}(v)$;
2. set $\mathcal{C}_{\mathcal{F}} := \mathcal{C}_{\mathcal{F}} \cup \{1 - x_{v:@_W^{owa}(C_1, \ldots, C_k)} = x_{v:\neg @_W^{owa}(C_1, \ldots, C_k)}\}$.

It is straightforward to see now that indeed also the inference rules for quantifier-guided OWA, namely rules $(qowa)$ and $(\neg qowa)$ for $\mathcal{P}(\mathbf{D})$, can be adapted to the fuzzy DL case in a similar manner as we did for the OWA.

Eventually, note that Remark 55 applies to OWA and quantifier-guided OWA as well.

Bibliography

[1] Daniel J. Abadi, Adam Marcus, Samuel Madden, and Kate Hollenbach. SW-Store: a vertically partitioned DBMS for semantic web data management. *VLDB Journal*, 18(2):385–406, 2009.

[2] Serge Abiteboul, Richard Hull, and Victor Vianu. *Foundations of Databases*. Addison Wesley Publ. Co., Reading, Massachussetts, 1995.

[3] G. Acampora and V. Loia. Using FML and fuzzy technology in adaptive ambient intelligence environments. *International Journal of Computational Intelligence Research*, 1(2):171–182, 2005.

[4] Sudhir Agarwal and Steffen Lamparter. Smart: A semantic matchmaking portal for electronic markets. In *CEC '05: Proceedings of the Seventh IEEE International Conference on E-Commerce Technology (CEC'05)*, pages 405–408, Washington, DC, USA, 2005. IEEE Computer Society.

[5] Teresa Alsinet and Lluís Godo. A complete calculus for possibilistic logic programming with fuzzy propositional variables with fuzzy propositional variables. In *Proceedings of the 16th Conference in Uncertainty in Artificial Intelligence (UAI-00)*, pages 1–10. Morgan Kaufmann, 2000.

[6] Teresa Alsinet and Lluís Godo. Towards an automated deduction system for first-order possibilistic logic programming with fuzzy constants. *International Journal of Intelligent Systems*, 17(9):887–924, September 2002.

[7] Teresa Alsinet, Lluís Godo, and Sandra Sandri. On the semantics and automated deduction of PLFC, a logic of possibilistic uncertainty and fuzzyness. In *Proceedings of the 15th Annual Conference on Uncertainty in Artificial Intelligence (UAI-99)*, 1999.

[8] S. Amarger, D. Dubois, and H. Prade. Constraint propagation with imprecise conditional probabilities. In *Proceedings UAI-1991*, pages 26–34. Morgan Kaufmann, 1991.

[9] Henrik R. Andersen. Local computation of simultaneous fixedpoints. Technical Report PB-420, DAIMI, 1992. See also http://www.itu.dk/people/hra/thesis.pdf.

[10] Renzo Angles and Claudio Gutierrez. The expressive power of SPARQL. In *Proceedings of the 7th International Conference on The Semantic Web (ISWC-07)*, volume 5318 of *Lecture Notes in Computer Science*, pages 114–129. Springer-Verlag, 2008.

[11] Carlos Areces and Balder ten Cate. Hybrid logics. In P. Blackburn, F. Wolter, and J. van Benthem, editors, *Handbook of Modal Logics*, pages 821–868. Elsevier, 2006.

[12] Alessandro Artale, Diego Calvanese, Roman Kontchakov, and Michael Zakharyaschev. The DL-Lite family and relations. *Journal of Artificial Intelligence Research*, 36:1–69, 2009.

[13] F. Baader, S. Brandt, and C. Lutz. Pushing the $\mathcal{EL}$ envelope. In *Proceedings of the Nineteenth International Joint Conference on Artificial Intelligence (IJCAI-05)*, pages 364–369, Edinburgh, UK, 2005. Morgan-Kaufmann Publishers.

[14] F. Baader, S. Brandt, and C. Lutz. Pushing the $\mathcal{EL}$ envelope. LTCS-Report LTCS-05-01, Chair for Automata Theory, Institute for Theoretical Computer Science, Dresden University of Technology, Germany, 2005. See http://lat.inf.tu-dresden.de/research/reports.html.

[15] F. Baader, C. Lutz, and B. Suntisrivaraporn. Efficient reasoning in $\mathcal{EL}^+$. In *Proceedings of the 2006 International Workshop on Description Logics (DL-06)*, CEUR-WS, 2006.

[16] F. Baader, M. Milicic, C. Lutz, U. Sattler, and F. Wolter. Integrating description logics and action formalisms for reasoning about web services. LTCS-Report LTCS-05-02, Chair for Automata Theory, Institute for Theoretical Computer Science, Dresden University of Technology, Germany, 2005. See http://lat.inf.tu-dresden.de/research/reports.html.

[17] Franz Baader. Terminological cycles in a description logic with existential restrictions. In *Proceedings of the 18th International Joint Conference on Artificial intelligence (IJCAI-03)*, pages 325–330, San Francisco, CA, USA, 2003. Morgan Kaufmann Publishers Inc.

[18] Franz Baader, Sebastian Brandt, and Carsten Lutz. Pushing the $\mathcal{EL}$ envelope further. In Kendall Clark and Peter F. Patel-Schneider, editors, *In Proceedings of the OWLED 2008 DC Workshop on OWL: Experiences and Directions*, 2008.

[19] Franz Baader, Diego Calvanese, Deborah McGuinness, Daniele Nardi, and Peter F. Patel-Schneider, editors. *The Description Logic Handbook: Theory, Implementation, and Applications*. Cambridge University Press, 2003.

[20] Franz Baader, Enrico Franconi, Bernhard Hollunder, Bernhard Nebel, and Hans-Jürgen Profitlich. An empirical analysis of optimization techniques for terminological representation systems or: Making KRIS get a move on. *Applied Artificial Intelligence. Special Issue on Knowledge Base Management*, 4:109–132, 1994.

[21] Franz Baader and Philipp Hanschke. A schema for integrating concrete domains into concept languages. In *Proceedings of the 12th International Joint Conference on Artificial Intelligence (IJCAI-91)*, pages 452–457, Sydney, 1991.

[22] Franz Baader, Bernhard Hollunder, Bernhard Nebel, and Hans-Jürgen Profitlich. An empirical analysis of optimization techniques for teminological representation systems. Technical report, DFKI Saarbrücken, Germany, 1992.

[23] Franz Baader, Bernhard Hollunder, Bernhard Nebel, Hans-Jürgen Profitlich, and Enrico Franconi. An empirical analysis of optimization techniques for terminological representation systems or "making KRIS get a move on". In B. Nebel, W. Swartout, and C. Rich, editors, *Principles of Knowledge Representation and Reasoning: Proceedings of the 3rd International Conference*, pages 270–281, San Mateo, 1992. Morgan Kaufmann.

[24] Franz Baader, Carsten Lutz, Maja Miličic, Ulrike Sattler, and Frank Wolter. Integrating description logics and action formalisms: first results. In *Proceedings of the 20th National Conference on Artificial intelligence - Volume 2*, pages 572–577. AAAI Press, 2005.

[25] Franz Baader, Carsten Lutz, and Boontawee Suntisrivaraporn. Is tractable reasoning in extensions of the description logic $\mathcal{EL}$ useful in practice. In *Proceedings of the 2005 International Workshop on Methods for Modalities (M4M-05)*, 2005.

[26] Franz Baader and Rafael Peñaloza. On the undecidability of fuzzy description logics with GCIs and product t-norm. In *Proceedings of the 8th International Conference on Frontiers of Combining Systems (FroCoS-11)*, pages 55–70, Berlin, Heidelberg, 2011. Springer-Verlag.

[27] Franz Baader and Rafael Peñaloza. Are fuzzy description logics with general concept inclusion axioms decidable? In *Proceedings of 2011 IEEE International Conference on Fuzzy Systems (Fuzz-IEEE 2011)*. IEEE Press, 2011.

[28] Franz Baader and Rafael Peñaloza. GCIs make reasoning in fuzzy DLs with the product t-norm undecidable. In *Proceedings of the 24th International Workshop on Description Logics (DL-11)*. CEUR Electronic Workshop Proceedings, 2011.

[29] J. F. Baldwin. Evidential support of logic programming. *Fuzzy Sets and Systems*, 24(1):1–26, 1987.

[30] J. F. Baldwin. A theory of mass assignments for artificial intelligence. *Lecture Notes in Computer Science*, 833:22–34, 1994.

[31] J. F. Baldwin, T. P. Martin, and B. W. Pilsworth. *Fril - Fuzzy and Evidential Reasoning in Artificial Intelligence*. Research Studies Press Ltd, 1995.

[32] J. F. Baldwin, T. P. Martin, and B. W. Pilsworth. Applications of fuzzy computation: Knowledge based systems: Knowledge representation. In E. H. Ruspini, P. Bonnissone, and W. Pedrycz, editors, *Handbook of Fuzzy Computing*. IOP Publishing, 1998.

[33] Francois Bancilhon, David Maier, Yehoshua Sagiv, and Jeffrey D Ullman. Magic sets and other strange ways to implement logic programs (extended abstract). In *Proceedings of the 5th ACM SIGACT-SIGMOD Symposium on Principles of Database Systems (PODS-86)*, pages 1–15, New York, NY, USA, 1986. ACM Press.

[34] Chitta Baral, Michael Gelfond, and Nelson Rushton. Probabilistic reasoning with answer sets. In *Proceedings of the 7th International Conference in Logic Programming and Nonmonotonic Reasoning (LPNMR-04)*, volume 2923 of *Lecture Notes in Artificial Intelligence*, pages 21–33, Fort Lauderdale, FL, USA, 2004. Springer Verlag.

[35] Chitta Baral and Matt Hunsaker. Using the probabilistic logic programming language p-log for causal and counterfactual reasoning and non-naive conditioning. In *Proceedings of the 20th International Joint Conference on Artificial Intelligence (IJCAI-07)*, pages 243–249, 2007.

[36] Bernhard Beckert, Reiner Hähnle, and Felip Manyá. Transformations between signed and classical clause logic. In *Proceedings of the 29th International Symposium on Multiple-Valued Logics*, pages 248–255. IEEE CS Press, Los Alamitos, 1999.

[37] Ramon Bejar, Reiner Hähnle, and Felip Manyá. A modular reduction of regular logic to classical logic. In *31st IEEE International Symposium on Multiple-Valued Logic (ISMVL 2001)*, pages 221–226. IEEE Computer Society, 2001.

[38] R.E. Bellmann and L.A. Zadeh. Decision-making in a fuzzy environment. *Management Sciences*, 17:141–164, 1970.

[39] Fernando Bobillo, Félix Bou, and Umberto Straccia. On the failure of the finite model property in some fuzzy description logics. *Fuzzy Sets and Systems*, 172(1):1–12, 2011.

[40] Fernando Bobillo, Miguel Delgado, and Juan Gómez-Romero. A crisp representation for fuzzy $\mathcal{SHOIN}$ with fuzzy nominals and general concept inclusions. In *Proceedings of the 2nd Workshop on Uncertainty Reasoning for the Semantic Web (URSW-06)*, November 2006.

[41] Fernando Bobillo, Miguel Delgado, and Juan Gómez-Romero. A crisp representation for fuzzy $\mathcal{SHOIN}$ with fuzzy nominals and general concept inclusions. In *Uncertainty Reasoning for the Semantic Web I*, volume 5327 of *Lecture Notes in Computer Science*, pages 174–188. Springer Verlag, 2008.

[42] Fernando Bobillo, Miguel Delgado, and Juan Gómez-Romero. Delorean: A reasoner for fuzzy OWL 1.1. In *Proceedings of the 4th International Workshop on Uncertainty Reasoning for the Semantic Web (URSW 2008)*, volume 423. CEUR Workshop Proceedings, 10 2008.

[43] Fernando Bobillo, Miguel Delgado, and Juan Gómez-Romero. Optimizing the crisp representation of the fuzzy description logic $\mathcal{SROIQ}$. In *Uncertainty Reasoning for the Semantic Web I*, volume 5327 of *Lecture Notes in Computer Science*, pages 189–206. Springer Verlag, 2008.

[44] Fernando Bobillo, Miguel Delgado, and Juan Gómez-Romero. Crisp representations and reasoning for fuzzy ontologies. *International Journal of Uncertainty, Fuzziness and Knowledge-Based Systems*, 17(4):501–530, 2009.

[45] Fernando Bobillo, Miguel Delgado, Juan Gómez-Romero, and Umberto Straccia. Fuzzy description logics under Gödel semantics. *International Journal of Approximate Reasoning*, 50(3):494–514, 2009.

[46] Fernando Bobillo, Miguel Delgado, Juan Gómez-Romero, and Umberto Straccia. Joining Gödel and Zadeh fuzzy logics in fuzzy description logics. *International Journal of Uncertainty, Fuzziness and Knowledge-Based Systems*, 20:475–508, 2012.

[47] Fernando Bobillo and Umberto Straccia. A fuzzy description logic with product t-norm. In *Proceedings of the IEEE International Conference on Fuzzy Systems (Fuzz-IEEE-07)*, pages 652–657. IEEE Computer Society, 2007.

[48] Fernando Bobillo and Umberto Straccia. fuzzyDL: An expressive fuzzy description logic reasoner. In *2008 International Conference on Fuzzy Systems (FUZZ-08)*, pages 923–930. IEEE Computer Society, 2008.

[49] Fernando Bobillo and Umberto Straccia. On qualified cardinality restrictions in fuzzy description logics under Łukasiewicz semantics. In Luis Magdalena, Manuel Ojeda-Aciego, and José Luis Verdegay, editors, *Proceedings of the 12th International Conference of Information Processing*

and Management of Uncertainty in Knowledge-Based Systems (IPMU 2008), pages 1008–1015, June 2008.

[50] Fernando Bobillo and Umberto Straccia. Towards a crisp representation of fuzzy description logics under Łukasiewicz semantics. In Aijun An, Stan Matwin, Zbigniew W. Raś, and Dominik Ślęzak, editors, *Proceedings of the 17th International Symposium on Methodologies for Intelligent Systems (ISMIS 2008)*, volume 4994 of *Lecture Notes in Computer Science*, pages 309–318. Springer Verlag, May 2008.

[51] Fernando Bobillo and Umberto Straccia. Extending datatype restrictions in fuzzy description logics. In *Proceedings of the 9th International Conference on Intelligent Systems Design and Applications (ISDA-09)*, pages 785–790. IEEE Computer Society, 2009.

[52] Fernando Bobillo and Umberto Straccia. Fuzzy description logics with fuzzy truth values. In João P. B. Carvalho, Didier Dubois, Uzay Kaymak, and João M. C. Sousa, editors, *Proceedings of the 13th World Congress of the International Fuzzy Systems Association and 6th Conference of the European Society for Fuzzy Logic and Technology (IFSA-EUSFLAT 2009)*, pages 189–194, July 2009.

[53] Fernando Bobillo and Umberto Straccia. Fuzzy description logics with general t-norms and datatypes. *Fuzzy Sets and Systems*, 160(23):3382–3402, 2009.

[54] Fernando Bobillo and Umberto Straccia. An OWL ontology for fuzzy OWL 2. In *Proceedings of the 18th International Symposium on Methodologies for Intelligent Systems (ISMIS-09)*, volume 5722 of *Lecture Notes in Computer Science*, pages 151–160. Springer-Verlag, September 2009.

[55] Fernando Bobillo and Umberto Straccia. Supporting fuzzy rough sets in fuzzy description logics. In *Proceedings of the 10th European Conference on Symbolic and Quantitative Approaches to Reasoning with Uncertainty (ECSQARU-09)*, volume 5590 of *Lecture Notes in Artificial Intelligence*, pages 676–687. Springer Verlag, 2009.

[56] Fernando Bobillo and Umberto Straccia. Finite fuzzy description logics: A crisp representation for finite fuzzy $\mathcal{ALCH}$. In Fernando Bobillo, Rommel Carvalho, Paulo C. G. da Costa, Claudia d'Amato, Nicola Fanizzi, Kathryn B. Laskey, Kenneth J. Laskey, Thomas Lukasiewicz, Trevor Martin, Matthias Nickles, and Michael Pool, editors, *Proceedings of the 6th ISWC Workshop on Uncertainty Reasoning for the Semantic Web (URSW 2010)*, volume 654, pages 61–72. CEUR Workshop Proceedings, November 2010.

[57] Fernando Bobillo and Umberto Straccia. Representing fuzzy ontologies in owl 2. In *Proceedings of the 19th IEEE International Conference on*

Fuzzy Systems (FUZZ-IEEE 2010), pages 2695–2700. IEEE Press, July 2010.

[58] Fernando Bobillo and Umberto Straccia. Aggregation operators and fuzzy OWL 2. In *Proceedings of the 20th IEEE International Conference on Fuzzy Systems (FUZZ-IEEE 2011)*, pages 1727–1734. IEEE Press, June 2011.

[59] Fernando Bobillo and Umberto Straccia. Fuzzy ontologies and fuzzy integrals. In *Proceedings of the 11th International Conference on Intelligent Systems Design and Applications (ISDA 2011)*, pages 1311–1316. IEEE Press, November 2011.

[60] Fernando Bobillo and Umberto Straccia. Fuzzy ontology representation using OWL 2. *International Journal of Approximate Reasoning*, 52:1073–1094, 2011.

[61] Fernando Bobillo and Umberto Straccia. Reasoning with the finitely many-valued Łukasiewicz fuzzy description logic $\mathcal{SROIQ}$. *Information Sciences*, 181:758–778, 2011.

[62] Fernando Bobillo and Umberto Straccia. Generalized fuzzy rough description logics. *Information Sciences*, 189:43–62, 2012.

[63] Harold Boley, Said Tabet, and Gerd Wagner. Design rationale of RuleML: A markup language for semantic web rules. In *Proceedings of the 1st Semantic Web Working Symposium (SWWS-01)*, pages 105–113, Stanford, 2001.

[64] P. Bonatti and A. Tettamanzi. Some complexity results on fuzzy description logics. In A. Petrosino V. Di Gesù, F. Masulli, editor, *WILF 2003 International Workshop on Fuzzy Logic and Applications*, LNCS 2955, Berlin, 2004. Springer Verlag.

[65] Piero A. Bonatti, Aidan Hogan, Axel Polleres, and Luigi Sauro. Robust and scalable linked data reasoning incorporating provenance and trust annotations. *Journal of Web Semantics*, 9(2):165–201, 2011.

[66] G. Boole. *An Investigation of the Laws of Thought, on which are Founded the Mathematical Theories of Logic and Probabilities*. Walton and Maberley, London, 1854. (reprint: Dover Publications, New York, 1958).

[67] Egon Börger. *Computability, Complexity, Logic*. North-Holland Studies in Logic and Foundations of Mathematics, North-Holland, 1988.

[68] Stefan Borgwardt, Felix Distel, and Rafael Peñaloza. How fuzzy is my fuzzy description logic? In *Proceedings of the 6th International Joint*

Conference on Automated Reasoning (IJCAR-12), volume 7364 of *Lecture Notes in Artificial Intelligence*, pages 82–96, Manchester, UK, 2012. Springer-Verlag.

[69] Stefan Borgwardt, Felix Distel, and Rafael Peñaloza. Non-Gödel negation makes unwitnessed consistency undecidable. In *Proceedings of the 2012 International Workshop on Description Logics (DL-2012)*, volume 846. CEUR-WS.org, 2012.

[70] Stefan Borgwardt and Rafael Peñaloza. Description logics over lattices with multi-valued ontologies. In *Proceedings of the Twenty-Second International Joint Conference on Artificial Intelligence (IJCAI-11)*, pages 768–773, 2011.

[71] Stefan Borgwardt and Rafael Peñaloza. Finite lattices do not make reasoning in $\mathcal{ALCI}$ harder. In *Proceedings of the 7th International Workshop on Uncertainty Reasoning for the Semantic Web (URSW-11)*, volume 778, pages 51–62. CEUR-WS.org, 2011.

[72] Stefan Borgwardt and Rafael Peñaloza. Fuzzy ontologies over lattices with t-norms. In *Proceedings of the 24th International Workshop on Description Logics (DL-11)*. CEUR Electronic Workshop Proceedings, 2011.

[73] Stefan Borgwardt and Rafael Peñaloza. A tableau algorithm for fuzzy description logics over residuated De Morgan lattices. In Markus Krötzsch and Umberto Straccia, editors, *Proceedings of the 6th International Conference on Web Reasoning and Rule Systems (RR-12)*, volume 7497 of *Lecture Notes in Computer Science*, pages 9–24. Springer, 2012.

[74] Stefan Borgwardt and Rafael Peñaloza. Undecidability of fuzzy description logics. In *Proceedings of the 13th International Conference on Principles of Knowledge Representation and Reasoning (KR-12)*, pages 232–242, Rome, Italy, 2012. AAAI Press.

[75] Félix Bou, Marco Cerami, and Francesc Esteva. Finite-valued Łukasiewicz modal logic is Pspace-complete. In *Proceedings of the 22nd International Joint Conference on Artificial Intelligence (IJCAI-11)*, pages 774–779, 2011.

[76] Ronald J. Brachman and Hector J. Levesque. The tractability of subsumption in frame-based description languages. In *Proceedings of AAAI-84, 4th Conference of the American Association for Artificial Intelligence*, pages 34–37, Austin, TX, 1984. [a] An extended version appears as [256].

[77] Dan Brickley and R.V. Guha. RDF Vocabulary Description Language 1.0: RDF Schema. W3C Recommendation, W3C, 2004. http://www.w3.org/TR/rdf-schema/.

[78] Nicolas Bruno, Surajit Chaudhuri, and Luis Gravano. Top-k selection queries over relational databases: Mapping strategies and performance evaluation. *ACM Trans. Database Syst.*, 27(2):153–187, 2002.

[79] F. Bueno, D. Cabeza, M. Carro, M. Hermenegildo, P. López-García, and G. Puebla. The Ciao prolog system. Reference manual. Technical Report CLIPS3/97.1, School of Computer Science, Technical University of Madrid (UPM), 1997. Available at http://www.cliplab.org/Software/Ciao/.

[80] Andrea Calì, Domenico Lembo, and Riccardo Rosati. Query rewriting and answering under constraints in data integration systems. In *Proceedings of the 18th International Joint Conference on Artificial Intelligence (IJCAI-03)*, pages 16–21, 2003.

[81] J. Calmet, J. Lu, M. Rodriguez, and J. Schü. Signed formula logic programming: operational semantics and applications. In Zbigniew W. Rás and Maciek Michalewicz, editors, *Proceedings of the 9th International Symposium on Foundations of Intelligent Systems*, volume 1079 of *Lecture Notes in Artificial Intelligence*, pages 202–211, Berlin, 1996. Springer.

[82] Diego Calvanese, Giuseppe De Giacomo, Domenico Lembo, Maurizio Lenzerini, and Riccardo Rosati. DL-Lite: Tractable description logics for ontologies. In *Proceedings of the 20th National Conference on Artificial Intelligence (AAAI-05)*, 2005.

[83] Diego Calvanese, Giuseppe De Giacomo, Domenico Lembo, Maurizio Lenzerini, and Riccardo Rosati. Data complexity of query answering in description logics. In *Proceedings of the Tenth International Conference on Principles of Knowledge Representation and Reasoning (KR-06)*, pages 260–270, 2006.

[84] Diego Calvanese, Giuseppe De Giacomo, and Maurizio Lenzerini. Conjunctive query containment in description logics with n-ary relations. In *Proceedings of the 1997 Description Logic Workshop (DL-97)*, pages 5–9, 1997.

[85] Diego Calvanese, Giuseppe De Giacomo, and Maurizio Lenzerini. On the decidability of query containment under constraints. In *Proceedings of the 17th ACM SIGACT SIGMOD SIGART Symposium on Principles of Database Systems (PODS-98)*, pages 149–158, 1998.

[86] Diego Calvanese, Giuseppe De Giacomo, and Maurizio Lenzerini. Description logics for information integration. In A. Kakas and F. Sadri, editors, *Computational Logic: Logic Programming and Beyond, Essays in Honour of Robert A. Kowalski*, volume 2408 of *Lecture Notes in Computer Science*, pages 41–60. Springer, 2002.

[87] Diego Calvanese, Giuseppe Giacomo, Domenico Lembo, Maurizio Lenzerini, and Riccardo Rosati. Tractable reasoning and efficient query answering in description logics: The DL-Lite family. *Journal of Automated Reasoning*, 39(3):385–429, 2007.

[88] Diego Calvanese, Giuseppe De Giacomo, Domenico Lembo, Maurizio Lenzerini, and Riccardo Rosati. EQL-Lite: Effective first-order query processing in description logics. In *Proceedings of the 20th International Joint Conference on Artificial Intelligence (IJCAI-07)*, pages 274–279. IJCAI, 2007.

[89] Diego Calvanese, Giuseppe De Giacomo, and Maurizio Lenzerini. Conjunctive query containment and answering under description logic constraints. *ACM Transaction on Computational Logic*, 9(3):1–31, 2008.

[90] True H. Cao. Annotated fuzzy logic programs. *Fuzzy Sets and Systems*, 113(2):277–298, 2000.

[91] Marco Cerami, Francesc Esteva, and Fèlix Bou. Decidability of a description logic over infinite-valued product logic. In *Proceedings of the Twelfth International Conference on Principles of Knowledge Representation and Reasoning (KR-10)*. AAAI Press, 2010.

[92] Marco Cerami and Umberto Straccia. On the undecidability of fuzzy description logics with gcis with lukasiewicz t-norm. Technical report, Computing Research Repository, 2011. Available as CoRR technical report at http://arxiv.org/abs/1107.4212.

[93] C. Chang and R.C. Lee. *Symbolic Logic and Mechanical Theorem Proving*. Academic Press, 1973.

[94] Kevin Chen-Chuan Chang and Seung won Hwang. Minimal probing: Supporting expensive predicates for top-k queries. In *SIGMOD Conference*, pages 346–357, 2002.

[95] Weidong Chen and David S. Warren. Tabled evaluation with delaying for general logic programs. *Journal of the ACM*, 43(1):20–74, 1996.

[96] Carlos Chesñevar, Guillermo Simari, Teresa Alsinet, and Lluís Godo. A logic programming framework for possibilistic argumentation with vague knowledge. In *Proceedings of the 20th Annual Conference on Uncertainty in Artificial Intelligence (UAI-04)*, pages 76–84, Arlington, Virginia, 2004. AUAI Press.

[97] Alexandros Chortaras, Giorgos B. Stamou, and Andreas Stafylopatis. Integrated query answering with weighted fuzzy rules. In *9th European Conference on Symbolic and Quantitative Approaches to Reasoning with Uncertainty (ECSQARU-07)*, volume 4724 of *Lecture Notes in Computer Science*, pages 767–778. Springer Verlag, 2007.

[98] Alexandros Chortaras, Giorgos B. Stamou, and Andreas Stafylopatis. Top-down computation of the semantics of weighted fuzzy logic programs. In *Web Reasoning and Rule Systems, First International Conference, (RR-07)*, pages 364–366, 2007.

[99] Simona Colucci, Tommaso Di Noia, Azzurra Ragone, Michele Ruta, Umberto Straccia, and Eufemia Tinelli. Informative top-k retrieval for advanced skill management. In *Semantic Web Information Management*, chapter 19, pages 449–476. Springer Verlag, 2010.

[100] Claudio Corona, Marco Ruzzi, and Domenico Fabio Savo. Filling the gap between OWL 2 QL and QuOnto: ROWLKit. In *Proceedings of the 22nd International Workshop on Description Logics (DL-09), Oxford, UK, July 27-30, 2009*, volume 477 of *EUR Workshop Proceedings*. CEUR-WS.org, 2009.

[101] B. Cuenca-Grau, I. Horrocks, B. Motik, B. Parsia, P.F. Patel-Schneider, and U. Sattler. OWL 2: The next step for OWL. *Journal of Web Semantics*, 6(4):309–322, 2008.

[102] C. V. Damásio and L. M. Pereira. Hybrid probabilistic logic programs as residuated logic programs. *Studia Logica*, 72(1):113–138, 2002.

[103] Carlos Viegas Damásio, J. Medina, and M. Ojeda Aciego. Sorted multi-adjoint logic programs: Termination results and applications. In *Proceedings of the 9th European Conference on Logics in Artificial Intelligence (JELIA-04)*, volume 3229 of *Lecture Notes in Computer Science*, pages 252–265. Springer Verlag, 2004.

[104] Carlos Viegas Damásio, J. Medina, and M. Ojeda Aciego. A tabulation proof procedure for residuated logic programming. In *Proceedings of the 6th European Conference on Artificial Intelligence (ECAI-04)*, 2004.

[105] Carlos Viegas Damásio, J. Medina, and M. Ojeda Aciego. Termination results for sorted multi-adjoint logic programs. In *Proceedings of the 10th International Conference on Information Processing and Managment of Uncertainty in Knowledge-Based Systems, (IPMU-04)*, pages 1879–1886, 2004.

[106] Carlos Viegas Damásio and Luís Moniz Pereira. A survey of paraconsistent semantics for logic programs. In D. Gabbay and P. Smets, editors, *Handbook of Defeasible Reasoning and Uncertainty Management Systems*, pages 241–320. Kluwer, 1998.

[107] Carlos Viegas Damásio and Luís Moniz Pereira. Antitonic logic programs. In *Proceedings of the 6th European Conference on Logic Programming and Nonmonotonic Reasoning (LPNMR-01)*, volume 2173 of *Lecture Notes in Computer Science*. Springer-Verlag, 2001.

[108] Carlos Viegas Damásio and Luís Moniz Pereira. Monotonic and residuated logic programs. In Salem Benferhat and Philippe Besnard, editors, *Symbolic and Quantitative Approaches to Reasoning with Uncertainty, 6th European Conference, ECSQARU 2001, Toulouse, France, September 19-21, 2001, Proceedings*, volume 2143 of *Lecture Notes in Computer Science*, pages 748–759. Springer, 2001.

[109] Carlos Viegas Damásio and Luís Moniz Pereira. Sorted monotonic logic programs and their embeddings. In *Proceedings of the 10th International Conference on Information Processing and Managment of Uncertainty in Knowledge-Based Systems, (IPMU-04)*, pages 807–814, 2004.

[110] C.V. Damásio, J. Medina, and M. Ojeda-Aciego. A tabulation procedure for first-order residuated logic programs. In *Proceedings of the 11th International Conference on Information Processing and Managment of Uncertainty in Knowledge-Based Systems, (IPMU-06)*, 2006.

[111] C.V. Damásio, J. Medina, and M. Ojeda-Aciego. A tabulation procedure for first-order residuated logic programs. In *Proceedings of the IEEE World Congress on Computational Intelligence (section Fuzzy Systems) (WCCI-06)*, pages 9576–9583, 2006.

[112] C.V. Damásio, J. Medina, and M. Ojeda-Aciego. Termination of logic programs with imperfect information: applications and query procedure. *Journal of Applied Logic*, 7(5):435–458, 2007.

[113] Evgeny Dantsin, Thomas Eiter, Georg Gottlob, and Andrei Voronkov. Complexity and expressive power of logic programming. *ACM Computing Surveys*, 33(3):374–425, 2001.

[114] Mathieu d'Aquin, Jean Lieber, and Amedeo Napoli. Towards a semantic portal for oncology using a description logic with fuzzy concrete domains. In Elie Sanchez, editor, *Fuzzy Logic and the Semantic Web*, Capturing Intelligence, pages 379–393. Elsevier, 2006.

[115] Alex Dekhtyar and Michael I. Dekhtyar. Possible worlds semantics for probabilistic logic programs. In *20th International Conference on Logic Programming*, volume 3132 of *Lecture Notes in Computer Science*, pages 137–148. Springer Verlag, 2004.

[116] Alex Dekhtyar and Michael I. Dekhtyar. Revisiting the semantics of interval probabilistic logic programs. In *8th International Conference on Logic Programming and Nonmonotonic Reasoning (LPNMR-05)*, volume 3662 of *Lecture Notes in Computer Science*, pages 330–342. Springer Verlag, 2005.

[117] Alex Dekhtyar, Michael I. Dekhtyar, and V. S. Subrahmanian. Temporal probabilistic logic programs. In Danny De Schreye, editor, *Logic Programming: The 1999 International Conference*, pages 109–123, 1999.

[118] Alex Dekhtyar and V.S. Subrahmanian. Hybrid probabilistic programs. *Journal of Logic Programming*, 43(3):187–250, 2000.

[119] Michael I. Dekhtyar, Alex Dekhtyar, and V. S. Subrahmanian. Hybrid probabilistic programs: Algorithms and complexity. In Kathryn B. Laskey and Henri Prade, editors, *Proceedings of the 15th Conference on Uncertainty in Artificial Intelligence (UAI-99)*, pages 160–169. Morgan Kaufmann Publishers, 1999.

[120] M. Denecker, V. Marek, and M. Truszczyński. Approximations, stable operators, well-founded fixpoints and applications in nonmonotonic reasoning. In J. Minker, editor, *Logic-Based Artifical Intelligence*, pages 127–144. Kluwer Academic Publishers, 2000.

[121] M. Denecker, N. Pelov, and M. Bruynooghe. Ultimate well-founded and stable semantics for logic programs with aggregates. In Philippe Codognet, editor, *17th International Conference on Logic Programming*, volume 2237 of *Lecture Notes in Computer Science*, pages 212–226. Springer, 2001.

[122] Marc Denecker, Victor W. Marek, and Mirosław Truszczyński. Uniform semantic treatment of default and autoepistemic logics. In A.G. Cohn, F. Giunchiglia, and B. Selman, editors, *Proceedings of the 7th International Conference on Principles of Knowledge Representation and Reasoning*, pages 74–84. Morgan Kaufman, 2000.

[123] Marc Denecker, Victor W. Marek, and Mirosław Truszczyński. Ultimate approximations. Technical Report CW 320, Katholieke Iniversiteit Leuven, September 2001.

[124] Marc Denecker, Victor W. Marek, and Mirosław Truszczyński. Ultimate approximations in nonmonotonic knowledge representation systems. In D. Fensel, F. Giunchiglia, D. McGuinness, and M. Williams, editors, *Principles of Knowledge Representation and Reasoning: Proceedings of the 8th International Conference*, pages 177–188. Morgan Kaufmann, 2002.

[125] Description Logics Web Site. *http://dl.kr.org*.

[126] Tommaso Di Noia, Eugenio Di Sciascio, Francesco M. Donini, Francesco di Cugno, and Eufemia Tinelli. A framework for content-based image retrieval fully exploiting the semantics of annotation. In *Proceedings of the 21st ACM Annual ACM (SIGAPP) Symposium on Applied Computing*, pages 1709–1710. ACM, 2006.

[127] Dzung Dinh-Khac, Steffen Hölldobler, and Dinh-Khang Tran. The fuzzy linguistic description logic $\mathcal{ALC}_{FL}$. In *Proceedings of the 11th International Conference on Information Processing and Managment of Un-*

certainty in Knowledge-Based Systems, (IPMU-06), pages 2096–2103. E.D.K., Paris, 2006.

[128] Guozhu Dong, Leonid Libkin, and Limsoon Wong. Incremental recomputation in local languages. *Information and Computation*, 181(2):88–98, 2003.

[129] Guozhu Dong and Jianwen Su. Space-bounded FOIES (extended abstract). In *Proceedings of the 14th ACM SIGACT-SIGMOD-SIGART Symposium on Principles of Database Systems (PODS-95)*, pages 139–150, New York, NY, USA, 1995. ACM Press.

[130] Guozhu Dong, Jianwen Su, and Rodney W. Topor. Nonrecursive incremental evaluation of datalog queries. *Annals of Mathematics and Artificial Intelligence*, 14(2-4):187–223, 1995.

[131] Francesco M. Donini and Fabio Massacci. Exptime tableaux for $\mathcal{ALC}$. *Artificial Intelligence*, 124(1):87–138, 2000.

[132] W.F. Dowling and J.H. Gallier. Linear-time algorithms for testing the satisfiability of propositional Horn formulas. *Journal of Logic Programming*, 3(1):267–284, 1984.

[133] D. Dubois and H. Prade. On fuzzy syllogisms. *Computational Intelligence*, 4(2):171–179, 1988.

[134] D. Dubois, H. Prade, L. Godo, and R. López de Màntaras. Qualitative reasoning with imprecise probabilities. *Journal of Intelligent Information Systems*, 2:319–363, 1993.

[135] D. Dubois, H. Prade, and J.-M. Touscas. Inference with imprecise numerical quantifiers. In Z. W. Ras and M. Zemankova, editors, *Intelligent Systems*, chapter 3, pages 53–72. Ellis Horwood, 1990.

[136] Didier Dubois, Laurent Foulloy, Gilles Mauris, and Henri Prade. Probability-possibility transformations, triangular fuzzy sets, and probabilistic inequalities. *Reliable Computing*, 10(4):273–297, 2004.

[137] Didier Dubois, Jérome Lang, and Henri Prade. Towards possibilistic logic programming. In *Proceedings of the 8th International Conference on Logic Programming (ICLP-91)*, pages 581–595. The MIT Press, 1991.

[138] Didier Dubois, Jerome Mengin, and Henri Prade. Possibilistic uncertainty and fuzzy features in description logic. A preliminary discussion. In Elie Sanchez, editor, *Capturing Intelligence: Fuzzy Logic and the Semantic Web*. Elsevier, 2006.

[139] Didier Dubois and Henri Prade. *Fuzzy Sets and Systems*. Academic Press, 1980.

[140] Didier Dubois and Henri Prade. Possibilistic logic. In Dov M. Gabbay and C. J. Hogger, editors, *Handbook of Logic in Artificial Intelligence*, volume 3, pages 439–513. Clarendon Press, Oxford, Dordrecht, NL, 1986.

[141] Didier Dubois and Henri Prade. When upper probabilities are possibility measures. *Fuzzy Sets and Systems*, 49:65–74, 1992.

[142] Didier Dubois and Henri Prade. Can we enforce full compositionality in uncertainty calculi? In *Proceedings of the 12th National Conference on Artificial Intelligence (AAAI-94)*, pages 149–154, Seattle, Washington, 1994.

[143] Didier Dubois and Henri Prade. Possibility theory, probability theory and multiple-valued logics: A clarification. *Annals of Mathematics and Artificial Intelligence*, 32(1-4):35–66, 2001.

[144] Rafee Ebrahim. Fuzzy logic programming. *Fuzzy Sets and Systems*, 117(2):215–230, 2001.

[145] Thomas Eiter, Magdalena Ortiz, and Mantas Simkus. Conjunctive query answering in the description logic sh using knots. *Journal of Computer and System Sciences*, 78(1):47–85, 2012.

[146] Charles Elkan. The paradoxical success of fuzzy logic. In *Proceedings of the 11th National Conference on Artificial Intelligence (AAAI-93)*, pages 698–703, 1993.

[147] M. H. Van Emden and R. A. Kowalski. The semantics of predicate logic as a programming language. *Journal of the ACM (JACM)*, 23(4):733–742, 1976.

[148] Francesc Esteva, Joan Gispert, Lluís Godo, and Carles Noguera. Adding truth-constants to logics of continuous t-norms: Axiomatization and completeness results. *Fuzzy Sets and Systems*, 158:597–618, March 2007.

[149] Francesc Esteva, Lluís Godo, and Carles Noguera. Expanding the propositional logic of a t-norm with truth-constants: completeness results for rational semantics. *Soft Computing - A Fusion of Foundations, Methodologies and Applications*, 14:273–284, 2010.

[150] Ronald Fagin. Combining fuzzy information: an overview. *SIGMOD Rec.*, 31(2):109–118, 2002.

[151] Ronald Fagin, Joseph Y. Halpern, and Nimrod Megiddo. A logic for reasoning about probabilities. *Information and Computation*, 87(1/2):78–128, 1990.

[152] Ronald Fagin, Amnon Lotem, and Moni Naor. Optimal aggregation algorithms for middleware. In *Symposium on Principles of Database Systems*, 2001.

[153] Fire. http://www.image.ece.ntua.gr/~nsimou/FiRE/.

[154] M. C. Fitting. The family of stable models. *Journal of Logic Programming*, 17:197–225, 1993.

[155] M. C. Fitting. Fixpoint semantics for logic programming - a survey. *Theoretical Computer Science*, 21(3):25–51, 2002.

[156] Melvin Fitting. A Kripke-Kleene-semantics for general logic programs. *Journal of Logic Programming*, 2:295–312, 1985.

[157] Melvin Fitting. Pseudo-Boolean valued Prolog. *Studia Logica*, XLVII(2):85–91, 1987.

[158] Melvin Fitting. *First-Order Logic and Automated Theorem Proving*. Springer-Verlag, 1990.

[159] Melvin Fitting. Bilattices and the semantics of logic programming. *Journal of Logic Programming*, 11:91–116, 1991.

[160] Christodoulos A. Floudas. *Nonlinear and mixed-integer optimization*. Oxford University Press, 1995.

[161] C. Forgy. Rete: A fast algorithm for the many pattern/many object pattern match problem. *Artificial Intelligence*, 19:17–37, 1982.

[162] A. M. Frisch and P. Haddawy. Anytime deduction for probabilistic logic. *Artif. Intell.*, 69(1–2):93–122, 1994.

[163] Norbert Fuhr. Probabilistic Datalog: Implementing logical information retrieval for advanced applications. *Journal of the American Society for Information Science*, 51(2):95–110, 2000.

[164] fuzzyDL. http://www.straccia.info/software/fuzzyDL/fuzzyDL.html.

[165] Fuzzy OWL 2 Web Ontology Language . *http://www.straccia.info/software/FuzzyOWL/*. ISTI - CNR, 2011.

[166] Hervé Gallaire, Jack Minker, and Jean-Marie Nicolas. An overview and intoduction to logic and data bases. In *Symposium on Logic and Data Bases*, pages 3–30, 1977.

[167] Jean H. Gallier. *Logic for Computer Science: Foundations of Automatic Theorem Proving*. Harper & Row Publishers, New York, 1986.

[168] Mingxia Gao and Chunnian Liu. Extending OWL by fuzzy description logic. In *Proceedings of the 17th IEEE International Conference on Tools with Artificial Intelligence (ICTAI-05)*, pages 562–567, Washington, DC, USA, 2005. IEEE Computer Society.

[169] Àngel García-Cerdaña, Eva Armengol, and Francesc Esteva. Fuzzy description logics and t-norm based fuzzy logics. *International Journal of Approximate Reasoning*, 51:632–655, July 2010.

[170] Birte Glimm, Ian Horrocks, Boris Motik, Rob Shearer, and Giorgos Stoilos. A novel approach to ontology classification. *Journal of Web Semantics*, 14:84–101, 2012.

[171] Birte Glimm and Yevgeny Kazakov. Role conjunctions in expressive description logics. In *Proceedings of the 15th International Conference on Logic for Programming, Artificial Intelligence, and Reasoning (LPAR-08)*, pages 391–405, Berlin, Heidelberg, 2008. Springer-Verlag.

[172] S. Gottwald. *A Treatise on Many-Valued Logics*. A Research Studies Press Book, 2000.

[173] Benjamin N. Grosof, Ian Horrocks, Raphael Volz, and Stefan Decker. Description logic programs: combining logic programs with description logic. In *Proceedings of the 12th International Conference on World Wide Web*, pages 48–57. ACM Press, 2003.

[174] N. Guarino and R. Poli. Formal ontology in conceptual analysis and knowledge representation. *International Journal of Human and Computer Studies*, 43(5/6):625–640, 1995.

[175] Dusan Guller. Procedural semantics for fuzzy disjunctive programs. In Matthias Baaz and Andrei Voronkov, editors, *Logic for Programming, Artificial Intelligence, and Reasoning 9th International Conference, LPAR 2002, Tbilisi, Georgia, October 14-18, 2002, Proceedings*, volume 2514 of *Lecture Notes in Computer Science*, pages 247–261. Springer, 2002.

[176] Dusan Guller. Semantics for fuzzy disjunctive programs with weak similarity. In Ajith Abraham and Mario Köppen, editors, *Hybrid Information Systems, First International Workshop on Hybrid Intelligent Systems, Adelaide, Australia, December 11-12, 2001, Proceedings*, Advances in Soft Computing, pages 285–299. Physica-Verlag, 2002.

[177] Claudio Gutierrez, Carlos Hurtado, and Alberto O. Mendelzon. Foundations of semantic web databases. In *Proceedings of the 23rd ACM SIGMOD-SIGACT-SIGART Symposium on Principles of Database Systems (PODS-04)*, pages 95–106. ACM Press, 2004.

[178] Christoph Haase and Carsten Lutz. Complexity of subsumption in the $\mathcal{EL}$ family of description logics: Acyclic and cyclic TBoxes. In Malik Ghallab, Constantine D. Spyropoulos, Nikos Fakotakis, and Nikos Avouris, editors, *Proceedings of the 18th European Conference on Artificial Intelligence (ECAI08)*, volume 178 of *Frontiers in Artificial Intelligence and Applications*, pages 25–29. IOS Press, 2008.

[179] A. Hadjali, S. Kaci, and H. Prade. Database preference queries — a possibilistic logic approach with symbolic priorities. In *Proceedings of the 5th International Symposium on Foundations of Information and Knowledge Systems (FoIKS-08)*, volume 4932 of *Lecture Notes in Computer Science*. Springer Verlag, 2008.

[180] Reiner Hähnle. Uniform notation of tableaux rules for multiple-valued logics. In *Proceedings of the International Symposium on Multiple-Valued Logic*, pages 238–245. IEEE Press, Los Alamitos, 1991.

[181] Reiner Hähnle. Efficient deduction in many-valued logics. In *Proceedings of the International Symposium on Multiple-Valued Logics (ISMVL-94)*, pages 240–249. IEEE CS Press, Los Alamitos, 1994.

[182] Reiner Hähnle. Many-valued logics and mixed integer programming. *Annals of Mathematics and Artificial Intelligence*, 3,4(12):231–264, 1994.

[183] Reiner Hähnle. Advanced many-valued logics. In Dov M. Gabbay and F. Guenthner, editors, *Handbook of Philosophical Logic, 2nd Edition*, volume 2. Kluwer, Dordrecht, Holland, 2001.

[184] Reiner Hähnle and Gonzalo Escalada-Imaz. Deduction in many-valued logics: a survey. *Mathware and Soft Computing*, IV(2):69–97, 1997.

[185] T. Hailperin. *Sentential Probability Logic: Origins, Development, Current Status, and Technical Applications*. Associated University Presses, London, UK, 1996.

[186] Petr Hájek. *Metamathematics of Fuzzy Logic*. Kluwer, 1998.

[187] Petr Hájek. Ten claims about fuzzy logic. *Soft Computing*, 2(1):14–15, 1998.

[188] Petr Hájek. Making fuzzy description logics more general. *Fuzzy Sets and Systems*, 154(1):1–15, 2005.

[189] Petr Hájek. What does mathematical fuzzy logic offer to description logic? In Elie Sanchez, editor, *Fuzzy Logic and the Semantic Web*, Capturing Intelligence, chapter 5, pages 91–100. Elsevier, 2006.

[190] Petr Hájek. On witnessed models in fuzzy logic. *Mathematical Logic Quarterly*, 53(1):66–77, 2007.

[191] Pierre Hansen, Brigitte Jaumard, Guy-Blaise Nguetsé, and Marcus Poggi de Aragão. Models and algorithms for probabilistic and bayesian logic. In *Proceedings of the 14th International Joint Conference on Artificial Intelligence (IJCAI-95)*, pages 1862–1868, Montreal, Canada, 1995. Morgan Kaufmann, Los Altos.

[192] C.J. Hinde. Fuzzy prolog. *International Journal Man.-Machine Studies*, 24:569–595, 1986.

[193] J. Hladik and J. Model. Tableau systems for SHIO and SHIQ. In V. Haarslev and R. Möller, editors, *Proceedings of the 2004 International Workshop on Description Logics (DL 2004)*. CEUR, 2004. Available from `ceur-ws.org`.

[194] Steffen Hölldobler, Tran Dinh Khang, and Hans-Peter Störr. A fuzzy description logic with hedges as concept modifiers. In Nguyen Hoang Phuong, Hung T. Nguyen, Nguyen Cat Ho, and Pratit Santiprabhob, editors, *Proceedings InTech/VJFuzzy'2002*, pages 25–34, Hanoi, Vietnam, 2002. Institute of Information Technology, Vietnam Center for Natural Science and Technology, Science and Technics Publishing House, Hanoi, Vietnam.

[195] Steffen Hölldobler, Nguyen Hoang Nga, and Tran Dinh Khang. The fuzzy description logic $\mathcal{ALC}_{FH}$. In *Proceeedings of the International Workshop on Description Logics (DL-05)*, 2005.

[196] Steffen Hölldobler, Hans-Peter Störr, and Tran Dinh Khang. The fuzzy description logic $\mathcal{ALC}_{FH}$ with hedge algebras as concept modifiers. *Journal of Advanced Computational Intelligence*, 2003.

[197] Steffen Hölldobler, Hans-Peter Störr, and Tran Dinh Khang. A fuzzy description logic with hedges and concept modifiers. In *Proceedings of the 10th International Conference on Information Processing and Managment of Uncertainty in Knowledge-Based Systems, (IPMU-04)*, 2004.

[198] Steffen Hölldobler, Hans-Peter Störr, and Tran Dinh Khang. The subsumption problem of the fuzzy description logic $\mathcal{ALC}_{FH}$. In *Proceedings of the 10th International Conference on Information Processing and Managment of Uncertainty in Knowledge-Based Systems, (IPMU-04)*, 2004.

[199] Bernhard Hollunder. An alternative proof method for possibilistic logic and its application to terminological logics. *International Journal of Approximate Reasoning*, 12:85–109, 1995.

[200] Matthew Horridge, Dmitry Tsarkov, and Timothy Redmond. Supporting early adoption of OWL 1.1 with Protege-OWL and FaCT. In *Proceedings of the Second OWL Experiences and Directions Workshop (OWLED-06)*, 2006.

[201] I. Horrocks and U. Sattler. Ontology reasoning in the $\mathcal{SHOQ}(D)$ description logic. In *Proceedings of the Seventeenth International Joint Conference on Artificial Intelligence*, 2001.

[202] Ian Horrocks. Using an expressive description logic: Fact or fiction? In *Proceedings of the 8th International Conference on the Principles of Knowledge Representation and Reasoning (KR-98)*, 1998.

[203] Ian Horrocks, Oliver Kutz, and Ulrike Sattler. The even more irresistible $\mathcal{SROIQ}$. In *Proceedings of the 10th International Conference on Principles of Knowledge Representation and Reasoning (KR-06)*, pages 57–67. AAAI Press, 2006.

[204] Ian Horrocks and Peter Patel-Schneider. Reducing OWL entailment to description logic satisfiability. *Journal of Web Semantics*, 1(4):345–357, 2004.

[205] Ian Horrocks, Peter F. Patel-Schneider, and Frank van Harmelen. From $\mathcal{SHIQ}$ and RDF to OWL: The making of a web ontology language. *Journal of Web Semantics*, 1(1):7–26, 2003.

[206] Ian Horrocks and Ulrike Sattler. A description logic with transitive and inverse roles and role hierarchies. *Journal of Logic and Computation*, 9(3):385–410, 1999.

[207] Ian Horrocks and Ulrike Sattler. A tableau decision procedure for $\mathcal{SHOIQ}$. *Journal of Automated Reasoning*, 39(3):249–276, 2007.

[208] Ian Horrocks, Ulrike Sattler, and Stephan Tobies. Practical reasoning for very expressive description logics. *Logic Journal of the IGPL*, 8(3):239–263, 2000.

[209] Ian Horrocks, Ulrike Sattler, and Stephan Tobies. Reasoning with individuals for the description logic $\mathcal{SHIQ}$. In David MacAllester, editor, *Proceedings of the 17th International Conference on Automated Deduction (CADE-17)*, volume 1831 of *Lecture Notes in Artificial Intelligence*, pages 482–496, Germany, 2000. Springer Verlag.

[210] Giovambattista Ianni, Thomas Krennwallner, Alessandra Martello, and Axel Polleres. Dynamic Querying of Mass-Storage RDF Data with Rule-Based Entailment Regimes. In *8th International Semantic Web Conference (ISWC-09)*, volume 5823 of *Lecture Notes In Computer Science*, pages 310–327. Springer Verlag, 2009.

[211] Giovambattista Ianni, Thomas Krennwallner, Alessandra Martello, and Axel Polleres. A rule system for querying persistent RDFS data. In *The Semantic Web: Research and Applications, 6th European Semantic Web Conference (ESWC-2009)*, pages 857–862, 2009.

[212] Ihab F. Ilyas, Walid G. Aref, and Ahmed K. Elmagarmid. Supporting top-k join queries in relational databases. In *Proceedings of 29th International Conference on Very Large Data Bases (VLDB-03)*, pages 754–765, 2003.

[213] Ihab F. Ilyas, Walid G. Aref, Ahmed K. Elmagarmid, Hicham G. El-mongui, Rahul Shah, and Jeffrey Scott Vitter. Adaptive rank-aware query optimization in relational databases. *ACM Transactions on Database Systems*, 31(4):1257–1304, 2006.

[214] Mitsuru Ishizuka and Naoki Kanai. Prolog-ELF: incorporating fuzzy logic. In *Proceedings of the 9th International Joint Conference on Artificial Intelligence (IJCAI-85)*, pages 701–703, Los Angeles, CA, 1985.

[215] B. Jaumard, P. Hansen, and M. Poggi de Aragão. Column generation methods for probabilistic logic. *ORSA Journal on Computing*, 3:135–147, 1991.

[216] Robert G. Jeroslow. *Logic-based Decision Support. Mixed Integer Model Formulation.* Elsevier, Amsterdam, Holland, 1989.

[217] Yuncheng Jiang, Hai Liu, Yong Tang, and Qimai Chen. Semantic decision making using ontology-based soft sets. *Mathematical and Computer Modelling*, 53(5–6):1140–1149, 2011.

[218] Yuncheng Jiang, Yong Tang, Qimai Chen, Ju Wang, and Suqin Tang. Extending soft sets with description logics. *Computers & Mathematics with Applications*, 59(6):2087–2096, 2010.

[219] Yuncheng Jiang, Yong Tang, Ju Wang, Peimin Deng, and Suqin Tang. Expressive fuzzy description logics over lattices. *Knowledge-Based Systems*, 23:150–161, March 2010.

[220] Yuncheng Jiang, Yong Tang, Ju Wang, and Suqin Tang. Reasoning within intuitionistic fuzzy rough description logics. *Information Sciences*, 179(2362–2378), 2009.

[221] Yuncheng Jiang, Yong Tang, Ju Wang, and Suqin Tang. Representation and reasoning of context-dependant knowledge in distributed fuzzy ontologies. *Expert Systems with Applications*, 37(8):6052–6060, 2010.

[222] Yuncheng Jiang, Ju Wang, Peimin Deng, and Suqin Tang. Reasoning within expressive fuzzy rough description logics. *Fuzzy Sets and Systems*, 2009.

[223] Yuncheng Jiang, Ju Wang, Suqin Tang, and Bao Xiao. Reasoning with rough description logics: An approximate concepts approach. *Information Sciences*, 179(5):600–612, 2009.

[224] P. Julian, J. Medina, G. Moreno, and M. Ojeda. Efficient thresholded tabulation for fuzzy query answering. In *Foundations of Reasoning Under Uncertainty*, volume 249 of *Studies in Fuzziness and Soft Computing*, pages 125–141. Springer Verlag, 2010.

[225] Cengiz Kahraman, editor. *Fuzzy Multi-Criteria Decision Making: Theory and Applications with Recent Developments*. Springer Verlag, 2008.

[226] Wolgang Kainz. Theory and practice of fuzzy sets in gis. In *Geoinformatics Paves the Highway to Digital Earth*, pages 49—54. gi-reports @ igf, Bd. 8, 2008.

[227] Dazhou Kang, Baowen Xu, Jianjiang Lu, and Yanhui Li. Reasoning for a fuzzy description logic with comparison expressions. In *Proceeedings of the International Workshop on Description Logics (DL-06)*. CEUR Workshop Proceedings, 2006.

[228] Yevgeny Kazakov. $\mathcal{RIQ}$ and $\mathcal{SROIQ}$ are harder than $\mathcal{SHOIQ}$. In *Proceedings of the Eleventh International Conference on Principles of Knowledge Representation and Reasoning (KR-08)*, pages 274–284, 2008.

[229] Yevgeny Kazakov, Markus Kroetzsch, and Frantisek Simancik. Practical reasoning with nominals in the $\mathcal{EL}$ family of description logics. In *Proceedings of the Thirteenth International Conference on Principles of Knowledge Representation and Reasoning: (KR-12)*. AAAI Press, 2012.

[230] Yevgeny Kazakov, Markus Krötzsch, and Frantisek Simancik. Concurrent classification of $\mathcal{EL}$ ontologies. In *10th International Semantic Web Conference (ISWC-10)*, volume 7031 of *Lecture Notes in Computer Science*, pages 305–320, 2011.

[231] Gabriele Kern-Isberner and Thomas Lukasiewicz. Combining probabilistic logic programming with the power of maximum entropy. *Artificial Intelligence*, 157(1-2):139–202, 2004.

[232] Kristian Kersting and Luc De Raedt. Bayesian logic programs. In James Cussens and Alan M. Frisch, editors, *ILP Work-in-progress reports, 10th International Conference on Inductive Logic Programming*, CEUR Workshop Proceedings. CEUR-WS.org, 2000.

[233] Kristian Kersting and Luc De Raedt. Bayesian logic programming: Theory and tools. In L. Getoor and B. Taskar, editors, *An Introduction to Statistical Relational Learning*, chapter 10. MIT Press, 2007.

[234] M.A. Khamsi and D. Misane. Disjunctive signed logic programs. *Fundamenta Informaticae*, 32:349–357, 1996.

[235] M.A. Khamsi and D. Misane. Fixed point theorems in logic programming. *Annals of Mathematics and Artificial Intelligence*, 21:231–243, 1997.

[236] M. Kifer and Ai Li. On the semantics of rule-based expert systems with uncertainty. In *Proceedings of the International Conference on Database*

Theory (ICDT-88), volume 326 of *Lecture Notes in Computer Science*, pages 102–117. Springer-Verlag, 1988.

[237] Michael Kifer and Georg Lausen. F-logic: a higher-order language for reasoning about objects, inheritance, and scheme. In *Proceedings of the 1989 ACM SIGMOD International Conference on Management of Data*, pages 134–146. ACM Press, 1989.

[238] Michael Kifer, Georg Lausen, and James Wu. Logical foundations of object-oriented and frame-based languages. *Journal of the ACM*, 42(4):741–843, 1995.

[239] Michael Kifer and V.S. Subrahmanian. Theory of generalized annotated logic programming and its applications. *Journal of Logic Programming*, 12:335–367, 1992.

[240] Frank Klawonn and Rudolf Kruse. A Łukasiewicz logic based Prolog. *Mathware & Soft Computing*, 1(1):5–29, 1994.

[241] Erich Peter Klement, Radko Mesiar, and Endre Pap. *Triangular Norms*. Trends in Logic - Studia Logica Library. Kluwer Academic Publishers, 2000.

[242] George J. Klir and Bo Yuan. *Fuzzy sets and fuzzy logic: theory and applications*. Prentice-Hall, Inc., Upper Saddle River, NJ, USA, 1995.

[243] Markus Krötzsch. Efficient inferencing for OWL EL. In *12th European Conference on Logics in Artificial Intelligence (JELIA-10)*, volume 6341 of *Lecture Notes in Computer Science*, pages 234–246, 2010.

[244] Markus Krötzsch. Efficient inferencing for the description logic underlying OWL EL. Technical Report 3005, Institute AIFB, Karlsruhe Instistute of Technology (KIT), 2010.

[245] Markus Krötzsch. Efficient rule-based inferencing for OWL EL. In *Proceedings of the 22nd International Joint Conference on Artificial Intelligence (IJCAI-11)*, pages 2668–2673. IJCAI/AAAI, 2011.

[246] Rudolf Kruse, Detlef Nauck, and Christian Borgelt. Data mining with fuzzy methods: Status and perspectives. In *Proceedings of The European Congress on Intelligent Techniques and Soft Computing (EUFIT-99)*, 1999.

[247] Peter Kulmann and Sandra Sandri. An annotaded logic theorem prover for an extended possibilistic logic. *Fuzzy Sets and Systems*, 144:67–91, 2004.

[248] Nicolas Madrid Labrador and Umberto Straccia. Monotonic mappings invariant linearisation of finite posets. Technical report, Computing Research Repository, 2010. Available as CoRR technical report at http://arxiv.org/abs/1006.2679.

[249] Laks Lakshmanan. An epistemic foundation for logic programming with uncertainty. In *Foundations of Software Technology and Theoretical Computer Science*, volume 880 of *Lecture Notes in Computer Science*, pages 89–100. Springer-Verlag, 1994.

[250] Laks V. S. Lakshmanan and Fereidoon Sadri. On a theory of probabilistic deductive databases. *Theory and Practice of Logic Programming*, 1(1):5–42, 2001.

[251] Laks V.S. Lakshmanan and Fereidoon Sadri. Uncertain deductive databases: a hybrid approach. *Information Systems*, 22(8):483–508, 1997.

[252] Laks V.S. Lakshmanan and Nematollaah Shiri. Probabilistic deductive databases. In *Proceedings of the International Logic Programming Symposium*, pages 254–268, 1994.

[253] Laks V.S. Lakshmanan and Nematollaah Shiri. A parametric approach to deductive databases with uncertainty. *IEEE Transactions on Knowledge and Data Engineering*, 13(4):554–570, 2001.

[254] Niels Landwehr, Kristian Kersting, and Luc De Raedt. nFOIL: Integrating naïve Bayes and FOIL. In *Proceedings of the 20th National Conference on Artificial Intelligence (AAAI-2005)*, pages 795–800. AAAI Press, 2005.

[255] Niels Landwehr, Kristian Kersting, and Luc De Raedt. Integrating naïve bayes and FOIL. *Journal of Machine Learning Research*, 8:481–507, 2007.

[256] Hector J. Levesque and Ronald J. Brachman. Expressiveness and tractability in knowledge representation and reasoning. *Computational Intelligence*, 3:78–93, 1987.

[257] Chengkai Li, Kevin Chen-Chuan Chang, and Ihab F. Ilyas. Supporting ad-hoc ranking aggregates. In *Proceedings of the 2006 ACM SIGMOD International Conference on Management of Data (SIGMOD-06)*, pages 61–72, USA, 2006. ACM Press.

[258] Chengkai Li, Kevin Chen-Chuan Chang, Ihab F. Ilyas, and Sumin Song. RankSQL: query algebra and optimization for relational top-k queries. In *Proceedings of the 2005 ACM SIGMOD International Conference on Management of Data (SIGMOD-05)*, pages 131–142, New York, NY, USA, 2005. ACM Press.

[259] Leonid Libkin and Limsoon Wong. On the power of incremental evaluation in SQL-like languages. *Lecture Notes in Computer Science*, 1949:17–30, 2000.

[260] Francesca Alessandra Lisi and Umberto Straccia. An inductive logic programming approach to learning inclusion axioms in fuzzy description logics. In *26th Italian Conference on Computational Logic (CILC-11)*, volume 810, pages 57–71. CEUR Electronic Workshop Proceedings, 2011.

[261] Francesca Alessandra Lisi and Umberto Straccia. Towards learning fuzzy dl inclusion axioms. In *9th International Workshop on Fuzzy Logic and Applications (WILF-11)*, volume 6857 of *Lecture Notes in Computer Science*, pages 58–66, Berlin, 2011. Springer Verlag.

[262] Ou Liu, Qijian Tian, and Jian Ma. A fuzzy description logic approach to model management in R&D project selection. In *Proceedings of the 8th Pacific Asia Conference on Information Systems (PACIS-04)*, 2004.

[263] John W. Lloyd. *Foundations of Logic Programming*. Springer, Heidelberg, RG, 1987.

[264] Nuno Lopes, Axel Polleres, Umberto Straccia, and Antoine Zimmermann. AnQL: SPARQLing up annotated RDF. In *Proceedings of the International Semantic Web Conference (ISWC-10)*, volume 6496 of *Lecture Notes in Computer Science*, pages 518–533. Springer-Verlag, 2010.

[265] Nuno Lopes, Antoine Zimmermann, Aidan Hogan, Gergely Lukacsy, Axel Polleres, Umberto Straccia, and Stefan Decker. Rdf needs annotations. In *Proceedings of W3C Workshop — RDF Next Steps*, http://www.w3.org/2009/12/rdf-ws/, 2010.

[266] Yann Loyer and Umberto Straccia. Uncertainty and partial non-uniform assumptions in parametric deductive databases. In *Proceedings of the 8th European Conference on Logics in Artificial Intelligence (JELIA-02)*, volume 2424 of *Lecture Notes in Computer Science*, pages 271–282, Cosenza, Italy, 2002. Springer-Verlag.

[267] Yann Loyer and Umberto Straccia. The well-founded semantics in normal logic programs with uncertainty. In *Proceedings of the 6th International Symposium on Functional and Logic Programming (FLOPS-2002)*, volume 2441 of *Lecture Notes in Computer Science*, pages 152–166, Aizu, Japan, 2002. Springer-Verlag.

[268] Yann Loyer and Umberto Straccia. The approximate well-founded semantics for logic programs with uncertainty. In *28th International Symposium on Mathematical Foundations of Computer Science (MFCS-2003)*, volume 2747 of *Lecture Notes in Computer Science*, pages 541–550, Bratislava, Slovak Republic, 2003. Springer-Verlag.

[269] Yann Loyer and Umberto Straccia. Default knowledge in logic programs with uncertainty. In *Proceedings of the 19th International Conference on*

Logic Programming (ICLP-03), volume 2916 of *Lecture Notes in Computer Science*, pages 466–480, Mumbai, India, 2003. Springer Verlag.

[270] Yann Loyer and Umberto Straccia. Epistemic foundation of the well-founded semantics over bilattices. In *29th International Symposium on Mathematical Foundations of Computer Science (MFCS-2004)*, volume 3153 of *Lecture Notes in Computer Science*, pages 513–524, Bratislava, Slovak Republic, 2004. Springer Verlag.

[271] Yann Loyer and Umberto Straccia. Any-world assumptions in logic programming. *Theoretical Computer Science*, 342(2-3):351–381, 2005.

[272] Yann Loyer and Umberto Straccia. Epistemic foundation of stable model semantics. *Journal of Theory and Practice of Logic Programming*, 6:355–393, 2006.

[273] James J. Lu. Logic programming with signs and annotations. *Journal of Logic and Computation*, 6(6):755–778, 1996.

[274] James J. Lu, Jacques Calmet, and Joachim Schü. Computing multiple-valued logic programs. *Mathware & Soft Computing*, 2(4):129–153, 1997.

[275] T. Lukasiewicz. Local probabilistic deduction from taxonomic and probabilistic knowledge-bases over conjunctive events. *International Journal of Approximate Reasoning*, 21(1):23–61, 1999.

[276] T. Lukasiewicz. Probabilistic deduction with conditional constraints over basic events. *Journal of Artificial Intelligence Research*, 10:199–241, 1999.

[277] T. Lukasiewicz. Weak nonmonotonic probabilistic logics. *Artificial Intelligence*, 168(1–2):119–161, 2005.

[278] Thomas Lukasiewicz. Many-valued first-order logics with probabilistic semantics. In *Proceedings of the Annual Conference of the European Association for Computer Science Logic (CSL-98)*, volume 1584 of *Lecture Notes in Computer Science*, pages 415–429. Springer Verlag, 1998.

[279] Thomas Lukasiewicz. Probabilistic logic programming. In *Proceedings of the 13th European Confenference on Artificial Intelligence (ECAI-98)*, pages 388–392, 1998.

[280] Thomas Lukasiewicz. Many-valued disjunctive logic programs with probabilistic semantics. In *Proceedings of the 5th International Conference on Logic Programming and Nonmonotonic Reasoning (LPNMR-99)*, volume 1730 of *Lecture Notes in Computer Science*, pages 277–289. Springer Verlag, 1999.

[281] Thomas Lukasiewicz. Probabilistic and truth-functional many-valued logic programming. In *The IEEE International Symposium on Multiple-Valued Logic*, pages 236–241, 1999.

[282] Thomas Lukasiewicz. Fixpoint characterizations for many-valued disjunctive logic programs with probabilistic semantics. In *Proceedings of the 6th International Conference on Logic Programming and Non-monotonic Reasoning (LPNMR-01)*, volume 2173 of *Lecture Notes in Artificial Intelligence*, pages 336–350. Springer-Verlag, 2001.

[283] Thomas Lukasiewicz. Probabilistic logic programming under inheritance with overriding. In *Proceedings of the 17th Conference in Uncertainty in Artificial Intelligence (UAI-01)*, pages 329–336, San Francisco, CA, USA, 2001. Morgan Kaufmann Publishers Inc.

[284] Thomas Lukasiewicz. Probabilistic logic programming with conditional constraints. *ACM Transactions on Computational Logic*, 2(3):289–339, 2001.

[285] Thomas Lukasiewicz. Fuzzy description logic programs under the answer set semantics for the semantic web. In *Second International Conference on Rules and Rule Markup Languages for the Semantic Web (RuleML-06)*, pages 89–96. IEEE Computer Society, 2006.

[286] Thomas Lukasiewicz. Fuzzy description logic programs under the answer set semantics for the semantic web. *Fundamenta Informaticae*, 82(3):289–310, 2008.

[287] Thomas Lukasiewicz and Umberto Straccia. Description logic programs under probabilistic uncertainty and fuzzy vagueness. In *Proceedings of the 9th European Conference on Symbolic and Quantitative Approaches to Reasoning with Uncertainty (ECSQARU-07)*, volume 4724 of *Lecture Notes in Computer Science*, pages 187–198. Springer Verlag, 2007.

[288] Thomas Lukasiewicz and Umberto Straccia. Tightly integrated fuzzy description logic programs under the answer semantics for the semantic web. In *Proceedings of the First International Conference on Web Reasoning and Rule Systems (RR-07)*, volume 4524 of *Lecture Notes in Computer Science*, pages 289—298. Springer Verlag, 2007.

[289] Thomas Lukasiewicz and Umberto Straccia. Top-k retrieval in description logic programs under vagueness for the semantic web. In *Proceedings of the 1st International Conference on Scalable Uncertainty Management (SUM-07)*, volume 4772 of *Lecture Notes in Computer Science*, pages 16–30. Springer Verlag, 2007.

[290] Thomas Lukasiewicz and Umberto Straccia. Managing uncertainty and vagueness in description logics for the semantic web. *Journal of Web Semantics*, 6:291–308, 2008.

[291] Thomas Lukasiewicz and Umberto Straccia. Tightly coupled fuzzy description logic programs under the answer set semantics for the semantic web. *International Journal on Semantic Web and Information Systems*, 4(3):68–89, 2008.

[292] Thomas Lukasiewicz and Umberto Straccia. Description logic programs under probabilistic uncertainty and fuzzy vagueness. *International Journal of Approximate Reasoning*, 50(6):837–853, 2009.

[293] C. Lutz, D. Toman, and F. Wolter. Conjunctive query answering in the description logic el using a relational database system. In *Proceedings of the 21st International Joint Conference on Artificial Intelligence (IJCAI-09)*. AAAI Press, 2009.

[294] Carsten Lutz. Reasoning with concrete domains. In *Proceedings of the Sixteenth International Joint Conference on Artificial Intelligence*, pages 90–95. Morgan Kaufmann Publishers Inc., 1999.

[295] Carsten Lutz. Description logics with concrete domains—a survey. In *Advances in Modal Logics Volume 4*. King's College Publications, 2003.

[296] Carsten Lutz. The complexity of conjunctive query answering in expressive description logics. In *Proceedings of the 4th International Joint Conference on Automated Reasoning (IJCAR-08)*, pages 179–193, Berlin, Heidelberg, 2008. Springer-Verlag.

[297] Despoina Magka, Yevgeny Kazakov, and Ian Horrocks. Tractable extensions of the description logic $\mathcal{EL}$ with numerical datatypes. *Journal of Automated Reasoning*, 47(4):427–450, 2011.

[298] P. Magrez and P. Smets. Fuzzy modus ponens: a new model suitable for applications in knowledge-based systems. *International Journal of Intelligent Systems*, 4:181–200, 1989.

[299] Theofilos P. Mailis, Giorgos Stoilos, and Giorgos B. Stamou. Expressive reasoning with horn rules and fuzzy description logics. In *Proceedings of the First International Conference on Web Reasoning and Rule Systems (RR-07)*, volume 4524 of *Lecture Notes in Computer Science*, pages 43–57, 2007.

[300] Zoran Majkic. Coalgebraic semantics for logic programs. In *18th Workshop on (Constraint) Logic Programming (WCLP-05)*, Ulm, Germany, 2004.

[301] Zoran Majkic. Many-valued intuitionistic implication and inference closure in a bilattice-based logic. In *35th International Symposium on Multiple-Valued Logic (ISMVL-05)*, pages 214–220, 2005.

[302] Zoran Majkic. Truth and knowledge fixpoint semantics for many-valued logic programming. In *19th Workshop on (Constraint) Logic Programming (WCLP-05)*, pages 76–87, Ulm, Germany, 2005.

[303] E. H. Mamdani and S. Assilian. An experiment in linguistic synthesis with a fuzzy logic controller. *International Journal of Man-Machine Studies*, 7(1):1–13, 1975.

[304] Frank Manola and Eric Miller. RDF Primer. W3C Recommendation, W3C, 2004. http://www.w3.org/TR/rdf-primer/.

[305] V. W. Marek and M. Truszczyński. Logic programming with costs. Technical report, University of Kentucky, 2000. Available at ftp://al.cs.engr.uky.edu/cs/manuscripts/lp-costs.ps.

[306] Amélie Marian, Nicolas Bruno, and Luis Gravano. Evaluating top-k queries over web-accessible databases. *ACM Transactions on Database Systems*, 29(2):319–362, 2004.

[307] Draltan Marin. A formalization of rdf. Technical Report TR/DCC-2006-8, Deptartment of Computer Science, Universidad de Chile, http://www.dcc.uchile.cl/cgutierr/ftp/draltan.pdf, 2004.

[308] Alberto Martelli and Ugo Montanari. An efficient unification algorithm. *ACM Trans. Program. Lang. Syst.*, 4:258–282, April 1982.

[309] T. P. Martin, J. F. Baldwin, and B. W. Pilsworth. The implementation of FProlog –a fuzzy prolog interpreter. *Fuzzy Sets and Systems*, 23(1):119–129, 1987.

[310] Trevor P. Martin. Soft computing, logic programming and the semantic web. In *Proceedings of the 10th International Conference on Information Processing and Managment of Uncertainty in Knowledge-Based Systems, (IPMU-04)*, pages 815–822, 2004.

[311] Cristinel Mateis. Extending disjunctive logic programming by t-norms. In *Proceedings of the 5th International Conference on Logic Programming and Nonmonotonic Reasoning (LPNMR-99)*, volume 1730 of *Lecture Notes in Computer Science*, pages 290–304. Springer-Verlag, 1999.

[312] Cristinel Mateis. Quantitative disjunctive logic programming: Semantics and computation. *AI Communications*, 13:225–248, 2000.

[313] Mauro Mazzieri. A fuzzy RDF semantics to represent trust metadata. In *Proceedings of the 1st Italian Semantic Web Workshop: Semantic Web Applications and Perspectives (SWAP 2004)*, 2004.

[314] Mauro Mazzieri and Aldo Franco Dragoni. A fuzzy semantics for semantic web languages. In *Proceedings of the ISWC Workshop on Uncertainty Reasoning for the Semantic Web (URSW-05)*, volume 173. CEUR Workshop Proceedings, 2005.

[315] Mauro Mazzieri and Aldo Franco Dragoni. A fuzzy semantics for the resource description framework. In *Uncertainty Reasoning for the Semantic Web I, ISWC International Workshops, URSW 2005-2007, Revised Selected and Invited Papers*, volume 5327 of *Lecture Notes in Computer Science*, pages 244–261. Springer Verlag, 2008.

[316] Jesús Medina and Manuel Ojeda-Aciego. Multi-adjoint logic programming. In *Proceedings of the 10th International Conference on Information Processing and Managment of Uncertainty in Knowledge-Based Systems, (IPMU-04)*, pages 823–830, 2004.

[317] Jesús Medina, Manuel Ojeda-Aciego, and Peter Vojtás. Multi-adjoint logic programming with continuous semantics. In *Proceedings of the 6th International Conference on Logic Programming and Nonmonotonic Reasoning (LPNMR-01)*, volume 2173 of *Lecture Notes in Artificial Intelligence*, pages 351–364. Springer Verlag, 2001.

[318] Jesús Medina, Manuel Ojeda-Aciego, and Peter Vojtás. A procedural semantics for multi-adjoint logic programming. In *Proceedings of the 10th Portuguese Conference on Artificial Intelligence on Progress in Artificial Intelligence, Knowledge Extraction, Multi-Agent Systems, Logic Programming and Constraint Solving*, pages 290–297. Springer-Verlag, 2001.

[319] Jesús Medina, Manuel Ojeda-Aciego, and Peter Vojtás. Similarity-based unification: a multi-adjoint approach. *Fuzzy sets and systems*, 1(146):43–62, 2004.

[320] Carlo Meghini, Fabrizio Sebastiani, and Umberto Straccia. A model of multimedia information retrieval. *Journal of the ACM*, 48(5):909–970, 2001.

[321] P. S. Mostert and A. L. Shields. On the structure of semigroups on a compact manifold with boundary. *Annals of Mathematics*, 65:117–143, 1957.

[322] Stephen Muggleton. Stochastic logic programs. In L. De Raedt, editor, *Proceedings of the 5th International Workshop on Inductive Logic Programming*, page 29. Department of Computer Science, Katholieke Universiteit Leuven, 1995.

[323] M. Mukaidono. Foundations of fuzzy logic programming. In *Advances in Fuzzy Systems – Application and Theory*, volume 1. World Scientific, Singapore, 1996.

[324] M. Mukaidono, Z. Shen, and L. Ding. Fundamentals of fuzzy prolog. *International Journal of Approximate Reasoning*, 3(2):179–193, 1989.

[325] Sergio Muñoz, Jorge Pérez, and Claudio Gutiérrez. Minimal deductive systems for RDF. In *4th European Semantic Web Conference (ESWC-07)*, volume 4519 of *Lecture Notes in Computer Science*, pages 53–67. Springer Verlag, 2007.

[326] Bernhard Nebel. Terminological reasoning is inherently intractable. *Artificial Intelligence*, 43:235–249, 1990.

[327] Raymond Ng and V.S. Subrahmanian. Probabilistic logic programming. *Information and Computation*, 101(2):150–201, 1993.

[328] Raymond Ng and V.S. Subrahmanian. Stable model semantics for probabilistic deductive databases. *Information and Computation*, 110(1):42–83, 1994.

[329] Liem Ngo. Probabilistic disjunctive logic programming. In *Uncertainty in Artificial Intelligence: Proceedings of the 12th Conference (UAI-1996)*, pages 397–404, San Francisco, CA, 1996. Morgan Kaufmann Publishers.

[330] Liem Ngo and Peter Haddawy. Answering queries from context-sensitive probabilistic knowledge bases. *Theoretical Computer Science*, 171(1-2):147–177, 1997.

[331] Pascal Nicolas, Laurent Garcia, and Igor Stéphan. Possibilistic stable models. In *Proceedings of the 19th International Joint Conference on Artificial Intelligence (IJCAI-05)*, pages 248–253. Morgan Kaufmann Publishers, 2005.

[332] Nils Nilsson. Probabilistic logic. *Artificial Intelligence*, 28:71–87, 1986.

[333] Natalya F. Noy, Michael Sintek, Stefan Decker, Monica Crubézy, Ray W. Fergerson, and Mark A. Musen. Creating semantic web contents with protégé. *IEEE Intelligent Systems*, 16(2):60–71, March 2001.

[334] Magdalena Ortiz, Diego Calvanese, and Thomas Eiter. Data complexity of query answering in expressive description logics via tableaux. *Journal of Automated Reasoning*, 41(1):61–98, 2008.

[335] Magdalena Ortiz, Sebastian Rudolph, and Mantas Simkus. Query answering in the Horn fragments of the description logics $\mathcal{SHOIQ}$ and $\mathcal{SROIQ}$. In *Proceedings of the 22nd International Joint Conference on Artificial Intelligence (IJCAI-11)*, pages 1039–1044. IJCAI/AAAI, 2011.

[336] Magdalena Ortiz, Mantas Simkus, and Thomas Eiter. Worst-case optimal conjunctive query answering for an expressive description logic without inverses. In *Proceedings of the 23rd AAAI Conference on Artificial Intelligence (AAAI-08)*, pages 504–510. AAAI Press, 2008.

[337] Maria Magdalena Ortiz de la Fuente, Diego Calvanese, Thomas Eiter, and Enrico Franconi. Data complexity of answering conjunctive queries over SHIQ knowledge bases. Technical report, Faculty of Computer Science, Free University of Bozen-Bolzano, 2005. Also available as CORR technical report at http://arxiv.org/abs/cs.LO/0507059/.

[338] OWL Web Ontology Language overview. *http://www.w3.org/TR/owl-features/*. W3C, 2004.

[339] OWL 2 RL in RIF. *http://www.w3.org/TR/rif-owl-rl/*. W3C, 2010.

[340] OWL 2 Web Ontology Language Document Overview. *http://www.w3.org/TR/2009/REC-owl2-overview-20091027/*. W3C, 2009.

[341] OWL 2 Web Ontology Language Profiles. *http://www.w3.org/TR/2009/REC-owl2-profiles-20091027/*. W3C, 2009.

[342] Jeff Z. Pan, Giorgos Stamou, Giorgos Stoilos, and Edward Thomas. Expressive querying over fuzzy DL-Lite ontologies. In *Twentieth International Workshop on Description Logics*, 2007.

[343] Jeff Z. Pan, Giorgos Stamou, Giorgos Stoilos, Edward Thomas, and Stuart Taylor. Scalable querying service over fuzzy ontologies. In *International World Wide Web Conference (WWW-08)*, 2008.

[344] Jeff Z. Pan, Edward Thomas, Yuan Ren, and Stuart Taylor. Exploiting tractable fuzzy and crisp reasoning in ontology applications. *IEEE Comp. Int. Mag.*, 7(2):45–53, 2012.

[345] Christos H. Papadimitriou. *Computational Complexity*. Addison Wesley Publ. Co., Reading, Massachussetts, 1994.

[346] Leonard Paulik. Best possible answer is computable for fuzzy SLD-resolution. In Petr Hájek, editor, *Gödel 96: Logical Foundations of Mathematics, Computer Science, and Physics*, volume 6 of *Lecture Notes in Logic*, pages 257–266. Springer Verlag, 1996.

[347] J. Pavelka. On fuzzy logic I,II,III. *Zeitschrift für Mathematik und Logik*, 25:45–52,119–134,447–464, 1979.

[348] Jorge Pérez, Marcelo Arenas, and Claudio Gutiérrez. Semantics and complexity of SPARQL. *ACM Transactions on Database Systems*, 34(3), 2009.

[349] David Poole. Probabilistic horn abduction and Bayesian networks. *Artificial Intelligence*, 64(1):81–129, 1993.

[350] David Poole. The independent choice logic for modelling multiple agents under uncertainty. *Artificial Intelligence*, 94(1-2):7–56, 1997.

[351] D. Mundici. R. L. O. Cignoli, I. M. L. D'Ottaviano. *Algebraic Foundations of Many-Valued Reasoning.* Kluwer, 2000.

[352] Luc De Raedt and Kristian Kersting. Probabilistic logic learning. *SIGKDD Explor. Newsl.*, 5(1):31–48, 2003.

[353] Luc De Raedt and Kristian Kersting. Probabilistic inductive logic programming. In *Proceedings of the Fifteenth International Conference on Algorithmic Learning Theory (ALT-2004)*, volume 3244 of *Lecture Notes in Computer Science*, pages 19–36. Springer Verlag, 2004.

[354] Luc De Raedt, Angelika Kimmig, and Hannu Toivonen. ProbLog: A probabilistic prolog and its application in link discovery. In *Proceedings of 20th International Joint Conference on Artificial Intelligence (IJCAI-07)*, pages 2462–2467, 2007.

[355] Azzurra Ragone, Umberto Straccia, Fernando Bobillo, Tommaso Di Noia, and Eugenio Di Sciascio. Fuzzy bilateral matchmaking in e-marketplaces. In *12th International Conference on Knowledge-Based & Intelligent Information & Engineering Systems - KES2008*, volume 5179 of *Lecture Notes in Artificial Intelligence*, pages 293–301. Springer, 2008.

[356] Azzurra Ragone, Umberto Straccia, Fernando Bobillo, Tommaso Di Noia, and Eugenio Di Sciascio. Fuzzy description logics for bilateral matchmaking in e-marketplaces. In *Proceedings of the 21st International Workshop on Description Logics (DL-08)*, volume 353. CEUR Workshop Proceedings, 2008.

[357] Azzurra Ragone, Umberto Straccia, Tommaso Di Noia, Eugenio Di Sciascio, and Francesco M. Donini. Extending datalog for matchmaking in p2p e-marketplaces. In Michelangelo Ceci, Donato Malerba, and Letizia Tanca, editors, *15th Italian Symposium on Advanced Database Systems (SEBD-07)*, pages 463–470, 2007.

[358] Azzurra Ragone, Umberto Straccia, Tommaso Di Noia, Eugenio Di Sciascio, and Francesco M. Donini. Vague knowledge bases for matchmaking in p2p e-marketplaces. In *4th European Semantic Web Conference (ESWC-07)*, volume 4519 of *Lecture Notes in Computer Science*, pages 414–428. Springer Verlag, 2007.

[359] Azzurra Ragone, Umberto Straccia, Tommaso Di Noia, Eugenio Di Sciascio, and Francesco M. Donini. Towards a fuzzy logic for automated multi-issue negotiation. In *Proceedings of the 5th International Symposium on Foundations of Information and Knowledge Systems (FoIKS-08)*, volume 4932 of *Lecture Notes in Computer Science*, pages 381–396. Springer Verlag, 2008.

[360] Azzurra Ragone, Umberto Straccia, Tommaso Di Noia, Eugenio Di Sciascio, and Francesco M. Donini. Fuzzy matchmaking in e-marketplaces of peer entities using Datalog. *Fuzzy Sets and Systems*, 160(2):251–268, 2009.

[361] RDF. *http://www.w3.org/RDF/*. W3C, 2004.

[362] RDF Semantics. *http://www.w3.org/TR/rdf-mt/*. W3C, 2004.

[363] Paul C. Rhodes and Sabah Merad Menani. Towards a fuzzy logic programming system: a clausal form fuzzy logic. *Knowledge-Based Systems*, 8(4):174–182, 1995.

[364] William C. Rounds and Guo-Qiang Zhang. Clausal logic and logic programming in algebraic domains. *Information and Computation*, 171:183–200, 2001.

[365] Rule Interchange Format (RIF). *http://www.w3.org/2001/sw/wiki/RIF*. W3C, 2011.

[366] Harvey Salkin and Mathur Kamlesh. *Foundations of Integer Programming*. North-Holland, 1988.

[367] Daniel Sanchez and Andrea G.B. Tettamanzi. Generalizing quantification in fuzzy description logics. In *Proceedings 8th Fuzzy Days in Dortmund*, 2004.

[368] Daniel Sanchez and Andrea G.B. Tettamanzi. Reasoning and quantification in fuzzy description logics. In *International Workshop on Fuzzy Logic and Applications (WILF-05)*, volume 3849 of *Lecture Notes in Artificial Intelligence*, pages 81–88, 2005.

[369] Daniel Sanchez and Andrea G.B. Tettamanzi. Fuzzy quantification in fuzzy description logics. In Elie Sanchez, editor, *Capturing Intelligence: Fuzzy Logic and the Semantic Web*. Elsevier, 2006.

[370] Klaus Schild. A correspondence theory for terminological logics: Preliminary report. In *Proceedings of the 12th International Joint Conference on Artificial Intelligence (IJCAI-91)*, pages 466–471, Sydney, 1991.

[371] Manfred Schmidt-Schauß and Gert Smolka. Attributive concept descriptions with complements. *Artificial Intelligence*, 48:1–26, 1991.

[372] Michael Schroeder and Ralf Schweimeier. Fuzzy argumentation and extended logic programming. In *Proceedings of ECSQARU Workshop Adventures in Argumentation*, 2001.

[373] Michael Schroeder and Ralf Schweimeier. Arguments and misunderstandings: Fuzzy unification for negotiating agents. In *Proceedings of the ICLP Workshop CLIMA02*. Elsevier, 2002.

[374] Michael Schroeder and Ralf Schweimeier. Fuzzy unification and argumentation for well-founded semantics. In *Proceedings of the Conference on Current Trends in Theory and Practice of Informatics (SOFSEM-04)*, volume 2932 of *Lecture Notes in Computer Science*, pages 102–121. Springer Verlag, 2004.

[375] Maria I. Sessa. Approximate reasoning by similarity-based sld resolution. *Theoretical Computer Science*, 275:389–426, 2002.

[376] Ehud Y. Shapiro. Logic programs with uncertainties: A tool for implementing rule-based systems. In *Proceedings of the 8th International Joint Conference on Artificial Intelligence (IJCAI-83)*, pages 529–532, 1983.

[377] Zuliang Shen, Liya Ding, and Masao Mukaidono. *Fuzzy Computing*, chapter A Theoretical Framework of Fuzzy Prolog Machine, pages 89–100. Elsevier Science Publishers B.V., 1988.

[378] Raymond M. Smullyan. *Fisrt-Order Logic*. Dover Publications, 1995.

[379] SPARQL 1.1 Entailment Regimes. *http://www.w3.org/TR/2011/WD-sparql11-entailment-20110512/*. W3C, 2011.

[380] SPARQL 1.1 Query Language. *http://www.w3.org/TR/sparql11-query/*. W3C, 2012.

[381] SPARQL Query Language for RDF. *http://www.w3.org/TR/rdf-sparql-query/*. W3C, 2008.

[382] G. Stoilos, G. Stamou, and J. Z. Pan. Fuzzy extensions of OWL: Logical properties and reduction to fuzzy description logics. *International Journal of Approximate Reasoning*, 51(6):656–679, July 2010.

[383] George Stoilos and Giorgos Stamou. Extending fuzzy description logics for the semantic web. In *3rd International Workshop of OWL: Experiences and Directions*, 2007.

[384] George Stoilos, Giorgos Stamou, Jeff Pan, Vassilis Tzouvaras, and Ian Horrocks. The fuzzy description logic f-SHIN. In *International Workshop on Uncertainty Reasoning For the Semantic Web*, 2005.

[385] Giorgos Stoilos, Nikolaos Simou, Giorgos Stamou, and Stefanos Kollias. Uncertainty and the semantic web. *IEEE Intelligent Systems*, 21(5):84–87, 2006.

[386] Giorgos Stoilos, Giorgos Stamou, Vassilis Tzouvaras, Jeff Z. Pan, and Ian Horrock. A Fuzzy Description Logic for Multimedia Knowledge Representation. In *Proceedings of the International Workshop on Multimedia and the Semantic Web*, 2005.

[387] Giorgos Stoilos and Giorgos B. Stamou. A framework for reasoning with expressive continuous fuzzy description logics. In *Proceedings of the 22nd International Workshop on Description Logics (DL-09)*, volume 477 of *CEUR Workshop Proceedings*. CEUR-WS.org, 2009.

[388] Giorgos Stoilos, Giorgos B. Stamou, and Jeff Z. Pan. Classifying fuzzy subsumption in fuzzy-el+. In *Proceedings of the 21st International Workshop on Description Logics (DL–08)*, volume 353 of *CEUR Workshop Proceedings*. CEUR-WS.org, 2008.

[389] Giorgos Stoilos, Giorgos B. Stamou, Jeff Z. Pan, Vassilis Tzouvaras, and Ian Horrocks. Reasoning with very expressive fuzzy description logics. *Journal of Artificial Intelligence Research*, 30:273–320, 2007.

[390] Giorgos Stoilos, Umberto Straccia, Giorgos Stamou, and Jeff Z. Pan. General concept inclusions in fuzzy description logics. In *Proceedings of the 17th Eureopean Conference on Artificial Intelligence (ECAI-06)*, pages 457–461. IOS Press, 2006.

[391] Umberto Straccia. A fuzzy description logic. In *Proceedings of the 15th National Conference on Artificial Intelligence (AAAI-98)*, pages 594–599, Madison, USA, 1998.

[392] Umberto Straccia. *Foundations of a Logic Based Approach to Multimedia Document Retrieval*. PhD thesis, Department of Computer Science, University of Dortmund, Dortmund, Germany, June 1999.

[393] Umberto Straccia. A framework for the retrieval of multimedia objects based on four-valued fuzzy description logics. In F. Crestani and Gabriella Pasi, editors, *Soft Computing in Information Retrieval: Techniques and Applications*, pages 332–357. Physica Verlag (Springer Verlag), Heidelberg, Germany, 2000.

[394] Umberto Straccia. Reasoning and experimenting within Zadeh's fuzzy propositional logic. Technical Report 2000-b4-011, Istituto di Elaborazione dell'Informazione, Consiglio Nazionale delle Ricerche, Pisa, Italy, 2000.

[395] Umberto Straccia. Reasoning within fuzzy description logics. *Journal of Artificial Intelligence Research*, 14:137–166, 2001.

[396] Umberto Straccia. Transforming fuzzy description logics into classical description logics. In *Proceedings of the 9th European Conference on Logics in Artificial Intelligence (JELIA-04)*, volume 3229 of *Lecture Notes in Computer Science*, pages 385–399, Lisbon, Portugal, 2004. Springer Verlag.

[397] Umberto Straccia. Uncertainty in description logics: a lattice-based approach. In *Proceedings of the 10th International Conference on Information Processing and Managment of Uncertainty in Knowledge-Based Systems, (IPMU-04)*, pages 251–258, 2004.

[398] Umberto Straccia. Description logics with fuzzy concrete domains. In Fahiem Bachus and Tommi Jaakkola, editors, *21st Conference on Uncertainty in Artificial Intelligence (UAI-05)*, pages 559–567, Edinburgh, Scotland, 2005. AUAI Press.

[399] Umberto Straccia. Fuzzy ALC with fuzzy concrete domains. In *Proceedings of the International Workshop on Description Logics (DL-05)*, pages 96–103, Edinburgh, Scotland, 2005. CEUR.

[400] Umberto Straccia. Query answering in normal logic programs under uncertainty. In *8th European Conferences on Symbolic and Quantitative Approaches to Reasoning with Uncertainty (ECSQARU-05)*, volume 3571 of *Lecture Notes in Computer Science*, pages 687–700, Barcelona, Spain, 2005. Springer Verlag.

[401] Umberto Straccia. Towards a fuzzy description logic for the semantic web (preliminary report). In *2nd European Semantic Web Conference (ESWC-05)*, volume 3532 of *Lecture Notes in Computer Science*, pages 167–181, Crete, 2005. Springer Verlag.

[402] Umberto Straccia. Uncertainty management in logic programming: Simple and effective top-down query answering. In Rajiv Khosla, Robert J. Howlett, and Lakhmi C. Jain, editors, *9th International Conference on Knowledge-Based & Intelligent Information & Engineering Systems (KES-05), Part II*, volume 3682 of *Lecture Notes in Computer Science*, pages 753–760, Melbourne, Australia, 2005. Springer Verlag.

[403] Umberto Straccia. Annotated answer set programming. In *Proceedings of the 11th International Conference on Information Processing and Managment of Uncertainty in Knowledge-Based Systems, (IPMU-06)*, pages 1212–1219. E.D.K., Paris, 2006.

[404] Umberto Straccia. Answering vague queries in fuzzy DL-Lite. In *Proceedings of the 11th International Conference on Information Processing and Managment of Uncertainty in Knowledge-Based Systems, (IPMU-06)*, pages 2238–2245. E.D.K., Paris, 2006.

[405] Umberto Straccia. Description logics over lattices. *International Journal of Uncertainty, Fuzziness and Knowledge-Based Systems*, 14(1):1–16, 2006.

[406] Umberto Straccia. A fuzzy description logic for the semantic web. In Elie Sanchez, editor, *Fuzzy Logic and the Semantic Web*, Capturing Intelligence, chapter 4, pages 73–90. Elsevier, 2006.

[407] Umberto Straccia. Fuzzy description logic programs. In *Proceedings of the 11th International Conference on Information Processing and Managment of Uncertainty in Knowledge-Based Systems, (IPMU-06)*, pages 1818–1825. E.D.K., Paris, 2006.

[408] Umberto Straccia. Query answering under the any-world assumption for normal logic programs. In *Proceedings of the 10th International Conference on Principles of Knowledge Representation (KR-06)*, pages 329–339. AAAI Press, 2006.

[409] Umberto Straccia. Towards top-k query answering in deductive databases. In *Proceedings of the 2006 IEEE International Conference on Systems, Man and Cybernetics (SMC-06)*, pages 4873–4879. IEEE, 2006.

[410] Umberto Straccia. Towards top-k query answering in description logics: the case of DL-Lite. In *Proceedings of the 10th European Conference on Logics in Artificial Intelligence (JELIA-06)*, volume 4160 of *Lecture Notes in Computer Science*, pages 439–451, Liverpool, UK, 2006. Springer Verlag.

[411] Umberto Straccia. Uncertainty and description logic programs over lattices. In Elie Sanchez, editor, *Fuzzy Logic and the Semantic Web*, Capturing Intelligence, chapter 7, pages 115–133. Elsevier, 2006.

[412] Umberto Straccia. Reasoning in Ł-$\mathcal{SHIF}$: an expressive fuzzy description logic under Łukasiewicz semantics. Technical Report TR-2007-10-18, Istituto di Scienza e Tecnologie dell'Informazione, Consiglio Nazionale delle Ricerche, Pisa, Italy, 2007.

[413] Umberto Straccia. A top-down query answering procedure for normal logic programs under the any-world assumption. In *Proceedings of the 9th European Conference on Symbolic and Quantitative Approaches to Reasoning with Uncertainty (ECSQARU-07)*, volume 4724 of *Lecture Notes in Computer Science*, pages 115–127. Springer Verlag, 2007.

[414] Umberto Straccia. Towards vague query answering in logic programming for logic-based information retrieval. In *World Congress of the International Fuzzy Systems Association (IFSA-07)*, volume 4529 of *Lecture Notes in Computer Science*, pages 125–134, Cancun, Mexico, 2007. Springer Verlag.

[415] Umberto Straccia. Fuzzy description logic programs. In C. Marsala B. Bouchon-Meunier, R.R. Yager and M. Rifqi, editors, *Uncertainty and Intelligent Information Systems*, chapter 29, pages 405–418. World Scientific, 2008.

[416] Umberto Straccia. Managing uncertainty and vagueness in description logics, logic programs and description logic programs. In *Reasoning Web, 4th International Summer School, Tutorial Lectures*, volume 5224 of *Lecture Notes in Computer Science*, pages 54–103. Springer Verlag, 2008.

[417] Umberto Straccia. Multimedia retrieval and reasoning. In *BOEMIE 2008 Workshop on Ontology Evolution and Multimedia Information Extraction*, 2008. Invited Presentation.

[418] Umberto Straccia. Multi-criteria decision making in fuzzy description logics: A first step. In *13th International Conference on Knowledge-Based & Intelligent Information & Engineering Systems - KES-09*, volume 5711 of *Lecture Notes in Artificial Intelligence*, pages 79–87. Springer, 2009.

[419] Umberto Straccia. Towards spatial reasoning in fuzzy description logics. In *2009 IEEE International Conference on Fuzzy Systems (FUZZ-IEEE-09)*, pages 512–517. IEEE Computer Society, 2009.

[420] Umberto Straccia. An ontology mediated multimedia information retrieval system. In *Proceedings of the the 40th International Symposium on Multiple-Valued Logic (ISMVL-10)*, pages 319–324. IEEE Computer Society, 2010.

[421] Umberto Straccia. Softfacts: A top-k retrieval engine for ontology mediated access to relational databases. In *Proceedings of the 2010 IEEE International Conference on Systems, Man and Cybernetics (SMC-10)*, pages 4115–4122. IEEE Press, 2010.

[422] Umberto Straccia. Fuzzy logic, annotation domains and semantic web languages. In *Proceedings of the 5th International Conference on Scalable Uncertainty Management (SUM-11)*, volume 6929 of *Lecture Notes in Computer Science*, pages 2–21. Springer Verlag, 2011.

[423] Umberto Straccia. *Foundations of Fuzzy Logic and Semantic Web Languages*. CRC Studies in Informatics Series. Chapman & Hall, 2012.

[424] Umberto Straccia. Top-k retrieval for ontology mediated access to relational databases. *Information Sciences*, 198:1–23, 2012.

[425] Umberto Straccia and Fernando Bobillo. Mixed integer programming, general concept inclusions and fuzzy description logics. In *Proceedings of the 5th Conference of the European Society for Fuzzy Logic and Technology (EUSFLAT-07)*, volume 2, pages 213–220, Ostrava, Czech Republic, 2007. University of Ostrava.

[426] Umberto Straccia and Fernando Bobillo. Mixed integer programming, general concept inclusions and fuzzy description logics. *Mathware & Soft Computing*, 14(3):247–259, 2007.

[427] Umberto Straccia, Nuno Lopes, Gergely Lukacsy, and Axel Polleres. A general framework for representing and reasoning with annotated semantic web data. In *Proceedings of the 24th AAAI Conference on Artificial Intelligence (AAAI-10)*, pages 1437–1442. AAAI Press, 2010.

[428] Umberto Straccia and Nicolas Madrid. A top-k query answering procedure for fuzzy logic programming. *Fuzzy Sets and Systems*, 205:1–29, 2012.

[429] Umberto Straccia, Manuel Ojeda-Aciego, and Carlos V. Damásio. On fixed-points of multi-valued functions on complete lattices and their application to generalized logic programs. *SIAM Journal on Computing*, 8(5):1881–1911, 2009.

[430] Umberto Straccia, Eufemia Tinelli, Tommaso Di Noia, Eugenio Di Sciascio, and Simona Colucci. Semantic-based top-k retrieval for competence management. In J. Rauch et al., editor, *Proceedings of the 18th International Symposium on Methodologies for Intelligent Systems (ISMIS-09)*, volume 5722 of *Lecture Notes in Artificial Intelligence*, pages 473–482. Springer Verlag, 2009.

[431] Umberto Straccia, Eufemia Tinelli, Tommaso Di Noia, Eugenio Di Sciascio, and Simona Colucci. A system for retrieving top-k candidates to job positions. In *Proceedings of the 22nd International Workshop on Description Logics (DL-09)*, volume 477 of *CEUR Workshop Proceedings*, 2009.

[432] Umberto Straccia, Eufemia Tinelli, Tommaso Di Noia, Eugenio Di Sciascio, and Simona Colucci. Top-k retrieval for automated human resource management. In *Proceedings of the 17th Italian Symposium on Advanced Database Systems (SEBD-09)*, pages 161–168, 2009.

[433] Umberto Straccia and Raphael Troncy. Towards distributed information retrieval in the semantic web. In *3rd European Semantic Web Conference (ESWC-06)*, volume 4011 of *Lecture Notes in Computer Science*, pages 378–392. Springer Verlag, 2006.

[434] Umberto Straccia and Giulio Visco. DL-Media: an ontology mediated multimedia information retrieval system. In *Proceeedings of the International Workshop on Description Logics (DL-07)*, volume 250, Insbruck, Austria, 2007. CEUR.

[435] Umberto Straccia and Giulio Visco. DLMedia: an ontology mediated multimedia information retrieval system. In *Proceedings of the Fourth International Workshop on Uncertainty Reasoning for the Semantic Web, Karlsruhe, Germany, October 26, (URSW-08)*, volume 423 of *CEUR Workshop Proceedings*. CEUR-WS.org, 2008.

[436] V.S. Subramanian. On the semantics of quantitative logic programs. In *Proc. 4th IEEE Symp. on Logic Programming*, pages 173–182. Computer Society Press, 1987.

[437] Rajshekhar Sunderraman. Datalog evaluation algorithms.

[438] Xinming Tang, Yu Fang, and Wolfgang Kainz. Fuzzy topological relations between fuzzy spatial objects. In *Third International Conference Fuzzy Systems and Knowledge Discovery, (FSKD-06)*, volume 4223 of *Lecture Notes in Computer Science*, pages 324–333, 2006.

[439] A. Tarski. A lattice-theoretical fixpoint theorem and its applications. *Pacific Journal of Mathematics*, 5:285–309, 1955.

[440] Herman J. ter Horst. Completeness, decidability and complexity of entailment for rdf schema and a semantic extension involving the owl vocabulary. *Journal of Web Semantics*, 3(2-3):79–115, 2005.

[441] Stephan Tobies. The complexity of reasoning with cardinality restrictions and nominals in expressive description logics. *Journal of Artificial Intelligence Research*, 12:199–217, 2000.

[442] Stephan Tobies. *Complexity Results and Practical Algorithms for Logics in Knowledge Representation*. PhD thesis, RWTH-Aachen, Germany, 2001.

[443] Vicenç Torra and Yasuo Narukawa. *Information Fusion and Aggregation Operators*. Cognitive Technologies. Springer Verlag, 2007.

[444] C. Tresp and R. Molitor. A description logic for vague knowledge. In *Proceedings of the 13th European Conference on Artificial Intelligence (ECAI-98)*, Brighton (England), August 1998.

[445] E. Triantaphyllou. *Multi-Criteria Decision Making Methods: A Comparative Study*. Kluwer Academic Publishers, Dordrecht, 2000.

[446] Hudson Turner. Signed logic programs. In Maurice Bruynooghe, editor, *Logic Programming: Proc. of the 1994 International Symposium*, pages 61–75. The MIT Press, 1994.

[447] Octavian Udrea, Diego Reforgiato Recupero, and V. S. Subrahmanian. Annotated RDF. In *The Semantic Web: Research and Applications, 3rd European Semantic Web Conference, ESWC 2006*, volume 4011 of *Lecture Notes in Computer Science*, pages 487–501. Springer Verlag, 2006.

[448] Octavian Udrea, Diego Reforgiato Recupero, and V. S. Subrahmanian. Annotated RDF. *ACM Transaction on Computational Logic*, 11(2):1–41, 2010.

[449] J. D. Ullman. *Principles of Database and Knowledge Base Systems*, volume 1,2. Computer Science Press, Potomac, Maryland, 1989.

[450] Vaneková V., Bella J., Gurský P., and Horváth T. Fuzzy RDF in the semantic web: Deduction and induction. In *Proceedings of Workshop on Data Analysis (WDA 2005)*, 2005.

[451] M.H. van Emden. Quantitative deduction and its fixpoint theory. *Journal of Logic Programming*, 4(1):37–53, 1986.

[452] M. Vardi. The complexity of relational query languages. In *Proceedings of the 14th ACM SIGACT Symposium on Theory of Computing (STOC-82)*, pages 137–146, 1982.

[453] M. Vardi. Querying logical databases. *Journal of Computer and System Sciences*, 33:142–160, 1986.

[454] T. Venetis, G. Stoilos, G. Stamou, and S. Kollias. f-DLPs: Extending description logic programs with fuzzy sets and fuzzy logic. In *IEEE International Conference on Fuzzy Systems (Fuzz-IEEE 2007)*, 2007.

[455] Joost Vennekens, Sofie Verbaeten, and Maurice Bruynooghe. Logic programs with annotated disjunctions. In *20th International Conference on Logic Programming (ICLP-04)*, volume 3132 of *Lecture Notes in Computer Science*, pages 431–445. Springer Verlag, 2004.

[456] Peter Vojtás. Fuzzy logic programming. *Fuzzy Sets and Systems*, 124:361–370, 2001.

[457] Peter Vojtás. Fuzzy logic aggregation for semantic web search for the best (top-k) answer. In Elie Sanchez, editor, *Fuzzy Logic and the Semantic Web*, Capturing Intelligence, chapter 17, pages 341–359. Elsevier, 2006.

[458] Peter Vojtás and Leonard Paulík. Soundness and completeness of non-classical extended SLD-resolution. In *5th International Workshop on Extensions of Logic Programming (ELP'96)*, volume 1050 of *Lecture Notes in Artificial Intelligence*, pages 289–301, Leipzig, Germany, 1996.

[459] Peter Vojtás and Marta Vomlelová. Transformation of deductive and inductive tasks between models of logic programming with imperfect information. In *Proceedings of the 10th International Conference on Information Processing and Managment of Uncertainty in Knowledge-Based Systems, (IPMU-04)*, pages 839–846, 2004.

[460] Gerd Wagner. Negation in fuzzy and possibilistic logic programs. In T. Martin and F. Arcelli, editors, *Logic programming and Soft Computing*. Research Studies Press, 1998.

[461] David S. Warren. Memoing for logic programs. *Commununications of the ACM*, 35(3):93–111, 1992.

[462] Beat Wüttrich. Probabilistic knowledge bases. *IEEE Transactions on Knowledge and Data Engineering*, 7(5):691–698, 1995.

[463] XML. *http://www.w3.org/XML/*. W3C.

[464] Ronald R. Yager. On ordered weighted averaging aggregation operators in multicriteria decisionmaking. *IEEE Transactions on Systems, Man, and Cybernetics*, 18:183–190, January 1988.

[465] Ronald R. Yager. Connectives and quantifiers in fuzzy sets. *Fuzzy Sets and Systems*, 40:39–75, March 1991.

[466] Ronald R. Yager. Families of owa operators. *Fuzzy Sets and Systems*, 59:125–148, October 1993.

[467] Ronald R. Yager. Constrained owa aggregation. *Fuzzy Sets and Systems*, 81:89–101, July 1996.

[468] Ronald R. Yager and Janusz Kacprzyk, editors. *The ordered weighted averaging operators: theory and applications*. Kluwer Academic Publishers, Norwell, MA, USA, 1997.

[469] Jianjiang Lu Yanhui Li, Baowen Xu and Dazhou Kang. Discrete tableau algorithms for $\mathcal{SHI}$. In *Proceeedings of the International Workshop on Description Logics (DL-06)*. CEUR, 2006.

[470] H. Yasui, Y. Hamada, and M. Mukaidono. Fuzzy prolog based on lukasiewicz implication and bounded product. *IEEE Transactions on Fuzzy Systems*, 2:949–954, 1995.

[471] John Yen. Generalizing term subsumption languages to fuzzy logic. In *Proceedings of the 12th International Joint Conference on Artificial Intelligence (IJCAI-91)*, pages 472–477, Sydney, Australia, 1991.

[472] L. A. Zadeh. Fuzzy sets. *Information and Control*, 8(3):338–353, 1965.

[473] L. A. Zadeh. Outline of a new approach to the analysis of complex systems and decision processes. *IEEE Transactions on Systems, Man and Cybernetics*, 3(1):28–44, 1973.

[474] Lei Zhang, Yong Yu, Jian Zhou, ChenXi Lin, and Yin Yang. An enhanced model for searching in semantic portals. In *WWW '05: Proceedings of the 14th international conference on World Wide Web*, pages 453–462, New York, NY, USA, 2005. ACM Press.

[475] Zhangquan Zhou, Guilin Qi, Chang Liu, Pascal Hitzler, and Raghava Mutharaju. Reasoning with fuzzy-$\mathcal{EL}^+$ ontologies using mapreduce. In *20th European Conference on Artificial Intelligence (ECAI-12)*, pages 933–934. IOS Press, 2012.

[476] Antoine Zimmermann, Nuno Lopes, Axel Polleres, and Umberto Straccia. A general framework for representing, reasoning and querying with annotated semantic web data. *Journal of Web Semantics*, 11:72–95, March 2012.

Index

L-function, 105
R-function, 105

ABox
    DLs, 33
    fuzzy DLs, 175
acyclic TBox
    DLs, 50
    fuzzy DLs, 180
aggregation operator, 121, 186
ancestor
    DLs, 49, 280
    fuzzy DLs, 204, 311, 315
answer
    DLs, 45
    fuzzy RDF, 167
    fuzzy SPARQL, 307
    RDF, 23, 88
answer set
    DLs, 45
    fuzzy DL query, 188
    fuzzy RDF, 167
    LPs, 78
    RDF, 23, 88
AO, 121
Archimedean t-norm, 114
arithmetic mean, 121
atomic formula
    RIF, 285
atoms
    LPs, 74

basic graph pattern, 91
    RDF, 91
bed
    fuzzy DLs, 176
    fuzzy FOL, 129

best entailment degree
    fuzzy DLs, 176
    fuzzy FOL, 129
    probability, 290
    prossibility, 294
best satisfiability degree
    fuzzy DLs, 176
    fuzzy FOL, 130
BGP
    RDF, 91
BL-logic, 132
blocking
    DLs, 53, 280
    fuzzy DLs, 207, 215, 312
boolean algebra, 102
boolean lattice, 102
bsd
    fuzzy DLs, 176
    fuzzy FOL, 130

cartesian product, 102
clash
    DLs, 280
    fuzzy, 143, 145
    fuzzy DLs, 204, 311
clash free
    DLs, 49, 280
    fuzzy, 143
    fuzzy DLs, 204
combined complexity, 85
complete completion-forest
    DLs, 49, 280
    fuzzy DLs, 204, 212
completion-forest
    DLs, 48, 280
    fuzzy DLs, 204, 211, 311, 313
concept, 32